from the
KITCHEN *of*

BON APPÉTIT

the

COUNTRY COOKING OF

FRANCE

by ANNE WILLAN

photographs by FRANCE RUFFENACH

CHRONICLE BOOKS

SAN FRANCISCO

LIBRARY OF CONGRESS CATALOGING-IN-PUBLICATION DATA AVAILABLE.

ISBN-10: 0-8118-4646-6

ISBN-13: 978-0-8118-4646-2

MANUFACTURED IN SINGAPORE.

DESIGNED BY SARA SCHNEIDER

PROP STYLING BY SARA SLAVIN

FOOD STYLING BY GEORGE DOLESE

ASSOCIATE FOOD STYLING BY ELISABET DER NEDERLANDEN

PHOTO ASSISTING BY CEDRIC GLASIER

TYPESETTING BY JANIS REED

DISTRIBUTED IN CANADA BY

RAINCOAST BOOKS

9050 SHAUGHNESSY STREET

VANCOUVER, BRITISH COLUMBIA V6P 6E5

10 9 8 7 6 5 4 3 2 1

CHRONICLE BOOKS LLC

680 SECOND STREET

SAN FRANCISCO, CALIFORNIA 94107

WWW.CHRONICLEBOOKS.COM

= ACKNOWLEDGMENTS =

This book is a celebration of many happy years spent in France, and my warm thanks go to those who have helped me capture its joy on these pages: writer and researcher Laura Calder, whose skill with words and ideas helped fire my imagination; test kitchen director Randall Price, whose instinct for transferring authentic flavors to the plate is unerring; and my husband, Mark Cherniavsky, who collects the books for us to read, masterminds our voyages of discovery around France, and helps shape the results. I also salute the wise guidance of my agent, Lisa Ekus.

Molly Stevens reviewed the first draft of the book, and Sharon Silva edited the final one. I am grateful for their expertise as well as that of indexer Alexandra Nickerson.

I would also like to recognize the skills and hard work of research associates Cori Doherty, Vivian Pei, Patricia Sinaiko, and Anna Watson, and the dedication of La Varenne trainees who helped in the office and test kitchen: Meredith Breen, Louisa Cooper, Michelle DiMaio-Pellegri, Clarice Dionot, Sydney Francis, Sue Lim, Caroline Markunas, Michelle Rodarte, and Natalya Sokolova. It has been an equal pleasure to work with the Chronicle Books team led by editor Bill LeBlond, associate editor Amy Treadwell, managing editors Doug Ogan and Evan Hulka, production coordinator Tera Killip, art director and designer Sara Schneider, and photographer France Ruffenach, whose images perfectly convey the magic of the French countryside.

= PHOTOGRAPHER'S ACKNOWLEDGMENTS =

Traveling through my country to document both its beauty and its food was an amazing gift. Thank you to all the passionate food artisans and growers I met along the way, who shared their craft. Their dedication to keeping and cultivating their knowledge is what makes France's cuisine so rich in tradition and taste.

The recipe photography in this book would never have happened without a spirited collaboration between many people. Thank you to the talented George Dolese, whose knowledge and approach to food are of the highest standards; Sara Slavin for her impeccable sensibility and creativity; and Cedric Glasier and Elisabet der Nederlanden for their irreplaceable contributions.

The entire photography team thanks Cary Nowell and Yasmine McGrane for sharing their lovely homes with us, and Sue Fisher King, San Francisco, CA, and Culinaire, One Ferry Building, San Francisco, CA, for graciously sharing their props. Special thanks from George Dolese to the following purveyors for providing many of the ingredients used in preparing the recipes for photography: Val Cipollone with Jenny & Francoise wine importers, Christopher Barry with Ports Seafood, Cowgirl Creamery, and pastry chef Amy Hatwig... *merci à tous!*

Thank you to author Anne Willan for writing such a substantial and authoratative manuscript, rich with visual possibility; Bill LeBlond, Amy Treadwell, and Tera Killip at Chronicle Books for their support of me and the images in this book; and finally, to Sara Schneider... I couldn't ask for a more loving and creative person to partner with on projects of all scales.

MERCI BEAUCOUP!

table of CONTENTS

I often ask myself "Why France?" Just why is the country cooking of France so compelling, and why does it exert such fascination and evoke so much respect? I was raised in the countryside (in Yorkshire, not in France) and grew up with fresh farm produce and the habit of snapping up the best in the nearby outdoor market. None of that prepared me for the riches of rural France, the sights, the smells, the relish with which everyone enjoys the diversity of ingredients that change with the seasons.

One key is *terroir*. When shopping for produce in French markets, everywhere you'll come across *produits du terroir*; almost any magazine article about a chef is bound to talk about the taste, or *goût du terroir*; and French cookbooks are full of what are called *recettes du terroir*. No English equivalent exists, but the French word has spread internationally—particularly in wine circles—over the past thirty years. What exactly does *terroir* mean?

In bald terms, *terroir* refers to the soil, climate, and topography of a microregion, and pinpoints what makes an ingredient grown in one place taste different from the same ingredient grown in another. The principle underlies the whole system of *appellation contrôlée*, or AOC, which recognizes a particular food as being unique to a specific area. For example, potatoes from the Ile de Ré, off the west coast of France, have AOC status (page 111) because the sandy soils and proximity to the salty sea give them unique flavor.

But *terroir* isn't merely rainfall, mineral content, and angles of exposure to sunlight. No matter where we're from, *terroir* is our cultural and historical link to the land, the expression of the land itself and of the people who live there. To the French—and to me—it is an emotionally charged term, for it is food that tells a story. Hence, a *recette du terroir* is a recipe that uses the ingredients and methods of a particular region. On the face of it, Boeuf Bourguignon (page 136) and Daube de Boeuf Provençale (page 139) are simply versions of wine-and-beef stew—one has baby onions, mushrooms, and smoky bacon, while the second is aromatic with olives, herbs, and zest of orange. Such distinctions may seem irrelevant to an outsider, but to locals who live in these provinces, they define what is, and is not, *du pays*.

Ah, that's another word loaded with meaning. Most French families feel they belong to a *pays*, a specific region that may be large, like Brittany, but is often quite small. Novelist Colette wrote wistfully of the Puisaye where she was raised, a meager landscape of one-story dwellings and thin soil. One of France's biggest TV series in recent years was a reality show in which celebrities were parachuted onto a nineteenth-century farm to see how they coped—quite well, as it turned out.

France is a jigsaw of *pays* that can change character within a few kilometers. Three bodies of water border the land—the Channel, the Atlantic, and the Mediterranean—each supplying different fish. Two great mountain ranges provide green summer pastures and fine cheese, with cool dry winds that are ideal for aging hams and sausages. And that's without counting the hump of the Massif Central that epitomizes *la France profonde*, the brooding heartland. As a final blessing, rivers lace France and were the highways that made the country prosperous in olden times. Hardly any region seriously lacks water, and many have alluvial plains full of fruits and vegetables.

The abstractions of *terroir* and *pays* would mean nothing without the intercession of country folk, the stewards of rural life. In the English-speaking world, nobody wants to be called a peasant, though the word derives from *pays*, the French word for country and countryside. In France, *paysan* is not a pejorative term; respect for artisan producers and tough outdoor work on land and at sea is long-standing. Country cooking is essentially comfort food, it nurtures, soothes, and reassures those around the table. In France it is often called *cuisine de femme*, the instinctive woman's cooking that is close to Mother Earth. Historically, women have been very active in French agriculture. Restaurants and *haute cuisine* have followed a separate track, with celebrated male chefs taking a precise, brilliant, intellectual approach that in many ways is the antithesis of regionalism; their food could come from anywhere.

Talking to country cooks and artisan producers, their passion is instantaneous. Feisty Martine Labro takes the ingredients of the day and melds them into astonishingly fragrant, pretty dishes that reflect the sun of her native Provence. "Beauty is important in the kitchen," she says. Pâtissier Eric Jubin has traveled the world, from China to Qatar, the United States, and Paris, but to open his own *chocolaterie* he has chosen to return to his roots in the little Breton town of Pont Aven. Jam-maker Roseline Fontaine searches old cookbooks for preserves such as paradise jelly and *gratte-cul* (scratch-your-backside). To ensure the very best bread for his customers, Dominique Jan chooses to bake from midnight to midday without a break, six days a week. They have earned a place in this book because they share a pride in their knowledge, and an eagerness to communicate and pass it to the next generation.

An attachment to the land can translate into hard cash, with restaurants offering *spécialités régionales* and farmers welcoming guests as part of the Fermes Auberges organization. Members pledge to serve only foods raised on the farm, and to open their activities to visitors, whether fattening ducks for foie gras, bee-keeping, cheese-making, or raising pedigree cattle. There's a return to regional recipes such as Soupe au Pistou (page 16) and Tartiflette (page 60), and an appreciation of local ingredients like espelette pepper. A friend once asked me what constituted the perfect ratatouille, and on reflection I was surprised how categoric I was. The permitted vegetables are onion, tomato, bell peppers, eggplant, and zucchini; possibly other summer squash, but nothing else. Garlic of course, Mediterranean herbs such as wild thyme and fennel, a whiff of coriander, but no chili pepper, let alone an alien Asian spice such as star anise. The country cooks I've talked to feel just the same way: there's a right way to cook traditional dishes, and all others are wrong.

Regionalism is back on the agenda in France and so are provincial languages such as Breton, Catalan, and Basque. Towns, even cities, also have a strong sense of place. I've picked out three—Bordeaux, Lille, and Lyon—where good drink, great chefs, a reverence for tradition, and a love of comfort add up to a passion for the table and an unwavering appreciation of the good life, despite the distractions of the modern world. "Oh, let me taste that, we don't have that back home!" I heard at the annual foodie trade fair in Paris, the Salon Saveur. Prick your ears and you'll hear the same sentiment in farmers' markets all over France. There are no less than 26,000 of them in city, town, and village—about 1 farmers' market for every 2,400 people. Stallholders rotate between regional markets Sunday through Saturday and turn over quality produce at speed.

How wonderful it would be if the France I describe in this book was a fixture in time and place. But it is not. People's lives can and must change and continue to improve, yet in doing so, precious traditions are disappearing. Artisan production requires strong support and mustachioed militants are not needed to make the point by trashing McDonald's. The European Union, with its one-size-fits-all approach, is stifling diversity, even at the home table. What Julia Child used to call the "food police" are constantly on the march, imposing regulations on our markets and our lands.

France leads the fight against conformity. Most Sundays I visit our modest local farmers' market, with its open stalls clustered around the soaring sixteenth-century church. The village, and probably its market too, dates back to Roman times. Among the dozen stands I find the widest choice of fresh produce in the area, with an array of cheeses to rival any in central Paris. Sausages and pâtés cooked by a retired policeman come from the next-door village, wines are from six kilometers away, with wild mushrooms picked that morning, and the occasional surreptitious leg of wild boar in season. Inspiration and indulgence for a whole week of feasting. No wonder so many of us migrate here.

VIVE LA BELLE FRANCE!

ANNE WILLAN
CHÂTEAU DU FEŸ

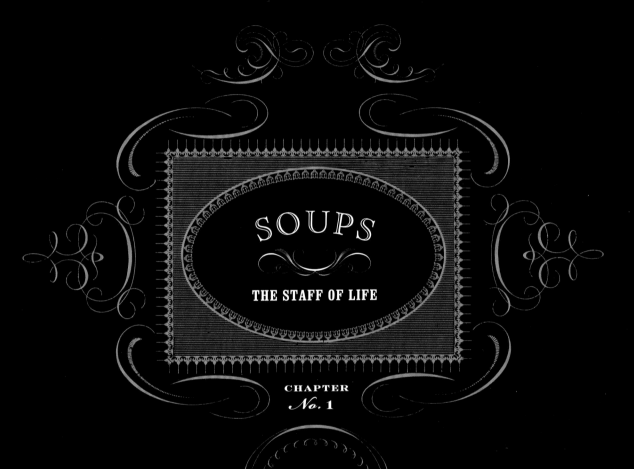

SOUPS

THE STAFF OF LIFE

CHAPTER
No. 1

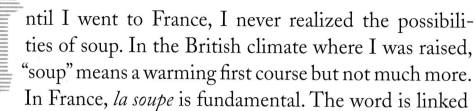

ntil I went to France, I never realized the possibilities of soup. In the British climate where I was raised, "soup" means a warming first course but not much more. In France, *la soupe* is fundamental. The word is linked to *souper* (supper), and you will still find some country households that end almost every day with a big bowl of broth and vegetables fortified with bacon or cheese, along with quantities of bread.

The umbrella term in French for what we call soup is *potage*, meaning "cooked in a pot." *Soupe* itself implies the presence of bread, whether baked or fried as croûtes or sliced baguette for dipping. Gratinée Lyonnaise (page 20), the onion soup that is almost a symbol of France, is a typical example. *Purée* means the soup has been sieved or worked through a food mill (the modern food processor is by no means universal in French kitchens, and does not remove chewy fiber in any case). Soupe de Poissons Provençale (page 18) is a combination of the two, first puréed and then served with croûtes, grated cheese, and a zippy chili mayonnaise. A *crème* is a richer, smoother edition of a purée containing cream or milk.

That brings us to *bouillon*, a humble broth that can be as simple as Nouzillards au Lait (page 24), with whole chestnuts crumbling in an aromatic broth, or as elastic as Provençal Soupe au Pistou (page 16), which combines a dozen different sliced or diced vegetables in a broth flavored with basil pesto. Broths go well with ravioli stuffed with meat or cheese, or with dumplings, whether based on cornmeal (as in the southwest) or liver (an Alsatian favorite). In wine-producing areas, an endearing custom is to *faire chabrol*, to rinse an almost-empty bowl of broth with a few spoonfuls of wine and then down the contents with their warm bouquet of the grape.

Regardless of its pedigree, a good soup has certain instantly recognizable characteristics. Its aroma is enticing, an invitation to lift the spoon and sip. Its color is cheerful, glinting orange with carrot or green with parsley, perhaps topped with a sprinkling of grated cheese. It has a sense of place, making the best use of fresh local ingredients. Basil, for example, is inappropriate north of the Loire, while olive oil replaces butter in the south. In the hands of a country cook, a soup, above all, is restorative, often a meal in itself, and, at the very least, a sustaining opening for things to come. *Mange ta soupe, chéri,* the ancient maternal admonition to a child, still echoes in French homes today.

POTAGE PICARD AU POIS

SPLIT PEA SOUP

serves 4

This soup comes from the cold northern plains of Picardy, though you will find it all over France. A bit of bacon provides meaty backing to the hearty purée of peas. In the days when pea soup was the entire meal, the purée would be stiff, known in England as pease pudding. This version is pourable.

I POUND/450 G GREEN SPLIT PEAS

5 CUPS/1.25 LITERS WATER, MORE IF NEEDED

5-OUNCE/140-G PIECE LEAN BACON

3 OR 4 SPRIGS FRESH THYME

SALT AND PEPPER

FRIED CROUTONS MADE WITH 6 SLICES WHOLE-WHEAT BREAD, CUBED AND FRIED IN 4 TABLESPOONS/60 G BACON FAT OR VEGETABLE OIL (SEE PAGE 374)

3 TABLESPOONS/45 G BUTTER, DICED

Rinse the peas well, then put in a bowl, add water to cover, and let soak for 1 hour. Drain the peas, put them in a soup pot, and add the water, bacon, thyme, and pepper. Cover, bring to a boil, reduce the heat to very low, and simmer until the peas are very tender and falling apart, 1¼ to 1½ hours. Add salt halfway through cooking, with more water if the pan seems dry. When the peas are done, most of the water should be absorbed and the peas should be soupy. If necessary, remove the lid toward the end of cooking so some of the water evaporates. Meanwhile, make the croutons.

Remove the piece of bacon from the soup and set it aside; discard the thyme sprigs. Work the soup through a food mill, or purée it in a food processor and then work it through a strainer to remove any fibers. Return the soup to the pot. Dice the bacon, discarding any rind or bits of cartilage, and add it to the soup. It may be refrigerated for up to 3 days, or frozen for 3 months.

To finish, bring the soup back to a boil. If it is very thick, add enough water so it pours easily from the spoon. It should still be thick and rich. Taste and adjust the seasoning. Stir in the butter until almost melted, and pour the soup into a tureen or spoon it into bowls. Sprinkle the croutons on top and serve.

CRÈME DE CRESSON TOURANGELLE

CREAM OF WATERCRESS SOUP

serves 4 to 6

My eyes light up whenever I see watercress soup, with its brilliant green color and slightly acidic bite that is delicious hot or chilled. However, watercress must be blanched and then thoroughly simmered in broth before any milk is added, or the acid in the watercress will cause the milk to curdle. This piquant green can be difficult to cultivate, prospering in currents of clean river water. It flourishes around Tours, where this soup originated. For Cream of Spinach Soup, substitute 1 pound/450 g spinach for the watercress. Decorate each serving with a spoonful of crème fraîche instead of the leaves.

I LARGE BUNCH WATERCRESS (ABOUT I POUND/450 G)

2 TABLESPOONS/30 G BUTTER

I VERY LARGE BAKING POTATO, PEELED AND THINLY SLICED

3 CUPS/750 ML CHICKEN BROTH (SEE PAGE 373) OR WATER

SALT AND PEPPER

I CUP/250 ML MILK, MORE IF NEEDED

¼ CUP/60 ML CRÈME FRAÎCHE (PAGE 374) OR HEAVY CREAM

GRATED NUTMEG

Wash the watercress, discard the stems, and reserve the sprigs, setting aside 12 leaves for decoration. Bring a large pot of water to a boil, add the watercress, and blanch for 1 minute. Drain, rinse under cold running water, then squeeze the watercress dry with your hands.

Melt the butter in a soup pot over low heat. Add the blanched watercress and cook, stirring, until the moisture has evaporated, 2 to 3 minutes. Add the potato and broth, season with salt and pepper, and bring to a boil. Cover and simmer, stirring occasionally, until the potato is tender, 15 to 20 minutes.

Purée the soup in a food processor or in the pot using an immersion blender. It can be prepared up to this point 2 days ahead and stored in the refrigerator.

To finish, stir the milk into the vegetable purée and reheat the soup almost to boiling. Stir in the crème fraîche and nutmeg and bring it just back to a boil. If the soup is too thick, thin it with a little milk. Taste and adjust the seasoning with salt, pepper, and nutmeg. This soup should be light and refreshing. Serve it hot, or let it cool, chill well, and serve in chilled bowls. Decorate each serving with the reserved watercress leaves.

SOUPE AU PISTOU
PROVENÇAL VEGETABLE SOUP WITH BASIL
serves 8 to 10

I once asked Simone Beck, coauthor (with Julia Child) of Mastering the Art of French Cooking, *what taste she thought most typical of Provence (she lived near Grasse). "Basil," she replied instantly. "Its perfume sums up Provence and the sun." And it does just that in this mixed vegetable soup simply known as pistou, the Provençal name for the pounded basil sauce that accompanies it. It can be made a day ahead; immediate freshness is lost, but I think the flavor of the soup deepens and blooms.*

1/3 CUP/60 G DRIED WHITE KIDNEY BEANS, PREFERABLY CANNELLINI

1 1/2 CUPS/375 ML PISTOU (PAGE 220)

1 LEEK, WHITE AND GREEN PARTS, THINLY SLICED (SEE PAGE 371)

3 TOMATOES (ABOUT 1 POUND/450 G TOTAL), PEELED, SEEDED, AND CHOPPED (SEE PAGE 372)

2 CARROTS, DICED

2 POTATOES, PEELED AND DICED

3 SMALL ZUCCHINI (ABOUT 1 POUND/450 G TOTAL), DICED

1 ONION, CHOPPED

1 HANDFUL OF GREEN BEANS, TRIMMED AND CUT INTO 2 OR 3 PIECES

1 BOUQUET GARNI (SEE PAGE 370)

2 QUARTS/2 LITERS WATER

SALT AND PEPPER

1 CUP/170 G SHELLED FRESH OR FROZEN PEAS

2 1/2 OUNCES/75 G DRIED SHORT NOODLES

GRATED PARMESAN CHEESE, FOR SERVING

In a heatproof bowl, pour boiling water over the kidney beans to cover, leave to soak for 30 minutes, and drain. Put the beans in a small saucepan with water to cover generously. Cover, bring to a simmer, and cook until nearly tender, about 1 hour, adding more water if the pan gets dry. Meanwhile, make the pistou.

Drain the beans and put them in a soup pot with the leek, tomatoes, carrots, potatoes, zucchini, onion, green beans, and bouquet garni. Add the water, season with salt and pepper, cover, bring to a simmer, and cook for 20 minutes. Add the peas, simmer for 5 minutes, and stir in the noodles. Continue simmering until the noodles are cooked and the vegetables are tender, 7 to 10 minutes longer. They should not be crunchy.

The soup should be quite thick, but if too much of the water has evaporated, thin it with a little boiling water. Take the soup from the heat, discard the bouquet garni, and stir in half of the pistou. Cover and set aside for 10 to 15 minutes for the flavor to mellow. You may also let it cool and then store it in the refrigerator for up to 24 hours.

To finish, if the soup has been made ahead, bring it back just to a boil. Taste and adjust the seasoning. Serve very hot, passing bowls of Parmesan cheese and the remaining pistou separately.

SOUPE SAVOYARDE
WINTER WHITE VEGETABLE SOUP
serves 6 to 8

The former kingdom of Savoy borders the Alps and includes Mont Blanc, the highest mountain in Europe. Appropriately, this hearty soup is creamy white and full of root vegetables, bolstered with plenty of cheese. The local Tomme de Savoie is an aged, slightly piquant cow's-milk cheese, good for cooking as well as for enjoying with bread. Gruyère can take its place here. Serve the soup as a vegetarian main course, in generous bowls and accompanied by country bread.

3 TURNIPS (ABOUT 12 OUNCES/330 G TOTAL)

1 SMALL CELERY ROOT (ABOUT 12 OUNCES/330 G)

2 LARGE POTATOES (ABOUT 1 POUND/450 G TOTAL), PEELED AND SLICED

2 TABLESPOONS/30 G BUTTER

1 LARGE ONION, CHOPPED

4 OR 5 LEEKS (ABOUT 1 1/2 POUNDS/675 G TOTAL), WHITE AND GREEN PARTS, THINLY SLICED (SEE PAGE 371)

SALT AND PEPPER

2 CUPS/500 ML WATER

2 1/2 CUPS/625 ML MILK

12 TO 16 FRIED CROÛTES, MADE WITH 1 SLIM BAGUETTE AND FRIED IN 4 TABLESPOONS/60 G BUTTER (SEE PAGE 374)

5 OUNCES/140 G TOMME DE SAVOIE OR GRUYÈRE CHEESE, RIND DISCARDED AND THINLY SLICED

Peel the turnips, quarter them, and then slice 1/2 inch/1.25 cm thick. Peel the celery root, cut into 8 wedges, and then slice the wedges crosswise 1/2 inch/1.25 cm thick. Peel the potatoes, cut them into small chunks 1/2 inch/1.25 cm thick, and put in a bowl of cold water to cover.

continued

SOUPE AU PISTOU

Melt the butter in a soup pot over medium heat. Add the onion and sauté until soft but not browned, 5 to 7 minutes. Stir in the turnips, celery root, and leeks, season with salt and pepper, and press a piece of aluminum foil down on the vegetables. Cover the pan, reduce the heat to very low, and sweat the vegetables, stirring occasionally, until translucent, about 20 minutes.

Drain the potatoes, stir them into the vegetables, and add the water. Cover the pot again and simmer until the vegetables start to get tender, 20 to 25 minutes. Bring the milk almost to a boil in a small saucepan, add it to the soup, and taste for seasoning. Cover and continue simmering gently until the vegetables are very tender, 15 to 20 minutes. If the milk is boiled hard, it will curdle. Taste again and adjust the seasoning. The soup may be kept for a day or two in the refrigerator, where the flavor will mellow nicely.

To finish, make the croûtes. Reheat the soup if necessary. Put the croûtes in warmed soup bowls and top with the cheese slices. Pour over the soup and serve at once so the cheese just melts and the croûtes remain crisp.

SOUPE DE POISSONS PROVENÇALE

PURÉED FISH SOUP

serves 6 as a first course

This soup, popular in Provence and on the island of Corsica, is a good way to use Mediterranean fish that are often full of bones. You will need a variety of small whole fish, both rich species such as smelt and mackerel and white-fleshed ones such as perch, hake, pollock, or whiting. Choose whatever is fresh and inexpensive. Puréeing is best done with a food mill fitted with the coarsest grid, or you can work the soup through a very coarse strainer or fine-mesh colander. (A food processor is no help here.) Like Bouillabaisse (page 99), Soupe de Poissons is flavored with orange zest and anise liquor, and in France it is usually served as a first course, though I find it plenty robust enough to be a main dish, too. The finished soup should be textured, intense, and lightly piquant—a breath of sea air.

2 POUNDS/900 G MIXED SMALL FISH, CLEANED AND WITH HEADS INTACT

¹/₄ CUP/60 ML OLIVE OIL

2 ONIONS, SLICED

I SMALL FENNEL BULB, TRIMMED AND CHOPPED

I POUND/450 G TOMATOES, COARSELY CHOPPED

3 GARLIC CLOVES, CHOPPED

I¹/₂ QUARTS/1.5 LITERS WATER, MORE IF NEEDED

I BOUQUET GARNI (SEE PAGE 370)

ZEST OF I ORANGE, PARED IN STRIPS

2 TABLESPOONS TOMATO PASTE

2 PINCHES OF SAFFRON THREADS, SOAKED IN 2 TABLESPOONS BOILING WATER

SALT AND BLACK PEPPER

2 TABLESPOONS ANISE LIQUOR SUCH AS PERNOD

GENEROUS PINCH OF CAYENNE PEPPER

ACCOMPANIMENTS

BAKED CROÛTES MADE WITH I BAGUETTE (SEE PAGE 374)

I¹/₂ CUPS/375 ML SAUCE ROUILLE (PAGE 219)

I CUP/100 G GRATED GRUYÈRE CHEESE

Cut off the fins and scale the fish if not already done. Wash and dry them, and then cut crosswise into slices 1 inch/2.5 cm thick.

Heat the olive oil in a soup pot over medium heat. Add the onions and fennel and sauté until soft but not brown, 8 to 10 minutes. Stir in the tomatoes, garlic, and fish pieces (including heads) and continue sautéing, stirring, for about 5 minutes. Add the water, bouquet garni, orange zest, tomato paste, and saffron with its liquid and season with salt and black pepper. If the fish are not fully covered with water, add more as needed. Cover, bring to a boil, and simmer, stirring often, until the fish flakes very easily, 40 to 50 minutes. Meanwhile, make the croûtes and sauce rouille.

Transfer the fish and vegetables to a tray with a draining spoon. Boil the cooking liquid until well flavored and reduced, 10 to 15 minutes. Meanwhile, discard the large fish bones, fish heads, and bouquet garni. Using a food mill fitted with the coarse grid, work the fish and vegetables into a large bowl. Stir the reduced cooking liquid into the fish purée and add the anise liquor and cayenne pepper. Taste and adjust the seasoning. The soup may be made up to 2 days ahead and refrigerated, or it may be frozen for up to 2 months.

To finish, return the soup to the pot and bring to a boil. Ladle it into bowls and serve piping hot with bowls of the croûtes, sauce rouille, and Gruyère on the side. Diners may stir the rouille into the soup, or spread it on the croûtes to soak in the soup. Lastly comes a sprinkling of cheese on top.

= PLACE NAMES IN COOKING =

Traditional French recipes often have a region or place in the title, which acts as shorthand for the ingredients in the dish. *Basquaise*, for instance, implies a flavoring of peppers and ham; anything *périgourdine* should contain truffles; and *lyonnaise* suggests a lot of onions. Many of these names date to the eighteenth century, when particular places became celebrated for the excellence of their ingredients, like the cheese of Savoy in *savoyarde*, or the combination of mushrooms, baby onions, lardons of bacon, and red wine sauce that adds up to *bourguignonne*. When used in cooking, these expressions are in the feminine singular: *pommes sarladaise* refers to the town of Sarlat in Périgord, and is shorthand for *pommes de terre à la façon sarladaise*.

There is a catch to these handy descriptions. Just like French grammar, they are full of exceptions. For example,

not only is the cooking of Burgundy infinitely more varied than is denoted by *à la bourguignonne* (think of snails in garlic butter), but often chefs elaborate on a regional theme until it would be scarcely recognizable on home ground. *Sole dieppoise*, for instance, with its garnish of mussels and mushrooms in white wine and cream sauce, is very much a restaurant creation; in Dieppe itself, the fish is much more likely to be a homey stew.

Just occasionally, regional descriptions are wildly misleading. *Sauce béarnaise* has nothing to do with Béarn, which sits on France's southwestern border with Spain. Rather, it was a nineteenth-century creation of the restaurant Henri IV at Saint-Germain-en-Laye, near Paris. The chef sought to honor the French king who originally ruled over Béarn and had rashly promised "a chicken in every pot" on Sundays.

= CULINARY COMMENTATORS: CURNONSKY =
(1872–1956)

Come, dear travelers and fellow gastronomes, walk or ride the beautiful roads of France.
But know when to pull over!

So wrote Curnonsky, the Prince of Gastronomes, one of the great French food writers of the first half of the twentieth century. Born Maurice Sailland, Curnonsky was an early foot soldier for the famed Michelin guide (see "French Restaurant Guides," page 194) and did much to put French country cooking on the map. Perhaps his greatest achievement was a multivolume series, *La France Gastronomique*, about regional produce and country restaurants. Curnonsky put his name to dozens of food guides and cookbooks after that, always linking tourism with gastronomy. He urged readers to sample dishes in their rightful place. "Don't eat bouillabaisse in Dunkerque! Nor quiche Lorraine in Quimper, nor a *garbure* in Rouen!" he cried. How right he was.

The Prince of Gastronomes loomed large, grew even larger, and was loved wherever he went. Curnonsky reveled in the countryside, and his grasp of French cooking was impressive. He distinguished four cuisines: *haute cuisine*, the stuff of starred restaurants; *cuisine bourgeoise*, home food cooked by skilled, middle-class housewives; *cuisine régionale*, traditional dishes and specialties from the provinces; and *cuisine à l'improviste*, be it fish tugged from the water and fried by the riverside, a hunter's stew made from a just-caught hare, or a fricassée of mushrooms stolen from the woods. In every case, Curnonsky reinforced what Escoffier had said before him: "Fine cooking is when things taste of what they are."

GRATINÉE LYONNAISE
FRENCH ONION SOUP
serves 6 to 8

Parisians have tried to hijack French onion soup, but Lyonnais cooks can plausibly claim title to this bistro classic. A local traveler once observed, "After a meal of onion soup, sausage, a good Saint-Marcellin cheese, and a bottle of Juliénas, nothing more is needed but a good night's sleep." The same four specialties remain typical of Lyon. There are two keys to good onion soup: use pungent yellow onions, and cook them to a dark, almost burnt caramel for good depth of flavor. In this recipe, I have added my personal tip: a cut onion charred in a dry pan to add particular intensity and color.

4 TABLESPOONS/60 G BUTTER

5 TO 6 YELLOW ONIONS (ABOUT 2 POUNDS/900 G TOTAL), THINLY SLICED

SALT AND PEPPER

1 YELLOW ONION, HALVED BUT NOT PEELED

1 TEASPOON SUGAR

1½ QUARTS/1.5 LITERS VEAL BROTH (SEE PAGE 373)

BAKED CROÛTES MADE WITH ½ BAGUETTE (SEE PAGE 374)

1 CUP/100 G GRATED GRUYÈRE CHEESE

Melt the butter in a soup pot over low heat. Stir in the sliced onions, season with salt and pepper, and press a piece of buttered aluminum foil down on the onions. Cover the pan and sweat the onions over very low heat, stirring occasionally, 20 to 25 minutes. Remove the lid and foil, raise the heat, and continue cooking, stirring occasionally to prevent scorching, until the onions are reduced, concentrated, and very dark brown, 8 to 10 minutes longer.

Meanwhile, char the halved onion. Heat an electric burner until hot, or heat a small sauté pan over a gas burner. Sprinkle the cut surfaces of the onion with the sugar and set the halves, cut side down, on the burner or pan. Cook until dark brown, 2 to 3 minutes.

When the sliced onions are ready, stir in the broth and add the charred onion. Cover, bring to a boil, and simmer to blend the flavors for 10 to 15 minutes. Discard the charred onion halves, taste the soup, and adjust the seasoning. The soup can be made 2 to 3 days ahead and stored in the refrigerator.

Preheat the broiler and reheat the soup if necessary. Put 4 to 6 deep flameproof soup bowls on a baking sheet and heat in the broiler. Set 2 or 3 croûtes in each bowl and ladle the soup on top. Sprinkle with the cheese and broil until the tops are browned. Serve at once—onion soup must be scalding hot.

LE THOURIN
TOMATO AND GARLIC SOUP
serves 4 to 6

Le Thourin is another soup from southwestern France, this time from Périgord. One white version is creamy and thick, based only on onion and milk spiked with garlic; another more closely resembles Gratinée Lyonnaise. The common denominator seems to be onion and garlic, here combined with tomato for a lively first course. It is quick to prepare but must stand an hour or two so the flavor develops. Need I say that fresh ripe tomatoes are essential?

3 TABLESPOONS/45 G GOOSE FAT OR LARD

2 ONIONS, CHOPPED

6 GARLIC CLOVES, THINLY SLICED

SALT AND BLACK PEPPER

2 TABLESPOONS/15 G FLOUR

1 POUND/450 G TOMATOES, PEELED, SEEDED, AND CHOPPED (SEE PAGE 372)

1 QUART/1 LITER WATER

1 BOUQUET GARNI (SEE PAGE 370)

TOASTED CROÛTES MADE WITH 1 SLIM BAGUETTE (SEE PAGE 374)

PINCH OF CAYENNE PEPPER

Melt the fat in a soup pot over low heat. Add the onions and garlic, season with salt and black pepper, and press a piece of aluminum foil down on the vegetables. Cover the pan and sweat the vegetables over very low heat, stirring occasionally, until soft, 15 to 20 minutes. Do not let them brown.

Stir in the flour, add the tomatoes, and leave to cook, uncovered, for 2 minutes. Stir in the water and bouquet garni, season with salt and pepper, and simmer gently, uncovered, until reduced by about one-third, 25 to 30 minutes. When the simmering is done, the broth should be well flavored but not too concentrated. Let the soup stand for an hour or two off the heat, so the flavor develops before serving, then discard the bouquet garni. The soup is even better stored in the refrigerator overnight.

To finish, make the croûtes. Bring the soup to a boil, and simmer for 5 minutes. Put 2 to 3 croûtes in each soup bowl. Add the cayenne pepper to the soup, taste, and adjust the seasoning. Spoon into the bowls and serve very hot.

═ GLORIOUS GARLIC ═

The French have long been convinced that garlic, like wine, is good for you. It was the primary ingredient in four thieves vinegar, sold in Marseille as a preventative against the Black Death. In his nineteenth-century novel *Tartarin de Tarascon*, Alphonse Daudet recounted how the local doctor dosed his patients with garlic soup. Even today, when you walk into a country market on a cold day, the aroma of garlic breath overwhelms that of tobacco.

There are three main kinds of garlic: white garlic is the mildest and keeps for about six months, violet garlic is of medium strength and stays good a bit longer, and rose or red garlic is the strongest, reputed to last for a year or more. It is *l'ail rose de Lautrec*, with its pretty pink-streaked knuckles, that fetches the highest price. Another sought-after variation is smoked garlic *(ail fumé)*, a specialty from near the Belgian border. Its rust-colored braids with faint aromas of wood and straw lend a mysterious, earthy pungency to potato dishes and soups. In the Bordelais region, green

garlic sprouts called *aillets* are used as a condiment, added to omelets, and even eaten raw as a crudité sprinkled with salt.

When cooked, the taste of garlic mellows agreeably. Recipes like garlic soup or *pistache de mouton*, a shoulder of lamb cooked not with pistachios but with up to fifty whole garlic cloves, is not the devilish threat that you might expect. The taste of uncooked garlic is a good deal stronger. Watch out, as some cooks still use two raw cloves per person in recipes such as Aïoli (page 219).

A basic rule is that fresh garlic is milder tasting. In winter, or when only dry garlic is available, less may be needed. A fresh bulb will be plump and firm when you pinch it. As it dries, it acquires wrinkles and a papery skin, until finally the cloves turn to dust and are unusable. Commercial garlic powder—acrid, often salty—and ready-peeled garlic cloves that are processed for storage are no substitute for the real thing.

APERITIFS AND DIGESTIFS

Country meals in France traditionally begin with a cheery little glass of aperitif and may end with a digestif. Vivid color catches the eye and a brisk whiff of herb, anise, orange, or simply fermented grapes titillates the nose. Who can resist? Heavily marketed commercial brands are available the world over, but it is the artisanal versions, ranging from light to dark, bitter to sweet, that evoke country France.

Centuries ago, French monks brewed elixirs and strong waters intended not as alcoholic stimulants but rather as potions to ensure long life. These potent and often efficacious eaux-de-vie were made with ingredients that could be distilled, such as bilberry, raspberry, aniseed, fennel, mint, juniper, orange, lavender, and thyme.

Two famous monkish medicines, Bénédictine and Chartreuse, are still named after their religious foundations. The first is made at Fécamp in Normandy, and the second by Carthusians at La Grande Chartreuse, their charterhouse in a remote Dauphiné valley. As with most medicines, the formula for Chartreuse is a closely held secret. Legend has it that only a single set of instructions survived the dissolution of the monastery during the Revolution. It was then that the Basques seized the opportunity to copy both yellow and green Chartreuse in their version, Izarra. Modern analysis has proved the mysterious concoction to be medicinal herbs, saffron threads, stick cinnamon, and mace. How unromantic!

Other regions have their own specialties. La Vieille Cure, made until twenty years ago at the Abbaye de Cernon near Bordeaux, contains several kinds of brandy mixed with herbs, as does the green Verveine du Velay from central France, which is based on verbena. There is also a whole family of aperitifs distilled from the yard-long root of the mountain gentian plant. Called *génépi* in Savoy and *enzian* in the Auvergne to the west, these gentian-flavored aperitifs, which taste like a cough remedy to the uninitiated, are most familiar as Suze. Wormwood gave its name to familiar vermouth, a slight surprise given that the wormwood root shares some similarities with absinthe, now banned for its poisonous nature. Absinthe would turn beguilingly cloudy when diluted with water, today a telltale sign of all anise and pastis drinks. Similar in taste to Greek ouzo and Arab arak, the bright yellow French varieties, best known under names like Pernod and Ricard, are found in the smallest bar, lined up alongside other brand-name aperitifs like Dubonnet, Lillet, Ambassadeur, and Amer Picon.

SOUPE DE POTIRON ET POIREAUX AU FOIE GRAS

PUMPKIN AND LEEK SOUP WITH FOIE GRAS

serves 6

The richness of pumpkin and the hearty onion flavor of leek have long been favorite partners in French soups. In 1766, Tobias Smollett, while traveling through Burgundy, wrote, "I observed a vast quantity of very large pompions [pumpkins] with the contents of which they thicken their soups and ragoûts." French pumpkins are larger than most of those sold in the United States, so here I call for a piece rather than a whole pumpkin. Now that duck liver is produced in farmhouses all over France, the festive addition of a sliver of foie gras is almost expected!

2-POUND/900-G PIECE PUMPKIN

2 BAKING POTATOES (ABOUT 12 OUNCES/330 G TOTAL)

4 LEEKS (ABOUT 1½ POUNDS/675 G TOTAL), WHITE PART ONLY, THINLY SLICED (SEE PAGE 371)

5 CUPS/1.25 LITERS WATER

SALT AND PEPPER

PINCH OF SUGAR (OPTIONAL)

6 OUNCES/170 G FRESH FOIE GRAS

4 TABLESPOONS/60 G BUTTER, CUT INTO PIECES

1 TABLESPOON CHOPPED FRESH CHIVES

Cut the peel from the pumpkin with a large knife and remove and discard the seeds and fibers, pulling them away with your hand. There should be about 1½ pounds/675 g flesh. Cut the flesh into 1-inch/2.5-cm chunks. Peel the potatoes and cut them into chunks the same size as the pumpkin. Put the pumpkin, potatoes, and leeks in a soup pot and add the water and salt. Bring to a boil, cover, and simmer until the vegetables are very soft, 30 to 40 minutes.

Working in 2 or 3 batches, purée the vegetables and liquid in a food mill or blender. Wipe out the soup pot and return the purée to it. Bring the soup to a boil. The consistency should be rich, but if it is very thick, add more water. Taste the soup and adjust the seasoning, adding the sugar if it seems bland. The soup keeps well in the refrigerator for up to 3 days, or it can be frozen for up to 3 months.

To finish, reheat the soup if necessary. Cut the foie gras into 6 thin slices, discarding any skin or membrane. Heat a small frying pan until very hot. Sprinkle the foie gras with salt and pepper and sear it quickly on each side, 30 seconds to 1 minute. Don't cook it too long, or it will melt into a pool of oil. Stir the butter into the hot soup a few pieces at a time and spoon the soup into bowls. Set a slice of foie gras on top, sprinkle with the chives, and serve.

NOUZILLARDS AU LAIT

CREAM OF CHESTNUT SOUP

serves 6

In much of rural France, you will find majestic avenues of edible-chestnut trees, often hundreds of years old. In the past, cooked chestnuts took the place of bread in years plagued by a bad harvest. For the evening meal, they were simply spooned into bowls and covered with boiling milk. This version from the Loire Valley, with a bit of onion and celery, is scarcely more complicated.

1½ POUNDS/675 G FRESH CHESTNUTS

2 TABLESPOONS/30 G BUTTER

1 ONION, CHOPPED

3 STALKS CELERY, CHOPPED

1 QUART/1 LITER VEAL OR CHICKEN BROTH (SEE PAGE 373)

SALT AND PEPPER

2 CUPS/500 ML MILK

Peel the chestnuts (see page 371). Melt the butter in a soup pot over low heat. Add the onion and celery and cook, stirring often, until softened, about 10 minutes. Add the chestnuts and broth and season with salt and pepper. Cover and bring to a boil. Reduce the heat to low and simmer, shaking the pot occasionally, until the chestnuts are nearly tender, about 15 minutes.

In a small saucepan, bring the milk almost to a boil. (If it is added cold to the soup, it may curdle.) Add the milk to the soup pot and continue simmering gently, still covered, until the chestnuts are very tender, 15 to 20 minutes more.

Taste the soup and adjust the seasoning. Spoon into warmed bowls and serve very hot.

NOUZILLARDS AU LAIT À LA MINUTE

QUICK CHESTNUT SOUP

Whole peeled chestnuts are available vacuum packed, saving a good deal of time on peeling, plus they are already tender, needing little cooking. Their flavor, however, cannot match that of fresh chestnuts. You will need about 12 ounces/330 g peeled chestnuts.

Make the soup as for Nouzillards au Lait, but add only half of the chestnuts to the broth. Simmer them for 10 minutes and then crush them with a fork against the sides of the pan. Add the remaining chestnuts with the boiled milk and continue simmering until the soup is well flavored, 5 to 10 minutes more.

= RESTAURANTS EN ROUTE =

How I love to eat out in France. Three of the most abundant choices are the bistro, the brasserie, and the café. Traditionally, bistros belong to the town rather than the country, and at their best are small, quaint establishments with menus serving classics, like *steak frites*, Confit de Canard (page 119), chocolate mousse, and crème caramel. Brasseries originated in Alsace as breweries-*cum*-eateries and are in a bigger, brighter, and busier belle époque style. They specialize in seafood (you may see carts outside overloaded with shellfish, and burly men shucking oysters) as well as Alsatian specialties, notably Choucroute Alsacienne (page 176) and an array of beers. Cafés are different because they open in early morning with coffee and croissants, but they often offer bistro menus at noon and all-day snacks, such as sandwiches, omelets, hearty salads, and Croque Monsieur (page 56).

In the regions, I keep an eye out for the local variety of bistro that may go by a different name. For example, in Lyon, *bouchon* is the historic name and the menus are classics of inverted chic. Here you will find local specialties like sausage and onions, or tripe with tomato à la mode. The northern equivalent is called *estaminet*, where you can rely on beer, braised rabbit, Carbonnade de Boeuf (page 137), and

spice cookies with your coffee. In Brittany, more-modern *crêperies* take over the landscape. They don't offer bistro fare, just crêpes—albeit with every conceivable sweet and savory filling—and, of course, cider. And then on the truck routes there are *relais routiers*, truck stops that have limited full-course menus and often very decent food at the best prices.

Finally, among my favorite places to stop when traveling are the unlikely roadside cafés, open for lunch only. Once, in a seemingly empty spot outside Beaune, I happened on Chez Jackie. Despite its isolation, the place filled up in an instant at noon; the clientele was scores of workers from nearby vineyards. Service was beyond speedy. The second I sat down, a carafe of wine and a basket of bread landed dead center on the table. In its wake came a big plate of pâtés and crudités, followed by beef stew with boiled potatoes, then green salad, next cheeses, after that an offering of fresh fruits and yogurts, and finally apple tart and coffee. Nobody had to order anything (it was one menu for all); everything was devoured as it appeared in sequence. I watched the assembled company wash their lunch down with rather alarming quantities of red wine. And then the entire space fell quiet on the dot of one-thirty. It was a hard day's work for Jackie, making her receipts well deserved.

GARBURE GASCONNE

GASCON VEGETABLE SOUP

serves 8

Garbure is an archetypal hearty country soup found in Gascony, the south-western region of France famous for its gourmandise. Almost any vegetable that can be simmered in broth can go into it. When ham, salt pork, or goose confit is added, it transcends mere soup, becoming a stew that is thick enough to support a spoon upright. Elaborate versions may be served in two stages: first comes a broth, then a gratin of simmered vegetables and meats. I enjoy this simpler version of beans and sliced vegetables flavored with duck confit, which is still substantial enough to form a complete meal. Vegetables vary with the season and everyone likes plenty of garlic in the pot. In Gascony, the beans would be thin-skinned and white, the same as those used for Cassoulet (page 178); haricot or navy beans are also fine. My recipe features golden brown, crisp croûtes of bread topped with the puréed vegetables and grated cheese, but you can omit them if you want to save time.

BEANS

3/4 CUP/275 G DRIED WHITE KIDNEY BEANS, PREFERABLY CANNELLINI

I ONION, STUDDED WITH 2 WHOLE CLOVES

I SMALL CARROT

I BOUQUET GARNI (SEE PAGE 370)

3 TABLESPOONS/45 G BUTTER

3 LEEKS (ABOUT I POUND/450 G TOTAL), WHITE PART ONLY, THINLY SLICED (SEE PAGE 371)

I TURNIP, THINLY SLICED

2 LARGE CARROTS, THINLY SLICED

1/4 HEAD GREEN CABBAGE (ABOUT I POUND/450 G), SHREDDED

2 OR 3 STALKS CELERY, THINLY SLICED

5 OR 6 GARLIC CLOVES, THINLY SLICED

2 WAXY POTATOES, PEELED AND THINLY SLICED

SALT AND PEPPER

2 LEGS CONFIT DE CANARD (PAGE 119)

2 QUARTS/2 LITERS VEAL OR CHICKEN BROTH (SEE PAGE 373) OR WATER, MORE IF NEEDED

TOASTED CROÛTES MADE WITH 1/2 SLIM BAGUETTE, BRUSHED WITH MELTED BUTTER (SEE PAGE 374)

I CUP/IOO G GRATED GRUYÈRE CHEESE

2 TABLESPOONS CHOPPED FRESH PARSLEY

For the beans, put the beans in a saucepan with water to cover and bring to a boil. Cover the pan, take it from the heat, and set it aside for 1 hour so the beans soften. Drain the beans and put them back in the pan with the clove-studded onion, carrot, bouquet garni, and water to cover. Bring to a simmer, cover, and cook until the beans are tender, 1½ to 2 hours, adding more water if the pan gets dry.

Meanwhile, melt 2 tablespoons of the butter in a soup pot over low heat. Add the leeks, turnip, carrots, cabbage, celery, garlic, and potato slices, season with salt and pepper, and press a piece of aluminum foil down on the vegetables. Cover the pan and sweat the vegetables over very low heat, stirring occasionally, until nearly tender, 25 to 30 minutes. Do not let them brown. Set them aside until the beans are ready. While the vegetables are cooking, coarsely shred the meat on the duck legs, discarding the skin and bones.

When the beans are done, drain them and add them to the vegetables along with the shredded confit, broth, and pepper (the confit will add salt). Cover and simmer until the vegetables are very tender, 20 to 30 minutes. While the soup simmers, make the croûtes. The soup and croûtes may be made up to 2 days ahead; keep the soup in the refrigerator and the croûtes in an airtight container.

To finish, heat the oven to 350°F/180°C. Lift about one-fourth of the vegetables from the soup with a draining spoon and purée them in a food processor. Melt the remaining 1 tablespoon butter in a small pan over medium heat, add the purée, and cook, stirring constantly, until it thickens to the consistency of mashed potatoes, 5 to 8 minutes. Taste and adjust the seasoning. Spread the purée on the croûtes, mounding it well, and sprinkle with the cheese. Set the croûtes on a baking sheet and bake until browned, 8 to 12 minutes.

When the croûtes are almost ready, reheat the soup, then taste and adjust the seasoning. Spoon into bowls, sprinkle with the parsley, and serve piping hot. Pass the vegetable croûtes separately.

GARBURE GASCONNE EN PURÉE

PURÉED GASCON VEGETABLE SOUP

Follow the recipe for Garbure Gasconne, but omit the croûtes and purée all the vegetables with the liquid in a food processor. Just before serving, reheat the soup, stir in the remaining 1 tablespoon butter and the parsley, and spoon the soup into heatproof serving bowls on a baking sheet. Cover the surface of each bowl with overlapping toasted thin baguette slices and sprinkle each bowl with 2 to 3 tablespoons grated Gruyère cheese. Bake in a 450°F/230°C oven until the tops are browned, or brown the cheese under the broiler.

= GASCONY: THE GOOD LIFE =

In caricature, Gascons are notorious braggarts, so much so that a *gasconnade* is an absurd boast. The reputation dates back to Gascony's warring past, against the English in particular. Gascon soldiers were belligerent, acquiring a cocky penchant for bravado, as in Alexandre Dumas's *The Three Musketeers*. I have to allow that if you visit this region, Gascons *do* have something to brag about. They weren't defending their homeland for nothing. Its lush river valleys and fertile plains make Gascony a cook's paradise.

Let's begin with foie gras, an icon of French cuisine. Traveling the backroads of the southwest, you almost trip over ducks and geese. Signs in shops and along the roadside point the way to *produits régionaux*, cottage industries tied to birds that quack and honk: Chef Chambrette's Terrine de Foie Gras (page 127), Confit de Canard (page 119), and Cassoulet (page 178) are known worldwide. Not surprisingly, goose or duck fat replaces oil or butter in many recipes.

Complementing this robust diet is a cornucopia of fruit from the Garonne Valley. The vineyards yield tiny white table grapes called Chasselas. In the orchards are quince, peaches, apricots, pears, apples, and the fat purple plums that are dried to become the famous black prunes known as *pruneaux d'Agen*. "Grown, dried, and packaged on the property" boast the labels. Gascons like prunes wrapped in bacon and served hot for aperitifs, or added to dishes like rabbit

sauté, or *matelote* of eel. For dessert, prunes are popular steeped in Gascony's eau-de-vie, Armagnac (page 328), or whirled into Glace aux Pruneaux (page 329).

The equally impressive lineup of Gascon vegetables—cauliflower, pumpkins, fava beans, tomatoes, white beans—helps explain the proliferation of vegetable soups. Many are water based and flavored with goose fat, garlic, and onion, Garbure (page 27) being the most famous. In Gascon hands, simple egg dishes suddenly sound out of the ordinary: *oeufs à la Vic* are eggs baked with local sausages (from Vic-Fezensac, to be precise), and *oeufs frits à la gasconne* come with Bayonne ham, eggplant slices, and tomato sauce. Omelets are frequently stuffed with foie gras.

I enjoy combing local pastry shops for unusual Gascon cakes. *Pastis* is a drum-shaped loaf of sweet brioche, rich with butter and flavored with rum. Rum is also the dominant note in Cannelés (page 338), a small, fluted bucket-shaped delicacy with a dark, crisp crust and curiously chewy center.

The Gascon repertoire also holds a few gastronomic wild cards, such as escargots grilled over an open fire or tossed into Armagnac-doused ragoût; *salmis de palombes*, wood pigeons from the coastal Landes region dressed in a dark, blood-thickened sauce; roast pork liver with plump fresh cèpes; and fish fried in goose fat. No wonder Gascons like to toot their own horn.

the
French Touch

FROGS
& SNAILS

CHAPTER
No. 2

The French eat some odd things, frogs being a notorious example. Indeed, the British have called the French "frogs" for centuries, and the French concede that the small amphibians are not everyone's cup of tea. "Frogs are a delicate dish, but they are not to everyone's taste," Grimod de la Reynière noted in his *Almanach des Gourmands* in 1806. To overcome resistance, Escoffier disguised frog's legs in a

whimsical pink sauce coated with Champagne aspic and called them *nymphes à l'aurore*.

The truth is, frog's legs are inoffensive. The greater problem is that their meat—white and delicate, much like chicken—can lack all taste, which is why recipes often compensate by adding white wine, garlic, herbs, and cream. In the Lyonnais and the Massif Central around Riom, frog's legs are deep-fried, while in the Jura, they turn up in soup (their carcasses make excellent broth). But most popular of all, they are sautéed in butter or oil with quantities of garlic, shallot, and parsley. Frog's legs used to be a favorite dish in Languedoc, where they were once cheaper than butchers' meat and where a frog seller walked the streets of Béziers crying, *"La gragnota, la gragnota."*

Historically, frogs were harvested wherever there were large stretches of shallow fresh water: in the marshes of Poitou, the streams of the Auvergne, and the ponds of the Dombes east of Lyon. However, today they are uniformly raised in artificial ponds; many are imported frozen from central Europe. If you thaw them in milk, they remain white and sweet.

The snail, which creeps and crawls rather than jumps, is another French delight. Nowadays, most of them are imported, though in season local varieties are available in the countryside. There are two main types: the big, beige *escargot de Bourgogne*, found well beyond the confines of Burgundy; and the smaller *petit-gris*, especially abundant in Provence and

Languedoc, and even inhabiting Paris gardens after a good rain! Strange as it may seem, some French still go hunting for live snails. A little implement is sold to measure each shell (it is illegal to harvest the smallest), and the long arm of the law will be after you if you trespass on land posted *Défense de Ramasser les Escargots*.

After that you have to purge, fatten, clean, simmer, and extract the snails before they are even edible. Needless to say, the whole operation is a lot of work, and most cooks cheat by buying prepared snails in the shell, cooked and stuffed, which need only to be reheated. Around the world, snails are most commonly bought in cans, ready to coat in garlic batter and fry, or to sauté in the time-honored herb and garlic butter (facing page).

In Languedoc, snails are served in a piquant sauce of anchovy, ham, and Cognac, with walnuts to add texture. Much touted on tourist postcards is *cargolade*, snails roasted in the shell over a fire of vine stocks. Tempting though this may sound, snails are easily overcooked, when they turn inedibly tough. Sometimes a huge pot of hot snails is set right on the table and guests are left to help themselves, spearing the snails from their shells and dipping them in Aïoli (page 219). They may make novices squeamish, but a seasoned enthusiast will get through dozens, even hundreds, to judge from the snail-eating contests held annually at country fairs.

GRENOUILLES SAUTÉES PROVENÇALE

SAUTÉED FROG'S LEGS WITH GARLIC AND SHALLOTS

serves 4 to 6 as a first course

In culinary shorthand, provençale means to sauté in butter and olive oil, laced with finely chopped garlic, shallots, and sometimes a bit of tomato. Almost any fish or shellfish, notably scallops and frog's legs, benefit from this treatment. In Bordeaux, cooks go lighter on the garlic; a topping of plain shallots and parsley is popular not just with frog's legs, but also with fish, shellfish, and grilled meats, particularly fish and steak. When serving frog's legs, I like to add an accompaniment of sautéed leeks or, better still, a few sautéed wild mushrooms.

24 PAIRS FROG'S LEGS (ABOUT 12 OUNCES/ 330 G TOTAL)

1/4 CUP/30 G FLOUR, SEASONED WITH SALT AND PEPPER

6 TABLESPOONS/90 G BUTTER

4 SHALLOTS (ABOUT 3 OUNCES/90 G TOTAL), FINELY CHOPPED

3 GARLIC CLOVES, FINELY CHOPPED, MORE TO TASTE

6 TABLESPOONS CHOPPED FRESH PARSLEY

If necessary, prepare the frog's legs by trimming the spines and tips of the feet. Wash and dry them. Roll the legs in the seasoned flour and shake off the excess. Melt half of the butter in a large frying pan over high heat. (The frog's legs will brown better if they are not crowded.) When the butter stops sputtering, add half of the legs and sauté until browned, 1 to 2 minutes. Turn and brown the other side. The butter should be quite brown to add flavor. Remove the frog's legs to a warmed plate, wipe out the pan, and sauté the remaining legs with butter in the same way. Remove the legs to the plate with the first batch.

Return the pan to the heat, add the shallots, garlic, and parsley, and sauté, stirring, for 30 seconds until fragrant. Replace the frog's legs and toss together over medium heat for another 30 seconds until very hot. Serve at once. The shallots should be slightly crunchy, in contrast to the tender frog's legs.

ESCARGOTS À LA BOURGUIGNONNE

SNAILS WITH HERB AND GARLIC BUTTER

serves 6

For French and foreigners alike, the herb and garlic butter of Escargots à la Bourguignonne is the authentic whiff of France. The snails are sold ready to bake in charcuteries everywhere, and for anyone into do-it-yourself, snails are sold in cans with a package of shells at the ready. There are also special dishes for holding the snail shells steady during baking, with the most attractive made of glazed earthenware. Or you can improvise in a regular baking dish, adding a layer of salt or thin slices of baguette to keep the shells level. Unfortunately, you will sacrifice the savory garlic butter that gathers at the bottom of the dish, just right for mopping with country bread. You may want tongs and forks for extracting the snails at table. Frankly, I prefer to forget the shells and simply bake the snails in ramekins with garlic butter. The same garlic butter treatment is delicious with mussels or clams: steam them open, extract them from their shells, and treat them like snails.

ONE 14-OUNCE/390-G CAN LARGE OR MEDIUM SNAILS

1 SHALLOT, CUT INTO PIECES

1 TO 2 GARLIC CLOVES, CUT INTO PIECES, MORE TO TASTE

1 CUP/250 G BUTTER, SOFTENED

3 TABLESPOONS/45 ML MARC OR COGNAC

SALT AND PEPPER

3 TABLESPOONS CHOPPED FRESH PARSLEY

36 TO 48 SNAIL SHELLS, 6 INDIVIDUAL BAKING DISHES, FORKS AND TONGS FOR SERVING

Drain and rinse the snails. For the butter, combine the shallot and garlic in a food processor and pulse to chop coarsely. Add the butter and pulse until the flavorings are finely chopped. Work in the marc with salt and pepper followed by the parsley. Taste and adjust the seasoning. If you want more garlic, chop it first so it mixes evenly. Add a small spoonful of butter to the appropriate number of shells. Stuff a snail into each shell and top with a bit more butter. The snails can be prepared up to 12 hours ahead and refrigerated.

To finish, heat the oven to 425°F/220°C. Set the snails in 6 individual baking dishes and bake until very hot and the butter bubbles, 3 to 5 minutes. Serve at once, very hot, with forks and tongs for extracting and eating the snails.

ESCARGOTS SUR UN CHAMP VERT

SNAILS ON A GREEN FIELD OF PARSLEY

serves 4 to 6

The delectable snails from my local snail producer are fattened on a diet of cabbage leaves and peppery greens, so to serve them on a field of puréed parsley seems a natural progression. A large can of snails holds 36 to 48 snails, an ideal number for serving 4 to 6. Be sure to serve them with plenty of country bread.

PARSLEY PURÉE

    2 LARGE BUNCHES PARSLEY (ABOUT 6 OUNCES/ 170 G TOTAL)

    2 TABLESPOONS VEGETABLE OIL

    1/4 CUP/60 ML CRÈME FRAÎCHE (PAGE 374) OR HEAVY CREAM

    SALT AND PEPPER

SNAILS

    ONE 14-OUNCE/390-G CAN MEDIUM OR LARGE SNAILS

    4 TABLESPOONS/60 G BUTTER

    2 SMALL SHALLOTS, FINELY CHOPPED

    1 SMALL GARLIC CLOVE, FINELY CHOPPED

For the parsley purée, bring a saucepan of salted water to a boil. Discard the parsley stems, add the leafy sprigs to the boiling water, and simmer until quite tender, 2 to 3 minutes. Drain the parsley, reserving ¼ cup (60 ml) of the liquid. Rinse with cold water and drain again thoroughly; the parsley will be bright green. Chop it coarsely and put it in a blender with the oil and reserved cooking liquid. Process until finely chopped, 1 to 2 minutes. Stir in the crème fraîche, taste, and season with salt and pepper. The purée may be made a day ahead and refrigerated.

To finish, warm the parsley purée in a small saucepan over low heat. Drain and rinse the snails. Melt the butter in a frying pan over medium heat. Add the shallots and garlic and sauté until soft and fragrant, 2 to 3 minutes. Add the snails, sprinkle with salt and pepper, and continue sautéing, stirring constantly, until the snails are very hot, 2 to 3 minutes. Spread the hot parsley purée on 4 warmed plates and dot with the snails. Serve at once.

ESCARGOTS LANGUEDOCIENNE

SNAILS WITH ANCHOVY AND WALNUT SAUCE

serves 4

Crunchy with walnuts and tingling with anchovy—that is how snails gathered in the garrigues, *the herb-covered hillsides of Languedoc, are served. Traditionally, they come as a first course in little bowls or ramekins, no shells needed! In more modern style, try snails cooked this way as an unusual topping for pasta.*

ANCHOVY AND WALNUT SAUCE

    10 ANCHOVY FILLETS, SOAKED IN MILK FOR A FEW MINUTES

    1/2 CUP/60 G CHOPPED WALNUTS OR ALMONDS

    1 GARLIC CLOVE, FINELY CHOPPED

    2 TABLESPOONS CHOPPED FRESH PARSLEY

    3 TABLESPOONS/45 ML OLIVE OIL

    2 THICK SLICES LEAN BACON (ABOUT 2 OUNCES/ 60 G TOTAL), CHOPPED

    1 THICK SLICE COOKED HAM (ABOUT 2 OUNCES/ 60 G), CHOPPED

    2 TABLESPOONS COGNAC

    1 TABLESPOON TOMATO PASTE

    1 CUP/250 ML VEAL OR BEEF BROTH (SEE PAGE 373)

SNAILS

    ONE 14-OUNCE/390-G CAN MEDIUM OR LARGE SNAILS

    SALT AND PEPPER

    2 TABLESPOONS FRESH BREAD CRUMBS

    LEAVES FROM 3 SPRIGS FRESH BASIL, SHREDDED

For the sauce, drain off the milk from the anchovies and chop finely on a cutting board. Add the walnuts, garlic, and parsley to the anchovies and briefly chop all the ingredients together. Put the mixture into a bowl and mix in 1 tablespoon of the olive oil. Heat the remaining 2 tablespoons oil in a large saucepan over medium heat. Add the bacon and ham and brown well, 3 to 5 minutes. Add the anchovy mixture and cook over low heat, stirring, for 2 minutes. Stir in the Cognac, tomato paste, and broth and bring to a boil.

Drain and rinse the snails. Stir them into the sauce and simmer gently for about 5 minutes. Salt will probably not be needed, as the anchovies are salty, but add plenty of freshly ground pepper. Stir in the bread crumbs to thicken the mixture slightly, transfer to warmed plates, and top with the basil. Serve at once.

ESCARGOTS SUR UN CHAMP VERT

LA CHASSE AUX ESCARGOTS

FIRST CATCH YOUR SNAIL

serves 6 to 8

The way to catch a snail (and let's face it, if there is a chase, we know who won't win) is to head out with a plastic bucket and a flexible back. In Burgundy, the little creatures flourish among the vines, and the best time to pick them is in late fall when they are hibernating and are fat, yet relatively clean. Elsewhere, even in the suburban gardens of Paris, snail maniacs gather the smaller petit-gris. *If you want to reuse the snail shells after the meat has been cooked and extracted, simmer them in salted water for 10 to 15 minutes, then drain, rinse, and dry.*

    1 BUCKETFUL OF SNAILS (9 TO 12 DOZEN TOTAL)

    ABOUT 2 CUPS/250 G FLOUR

    1½ CUPS/430 G COARSE SALT

COURT BOUILLON

    2 ONIONS, THINLY SLICED

    1 LARGE BOUQUET GARNI (SEE PAGE 370)

    1 TEASPOON SALT

    1 TEASPOON PEPPERCORNS

    1 CUP/250 ML WHITE WINE VINEGAR

    3 CUPS/750 ML WATER, MORE IF NEEDED

First the snails must be purged of any poisonous herbs for a week. Wash them thoroughly in cold running water and drain. Put them in a large ventilated cage or box, such as a cardboard carton with holes poked in the sides, and set them in a cool place outdoors. If you have a large yard, you may instead sprinkle wood ash from the fireplace in a circle 3 feet/1 m or more across. Set the snails inside the circle; they cannot crawl through the ashes. Spray the snails with water once or twice a day to keep them moist. During the last 2 days, sprinkle them with flour to plump them.

Then, the snails need a good soak. Cover them with water, let them sit for 10 minutes, and then drain them. Live snails will peep out from their shells; discard the rest. Toss the live snails in a large bowl with the coarse salt and leave them for 15 minutes. This will draw out their sticky juices. Rinse thoroughly again.

For the court bouillon, put the onions, bouquet garni, salt, peppercorns, vinegar, and water in a large saucepan. Bring to a boil, lower the heat and simmer for about 10 minutes. Add the snails, cover the pan, and simmer until tender, 2 to 3 hours, depending on their size. Add more water if necessary so the snails remain covered at all times. To test if they are tender, lift out a snail from the pan, pull it from its shell with a large pin, and cut it with a knife.

When the snails are ready, let them cool in the court bouillon until tepid, then drain them and pull off and discard the operculum (the hard disk covering the meat). Pull out the meat using a crab pick or large pin, and cut off the soft, dark stomach at the extremity. The snails are now ready to be reheated with age-old garlic butter à la bourguignonne (page 33), or another sauce. The snails can be prepared up to 2 days ahead: strain the court bouillon, pour enough over the snails to cover them, cover tightly, and store in the refrigerator.

INDISPENSABLE

EGGS & CHEESE

CHAPTER
No. 3

It's hard to imagine a French country kitchen without eggs and cheese. Simply cooked, they are the answer to many a light meal and quick supper. There's even a word for it, *grignoter*, "to nibble."

Hens are long gone from most country households, but fresh farm eggs are sold in French farmers' markets, easily identified by their motley sizes and unwashed shells. Here you have the best hope of an egg with a golden yolk to add color to egg dishes and cakes, though, to be candid, color depends as much on the breed of hen as how it was fed. More important is flavor—the taste of a fresh egg from a hen that has led an outdoor life is instantly recognizable when soft boiled, baked *en cocotte*, or whisked in an omelet. Most portions in France are modest by American standards, but eggs are an exception. Two eggs are a minimum serving, even three when scrambled or in an omelet. If a single baked or poached egg were to be offered, even in a rich *sauce meurette* (facing page), the cook would be regarded as stingy.

Just occasionally you'll see duck and quail eggs in the market, too. A duck egg is somewhat larger than a hen's, and reputedly richer, though I find little difference. Quail eggs, an offshoot of farmed quail, are popular in gourmet restaurants for finicky hors d'oeuvre. To cook raw ones, put them in cold water, bring them to a boil and simmer 2 minutes. They are best served hard boiled with sea salt, to be shelled by your guests at the table.

When it comes to a seriously good meal, no French patriot passes over the cheese platter, with its mind-boggling display. Key to the quality of all these cheeses is the use of unpasteurized (a.k.a. raw) milk. Pasteurization destroys not only bacteria, but also many of the native enzymes in milk that give fine cheese its aroma and flavor. Some survive pasteurization better than others, notably the aged types such as Gruyère. Soft-paste cheeses such as Saint Nectaire, and those with a blooming rind such as Brie, suffer the most, becoming faded and bland. Whether made with cow's, sheep's, or goat's milk, most French unpasteurized cheeses are made in pasteurized versions that bear the same name, so keep a close eye on what the label says.

Cheeses for cooking are a different story from those laid out on a cheese platter. For one thing, after heating, the distinction between the use of unpasteurized and pasteurized milk is less crucial. And for cooking, most French kitchens rely only on a few cheeses. Number one is Gruyère, available grated or sliced everywhere and valued for its nutty flavor and the ease with which it melts and enriches sauces, or browns to a crusty topping. Comté is a superior, aged version, while Emmental, pitted with holes, is blander and less expensive. For truly intense flavor, French cooks have to admit that Italian Parmesan is irreplaceable. Its dryness makes it less likely to cook into strings, a hazard with more fatty, moist cheeses. (Strings result from the protein and fat getting too hot; that's why a cheese mixture or sauce must never boil.)

Blue cheeses—particularly piquant, salty Roquefort—are often crumbled to flavor stuffings and quiches, or to enhance a sauce for topping meats. Likewise, goat cheeses are invaluable crumbled in salads or sprinkled as a trendy pizza topping. However, goat cheese resists melting and I find it curiously tasteless in a sauce. But perhaps that's my prejudice, as it tastes so delicious plain on the plate.

OEUFS EN MEURETTE

POACHED EGGS IN RED WINE SAUCE

serves 4 as a main course, or 8 as a light first course

Poached eggs en meurette, *coated in the magnificent red wine sauce garnished with bacon lardons, baby onions, and mushrooms, is one of the supreme dishes of Burgundy, a province renowned for good living. The use of Pinot Noir, the red wine grape of the region, is a surprise. The eggs acquire a winey flavor and an odd purple color that is later concealed by a glossy brown veil of sauce. Each detail is important, from the mushrooms that are quartered to match the size of the baby onions and the flavoring of smoked rather than salted bacon to the crisp accompaniment of fried croûtes. The sauce is bound at the end of cooking with beurre manié (kneaded butter) that gives a lighter consistency than the more common roux of butter and flour used at the start of a sauce. My version has a secret ingredient, a nut of bittersweet chocolate that adds yet one more layer of taste.*

1 BOTTLE (750 ML) PINOT NOIR

2 CUPS/500 ML VEAL BROTH (SEE PAGE 373), MORE IF NEEDED

8 EGGS

1 ONION, THINLY SLICED

1 CARROT, THINLY SLICED

1 STALK CELERY, THINLY SLICED

1 GARLIC CLOVE, CHOPPED

1 BOUQUET GARNI (SEE PAGE 370)

1/2 TEASPOON PEPPERCORNS

FRIED CROÛTES MADE WITH 8 SLICES WHITE BREAD, CUT INTO ROUNDS AND FRIED IN 2 TABLESPOONS VEGETABLE OIL AND 2 TABLESPOONS/30 G BUTTER (SEE PAGE 374)

1 HAZELNUT-SIZED PIECE BITTERSWEET CHOCOLATE, CHOPPED (OPTIONAL)

SALT AND PEPPER

GARNISH

2 TABLESPOONS/30 G BUTTER

6 OUNCES/170 G BUTTON MUSHROOMS, TRIMMED AND QUARTERED

6-OUNCE/170-G PIECE LEAN BACON, CUT INTO LARDONS (SEE PAGE 371)

20 TO 24 BABY ONIONS (ABOUT 12 OUNCES/330 G TOTAL)

BEURRE MANIÉ

2 TABLESPOONS/30 G BUTTER

3 TABLESPOONS/22 G FLOUR

Bring the wine and broth to a vigorous boil in a large sauté pan. Break 4 eggs, one by one, into the places where the liquid is bubbling so the bubbles spin the eggs. Lower the heat and poach the eggs at a very gentle simmer until the yolks are fairly firm but still soft to the touch, 3 to 4 minutes. Carefully lift out the eggs with a draining spoon and immerse them in a bowl of cool water. Poach the remaining eggs in the same way. Trim the stringy edges from the eggs with scissors, leaving the eggs in the water. Add the onion, carrot, celery, garlic, bouquet garni, and peppercorns to the wine mixture and simmer until it is concentrated and reduced, 20 to 25 minutes.

Meanwhile, cook the garnish. Melt 1 tablespoon of the butter in a large saucepan over medium heat, add the mushrooms, and sauté until they are tender, 2 to 3 minutes. Remove the mushrooms to a bowl. Add the lardons and the remaining 1 tablespoon butter to the pan and fry until brown but still soft. Transfer the lardons to the mushrooms using a draining spoon. Lastly, add the onions to the pan and lower the heat to low. Cook gently, shaking the pan often so they color evenly, until browned and tender, 10 to 15 minutes. Drain off all the fat, replace the mushrooms and lardons, and set the pan aside. Make the croûtes.

For the beurre manié, crush the butter on a plate with a fork and work in the flour to form a soft paste. To thicken the sauce, bring the wine mixture to a boil and whisk in the beurre manié a piece or two at a time until the sauce coats a spoon lightly. You may not need all of the paste. Strain the sauce over the mushroom garnish, pressing the vegetables in the strainer to extract all the liquid and flavor. Stir in the chocolate (if using) and bring the sauce back to a simmer. Taste and adjust the seasoning with salt and pepper. The sauce, eggs in water, and croûtes can be prepared to this point and stored for up to 12 hours in the refrigerator.

To finish, warm the croûtes in a low oven. If necessary, reheat the sauce and garnish over medium heat, thinning the mixture with a little broth if it is heavy. Warm the eggs by transferring them to a bowl of hot water for about 1 minute. Lift the eggs out with a draining spoon, blot briefly on paper towels, and set them on the croûtes on warmed plates. Spoon over the sauce and garnish, and serve at once.

OEUFS EN COCOTTE LYONNAISE

BAKED EGGS IN RAMEKINS WITH ONIONS

serves 4 as a first course

The flavor and texture of an egg is subtly different when baked en cocotte, in a small, deep dish such as a ramekin, rather than flat, as in Oeufs au Plat (page 261). When served, the egg white should just be set and the yolk soft. Oeufs en Cocotte are rarely offered outside a home, as they overcook too easily for restaurant fare. When seasoning, sprinkle the salt and pepper into the ramekin before you drop in the egg, not after, or its surface will be spotty. Oeufs en Cocotte can be served plain but are usually picked up with a little garnish. Fresh herbs are a light, colorful touch; truffle shavings or a slice of foie gras add a whiff of luxury; and a spoonful of ham, bacon, or other typical omelet filling is a simple, savory addition. A tablespoonful of cream on top keeps the egg moist. Serve the egg in the ramekin, set on a napkin or doily on a small plate, with a teaspoon for eating.

I TABLESPOON/15 G BUTTER, MORE FOR THE
RAMEKINS

6 TO 8 SCALLIONS OR BABY ONIONS, SLICED

SALT AND PEPPER

FRIED CROUTONS MADE WITH 2 SLICES COUNTRY
BREAD OR BAGUETTE, CUBED AND FRIED IN
2 TABLESPOONS/30 G BUTTER (SEE PAGE 374)

4 EGGS

1/4 CUP/60 ML HEAVY CREAM

FOUR 1/2-CUP/125-ML RAMEKINS

Heat the oven to 350°F/180°C. Butter the ramekins. Melt the butter in a small frying pan over medium heat. Add the scallions and fry, stirring often, until golden brown, 5 to 7 minutes. Season with salt and pepper and spread them in the ramekins. Make the croutons. Scatter them on the scallions with a bit more salt and pepper. This garnish can be prepared 3 to 4 hours ahead and kept at room temperature.

Break an egg into each ramekin and then spoon 1 tablespoon of the cream over each egg to coat it lightly. Line a roasting pan with a dish towel, set the ramekins in it, and pour in boiling water to make a water bath (see page 373). Bring the water just back to a boil on the stove top and transfer the pan to the oven. Bake the eggs until the whites are almost set, 10 to 11 minutes, depending on the thickness of the ramekins. The eggs will continue cooking for a minute or two in the hot dishes when you take them from the oven.

OEUFS BROUILLÉS AUX CHAMPIGNONS SAUVAGES

SCRAMBLED EGGS WITH WILD MUSHROOMS

serves 4

In France as everywhere else, cooks are spending less time in the kitchen, and dishes like scrambled eggs and soft-boiled eggs are right in style. In the foothills of the Alps and Savoy in spring, you will find local morels in a brouillade of scrambled eggs, and later in the year, the full range of chanterelles, oyster mushrooms, hedgehogs, and cèpes (see "Mushrooms," page 250) will be joined together with butter and herbs in one glorious scramble. Serve the eggs with crusty country bread or on a slice of toast.

8 OUNCES/225 G MIXED WILD MUSHROOMS

4 TABLESPOONS/60 G BUTTER

I TABLESPOON CHOPPED FRESH PARSLEY

I TABLESPOON CHOPPED FRESH CHIVES

SALT AND PEPPER

8 EGGS

Clean the mushrooms (see page 373). Melt 2 tablespoons of the butter in a frying pan over high heat. Add the mushrooms and sauté, stirring often, until they are tender and all the liquid they released has evaporated, 5 to 7 minutes. Stir in the parsley and chives and season with salt and pepper. The mushrooms can be cooked an hour or two ahead and left at room temperature.

If necessary, warm the cooked mushrooms. To scramble the eggs, whisk them in a bowl with salt and pepper. Melt the remaining 2 tablespoons butter in a heavy saucepan over low heat. Add the eggs and cook, stirring constantly with a wooden spoon, until they begin to thicken. This should take at least 5 minutes. Continue stirring, lifting the pan from the heat as necessary so the eggs thicken smoothly and form quite small curds. In France, scrambled eggs are served soft, but you may prefer them almost set. When cooked to your taste, stir in the mushrooms. Taste, adjust the seasoning, and serve at once on warmed plates.

OEUFS BROUILLÉS AUX CHAMPIGNONS SAUVAGES

The hilly, chilly regions that border the Alps from the Dauphiné north through Savoy and the Franche-Comté have always been frontier territories. In the past, they were semi-autonomous, and in fact Savoy only became French in 1860. All three share lakes, green pastures, chalets, ski resorts, and a sturdy cuisine. You need to eat well in a harsh mountain climate. "*Cuisine savoyarde* is simple, generous, full of hearty soups, charcuterie, cheese, and potatoes," says Jean-Michel Bouvier, chef of L'Essentiel, the leading restaurant in Chambéry, where he was born and raised. "*C'est une belle cuisine!*"

A whole culinary culture has built up around ski resorts, with energizing dishes such as Raclette (page 56), melted cheese served with pickles and boiled potatoes in their skins, downed with a jug of mulled wine. The cow counts for a lot around here. Beef or veal is the meat of choice, and cheese is important. In the lakeside market of Annecy in Savoy, I saw a dozen or more hard cheeses on display, the good ones marked *montagne*, signaling those from high pastures where the cows crop the lush summer grass. I could choose my cheese at three months, twelve months, even eighteen months of age, either *salé* (piquant) or *fruité* (aromatic). Milk forms the basis of soups such as Soupe Savoyarde (page 16) and of the legendary Gratin Dauphinois (page 225), potato simmered in milk and cream, then browned with a whisper of cheese. It is said that chef Fernand Point, a founder of modern French cuisine, was arrested during World War II for buying a black-market bucket of crème fraîche. "It's for my gratin!" he protested, and the judge let him free.

Around the lakes the cooking is lighter, with trout, crayfish, and the famous *omble chevalier* (a type of arctic char) that exists nowhere else. Chef Marc Veyrat has earned an international reputation for his inspired play on traditional dishes. I love his tiny jars of forgotten root vegetables, and his scrambled eggs flavored with intense, tongue-tingling alpine herbs such as *serpolet*, a wild thyme; *livèche* (lovage); and bitter gentian root.

Veyrat leads a movement back to mountain foods. Mushrooms from the hillsides (see "Mushrooms," page 250), particularly morels and cèpes, are eaten fresh and dried for the winter. Walnuts and hazelnuts somehow have a more astringent bite when grown in mountain air. Wild raspberries, bilberries, rose hips, and tiny semiwild apples punctuate desserts, while sour preserves transform slabs of dark bread cut from mountain-sized crusty loaves. In the Franche-Comté, dark cherry jam is served with cheese.

Much is served in pottery bowls in warm, woodsy colors and splashed with dots, alpine flowers, or the occasional cow. They look like kids' stuff, as does much of the cooking. Mountain food is easy to enjoy.

= CHEFS: MÈRE POULARD, THE MOTHER HEN =
(1851–1931)

Travelers flocked to her table from around the world. Connoisseurs and food writers racked their brains to uncover the secret to her recipe. What did Annette Poulard *do*, they agonized, that made her omelet so light and delicious? Some surmised she added water. Others suspected crème fraîche or foie gras. One cookbook theorized that she increased the proportion of egg whites to yolks. Finally, to clear up the matter once and for all, Madame Poulard wrote to the French Académie des Gastronomes.

Here is the recipe for the omelet: I break some good eggs into a bowl, I beat them well, I put a good lump of butter into the pan, I pour the eggs into it, and I stir it constantly. I am happy, monsieur, if this recipe pleases you.
—Madame Poulard, June 6, 1922

Madame Poulard's omelets live on. The eponymous restaurant is still a destination at Mont-Saint-Michel in Normandy.

OMELETTE SANTÉ

FLAT OMELET WITH MUSHROOMS, TOMATO, AND HERBS

serves 2 or 3

Most regions of France have a favorite omelet, often a substantial affair including potato or bread croutons, with ham or cheese. I am partial to this lighter version from the Loire, with mushrooms, tomato, and plenty of fresh herbs that lead to its title santé, *meaning "healthy." When cooked like this as a flat cake, instead of being folded, it can be eaten hot or left to cool and cut into wedges—perfect for a picnic.*

5 EGGS

SALT AND PEPPER

3 TABLESPOONS/45 G BUTTER

4 BUTTON MUSHROOMS (ABOUT 6 OUNCES/170 G TOTAL), TRIMMED AND SLICED

1 TOMATO, PEELED, SEEDED, AND CHOPPED (SEE PAGE 372)

1 TABLESPOON CHOPPED FRESH PARSLEY

2 TABLESPOONS CHOPPED MIXED FRESH HERBS SUCH AS SORREL, BASIL, OREGANO, AND/OR CHIVES

9-INCH/23-CM OMELET PAN

In a bowl, whisk the eggs until frothy with salt and pepper and set aside. Melt the butter in the omelet pan over medium heat. Add the mushrooms, season with salt and pepper, and sauté until they are tender and all the liquid they released has evaporated, 2 to 3 minutes. Stir in the tomato, parsley, and mixed herbs, increase the heat to high, and cook until very hot, about 1 minute.

Pour in the eggs and stir briskly with the flat of a large fork until the omelet is almost as thick as scrambled eggs. Leave it to cook for 2 to 3 minutes. It should be well browned on the bottom and almost firm on top. Take the pan from the heat, invert a heatproof plate on top, and turn out the omelet onto the plate. Slide the omelet back into the pan, browned side up, and quickly brown the bottom over medium heat, about 30 seconds. Slide the omelet onto a warmed plate and serve hot or at room temperature, cut into wedges.

OMELETTE AUVERGNATE

FLAT OMELET WITH HAM, POTATO, AND CHEESE

This particular flat omelet comes from central France, where the local pungent Cantal cheese is an excellent counterpoint to eggs; Gruyère can take its place.

Whisk the eggs as for Omelette Santé. Finely dice 3 ounces/90 g thinly sliced cured raw ham, and then peel and dice 2 potatoes. Heat 3 tablespoons/45 g lard or vegetable oil in the omelet pan over medium heat. Add the potatoes and fry, stirring often, until tender and browned, 8 to 10 minutes. Stir in the ham, then the eggs. Cook the omelet on the first side as for omelette santé. After turning it, spoon 2 tablespoons crème fraîche or heavy cream over the top and sprinkle with ½ cup/50 g grated Cantal or Gruyère cheese. Brown the bottom of the omelet, slide the omelet onto a warmed plate, and serve it hot or at room temperature for 2 or 3 people.

OEUFS MAYONNAISE

HARD-BOILED EGGS WITH MAYONNAISE

serves 4

It can't just be coincidence that the world's two top salad dressings, mayonnaise and vinaigrette, are originally French. The French could not do without either one of them, and the country-wide popularity of Oeufs Mayonnaise as a cold first course is proof. Often the hard-boiled eggs are served plain, accompanied only by a few baguette slices and not even a lettuce leaf for contrast. You can, of course, add herbs to the mayonnaise, or a few sprigs of watercress on the side. I like to sieve a bit of egg yolk to scatter on top as "mimosa," an echo of the fluffy yellow flowers.

MAYONNAISE

2 EGG YOLKS

SALT AND WHITE PEPPER

1 TABLESPOON VINEGAR OR FRESH LEMON JUICE, MORE TO TASTE

1 TEASPOON DIJON MUSTARD, MORE TO TASTE

3/4 CUP/175 ML OLIVE OIL

8 HARD-BOILED EGGS

Make the mayonnaise (see page 374). Peel the eggs and halve them lengthwise. Arrange 3 halves, points inward, on each of 4 individual plates. Coat each half with a generous spoonful of mayonnaise. Separate the remaining egg yolks from the whites. Chop the whites and divide them evenly among the plates, piling them in the center of the coated eggs. Push the egg yolks through a strainer so the fluffy purée falls on top of the eggs, again dividing evenly. Serve within an hour or the surface of the mayonnaise will discolor.

QUICHE LORRAINE

serves 6 to 8

The word quiche *comes from the German* kuchen, *or "cake," and Quiche Lorraine is the mother of them all. The name gets appropriated by pretenders, but it truly belongs to only one dish: a flat, open tart filled with lardons cut from lean smoked bacon and a combination of crème fraîche and eggs (known in Lorraine as* migaine).

The recipe dates back to at least the sixteenth century. Originally Quiche Lorraine was made with bread dough, but today pie pastry is the norm, with puff pastry an occasional alternative. Few other variations are legitimate. Foreigners often add Gruyère cheese, but in France this version is authentic only in the area around Metz. Even then the Gruyère must be sliced into strips or diced, not grated. Chopped chives are found here and there in Lorraine, or sometimes some minced onion. Milk is widely scorned as a replacement for crème fraîche, though a little can be used to dilute the cream. Locals insist that crème fraîche must fall from the spoon, neither too thick nor too thin (see "Inimitable Crème Fraîche," page 320). To my mind, the best texture is achieved when the eggs play second fiddle to the cream.

I have a few more tips of my own: The pastry shell must first be baked blind (empty) so the custard filling does not make it soggy. The bacon should be the best, not too salty, and cut from the piece in true lardons, or strips, not dice. The lardons should be fried in butter (not on their own or in oil) until just starting to brown; if overdone, they will be hard. Finally, check the consistency of the crème fraîche. It is often too thick to pour, so it may need thinning with heavy cream.

PÂTE BRISÉE

1²/₃ CUPS/200 G FLOUR

I EGG YOLK

³/₄ TEASPOON SALT

3 TABLESPOONS/45 ML WATER, MORE IF NEEDED

6 TABLESPOONS/90 G BUTTER, MORE FOR THE PAN

FILLING

I TABLESPOON/15 G BUTTER

7-OUNCE/200-G PIECE LEAN SMOKED BACON, CUT INTO LARDONS (SEE PAGE 371)

2 EGGS

I CUP/250 ML CRÈME FRAÎCHE (PAGE 374), THINNED WITH HEAVY CREAM

SALT AND PEPPER

PINCH OF GRATED NUTMEG

9- TO 10-INCH/23- TO 25-CM TART PAN WITH REMOVABLE BASE (SEE PAGE 372)

Make the pâte brisée (see page 375) and chill it until firm, 15 to 30 minutes. Heat the oven to 375°F/190°C and set a baking sheet on a low shelf to heat. Roll out the dough and line the tart pan, then bake it blind (see page 372) on the hot baking sheet. Let the tart shell cool, and leave the baking sheet in the oven and the oven on.

For the filling, melt the butter in a small frying pan over medium heat, add the lardons, and sauté until lightly browned but still tender, 5 to 7 minutes. Lift them out with a draining spoon and spread them evenly in the tart shell. In a bowl, whisk together the eggs and crème fraîche, and season with salt, pepper, and nutmeg.

Set the tart shell in its pan on the hot baking sheet and pour the custard into the shell. Bake until the filling is set and golden brown, 30 to 35 minutes. Do not overcook it or the filling will curdle.

One authority maintains that the perfect quiche Lorraine should be eaten scalding hot while it is still puffed up. I prefer it warm or at room temperature, so the texture is soft and velvety. It can be baked ahead and reheated the following day but will always be best warm from the oven.

QUICHE AU ROQUEFORT ET AUX OIGNONS
ROQUEFORT AND CARAMELIZED ONION TART

Once a specialty of the remote, sunbaked mountains where Roquefort is made, this quiche has become a favorite throughout France.

Follow the recipe for Quiche Lorraine, blind baking the tart shell. Thinly slice 3 onions (about 1 pound/450 g). Melt 2 tablespoons/30 g goose fat or vegetable oil in a frying pan over low heat and stir in the onions. Press a piece of aluminum foil down on the onions, cover the pan, and sweat the onions over very low heat, stirring occasionally, until very soft, 20 to 25 minutes. Remove the lid and foil, increase the heat to medium, and cook, stirring often, until the onions brown, 6 to 8 minutes more. Stir in 4 ounces/110 g Roquefort cheese, crumbled, with 2 teaspoons chopped fresh thyme and plenty of pepper. Spread the onions in the prebaked tart shell and top with a custard made of 1 whole egg, 1 egg yolk, and 1 cup/250 ml heavy cream. Bake as for quiche Lorraine, but reduce the time to 20 to 25 minutes.

= NOBLE MOLD =

The rocky, windswept plateaus of central France are known as the Causses. According to legend, it was there, in a great limestone cave, that a shepherd boy mislaid his lunch of bread and white curd cheese. A few weeks later, hungry yet optimistic, he returned to collect it. His abandoned cheese had become lined with veins of blue-green mold: the first Roquefort!

Little is left to chance with Roquefort today. Technology has taken over and cheese curd from ewes' milk is injected with *Penicillium roquefortii*, a mold made from rye bread crumbs. The damp and drafty caves of the Causses are still used for the ripening process, however. The cheese must be made with milk from specified areas of southern France, including Corsica, where the rugged terrain makes the ewes' milk exceptionally fat and sweet. It was a favorite cheese of French rulers, and the name Roquefort has been protected since 1411, when Charles VI decreed that "bastard cheese

made in bastard caves" did not qualify. Roquefort was granted AOC status in 1979.

There are many other excellent French blue cheeses, sometimes called *persillé* because their stippled mold is suggestive of chopped parsley. Blue cheese melted with cream for pasta sauce, incorporated into salad dressing, or served in salads has become a popular standby. But for me, the best way to eat blue cheese is still just as it comes, with bread or fruit.

BLUE CHEESES AT A GLANCE

Bleu d'Auvergne: Dense cow's milk blue.
Bleu de Bresse: Burgundian cow's milk blue, widely commercialized.
Bleu des Causses: Foil-wrapped wheels of cow's milk blue.
Fourme d'Ambert or *Montbrison:* Cylindrical cow's milk blue.
Roquefort: Sheep's milk blue with a salty tang.

= BLOOMING CHEESES =

Generally speaking, blooming cheeses are made by salting fresh cheese and leaving it to develop a velvety, white rind. They represent a third of French production and include some of the most famous, notably Camembert and Brie. Unfortunately, the production of both these cheeses is driven by quantity rather than quality. Camembert is the better-known of the two, but not because it is superior. Camembert is now 90 percent industrialized and produced as far away as Japan and Argentina. These sterile, white disks are a far cry from the rare, old-style Camemberts still produced by a few traditionalists in Normandy. Unfortunately, the AOC Camembert de Normandie label is so loosely defined that it carries little guarantee of quality (see "AOC," page 111).

Tasteless, rubbery knockoffs of Brie abound, too, but two originals from southeast of Paris stand out for their excellence: Brie de Meaux and the slightly more rustic Brie de Melun. These cheeses have a short lifespan and must be eaten at just the right time: too young and they are chalky; overripe, they are runny and strong. In their perfect state, they bulge, rather than flow, and are creamy and pleasantly pungent in taste.

Other soft-bloom cheeses worth trying include small, creamy Saint-Marcellin from the Dauphiné; firmer but still creamy Chaource from Champagne; and Normandy's triple-cream Brillat-Savarin. Gratte-paille and Explorateur are other butterfat bonanzas. Even when carefully stored, these cheeses are at their peak for only a few days. Seek them out.

SOFT, BLOOMY-RIND CHEESES AT A GLANCE

All are made with cow's milk.
Brie de Meaux or *Brie de Melun:* Flat, creamy wheels.
Brillat-Savarin: Triple-cream Norman cheese, best eaten fresh.
Camembert de Normandie: The only AOC of the Camemberts.
Chaource: Squat tart drums with even more butterfat than Brie.
Coulommiers: Rustic, flat disks with Brie-like characteristics.
Explorateur: Cylindrical cheese with a soft, unpressed paste.
Pierre Robert: Simple-tasting, cream-enriched cow's milk cheese.
Saint-Félicien: Small, richly flavored disks from the Drôme.
Saint-Marcellin: Small, soft cheeses best eaten runny.

The smelliest cheeses in France all have something in common: ironically, they are washed. It is a trick that helps cheese last longer: they start out as fresh cheese made from cow's milk, then during ripening they are rubbed, rinsed, or immersed in brine, wine, or eau-de-vie. Washing young cheese inhibits the growth of bloom while encouraging bacteria, which is why these cheeses develop strong flavor and smell, as well as rinds that help preserve them. Some soft, washed-rind cheeses are also brushed or dry-salted, so that they acquire an attractive orange hue. All are potent, perfect endings to a country meal.

Normandy boasts two of these strong cheeses, which if left to ripen naturally would be much like Camembert. Brine-washed Livarot, which dates back to the thirteenth century, comes from Calvados and has five red bands encircling it like a corset. Livarot can be magical, especially served with apples or pears. But if it is too young, it will be chalky and tart, and if too old, it will smell positively rank. Square-shaped Pont-L'Évêque, packed in a wooden box, is higher in fat but much like Livarot and has a brushed, washed rind and slightly less barnyard aroma.

The stinkiest of the lot may well be Munster, named for its native village in Alsace. Reflecting its Germanic origins, this sharp cheese is served on seed-strewn dark bread. In fact, anise, caraway, cumin, or fennel seeds are often found in the cheese itself. Move down to Burgundy and the aromatic cheese of choice is Époisses, wrapped in an emblematic vine leaf and packed in a wooden box. Remember, if a boxed cheese is shrunken and rattling, you can be sure it is past its prime.

Another famous cheese, less stinky but no less tasty, is Vacherin from the Jura. There are several types, all of them delicious, with Mont d'Or the most famous. Vacherin is unusual, the best being made from winter milk, when cattle feed on hay and silage rather than grazing outdoors. The cheese is banded with a strip of spruce bark, which imparts a hint of pine, before going into its box. At its peak of ripeness, Vacherin is so runny you will need a spoon!

The cheese called Reblochon, made in Savoy, is also relatively mild. Centuries ago, landowners taxed local peasants by demanding a share of milk production. The farmers were no fools, however, and only half-milked their cows when the bailiffs came, which meant they paid less. Once the bailiffs were out of sight, the cows were milked a second time, *rebloché,* or "stripped," in the local language. In fact, that was the richest milk, ideal for this farmhouse cheese. With an herb and hazelnut flavor, Reblochon is quickly made and is a key ingredient in Tartiflette (page 60), a Dauphiné specialty.

WASHED-RIND CHEESES AT A GLANCE
All are made from cow's milk.

Époisses: Full-fat disks in a box, usually washed in Marc de Bourgogne.

Langres: Small, orange concave drums from Champagne with a big flavor and aroma.

Livarot: Small, orange barrels from Normandy packed in a wooden box; very strong taste and smell.

Maroilles: Boxed cheese from Picardy, Flanders, and Artois, with an inedible gritty rind.

Munster: Very pungent Alsatian disks with russet-colored rind.

Pont-L'Évêque: Rich, soft squares in wooden boxes from Normandy.

Reblochon: Soft cheese from Savoy with a toasted flavor; packaged between wooden disks.

Saint-Florentin: Soft, creamy, rich flat drums from northern Burgundy; aged in a box.

Soumaintrain: Yellowish double-cream disks, also from Burgundy, eaten fresh and also aged and quite strong.

Vacherin: Variously sized round washed-rind cheeses, banded with a strip of bark, in wooden boxes from the Franche-Comté; runny when ripe.

PIPÉRADE BASQUAISE

PEPPER AND TOMATO PURÉE WITH EGGS

serves 4

Pipérade is a mainstay of the Basque country, a delectable purée of peppers and scrambled egg with a bit of tomato thrown in. The favorite pepper is the rust red Espelette, a mild chili with a touch of sweetness. Here, I am suggesting a combination of red bell peppers and dried ground Espelette pepper (paprika with a pinch of cayenne pepper is a good substitute). I have come across the dish in several guises, including a rolled omelet filled with peppers and tomatoes, a flat omelet, and this vegetable purée thickened with eggs, my top choice. The vegetables must be cooked until they are quite dry, holding the trail of the spoon.

2 TABLESPOONS OLIVE OIL

I ONION, CHOPPED

I¹/₂ TEASPOONS GROUND DRIED ESPELETTE PEPPER, OR I¹/₂ TEASPOONS PAPRIKA AND A LARGE PINCH OF CAYENNE

I GARLIC CLOVE, CHOPPED

SALT

2 BELL PEPPERS (I RED, I GREEN), CORED, SEEDED, AND CHOPPED (SEE PAGE 370)

I POUND/450 G TOMATOES, PEELED, SEEDED, AND CHOPPED (SEE PAGE 372)

FRIED CROÛTES MADE WITH 4 SLICES COUNTRY BREAD, FRIED IN 2 TABLESPOONS OLIVE OIL AND I TABLESPOON/15 G BUTTER (SEE PAGE 374)

5 EGGS

Heat the oil in a deep frying pan over low heat. Add the onion and cook, stirring often, until soft but not brown, 3 to 5 minutes. Stir in the Espelette pepper, garlic, and salt and continue cooking, stirring, until fragrant, about 1 minute. Stir in the bell peppers and tomatoes and continue cooking over quite low heat, stirring often, until the vegetables soften and reduce to a thick purée, 25 to 30 minutes. Taste and adjust the seasoning. The purée can be prepared 1 or 2 days ahead and stored in the refrigerator.

To finish, make the croûtes. If necessary, reheat the vegetable purée in the frying pan. In a bowl, whisk the eggs until blended with salt. Stir the eggs into the warm vegetable purée and cook over very low heat like scrambled eggs, stirring constantly so the eggs thicken evenly, forming small curds—the mixture should remain moist and lightly thickened—5 to 7 minutes. Do not let the pipérade get too hot or it will separate and be watery. Taste and adjust the seasoning. Set the croûtes on warmed plates, spoon the pipérade on top, and serve at once.

GOUGÈRES

CHEESE PUFFS

makes about thirty 2¹/₂-inch/6-cm puffs

Burgundians relish a little snack with a glass of wine, and many variations on these choux puffs flavored with cheese are sold in local pastry shops. Gougères sometimes come stuffed with goat cheese or a creamy filling, and in one inventive version, Gougère Plate au Fromage de Chèvre, the dough is spread flat and topped like pizza with sliced tomato and herbs.

PÂTE À CHOUX

I CUP/250 ML WATER

³/₄ TEASPOON SALT

¹/₂ CUP/110 G BUTTER, CUT INTO CUBES

I CUP/125 G FLOUR

4 TO 5 EGGS

4 OUNCES/110 G GRUYÈRE CHEESE

I EGG, BEATEN TO MIX WITH ¹/₂ TEASPOON SALT, FOR GLAZE

2 TO 3 TABLESPOONS GRATED GRUYÈRE CHEESE

Heat the oven to 400°F/200°C and lightly butter a baking sheet. Make the pâte à choux (see page 374). Cut the Gruyère cheese in tiny dice, or coarsely grate it, and beat it into the dough. Transfer the dough to a pastry bag fitted with a ½-inch/1.25-cm plain tip and pipe 1½-inch/4-cm mounds on the baking sheet, spacing them well apart as they will puff during baking. Alternatively, drop mounds of dough on the baking sheet using 2 small spoons. Brush the mounds with the egg glaze and sprinkle with grated Gruyère.

Bake the puffs until golden brown and crisp, 25 to 30 minutes. The puffs often seem done too soon, so take out a puff and let it cool for a minute or two to check if it is ready before removing the rest. The puff should stay crisp on the outside and slightly soft inside. Gougères are at their best warm from the oven, but they can be baked ahead, or stored in the freezer, and reheated in a low oven.

GOUGÈRE PLATE AU FROMAGE DE CHÈVRE
FLAT GOAT CHEESE GOUGÈRE

When cheese pâte à choux is spread flat, it invites the same toppings as pizza, a perfect light supper dish with a green salad.

Heat the oven to 375°F/190°C and butter a baking sheet. Make the pâte à choux (see page 374) and mix in the Gruyère cheese as for Gougères. Using the back of a spoon, spread the dough in a 10-inch/25-cm round on the baking sheet. Sprinkle the dough with 1 tablespoon chopped mixed fresh herbs such as thyme, rosemary, and parsley and 1 garlic clove, chopped. Top the herbs evenly with 6 thick slices (5 ounces/140 g total) goat cheese (about three-fourths of a log). Brush the cheese rounds with olive oil. Bake the gougère until the dough is crusty and brown and the goat cheese is toasted, 45 to 50 minutes. The gougère will puff, then deflate slightly as it cools. Serve warm, cut into wedges for 6.

SOUFFLÉ AU FROMAGE DE FRANÇOISE

FRANÇOISE'S CHEESE SOUFFLÉ

serves 5 or 6

A plain cheese soufflé like this one from Françoise Samson is a country standby. Françoise is Norman and a born cook; her sole meunière *tastes triumphantly buttery, with that golden sheen that professionals strive to achieve, while her* coquilles Saint-Jacques parisienne *is unfailingly fragrant and tender. This cheese soufflé is also infallible, rising to a rich, fluffy tower every time. Rush it to the table and break into it at once, using two spoons to get the crisp outside and soft, saucelike center onto warm plates.*

5 TABLESPOONS/75 G BUTTER, MORE FOR THE
SOUFFLÉ DISH

$^1/_4$ CUP/30 G FLOUR

1$^1/_2$ CUPS/375 ML MILK

SALT AND PEPPER

GRATED NUTMEG

5 EGGS, SEPARATED

1$^1/_2$ CUPS/150 G GRATED GRUYÈRE CHEESE

3 EGG WHITES

2-QUART/2-LITER SOUFFLÉ DISH (SEE PAGE 377)

To make a béchamel sauce, melt the butter in a saucepan over medium heat, whisk in the flour, and cook until foaming. Add the milk and bring to a boil, whisking constantly until the sauce thickens. Season with salt, pepper, and nutmeg and simmer for 1 minute.

Take the pan from the heat and whisk the egg yolks into the hot sauce so that they cook and thicken slightly. Stir in the cheese, reserving a tablespoonful for topping. Taste and adjust the seasoning. The mixture should be highly seasoned to compensate for the bland egg whites. Press a piece of plastic wrap directly onto the surface of the sauce to prevent a skin from forming. It may be prepared up to 5 hours ahead and kept at room temperature.

To finish, position a shelf in the lower third of the oven and remove the shelves above. Heat the oven to 425°F/220°C. Thickly butter the soufflé dish, particularly around the rim. Reheat the cheese mixture until hot to the touch but do not let it boil, or it will cook into strings. Whisk the egg whites until stiff using a stand mixer and adding a pinch of salt to help the whites stiffen. Add about one-fourth of the egg whites to the hot cheese mixture and stir them together thoroughly. This lightens the mixture and makes it easier to fold. Add this mixture to the remaining egg whites and fold them together as lightly as possible. Spoon the mixture into the prepared dish; it should fill almost to the rim. Sprinkle the reserved cheese on top, and then run your thumb around the inside rim of the dish so the soufflé rises evenly.

Bake the soufflé until puffed and brown, 20 to 25 minutes. If you like the center soft (as I do), remove the soufflé when it still wobbles slightly if gently shaken. If you prefer it firm, leave it for another 3 to 5 minutes. Set the dish on a plate lined with a napkin, so the dish cannot slip. Take the soufflé to the table at once.

CAMEMBERT FONDUE EN BOÎTE

MELTED CAMEMBERT IN A BOX

serves 3 or 4

This rustic recipe for whole Camembert, baked in its wood-chip box, is perfect for country weekends. The melted cheese forms a quick fondue in which to dip slices of bread or sticks of celery and carrot—or, perhaps best of all, crescents of crisp, tart apple that marry well with the Calvados sprinkled on the cheese. Here, I bake the Camembert in the oven, but you can also cook it in the fireplace: wrap the box tightly in aluminum foil, push it into the hot embers, and leave it until it is quite runny. Eat it beside the fire.

ONE 9-OUNCE/250-G CAMEMBERT CHEESE

2 TABLESPOONS CALVADOS OR WHITE WINE

COUNTRY BREAD SLICES

Heat the oven to 400°F/200°C. Remove the Camembert from its box, discard the wrapping, and return the cheese to the box. Prick the cheese with a fork, then sprinkle with the Calvados, letting it trickle into the holes. Put the lid back on the box. Bake the cheese until it feels soft and melting when you press it with a finger, 12 to 15 minutes.

Remove the box to a plate, surround it with bread slices, and take off the lid. Let everyone dip in.

= PORTRAIT OF A CHEESE AFFINEUR =

As one who eats cheese every day for lunch (our platter always has three or four choices), I make it my business to know my cheesemonger well. At my local market, it is Pascal LeRoux, who is in business with his father and has an impressive stand. He is one of a select band of *affineurs* who buy cheese directly from artisanal producers, age it to just the right stage, and then take it to market.

As I wait in line behind the locals with their produce-laden baskets, I run my eyes over his offerings: heavy wedges of Comté, several blues, small rounds of Basque sheep's milk cheese, buttons of goat cheese—what to choose? I can be sure that if a cheese isn't quite ripe, Monsieur LeRoux won't let me have it. "You want a Brie that will be ready for lunch?" he has been known to ask. "Yes, you can buy it now, but it will be ready only in a couple of days. Can I recommend something else?" Neither will he let me buy a cheese out of season. "It's not the time for Mont d'Or," he says. "Wait until late autumn." He considers educating his clientele an important part of his job. In other words, he is not just there to sell. This, and the quality of the cheese, is what sets an *affineur* apart from an average grocery counter.

Monsieur LeRoux sells only raw milk cheeses and has no use for pasteurized industrial products. "Pasteurized cheese is dead," he says, frankly. "Cheese made of raw milk is a living thing. Each one is different and evolves over time. That's what makes cheese so interesting." Industrial cheeses far outnumber France's artisanal production, but fine cheese is still in high demand. "My clients are people who like to eat," says Monsieur LeRoux. "They come to me because they want something superior to what's at the grocery store." On his counter, for example, I often find Soumaintrain, our local washed-rind cheese. He collects it from producers when it is about eight days old, and brings it to maturity in his own *caves* by turning the rounds regularly and washing the rinds so they develop their characteristic orange hue, soft and slippery.

"How should I store this?" a client with a foreign accent asks. "Don't store it; eat it!" Monsieur LeRoux jokes, and then: "Well, if you *must* store it, just don't wrap in plastic; that's the worst. Keep it wrapped in its paper so it can breathe. In the refrigerator, it stops aging. You won't ruin it, but after a few days it will be stifled." I typically buy cheeses only a few days ahead, but not because I worry about storage. I just want an excuse to come back for more.

THE PERFECT CHEESE PLATTER

Say "cheese" and a Frenchman thinks at once of table cheeses, the unending variety of cow's, goat's, and sheep's milk cheeses that perfume the markets of France. "Some people say there are 365 French cheeses, one for every day of the year!" I brightly remarked to one of our local cheese vendors, Gilbert Parret. He looked shocked. "There are many more than that," he protested. And surveying the seasonal parade in the weekly market of our small town, he is right. Midday lunch, still a leisurely fixture in country areas, often ends with cheese and fruit rather than dessert, and no celebration, least of all a Sunday lunch, would be without a cheese platter.

In France, cheese is served between the main course and dessert, sometimes following green salad, and always with a generous basket of bread. Choose a wooden or marble board for serving (not metal or plastic, which affects taste). You can also use flat basket trays, but always line them with doilies, paper napkins, or, best of all, vine leaves. In fact, almost any garden leaf that is flat, nontoxic, and not bitter is a pleasing substitute.

At home, the ideal cheese board has three or four large pieces of different cheeses of contrasting texture and taste. France follows the rule of three: cheeses that are soft and velvety (chèvres, Saint-Nectaire, or Tommes, for example); cheeses that are aromatic, ranging from Cantal to Camembert; and strong cheeses (blue and sheep cheeses, for instance, or smelly Époisses). With their contrasting textures, one from each category suffices. It is also fun, for the sake of comparison, to serve a variety of the same cheese type, such as different chèvres at varying stages of ripeness. Nor is there any shame in serving just one single cheese at its peak; a Brie or a Mont d'Or can be perfect alone. Yet another

alternative, typical of Burgundy, is a bowl of fresh cow's or goat's milk cheese, scarcely a day old, served with sugar, or with chopped herbs and garlic. When choosing any of them, remember that the use of raw rather than pasteurized milk makes all the difference between a fine, artisanal product and a bland stereotype.

Space your cheeses well apart on a serving board so their flavors do not mingle, and make sure that they are at room temperature. There is no rule on amounts, but I find 3 ounces/90 grams per person about right. The board gets passed around the table and diners serve themselves, cutting off a piece of cheese so as to preserve its original shape. A wedge-shaped cheese should be cut in slim wedges so that each piece includes some rind or, in the case of blue cheeses, a section of both the ripe, veined center and the firmer outside. Small, round or square cheeses are cut in wedges like a cake; a rolled cheese is sliced like a loaf. These rules ensure that everyone gets a bit of the best. I still have trouble stopping my son from cutting off the "nose" of a wedge of Brie when he thinks no one is looking.

A mouthful of Roquefort eaten first will stun the palate for anything that comes afterward, so cheeses are tasted in order of mildest to strongest. As for the rinds, it is a matter of taste. Once it was correct to trim and discard them, but not so now, as cheese is expensive. I suggest that you serve cheese with its rind so that guests can decide for themselves. I am partial to the outsides of fresh or mild cheeses, including goat's milk cheeses. Aged or washed-rind cheeses can be more of a challenge, and I will grant that the rind on hard cheese is virtually inedible. However, the cheese man at our local market insists that his sister will eat nothing but!

= JUST PLAIN CHEESE =

Nothing accompanies a carafe of country wine better than a wooden board of *saucisson*, cornichons, and cubes of a simple cheese of the pressed, uncooked type (uncooked in the sense that the curds are not heated). There are endless variations of these semihard, cake-shaped loaves with rustic rinds, almost all quite mild and milky tasting and many originally made by monks. One of the most ancient of these cheeses is Saint-Nectaire, from the highest part of the Massif Central and made from the summer and autumn milk of cows that have grazed on mountain pastures.

Perhaps the most impressive-looking cheese in this plain family is Morbier from the Jura. Originally, half the curds came from the morning milk and the other half from the evening milk, with the two separated by a layer of ash. It was Gruyère cheesemakers who invented this softer, brine-washed cheese, using ash to stop the first lot of curds from drying out before the next batch of milk. Today, virtually all Morbier is from a single daily milking and the ash is synthetic, but it is still a fine cheese, perfect for picnics.

Little sisters in this family include Tommes, often made from milk coming from more than one herd. Tomme de Savoie is perhaps the best known, made mostly with skim milk. A lot of it comes from outside the region and is simply aged in Savoy, so watch for *fabriqué en Savoie* on the label for the genuine article.

MILD CHEESES AT A GLANCE

Abondance: Buttery, nut-tasting rounds of cow's milk cheese from Savoy.

Mimolette: Bright orange rounds of cow's milk cheese from Flanders and Normandy, quite hard and best when thoroughly aged.

Morbier: Mild, ivory cow's milk cheese from the Franche-Comté, with a sandwichlike central layer of ash.

Ossau-Iraty: Firm sheep's milk cheese with nutty-fruity taste, from the Basque region of the Pyrenees.

Saint-Nectaire: Earthy-tasting rounds of cow's milk cheese from the Auvergne.

Tomme de Savoie: Disks or barrels of cow's milk cheese with fuzzy, fawn-colored rind.

FONDUE SAVOYARDE

CHEESE FONDUE

serves 4

Classic fondue comes from the foothills and higher mountains of the Jura and Savoy, cheese country where cows flourish and the brisk air gives just the right nip to a ripening cheese. Fondue can be made with a combination of cheeses, such as piquant Tomme de Savoie and meltingly rich Vacherin, or simply with Gruyère, as here. It is usually prepared in a shallow earthenware saucepan called a caquelon, or in an enameled cast-iron fondue pot. The mixture must be heated gently but steadily, and stirred in a figure eight, the superstitious say, so that the cheese melts in the wine without cooking into strings. (Alcohol lowers the boiling point of the fondue, making strings less likely.) If a man drops any of his bread into the fondue, he must buy the party a bottle of wine; the penalty for women is a kiss all around.

I UNPEELED GARLIC CLOVE, HALVED

I TABLESPOON/15 G BUTTER, SOFTENED

I CUP/250 ML DRY WHITE WINE

I POUND/450 G GRUYÈRE CHEESE, CUT INTO THIN STRIPS

SALT AND PEPPER

3 TABLESPOONS/45 ML KIRSCH

I BAGUETTE OR LOAF COUNTRY BREAD, CUT INTO SMALL CHUNKS

CAQUELON OR FONDUE POT, 4 LONG FONDUE FORKS

Rub the inside of the *caquelon* or fondue pot with the cut garlic clove, then spread the pot with the butter. Add the wine and bring to a boil over very low heat. Stir in the cheese, handful by handful, stirring constantly with a wooden spoon in a figure eight, until the cheese is completely melted. Add pepper and the kirsch, taste, and season with salt if needed. It is important not to pause in the melting process, or the fondue may form strings.

Transfer the pot to a burner in the middle of the table and let guests help themselves, spearing pieces of bread on the forks and dipping them in the fondue.

FONDUE FRANCHE-COMTOISE

This version of fondue, fortified with eggs, is lighter than plain cheese fondue and is served in the same style.

Beat 4 eggs with a whisk until frothy and stir in 4 tablespoons/ 60 g butter, cut into small dice. Stir the eggs into the prepared fondue and heat gently, stirring constantly, until the fondue thickens, 2 to 3 minutes. Serves 4.

RACLETTE

A recipe for the ski-resort favorite, Raclette, scarcely exists, as the dish consists simply of melted cheese served with boiled potatoes, usually in their skins; cornichons; pickled onions; and sometimes wafer-thin slices of smoked ham. The cheese itself, usually referred to simply as *fromage à raclette*, is mild, creamy, and melts easily. Morbier, a cheese with a characteristic streak of gray ash in the center, is a good substitute, and 5 ounces/140 grams is a generous portion. Various devices exist for melting the cheese, or a hunk can be set beside an open fire until it melts sufficiently to scrape in creamy layers. Even easier is to line heatproof plates with slices of cheese (rind removed) and heat the plates in a 450°F/230°C oven for a few minutes until melted. The accompanying potatoes and cornichons are passed separately.

CROQUE MONSIEUR

serves 4

If anything could claim to be the hamburger of France, it is the Croque Monsieur, the ham and cheese sandwich found in bistros and roadside cafés from Calais to Marseille. As with all simple recipes, a Croque Monsieur is only as good as the ingredients that go into it. If you use slices of Comté (a type of Gruyère) or creamy Morbier, you will be tasting the real France. For Croque Madame, a more substantial snack, perch an egg fried in butter on top of Monsieur's sandwich.

2 TABLESPOONS/30 G BUTTER

2 SLICES WHITE BREAD (NOT BAGUETTE)

2 SLICES GRUYÈRE CHEESE

I SLICE HIGH-QUALITY COOKED HAM

Heat the oven to 400°F/200°C. Melt the butter in a small saucepan over low heat. Brush both sides of each bread slice with the butter. Lay 1 slice of cheese on each piece of bread. Top the cheese on 1 slice with the ham. Clap the sandwich together, press it firmly, and set it on a baking sheet.

Bake, turning once at the midway point, until crisp and brown, 8 to 10 minutes. Alternatively, toast the sandwich in a sandwich grill. Be sure to eat while hot.

The largest French cheeses come from the Alps and the Massif Central. They are colossal hard and semihard rounds that age well—essential for isolated mountain life—and melt well, making them ideal for cooking. Best known is Gruyère, whose family also includes Comté, Beaufort, and Emmental. In the old days, cheeses were taxed by number rather than weight, so producers made the wheels as large as possible. These Gruyères are ubiquitous in alpine soups, fondues, gratins, and omelets. There is even a *salade de Gruyère* that features matchsticks of the cheese tossed with walnuts, lettuce, tarragon, and walnut oil dressing.

Emmental is the everyday version of Gruyère, a supersized champion, weighing up to two hundred twenty pounds (one hundred kilograms). Straw colored with walnut-sized holes, its picture-book appearance makes it the most recognizable of hard cheeses. The best, Emmental Français Grand Cru, is made from partially skimmed raw cow's milk. Young, it belongs in fondue; middle-aged, it can also make its way into a sandwich; and extra-aged, it is finally sharp enough to add character to gratins and soups. Comté, weighing in at eighty pounds (thirty-six kilograms), is one up on the quality scale. As it ages from four to thirty-six months, its taste progresses from herbaceous to fruity to nutty to almost toffeelike. My lunchtime cheese platter is rarely without some Comté, and I always have some on hand for savory tarts, gratins, and onion soup (page 20). Even better is Beaufort, so famous for its longevity that during the French Revolution the Committee of Public Safety ordered one thousand tons of it to feed Paris—that's about twenty-five thousand wheels!

It always surprises me that these cheeses, so plain to the eye, have a high fat content averaging 44 percent. Of course, for quality, you need the AOC versions (page 111). Industrial knockoffs of these famous names bear no comparison. The AOC Beaufort d'Alpage, for example, must be made from raw summer milk from a single herd of cows that graze in mountain pastures above 4,500 feet (1,500 meters). Another famous AOC, Gruyère de Comté,

is made exclusively from the raw milk of the Montbéliard breed, cows with distinctive red and white patches and lugubrious fat faces. They must be fed on mountain herbs and grasses. Winter milk, even from the very same cows, doesn't pass muster; neither does lowland milk. Cow bells are not merely decorative, but make it easier to find straying animals. The lead cow of a herd sports the biggest bell, earned in at least one valley by engaging her rivals in a display of horned combat.

In the Massif Central, the texture of the biggest wheels is more crumbly than their alpine cousins because the cheese curds are not heated before they are pressed. Of these, Cantal, one of the oldest cheeses in France, is the best known and most widely commercialized. Even the AOC variety can be unreliable because it may be made with pasteurized milk. A better bet is to buy Salers, which has the same semifirm, slightly sour characteristics and comes from the raw summer milk of Salers cattle, which consume gentian, violet, fennel, and thyme in the herbage. Lesser-known Laguiole is similar to Cantal and Salers but has been aged longer, which makes it firmer and sharper. Rarely found outside its own region, Laguiole is used just like Cantal and Salers to make Aligot (page 225) of puréed potatoes and cheese, as well as to enrich potato gratins and omelets.

BIG CHEESES AT A GLANCE
All are made with cow's milk.

Beaufort: Smooth, beige rounds from Savoy, with layered, fruity flavor.

Cantal: Tall drums of cheese from the Auvergne, with a sourish, buttery taste.

Comté: Fruity, toffee-flavored cheese from the Franche-Comté.

Emmental Français Grand Cru: Buttery, nutty, fruity cheese with holes.

Laguiole: Fat barrels of complex-tasting cheese from the Auvergne.

SALADE DE FROMAGE DE CHÈVRE MARINÉ

MARINATED GOAT CHEESE SALAD

serves 4

The country habit of marinating little goat cheeses in herbs and oil (olive oil along the Mediterranean or nut oil where walnuts do well) has recently gone global. It is hard to resist when the cheese is toasted to a bubbling brown, then served on a salad dressed with the oil from the marinade. Tart salad greens such as arugula stand up best to its lively taste.

6 OUNCES/170 G ARUGULA OR OTHER TART SALAD
GREENS

MARINATED GOAT CHEESES (RECIPE FOLLOWS)

8 SLICES WHOLE-WHEAT BREAD

OIL FROM MARINATING THE CHEESE, FOR BRUSHING

VINAIGRETTE

2 TABLESPOONS RED WINE VINEGAR

SALT AND PEPPER

6 TABLESPOONS/90 ML OIL FROM MARINATING

Wash and dry the salad greens, discarding any wilted leaves. Slice each cheese in half horizontally. Using a 2- to 3-inch/5- to 7-cm round cookie cutter, stamp a round from each bread slice slightly larger than the rounds of cheese. Brush the bread rounds with the oil, and set a round of cheese, cut side down, on top.

For the vinaigrette, whisk together the vinegar, salt, and pepper in a small bowl until the salt dissolves. Gradually add the oil, whisking constantly so the dressing emulsifies and thickens slightly. Taste and adjust the seasoning. The greens, cheese, and dressing may be prepared an hour or two ahead.

To finish, heat the broiler. Arrange the cheeses on a baking sheet and broil them about 3 inches/7.5 cm from the heat until bubbling and browned, 5 to 7 minutes. Meanwhile, toss the greens with the vinaigrette, then taste a leaf and adjust the seasoning. Pile the greens on 4 plates. Set 2 rounds of cheese on each plate and serve while still warm.

FROMAGES DE CHÈVRE MARINÉ

MARINATED GOAT CHEESES

Marinating adds depth of flavor to goat cheeses, which are delicious in any recipe calling for goat cheese or served on their own with country bread. Small goat cheeses are best for marinating, and they should be firm. Leftover olive oil is great for grilling.

Put 4 small round goat cheeses (about 2½ ounces/75 g each) in a 1 quart/1 liter jar with a lid. Add 3 dried bay leaves, 2 teaspoons peppercorns, 3 sprigs fresh thyme, 3 or 4 tiny dried chiles, and 1½ cups/375 ml olive or walnut oil, or enough to cover the cheeses generously. Cover with the lid and leave in a cool place for at least 2 weeks before using. The cheeses are good for 3 to 4 weeks, but will soften if kept too long. As you use them, more cheeses may be added to the oil. Makes 4 cheeses to serve 4, with salad.

TARTIFLETTE

POTATO AND REBLOCHON CHEESE MELT

serves 6 to 8

Here is another of the mountain cheese dishes that have become part of the ski culture and the French winter vacation. All you need is a sauté pan, potatoes, a bit of bacon, and the right kind of cheese, preferably Reblochon with its nutty, soft-paste interior, though Vacherin or Morbier may be used in its absence. You should use waxy potatoes that won't crumble during frying. For best effect, serve Tartiflette with a generous salad of bitter greens.

2 TABLESPOONS VEGETABLE OIL

6-OUNCE/170-G PIECE LEAN SMOKED BACON, CUT
INTO LARDONS (SEE PAGE 371)

2 ONIONS, SLICED

2 TABLESPOONS/30 G BUTTER

6 TO 8 WAXY POTATOES (ABOUT 3 POUNDS/1.35 KG
TOTAL), PEELED AND CUT INTO 1-INCH/2.5-CM CHUNKS

1 POUND/450 G REBLOCHON CHEESE

Heat 1 tablespoon of the oil in a sauté pan or deep frying pan over medium heat. Add the lardons and fry until lightly browned, 3 to 5 minutes. Lift them out with a draining spoon and set aside. Add the onions and fry over medium heat until lightly browned, 5 to 7 minutes.

Add the remaining 1 tablespoon oil and the butter to the pan and heat until a piece of potato sizzles when added. Stir in the remaining potatoes and spread them in an even layer. Cover the pan with a large lid and cook over medium heat, stirring occasionally, until tender and browned, 20 to 25 minutes. For the last 10 minutes of cooking, remove the pan lid so the potatoes become crisp. Meanwhile, trim away the rind and then thinly slice the cheese.

When the potatoes are done, stir in the lardons. Cover the mixture with the cheese slices and continue cooking over medium heat, without stirring, until the cheese has melted, 5 to 7 minutes. Turn the heat to high and give a quick hot burst to the pan for 1 minute. Serve at once.

SALADE DE FROMAGE DE CHÈVRE MARINÉ

= CAPRICIOUS GOATS =

The French call a goat a poor man's cow because it needs no more than roadside herbage to survive. The variety of goat cheeses, or chèvres, seems endless—a small miracle considering that they all are made in more or less the same way. Chèvres share a unique and invaluable quality, which distinguishes them from cow's milk cheeses: they can be enjoyed at every stage of their development. The goat cheeses you find on Provençal stands are a good example: tiny potent picodons and pelardons; logs cloaked in gray ash; anonymous disks tossed in dried wild herbs or perhaps a spice. To me, the hardening that comes with age is a plus: the cheese becomes drier, firmer, and more piquant, until at about three months it crumbles at the touch of a knife.

For better or worse, chèvre has become a mass-market item in a tight, transparent wrapper. More than 80 percent of production is industrial: dry, chalky, and monotonous. Superior artisanal production comes from farmsteads with a few dozen goats, and by far the most gambol in Poitou and Charentes, running down from the Loire. Local markets are the place to find good goat cheese, or if you venture along quiet country roads, you may spot a hand-painted sign that bleats *Fromages de Chèvre* and sometimes other goodies, too, such as rabbits.

Goat meat is another story. *Chevreau,* or "kid," does well in stews, although the female is palatable longer than the male. It is a springtime dish, and in the Poitou it is cooked with green garlic for traditional May Day repasts. In Corsica, where the goat is particularly suited to the terrain, roasted *chevreau* is enjoyed with garlic bread to mop up the drippings.

Goat Cheeses at a Glance

Chabichou: A small, cylindrical cheese that acquires a beige rind as it ages.

Crottin de Chavignol: Small barrels, made in the Berry.

Picodon: Thick disks, sometimes soaked in spirits, from the Dauphiné.

Pouligny Saint-Pierre: Tall, white pyramids from the Berry that develop a blue exterior with age.

Rocamadour: Tiny buttons from Quercy; best aged for a few weeks, when they turn chewy and brown.

Saint-Maure: Log-shaped with a straw running through the middle and a blue exterior; from Touraine, Berry, and Poitou.

Selles-dur-Cher: Slightly conical disks, powdered with charcoal, from the Loire Valley.

A GREAT CATCH

FISH & SHELLFISH

CHAPTER
No. 4

A glance at the map explains why the French are such lovers of fish. Three sides of *l'héxagone*, as France is habitually called, border three very different waters. In the south, the warm waters and shallow depths of the Mediterranean welcome the likes of swordfish, tuna, conger eel, and smaller spiny fish like *rascasse* (scorpion fish). On the French Riviera near Italy, the coastline is rocky, while at the other end in Languedoc, vast sandy beaches overlook shallow lagoons. In these still waters, plump mussels grow outsize, just right for stuffing or soup. You also find squid and a wide range of clams, such as *palourdes* and the little *clovisses* that are so good with rice and pasta, or simmered with garlic, herbs, and white wine.

To the west of France, the chilly waters of the Atlantic stretch all the way to the New World, once a hunting ground for whales and for cod (now so sadly depleted) and its cousins, haddock and hake. Nearer home, boats from Basque and Breton ports venture as far as Senegal in search of anchovies, sardines, mackerel, and red mullet. The rocky promontory of Brittany is slashed with great estuaries like Brest, home of the French navy, while Brittany's smaller inlets are famous for shellfish, particularly the costly lobsters that resurface at Rungis, the wholesale market outside Paris.

Rounding the bend of Brittany, you reach a third marine world, the English Channel. The waters are shallow again, but a very different temperature from the Mediterranean. Here, I think of Dover sole, turbot, scallops, gray shrimp, and tiny piquant mussels raised on ropes (*bouchots*) washed clean by the tide.

France is also a land of rivers that twine from the mountains and lace the plains. Freshwater fishing is carefully controlled, but during the short open seasons you will find every lakefront and riverbank lined with avid fishermen, to a man eager to win the prize for the biggest fish. Commercially, of course, as in all developed countries, fish farming has revolutionized both supplies and prices of a few major species. Farmed fish come standardized in convenient sizes, looking far more appetizing than they taste.

No matter the region, the recipes remain timeless, endowing even a farmed fish with a strong sense of place. The *meunière* treatment of dusting with flour and then sautéing in butter is still top choice for small whole fish and white fish fillets. Salmon gets robust treatment with horseradish and bacon in Alsace (salmon were once plentiful in the Rhine River), and bathed in *sauce meurette* (red wine sauce) in Burgundy. Mackerel are marinated in vinegar in the north, and red mullet is served with a tomato vinaigrette in the south. Both inland and on the sea you will find *friture*, tiny fish that are deep-fried to serve in a savory, crisp mound with a wedge of lemon.

Shellfish for most of France is a luxury set aside for anniversaries and fêtes (see "Food Fêtes and Festivals," page 232). Country cooks favor a simple approach, doing little more than steaming mussels *à la marinière* (with white wine) or simmering crayfish *à la nage* (in court bouillon). The French love to get in there, hands-on, gulping down oysters and their juice from the half shell. The habit starts young. I had thought our children would shudder at the idea of prizing cooked mussels from their shell, but not at all. The fun of extracting them, using a discarded shell as pincers and chunks of bread to soak up the juices, has proved addictive.

BAUDROIE RÔTIE AU BEURRE DE MONTPELLIER

ROAST MONKFISH WITH HERB BUTTER

serves 6

Baudroie *is the Provençal name for monkfish, known elsewhere as* lotte, *a firm-fleshed white fish with no lateral bones and a primitive spinal column that yields generous fillets of solid meat. It also has a curious double skin, so be sure your supplier trims it thoroughly. Cod is an excellent alternative to monkfish. Montpellier butter is a classic accompaniment to roast fish, a cross between herb butter and an herb mayonnaise and better than either, in my opinion. Olive oil prevents the butter from setting, so it stays light, creamy, and deliciously piquant with cornichons and fresh herbs. Grilled vegetables are the best accompaniment.*

2 POUNDS/900 G MONKFISH FILLETS, TRIMMED

2 TABLESPOONS OLIVE OIL

SALT AND PEPPER

1 BUNCH FRESH THYME (ABOUT 1 OUNCE/30 G)

1 BUNCH FRESH OREGANO OR MARJORAM
(ABOUT 1 OUNCE/30 G)

SALAD GREENS, FOR SERVING

MONTPELLIER BUTTER

1 BUNCH WATERCRESS (ABOUT 2 OUNCES/60 G)

1 HANDFUL OF SPINACH LEAVES (ABOUT 1 OUNCE/30 G)

1 BUNCH FRESH PARSLEY (ABOUT 2 OUNCES/60 G)

1 BUNCH FRESH CHERVIL (ABOUT 1 OUNCE/30 G),
OPTIONAL

4 ANCHOVY FILLETS, SOAKED IN WATER OR MILK
FOR A FEW MINUTES

2 CORNICHONS

1 TABLESPOON CAPERS, RINSED AND DRAINED

1 GARLIC CLOVE, CUT INTO PIECES

3/4 CUP/170 G BUTTER, SOFTENED

1/2 CUP/125 ML OLIVE OIL

2 TEASPOONS DIJON MUSTARD

SQUEEZE OF FRESH LEMON JUICE

Wash the fish fillets and dry well. Brush them with the olive oil and sprinkle with salt and pepper. Spread the thyme and oregano in a baking dish and set the fillets on top, burying them in the herbs. Cover and leave to marinate in the refrigerator for at least 1 hour and up to 4 hours.

For the Montpellier butter, discard the stems from the watercress and spinach, and the large stalks from the parsley and chervil. Bring a saucepan of water to a boil, add the greens and herbs, and blanch for 1 minute. Drain, rinse with cold water, and squeeze dry in a cloth. Drain the anchovies, put them in a food processor with the cornichons, capers, and garlic, and pulse until finely chopped. Add the butter gradually, pulsing until the mixture is smooth. Add the greens and process until finely chopped. With the blades turning, slowly pour in the olive oil and then add the mustard, lemon juice, salt, and pepper. Taste and adjust the seasoning. Transfer the butter to a serving bowl. The butter may be set aside for up to 12 hours, but don't chill it or it will lose its attractive soft texture. The monkfish is best roasted just before serving.

To finish, heat the oven to 450°F/230°C. Uncover the baking dish, leaving the fish buried in the herbs, and roast for 8 to 10 minutes. Turn the fillets over and continue roasting for 2 to 3 minutes longer for small fillets and up to 10 minutes longer for larger ones. The fish should be firm to the touch, but remain slightly translucent in the center when you flake it with a fork.

For serving, cut small fillets on the diagonal into 2 or 3 pieces, or cut large fillets into 4 or 5 pieces. Set the pieces on a bed of salad greens and pass the Montpellier butter at the table.

LOUP FLAMBÉ AU FENOUIL

WHOLE SEA BASS FLAMBÉED WITH FENNEL

serves 6

From picnic barbecues to select restaurants, fresh fish grilled over fennel twigs until the skin is crisp and slightly charred is a summer tradition along the Riviera. Wild fennel is one of the many aromatic herbs of the maquis, the underbrush that carpets the mountains, perfuming not only the hillsides but also the local bistros. Both herb- and anise-flavored liquors such as Pernod add to the ensemble. Sea bass (known as loup de mer *locally and as* bar *elsewhere) is highly prized for grilling, as are bream* (dorade) *and sea trout* (truite de mer)*; both can be substituted for sea bass in this recipe. The fish should be cleaned and scaled, with the head and tail left on.*

To arrive at the cooking time for a whole fish, measure the fish at its thickest point. Allow 10 minutes' grilling or broiling time per 1 inch/ 2.5 centimeters of thickness. If you cannot find dried fennel, sprinkle dried vine cuttings or your favorite barbecue wood chips with fennel seeds. At table, a drizzle of olive oil and a squeeze of lemon are the classic condiments, and I recommend some grilled zucchini and eggplant on the side.

ONE 5-POUND/2.25-KG WHOLE SEA BASS
OR 2 SMALLER FISH, CLEANED AND SCALED

1/2 CUP/125 ML OLIVE OIL, MORE FOR BRUSHING

SALT AND PEPPER

1 LARGE BUNCH DRIED WILD FENNEL TWIGS

3 TO 4 TABLESPOONS PERNOD OR OTHER ANISE
LIQUOR

OLIVE OIL AND LEMON WEDGES, FOR SERVING

Light the grill or heat the broiler. Cut the fins from the fish and trim the tail to a V. Wash and dry the fish. Make 3 or 4 deep diagonal slashes on each side, brush both sides with the oil, and sprinkle with salt and pepper. Insert 2 or 3 fennel twigs in the stomach cavity.

Position the grill rack or broiler rack 4 to 5 inches/10 to 13 cm from the heat. Brush the grill rack with oil and lay the fish on it. Grill or broil the fish, brushing occasionally with more oil and turning once, until it just flakes at the thickest part when tested with a fork. Allow 10 to 12 minutes on each side for a large fish, or 8 to 10 minutes on each side for smaller ones, and brush the fish occasionally with more oil while cooking.

Meanwhile, put the remaining fennel on a long heatproof platter and warm it in a low oven or on a corner of the grill until very dry. Lay the cooked fish on top while it is still very hot. Heat the Pernod in a small saucepan. In front of guests, flambé (see page 371) the Pernod with a long match and pour it while flaming onto the hot platter; the fennel twigs will ignite.

Serve the fish at once. To remove the fillets, cut the skin at each side of the fish with scissors, working from head to tail, and carefully peel it away. Scrape out and discard the bones lying along the back. Divide the flesh into 2 fillets by cutting with a knife from head to tail, following the natural central line. With a spoon and fork, ease both fillets onto the edge of the plate. Snap the backbone at the head and tail, slide the knife underneath it, and remove it. Replace the 2 top fillets on the bottom ones and serve with a small pitcher of olive oil and the lemon wedges.

SARDINES GRILLÉES

GRILLED SARDINES

Sardines are even simpler to grill than whole bass, as they need little preparation.

Light the grill. Wash 2 pounds/900 g very fresh sardines and dry well (they should already be cleaned). Put a small sprig of dried fennel in the cavity of each sardine and thread one-fourth of the sardines onto 2 wooden skewers, threading 1 skewer through the tails and the second one through the heads. Repeat with the remaining sardines and 6 more skewers. Brush the sardines on both sides with olive oil. Set the grill rack about 3 inches/7.5 cm from the heat, brush the rack with oil, and grill the sardines, turning once, until the flesh just flakes easily, 3 to 5 minutes on each side. Flambé the sardines with Pernod or another anise liquor as directed in Loup Flambé au Fenouil. Serve the sardines on the skewers to 4 diners, leaving them to detach the meat from the bones.

LOUP FLAMBÉ AU FENOUIL

= WINE IN THE COUNTRY KITCHEN =

Wine is a staple in French kitchens and its distinctive attributes are appreciated as a matter of course. For example, Coq au Vin (page 113) can be generic, but call it *coq au Beaujolais* and you know the bird is Burgundian, *coq au vin jaune* and you are off in the Jura, Coq au Riesling (page 114) in Alsace, and so on all around the country. There is nothing precious or fancy about how wine is used in the pot; the home cook will use yesterday's half-drained bottle to deglaze a pan of fried steaks, or take a simple white wine from the refrigerator door to top up a court bouillon for poaching fish. Wine is a very friendly kitchen companion.

However, a few dos and don'ts are important. The first is never to cook with a wine that you would not drink. I am not suggesting you squander a great vintage on a rump of beef, but wine for cooking must be drinkable. If it tastes like vinegar in the glass, it will be no different on the plate. Next, what you taste in the glass—fruit, spice, acidity—will come across in the dish. A light wine generates a light sauce. White partners well with eggs, fish, and white meats, while red wine goes with duck, red meats, and game. Chicken is right in the middle and is commonly cooked with either.

Of course, rules are made to be broken. Burgundians like to poach eggs *en meurette* (in a red wine sauce, page 41), while Alsatians add white Riesling to their game dishes. Sweet white wines are best for desserts, yet terrine of foie gras macerated in Sauternes is classic. Champagne, in my opinion, is best added at the last minute to chilled dishes, such as cold fruit soups, to maximize the fizz. Forget the magic of the name. Any acceptable sparkling wine will do equally well.

Most of the time, wine gets cooked, but not always. Wine straight from the bottle is good in marinades because it acts as a tenderizer and mild preservative, as well as adding flavor. When combined simply with sugar, red wine is ideal for macerating fruits such as strawberries or peaches. Once heated, however, most wines should be cooked until they reduce by at least half, concentrating flavor and mellowing acid. This should happen as part of the cooking process, but don't hesitate to simmer a dish longer if a wine sauce tastes acid or raw. When deglazing pan juices, wine performs better than water or stock because it dissolves fat and breaks down starch, so the result will be much lighter. One or two effects of wine in food are less expected: a little wine in pastry and pasta doughs cuts gluten and yields a pliable dough that is easier to work. In cheese fondue, the alcohol content of wine lowers the boiling point so that hard cheeses melt without becoming stringy.

Versatile as wine is—for poaching, stewing, glazing and deglazing, flambéing, macerating, marinating—certain ingredients are not wine-friendly. Root vegetables are toughened by wine and can take twice as long to cook in a wine broth as in water. The skins of legumes are toughened by wine, as are unhusked grains like brown rice. Dried mushrooms and other porous ingredients may absorb wine so quickly that their intrinsic flavor disappears. But these are exceptions. In general, you can trust the principle that a little bit of wine in a dish can do a world of good.

TRUITE AU JAMBON DE BAYONNE

SAUTÉED TROUT WITH CURED HAM

serves 4

In the high mountains of the Pyrenees, wild trout are occasionally still landed and rushed home to the pan. Bacon fat or lard is preferred to butter for frying, and lardons of the local Bayonne ham add a character-istic salty bite. Don't hesitate to try this same recipe with fillets of robust fish such as tuna or shark, and add some crispy potatoes, fried in the same fat, for serving.

4 WHOLE TROUT (ABOUT 10 OUNCES/280 G EACH), CLEANED

$^1/_4$ CUP/30 G FLOUR, SEASONED WITH SALT AND PEPPER

4 TABLESPOONS/60 G LARD OR BUTTER

7-OUNCE/200-G PIECE CURED RAW HAM, CUT INTO LARDONS (SEE PAGE 371)

2 GARLIC CLOVES, CHOPPED

2 TABLESPOONS RED WINE VINEGAR

2 TABLESPOONS CHOPPED FRESH PARSLEY

Cut the fins off the trout and trim the tails to a V. Wash the fish and dry well. Coat them with the seasoned flour, patting off the excess with your hands.

Melt the lard in a large frying pan over medium heat. Add the ham and fry just until the fat runs, about 1 minute. Do not allow it to brown or it will be tough. Remove the ham to a plate with a draining spoon and set aside. Add the trout to the hot pan and sauté until browned, 4 to 5 minutes. Turn and brown the other side, 3 to 4 minutes longer. The flesh near the gills should just flake easily when tested with a fork.

Transfer the trout to warmed plates or a platter, heads to the left and stomach nearest you, so the flesh is easy for the diner to remove from the bones. Scatter the ham on top and keep the fish warm.

Return the pan to the heat, add the garlic, and sauté just until fragrant, about 30 seconds. Take the pan from the heat and add the vinegar, standing back as it will splatter. Stir in the parsley and, while still foaming, pour the sauce over the trout. Serve at once.

TRUITES AUX NOISETTES

SAUTÉED TROUT WITH HAZELNUTS

Legend has it that Hannibal enjoyed the local trout from moun-tain streams when he crossed the Dauphiné before climbing the Alps with his elephants.

Cut the peel from a lemon, removing all the white pith as well, and then cut the flesh crosswise into slices, discarding any seeds. Substitute ½ cup/70 g peeled hazelnuts for the ham and use 6 tablespoons/90 g butter instead of lard. Fry the hazelnuts in 2 tablespoons of the butter until browned and set them aside. Sauté the trout in the remaining 4 tablespoons/60 g butter as described in Truite au Jambon, arrange them on plates or a platter, and top with the lemon slices. Make the sauce with 2 tablespoons fresh lemon juice instead of vinegar.

THON À LA MARSEILLAISE

ROAST TUNA WITH LETTUCE, ONIONS, AND TOMATO

serves 6

The first lettuce reportedly arrived in France from Italy with the Avignon popes in the fourteenth century, hence the name romaine, or Roman, let-tuce. Firm lettuce of this type is excellent cooked, losing its crispness but gaining an acidity that nicely balances the richness of tuna. You do not need expensive sushi-grade tuna for this recipe; other robust fish, such as swordfish and halibut, will do. On a hot day, this dish is good served at room temperature, so it can be cooked an hour or two ahead.

6 TUNA STEAKS (ABOUT 2 POUNDS/900 G TOTAL)

3 TABLESPOONS/45 ML RED WINE VINEGAR

3 TABLESPOONS/45 ML WATER

1 LARGE HEAD ROMAINE LETTUCE (ABOUT 12 OUNCES/330 G)

1 LEMON

$^3/_4$ CUP/175 ML OLIVE OIL, MORE FOR THE ROASTING PAN

4 ONIONS (ABOUT 1$^1/_2$ POUNDS/675 G TOTAL), SLICED

2 POUNDS/900 G TOMATOES, PEELED, SEEDED, AND CHOPPED (SEE PAGE 372)

3 GARLIC CLOVES, CHOPPED

SALT AND PEPPER

Put the tuna steaks in a shallow dish and sprinkle them with the vinegar, then the water. Leave them to soak for about 30 minutes.

Separate the lettuce leaves and wash and dry them. Reserve 5 or 6 of the largest leaves and coarsely shred the rest. Cut the peel from the lemon, removing all the white pith as well, and then cut the flesh crosswise into slices, discarding any seeds. Heat the oven to 325°F/160°C.

Drain the tuna steaks, discarding the liquid, and pat them dry. Oil a roasting pan or a flameproof baking dish and spread half of the shredded lettuce in it. Top with half of the onions, tomatoes, garlic, and lemon slices. Sprinkle with salt and pepper, put the tuna steaks on top, and season them also. Top with the remaining onions, tomatoes, garlic, and lemon slices. Cover with the remaining shredded lettuce and then with the reserved whole leaves. Moisten with the olive oil. Roast until the tuna is cooked but still rosy in the center when poked with a knife, 55 to 65 minutes.

Discard any scorched lettuce leaves, transfer the tuna to a platter, cover, and keep warm. Put the pan on the stove top over high heat and continue cooking the vegetables, stirring often, until they are quite tender and almost all the liquid has evaporated, 5 to 10 minutes. Spoon the vegetables over and around the tuna. Serve hot or at room temperature.

SAUMON LARDÉ AU RAIFORT

ROAST SALMON WITH BACON AND HORSERADISH CREAM

serves 6

Bacon, horseradish, and a bed of lentils sound like strong stuff for salmon, but not in Alsace, where German traditions blend with the French. The mix of rosy pink salmon with earthy lentils and creamy sauce makes for a stunning presentation of texture and color. Fresh ginger can be used in place of the horseradish if you prefer. The salmon can be prepared several hours ahead and refrigerated, but is best roasted just before serving.

LENTILS

    1¹⁄₄ CUPS/225 G GREEN OR BROWN LENTILS

    1 ONION, STUDDED WITH 1 WHOLE CLOVE

    1 GARLIC CLOVE

    1 BOUQUET GARNI (SEE PAGE 370)

    SALT AND PEPPER

    2 CUPS/500 ML WATER, MORE IF NEEDED

SALMON

    2 TABLESPOONS/30 G BUTTER, SOFTENED, MORE
    FOR THE BAKING DISH

    1 LARGE SALMON FILLET (2 POUNDS/900 G),
    WITHOUT SKIN

    4-OUNCE/110-G PIECE LEAN BACON, CUT INTO
    LARDONS (SEE PAGE 371)

    1 CUP/250 ML CRÈME FRAÎCHE OR HEAVY CREAM

    2 TABLESPOONS GRATED FRESH HORSERADISH, OR
    3 TO 4 TABLESPOONS BOTTLED HORSERADISH

    2 SHALLOTS, FINELY CHOPPED

    8-BY-11-INCH/20-BY-28-CM FLAMEPROOF BAKING
    DISH OR ROASTING PAN

Pick over the lentils, discarding any stones, and wash them well. Put them in a saucepan with the onion, garlic, bouquet garni, and water to cover generously. Season with pepper, cover, bring to a boil, and then simmer until the lentils are tender, 45 minutes to 1 hour. Add a large pinch of salt halfway through the cooking, along with more water if the pan seems dry. When done, the lentils should be soupy, but most of the water should be absorbed. If necessary, remove the lid toward the end of cooking so the water evaporates. Discard the onion, bouquet garni, and garlic and taste the lentils for seasoning. They may be covered and refrigerated for a couple of days.

Heat the oven to 350°F/180°C. Butter the flameproof baking dish or roasting pan. Wash and dry the salmon, cut the fillet in half crosswise, and lay the tail piece skinned side down on a work surface. Poke holes in the flesh with the point of a knife and poke a lardon in each hole (called larding), using about half the lardons. Lay the tail piece of salmon, bacon side down, in the prepared dish and set the remaining fillet half on top, skinned side down, with the thicker end over the tail to form an even layer. Lard the upper piece of salmon with the remaining lardons. Spread the salmon with the butter and sprinkle it with pepper. Roast, basting often with the pan juices, 20 to 30 minutes, until a skewer inserted in the center is hot to the touch when withdrawn after 30 seconds.

To finish, reheat the lentils on the stove top if necessary. Transfer the salmon to a platter, cover it loosely with aluminum foil, and keep warm. Skim off and discard the fat from the baking dish. Add the crème fraîche and bring to a boil, stirring to dissolve the pan juices. Strain the mixture into a small saucepan, whisk in the horseradish, shallots, salt, and pepper, and bring back to a boil. Taste the sauce, adjust the seasoning, and pour into a sauce bowl. Spoon the lentils around the salmon, coat it with a little of the sauce, and serve immediately. Pass the rest of the sauce at the table.

ROUGETS SAUTÉS À LA VINAIGRETTE DE TOMATES

ROUGETS SAUTÉS À LA VINAIGRETTE DE TOMATES

SAUTÉED RED MULLET WITH TOMATO VINAIGRETTE

serves 4

Red mullet is prized in France, as much for its brisk, almost gamey taste as for its brilliant skin. It is a small fish, so more than one may be needed per person. Any small whole fish, particularly bream, can be used instead. The regional twist comes with local oils: olive oil in the south, or walnut or hazelnut oil farther north. Vinegars range from artisanal brews using red or white wine, or perhaps Champagne, to the cider vinegar that has long been a part of fish dishes in Normandy and Brittany. With its pink skin and bright tomato garnish, this is one of the prettiest fish dishes I know.

TOMATO VINAIGRETTE

> 2 TABLESPOONS RED WINE VINEGAR
>
> SALT AND PEPPER
>
> 6 TABLESPOONS/90 ML OLIVE OR WALNUT OIL
>
> 3 TOMATOES (ABOUT 1 POUND/450 G TOTAL), PEELED, SEEDED, AND CHOPPED (SEE PAGE 372)
>
> 1 TABLESPOON CHOPPED FRESH CHIVES

> 4 WHOLE RED MULLET (ABOUT 10 OUNCES/280 G EACH), CLEANED AND SCALED
>
> 3 TO 4 TABLESPOONS FLOUR, SEASONED WITH SALT AND PEPPER
>
> 3 TABLESPOONS/45 ML OLIVE OR VEGETABLE OIL

For the vinaigrette, whisk the vinegar with salt and pepper to taste in a small bowl until the salt dissolves. Gradually add the oil, whisking constantly so the dressing emulsifies and thickens slightly. Stir in the tomatoes and chives, taste, and adjust the seasoning. The dressing may be prepared an hour or so in advance.

Trim off the fins from the mullet and cut the tails in a V. Wash the fish and dry well, handling them as lightly as possible. Coat them with the seasoned flour, patting off the excess with your hands. Heat the oil in a large frying pan over medium heat. Add the fish, with their backs toward you and their heads facing to the left (this ensures their best side is upward for serving), and sauté until lightly browned, 4 to 5 minutes. Turn and brown the other side, 3 to 4 minutes longer, depending on size. The flesh should just flake easily when tested with a fork.

Transfer the fish to warmed plates, placing them with heads to the left and stomachs nearest the diner, so the flesh is easy to lift from the bones. Stir the dressing again briefly, spoon the cool vinaigrette over the hot fish as a contrast, and serve at once.

BAR EN CROÛTE DE SEL

SEA BASS IN A SALT CRUST

serves 4

Cooking in a salt crust has long been popular in salt-producing areas like the Île de Ré on the Atlantic coast, where this recipe originates. The salt is combined with whole-wheat flour to make a pliable crust for wrapping fillets of fish, such as sea bass. Salmon is a good choice, too. Your guests will enjoy breaking open the crust, but you must warn them not to eat it. I like to serve the bass with boiled baby potatoes (another product of the Île de Ré) and a Sauce Beurre Blanc (page 221), which was invented in Charentes, just down the coast.

SALT CRUST

> 5 EGG WHITES, MORE IF NEEDED
>
> 1 CUP/250 G COARSE SEA SALT
>
> 1½ CUPS/185 G WHOLE-WHEAT FLOUR

> 1½ POUNDS/675 G SEA BASS FILLETS, WITH SKIN
>
> 4 SPRIGS FRESH THYME
>
> 1 EGG, BEATEN TO MIX, FOR GLAZE

For the salt crust, whisk the egg whites in a small bowl until frothy. Put them in a food processor with the salt and flour and pulse until the mixture forms crumbs. If they feel dry, work in a bit more egg white. Turn the crumbs onto a work surface and press them into a ball. Wrap the dough in plastic wrap and chill for 15 to 30 minutes. It may be made up to 2 hours ahead.

Heat the oven to 400°F/200°C and put a baking sheet in the oven to heat. Wash and dry the fish fillets. Cut them into 4 portions, if necessary, and fold over each portion, skin side outward, to form a square. Divide the dough into 4 equal pieces. Roll out a piece to a 7-inch/18-cm square. Put a sprig of thyme in the center of the square and top with a piece of fish, skin side down, placing it kitty-corner. Brush the surrounding dough with the glaze. Fold the dough corners to the center to enclose the fish, and pinch the edges together to make a package. Repeat with the remaining fish and dough pieces.

Put the fish packages, seam side down, on the hot baking sheet, and brush the tops with the egg glaze. Using the tip of a paring knife, decorate each package with 2 curved lines to form a fish. Bake for 10 to 12 minutes, depending on the thickness of the fish. Take out the packages and let them rest at room temperature for 10 minutes before serving. Do not leave them longer or they will become too salty. Let guests break open the crust at the table.

= A PINCH OF SALT =

Today we take salt for granted as a cheap staple, readily available to everyone, but it was not always so. In medieval times, salt was precious, occupying pride of place at the table, where it was piled in great cellars of silver or gold. To be seated below the salt signified you were a commoner; dignitaries were placed above. The salt trade was widely used to levy taxes, and from the fourteenth century onward in France, most citizens were required to buy a specified amount of heavily taxed salt every year. The *gabelle*, as this tax was called, was hated but was not entirely abolished until 1790, following the Revolution.

In France, three types of salt predominate. Coarse salt, refined or not (unrefined crystals are gray), is used to boil pasta, for example, or to make salt crusts. Kitchen salt has much smaller crystals, more suitable for seasoning dishes during cooking. Fine salt, also called table salt, dissolves rapidly and is best for baking and for seasoning foods that are already cooked, or will be eaten raw, such as salads. Table salt gets a bad rap because it contains tiny amounts

of anticaking additives that add a tinge of bitterness to the taste of sodium chloride. Try a few grains on the tongue to detect it. Whichever salt you use, the volume varies enormously with the size of the crystals, so it is best to go by weight—and taste—when measuring.

The most highly prized salt in France is *fleur de sel*, a delicate white salt that forms on the surface of seawater. The best comes from a handful of salt basins on the Atlantic, such as those at Guérande, the Île de Ré, Noirmoutier, and off the Île d'Oléron. The salt crystals are extracted naturally—by the sun, the wind, and the tides—unlike the *fleur de sel* from Camargue on the Mediterranean, which is harvested through a mechanized pumping system. Look for place names on *fleur de sel* boxes in shops, and don't waste the salt in cooking where nuances of taste and crunchy texture are lost. Save it for seasoning meats and vegetables at the table, especially dishes like Pot-au-Feu (page 142) and boiled new potatoes.

BRANDADE DE MORUE DE NÎMES

PURÉE OF SALT COD

serves 6 to 8

Salt cod is found in many French regions, even those inland. The Basques like it with peppers, tomatoes, and plenty of garlic; the Bretons prefer it with beans, onions, and potatoes; in the Languedoc, cooks serve it with chickpeas as a Lenten dish; and during the same period in the Auvergne, it is cooked with walnut oil, garlic, parsley, and cream. But the most famous recipe by far, popular throughout southern France as well as in Paris bistros, is Brandade de Morue de Nîmes, a purée of salt cod, olive oil, milk, and sometimes potato.

Brandade is at its best piping hot, creamy white, and fluffy, with the cod thoroughly blanched of its salt and highlighted by fruity olive oil. It is easy to make in a food processor, provided the salt cod has been gently poached, not boiled into strings. Oil and hot milk are beaten in slowly to form a light emulsion, and I like to include potato to lighten the purée, though it can also be made with cod only. If you prefer to beat by hand in the traditional way from start to finish, your brandade will be less fluffy and more robust. I give both methods here.

Brandade is served with fried garlic croûtes and a jet black garnish of ripe olives, or, at Christmas, a celebratory shower of chopped truffle. The controversial ingredient is more garlic. The Provençal poet Frédéric Mistral said that crushed garlic is permissible, but most cooks prefer to rub the mixing bowl with a cut clove, while some don't add any garlic at all. Take your pick.

1½ POUNDS/675 G SALT COD

I LARGE BAKING POTATO, PEELED AND CUT INTO
2 OR 3 CHUNKS

SALT AND WHITE PEPPER

FRIED CROÛTES MADE WITH I BAGUETTE, SLICED,
FRIED IN 4 TO 5 TABLESPOONS OLIVE OIL, AND
RUBBED WITH A CUT GARLIC CLOVE (SEE PAGE 374)

I CUP/250 ML OLIVE OIL

I CUP/250 ML MILK, MORE IF NEEDED

I GARLIC CLOVE (OPTIONAL)

GRATED NUTMEG

SQUEEZE OF FRESH LEMON JUICE

½ CUP/100 G SALTED (DRY-CURED) BLACK OLIVES

Soak the salt cod in cold water to cover for a day, changing the water several times. Drain, put the cod in a deep frying pan, and cover with cold water. Add the lid and heat gently until nearly simmering. Lower the heat and cook just below the simmering point (about 160°F/70°C) until the cod flakes easily, 10 to 15 minutes, depending on its dryness. Remove it and drain on paper

towels, letting it cool to tepid. Flake the fish with your fingers or a fork, discarding skin and bone.

Put the potato in a small saucepan, add salted water to cover, cover the pan, and bring to a boil. Lower the heat to a simmer and cook until very tender when poked with a knife, 15 to 20 minutes. Drain, return the potato to the pan over low heat, and dry it for 1 to 2 minutes, shaking the pan often. Make the croûtes.

To make brandade in a food processor, heat the oil in a saucepan until very hot. Scald the milk in another saucepan. Finely chop the garlic clove and put it in the processor, or cut the clove in half and rub the work bowl with it. Add the flaked cod to the bowl. With the blades turning, slowly pour in the hot oil, alternating with the hot milk. Finally, drop the potato pieces into the cod mixture with the machine running and purée just until the mixture is smooth, 30 seconds to 1 minute (if overworked, the potato will become sticky).

To make brandade by hand, heat ⅔ cup/150 ml of the oil in a large saucepan until very hot. Scald the milk in another saucepan. Finely chop the garlic, if using. Add the flaked cod to the oil and beat vigorously with a wooden spoon over low heat, crushing and separating the fibers. Move the pan on and off the heat as you beat so the cod does not brown. Beat in the chopped garlic, if using. Work the cooked potato through a ricer, or crush it to a purée with a potato masher. Add it to the puréed cod. Beat in a tablespoon of milk and then a tablespoon of the remaining oil. Continue until all the milk and all the remaining oil are added.

Whether made in a food processor or by hand, the finished purée should be white, smooth, and stiff enough to hold its shape. If very stiff, beat in a little more milk. Taste and adjust the seasoning with nutmeg, lemon juice, and pepper—salt may not be needed. Pile the brandade in a warmed serving bowl and decorate around the edge with the croûtes and small mounds of the olives. Serve very hot.

Traditionalists would not approve, but brandade may in fact be made 2 to 3 days ahead and stored in the refrigerator. Let it come to room temperature, then put it in a heatproof bowl. Line a roasting pan with a dish towel, set the bowl in it, and pour in boiling water to make a water bath (see page 373). Bring the water back to a boil on the stove top, beating the brandade often so it stays fluffy and emulsified.

TURBOT VALLÉE D'AUGE
TURBOT WITH APPLE AND CIDER SAUCE
serves 4 to 6

In the Auge Valley of Normandy, home of the finest cider apples, the grass is said to grow so fast that a stick left lying out at night is covered by morning. All sorts of ingredients, from fish, chicken, and veal to pheasant, are given the Auge Valley treatment, a pale and utterly delicious sauce of apple, apple cider (it must be alcoholic, or hard, cider), and crème fraîche, often with mushrooms. Most white fish take kindly to the sauce, with sole, flounder, and John Dory immediately springing to mind.

4 TURBOT FILLETS (ABOUT 1½ POUNDS/675 G TOTAL), WITHOUT SKIN

SALT AND PEPPER

2 TABLESPOONS/30 G COLD BUTTER, CUT INTO PIECES, MORE FOR THE SAUTÉ PAN

1 LEEK, WHITE PART ONLY, SLICED (SEE PAGE 371)

1 TART APPLE, PEELED, CORED, AND THINLY SLICED

1½ CUPS/375 ML DRY (ALCOHOLIC) CIDER

1½ CUPS/375 ML FISH STOCK (SEE PAGE 376)

8 OUNCES/225 G MUSHROOMS, TRIMMED AND SLICED

SQUEEZE OF FRESH LEMON JUICE

2 TO 3 TABLESPOONS WATER

1 CUP/250 ML CRÈME FRAÎCHE (PAGE 374) OR HEAVY CREAM

Heat the oven to 375°F/190°C. Wash and dry the fish fillets. Sprinkle them with salt and pepper and fold each one in half, skinned side in. Butter an ovenproof sauté pan or deep frying pan and spread the leek and apple slices in it. Set the turbot on top, and pour over the cider and stock. Cover the dish with buttered parchment paper, buttered side down, and bring to a simmer. Transfer to the oven and poach until the fish just flakes easily when tested with a fork, 10 to 12 minutes.

Meanwhile, put the mushrooms in a frying pan and sprinkle with the lemon juice, salt, pepper, and water. Cover and cook over high heat, stirring occasionally, until tender, 5 to 7 minutes.

Transfer the fish to a platter with a draining spoon and cover loosely with aluminum foil to keep warm. Pour the liquid from the mushrooms into the sauté pan, reserving the mushrooms. Boil the liquid until reduced to about ½ cup/125 ml, 15 to 20 minutes. The apples may soften and thicken the liquid or they may hold their shape—either is fine. Stir in the crème fraîche, lower the heat, and simmer until reduced by about one-fourth and thick

enough to coat a spoon lightly, 3 to 5 minutes. Whisk in the butter a piece at a time, keeping the pan sometimes over low heat and sometimes off the heat so the butter softens and enriches the sauce. Stir in the mushrooms, along with any liquid released by the fish. Taste and adjust the seasoning. Add the fish back to the sauce and warm gently over low heat, about 2 minutes. Serve at once.

MAQUEREAUX MARINÉS
MARINATED MACKEREL
serves 4 to 6

Spiced white wine with vinegar is an excellent marinade for rich fish such as mackerel and herring, yielding an appetizer popular along the north coast of France and into Belgium. Upping the ante, a tablespoon of juniper berries may be added to the wine for maquereaux marinés aux baies de genièvre. *In Normandy, wine is often replaced with hard (alcoholic) cider.*

2½ CUPS/625 ML MEDIUM-DRY WHITE WINE

2 CARROTS, SLICED

2 ONIONS, SLICED

1 LARGE BOUQUET GARNI (SEE PAGE 370)

1 TEASPOON PEPPERCORNS

1 WHOLE CLOVE

SALT

4 TO 6 SMALL WHOLE MACKEREL (ABOUT 2 POUNDS/ 900 G TOTAL), CLEANED AND SCALED

⅔ CUP/150 ML WHITE WINE VINEGAR

Combine the wine, carrots, and onions in a saucepan and bring to a boil. Tie the bouquet garni, peppercorns, and clove in a piece of cheesecloth and add to the pan with a pinch of salt. Cover and simmer until the vegetables are tender, about 30 minutes.

Meanwhile, prepare the mackerel. Cut off the fins and trim the tails to a V. Wash the fish, dry well, and then lay them in a flameproof baking dish or a roasting pan. Set the baking dish on the stove top. Add the vinegar to the wine and vegetables, bring just back to a boil, and pour the hot liquid over the fish, discarding the spice bag. Return the liquid just to a boil, cover, and simmer for 2 minutes. Turn off the heat and leave the fish to continue cooking gently in the heat of the liquid.

When the fish is at room temperature, store in the refrigerator for at least 2 days and up to 4 days. The liquid will set to a light aspic. Serve the fish at room temperature, with the vegetable aspic.

QUENELLES NANTUA

FISH DUMPLINGS WITH CRAYFISH SAUCE

serves 6

Nantua, a gray, chilly town in Savoy, achieved gastronomic fame through its fish dumplings, bathed in an intense sauce of freshwater crayfish from the lake and mountain streams nearby. Quenelles Nantua is a legendary dish, one of the highlights of French regional cooking that chefs strive to perfect, knowing their career will look up if they can get it just right. Even today, the crayfish sauce must still be made the old-fashioned way, though a food processor provides an excellent shortcut for the dumplings. Pike is the traditional fish for the quenelles, but a white fish such as whiting or bream does well, too. Don't use frozen fish, or the quenelle dough, even though bound with pâte à choux, will fall apart during cooking. However, frozen crayfish are fine for the sauce. Believe me, getting this dish right pays off with your friends!

PÂTE À CHOUX

  ½ CUP/125 ML WATER

  ½ TEASPOON SALT

  3 TABLESPOONS/45 G BUTTER, CUT INTO CUBES

  ½ CUP/60 G FLOUR

  2 EGGS

QUENELLES

  1 POUND/450 G FIRM WHITE FISH FILLETS, WITHOUT SKIN

  3 EGG WHITES, WHISKED UNTIL FROTHY, MORE IF NEEDED

  1 CUP/250 ML CRÈME FRAÎCHE (PAGE 374) OR HEAVY CREAM

  SALT AND BLACK PEPPER

  GRATED NUTMEG

SAUCE NANTUA

  ½ CUP/110 G BUTTER

  ½ ONION, FINELY CHOPPED

  ½ CARROT, FINELY CHOPPED

  12 TO 16 LIVE OR THAWED FROZEN CRAYFISH (ABOUT 1½ POUNDS/675 G TOTAL)

  2 TABLESPOONS COGNAC, MORE TO FINISH

  ¼ CUP/60 ML DRY WHITE WINE

  3 CUPS/750 ML FISH STOCK (SEE PAGE 376), MORE IF NEEDED

  1 BOUQUET GARNI (SEE PAGE 370)

  ¼ CUP/30 G FLOUR

  1¼ CUPS/300 ML CRÈME FRAÎCHE (PAGE 374) OR HEAVY CREAM

  ½ TEASPOON TOMATO PASTE (OPTIONAL)

  PINCH OF CAYENNE PEPPER

  BUTTER, FOR THE BAKING DISH(ES)

  6 INDIVIDUAL BAKING DISHES OR 1 LARGE BAKING DISH

For the quenelle mixture, first make the pâte à choux (see page 374). Wash and dry the fish fillets, and cut them into pieces. Purée them in a food processor. With the blades running, gradually add the egg whites, taking 1 to 2 minutes. Transfer the mixture to a metal bowl and set it over an ice bath. Chill, stirring occasionally, until very cold, 15 to 20 minutes. Return the mixture to the food processor and beat in the pastry dough. Gradually beat in the crème fraîche, followed by salt, black pepper, and nutmeg. If the quenelle mixture is soft, you will find the salt will stiffen it slightly. Return the mixture to the metal bowl and chill again over ice until very cold.

To poach the dumplings, fill a large sauté pan or shallow saucepan with water to a depth of 3 inches/7.5 cm. Add salt and bring to a simmer. Hold a tablespoon in each hand, dip them in the pan of hot water, scoop up a spoonful of the quenelle mixture, and use both spoons to shape and turn it into an oval. Drop the dumpling into the simmering water and simmer for 2 to 3 minutes. If this test dumpling starts to break up, add another lightly beaten egg white to the remaining mixture and beat for 2 to 3 minutes over ice. Also, taste the cooked quenelle and adjust the seasoning of the mixture. Shape more ovals and drop them into the simmering water. Poach until they are firm when you press them with a fingertip, 10 to 15 minutes, depending on size. Lift them out with a draining spoon and drain on paper towels.

Meanwhile, begin the Nantua sauce. Divide the butter into 3 equal portions. Melt 1 portion in a sauté pan or large, shallow saucepan over medium heat. Add the onion and carrot and sauté for about 2 minutes. Increase the heat to high, add the crayfish, and sauté, stirring often, for 2 to 3 minutes. Add the Cognac and flambé it (see page 371). Add the wine, stock, bouquet garni, salt, and black pepper. The crayfish should be partly submerged; add more stock if necessary. Cover and simmer the crayfish until they turn red, 8 to 10 minutes, depending on their size.

Remove the crayfish from the pan with the draining spoon and leave them until cool enough to handle. Pull the heads from the tails, and shell the tails like shrimp, discarding the intestinal vein. Set the tail meat aside. Put the shells in a heavy-duty plastic bag and pound with a rolling pin to crush them. Return them to the cooking liquid, cover, and simmer for 10 to 12 minutes. Strain the liquid into a bowl, pressing hard on the shells to extract maximum flavor, and set the liquid aside.

Melt a second portion of the butter in a saucepan over medium heat. Whisk in the flour and cook until foaming. Whisk in the crayfish liquid and bring to a boil, whisking constantly until the sauce thickens. Whisk in the crème fraîche, bring back just to a boil, and, if you like, add the tomato paste to deepen the color. Season to taste with salt, black pepper, cayenne pepper, and a trickle of Cognac. Take it from the heat and whisk in the remaining butter portion, cut into small pieces.

Butter the individual baking dishes or single dish. Arrange the quenelles in the dish(es) and scatter the reserved crayfish tails over them. Coat the quenelles generously with the sauce, bathing them in it. They can be prepared up to this point and stored in the refrigerator for 1 day.

To finish, heat the oven to 375°F/190°C. Bake the quenelles until bubbling and slightly puffed, 10 to 15 minutes. Serve very hot.

COQUILLES SAINT-JACQUES NANTAISE

SAUTÉED SCALLOPS WITH SPICES

serves 6 as a first course

In the seventeenth and eighteenth centuries, the Breton port of Nantes, at the mouth of the Loire, was a center of French trade with Asia, and a taste for spices still lingers. Muscadet white wine, light and dry, comes from the same region, while Cognac, somewhat of a surprise with these scallops, is made well to the south. Shrimps Nantaise are also a favorite of mine. Allow about 2 pounds/900 g raw shrimp and peel them before cooking.

1½ POUNDS/675 G SEA SCALLOPS

¼ CUP/30 G FLOUR, SEASONED WITH SALT AND BLACK PEPPER

2 TEASPOONS CURRY POWDER, MORE TO TASTE

¼ TEASPOON CAYENNE PEPPER, MORE TO TASTE

4 TABLESPOONS/60 G BUTTER

1 LARGE ONION, FINELY CHOPPED

⅔ CUP/150 ML DRY WHITE WINE

1 POUND/450 G TOMATOES, PEELED, SEEDED AND CHOPPED (SEE PAGE 372)

SALT AND BLACK PEPPER

2 TABLESPOONS COGNAC

2 TO 3 TABLESPOONS BROWNED BREAD CRUMBS (SEE PAGE 373)

2 TABLESPOONS/30 G BUTTER, MELTED

6 SCALLOP SHELLS OR INDIVIDUAL FLAMEPROOF BAKING DISHES

Wash the scallops, pat dry, and discard the tough, crescent-shaped muscle adhering to one side. If the scallops are large, slice them in half horizontally to create 2 disks. In a bowl, mix together the seasoned flour, curry powder, and cayenne pepper. Add the scallops and toss to coat them evenly.

Melt 3 tablespoons of the butter in a sauté pan or deep frying pan over high heat until foaming. Add the scallops and sauté until brown, 1 to 2 minutes. Turn them and brown the other side, 1 to 2 minutes longer. Lift them out and divide evenly among the scallop shells or baking dishes.

For the sauce, add the remaining 1 tablespoon butter to the pan. Reduce the heat to medium, add the onion, and sauté until soft, 5 to 7 minutes. Pour in the wine and simmer until reduced by about half. Stir in the tomatoes, season with salt and black pepper, and cook just until the tomatoes are pulpy, 5 to 7 minutes. Stir in the Cognac, taste, and adjust the seasoning, adding more curry powder and cayenne pepper if you like.

Spoon the sauce over the scallops. Sprinkle with the bread crumbs and melted butter. The scallops may be prepared to this point up to 6 hours ahead and refrigerated.

To finish, heat the broiler. Broil the scallops about 4 inches/ 10 cm from the heat until very hot and browned, taking care not to overcook them or they will toughen. Serve at once.

═ PORTRAIT OF A FISHERMAN ═

For several happy years we had a summer house in Normandy, near the little fishing village of Veules-les-Roses. Each day except Sunday, rowboats returned on the incoming tide with the catch of the day. You took what you could, large or small, cod, hake, luxury Dover sole or despised dogfish, first come, first served. Today it is different. *"La mer est vide!"* ("The sea is empty!") laments fisherman Denis Dufour. We have just walked along the modest seafront lined with beach huts, so evocative of an Impressionist painting. The glittering sea is full of bathers but no longer, apparently, of fish.

Denis first went to sea in the mid-1960s, age fourteen, rowing the boat while the skipper fished. "It was hard," he says, "but easy, too. The sea was full of fish—we would catch cod of eight kilos [over seventeen pounds], sometimes dozens—but now you're lucky to have one or two of two kilos [less than five pounds]." The boats were heavy, made of wood, and each day had to be dragged with a windlass across the cobbles. "They were shaped like a banana, a bow at each end," he explains, "modeled on the dories that were packed upside down like salad bowls on the mother ship,

then sent out in search of Newfoundland cod. They were wonderful in a high sea, but in fact here in Veules-les-Roses we never had to go more than a mile or two from shore to find a catch."

The first breakthrough came in the 1970s with outboard motors, the passport to deeper waters, and more fish. The three or four fishermen of Veules-les-Roses gained repute and a little crowd would assemble to buy the catch, still flapping in the bottom of the boats. Later the boats were aluminum, double the size of the old wooden dories and with two powerful outboards for safety. The tiny cabin, just three feet across, acts as little more than a windbreak, but these boats can handle up to twenty miles (thirty-two kilometers) of net that is suspended from buoys and trawls the ocean bed. (The Channel is shallow, rarely more than seventy-five feet [twenty-five meters] deep.) Today, Denis Dufour confronts an ocean that has been swept clean. He is glad he has retired. "Sometimes there is not a single cod, and they're fishing tiny fish. They're destroying the nursery," he says.

HOMARD À L'AMÉRICAINE

LOBSTER WITH TOMATOES AND GARLIC

serves 2

Lobster Américaine is an ideal combination of rich lobster, fruity tomatoes, the anise whiff of tarragon, and a hint of Cognac, a quiet classic that never dies. Part of the mystery is in the adjective: should the dish be called amoricaine *or* américaine? *Is it inspired by Armor, the ancient name for Brittany, and home of the finest lobsters in France? Or does it come from southern France, through a Provençal chef who invented the dish for an American customer? The second seems to me the more likely, since we find olive oil, tomatoes, and garlic in the dish, all so typical of the cuisine of the sun. This recipe is not for the fainthearted, as the live lobster must be cut up in the kitchen. But the burst of pure lobster flavor served in a complex coulis of tomato is worth the assault. Serve it on a bed of rice.*

2 LIVE LOBSTERS (ABOUT 1½ POUNDS/675 G EACH)

BOILED RICE, FOR SERVING

COOKING LIQUID

3 TABLESPOONS/45 ML OLIVE OIL

1 ONION, CHOPPED

3 SHALLOTS (ABOUT 2 OUNCES/60 G TOTAL), CHOPPED

1 GARLIC CLOVE, CHOPPED

6 TABLESPOONS/90 ML COGNAC

1 CUP/250 ML DRY WHITE WINE

1 CUP/250 ML FISH STOCK (SEE PAGE 376) OR WATER

1 BOUQUET GARNI (SEE PAGE 370)

1 SMALL BUNCH FRESH TARRAGON (ABOUT 1 OUNCE/30 G), LEAVES AND STEMS SEPARATED

PINCH OF CAYENNE PEPPER

SALT AND BLACK PEPPER

SAUCE

1 POUND/450 G TOMATOES, PEELED, SEEDED, AND CHOPPED (SEE PAGE 372)

2 TABLESPOONS TOMATO PASTE

4 TABLESPOONS/60 G BUTTER

2 TABLESPOONS CRÈME FRAÎCHE (PAGE 374) OR HEAVY CREAM

PINCH OF CAYENNE PEPPER, IF NEEDED

For this classic dish, the lobsters must be cut into pieces. Lay a lobster flat on a board, hard shell up, head facing right; cover the tail with a cloth and hold it firmly in place with one hand. Holding a sharp, heavy knife in the other, pierce down to the board through the cross mark at the center of the head. Turn the lobster

so the tail faces the other way and cover the body with the cloth. Starting where you pierced the shell, continue splitting the body lengthwise to the tail, then cut the tail off in one piece. Save the liquid that runs from the lobster. Scoop out the soft green meat (tomalley) and any black coral from the body and reserve them. Discard the head sac (just behind the eyes). Cut the lobster tail, including the shell, into thick slices, discarding the intestinal tract. Crack the claws. Repeat with the second lobster.

For the cooking liquid, heat the oil in a sauté pan or deep frying pan over high heat and add the cracked claws and tail pieces, cut sides down. Sauté for 1 minute, turn, and continue cooking until the shells turn red, 1 to 2 minutes. Take out the pieces, add the body and legs, cook until they turn red, about 2 minutes and remove.

Lower the heat to medium, add the onion, shallots, and garlic, and sauté until soft but not brown, 5 to 7 minutes. Replace all the lobster pieces, including the claws and tails, and add the Cognac and flambé it (see page 371). Add the wine, reserved liquid from cutting up the lobster, fish stock, bouquet garni, tarragon stems (reserve the leaves for the tomato sauce), and cayenne pepper and season with salt and black pepper. Cover and simmer until the lobster meat is no longer translucent and starts to pull from the shells, 8 to 10 minutes.

Take the lobster tails and claws from the cooking liquid, remove the meat, and set it aside. Set aside the legs for garnish. Crush all the shells in a large mortar with a pestle, or pound them in a heavy bowl with the end of a rolling pin. Return them to the cooking liquid and simmer until the liquid is well reduced and the maximum flavor has been extracted from the shells, 8 to 10 minutes. Strain the liquid into a bowl, pressing hard on the lobster shells to extract maximum flavor.

For the sauce, return the strained liquid to the sauté pan and stir in the tomatoes and tomato paste. Bring the sauce to a boil and simmer until well reduced and the tomatoes are pulpy, 12 to 15 minutes. Meanwhile, crush the butter and work in the tomalley and coral. Coarsely chop the tarragon leaves.

To finish, add the lobster tail meat to the sauce, reserving the claw meat for garnish. Gently heat the tail meat for about 1 minute. Stir in the chopped tarragon and crème fraîche, then the tomalley-flavored butter so it blends with the sauce. Off the heat, taste and adjust the seasoning with salt and black pepper, adding cayenne pepper to brighten the flavor if needed.

Spread a bed of rice on 2 warmed plates and spoon the lobster and sauce over the rice. Top each plate with the shelled lobster claws and arrange the legs around the edge. The lobster in its sauce can be prepared ahead and refrigerated for a few hours, but it must be reheated very carefully or the meat will be tough.

= A SUMPTUOUS SEAFOOD PLATTER =

The favorite opening to a good meal all along the coasts of France (and in brasseries inland, too) is a seafood platter. Great mounds of colorful claws and shells arrive heaped on a wire stand, along with crab pickers, nutcrackers, pins for the winkles, and fingerbowls. Extracting recalcitrant tidbits from the shells is messy work, but that's part of the fun.

The contents of a seafood platter range from a modest handful of winkles and baby shrimp to a gala display of eight or ten different shellfish, their subtle hues offset by a background of crushed ice and dark seaweed. Eaten raw on the half shell, oysters, clams, mussels, and baby scallops must be scrupulously fresh. A couple of sea snail varieties—winkles and whelks—are always included, having been boiled in a concentrated court bouillon to make them edible. More exceptional platters include some large pink shrimp along with some baby gray ones. The best platters have a few frail, pale pink langoustines draped over the edge, plus a crab or two, with cracked claws and split down the middle so the meat is easy to remove. The hard-earned morsels are then eaten with mayonnaise, onion- or shallot-flavored vinaigrette, thinly sliced brown bread, butter, and plenty of chilled white or rosé wine.

Here is a guide to seafood names you will find on restaurant menus:

araignée – spider crab
bigorneau – winkle
bulot – periwinkle
crevette or *bouquet* – shrimp
gamba – jumbo prawn or shrimp
huître – oyster
langouste – crayfish, spiny lobster, or rock lobster
langoustine – scampi or Dublin Bay prawn
moule – mussel
oursin – sea urchin
palourde – carpetshell clam
pétoncle – baby scallop
pouce-pied – goose barnacle
praire – littleneck clam
tourteau – crab (similar to Dungeness)

LA MOUCLADE VENDÉENE

MUSSELS WITH SAFFRON AND CREAM

serves 4 as a main course, or 8 as a first course

Tradition has it that the farming of mussels in the Vendée, south of the Loire, dates back to 1237, when an Irish sea captain was shipwrecked on the coast. He managed to swim ashore and set bird traps in the water. The sticks supporting the nets were soon covered with huge moules *(mussels), much larger than those growing on the rocks. Even now, mussels are still cultivated on stakes in much the same way.*

On part of the Atlantic coast, moucle *is the local name for mussel, and a* mouclade *can be made in many ways, with or without spices, some with cream. Here, a good pinch of saffron (be sure to use saffron threads rather than powder) perfumes the wine sauce and colors it a vivid gold. As a first course, serve the mussels with a spoon and lots of crusty bread to soak up the sauce. For a main course, add crisp* pommes frites—*memorable when dipped in the salty mussel-flavored sauce. The local white wine used in this recipe would be a Muscadet, light and dry.*

6 POUNDS/2.7 KG MUSSELS

1 CUP/250 ML DRY WHITE WINE

3 TABLESPOONS/45 G BUTTER

3 ONIONS (ABOUT 1 POUND/450 G TOTAL), CHOPPED

1 GARLIC CLOVE, CHOPPED

PINCH OF CAYENNE PEPPER

SALT AND BLACK PEPPER

2 TABLESPOONS COGNAC, MORE TO TASTE

LARGE PINCH OF SAFFRON THREADS, SOAKED IN 2 TO 3 TABLESPOONS BOILING WATER

1/2 CUP/125 ML CRÈME FRAÎCHE (PAGE 374) OR HEAVY CREAM

BEURRE MANIÉ

3 TABLESPOONS/45 G BUTTER

3 TABLESPOONS/22 G FLOUR

Clean the mussels (see page 372). Put them in a large pot and pour in the wine. Cover and cook over high heat, stirring once, until they open, about 5 minutes. Transfer the mussels with a draining spoon to a warmed bowl, cover, and keep warm. Reserve the cooking liquid.

For the sauce, melt the butter in a saucepan over medium heat. Add the onions and cook, stirring often, until soft and lightly browned, 8 to 10 minutes. Stir in the garlic, cayenne pepper, and a little black pepper and cook for another 30 seconds. Stir in the Cognac and the saffron with its liquid. Pour the reserved mussel liquid into the onions, leaving any grit behind.

To thicken the sauce, bring the liquid to a boil and simmer for 1 to 2 minutes until well flavored. For the beurre manié, crush the butter on a plate with a fork and work in the flour to form a soft paste. Whisk the paste into the simmering liquid a piece or two at a time until the sauce coats a spoon lightly. You may not need all of the paste. Whisk in the crème fraîche, bring the sauce to a boil, and simmer for 1 to 2 minutes. Taste and adjust the seasoning with black pepper, cayenne pepper, and Cognac; salt may not be needed, as the mussels are salty.

Pile the mussels in warmed soup bowls, spoon the sauce over them, and serve at once, very hot.

GAMBAS GRILLÉS AU SEL DE MER

SEARED PRAWNS WITH SEA SALT

serves 2 or 3 as a main course, or 4 as a first course

This recipe suits many sizes of prawns, from giant gambas *(jumbo prawns) on down, including langoustines (scampi or Dublin Bay prawns). The prawns must be large, raw, and in their shells, with or without heads. Don't use small shrimp, as they will absorb too much salt. Here is the place to use your special* fleur de sel. *You will find that your guests will jump right in, peeling the shellfish at the table as a first course or luxurious main course.*

1 1/2 TO 2 POUNDS/675 TO 900 G JUMBO PRAWNS

1/4 CUP/30 G CORNSTARCH

1 TABLESPOON/18 G COARSE SEA SALT

2 TABLESPOONS VEGETABLE OIL, MORE IF NEEDED

PEPPER, FOR SERVING

Peel and devein the prawns. Mix the cornstarch and salt in a bowl, add the prawns, and toss them until coated. Heat the oil in a sauté pan or deep frying pan over medium heat. When almost smoking, add half the prawns, spreading them flat in a single layer. Put a heavy pan on top of the prawns to press them down. Fry until lightly browned, 1 to 2 minutes, depending on their size. Remove the top pan, turn the prawns, press again, and brown the other side, 1 to 2 minutes longer. Remove the prawns from the pan and repeat with the remaining prawns, adding more oil if necessary.

Serve the prawns at once, very hot, passing the pepper mill for a topping of freshly ground pepper.

GAMBAS GRILLÉS AU
SEL DE MER

MOULES MARINIÈRE
serves 4 as a first course

Small, piquant moules de bouchot *are a specialty of Dieppe, traditionally the nearest fishing port to Paris, one hundred miles (160 kilometers) distant. As early as the sixteenth century, caravans of packhorses known as the* chasse marée *(marine express) raced from Dieppe with barrels of live fish, their route cleared by a bellman until they reached Boulevard Poissonnière (Fish Boulevard) in Paris. Moules Marinière is a foundation recipe, an invitation for all sorts of additions, such as crème fraîche, saffron threads, dried chili, tomato, or spicy sausage.*

6 POUNDS/ 2.7 KG SMALL MUSSELS

1 CUP/250 ML DRY WHITE WINE

3 SHALLOTS (ABOUT 2 OUNCES/60 G TOTAL), VERY FINELY CHOPPED

1 BOUQUET GARNI (SEE PAGE 370)

SALT AND PEPPER

2 TABLESPOONS COARSELY CHOPPED FRESH PARSLEY

Clean the mussels (see page 372). Put the wine, shallots, bouquet garni, and plenty of pepper in a soup pot. Bring it to a boil and then simmer for 2 minutes. Return the heat to high, add the mussels, cover, and cook, stirring once, until they open, about 5 minutes. Take care not to overcook them or they will be tough. Take the pan from the heat, sprinkle the mussels with the parsley, and stir. Discard the bouquet garni, taste, and adjust the seasoning of the cooking liquid. Salt may not be needed, as the mussels themselves are salty.

Serve the mussels very hot in large soup bowls. Spoon the cooking liquid over them, leaving behind any grit that has fallen to the bottom of the pot. You will need to provide spoons for the liquid, but no forks. An empty mussel shell forms handy pincers for pulling other mussels from their shells.

MOULES À LA CRÈME
MUSSELS WITH CREAM

This variation of Moules Marinière is popular in northern France.

Follow the recipe for Moules Marinière, and when the mussels are cooked, transfer them to serving bowls and keep warm. Discard the bouquet garni and carefully pour the cooking liquid into a saucepan, leaving any grit behind. Whisk in ½ cup/125 ml crème fraîche or heavy cream and bring just to a boil. Make a beurre manié by crushing 2 tablespoons/30 g butter with a fork and working in 2 tablespoons/15 g flour to make a soft paste. Whisk the paste into the cream mixture a piece or two at a time until the liquid thickens to a light sauce. You may not need all of the paste. Take from the heat and whisk in the parsley. Taste, adjust the seasoning, and pour the sauce over the mussels. Serve at once, steaming hot.

BEIGNETS D'HUÎTRES AU CHAMPAGNE

OYSTER FRITTERS IN CHAMPAGNE BATTER

serves 4 as a first course

You will find a treat like this only in areas of oyster production such as Arcachon, near Bordeaux, and Cancale, on the northern border of Brittany (see facing page). The oysters are opened on the spot, drained, dipped quickly in batter, and fried to rush to the table. Crisp and golden outside, moist and juicy inside, no accompaniment is needed except a sprinkling of fresh lemon juice or vinegar. The oysters may be large or medium, and any dry sparkling white wine can take the place of Champagne in the batter.

CHAMPAGNE BATTER

 1 CUP/125 G FLOUR

 1/2 CUP/60 G CORNSTARCH

 1 CUP/250 ML CHAMPAGNE OR DRY SPARKLING WHITE WINE, MORE IF NEEDED

24 OYSTERS IN THE SHELL

VEGETABLE OIL FOR DEEP-FRYING

LEMON WEDGES OR RED WINE VINEGAR, FOR SERVING

DEEP-FRYER

For the Champagne batter, sift the flour and cornstarch into a bowl. (No salt is needed, as the oysters are salty.) Make a well in the center and add the Champagne. Stir with a whisk, gradually drawing in the flour and cornstarch to make a smooth batter. Let stand for 15 to 30 minutes so the starches expand and the batter thickens slightly.

To shuck the oysters, take an oyster knife in one hand, cover your other hand with a thick glove or cloth, and grip the shell in your protected palm. Keeping the oyster level with the knife, insert the point of the blade next to the hinge and twist to pry open the shell. Scrape the top shell to loosen the oyster meat and discard the shell. Loosen the meat from the lower shell and tip it into a strainer set over a bowl. Repeat with the remaining oysters. The batter can be made and the oysters shucked 2 to 3 hours ahead, but dipping and frying must be done at the last minute; keep the oysters chilled, with their juices separate. If the batter seems too thick when you are ready to fry, thin it with a bit of the oyster juices.

To fry the oysters, heat the oil to 375°F/190°C in a deep-fryer. A drop of batter should sizzle at once. Dip an oyster into the batter, let the excess drip back into the bowl for a few seconds, and then lower the oyster into the oil. Continue with more oysters, frying about 6 oysters in each batch. Fry, stirring once or twice so the oysters do not stick together, until golden, 3 to 4 minutes. Transfer them to a rack lined with paper towels and let them drain while you fry the rest.

Serve the oysters at once, while still hot and crisp. Pass the lemon wedges at the table.

= OPULENT OYSTERS =

Before the nineteenth century, great numbers of oysters were harvested from the wild, but in Europe today virtually all are farmed. "The quality of an oyster depends on how it is grown," says Jérôme Delarue, winner of a national Prix d'Excellence. "It's just like making good wine. Oysters need clean water, space, and we sort them as they grow, discarding any shells that are misshapen or have parasites." Monsieur Delarue raises oysters in Arcachon, a fishing port on the edge of a vast, shallow bay south of Bordeaux that yields over four hundred thousand tons a year. As we talk, a rattling piece of machinery sorts his shells by size, before they are reimmersed in *claires*, or parks, where they will clean and fatten for sale. "We sell 30 percent of our yearly production in the week before Christmas. It's quite a challenge!" The traditional ban on selling oysters in months without an *r* is no longer necessary, says Delarue. It was a health precaution in hot weather before the days of refrigeration. Nonetheless, I still rarely see a Frenchman eating an oyster in summer.

Flat, round native oysters (*Ostrea edulis*), known as *huîtres plates*, which include the prized belon oysters of Brittany (called *gravettes* in Arcachon), represent less than 10 percent of production. The rest are concave and elongated (*huîtres creuses*) and are known as Portuguese oysters (*Crassostrea angulata*), or Japanese oysters when they are from the Pacific. The story goes that, in the 1860s, a Portuguese ship carrying these oysters foundered off France in a storm. Apparently, the creatures multiplied in their new home, until in the 1920s they outnumbered French oysters, which had been decimated by an epidemic. In fact, successive waves of disease have long plagued France's oyster beds, and now the resistant Japanese variety is the most common.

Habitat is crucial to how an oyster tastes. The oysters of Marennes, north of Bordeaux, are especially delicate with a greenish tinge, Normandy oysters are notably salty, while those from the Île de Ré taste distinctly of algae. In restaurants I recommend you order a platter of several different kinds, all raw, and accompany it with a glass of cool dry white wine. At home, I sometimes deep-fry oysters in batter or serve them gratinéed on the half shell, both typical country preparations. But when looking at the best raw belons, I wouldn't dream of adding more than a squeeze of fresh lemon or, at a stretch, the quintessential *mignonette* dressing of shallot and vinegar.

Oysters must be tightly shut when opened; if any shells are gaping, tap them briskly on the counter and discard them if they do not close at once. Most authorities recommend opening the hinge end first, with a sharp, stubby knife. Be sure to protect your grasping hand with a glove. Surprise is the key to success. Once the oyster tightens its muscle, it is doubly hard to pry open.

ÉCREVISSES À LA NAGE

CRAYFISH IN WHITE WINE COURT BOUILLON

serves 4 as a first course

A great bowl of crayfish served in their court bouillon *(literally "quick broth") is a rare treat still found occasionally in Savoy and the Dauphiné. Cooks in Normandy make a similar broth to poach their baby lobsters, a dish known as* les demoiselles de Cherbourg, *flavoring it with Calvados instead of vermouth. A dry white wine such as a Sauvignon Blanc is good for the bouillon. I am suggesting a white butter sauce based on a reduction of the cooking liquid for dipping the crayfish tails, but simple melted butter would be fine, too.*

24 LARGE CRAYFISH, LIVE OR THAWED FROZEN
(ABOUT 3 POUNDS/1.35 KG TOTAL)

COURT BOUILLON

3 CARROTS (ABOUT 9 OUNCES/250 G TOTAL),
THINLY SLICED

2 ONIONS, THINLY SLICED

1 BOUQUET GARNI (SEE PAGE 370)

1 BOTTLE (750 ML) DRY WHITE WINE

3 CUPS/750 ML WATER

PINCH OF CAYENNE PEPPER

SALT AND BLACK PEPPER

3 TABLESPOONS/45 ML DRY WHITE VERMOUTH

2 TABLESPOONS CHOPPED FRESH PARSLEY

SAUCE

1 TABLESPOON CRÈME FRAÎCHE (PAGE 374) OR
HEAVY CREAM

3/4 CUP/170 G COLD BUTTER, CUT INTO CUBES

FEW DROPS WHITE VERMOUTH

Wash the crayfish and, if they are live, discard any that are not moving. To remove the intestinal vein, wear a glove or use a cloth (for protection from the claws) to hold the crayfish body firmly in one hand. With your other hand, twist the central flange of the tail and pull out the vein attached to it. Repeat with the remaining crayfish.

For the court bouillon, put the carrots, onions, bouquet garni, wine, water, cayenne pepper, salt, and black pepper in a soup pot and bring to a boil. Add the crayfish, pushing them down under the liquid. Cover the pan and simmer until the crayfish are bright red, 6 to 8 minutes. Transfer the crayfish to a bowl with a draining spoon and cover to keep warm.

For the sauce, strain about one-third of the bouillon into a small saucepan and boil until reduced to about 3 tablespoons/ 45 ml, 15 to 20 minutes. Add the crème fraîche and boil again to reduce to about 3 tablespoons. Take the pan from the heat and whisk in a few cubes of the butter until softened. Continue adding the butter a few pieces a time, working on and off the heat so that it softens without melting to oil. Do not let the sauce get too hot or it will separate. Taste the sauce, seasoning it with salt, black pepper, and a few drops of vermouth. Set it on a rack over a pan of steaming water to keep warm.

Meanwhile, simmer the remaining bouillon until the vegetables are tender, 10 to 15 minutes. Stir in the 3 tablespoons of vermouth and the parsley, taste, and adjust the seasoning.

To serve, spoon the bouillon and vegetables into warmed bowls, discarding the bouquet garni. Pile the crayfish in the center and serve at once. Provide guests with individual bowls of the butter sauce for dipping, scissors, crab picks, and finger bowls. Some people like to drink the bouillon, so they will also need soup spoons.

MARÉE DE PETITS CALAMARS ET CREVETTES

SEA SALAD OF BABY SQUID AND SHRIMPS

serves 4 as a main course

It is hard to match the favorite Mediterranean salad of perfectly fresh seafood dressed with a little virgin olive oil and a squeeze of fresh lemon juice. Note the careful wording: the oil must be "virgin," or cold pressed, and it must be a "squeeze" of lemon, so the fragrant natural oils present in the peel mingle with the juice. These are the kinds of details that make so much difference when putting together simple dishes. You will need crusty bread to mop up the dressing.

1 POUND/450 G BABY SQUID, CLEANED

2 LEMONS, FOR SERVING

1 QUART/1 LITER WATER

3 TO 4 TABLESPOONS SALT

1 POUND/450 G COOKED PEELED SMALL SHRIMP

1 GARLIC CLOVE, CHOPPED

3 TO 4 TABLESPOONS CHOPPED FRESH PARSLEY

JUICE OF 1 LEMON

6 TABLESPOONS/90 ML EXTRA-VIRGIN OLIVE OIL

BLACK PEPPER

Cut the squid bodies into rings ¼ inch/6 mm wide and the tentacles into 1-inch/2.5-cm pieces. Rinse them thoroughly. Halve the lemons crosswise, cutting them in decorative "wolf's teeth," if you like, and slice a small piece from the base of each half so it will stand flat.

Put the water and salt in a saucepan and bring to a boil, stirring to dissolve the salt. Add the squid and cook just until firm, 1 to 2 minutes. Be careful not to overcook them or they will be tough. Lift them out with a draining spoon and set aside. To take the chill off the shrimp, immerse them in the boiling salted water for 5 seconds and drain them at once.

Put the squid and shrimp in a bowl and toss with the garlic, parsley, lemon juice, oil, salt, and plenty of freshly ground pepper. Taste and adjust the seasoning. Pile on individual plates and add a lemon half to each one. Serve at warm room temperature.

ENCORNETS FARCIS
STUFFED SQUID
serves 4 as a main course

Most kinds of squid can be stuffed, provided they have a large natural pouch. Encornet is a common type on the Mediterranean, and the good-sized calamar is another possibility. Languedoc white wines tend to be full-bodied from the sun, just right for this dish, which is lively with lemon and green olives and is good served at room temperature on a hot day.

8 WHOLE SQUID (ABOUT 2 POUNDS/900 G TOTAL), CLEANED AND DIVIDED INTO POUCH AND TENTACLES

OLIVE OIL, FOR THE DISH

I LEMON

½ BUNCH FRESH THYME (ABOUT ½ OUNCE/15 G)

STUFFING

6 SLICES WHITE BREAD (ABOUT 5½ OUNCES/150 G TOTAL)

¾ CUP/175 ML MILK

3 TABLESPOONS/45 ML OLIVE OIL

I SMALL ONION, CHOPPED

I POUND/450 G TOMATOES, PEELED, SEEDED, AND CHOPPED (SEE PAGE 372)

SALT AND BLACK PEPPER

½ CUP/100 G SALTED (DRY-CURED) OR BRINED GREEN OLIVES, PITTED AND CHOPPED

2 GARLIC CLOVES, CHOPPED

2 TABLESPOONS CHOPPED FRESH PARSLEY

2 EGG YOLKS

WHITE WINE SAUCE

2 TABLESPOONS OLIVE OIL

I ONION, CHOPPED

I GARLIC CLOVE, CHOPPED

I DRIED BAY LEAF

I TABLESPOON/7 G FLOUR

¾ CUP/175 ML FULL-BODIED WHITE WINE

½ CUP/125 ML WATER

JUICE OF ½ LEMON, MORE TO TASTE

Give the squid a good rinse, remove the fins, and chop the fins and tentacles. Set aside the pouches separately. Heat the oven to 350°F/180°C. Oil a baking dish.

For the stuffing, soak the bread in the milk. Heat the oil in a sauté pan or deep frying pan over medium heat. Add the onion and sauté, stirring occasionally, until soft, about 3 minutes. Stir in the chopped squid and tomatoes, season with salt and pepper, and continue cooking, stirring often, until all moisture has evaporated, 12 to 15 minutes. Squeeze as much moisture as possible from the bread and pull it into coarse crumbs with your fingers. Stir the bread into the tomato mixture with the olives, garlic, and parsley. Taste and adjust the seasoning. Take the pan from the heat and stir in the egg yolks.

Meanwhile, make the wine sauce. Heat the oil in a saucepan over low heat. Add the onion and sauté, stirring occasionally, until soft, about 5 minutes. Add the garlic, bay leaf, and flour and stir constantly for about 1 minute. Whisk in the wine, water, lemon juice, salt, and pepper. Bring to a boil over medium heat, whisking constantly until the sauce thickens, and then simmer for 8 to 10 minutes to develop the flavor. Taste and adjust the seasoning.

Cut the peel from the lemon, removing all the white pith as well; cut the flesh crosswise into 8 thin slices, discarding any seeds. Using a teaspoon, fill the squid pouches with the stuffing. Take care not to overfill them, or they may burst during cooking. Lay the squid in the prepared baking dish, overlapping them as they will shrink during cooking. Strain the wine sauce over the squid and top each one with a lemon slice. Tuck in the thyme sprigs among them.

Cover and bake until the squid lose their translucence and are tender when pricked with a skewer, 20 to 25 minutes. Serve them directly from the baking dish, hot or at room temperature.

Lace caps and lighthouses, butter and buckwheat, fishermen and farmers, oysters, artichokes, and sardines—the province of Brittany, jutting into the Atlantic from the northwest corner of France, is by nature a land of contrasts. The seas and coastline of Brittany are some of the most traveled in the world, but the rocky, forested interior remains remote. Here, within the family, the older generation still speaks Breton, a Celtic language very different from French, and road signs are bilingual.

The seas once held all the wealth, though supplies are increasingly stretched. Today, oysters are one of the most profitable local shellfish, bred on both northern and southern coasts (see "Opulent Oysters," page 91). Lobsters are so expensive now that they are almost beyond local reach, priced for fancy restaurants in far-off places. *Coquilles Saint-Jacques* (sea scallops) are a seasonal treat lasting from October to May, commonly served with their coral still attached, like an orange crescent moon. More affordable are mussels, steamed *à la marinière* (with onion, parsley and white wine), or broiled with garlic butter and bread crumbs, a style that also suits the indigenous clams, *palourdes*, at their peak in the spring. It is a miserly café that does not offer a gratis bowl of winkles or periwinkles with a glass of cider.

The list of Breton fish is equally impressive. Halibut, turbot, sea bass, and Dover sole swim alongside cod and hake, with the line-caught catch superior to trawled. Humbler varieties, such as whiting, eel, and mackerel, are often relegated to the stew pot for the local fish soup, Cotriade (page 100), the Atlantic's answer to Mediterranean Bouillabaisse (page 99). The warm Gulf Stream current also brings tuna close to Brittany's shores, along with anchovies, mullet, and sardines. Indeed, the pride of the long-established Breton canning industry is *sardines à l'huile*, which are aged for up to ten years in olive oil and salt and must be turned from time to time, like a good cheese. The most expensive are branded by vintage. Canned tuna is another flourishing, if less quaint, industry, along with (I hate to mention) frozen fish sticks and vacuum-packed fillets in sauce.

The endless coastline is what makes Brittany famous and prosperous, but the interior is now pulling its weight, too. Brightly colored trucks full of pigs trundle the roads, and today Brittany produces half of France's pork and three-fourths of its chickens. Thanks to a climate where frost is rare, Brittany is also a vegetable paradise, growing almost all the French cauliflowers and artichokes (a Breton emblem), alongside Plougastel strawberries, pink Roscoff onions, and little carrots cultivated in the sand dunes of Finistère (World's End). Here, whitewashed houses huddle to the ground, their slate roofs almost touching the earth on the windward side. The roads are lined with little fields protected by *bocage*, an ingenious system of enclosures, part wall, part hedge, rising to at least six feet (two meters) and sometimes topped by bushes of scarlet-flowered fuchsia, and by tall trees that provide shelter from the storm and wind.

Bretons are idiosyncratic about their cheese, preferring fresh dairy products to the aged cheeses found in the rest of France. They appreciate buttermilk (*lait ribot*) and *gros lait*, a local specialty that resembles soft yogurt. The province's cowherds watch over one-third of the milking cows in France, which means Bretons make plenty of butter, key to their baking (see "The Very Best Butter," page 303). *Kouign-aman* is Breton for butter cake, but to describe it as a croissant dough layered with caramelized sugar gives only an inkling of this luscious, tricky pastry. Gâteau Breton (page 293), a version of pound cake so rich it resembles shortbread, can include apples, raisins, and candied cherries. The *cornic* of Douarnenez (a type of croissant) and the rich, crispy *galettes de Pont Aven* have become household names. And let's not forget the most famous Breton specialty of all: Crêpes (page 238), which have spread far beyond the shores of this proud, quirky province.

the
French Touch

FAVORITE
FISH STEWS

CHAPTER
No. **5**

In France, wherever there is water, you will find fish stew. In the north, along the Channel coast, white fish such as cod is simmered with mussels in Chaudrée (page 100), the ancestor of American chowder. On the Atlantic, Basque fishermen take the same cod and spice it with chili and plenty of garlic in Ttoro (page 103). I will always remember the amazing Bouillabaisse (facing page) I enjoyed on the waterfront in Marseille, a banquet of a dozen different fish and shellfish moistened with a red-gold broth perfumed with saffron. On the side came croûtes fried in olive oil, a crisp contrast to the fish, with glowing, almost fiery Sauce Rouille (page 219).

Freshwater fish are a less happy story. Welcoming stews of pike and perch once proliferated under names like *pochouse* in Burgundy and *matelote* on the Loire. Today such fish have almost disappeared from French rivers, and with them fish stew. However, I have come across eel cooked in Touraine with red wine and bacon, and in Picardy with herbs and cream as *waterzoï*.

To me, fish stew is the happy finale for fish that might otherwise never reach the market because they are too small, too bony, or too ugly to sell (like eel). All fish stews follow the same principles: fresh fish; a flavorful broth packed with wine, herbs, garlic, or whatever is to local taste; and lively accompaniments (including croûtes). Many seaside markets sell piles of mixed whole fish for stew. They come with their heads for the cook to make fish fumet, a key to so many marine dishes. Expect fish bones in your soup bowl unless the cook has gone to great lengths to remove them, which is unlikely in the countryside.

When serving, you will need forks as well as spoons for broth, and possibly picks for shellfish. A single type of fish may anchor a particular stew. For example, cod is essential to Cotriade (page 100), and *rascasse* (scorpion fish) to Bouillabaisse. Apart from that, the more varied the mix the better, so that rich, oily fish are balanced by lighter, white varieties. In any of the recipes here, don't hesitate to substitute what is fresh and available. The point of fish stew is to make the most of the day's catch. I also think it is important to serve fish stew straight from the stove. When reheated, the lively, briny taste of fresh fish fades and the broth is flat. A dose of chopped herbs and a squeeze of lemon juice help.

BOUILLABAISSE

serves 8 to 10

Bouillabaisse, once a simple fish stew enjoyed along the coast of Provence, has expanded to become a cult. A serious Bouillabaisse calls for up to a dozen varieties of fish that must be skinned and deboned at table, to be enjoyed with a heady broth laden with fennel and saffron, with crisp croûtes and nippy Sauce Rouille on the side.

The name Bouillabaisse *is probably a compound of* bouillon abaissé, *or "broth reduced," a reminder that rapid boiling is needed to emulsify the large amount of olive oil in the cooking broth so it does not float on top of the stew. In theory, only Mediterranean fish qualify for a bouillabaisse:* rascasse *(an unpleasantly bony, though tasty, white-fleshed fish), John Dory, red mullet, and monkfish take the lead, with obscure types such as sea cicada (also known as a slipper lobster), and the* vive *(weever) with its poisonous spines, rounding out the flavor and complexity of the stew. Firm-fleshed fish may include conger eel, moray eel, and mackerel.*

These days, a wide variety of non-native fish are often substituted in Bouillabaisse, including whiting, flounder, bass, red snapper, perch, cod, and striped bass—whatever is plentiful is good for the pot.

3 POUNDS/1.35 KG WHITE FISH, WITH HEADS

2 POUNDS/900 G RICH FISH, WITH HEADS

8 TO 10 SMALL CRABS (OPTIONAL)

8 TO 10 SCAMPI (LANGOUSTINES), WITH HEADS (OPTIONAL)

MARINADE

6 TABLESPOONS/90 ML OLIVE OIL

2 GARLIC CLOVES, FINELY CHOPPED

PINCH OF SAFFRON THREADS, SOAKED IN 1 TO 2 TABLESPOONS BOILING WATER

1 LARGE BOUQUET GARNI (SEE PAGE 370)

4 OR 5 GARLIC CLOVES, CRUSHED

ZEST OF 1 ORANGE, PARED IN STRIPS

1 SMALL BUNCH FRESH FENNEL FRONDS, OR 2 TEASPOONS DRIED FENNEL SEEDS

3/4 CUP/175 ML OLIVE OIL

2 ONIONS, SLICED

2 LEEKS, WHITE PART WITH SOME GREEN PART, SLICED (SEE PAGE 371)

2 STALKS CELERY, SLICED

1 POUND/450 G TOMATOES, PEELED, SEEDED, AND CHOPPED (SEE PAGE 372)

LARGE PINCH OF SAFFRON THREADS, SOAKED IN 1 TO 2 TABLESPOONS BOILING WATER

SALT AND PEPPER

BAKED CROÛTES MADE WITH 2 BAGUETTES (SEE PAGE 374)

1 1/2 CUPS/375 ML SAUCE ROUILLE (PAGE 219)

1 TABLESPOON TOMATO PASTE

1 TABLESPOON PERNOD OR OTHER ANISE LIQUOR, OR TO TASTE

3 TO 4 TABLESPOONS CHOPPED FRESH PARSLEY

If not already done, clean and scale the fish, cutting off the fins with scissors. Wash and dry the fish. Remove the heads and tails and set aside. Cut the bodies into 2-inch/5-cm chunks. Cut the gills out of the fish heads (they can make the broth bitter) and put the heads in a saucepan along with the tails. Add water to barely cover and simmer over medium heat for 15 minutes. Strain and set aside the broth, discarding the heads and tails. There should be 2 to 3 quarts/2 to 3 liters broth (exact quantities are not important).

Meanwhile, wash and dry the crabs and scampi, if using. For the marinade, mix the oil, garlic, and saffron and its liquid in a large bowl. Add the fish and turn the pieces so they are coated.

Tie the bouquet garni, crushed garlic, orange zest, and fennel in a piece of cheesecloth. Heat the oil in a large soup pot over medium heat. Add the onions, leeks, and celery and sauté until soft but not brown, 8 to 12 minutes. Add the tomatoes and the cheesecloth bag of flavorings, and pour in the fish broth with the saffron and its liquid. Season with salt and pepper, cover, and bring to a boil. Simmer over medium heat for 30 to 40 minutes to create a flavorful broth. Meanwhile, make the croûtes and sauce rouille.

Add the rich fish and the crabs and scampi, if using, to the pot, pushing them well down into the liquid. Increase the heat to high, bring the liquid to a rolling boil, and cook the fish, uncovered, for 7 to 10 minutes. Don't stir, but shake the pan from time to time to prevent sticking. Put the white fish on top and boil until they just flake easily, 5 to 8 minutes longer. Add more water if needed during cooking to keep all the fish pieces bathed in broth. It is important to keep the liquid boiling fast so that the oil emulsifies with the broth.

Take the pot from the heat. Using a draining spoon, transfer the fish and shellfish to a warmed deep platter, arranging them so the different types are separated. Cover the platter with aluminum foil to keep warm. Discard the bag of flavorings. Whisk the tomato paste and Pernod into the hot broth, taste, and adjust the seasoning. Pour it into a warmed soup tureen.

Sprinkle the broth and seafood with the parsley and serve both at the same time, leaving guests to spoon a selection of seafood into large soup bowls and ladle broth on top. Serve the croûtes and rouille in separate dishes.

LA CHAUDRÉE

FISH CHOWDER

serves 4

At sea in the old days, fishermen cooked their meals in a chaudière *(casserole), hence the word* chaudrée *for fish stew. The term migrated with cod fishermen to the Grand Banks off Nova Scotia, and from there to the New World as* chowder. Chaudrée *was once as important on the Atlantic coast of France as* Bouillabaisse *along the Mediterranean. Like* Bouillabaisse, *it is a whole meal, with many versions. This simple recipe from the port of Fouras, near La Rochelle, contains plenty of onions, butter (a regional specialty), and a variety of fish, such as whiting, pollack, conger eel, and always including cod.*

The secrets of a good Chaudrée *are described in* La Cuisine du Poitou, *a local cookbook originally published in 1932: "To any recipe, add a thread of lemon juice toward the end of cooking, another while eating. Serve in a deep dish, heated and as thick as possible. Before pouring in the* chaudrée, *garnish the bottom with little pieces of good fresh butter." Just follow this advice!*

2 POUNDS/900 G MIXED FISH FILLETS, WITHOUT SKIN

1/2 CUP/110 G BUTTER

4 ONIONS (ABOUT 1 1/2 POUNDS/675 G TOTAL), QUARTERED

5 GARLIC CLOVES, CHOPPED

2 WHOLE CLOVES

2 CUPS/500 ML DRY WHITE WINE

3 CUPS/750 ML WATER, MORE IF NEEDED

1 SMALL BUNCH FRESH PARSLEY (ABOUT 1 OUNCE/30 G)

1 LARGE BOUQUET GARNI (SEE PAGE 370)

SALT AND PEPPER

BAKED CROÛTES MADE WITH 1 BAGUETTE (SEE PAGE 374)

1 LEMON

Wash and dry the fish, and cut into 2-inch/5-cm chunks. Melt half of the butter in a large flameproof casserole or soup pot. Spread the onions and garlic over the bottom, and press the cloves into an onion quarter. Lay the fish on top, putting firmer fish in first and more delicate ones on top. Pour in the wine and then add water just to cover the fish. Pull the parsley stems from the sprigs, and set the sprigs aside. Tie the parsley stems with the bouquet garni, add it to the casserole, and then season the contents with salt and pepper. Bring to a boil over medium heat, skimming often. Lower the heat and simmer, uncovered, for 4 to 6 minutes, or until the fish are just tender.

Transfer the fish with a draining spoon to a tray and set aside. Increase the heat and boil the broth until well flavored and reduced by about half, 25 to 30 minutes. Meanwhile, make the croûtes and keep them warm. Chop the reserved parsley sprigs. Cut the lemon in half lengthwise, and divide one-half into 4 wedges.

When the broth is ready, discard the bouquet garni and cloves, leaving the quartered onions. Squeeze in the juice from the remaining lemon half, taste, and adjust the seasoning. Return the fish to the broth and warm it briefly. Dice the remaining butter and divide it among 4 warmed soup bowls. Spoon in the chowder and sprinkle with the parsley. Perch a lemon wedge on the edge of each bowl. Serve very hot, with the croûtes passed separately.

COTRIADE BRETONNE

FISH STEW WITH SORREL AND LEEK

serves 6

Leek and sorrel add an agreeably acid bite to this Breton stew of white fish, dramatically topped with salty black mussels. Cotriade *is fortified with potatoes and made with white fish, like cod, haddock, hake, or whiting, plus a bit of rich fish, such as eel or mackerel. American alternatives are bluefish, red snapper, and flounder. Arugula can take the place of sorrel.*

1 POUND/450 G RICH FISH FILLETS, WITHOUT SKIN

1 POUND/450 G WHITE FISH FILLETS, WITHOUT SKIN

1 1/2 POUNDS /675 G MUSSELS

1 POUND/450 G SORREL OR ARUGULA, STEMS REMOVED

2 TABLESPOONS/30 G BUTTER

FRIED CROÛTES MADE WITH 1 BAGUETTE, SLICED, FRIED IN 4 TABLESPOONS/60 G BUTTER, AND RUBBED WITH A CUT GARLIC CLOVE (SEE PAGE 374)

COOKING LIQUID

2 TABLESPOONS/30 G BUTTER

2 ONIONS, CHOPPED

2 LEEKS, WHITE AND GREEN PARTS, CHOPPED (SEE PAGE 371)

2 GARLIC CLOVES, FINELY CHOPPED

1 QUART/1 LITER FISH STOCK (SEE PAGE 376)

1 POUND/450 G POTATOES, PEELED, QUARTERED, AND THINLY SLICED

1 BOUQUET GARNI (SEE PAGE 370)

SALT AND PEPPER

1 CUP/250 ML CRÈME FRAÎCHE (PAGE 374) OR HEAVY CREAM

JUICE OF 1 LEMON

continued

Wash and dry the fish, and cut into 2-inch/5-cm pieces. Clean the mussels (see page 372). Strip the stems from the sorrel, wash the leaves thoroughly, and drain them. Melt the butter in a large saucepan over medium heat. Add the sorrel, cover, and cook until the greens are wilted, 2 to 3 minutes. Remove the lid and continue cooking until all the moisture has evaporated. Sorrel will have dissolved to a purée; arugula will need to be chopped. Make the croûtes and set them aside.

For the cooking liquid, melt the butter in a large flameproof casserole or soup pot over medium heat. Add the onions, leeks, and garlic and cook, stirring often, until soft but not brown, 5 to 8 minutes. Add the stock, potatoes, bouquet garni, salt, and pepper and simmer until the potatoes are partially cooked, about 5 minutes.

Add the rich fish to the cooking liquid, pushing the pieces down into the liquid, and simmer for 2 minutes. Add the remaining fish and simmer until all the fish are nearly tender, 3 to 5 minutes longer. Add the sorrel or arugula and crème fraîche, shaking the pan so they mix into the liquid. Top with the mussels, cover, and continue simmering until the mussels open, 3 to 5 minutes.

Discard the bouquet garni, add the lemon juice, taste, and adjust the seasoning. Salt may not be needed, as the mussels are salty. Serve the cotriade directly from the pot, with the croûtes in a separate bowl. If you have guests, you may want to lift out the cooked mussels, shell them, and put the meats back in the stew before serving so they are easier to eat.

LA BOURRIDE

GARLIC FISH STEW

serves 4 to 6

Bourride is Languedoc's answer to the Bouillabaisse of Provence, and who knows which is the more popular of the two with the beach crowd. Favorite fish for Bourride are sea bass, sea bream, John Dory, and whiting, with monkfish and conger eel among firmer varieties. Provided you have the fish stock ready ahead, Bourride is quick to make. If the stew is to be kept warm for more than a minute or two, omit the egg yolk thickener and serve the Aïoli separately.

2 POUNDS/900 G MIXED FISH FILLETS, WITHOUT SKIN

1 CUP/250 ML AÏOLI (PAGE 219)

BAKED CROÛTES MADE WITH 1 BAGUETTE (SEE PAGE 374)

1 LARGE BOUQUET GARNI (SEE PAGE 370)

$^{1}/_{2}$ TEASPOON FENNEL SEEDS

2 STRIPS OF ORANGE ZEST

2 GARLIC CLOVES, UNPEELED AND CRUSHED

1$^{1}/_{2}$ QUARTS/1.5 LITERS FISH STOCK (SEE PAGE 376)

1 ONION, SLICED

1 TABLESPOON OLIVE OIL

SALT AND PEPPER

3 EGG YOLKS

Wash and dry the fish, and cut on the diagonal into slices ¾ inch/ 2 cm thick. Make the aïoli and croûtes.

Tie the bouquet garni, fennel seeds, orange zest, and garlic in cheesecloth, and put the bag in a soup pot with the stock, onion, oil, salt, and pepper. Bring to a boil, add the firm fish, and simmer over medium heat for 3 minutes. Add the remaining fish, lower the heat, and simmer very gently until all the fish just flake easily, 5 to 8 minutes. Transfer the fish to a platter with a draining spoon, cover with aluminum foil, and keep warm.

Whisk the aïoli with the egg yolks in a large bowl. Whisk in some of the hot fish broth and stir the mixture back into the pot. Stir the broth over very low heat, whisking constantly, until it thickens to the consistency of thin cream, 1 to 2 minutes. Do not let it get too hot or it will curdle.

Ladle some of the broth into 6 warmed bowls, add some pieces of fish, and set a croûte on top. Pour the remaining broth into a warmed tureen. Serve the bourride at once, passing a platter of the remaining fish, the tureen of broth, and the remaining croûtes separately.

TTORO

BASQUE PEPPERY FISH STEW

serves 4

Like all fish stews, Ttoro from the Basque country was originally designed to use flaky inexpensive fish with too many bones, such as hake, conger eel, mullet, and particularly gurnard, valued for its red skin. In the United States, I would suggest a mix of red snapper, jack, bream, pompano, and/ or mackerel. At its simplest, Ttoro includes garlic, tomatoes, mussels for a salty bite, and the lively Espelette pepper of the Basque region (I find paprika laced with a generous pinch of cayenne to be a good substitute). As a final fillip, this particular recipe is green with fresh herbs and has a whole langoustine perched on top of each serving bowl, as if trying to claw its way out. Fish such as eel, which cook more slowly than others, should be cut into smaller pieces.

BROTH

1 POUND/450 G FISH HEADS AND BONES

2 TABLESPOONS OLIVE OIL

2 ONIONS, SLICED

1 STALK CELERY, SLICED

3 GARLIC CLOVES, CHOPPED

1 BOUQUET GARNI (SEE PAGE 370)

1½ CUPS/375 ML MEDIUM-DRY WHITE WINE

1½ QUARTS/1.5 LITERS WATER

1 TOMATO, PEELED, SEEDED, AND CHOPPED (SEE PAGE 372)

2 TEASPOONS GROUND DRIED ESPELETTE PEPPER, OR 2 TEASPOONS PAPRIKA WITH A LARGE PINCH OF CAYENNE PEPPER, MORE TO TASTE

SALT

SEAFOOD

1½ POUNDS/675 G MUSSELS

1½ POUNDS/675 G MIXED FISH FILLETS, WITH SKIN

¼ CUP/30 G FLOUR, SEASONED WITH SALT AND PEPPER

2 TABLESPOONS OLIVE OIL

4 LARGE SCAMPI (LANGOUSTINES), WITH HEADS

GARNISH

FRIED CROÛTES MADE WITH 1 BAGUETTE, SLICED, FRIED IN 4 TO 5 TABLESPOONS OLIVE OIL, AND RUBBED WITH A CUT GARLIC CLOVE (SEE PAGE 374)

½ CUP CHOPPED FRESH PARSLEY

2 TABLESPOONS CHOPPED FRESH TARRAGON

2 TABLESPOONS CHOPPED FRESH CHIVES

For the broth, cut the gills out of the fish heads (they can make the broth bitter). Rinse the heads and bones, and cut the bones into 2 or 3 pieces. Heat the oil in a large flameproof casserole over low heat. Add the onions, celery, garlic, and bouquet garni and cook, stirring occasionally, until the onions are soft, 5 to 7 minutes. Add the wine, increase the heat, and boil until reduced by half, 3 to 5 minutes. Stir in the water, fish heads and bones, tomato, Espelette pepper, and salt. Bring to a boil, skim the surface, cover, and simmer, stirring occasionally, for 40 to 50 minutes. Strain the broth, pressing hard on the bones and vegetables to extract all the liquid, and then discard the solids. There should be about 1½ quarts/1.5 liters broth. It may be made up to 2 days in advance and refrigerated. Wash and dry the casserole to use later.

Make the croûtes and reserve for garnish. For the seafood, clean the mussels (see page 372). Cut the fish into 1½-inch/4-cm chunks, wash, and dry them. Coat the fish pieces with the seasoned flour, patting off the excess with your hands. Heat the oil in the casserole over high heat. Working in 2 or 3 batches, add the fish and brown quickly on all sides, transferring it to a plate with a draining spoon. When the last batch has been fried, discard any excess oil in the pot.

Return the fish to the pot, pour in the broth, and bring to a boil. Add the scampi, pushing them down into the broth, and set the mussels on top. Cover and simmer just until the mussels open, about 5 minutes. The fish should just flake easily when tested with a fork. Taste and adjust the seasoning. The broth should be quite peppery, but salt may not be needed, as the mussels are salty.

Lift out the scampi and set aside. Spoon the fish, mussels, and broth into warmed bowls and sprinkle with the parsley, tarragon, and chives. Add a scampi to each bowl. Arrange some of the croûtes around the edge of each bowl and serve the rest separately.

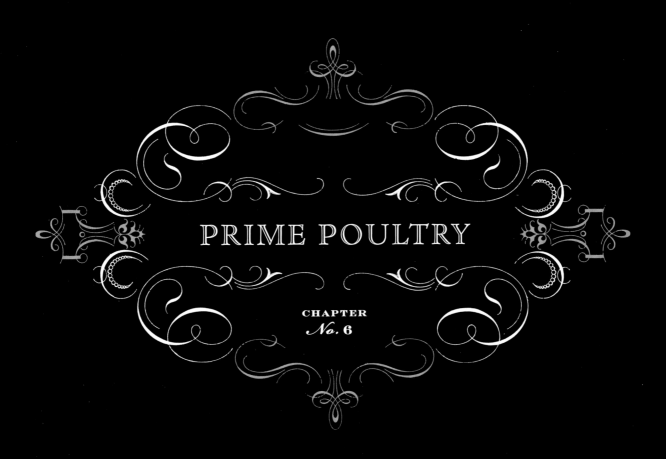

PRIME POULTRY

CHAPTER
No. 6

I am always happy to see chickens running around the backyard, and it is a common sight in rural France. Many are there just to provide a few eggs for the table, but some farming families still raise poultry in the open air, with no battery houses in sight. Retail farm poultry, or *volaille fermier*, which includes turkeys, ducks, geese, and guinea hens in addition to chickens, will have spent at least some of their life outdoors, as evidenced by the calluses on their feet. Most French supermarkets carry both *volaille fermier* and standard battery birds, and, in my experience, both are excellent.

Chickens come in at least half a dozen distinct categories. Most popular is *poulet*, a tender bird that is ideal for roasting whole or for cutting up for sautés, such as Poulet Sauté Basquaise (page 109). When carefully fattened (many producers grow their own corn), the bird becomes a plump *poularde* with generous breast meat, ideal with slices of jet black truffle in Poularde Demi-deuil (page 108). After laying eggs for a year or two, a mature hen becomes a *poule*, known in the United States as stewing hen or fowl and best simmered as Poule-au-Pot (facing page), a Gascon trademark. At the other end of the scale, one-portion chickens end a short life as *poussins* or *coquelets*, available in many supermarkets. I think they do best when split and grilled on skewers, but they make a handy individual roast, too.

Male birds also have their place, neutered young and fattened as *chapon* (capon), reaching up to a formidable ten pounds (four and one-half kilograms). A few privileged males get to lord it over the farmyard before they are marinated in wine, then simmered for several hours to tenderize their dark, gamey meat, as with the famed Coq au Vin (page 113). Equally sought after in specialty shops and a few large markets are *poulets de Bresse*, the aristocrats of the poultry world, with their blue feet, white feathers, and red crests. Graded AOC (page 111), they are a specific breed raised outdoors within the region of Bresse, fed on a defined diet until almost double the age of a supermarket chicken. A few other regions of France produce poultry of similar AOC quality.

There are two common varieties of duck: plump, white-skinned *canard Nantais* that are perfect for roasting, and darker, meaty *canard de Barbarie* (also known as Muscovy duck), good cut into pieces and braised in dishes like Canard aux Olives. Both are less fatty than the American Pekin breed. A foie gras duck is a third type, a crossbreed that is sold cut into legs and magrets (boneless breasts) after the valuable liver has been removed. When it comes to goose, breed is less important than appearance. You want white skin and buxom breast meat. A farm-raised French turkey may look skinny by American standards but will have far more taste. You will routinely find pieces and whole boned roasts as well as whole birds.

In this chapter I am also including one of the legendary specialties of France: foie gras (page 127). This is the liver of a fattened duck or goose, and production is now a cottage industry on farms throughout the country. As a result, a slice of foie gras is commonly used to top a steak or to garnish soups or vegetables, or is whisked into a special sauce for roast chicken. However, the most popular way to enjoy foie gras is solo in a terrine, where the intense richness of the liver can be fully appreciated.

POULE-AU-POT

serves 6 to 8

Poule-au-Pot is the stuff of legend, a dish that gathers families together with a big smile. In the early 1600s, Henri IV rashly vowed to put a chicken in the pot of every French household on Sundays. The Poule-au-Pot tradition comes from Béarn, the king's home province, but there is no standard recipe. In some versions, the chicken is cooked simply with vegetables, leaving out the ham stuffing I suggest here. Or to make the bird go further, you can add extra packages of stuffing, wrapped in blanched cabbage leaves. Part of the broth may be used to cook rice as an accompaniment, as in Poule au Riz au Safran (page 109), or the broth may be thickened as a sauce, perhaps with olives and baby onions added as a garnish.

STUFFING

3 CHICKEN LIVERS (ABOUT 3 OUNCES/90 G TOTAL)

1 TABLESPOON/15 G BUTTER

1 CUP/50 G FRESH BREAD CRUMBS (SEE PAGE 373)

1 CUP/250 ML MILK

6 OUNCES/170 G CURED RAW HAM, CHOPPED

1 GARLIC CLOVE, FINELY CHOPPED

1/4 CUP CHOPPED FRESH PARSLEY

SALT AND PEPPER

1 TEASPOON QUATRE ÉPICES (SEE PAGE 370)

1 EGG, BEATEN TO MIX

CHICKEN

ONE 6-POUND/2.7-KG STEWING HEN OR LARGE ROASTING CHICKEN

6 QUARTS/6 LITERS WATER, MORE AS NEEDED

1/2 TEASPOON SALT

1 ONION, STUDDED WITH 2 WHOLE CLOVES

1 LARGE BOUQUET GARNI (SEE PAGE 370)

10 PEPPERCORNS

1 STALK CELERY, CUT INTO PIECES

1 CINNAMON STICK

8 LEEKS (ABOUT 2 1/2 POUNDS/1.2 KG), WHITE AND GREEN PARTS, CUT INTO 4-INCH/10-CM LENGTHS

2 POUNDS/900 G BABY CARROTS, OR MEDIUM CARROTS, CUT INTO 4-INCH/10-CM LENGTHS

1 1/2 POUNDS/675 G TURNIPS, QUARTERED

1/2 CUP/100 G LONG-GRAIN RICE, OR 1 HANDFUL OF ANGEL HAIR PASTA

SEA SALT, FOR SERVING

To begin, make the stuffing. Chop the chicken livers, discarding any membrane. Melt the butter in a small pan over medium heat. Add the livers and sauté, stirring, until they are just cooked, 1 to 2 minutes. Set them aside. Soak the bread crumbs in the milk and then squeeze them dry, discarding the milk. Put the crumbs in a bowl, add the liver, ham, garlic, parsley, salt, pepper, and the *quatre épices*, and mix with a wooden spoon. Taste and adjust the seasoning, then stir in the egg.

Wipe the chicken inside and out with paper towels. Fill it with the stuffing, and truss it (see page 371). Put the bird in a stockpot or soup pot and add the water and salt. Wrap the onion, bouquet garni, peppercorns, celery, and cinnamon stick in cheesecloth and add the cheesecloth bag to the pot. Cover and bring slowly to a boil, skimming often. Lower the heat and poach the bird, uncovered, for 30 minutes. A very gentle simmer, with the pot uncovered so the broth gradually reduces, is important.

After the first 30 minutes, tie the leeks in bundles with string and add them to the pot with the carrots and turnips. Add water to cover the chicken and vegetables. Adjust the salt to taste. Continue simmering until the bird and vegetables are very tender, about 1 hour longer, adding hot water to cover as needed. A hen may take up to an hour longer to cook than a chicken. When done, the leg meat of the bird should be pulling from the bones and no pink juice should run from the thigh when it is pierced with a two-pronged fork.

Lift the bird with the fork onto a board, cover loosely with aluminum foil, and keep warm. Transfer the vegetables to a bowl using a draining spoon, cover, and keep them warm also. Boil the broth until it is concentrated and reduced by about one-third (you should end up with about 2½ quarts/2.5 liters), 15 to 25 minutes. Discard the bag of aromatics, taste the broth, and adjust the seasoning. Poule-au-pot may be prepared up to 2 days ahead and the flavor will mellow. To store it, let everything cool to room temperature, then return the cooked chicken and vegetables to the pot with the reduced broth, cover, and refrigerate.

To finish, if necessary, reheat the Poule-au-Pot on the stove top, 15 to 20 minutes. Transfer the bird to a board, discard the trussing strings, and carve it (see page 370). Pile the stuffing from the cavity on a very large platter, set the chicken pieces on top, and arrange the vegetables around the sides. Cover with foil.

Strain the reduced broth into a smaller pan, add the rice or pasta, and simmer until just tender, allowing about 10 minutes for the rice and only 2 minutes for the pasta. Serve the broth as a first course. The chicken and vegetables form the main course. Accompany them with sea salt.

POULARDE EN DEMI-DEUIL

CHICKEN IN HALF-MOURNING

serves 5 or 6

Poularde en Demi-deuil was a specialty of Mère Brazier, a legendary cook who began her working career in the early 1900s, age ten, minding chickens on a farm in Bresse. In the 1950s and 1960s, she was internationally famous for her rigorously simple cooking and menus such as salade aux artichauts aux truffes, quenelles au gratin, volaille demi-deuil, fromages, *and* galette Bressanne *(a sweet yeast bread). She accepted Paul Bocuse as a young apprentice because he climbed the mountain pass to her restaurant on a bicycle, seeking work. Inspiration to a generation of chefs, Bocuse continues to be chef emeritus to today's cooks.*

I have only once in my life been offered Poularde en Demi-deuil, and I remember every sumptuous moment: the pungent intensity of fresh truffle, and the dramatic contrast of the thin black slices against the plump white chicken breast. Even one fresh truffle can go a long way, permeating the meat of the chicken as well as the rich cream sauce made from the cooking broth. Cheaper canned truffles are also good, though less intense. To display the luxury of real truffles, a full-breasted bird is important. In fact, this recipe suits a small turkey as well as a chicken. Best of all, however, is a capon (a neutered male bird), a Christmas specialty. A perfect accompaniment no matter which bird is used is the rice pilaf in Poule au Riz au Safran (facing page), omitting the saffron.

1 OR 2 FRESH TRUFFLES, OR 1 SMALL JAR TRUFFLES (ABOUT 1 OUNCE/30 G)

ONE 4- TO 5-POUND/2-KG ROASTING CHICKEN

1 ONION, STUDDED WITH 2 WHOLE CLOVES

2 CARROTS, QUARTERED

1 STALK CELERY, CUT INTO PIECES

2 GARLIC CLOVES

1 BOUQUET GARNI (SEE PAGE 370)

1½ CUPS/375 ML DRY WHITE WINE

1½ QUARTS/1.5 LITERS CHICKEN BROTH OR WATER, MORE IF NEEDED

SALT AND PEPPER

TRUFFLE VELOUTÉ SAUCE

½ CUP/110 G BUTTER

¼ CUP/30 G FLOUR

½ CUP/125 ML CRÈME FRAÎCHE (PAGE 374) OR HEAVY CREAM

1 TEASPOON COGNAC, MORE TO TASTE

If using fresh truffles, scrub them with cold water and dry them. With a small knife, cut away the peel and reserve the peel and truffles separately. If using canned truffles, drain them, reserving the liquid. Cut fresh or canned truffles into 8 to 10 thick slices. Chop the rest of the truffle along with any reserved peel and set aside for the sauce.

Wipe the chicken inside and out with paper towels. Lay the bird on its back, with the drumsticks facing you, on a work surface. Gently slide your fingers under the skin that covers the breast, being careful not to tear it. Arrange most of the truffle slices on the breast meat, and then let the skin fall to hold them in place. Insert the remaining slices under the skin on the legs. Truss the chicken (see page 371).

Put the bird, breast down, in a pot just large enough to hold it. Add the onion, carrots, celery, garlic, and bouquet garni. Pour in the wine and enough water so that about three-fourths of the bird is immersed. The breast meat should be completely immersed. Season with salt and pepper and bring just to a boil. Cover the pan and simmer gently until the chicken is tender and no pink juice runs out when the thigh is pierced with a skewer, 1½ to 2 hours. Skim occasionally, and turn the bird halfway through poaching, using a two-pronged fork. The cooked chicken may be refrigerated in the broth for up to 2 days. However, the sauce is best made just before serving.

To finish, if necessary, reheat the chicken gently in its broth on the stove top, 15 to 20 minutes. Remove it from the cooking liquid, cover it loosely with aluminum foil, and keep warm. Boil the broth until reduced to about 3 cups/750 ml, 20 to 30 minutes.

For the truffle velouté sauce, melt half of the butter in a saucepan over medium heat, whisk in the flour, and cook until foaming. Strain in the reduced broth and bring the sauce to a boil, whisking constantly until it thickens. Simmer until the sauce is thick enough to coat a spoon lightly, about 2 minutes. Stir in the crème fraîche and the liquid from canned truffles, if using, and bring the sauce just back to a boil. Whisk in the chopped truffle and Cognac. Take from the heat and whisk in the remaining butter in small pieces. Taste and adjust the seasoning.

To finish, discard the trussing strings and set the chicken on a platter. Spoon a little sauce over the bird and around the base of the dish. The truffle slices should show clearly through the skin. Serve the remaining sauce separately. Carve the chicken at the table (see page 370).

POULE AU RIZ AU SAFRAN

POACHED CHICKEN WITH SAFFRON RICE

The method for poaching chicken in Poularde en Demi-deuil also leads to this favorite country recipe for a tough yet full-flavored stewing hen or a large roasting chicken. Some of the cooking broth becomes a rich cream sauce, while the rest is diverted to make saffron-perfumed rice pilaf. Without the saffron, the recipe becomes *poule au riz*, an age-old family standby.

In the recipe for Poularde en Demi-deuil, omit the truffles. Poach the bird as described. If possible, use a stewing hen, which will need an extra 30 minutes or more to be tender. After poaching, set the bird aside and keep it warm. Measure 3 cups/750 ml of the broth and reserve it for the rice. Boil the rest of the broth until reduced to 2 cups/500 ml.

Meanwhile, make the rice pilaf. Melt 2 tablespoons/30 g butter in a flameproof casserole over medium heat. Add 1 onion, chopped, and sauté until soft but not brown, 3 to 5 minutes. Stir in 1¾ cups/350 g long-grain rice and cook, stirring constantly, until the grains are opaque, 2 to 3 minutes. Strain in the reserved 3 cups/750 ml broth and add a large pinch of saffron threads with salt and pepper. Bring to a boil, cover, and then simmer until the broth is absorbed and the rice is tender, 18 to 20 minutes. Taste and adjust the seasoning.

To finish, make the cream sauce as described for Poularde en Demi-deuil, omitting the truffles and Cognac. Season with salt, pepper, and a squeeze of lemon juice. Spread the pilaf on a warmed platter and set the chicken on top. Spoon a little sauce over the chicken, and serve the rest separately. Serves 5 or 6.

POULET SAUTÉ BASQUAISE

SAUTÉ OF CHICKEN WITH BELL PEPPERS

serves 4

Poulet Basquaise is a native to the southwest, but like Coq au Vin (page 113), you will find it on menus throughout France. A cheerful mix of bell peppers and ham (Bayonne, capital of the French Basque country, is the home of prime cured ham), the regional touch is provided by Espelette pepper, a relative of paprika that adds depth and a bit of heat. As a fall-back, you can combine paprika with a pinch of cayenne pepper.

3 TABLESPOONS/22 G FLOUR

1 TEASPOON GROUND DRIED ESPELETTE PEPPER

SALT AND PEPPER

ONE 3½- TO 4-POUND/1.5-KG CHICKEN, CUT INTO 8 PIECES (SEE PAGE 371)

¼ CUP/60 ML OLIVE OIL

4 OUNCES/110 G BAYONNE OR OTHER CURED RAW HAM, DICED

2 GARLIC CLOVES, CHOPPED

1 CUP/250 ML CHICKEN BROTH (SEE PAGE 373)

2 RED BELL PEPPERS, CORED, SEEDED, AND SLICED (SEE PAGE 370)

2 GREEN BELL PEPPERS, CORED, SEEDED, AND SLICED (SEE PAGE 370)

1 TABLESPOON CHOPPED FRESH PARSLEY

Mix the flour and Espelette pepper with salt and pepper on a plate. Dip the chicken pieces in the mixture, patting off the excess with your hands. Heat the oil in a sauté pan or deep frying pan over medium heat. Add the chicken pieces, skin side down, and fry until thoroughly browned, 5 to 7 minutes. Turn and brown the other side, 2 to 3 minutes longer. Cover tightly, reduce the heat to low, and cook the chicken for 20 minutes.

Add the ham, garlic, and broth and stir to mix. Cover again and continue cooking for 10 minutes. Add the bell peppers to the pan, lifting the chicken pieces so the peppers fall to the bottom. Cover and continue cooking until the chicken is tender and falls easily from a two-pronged fork, 20 to 30 minutes longer. If some pieces are tender before the others, remove and set them aside while the rest continue to cook. At the end of cooking, the peppers will have wilted; taste them and adjust the seasoning. The chicken may be prepared up to 2 days ahead and refrigerated.

To finish, if necessary, reheat the chicken and peppers on the stove top. Transfer the chicken to a platter with the peppers, ham, and sauce. Sprinkle with the parsley.

= THE BASQUE COUNTRY: PEPPERY AND PROUD =

Most of the Basque country lies on the Spanish side of France's southwestern border. The French Basques are left an almost triangular region bordering the Atlantic on the west, and the Pyrenees to the south, with the port of Bayonne as its capital. The geography is certainly diverse, but the people are united by their obscure origins, unique language, and distinct culture.

"Peppery as the Welsh, proud as Lucifer, and combustible as his matches" is how Richard Ford described the Basques in his classic *Handbook to Spain*. Indeed, flaming red is the Basque color, found on their tiled roofs and scarlet berets. Red, too, is the theme of Basque cooking, which gives pride of place to peppers. The most common are sweet peppers called *piment doux d'Anglet* (or *piment Basque*), harvested green and often pickled in brine. A more piquant variety named after a village in the hills behind Biarritz is *piment d'Espelette*, dried and ground for use like a spice.

The Basque culinary repertoire resembles no other region, with dishes like *elzekaria* (vegetable soup); *merluza, salsa verde* (hake with a green sauce made of peas and asparagus); and *tripoxa* (tripe sausages) served with the local hot sauce that comes in a bottle, like Tabasco. *Axoa* is a ubiquitous Basque stew flavored with green and red peppers, often made with veal, but more familiar with chicken as Poulet Basquaise (page 109). Pipérade is a tricky mixture of sautéed green and red peppers, onions, and tomatoes thickened with eggs to form a purée (page 50). For dessert, you can find sheep's milk yogurt, various beignets and flans, and Gâteau Basque, a sweet dough sandwiched with a light rum-scented pastry cream, or, even better, with a layer of fresh plums, apricots, or cherries (page 351).

Anchovies and salt cod are staples in Basque cooking, and Bayonne is home to a piquant, raw dry-cured ham that is eaten in slivers as a first course or in a sandwich, as well as used for flavoring. Pyrenean charcuteries boast strings of dry mountain sausages, some spiced with chili powder like Spanish chorizo. And, along the coast, fishing plays a major role, the main catch being anchovies, small squid called *chipirones*, hake, red tuna, sardines, and baby eels called *pibales*. In the mountains, shepherding remains a hallmark of Basque culture, exemplified in sheep's cheese. Nutty and fruity, oily yet firm, the Basques call it *ardi-gasna*, dialect for "our cheese," whereas the French simply call it Brebis Basque, or Brebis des Pyrenees. You're on true Basque territory when you find it served with cherry preserves at the end of a meal. It may not be intentional, but there's that stroke of red appearing again, like a subtle declaration of Basque pride.

= CULINARY COMMENTATORS: BRILLAT-SAVARIN =
(1755–1826)

It is never too late to become a famous gastronome, at least by the lights of Jean-Anthelme Brillat-Savarin, a French magistrate and politician whose great work, *The Physiology of Taste*, was published only months before his death. True, his reputation as an epicure was already established, and his aphorisms about wine, food, and dining echoed in high circles. But Brillat-Savarin also enjoyed country life and country produce. One of many legends involves his arrival for dinner at an inn. When he demanded the house specialty, roast turkey, he was told that all the *dindes* in the house were set aside for a single diner. Indignant, Brillat-Savarin burst in on the culprit only to find his own son, in majestic solitude, at the table. Inspired by his father's example, the young man was picking only the best bit from each turkey, the "oysters" that lie along the backbone.

The Physiology of Taste was given a new breath of life in America with M. F. K. Fisher's 1949 translation, which put the best of Brillat-Savarin on our lips: "Tell me what you eat and I will tell you what you are. . . . The discovery of a new dish does more for human happiness than the discovery of a new star. . . . The destiny of nations depends on how they nourish themselves." Tasty tidbits of truth!

= AOC (APPELLATION D'ORIGINE CONTRÔLÉE) =

Trust the French to be first into the business of controlling the quality of what they eat and drink. It started in 1855, with the ranking of some of the best Bordeaux wines into five categories. Today, France, with its prestigious AOC (Appellation d'Origine Contrôlée) system, leads the European pack in classifying top-quality artisanal foods. To earn AOC status, a product must have not only a specific place of origin but also distinguishing characteristics that reflect "local, faithful, and constant methods" of production. A lengthy, rule-ridden process with plenty of red tape and inspections makes the AOC label hard to achieve.

In recent times, the AOC label has been extended to cover dozens of products, especially cheese and dairy. Roquefort was the first cheese to earn controlled status in 1925, and thirty-one others have been added to the list, mostly since 1980. They include Brie from the Parisian basin, Gruyère from the Franche-Comté, and crottin de Chavignol from the Berry. Other AOC dairy products include butters from Poitou and Charente, and crème fraîche from Isigny. The list of meat, fruits, grains, and vegetables is eclectic: walnuts from Grenoble, olives and olive oil from Nyons, green lentils from Le Puy, chickens from Bresse, white beans from Paimpol, bull meat from the Camargue, and prunes from Agen.

Consumers trust the label and all that it implies, so AOC products sell. A Bresse chicken commands up to three times the price of a regular supermarket bird. Not surprisingly, a high-ranking AOC status is invaluable in the wine world, though a number of blessed properties no longer fully deserve it. On the other hand, some renegade producers, planting grape varietals or using vinification methods that are not authorized under the AOC system, are making stellar but unclassified wines.

Both France and the European Union have introduced new quality labels to complement the AOC system and guarantee regional origins in a more pragmatic way. The E.U. Indication Géographique Protegée identifies particular products from specific areas, such as pork from Gascony and sea salt from Guérande. In France, the most important is *label rouge*, a distinctive red label that covers hundreds of products, notably poultry, as well as certain fruits, vegetables, cheeses, meat and charcuterie, and even seeds and wheat varieties. Coming from a different direction is the *agriculture biologique* label, indicating organic produce. There is even a *label monastique* to authenticate what monasteries sell for profit—a new twist on privatization! These designations are in constant flux as the E.U. drafts new standards.

LE VRAI COQ AU VIN

THE REAL COQ AU VIN

serves 6 to 8

Coq au Vin comes in many styles, taking on character from whatever regional wine in which you choose to cook it. Coq au Beaujolais, *for instance, with a light tawny sauce made with the local Gamay, is quite different from the dark, almost mahogany version of the dish found downriver in the Rhône Valley, where Syrah is the preponderant grape. Over in Alsace, it is made with white wine, another story again. However, there is only one authentic way to cook Coq au Vin. It takes several days of marinating, gentle simmering, and then letting the sauce mellow before you think of serving it. Muscle means flavor, so first look for a fine old cock (not the politest expression, but a favorite of Julia Child's); next marinate it in the wine for at least twenty-four hours, or even up to three days for a truly vinous effect; and lastly simmer, or rather poach, the bird very, very slowly until the meat is just shy of falling off the bone. The garnish of bacon lardons, baby onions, and mushrooms is added at the end of cooking. You will need a starch to accompany it, usually mashed or small fried potatoes, or the noodles or Spaëtzli (page 230) popular in Alsace.*

MARINADE

- I ONION, SLICED
- I CARROT, SLICED
- 2 STALKS CELERY, SLICED
- I GARLIC CLOVE
- I TEASPOON PEPPERCORNS
- I BOTTLE (750 ML) RED WINE
- I TABLESPOON OLIVE OIL

CHICKEN

- ONE 5- TO 6-POUND/2.5-KG STEWING HEN OR LARGE ROASTING CHICKEN, CUT INTO 8 PIECES (SEE PAGE 371)
- I TABLESPOON VEGETABLE OIL
- 6-OUNCE/170-G PIECE LEAN SMOKED BACON, CUT INTO LARDONS (SEE PAGE 371)
- 3 TABLESPOONS/22 G FLOUR
- 2 CUPS/500 ML CHICKEN BROTH (SEE PAGE 373), MORE IF NEEDED
- 2 SHALLOTS, CHOPPED
- 2 GARLIC CLOVES, CHOPPED
- I LARGE BOUQUET GARNI (SEE PAGE 370)

GARNISH

- 2 TABLESPOONS/30 G BUTTER, MORE IF NEEDED
- 16 TO 18 BABY ONIONS (ABOUT 8 OUNCES/225 G), PEELED
- 8 OUNCES/225 G BUTTON MUSHROOMS, TRIMMED AND QUARTERED IF LARGE
- SALT AND PEPPER
- I TABLESPOON CHOPPED FRESH PARSLEY

For the marinade, combine the onion, carrot, celery, garlic, peppercorns, and wine in a saucepan, bring to a boil, and simmer for 5 minutes. Let the marinade cool completely.

Pack the chicken pieces in a deep, nonmetallic bowl and pour the cooled marinade over them. Spoon the olive oil on top to keep the chicken moist. Cover and leave the pieces to marinate in the refrigerator for at least a day, turning them from time to time, and up to 3 days if you like a full-bodied wine flavor.

Take the chicken pieces from the marinade and pat them dry with paper towels. Strain the marinade, reserving the liquid and the vegetables separately. Heat the oven to 325°F/160°C.

To cook the chicken, heat the vegetable oil in a sauté pan or flameproof casserole over medium heat. Add the lardons and sauté until browned and the fat runs, about 5 minutes. Transfer them to a bowl using a draining spoon and set aside. Add the chicken pieces, skin side down, to the pan and sauté over medium heat until thoroughly browned, at least 10 minutes. Turn them and brown the other side, 3 to 5 minutes longer. Remove the chicken pieces and set aside.

Add the reserved marinade vegetables to the sauté pan over medium heat and fry until they start to brown, 5 to 7 minutes. Stir in the flour and cook over high heat, stirring, until it browns, 2 to 3 minutes. Pour in the marinade liquid and bring to a boil, stirring constantly until the sauce thickens. Simmer for 2 minutes, then stir in the broth, shallots, garlic, and bouquet garni. Replace the chicken, pushing the pieces down under the sauce. Cover the pan, transfer to the oven, and cook, turning the chicken occasionally, until the pieces are tender and fall easily from a two-pronged fork, 1 to 1¼ hours for a roasting chicken and at least 30 minutes longer for a stewing hen. If some pieces are tender before the others, remove them and set aside while the rest continue to cook.

Meanwhile, cook the garnish. Melt the butter in a frying pan over medium heat. Add the onions and brown them, shaking the pan from time to time so they color evenly, 5 to 7 minutes. Lower

continued

the heat, cover, and cook the onions, shaking the pan occasionally, until just tender, 8 to 10 minutes more. Lift them out with the draining spoon and add to the reserved lardons. Put the mushrooms in the pan, with a little more butter if needed, and sauté until tender, 3 to 5 minutes. Add them to the lardons and onions.

When the chicken is cooked, remove the pieces and set them aside. Wipe out the sauté pan, add the garnish, and strain the sauce on top, discarding the vegetables and seasonings. Reheat the garnish and sauce on the stove top over medium heat. If the sauce seems thick, add a little more broth, taste, and adjust the seasoning. Add the chicken pieces, pushing them well down into the sauce, and heat gently for 3 to 5 minutes so the flavors blend. Coq au vin improves if you keep it, well covered, in the refrigerator for at least 1 day and up to 3 days so the flavors mellow.

To serve, reheat the chicken with the garnish and sauce on the stove top if necessary. Transfer the chicken pieces to a serving dish or individual plates, and spoon the garnish with a little sauce over them. Sprinkle the chicken with the parsley and serve the remaining sauce separately.

COQ AU RIESLING
WHITE WINE COQ AU VIN

A dry Riesling is the ideal white wine for cooking a chicken (or a cock, if you can find one), as its body and acid lend structure to the sauce. I think of it as a summer version of red wine *coq au vin*, lighter, fresher, and, yes, quicker to make.

In the recipe for Le Vrai Coq au Vin, substitute 1 bottle (750 ml) dry Riesling for the red wine and marinate the bird for only 12 to 24 hours. Omit the bacon and baby onions, keeping only mushrooms in the garnish and increasing the vegetable oil if needed to brown the chicken pieces. When finishing the sauce, whisk in ½ cup/125 ml crème fraîche or heavy cream and bring it back to a boil before adjusting the seasoning.

PETITS COQUELETS DIJONNAISE
CORNISH HENS IN A MUSTARD CREAM SAUCE
serves 4

The simplest French sauce is a brushing of Dijon mustard with a dollop of cream, sufficient to add zip to roast rabbit, pork chops, and small birds such as these coquelets. *In the United States, Cornish hens do well. I like to serve the birds with hearty greens, such as kale or Savoy cabbage, sautéed with bacon lardons. This recipe says Burgundy or more particularly Dijon, its historic capital.*

- 4 COQUELETS OR SMALL CORNISH HENS (ABOUT 1½ POUNDS/675 G EACH)
- 3 TABLESPOONS/60 G DIJON MUSTARD, MORE IF NEEDED
- SALT AND PEPPER
- ½ CUP/125 ML CRÈME FRAÎCHE (PAGE 374) OR HEAVY CREAM
- 3 TABLESPOONS/45 ML RED WINE
- FEW SPOONFULS OF CHICKEN BROTH (OPTIONAL; PAGE 373)

GREENS

- 1 POUND/450 G HEARTY GREENS
- 2 TABLESPOONS VEGETABLE OIL
- 4 THICK SLICES (ABOUT 6 OUNCES/170 G TOTAL) LEAN BACON, CUT INTO LARDONS (SEE PAGE 371)
- 3 GARLIC CLOVES, CHOPPED
- SPLASH OF RED WINE VINEGAR

Heat the oven to 400°F/200°C. Wipe the birds inside and out with paper towels, and truss them (see page 371). Brush each one with mustard and set them in a roasting pan. Sprinkle the birds with salt and pepper and spoon the crème fraîche over them. Roast the birds, brushing often toward the end of cooking with the juices that run from the cavity, 1 to 1¼ hours. When the chickens are very brown and the meat starts to pull from the leg joints, test cooking by lifting each bird with a two-pronged fork and tipping the juices from the cavity. The juices should run clear, not pink.

Meanwhile, cook the greens. Bring a large pan of salted water to a boil. Discard the stems from the greens, stack the leaves, roll up lengthwise, and cut crosswise to shred them as finely as possible. Boil the greens until just tender, 8 to 12 minutes, depending on the type. Drain, rinse them with cold water, and drain again thoroughly.

Heat the oil in a sauté pan over medium heat. Add the lardons and fry until lightly browned and the fat runs, about 5 minutes. Stir in the garlic. Add the greens, toss them until well coated with fat, and season with salt and pepper. Cover and cook over low heat until the greens are very tender and flavored with bacon, 5 to 10 minutes. They may be cooked up to 2 hours ahead and reheated. Just before serving, sprinkle on a few drops of vinegar, taste, and adjust the seasoning.

Transfer the birds to a platter, cover with aluminum foil, and keep warm. For the sauce, skim the excess fat from the roasting pan. Add the wine, and bring to a boil on the stove top, stirring to dissolve the juices. There will be 2 to 3 spoonfuls sauce per person; if you want more, add a bit of broth. Taste, adjust the seasoning, and pour the sauce into a bowl. Pile the greens on the platter with the birds. Pass the sauce at the table.

SAUTÉ DE POULET AU VINAIGRE DE VIN
SAUTÉ OF CHICKEN WITH VINEGAR, GARLIC, AND TOMATO
serves 4 to 6

*I think you will be surprised by the mildly provocative tang of this Burgundian chicken recipe, which uses vinegar and lots of garlic that mellows and softens as it cooks and thickens the sauce. Vinegar—*vin aigre *or* acid wine*—is the natural by-product of any wine region, and at home I brew my own in a big crock in a quiet corner of the kitchen, feeding it from time to time with leftover red wine. I like to serve Poulet au Vinaigre de Vin with glazed root vegetables such as turnips, root celery, or carrots.*

ONE 3½- TO 4-POUND/1.5-KG CHICKEN, CUT INTO 8 PIECES (SEE PAGE 371)

SALT AND PEPPER

3 TABLESPOONS/45 G BUTTER

1 LARGE HEAD GARLIC, SEPARATED INTO CLOVES, UNPEELED

1 CUP/250 ML RED WINE VINEGAR

3 TOMATOES (ABOUT 1 POUND/450 G TOTAL), CHOPPED

1 TABLESPOON TOMATO PASTE

1 BOUQUET GARNI (SEE PAGE 370)

1 CUP/250 ML CHICKEN BROTH (SEE PAGE 373), MORE IF NEEDED

1 TABLESPOON CHOPPED FRESH PARSLEY

Season the chicken pieces with salt and pepper. Melt half of the butter in a sauté pan or deep frying pan over medium heat until it stops foaming. Add the chicken pieces, skin side down, and brown thoroughly, 5 to 7 minutes. Turn and brown the other side, 2 to 3 minutes longer.

Add the garlic cloves, cover, and cook over low heat for 10 minutes. Drain off the excess fat, holding the lid on the pan to trap the chicken pieces. Return the pan to the heat, add the vinegar, and continue simmering, uncovered, until well reduced, 10 to 15 minutes.

Add the tomatoes—they don't need to be skinned or peeled because the sauce is strained later—to the chicken with the tomato paste and bouquet garni. Cover the pan again and continue cooking until the chicken is tender and falls easily from a two-pronged fork, 10 to 15 minutes longer. If some pieces are tender before the others, remove and set them aside while the rest continue to cook.

Transfer the chicken pieces to a serving dish, cover with aluminum foil, and keep warm. Add the broth to the pan and simmer the sauce, uncovered, until it is concentrated and lightly thickened, 5 to 8 minutes. Work the liquid and vegetables through a strainer into a saucepan, pressing hard to extract all the garlic and tomato pulp. Bring the sauce to a boil, take it off the heat, and whisk in the remaining butter in small pieces. Taste and adjust the seasoning. Spoon the sauce over the chicken, sprinkle with the parsley, and serve.

SAUTÉ DE POULET AUX QUARANTE GOUSSES D'AIL
SAUTÉ OF CHICKEN WITH FORTY GARLIC CLOVES

Before you recoil in alarm, be assured that garlic mellows in fine style to flavor the sauce of this popular recipe. The younger the garlic, the milder the sauce will be.

In the recipe for Sauté de Poulet au Vinaigre de Vin, omit the vinegar, tomatoes, and tomato paste. Increase the amount of garlic to 3 to 4 heads and include generous amounts of thyme in the bouquet garni. Increase the amount of chicken broth to 2 cups/500 ml, adding it with the garlic cloves. When the chicken is tender, remove the pieces and set them aside with half the garlic cloves (leave them unpeeled for guests to squeeze out the soft pulp at table). Strain and finish the sauce with butter as for Sauté de Poulet au Vinaigre de Vin. Serves 4.

═ PÉRIGORD: RUSTIC LUXURY ═

As far as the French are concerned, Périgord, well inland to the east of Bordeaux, comes in four colors. They label the grassy upper part of the region green, the lower part around Bergerac purple (where the wine grapes are), the middle section white (for the chalky plateaus in the west), and the thickly forested area black.

For the great chronicler of French country cooking, Curnonsky, the Périgord (a.k.a. Dordogne) was "one of the regions where we eat the best, and have done so for centuries." I heartily agree. I once stayed near Périgueux in a modest hotel with the not-so-modest name France et Russie, so-called because the czar's agents stayed there when stocking up on provisions for the court.

It amuses me, browsing through one of the region's many cookbooks, to read that Périgord cooks are "born with a cooking pot in their hands, and know instinctively what to put in it." A bit over-the-top, but when you take into account the ingredients available, it is no wonder that, with a bit of skill and experience, local cooks do wonders. They have (or had) carp, trout, salmon, eel, and crayfish from the rivers, corn-fed poultry, ducks, and geese (whose necks they stuff and slice like sausage); forests of mushrooms and game; excellent pork, fruits, and vegetables; and chestnuts and walnuts galore. It seems appropriate that the main

city of Périgueux has given its name to the classic sauce made of truffles and Madeira, and that Pommes Sarladaise (page 226), potatoes sautéed in goose fat and generously tossed with chopped truffles and parsley, are named after the town of Sarlat.

What gives all the savory dishes of Périgord a special character are fats: lard, goose fat, duck fat, and walnut oil. Personally, I never leave the place without stocking up on walnuts to add to salads or grind for a Gâteau Périgourdin (page 300), a characteristic local recipe. Some farmers sell sacks of nuts in the shell right out of their barns, along with walnut oil for use in vinaigrettes and even for frying fish. Cooks are clever with green walnuts, too, using them for *vin aux noix*, the regional aperitif, and pickling them in verjuice, the acidic juice pressed from unripe grapes.

Settled millennia ago by prehistoric man, the Périgord, more than most parts of France, has ageless, rural qualities. Perhaps it is natural that the entire area has become a favorite nesting ground for foreigners. I like the faraway-from-it-all, inland feel of the place: the rocky outcroppings, the misty rivers, the grazing cows and pigs, the narrow roads that wind on forever over the hills. And no, I never mind getting stuck behind a tractor in the Périgord.

COQ À LA BIÈRE
CHICKEN WITH BEER
serves 4 to 6

This classic northern dish, which is typically Flemish, demands a large, meaty bird. The sauce is a tempting golden brown, laced with dark beer and juniper white alcohol called genièvre *(gin with a few crushed juniper berries can be used instead). I enjoy a purée of root celery or lentils on the side, but the traditional accompaniment is mashed or boiled potatoes.*

ONE 4- TO 5-POUND/2-KG CHICKEN, CUT INTO 8 PIECES (SEE PAGE 371)

3 TABLESPOONS/22 G FLOUR

SALT AND PEPPER

1 TABLESPOON VEGETABLE OIL

2 TABLESPOONS/30 G BUTTER

3 TABLESPOONS/45 ML JUNIPER WHITE ALCOHOL, MORE TO TASTE

3 SHALLOTS (ABOUT 2 OUNCES/60 G TOTAL), CHOPPED

9 OUNCES/250 G BUTTON MUSHROOMS, TRIMMED AND HALVED IF LARGE

1 CUP/250 ML DARK BEER

1 BOUQUET GARNI (SEE PAGE 370)

$^1/_4$ CUP/60 ML CRÈME FRAÎCHE (PAGE 374) OR HEAVY CREAM

1 TO 2 TEASPOONS WHITE WINE VINEGAR

1 TABLESPOON CHOPPED FRESH PARSLEY

Sprinkle the chicken pieces with the flour, salt, and pepper. Heat the oil and butter in a sauté pan over medium heat until they stop foaming. Add the chicken pieces, skin side down, and brown thoroughly, 5 to 7 minutes. Turn them and brown the other side, 2 to 3 minutes longer. Add the juniper alcohol and flambé it (see page 371), standing back as the flames may rise high.

Remove the chicken pieces and set aside. Lower the heat, add the shallots, and cook until soft, about 1 minute. Spread the mushrooms on top, pour in the beer, and add the bouquet garni. Replace the chicken pieces, pushing them down among the mushrooms. Cover and simmer the chicken pieces, turning them occasionally, until they are tender and fall easily from a two-pronged fork, 40 to 50 minutes. If some pieces are tender before the others, remove and set them aside while the rest continue to cook. The chicken may be prepared up to 3 days ahead and stored in the sauce in the refrigerator, or it may be frozen for up to 3 months.

To finish, reheat the chicken and mushrooms on the stove top if necessary. Remove the chicken pieces to a platter, cover with aluminum foil, and keep warm. Discard the bouquet garni from the pan, add the crème fraîche, and bring to a boil, stirring to mix it into the sauce. Take the pan from the heat, whisk in the vinegar to sharpen the flavor of the sauce, taste, and adjust the seasoning. This is a rustic dish, fine served directly from the pan, or you may serve the chicken with the sauce and mushrooms on a platter. Sprinkle with the parsley.

SUPRÊME DE POULARDE AUX ÉCREVISSES
CHICKEN BREASTS WITH CRAYFISH
serves 4

Chicken with shellfish may sound odd, but in Bresse, home to the world's most famous chickens, the combination is an old friend. Bresse borders Savoy and the Alps, with mountain streams for crayfish that transform simple chicken breasts into a celebratory dish. If you cannot get live or frozen crayfish, substitute large shrimp in their shells. The roux for thickening the sauce is a mélange of several ingredients in the style of New Orleans. To soak up the rich sauce, the dish begs for an accompaniment of croûtes (see page 374) and boiled rice.

2 TABLESPOONS VEGETABLE OIL

4 TABLESPOONS/60 G BUTTER

12 LARGE CRAYFISH, LIVE OR THAWED FROZEN (ABOUT 1$^1/_2$ POUNDS/675 G TOTAL)

4 SKINLESS, BONELESS CHICKEN BREASTS (ABOUT 1$^1/_4$ POUNDS/625 G TOTAL)

3 TABLESPOONS/45 ML MARC OR COGNAC

SAUCE

2 TABLESPOONS/30 GRAMS BUTTER

1 SMALL ONION, CHOPPED

2 SHALLOTS, CHOPPED

2 GARLIC CLOVES, CHOPPED

1 TABLESPOON TOMATO PASTE

$^1/_4$ CUP/30 G FLOUR

1$^1/_2$ CUPS/375 ML DRY WHITE WINE

2 CUPS/500 ML CHICKEN BROTH (SEE PAGE 373)

SALT AND PEPPER

1 BOUQUET GARNI (SEE PAGE 370)

1 CUP/250 ML CRÈME FRAÎCHE (PAGE 374) OR HEAVY CREAM

Heat the oven to 350°F/180°C. Heat the oil and butter in a sauté pan or flameproof casserole over high heat. Add the crayfish and sauté them until they turn red, 4 to 5 minutes. Take them out with a draining spoon and set aside. Lower the heat, add the chicken breasts, and sauté gently until lightly browned, 2 to 3 minutes. Turn them and brown the other side, 2 to 3 minutes longer. Return the crayfish to the pan and flambé (see page 371) with the marc. Remove both chicken and crayfish and set them aside.

For the sauce, melt the remaining butter in the sauté pan over low heat. Add the onion, shallots, garlic, tomato paste, and flour and cook, stirring constantly, until the onion is soft but not brown, 4 to 5 minutes. Stir in the wine and bring to a boil, whisking constantly until the sauce thickens. Whisk in the broth and season with salt and pepper. Return the chicken and crayfish to the pan, add the bouquet garni, and simmer, uncovered, for 5 minutes.

Remove the crayfish and set them aside. Cover the pan, transfer it to the oven, and cook until the chicken is very tender when pierced with a two-pronged fork, 20 to 30 minutes, depending on the size of the chicken breasts. The chicken and crayfish may be cooked a day ahead and stored with the sauce in the refrigerator.

To finish, reheat the chicken breasts in the sauce on the stove top if necessary. Remove them, cover, and keep warm. The sauce should be well flavored and coat the back of a spoon. If it is thin, boil it for a few minutes to reduce it. Strain the sauce into a large, shallow pan, bring to a boil, and whisk in the crème fraîche. Return the chicken breasts to the sauce and simmer for 2 minutes. Add the crayfish, reheat briefly, taste, and adjust the seasoning.

Arrange the chicken breasts on warmed plates. Coat with some of the sauce and set the crayfish around them. Serve the remaining sauce separately. You will need to provide your guests with crab picks and finger bowls.

SUPRÊME DE POULET À L'ESTRAGON
CHICKEN BREASTS IN TARRAGON CREAM SAUCE

Bushy stems of tarragon sprout in my garden in early summer, perfect for pairing with chicken breasts in a rich cream sauce. The cooking method is the same as for Suprême de Poularde aux Écrevisses, but the results are very different.

In the recipe for Suprême de Poularde aux Écrevisses, omit the crayfish and tomato paste. Strip the leaves from a large bunch of tarragon (about 2 ounces/60 g) and add the stems and half of the leaves to the sauce after flambéing the chicken breasts. Coarsely chop the remaining tarragon leaves and set them aside. Simmer the chicken breasts and make the sauce as directed. Add the chopped tarragon to the sauce with the cream. Serves 6.

CONFIT DE CANARD
DUCK CONFIT
serves 4

Most often, Confit de Canard is served alone as I suggest here, cooked gently in a little of its fat until it is hot and brown, with the skin crisp. Drained of the preserving fat, duck or goose confit is also used to enrich soups and stews, particularly those based on vegetables. It is excellent warmed gently, pulled into slivers, and served as a salad with dandelion greens or frisée, dressed in tarragon vinegar and walnut oil. Sautéed potatoes are a standard accompaniment—I particularly like them wafer-thin and crisp with a hint of garlic—but each region has its own seasonal accompaniment: cèpes in the Basque country, for instance, or puréed sorrel in the Périgord. Elsewhere white beans or lentils are popular, and I find sautéed winter greens pretty good, too.

4 LARGE DUCK LEGS (ABOUT 1 1/2 POUNDS/675 G TOTAL)

3 TABLESPOONS/60 G KOSHER OR COARSE SALT

1 TEASPOON PEPPERCORNS

2 OR 3 SPRIGS FRESH THYME

2 OR 3 DRIED BAY LEAVES, BROKEN INTO PIECES

3 POUNDS/1.35 KG DUCK FAT OR LARD, MELTED, MORE IF NEEDED

Rub each duck leg with some of the salt and put them in a bowl. Sprinkle with the remaining salt and add the peppercorns, thyme, and bay leaves. Cover and keep in the refrigerator, turning the pieces occasionally, for 6 to 12 hours, depending on how strong a salt cure you want.

Rinse the salt from the duck legs and dry on paper towels. Heat the oven to 300°F/150°C. Lay the duck legs, skin side down, in a frying pan over low heat and fry gently, turning them once, until the fat runs and the pieces brown evenly, 15 to 20 minutes. Transfer the legs to a small flameproof casserole and add enough melted fat to cover them. Cover tightly with a lid and cook in the oven until the duck has rendered all of its fat and is so tender that it is almost falling from the bone, 2 to 2½ hours.

To preserve the duck, pour a layer of the rendered fat from the casserole into the base of a preserving jar or small terrine. Pack the duck pieces on top and pour over enough fat to cover and seal them completely, adding more melted fat if necessary. Be sure there are no air bubbles. Cover and refrigerate for at least 1 week to allow the flavor to mellow. If you seal the jar with a cloth sprinkled with salt and then tightly cover it, the confit will keep for several months in a cool place. The longer it is left to mature, the better it will be.

continued

To serve the confit, heat the oven to 400°F/200°C. Line a roasting pan with a dish towel, set the jar of confit in it, and pour in boiling water to make a water bath (see page 373). Bring the water back to a boil on the stove top to melt the fat. Lift out the duck pieces, wiping off excess fat, and put them in a shallow baking dish. Bake the duck pieces in the oven until very hot and the skin is crisp, 12 to 15 minutes. Serve hot and crisp.

CONFIT DE PORC
PORK CONFIT

Pork that has been preserved as confit is often served with braised lentils or kidney beans. It may also be one of the meats included in Cassoulet (page 178).

Follow the recipe for Confit de Canard, substituting 3 pounds/1.35 kg boneless lean pork shoulder for the duck legs. Cut the meat into 6 equal pieces and tie each in a bundle. Put them in a shallow dish and sprinkle with the salt and flavorings. Cover and keep in the refrigerator, turning the pieces occasionally, for 24 to 36 hours. Cook as directed for the duck legs, substituting lard for the duck fat and allowing 2½ to 3 hours' cooking time. To serve pork confit, heat the pieces in a frying pan, pour off the excess fat, and fry the meat over low heat until very hot and brown on all sides, 10 to 12 minutes. Serves 4 to 6.

MAGRET DE CANARD AUX CERISES
DUCK BREAST WITH CHERRIES

serves 2 or 3

Thanks to the popularity of foie gras, we have magret—the robust breast meat of a fattened duck (the legs go for Confit de Canard). Magret has become an upmarket steak, particularly in southwestern France, and in the pan it behaves very much the same way. When pleasantly pink, the meat is rich and juicy, but be warned that overcooked magret tastes, and cuts, like shoe leather. I like it best with a sauce of seasonal fruit, starting with springtime cherries, moving through apricots and tart berries such as black currants, and on to apples, figs, and winter dried fruits. All of them can be substituted for cherries in this recipe. An appropriate wine would be a fruity Merlot or Gamay. In general, a magret serves one person, but a very large one can sometimes be enough for two.

CHERRY SAUCE

    8 OUNCES/225 G CHERRIES, PITTED

    1 CUP/250 ML FRUITY RED WINE

    2 TABLESPOONS RED CURRANT OR RASPBERRY JELLY

    $^{1}/_{3}$ CUP/75 ML RED WINE VINEGAR

    2 GARLIC CLOVES, FINELY CHOPPED

    2 TABLESPOONS TOMATO PASTE

    3 TABLESPOONS/45 G BUTTER, CUT INTO CUBES

2 DUCK MAGRETS (ABOUT 12 OUNCES/330 G TOTAL)

SALT AND PEPPER

ARUGULA LEAVES, FOR SERVING

To begin the sauce, put the cherries in a small saucepan with the wine and jelly. Simmer, stirring occasionally, until the cherries are just tender, 3 to 5 minutes. Set the pan aside.

Trim the excess fat from the magrets, then crosshatch the skin, cutting down almost to the meat so fat can escape. Sprinkle the breasts with salt and pepper.

Heat a heavy, dry frying pan over medium heat. Add the magrets, skin side down, and fry until the skin is very brown and crisp to extract as much fat as possible, 5 to 7 minutes or longer if necessary. Turn and brown the other side, 2 to 3 minutes longer. Test a magret by poking the center with the point of a knife to see the color of the meat. If it is too rare for your taste, continue cooking for 1 to 2 minutes, but remember that it will be very tough if overcooked. When done, set the magrets aside, skin side up, on a carving board. Cover them loosely with aluminum foil to keep warm.

To finish the sauce, discard the excess fat from the frying pan. Add the vinegar and boil, stirring to dissolve the pan juices, until reduced to about 1 tablespoon. Whisk in the garlic and tomato paste. Pour in the wine from the cherries, keeping back the cherries with a pan lid. Boil until the wine is slightly syrupy and reduced by more than half, 2 to 3 minutes. Stir in the cherries and heat them gently. Take the pan from the heat and stir in the butter a piece at a time. Taste, adjust the seasoning, and set the sauce aside.

Carve the magrets on the diagonal into thin slices. (You can discard the crisp skin if you must, but what a pity!) Pile a mound of arugula leaves at the side of 2 or 3 plates. Arrange the duck slices, overlapping them, on the plates. Using a draining spoon, pile the cherries on the plates. Spoon the sauce over the duck and serve at once.

MAGRET DE CANARD AUX CERISES

CANARD EN COCOTTE
AUX NAVETS DE MON JARDIN

DUCK WITH TURNIPS FROM MY GARDEN

serves 3 or 4

We get a nice little crop of purple-skinned, zesty turnips in the spring, just right with a rich, plump duck. Cooked in a casserole like this, the bird emerges well-done with a dark, Madeira-tinged sauce, just the way I like it!

ONE 5-POUND/2.25-KG DUCK

SALT AND PEPPER

1 TABLESPOON VEGETABLE OIL

1 TABLESPOON/15 G BUTTER

2 TABLESPOONS/15 G FLOUR

3/4 CUP/175 ML MEDIUM-DRY WHITE WINE

1 1/2 CUPS/375 ML CHICKEN BROTH (SEE PAGE 373),
MORE IF NEEDED

1 BOUQUET GARNI (SEE PAGE 370)

1 POUND/450 G ONIONS, SLICED

1 POUND/450 G SMALL TURNIPS, UNPEELED,
QUARTERED OR CUT INTO EIGHTHS

1 TEASPOON/15 G SUGAR

1/4 CUP/60 ML MADEIRA

1 TABLESPOON CHOPPED FRESH PARSLEY

Heat the oven to 400°F/200°C. Wipe the duck inside and out with paper towels, sprinkle with salt and pepper, and truss it (see page 371). Prick it all over with a fork so the fat can escape. Heat the oil and butter in a flameproof casserole over medium heat. Add the duck and brown it on all sides, taking at least 20 to 25 minutes or longer if necessary so the fat under the skin is melted. (You can expect anything from a few tablespoons up to 1 cup/250 ml fat.)

Remove the duck and pour off all but about 2 tablespoons of the fat from the pan, reserving the excess. Return the pan to medium heat, stir in the flour, and cook, stirring, until browned, about 1 minute. Whisk in the wine and broth and bring to a boil, whisking until the sauce thickens. Add the bouquet garni and replace the duck, breast down. Cover, put in the oven, and cook for 20 minutes.

Meanwhile, heat 2 tablespoons of the reserved duck fat in a frying pan over medium heat. Add the onions, season with salt and pepper, and sauté, stirring often, until they start to brown but are still firm, 5 to 7 minutes. Remove the onions and set aside. Heat 2 tablespoons more fat in the pan, add the turnips, and sprinkle

with the sugar and with salt and pepper. Sauté, stirring often, until browned on all sides, 4 to 5 minutes. Add them to the onions.

Remove the casserole from the oven, turn the duck breast up, and spread the onions and turnips around the duck. Baste the vegetables with the sauce. Return, uncovered, to the oven and continue to cook until the duck is tender and the meat pulls from the leg joints and the vegetables are tender, 20 to 30 minutes. A thermometer inserted into a thigh away from bone should register 165°F/74°C. If the sauce gets too thick during cooking, add more broth. The duck may be cooked up to 2 days ahead and kept covered in the refrigerator.

To finish, if necessary, reheat the duck on the stove top, 10 to 15 minutes. Discard the trussing strings and set the duck on a platter. Spoon the vegetables around it, cover with aluminum foil, and keep everything warm. Skim any fat from the surface of the sauce, add the Madeira, and bring just to a boil. Taste and adjust the seasoning. Spoon a little sauce over the duck and sprinkle the vegetables with parsley. Carve the duck and pass the remaining sauce at the table.

RAGOÛT DE CUISSES DE CANARD AUX NAVETS

RAGOÛT OF DUCK LEGS WITH TURNIPS

Here is a simple alternative to Confit de Canard for using the duck legs that are often left over when magrets are cut from the carcass of a duck.

Follow the recipe for Canard en Cocotte aux Navets, substituting 4 duck legs for the whole bird. Brown the duck legs as for the whole duck, using a large sauté pan or shallow flameproof casserole and allowing 10 to 15 minutes. Remove them, make the sauce, and replace the duck legs. Cover and simmer on the stove top for 15 to 20 minutes while you brown the onions and turnips. Stir the vegetables into the duck legs and sauce. Continue simmering until the duck legs and turnips are very tender, 15 to 20 minutes longer. Like Canard en Cocotte, these duck legs keep well for a couple of days in the refrigerator, and they may be frozen for up to 3 months. Serves 4.

DINDE AUX MARRONS BOURGUIGNONNE

BURGUNDIAN ROAST TURKEY WITH
CHESTNUTS AND WILD MUSHROOMS

serves 8 to 10

Most country cooks have their own time-honored way of roasting the Christmas turkey. This recipe comes from a Burgundian neighbor, Berthe Fournillon, whose farm has passed from daughter to daughter for a century.

ONE 8- TO 10-POUND/ABOUT 4-KG TURKEY

2 LEMONS, HALVED

¹/₂ CUP/110 G BUTTER, SOFTENED

MARINADE

    3 GARLIC CLOVES, CHOPPED

    2 TEASPOONS SALT

    ¹/₂ TEASPOON PEPPER

    ¹/₂ TEASPOON GRATED NUTMEG

    1 CUP/250 ML DRY WHITE WINE

    ¹/₄ CUP/60 ML VEGETABLE OIL

CHESTNUTS

    2 POUNDS/900 G FRESH CHESTNUTS

    2 CUPS/500 ML MILK, MORE IF NEEDED

    SALT AND PEPPER

    2 TO 3 TABLESPOONS DRIPPINGS FROM THE PAN

MUSHROOMS

    1¹/₂ POUNDS/675 G WILD MUSHROOMS

    ¹/₂ CUP/110 G BUTTER, SOFTENED

    2 SHALLOTS, VERY FINELY CHOPPED

    1 GARLIC CLOVE, VERY FINELY CHOPPED

    2 TABLESPOONS CHOPPED FRESH PARSLEY

GRAVY

    1 CUP/250 ML FULL-BODIED RED WINE

    2 CUPS/500 ML CHICKEN BROTH (SEE PAGE 373)

    ¹/₂ CUP/125 ML CRÈME FRAÎCHE (PAGE 374) OR
    HEAVY CREAM

    LARGE ROASTING PAN

Wipe the turkey inside and out with paper towels. Rub the skin thoroughly with the cut lemons. For the marinade, mix the garlic, salt, pepper, and nutmeg in a bowl and whisk in the wine. Gradually whisk in the oil. Rub some of the marinade over the inside and outside of the turkey, reserving the rest. Truss the bird (see page 371), cover, and let stand at room temperature for 30 minutes. Heat the oven to 350°F/180°C.

Set the turkey in the roasting pan, spread it with the butter, and pour over the remaining marinade. Roast until the breast is brown, 25 to 30 minutes. Baste well with the pan juices, cover loosely with aluminum foil, and continue roasting, basting often, for about 2 hours longer. The turkey is done when the meat starts to pull from the leg bones, the juices run clear, not pink, when the thigh is pierced with a skewer, and a thermometer inserted in the thigh registers 165°F/74°C. If the juices start to scorch during cooking, add 1 cup/250 ml water to the pan.

Meanwhile, peel the chestnuts (see page 371) and put them in a pan with enough milk to cover. Cover, bring to a boil, and simmer until the chestnuts are almost tender, 15 to 20 minutes. Do not let them get too soft or they will fall apart when roasted. Drain the chestnuts and put them in a baking dish. Add the drippings with salt and pepper and stir until the chestnuts are coated. Roast in the oven with the turkey until the chestnuts are glazed and very tender, 20 to 30 minutes. Set them aside. The chestnuts may be cooked up to a day ahead and reheated before serving.

For the mushrooms, clean them (see page 373) and cut into pieces if large. Melt 1 tablespoon of the butter in a frying pan over low heat. Add the mushrooms and salt and pepper, cover tightly, and cook gently until the juices run, 5 to 8 minutes. Remove the lid, raise the heat, and continue cooking, stirring occasionally, until the liquid evaporates. Cooking time will vary from 5 to 10 minutes, depending on the type of mushroom. Cream the remaining butter in a small bowl with the shallots, garlic, parsley, salt, and pepper and set it aside.

When the turkey is cooked, transfer it to a platter, cover it loosely with aluminum foil, and keep it warm. For the gravy, pour or spoon off the fat from the roasting pan, leaving the pan juices. Add the wine to the roasting pan and simmer on the stove top, stirring to dissolve the juices, until reduced to 2 to 3 tablespoons glaze. Add the broth and continue simmering until reduced by half, 6 to 8 minutes. Strain the gravy into a small saucepan, whisk in the crème fraîche, and bring just to a boil. Taste and adjust the seasoning.

To finish, reheat the chestnuts and mushrooms on the stove top if necessary. Discard the trussing strings from the turkey and pile the chestnuts around it on the platter, ready to carve at the table (see page 370). Stir the shallot butter into the mushrooms, taste, and adjust the seasoning. Pile the mushrooms in a warmed serving dish. Reheat the gravy, spoon a little over the turkey to moisten it, and serve the rest separately.

L'OIE RÔTIE DE NOËL

ROAST GOOSE WITH APPLES AND VEGETABLES

serves 5 or 6

Roast goose is a reason to celebrate, and here is a splendid Alsatian recipe in which the bird is basted with beer so the skin darkens and the gravy toasts to a deep caramel. Whole apples cooked in the cavity add unexpected flavor and emerge tasty and hot, ready to serve with the accompanying rutabagas and Brussels sprouts. I look for a goose with creamy white skin and plump breast meat that almost conceals the breastbone. Even then, a bird weighing ten pounds (four and one-half kilograms) serves only six people. In compensation, a goose renders quantities of superb fat for frying potatoes.

ONE 9- TO 10-POUND/4.5-KG GOOSE

SALT AND PEPPER

5 TART APPLES (ABOUT 2 POUNDS/900 G TOTAL)

1 CUP/250 ML DARK BEER

$1^1/_2$ POUNDS/675 G RUTABAGAS, CUT INTO $^3/_4$-INCH/
2-CM CHUNKS

$1^1/_2$ POUNDS/675 G BRUSSELS SPROUTS, TRIMMED
AND HALVED IF LARGE

2 TABLESPOONS/30 G BUTTER

GRAVY

1 CUP/250 ML MEDIUM-DRY WHITE WINE

2 CUPS/500 ML CHICKEN BROTH (SEE PAGE 373)

LARGE ROASTING PAN

Heat the oven to 450°F/230°C. Wipe the goose inside and out with paper towels, and season it inside and out with salt and pepper. Peel and core the apples, leaving them whole. Put them inside the bird, and truss it (see page 371). Put the goose on a rack in the roasting pan and pour over the beer, rubbing it well into the skin.

Roast the goose until it starts to brown, about 40 minutes. Prick the skin to release the fat underneath it, then turn the bird breast down and baste it. Lower the heat to 350°F/180°C and continue roasting, basting often, for 1 hour. Generous amounts of fat will accumulate in the bottom of the pan, so drain and reserve it. Finally, turn the goose once more, breast up. Continue roasting and basting until the bird is very brown, the meat pulls away from the drumstick, and the juices run clear when you prick the thigh with a skewer, 1 to 1¼ hours longer. A thermometer inserted in the thigh away from bone should register 165°F/74°C. If the skin starts to brown too much during cooking, cover the goose loosely with aluminum foil.

Meanwhile, prepare the vegetable garnish. Put the rutabagas in a saucepan with cold salted water to cover, bring to a boil, cover, and simmer until tender but still firm, 10 to 15 minutes. Drain and set aside. Put the Brussels sprouts in a saucepan with cold salted water to cover, bring to a boil, and cook, uncovered, just until tender, 8 to 10 minutes. Drain, rinse with cold water, and set aside.

When the goose is cooked, remove it from the oven. Turn the oven heat back up to 450°F/230°C. Line a baking sheet with aluminum foil and set the bird, breast side up, on the foil, setting the roasting pan aside. Rub the goose with the butter and return it to the oven for 5 to 10 minutes to crisp the skin. Transfer the goose to a large platter, and cover loosely with foil to keep warm. Set it aside while heating the vegetables and making the gravy.

To heat the vegetables, heat about 4 tablespoons/60 g of the reserved goose fat in a large frying pan. Add the vegetables with salt and pepper and sauté briskly until lightly browned. Spoon them around the goose and continue keeping it warm.

For the gravy, pour off all but 2 tablespoons fat from the roasting pan (keep the fat for another use). Add the wine to the pan, bring to a boil on the stove top, and simmer, stirring constantly to dissolve the pan juices, until reduced by at least half. Add the broth and simmer the gravy until well flavored and concentrated, 3 to 5 minutes. Taste it, adjust the seasoning, and strain into a bowl.

Carve the bird at the table (see page 370), spooning the apples from the inside like stuffing. Pass the gravy at the table.

= A FEAST ON THE FARM =

Some of the most satisfying dining to be experienced in France is, not surprisingly, in country homes. Luckily, there is no need to wait for a personal invitation to the table. Anyone touring the countryside can track down farms offering table d'hôte meals through an organization called Fermes Auberges (Farm Inns). At the associated Fermes de Séjour, accommodations are available as well, sometimes with extras like cooking lessons. Ideally, you enjoy regional dishes and local products, many grown right out the back door. I have long enjoyed inspired meals at *fermes auberges*, such as *coq au vin* and cherry gratin in Burgundy, and oysters and crêpes in Brittany, brought to the table aflame with Calvados. It is always very rustic: big wooden tables with everyone seated around, carafes of country wine, and a friendly welcome that reminds me of a Sunday lunch with cousins. However, until recently, I had never stayed at a *ferme de séjour*.

It was in the Périgord one November, and finding a place to sleep off-season was not easy. By the time I reached La Ferme de Laubicherie, the last house at the end of a lane very much at the back of beyond, it was pitch dark. I excused my unannounced appearance to the proprietors, Gerolf Jacobs and Jacqueline Garcia. "It's no trouble," they

assured me. "We're just sorry we didn't know in advance, or we'd have cooked a proper dinner and made you our walnut cake." Gerolf boasts that his walnut cake is legendary— dense, moist, and mysteriously walnutty—but he refused outright to share his recipe.

When not concocting culinary secrets, Gerolf grows fruits and vegetables; raises foie gras geese, black Basque pigs, lamb, and rabbits; and brews his own beer, some of it enhanced with aromas of truffle or chestnut. He is a true gourmand, with a cookbook collection and a mighty girth to prove it. That night's dinner was one he considered simple and ordinary, beginning with wonderfully rough pâté cooked by Jacqueline and a green salad. Next came a great platter of duck confit, surrounded by green beans and boiled potatoes. We finished with a local cheese, then chocolate mousse, made that morning by a visiting family friend and served with honey-drizzled fruits.

In the morning after breakfast (tea, toast, and pots of jams by Jacqueline), I took a stroll down the lane through the apple orchards. The ground was wet and carpeted with rotting leaves, the air fresh and misty. A few laps around here, I thought, and I might convince myself to stay for lunch.

CHEF CHAMBRETTE'S TERRINE DE FOIE GRAS

serves 6 to 8

The best foie gras I ever ate was made by Fernand Chambrette, a chef celebrated by James Beard for his Quiche Lorraine (page 46), Babas au Rhum (page 292), and, yes, foie gras. "The success of a terrine depends very much on the quality of the livers and how they were fattened," says Chambrette. "Do not choose livers that are too large, as that makes them more likely to melt into fat. A perfectly fattened liver should be firm but can vary in color from pink to yellow ocher." It is a chancy affair; even the most expert eye can be fooled by a liver that simply dissolves during cooking. All the same, I urge you to try, as a home-cooked terrine is far superior to canned or vacuum-packed foie gras, which has to be sterilized at too high a temperature. Here is Fernand Chambrette's recipe.

First the lobes of the fattened livers must be carefully trimmed of veins and membrane, a tricky job. Delicate seasoning and slow cooking are also key. If the cooking temperature rises above 190°F/90°C, even for a few moments, the liver literally melts away. For this reason, Chambrette prefers a ceramic mold, which conducts heat more gently than a metal one. And he finds that two foie gras livers do best in a larger terrine, rather than baking one liver in a smaller mold. Before cooking, the livers are seasoned and marinated in port. And on no account should you let the cooking go too far. The finest terrine of foie gras is always faintly pink.

At the table, slices of chilled terrine should be generous, and accompanied by chunks of toasted country bread or pain brioché *(light egg bread). You may want to serve sea salt for sprinkling on the terrine, and perhaps pass around a bowl of Confit d'Oignons (page 268). That's about it, barring a glass of late-picked sweet white wine, whether from Sauternes in Bordeaux or a taste-alike from elsewhere.*

2 FRESH FOIE GRAS DUCK LIVERS (ABOUT 2¼ POUNDS/
1 KG TOTAL)

1½ TEASPOONS/11 G FINE SALT

½ TEASPOON WHITE PEPPER

LARGE PINCH OF GRATED NUTMEG

½ CUP/125 ML PORT

SEA SALT, FOR SPRINKLING

5-CUP/1.25-LITER CERAMIC OR EARTHENWARE TERRINE

Put the livers in a large bowl with cold water to cover and soak them for 5 to 6 hours in the refrigerator to clean (*dégorger*) them. Remove the livers from the water and drain on paper towels, leaving them for 15 minutes at room temperature so they are easier to handle.

Next comes the most delicate operation: with your hands, gently separate each liver into 2 lobes, a large one and the other a little smaller. With a knife, slash each lobe horizontally in half along the length of its inner side (but do not cut them in two). Then, gently pull the arteries from the livers along with a maximum of membrane, being careful not to tear the lobes. The less the livers are handled, the better (there is always the risk of melting). Mix the salt, pepper, and nutmeg together, and season the livers with the mixture. Reshape them and put them in the terrine. It should be just large enough to hold them. Pour the port over the livers, cover, and marinate in the refrigerator for 12 hours.

Heat the oven to 350°F/180°C. Line a roasting pan with a dish towel. Cover the terrine with its lid, put it in the roasting pan, and pour in boiling water to make a water bath (see page 373). Bring the water back to just below a boil on the stove top and transfer the pan to the oven. Poach the terrine for 35 to 45 minutes. The terrine should register 100°F/39°C when tested at the center with a thermometer. While the terrine cooks, it is vital that the water remain below the boiling point without bubbling, 185°F/85°C on the thermometer, so the liver does not melt. Remove the terrine from the water and set it aside to cool for 2 hours. Its temperature will rise to around 120°F/50°C before it starts to cool.

Carefully transfer the cooled livers to a strainer set over a bowl to catch the cooking liquid and fat. Replace the livers in the terrine, spreading them flat; they will be quite soft and may fall apart somewhat. Cut a piece of cardboard to fit just inside the rim of the terrine, wrap it in aluminum foil, and set it on the livers. Top with a can as a weight. Chill the terrine for 24 hours. Also chill the reserved juices.

Lift off the fat that has solidified on the cooking juices, melt it, and set aside. Remove the cardboard from the terrine and pour enough melted fat over the livers to seal the surface completely. Replace the lid and store the terrine in the refrigerator. It will be much, much improved if you keep it for at least 3 days, or up to 10 days if you seal it carefully. Use the cooking juices to make a little sauce for steak, and any leftover fat to fry some potatoes.

At serving time, warm the terrine mold for about 20 seconds in hot water. Run a knife around the edge and turn the terrine onto a chopping board. With a thin knife dipped in hot water, cut the terrine into sturdy slices. Serve with toasts of country bread or brioche, and sea salt for sprinkling.

FOIE GRAS À LA RHUBARBE

SAUTÉED FOIE GRAS WITH RHUBARB COMPOTE

serves 6

A rich slice of sautéed foie gras begs for the contrasting bite of a fruit such as rhubarb. This compote cooks in less than fifteen minutes and also adds color to the plate. Meanwhile, the foie gras is sautéed in a dry pan for literally seconds to brown it on each side, then the pan is deglazed with a trickle of sherry vinegar and walnut oil, an ideal last-minute treat. Foie gras would normally be a first course, but you can upgrade it to a main dish with a rice pilaf on the side. You will find foie gras available on the Internet, and I have also made this recipe with great success using thinly sliced calf's liver, or whole duck magrets. Toasted spice bread (or gingerbread that is not too sweet) is a superb accompaniment.

1 LARGE FRESH FOIE GRAS DUCK LIVER (ABOUT 1½ POUNDS/675 G)

SALT AND PEPPER

1 SHALLOT, FINELY CHOPPED

2 TABLESPOONS/30 G SUGAR

6 TABLESPOONS/90 ML SHERRY VINEGAR

6 TABLESPOONS/90 ML WALNUT OIL

2 TABLESPOONS WALNUT PIECES, COARSELY CHOPPED

COMPOTE

1 POUND/450 G RHUBARB

1 PINT/225 G STRAWBERRIES, HULLED AND SLICED

2 TABLESPOONS/30 G SUGAR, MORE IF NEEDED

2 TABLESPOONS/30 G BUTTER, CUT INTO PIECES

3 TABLESPOONS HONEY

Chill the foie gras thoroughly before you start. For the compote, trim the rhubarb stalks, and if they are tough on the outside, peel them with a vegetable peeler. Thickly slice them and spread them in a heavy saucepan with the strawberries. Add 2 tablespoons water to prevent sticking and sprinkle the sugar on top. Cover tightly and cook over low heat, stirring occasionally, until the rhubarb softens to a purée, 10 to 15 minutes, depending on its toughness. Remove the lid and continue cooking, stirring constantly, until the purée just falls from the spoon. Stir in the butter and honey. Taste and adjust the sweetness with more sugar, if needed. Keep the rhubarb warm.

Meanwhile, gently separate the liver with your hands into 2 lobes, one large and the other a little smaller. With a small knife, carefully cut and pull the arteries from the lobes along with a maximum of membrane, being careful not to tear the lobes. The less the lobes are handled, the better (there is always the risk of melting). Cut the lobes on the diagonal into 6 slices, each about ⅜ inch/1 cm thick. Cut out any visible membranes, taking care to keep the slices whole. Sprinkle the slices on both sides with salt and pepper.

Heat a large frying pan over high heat until a drop of water flicked into the pan bounces back off the surface, showing it is very hot. Add the foie gras—its fat will melt at once and prevent it sticking—lower the heat to medium and sauté just until brown, less than 1 minute. Turn and brown the other side, again allowing less than 1 minute so the liver remains pink in the center. Transfer the foie gras to a plate and keep warm at the side of the stove.

To make a sauce, pour off all but 1 tablespoon of the foie gras fat from the frying pan and return to medium heat. Add the shallot, sprinkle with the sugar, and sauté, stirring often, until the sugar caramelizes, 1 to 2 minutes. Pour in the vinegar and bring to a boil, stirring to deglaze the pan juices. When reduced by half, add the walnut oil and heat for 1 minute. Remove from the heat, stir in the walnuts, taste, and adjust the seasoning. Spoon the rhubarb onto 6 warmed plates, top with the foie gras, spoon over the sauce, and serve at once. As you can see, this recipe moves fast.

GÂTEAUX DE FOIES DE VOLAILLE, COULIS DE TOMATES AUX HERBES

WARM CHICKEN LIVER MOUSSES WITH
FRESH HERBED TOMATO COULIS

serves 8

Where chickens are raised, dishes pop up to make good use of the livers. These chicken liver gâteaux are a specialty of Bresse, the home of little white birds with the elite AOC label (page 111). Gâteaux de Foies de Volaille are unusual in always being served warm, unlike chicken liver pâté. In winter in Bresse, you might be lucky enough to find a Sauce Nantua (page 80) made from a coulis of crayfish. In summer, I prefer this warm coulis of fresh tomatoes, flavored with a mixture of chives, oregano, parsley, and basil, or whatever mix of herbs you enjoy most. Traditionally, these gâteaux are an appetizer, but I find that with salad greens and perhaps some Céleri Remoulade (page 246) on the side, they add up to a light main course.

8 OUNCES/225 G CHICKEN LIVERS

I GARLIC CLOVE, CHOPPED

4 WHOLE EGGS, BEATEN TO MIX

4 EGG YOLKS

$^{1}/_{4}$ CUP/60 ML CRÈME FRAÎCHE (PAGE 374) OR
HEAVY CREAM

I$^{1}/_{2}$ CUPS/375 ML MILK

I TABLESPOON COGNAC

LARGE PINCH OF GRATED NUTMEG

SALT AND PEPPER

VEGETABLE OIL, FOR THE RAMEKIN

TOMATO COULIS

2 POUNDS/900 G TOMATOES, PEELED, SEEDED, AND
CHOPPED (SEE PAGE 372)

3 TO 4 TABLESPOONS CHOPPED MIXED FRESH HERBS

3 TABLESPOONS/45 ML WALNUT OIL

JUICE OF $^{1}/_{2}$ LEMON

TOASTED CROÛTES MADE WITH 8 SLICES WHITE BREAD,
CUT THE SIZE OF THE GÂTEAUX (SEE PAGE 374)

8 SPRIGS FRESH OREGANO, PARSLEY, OR BASIL

EIGHT $^{1}/_{2}$-CUP/125-ML RAMEKINS

Heat the oven to 350°F/180°C. Trim membrane and any green spots from the chicken livers. Put the livers and garlic in a food processor and purée until smooth, 20 to 30 seconds. Add the whole eggs and egg yolks and work again until smooth. Add the crème fraîche, milk, Cognac, nutmeg, salt, and pepper and work until thoroughly mixed, about 30 seconds. Fry a teaspoonful of the mixture in a small pan, taste, and adjust the seasoning.

Brush each ramekin with oil and line the bottom with a round of parchment paper. Work the liver mixture through a bowl strainer placed over a large measuring jug, then pour it into the ramekins. Line a roasting pan with a dish towel, set the ramekins in it, and pour in boiling water to make a water bath (see page 373). Bring the water just back to a boil on the stove top and transfer the pan to the oven. Cook the gâteaux just until firm and a wooden toothpick inserted in the center comes out clean, 15 to 18 minutes. Lift the ramekins from the water bath and let them cool for a few minutes. They may be stored for a day in the refrigerator.

Meanwhile, make the coulis. Put the tomatoes in a strainer and season with salt and pepper. Leave them for 20 minutes to drain excess liquid. Transfer them to a saucepan and stir in the herbs, oil, lemon juice, salt, and pepper. Taste and adjust the seasoning, then warm the coulis over very low heat until tepid. Make the croûtes.

To finish, reheat the gâteaux in a water bath on the stove top if necessary, allowing 10 to 15 minutes. Run a knife around the edge of each gâteau and turn out onto individual plates. Spoon the warm tomato coulis around the edge and top each gâteau with an herb sprig.

FOIE GRAS, A GLOBAL DELICACY

Foie gras, the enlarged liver of a force-fed goose or duck, is among the most ancient of French delicacies. The Romans force-fed geese with figs to fatten their livers three- or fourfold; nowadays the same effect is achieved with corn. The tradition is said to have begun with the Jews, who found goose fat a good alternative to lard from the forbidden pig. Israel, along with central Europe, still supplies France with many of the fattened livers used to make the "French" canned terrines and pâtés that are exported throughout the world.

Although Alsace, like Périgord, has always been famous for its goose and duck dishes, it was only in the late eighteenth century that foie gras became fashionable. At first, it was commonly baked in a pie crust with a layer of chopped pork surrounding the truffle-studded liver. Today, it is more often simply baked whole in a terrine with a port or Sauternes marinade, perhaps studded with slivers of fresh truffle if the budget permits. Of course, raw foie gras can also be sliced and seared to serve warm with sautéed apples, figs, or a tart fruit such as rhubarb. To make the livers go further, they may be puréed as a mousse, which is often sold in cans. Mousse of foie gras is much less expensive than *bloc* or *rouleau* cans of solid liver, and it has an airier texture, melting if it is heated.

Today, the sales of duck foie gras far outstrip those of goose. The foie gras from a duck is less expensive and the flavor less rich; some connoisseurs think it has more finesse (personally I do not agree). Thanks to air-conditioning, birds can be fattened year-round, but early December remains peak for the Christmas market. No New Year's *réveillon* would be complete without a festive slice.

CONFIT CONFIDENTIAL

The term *confit* was once exclusively French, but now it has gone international. The nearest English equivalent, "preserved," does not capture its essence. Technically, *confire* means to conserve, either by curing in salt and then slowly cooking foods in fat, as in Confit de Canard (page 119), or by pickling in salt, vinegar, or alcohol, as in Confit d'Oignons (page 268), or by candying in sugar or sugar syrup, as in Fruits Confits (page 352). The noun *confiture* means "jam."

These days, *confit* is applied ever more loosely, extending to vegetables and fruits cooked to a melting texture. *Confit de pommes* is a slow-cooked apple dessert. *Confit de tomates* refers to slowly caramelized tomatoes, usually for poultry or pork. If you see *confit de poireaux* on a menu, expect leeks cooked in butter until they are soft. A French home cook might advise you to cook a particular lamb dish until it is confit. She doesn't mean you should smother it in fat, but that you should roast the meat until it falls apart at the touch of spoon.

The best-known confit is made with the succulent legs of duck or goose, salted and then cooked in its own fat for hours. A southwest speciality, Confit de Canard is now everywhere—indeed, cans of it are almost a staple in French kitchens. My first encounter with confit was at age thirteen in Gascony with my parents. I was presented with a nondescript piece of brown meat on my plate, totally unadorned. I tasted it—was it ham? If so, it was the most delicious ham I had ever tasted. From that moment on, I was a confit convert.

the best of

BEEF, LAMB & VEAL

CHAPTER
No. 7

Buying meat in country France is a pleasure and something of a social exercise. In even small towns, you will find a specialty butcher who offers advice on cooking his meats, down to timing and recommended accompaniments. Waiting customers will join in discussion of the merits of shoulder versus ribs in Blanquette de Veau (page 147), or how many types of sausage should be included in an authentic Choucroute Alsacienne (page 176). The supermarket in the nearby town of ten thousand does brisk trade, and when I asked at the meat counter about the staff, I was told, "We're six in the department and we're kept busy with special requests."

Braises and stews take pride of place in France. Tough cuts and bones are valued for their depth of flavor and for the rich, gelatinous sauces that are extracted during slow cooking. Shanks, ribs, neck, and other meats on the bone are sought after, and to be sure of securing bones to make broth, I must order in advance. Many of the traditional stews, ragoûts, daubes, and pot roasts include lots of vegetables, creating a one-pot meal. It is the garnish that bestows the regional character, be it red wine, bacon, mushrooms, and onions for Boeuf Bourguignon (page 136), the beer and onions in Carbonnade de Boeuf (page 137), or the white beans, tomato, and garlic in Gigot d'Agneau à la Bretonne (page 155).

French steak and roasts are less marbled with fat than in the United States, making them relatively tough, and cuts such as fillet are large, as they often come from huge cattle that can each weigh one ton and up. I can tell where I am in France just by looking at cows in the fields. When they are black and white, they are the milking cows of Normandy; central France is marked by the ginger-haired, feisty Limousin breed; and when I see great horned black bulls, I know I am in the Camargue, the Mediterranean delta of the Rhône. Bull meat is something else again, dark, gamy, and surprisingly tender as a steak or in recipes like Daube de Boeuf Provençale (page 139).

Sheep are only slightly less distinguished, with many regional breeds, such as the Berrichon, reputed as baby lamb; the Bleu du Maine, its wool misleadingly white; and the hardy, rustic Caussenard of the south. Mountain sheep that have grazed on the wild southern herbs of the *garrigues*, and animals from the salt marches (*prés salés*) on the coast, are particularly prized for their zesty meat. On the butcher's counter, spring lamb can be tiny, known as *agneau primeur* when only weeks old. Both the meat and fat darken with age, but as *agneau* it should still make a tender lamb chop or roast. Over a year old, *agneau* becomes *mouton* (mutton), a robust meat that is hard to find but still appreciated in mountain areas such as the Pyrenees. Leisurely recipes like Gigot de Sept Heures (page 153), which braises for up to seven hours, were originally designed to make tough mutton edible, though now they are made with lamb.

In these days of contamination scares, France leads the way in tracking animals, so that even a supermarket knows the pedigree of each carcass of beef or lamb, who raised it, and where it was slaughtered. The provenance of veal and whether the calf has been milk fed are particularly scrutinized. In specialty butchers, it can all get a bit close and personal, with prize badges and pictures of calves gamboling like pets. I have to restrain myself from asking their names.

GRILLADE MARINIÈRE DE VALENCE

BRAISED SAILOR'S STEAK WITH ANCHOVIES

serves 4

In the days before railroads, the towpath along the Rhône River was a busy thoroughfare, acting as highway from the Mediterranean to Burgundy and the north. Robust draft horses pulled the barges upstream, but the river current took care of the return journey, so horses were sometimes converted to steak by the marins *(sailors), who favored robust seasonings, such as anchovy and garlic, and a bit of vinegar to tenderize the meat. Today, hearty cuts of stew beef are given the same treatment. Cooked very slowly on top of the stove, the steaks form a light, concentrated sauce, ideal with potatoes boiled in their skins or crushed to a purée. If you are not a fan of anchovy, you could consider substituting chopped olives or a couple of chopped tomatoes. This is a workingman's dish, served straight from the pan.*

4 PIECES BONELESS CHUCK OR OTHER STEW STEAK, CUT
1/2 INCH/1.25 CM THICK (ABOUT 1 1/2 POUNDS/675 G TOTAL)

SALT AND PEPPER

1/4 CUP/60 ML OLIVE OIL

2 ONIONS, THINLY SLICED

2 TABLESPOONS/30 G BUTTER

1 TABLESPOON/7 G FLOUR

2 TABLESPOONS RED WINE VINEGAR

5 ANCHOVY FILLETS, SOAKED IN MILK FOR A FEW
MINUTES, CHOPPED

3 OR 4 GARLIC CLOVES, CHOPPED

2 TABLESPOONS CHOPPED FRESH PARSLEY

Season the steaks lightly on both sides with salt and pepper (remember that the anchovies will add salt). Spread about 1 tablespoon of the oil in a sauté pan or frying pan and top with half of the onions. Lay the steaks on top and cover them with the remaining onions. To make a beurre manié, crush the butter on a plate with a fork and work in the flour to form a paste. Dot it in pieces on the onions. Cover the pan, set over low heat, and cook for 30 minutes. The meat will steam gently in its own juices. Loosen the steaks from time to time so they do not stick.

Mix the remaining 3 tablespoons oil with the vinegar, anchovies, garlic, parsley, and pepper in a small bowl. Spread the mixture on the meat, on top of the onions, stirring to distribute the flour paste (this binds the onions). Re-cover and continue cooking over very low heat until the steaks are very tender, 1¼ to 1½ hours longer. They will shrink during cooking, and this is normal; the seasonings will blend to form a thick, piquant sauce. Serve the steaks and sauce from the pan.

STEAK MARCHAND DE VIN

WINEMAKER'S STEAK

serves 4

Steak rivals omelet for speed, but all French cooks believe that good meat deserves a sauce. Hence Marchand de Vin, a two-minute jus of wine and fresh herbs made by deglazing pan juices. Nowadays, you may also come across such spices as coriander or cumin, and possibly a touch of dried red chili. Any cut of steak from fillet to T-bone, including entrecôte *(rib steak), the French favorite, does well. The steak is best served simply with a generous mound of frites or the plump, squat fries called* pommes Pont Neuf.

4 STEAKS, CUT 3/4 INCH/2 CM THICK (ABOUT
1 1/2 POUNDS/675 G TOTAL)

SALT AND PEPPER

4 TABLESPOONS/60 G BUTTER

2 SHALLOTS, FINELY CHOPPED

1 GARLIC CLOVE, FINELY CHOPPED

1 CUP/250 ML FULL-BODIED RED WINE

LEAVES FROM 3 OR 4 SPRIGS FRESH TARRAGON,
CHOPPED

3 OR 4 FRESH CHIVE BLADES, CHOPPED

3 OR 4 SPRIGS FRESH PARSLEY, CHOPPED

Season the steaks on both sides with salt and pepper. Melt half of the butter in a frying pan over high heat until it stops foaming. Add the steaks and fry until well browned, 2 to 3 minutes. Turn them, lower the heat slightly, and continue frying until brown and cooked to your taste, 2 to 3 minutes for rare steak, 3 to 5 minutes if you prefer it more done. Lift out the steaks and set on warmed plates; keep warm.

Pour off all but 1 tablespoon of the fat from the pan and return to high heat. Add the shallots and garlic and sauté until soft, about 2 minutes. Add the wine and boil rapidly until reduced by half. Take from the heat and whisk in the remaining butter in small pieces. Stir in the herbs, taste, and adjust the seasoning. Spoon the sauce over the steaks and serve at once.

BOEUF BOURGUIGNON

serves 6

Boeuf Bourguignon is the king of stews, the benchmark against which all others are judged, even in France. Dark, complex, rich but not cloying—when the balance of ingredients is just right, a Bourguignon is sublime. Well-aged beef (locals would specify from Charolais cattle), with plenty of cartilage to dissolve and enrich the sauce during long, slow cooking, is the foundation. My French butcher advises paleron, and in the United States the closest equivalent would be blade or chuck with a slice or two of shank. The beef is both marinated and simmered in red wine, a soft, fruity Pinot Noir if you are in Burgundy, with Merlot a good substitute.

Two groups of vegetables are used in the classic Boeuf Bourguignon: onions, carrots, and celery that add depth to the sauce during cooking and are then strained out, and the traditional garnish of baby onions, mushrooms, and bacon lardons that is added toward the end of cooking. Thorough browning of both meat and vegetables is important for the sauce to color to a lustrous chestnut. Above all, Boeuf Bourguignon must be cooked slowly, never at more than a simmer, for three to four hours if need be, until the meat is very tender but not quite falling apart to the prod of a fork. Fried croûtes are the traditional accompaniment, but now you will more commonly find pasta, or a potato cake sautéed in butter—as if the sauce were not rich enough!

2 POUNDS/900 G BONELESS BEEF CHUCK OR OTHER STEW MEAT

I POUND/450 G BONELESS SHANK MEAT

3 TABLESPOONS/45 ML VEGETABLE OIL, MORE IF NEEDED

3 TABLESPOONS/22 G FLOUR

2 CUPS/500 ML VEAL BROTH (SEE PAGE 373), MORE IF NEEDED

SALT AND PEPPER

MARINADE

2 ONIONS, SLICED

2 CARROTS, SLICED

I STALK CELERY, SLICED

I BOUQUET GARNI (SEE PAGE 370)

2 GARLIC CLOVES, CRUSHED

1/2 TEASPOON PEPPERCORNS

2 WHOLE CLOVES

I BOTTLE (750 ML) RED WINE

2 TABLESPOONS VEGETABLE OIL

GARNISH

2 TABLESPOONS/30 G BUTTER

8-OUNCE/225-G PIECE LEAN BACON, CUT INTO LARDONS (SEE PAGE 371)

20 TO 24 BABY ONIONS (ABOUT 330 G/12 OUNCES TOTAL), PEELED

12 OUNCES/330 G BUTTON MUSHROOMS, TRIMMED AND QUARTERED IF LARGE

FRIED CROÛTES MADE WITH 4 SLICES WHITE BREAD, CUT INTO HEARTS OR TRIANGLES, AND FRIED IN 4 TABLESPOONS/60 G BUTTER (SEE PAGE 374)

2 TABLESPOONS CHOPPED FRESH PARSLEY

A day or two ahead, marinate the beef. Trim the excess fat and cartilage from the meat. The shank will contain streaks of cartilage and collagen that will gradually dissolve, becoming tender at the end of cooking. Cut the meat into 2-inch/5-cm cubes and put the cubes in a deep bowl. For the marinade, add the onions, carrots, and celery to the bowl and stir to mix. Tie the bouquet garni, garlic, peppercorns, and cloves in a piece of cheesecloth and bury the bag in the meat and vegetables. Pour in the wine and spoon the oil on top. Cover and refrigerate for 12 to 24 hours, stirring once or twice.

Heat the oven to 325°F/160°C. Drain the contents of the bowl into a strainer placed over a bowl to capture the wine. Remove the beef, vegetables, and bouquet garni from the strainer. Separate the pieces of meat and pat them dry with paper towels. Heat the 3 tablespoons oil in a large flameproof casserole over high heat. Add a few pieces of the meat and brown thoroughly on all sides, taking about 4 to 5 minutes. Remove them with a draining spoon and set aside. Fry the remaining meat in batches, adding more oil if the pan seems dry.

Add the drained vegetables to the pan and fry them until starting to brown, 5 to 7 minutes. Stir in the flour and cook, stirring, until lightly browned, 1 to 2 minutes. Stir in the reserved wine, bring to a boil, and simmer for 1 minute. Return the beef to the pan and pour in enough broth to cover the meat. Cover the casserole and bring the contents to a boil. Transfer to the oven and simmer until the beef is tender and falls easily from a two-pronged fork, 2½ to 4 hours, depending on the meat. Stir the stew from time to time during cooking and add more broth if the sauce gets too thick.

Meanwhile, make the garnish. Melt half of the butter in a frying pan over medium heat. Add the lardons and fry until the fat runs and they start to brown, 2 to 3 minutes. Lift them out with the draining spoon and set them aside in a bowl. Add the baby onions to the pan with salt and pepper and sauté over low heat, shaking often so they color evenly, until browned and tender, 15 to 20 minutes. Add them to the lardons. Add the remaining butter to the pan with the mushrooms, salt, and pepper. Cook gently, stirring often, until tender, 3 to 5 minutes. Stir in the onions and lardons and transfer to a large bowl.

When the beef is tender, lift out the pieces with the draining spoon and add them to the garnish. Discard the bouquet garni and skim the excess fat from the sauce. Strain the sauce over the beef and garnish, pressing hard on the onions and carrots to extract maximum flavor. Stir to mix the beef and garnish with the sauce and put everything back into the casserole. Reheat the boeuf bourguignon gently on the stove top for 5 to 8 minutes to blend the flavors. Taste the sauce and adjust the seasoning. Here is another stew that benefits from being made ahead to reheat after 2 to 3 days in the refrigerator; it also freezes well for up to 3 months.

To finish, reheat the bourguignon on the stove top if necessary. Fry the croûtes and keep them in a warm place. Transfer the stew to a deep serving dish. Dip the point of each croûte into the sauce, then into chopped parsley, and set the croûtes around the edge of the dish.

CARBONNADE DE BOEUF

BEEF WITH BEER AND ONIONS

serves 4 to 6

Carbonnade is a hearty Flemish recipe, just right for cold winds and wet weather. The name comes from charbon, *or "charcoal," and this dish was once a grilled steak flavored with mustard. More to my taste is this version stewed in the oven with beer, then topped with mustard-flavored croûtes. I like to pick up color by serving it with braised red cabbage. Northerners prefer their mustard feisty, so hot rather than milder Dijon mustard is correct here.*

2 POUNDS/900 G BONELESS CHUCK OR OTHER STEW BEEF

SALT AND PEPPER

2 TABLESPOONS VEGETABLE OIL

1 TABLESPOON/15 G BUTTER

4 LARGE ONIONS (ABOUT 1 1/2 POUNDS/675 G TOTAL), THINLY SLICED

1 TABLESPOON/15 G SUGAR

2 TABLESPOONS/15 G FLOUR

3 CUPS/750 ML DARK BEER

1 CUP/250 ML BEEF OR VEAL BROTH (SEE PAGE 373), MORE IF NEEDED

1/2 TEASPOON GRATED NUTMEG

1 BOUQUET GARNI (SEE PAGE 370)

BAKED CROÛTES MADE WITH 3 OR 4 CRUSTY ROLLS (SEE PAGE 374)

1 TO 2 TABLESPOONS HOT DIJON MUSTARD

Heat the oven to 350°F/180°C. Trim the beef of all but a little fat and cut it into 2-inch/5-cm cubes. Season them with salt and pepper. Heat 1 tablespoon of the oil with the butter in a large flameproof casserole over high heat. Add half of the beef cubes and fry until well browned on all sides, taking 4 to 5 minutes. Remove them with a draining spoon, add the rest of the cubes, brown them also, and then set them aside.

Add the remaining 1 tablespoon oil to the pan along with the onions, salt, and pepper and cook over low heat, stirring often, until the onions are very soft, 15 to 20 minutes. Increase the heat to medium, add the sugar, and continue frying until the onions are caramelized, 3 to 5 minutes more. Stir in the flour and cook for 1 minute. Add the beer and bring to a boil, stirring constantly. Stir in the broth, nutmeg, and bouquet garni. Return the beef to the pan, pushing it well down into the liquid, and bring just back to a boil.

Cover the casserole, put it in the oven, and cook until the beef is very tender when you pinch it between your finger and thumb or poke it with a two-pronged fork, 2 to 2½ hours. Stir from time to time during cooking and add more broth if the pan gets dry. The sauce should be well reduced, dark, and concentrated. If it is thin, boil it on the stove top to reduce it. Discard the bouquet garni, taste, and adjust the seasoning. The longer you keep a complex stew like this, the better it will be. It can be refrigerated for up to 3 days and it freezes well for up to 3 months.

To finish, reheat the carbonnade if necessary on the stove top. Make the croûtes and spread them thinly with the mustard. Heat the broiler. Arrange the croûtes on top of the beef and baste them with the pan sauce. Broil about 3 inches/7.5 cm from the heat until the top is browned, 3 to 5 minutes. Serve the carbonnade very hot.

DAUBE DE BOEUF PROVENÇALE

BEEF STEW WITH VEGETABLES AND OLIVES

serves 8 to 10

Daube is the ultimate one-pot meal of meat, vegetables, and broth, bathed in a generous marinade of wine. There are many versions of daube, some with beef, others with lamb, still others with pungent bull meat. All of them are moistened with wine of some kind. In winter, I like to use a rich, dark red wine, with black olives for balance, while summer calls for green olives and the refreshing, softer finish of white wine.

The gremolata *relish of chopped lemon zest, garlic, and parsley is a recent import from Italy. Adding some small potatoes to the stew or serving it with your favorite country bread is a pleasant alternative.*

3 POUNDS/1.35 KG BONELESS CHUCK OR OTHER
STEW BEEF

1 PIG'S FOOT, SPLIT (OPTIONAL)

3/4 CUP/150 G BRINED GREEN OLIVES

3/4 CUP/150 G BRINED BLACK OLIVES

1 TABLESPOON OLIVE OIL

12-OUNCE/330-G PIECE LEAN BACON, CUT INTO
LARDONS (SEE PAGE 371)

4 ONIONS (ABOUT 1¹/₂ POUNDS/675 G TOTAL),
THINLY SLICED

6 LARGE CARROTS (ABOUT 1¹/₂ POUNDS/675 G
TOTAL), THICKLY SLICED

6 TOMATOES (ABOUT 2 POUNDS/900 G TOTAL),
PEELED, SEEDED, AND CHOPPED (SEE PAGE 372)

4 OR 5 GARLIC CLOVES, CHOPPED

1 CUP/250 ML VEAL BROTH (SEE PAGE 373)

SALT AND PEPPER

MARINADE

ZEST OF 1 ORANGE, PARED IN STRIPS

1 LARGE BOUQUET GARNI (SEE PAGE 370)

2-INCH PIECE CINNAMON STICK

3 WHOLE CLOVES

1 TEASPOON PEPPERCORNS

1 BOTTLE (750 ML) FULL-BODIED RED WINE

GREMOLATA

2 GARLIC CLOVES

SPRIGS FROM 1 SMALL BUNCH FRESH PARSLEY
(1¹/₂ OUNCES/45 G), CHOPPED

1 TABLESPOON FINELY CHOPPED LEMON ZEST

DAUBIÈRE OR LARGE FLAMEPROOF CASSEROLE;
CHEESECLOTH

Start preparing the daube a day ahead. Trim the excess fat from the beef, leaving most of the cartilage and collagen, as they will gradually dissolve to become tender at the end of stewing, contributing valuable gelatin to the cooking juices in the process. Cut the beef into 1½-inch/4-cm cubes. To blanch and clean the pig's foot (if using), put it in a pan of cold water, bring to a boil, and simmer, skimming often, for about 10 minutes. Drain and set aside. Pit the olives if you wish (the pits add flavor to the sauce).

Add the oil to a *daubière* (Provençale earthenware pot) or a large flameproof casserole. Layer the ingredients on top in the following order: beef, bacon lardons, green and black olives, onions, carrots, tomatoes, and garlic. For the marinade, tie the orange zest, bouquet garni, cinnamon stick, cloves, and peppercorns in a piece of cheesecloth and bury the bag in the meats and vegetables. Pour in the wine. Cover and refrigerate for 12 to 24 hours.

Heat the oven to 400°F/200°C. Pour enough broth into the *daubière* just to cover the ingredients and top them with freshly ground pepper. Cover tightly and bring to a simmer in the oven. This will take about 30 minutes, depending on the thickness of your *daubière*. Once the daube is simmering, lower the oven heat to 325°F/160°C and cook until the beef is tender enough to crush easily between your finger and thumb, 2 to 2½ hours. If the ingredients are swimming in liquid toward the end of cooking, remove the lid to allow the moisture to evaporate.

When the meat is done, take the pot from the oven. If you are using a pig's foot, it must be cooked further, so transfer it to a saucepan. Drain off enough cooking juices from the daube to cover the foot, top with a lid, and simmer until tender and the meat is falling from the bones, 2 to 2½ hours longer. Let the foot cool in the broth, then lift it out. The broth will be deliciously concentrated, so strain it back into the pot with the beef.

Pull the pig skin and meat from the bones and chop them, discarding the bones. Add the skin and meat to the daube, stirring them in gently. Taste the broth and adjust the seasoning. Salt may not be needed because the olives and bacon are salty. The finished daube may be kept a day or two in the refrigerator before serving. During this time, the flavor will mellow wonderfully.

At serving time, reheat the daube on the stove top if the *daubière* is flameproof. If not, reheat the daube in a 350°F/180°C oven; it will take an hour or more. Meanwhile, make the *gremolata*: Finely chop the garlic, then chop it together with 3 tablespoons of the parsley. Mix in the lemon zest. When the daube is hot, stir in the rest of the parsley and check the seasoning once more. Serve directly from the pot, and pass the *gremolata* for guests to help themselves.

BOULES DE PICOLAT
CATALONIAN MEATBALLS

serves 5 or 6

Barcelona so epitomizes Catalonia that most people forget that a small part of this historic province is in France. Here, local dishes teem with dark, pungent flavors that date back to the Phoenicians. The Arabs came later, adding spices like saffron, cinnamon, and nutmeg to savory and sweet dishes, such as the popular Crème Catalane topped with caramel (page 313). Catalan is very much a second language around Perpignan, the regional capital, and Paris seems a long way away. "We love anchovies," a local nationalist told me, "sardines, tuna, lots of fish, and game such as partridge and wild boar. I can tell you firsthand that wild boar liver is an acquired taste!" Garlic is a passion. "Our meatballs are half beef, half garlic."

As in many Mediterranean countries, Catalan cooks favor shallow earthenware dishes, known locally as a cassola, for recipes like these savory Boules de Picolat, simmered and served with a rust-colored sauce of tomato and green olives. Most earthenware dishes are resistant to low heat on the stove top, but if in doubt, you should simmer the meatballs in a 350°F/180°C oven. Given the strong Arab influence in this region, an accompaniment of saffron pilaf (page 109) or couscous would be perfect.

I POUND/450 G LEAN GROUND BEEF

8 OUNCES/225 GROUND PORK

3 OR 4 GARLIC CLOVES, FINELY CHOPPED

I EGG

I EGG YOLK

SALT AND BLACK PEPPER

¹/₄ CUP/30 G FLOUR

¹/₄ CUP/60 ML OLIVE OIL

3-OUNCE/90-G PIECE LEAN BACON, CUT INTO LARDONS (SEE PAGE 371)

SAUCE ROUSSE

I ONION, FINELY CHOPPED

2 TABLESPOONS/15 G FLOUR

2 CUPS/500 ML WATER

I CUP/200 G PITTED SALTED GREEN OLIVES

I THICK SLICE CURED RAW HAM (ABOUT 2 OUNCES/60 G), CUT INTO ³/₈-INCH/I-CM DICE

I TABLESPOON TOMATO PASTE

¹/₂ TEASPOON GROUND CINNAMON

LARGE PINCH OF CAYENNE PEPPER

2 TABLESPOONS CHOPPED FRESH PARSLEY

IO-INCH/25-CM CASSOLA OR FLAMEPROOF ROUND EARTHENWARE BAKING DISH

In a bowl, combine the ground meats, garlic, egg, egg yolk, salt, and black pepper. Beat the mixture with a wooden spoon until it pulls from the sides of the bowl, 2 to 3 minutes. Sauté a nugget of the mixture, taste it, and adjust the seasoning of the rest.

Spread the flour on a sheet of parchment paper and season it with salt and pepper. Dampen your hands and roll the meat mixture into balls the size of very large walnuts. Roll the meatballs, a few at a time, in the flour until well coated. Heat the oil in a large frying pan over medium heat. Add the bacon lardons and fry until golden, about 5 minutes. Lift them out with a draining spoon and set them aside. Add the meatballs to the pan—if they seem crowded, work in 2 batches—and brown them all over, 5 to 8 minutes. Using the draining spoon, transfer them to the *cassola* or other baking dish and set aside.

For the sauce, add the onion to the same pan and cook over medium heat, stirring occasionally, until soft, 3 to 5 minutes. Sprinkle the flour over the onions and cook, stirring, until lightly browned, 1 to 2 minutes. Add the water and bring to a boil, stirring to dissolve the pan juices. Stir in the lardons, olives, ham, tomato paste, cinnamon, cayenne pepper, and some black pepper. Taste and adjust the seasoning, remembering that the sauce should be quite hot and the olives and ham will contribute salt during further cooking.

Spoon the sauce over the meatballs and cover with a lid or aluminum foil. Set the dish over very low heat and simmer until the meatballs are no longer pink in the center, 20 to 25 minutes. The sauce should be thick and rich, so remove the cover if necessary toward the end of cooking. Serve the meatballs directly from the dish, sprinkled with a shower of parsley. Almost any kind of meatball reheats well, and Boules de Picolat may be refrigerated for up to 3 days, though freezing tends to toughen them. Reheat gently on the stove top.

BACKOËFE

MEAT AND POTATO CASSEROLE

serves 8 to 10

Backoëfe, *which means "baker's oven" in Alsatian dialect, includes a range of meats with potato and onion. A variant called* schnitzen *features more potatoes and is flavored with bacon and dried fruits that make a temptingly syrupy jus at the bottom of the dish. In a traditional household, Monday was laundry day (and still was in northern England when I was a child) and too busy for cooking at home. So on Sunday night the meats for Backoëfe would be left to marinate, and early the next morning all the ingredients would be layered into a large earthenware dish and carried to the village bakery, where it would cook in the oven until noon. The unusual mix of meats shows the recipe was a catchall for oddments, and you can treat it the same way, adding more or less beef, lamb, or pork, and including bits of ham and even chicken. You will need a dry white wine for marinating, but not too dry—a Riesling would be just right.*

1½ POUNDS/675 G BONELESS PORK LOIN

1½ POUNDS/675 G BONELESS LAMB SHOULDER

1½ POUNDS/675 G BONELESS CHUCK OR STEW BEEF

2 TABLESPOONS/30 G LARD OR VEGETABLE OIL

3 ONIONS (ABOUT 1 POUND/450 G TOTAL), THINLY SLICED

4 POUNDS/1.8 KG BAKING POTATOES, PEELED AND THINLY SLICED

SALT AND PEPPER

2 CUPS/500 ML WATER, MORE IF NEEDED

MARINADE

2 CARROTS, THINLY SLICED

2 ONIONS, THINLY SLICED

1 LARGE BOUQUET GARNI (SEE PAGE 370)

2 GARLIC CLOVES, CRUSHED

1 BOTTLE (750 ML) DRY WHITE WINE

1 TABLESPOON VEGETABLE OIL

Start preparing the casserole a day ahead. Trim the excess fat and any sinew from all the meats. Cut the pork and lamb into 1½-inch/4-cm cubes, and the beef into 1-inch/2.5-cm cubes, and put all the meats in a large bowl. For the marinade, add the carrots, onions, bouquet garni, and garlic to the bowl and stir to mix with the meats. Pour in the wine and top with the oil. Cover and refrigerate for 12 to 24 hours, stirring occasionally.

Heat the lard in a large, shallow flameproof casserole over medium heat. Add the onions and cook, stirring often, until

browned, 7 to 10 minutes. Take the pan from the heat, spread half of the potatoes over the onions and sprinkle with salt and pepper. Top with the marinated meat, lifting it out of the marinade with a draining spoon. Cover the meat with the remaining potato slices, pressing them down lightly, and season them with salt and pepper. Strain the marinade through a strainer held over the meat and vegetables and then add the water almost to cover them. (Discard the marinade vegetables and bouquet garni.)

Heat the oven to 325°F/160°C. Cover the casserole and heat it gently on the stove top until the liquid simmers, 10 to 15 minutes. Transfer the pan to the oven and cook until the meats are tender when pierced with a two-pronged fork, 1 to 1¼ hours. Backoëfe reheats well so it may be prepared a day or two ahead and kept in the refrigerator.

To finish, heat the oven to 400°F/200°C. Uncover the casserole and continue cooking until the potatoes brown and the cooking juices are concentrated, 15 to 20 minutes if the casserole is already hot, or up to 30 minutes if it has been refrigerated. Serve the meat and vegetables directly from the casserole.

CÔTES D'AGNEAU CHAMPVALLON

LAMB CHOPS WITH POTATO AND ONION

Even simpler than Backoëfe, this bistro favorite calls for only three main ingredients.

Heat the oven to 350°F/180°C. Sprinkle 4 thick-cut lamb chops on both sides with salt and pepper. Heat 2 tablespoons vegetable oil in a sauté pan over high heat and brown the chops thoroughly on each side. Remove them, add 3 onions (about 1 pound/450 g total), sliced, to the pan and sauté them until starting to brown, 5 to 7 minutes. Peel and thinly slice 6 baking potatoes (about 3 pounds/1.35 kg total) and toss them with the onions; 1 garlic clove, chopped; 3 tablespoons chopped fresh parsley; 1 tablespoon chopped fresh thyme; salt; and pepper. Spread half of the potato mixture in a deep baking dish and push the chops down into it. Cover them with the remaining potatoes. Pour in enough veal broth (see page 373) to almost cover the potatoes and dot with 1 tablespoon/15 g butter. Bake in the oven, uncovered, until the potatoes and chops are tender when poked with a two-pronged fork, 45 minutes to 1¼ hours. The top of the potatoes should be golden brown and most of the broth should have been absorbed. Serves 4.

POT-AU-FEU

serves 8

To achieve perfection with Pot-au-Feu, you must follow the rules. Don't be tempted to improve the basic recipe that includes several cuts of beef simmered with marrowbones and vegetables. The dozen or more ingredients should be carefully balanced and, more important, the cooking liquid should bubble at scarcely a simmer. If Pot-au-Feu boils for even a few minutes, the broth clouds, the vegetables break up, and disaster strikes!

I urge you to start cooking the meat in cold water, heating slowly and skimming to achieve the clear, intense broth that is the hallmark of a successful Pot-au-Feu.

This dish must be presented in style. Correct form is to serve the concentrated broth first, accompanied by toasted croûtes spread with marrow. The meats and vegetables are the second course. A great platter is obligatory, with room for all the vegetables to be set in neat piles around the edge and the lavishly sliced meats overlapping down the center. Lively condiments may include different types of mustard, tomato, or horseradish sauce; coarse salt; and cornichons—a feast for a family or a baronial hall.

2-POUND/900-G PIECE BEEF CHUCK OR BRISKET

3-POUND/1.35-KG PIECE BEEF OR VEAL SHANK, WITH BONE

2 POUNDS/900 G BEEF SHORT RIBS

8 QUARTS/8 LITERS WATER, MORE AS NEEDED

3 POUNDS/1.35 KG BEEF MARROWBONES, SAWN IN 4-INCH/10-CM LENGTHS

1 STALK CELERY, CUT INTO PIECES

1 LARGE BOUQUET GARNI (SEE PAGE 370)

1 CINNAMON STICK

1 TABLESPOON PEPPERCORNS

1 TABLESPOON SALT

1 ONION, UNPEELED

4 WHOLE CLOVES

2 POUNDS/900 G CARROTS, QUARTERED

8 TO 10 LEEKS (ABOUT 3 POUNDS/1.35 KG TOTAL), BOTH WHITE AND GREEN PARTS, HALVED LENGTHWISE AND CUT INTO 3-INCH/7.5-CM PIECES (SEE PAGE 371)

1½ POUNDS/675 G TURNIPS, CUT INTO EIGHTHS

1 SMALL CELERY ROOT (ABOUT 12 OUNCES/330 G), CUT INTO 3-INCH/7.5-CM PIECES

BAKED CROÛTES MADE WITH 1 BAGUETTE (SEE PAGE 374)

1 TABLESPOON CHOPPED FRESH PARSLEY

SEA SALT, MUSTARD, AND CORNICHONS, FOR SERVING

LARGE STOCKPOT

Tie the beef chuck, shank, and short ribs each in its own tight bundle with string (see page 371). Put them in the pot and pour in the water to cover generously. Wrap the marrowbones in cheesecloth and tie with string (this keeps the marrow in place during the long cooking) and add them to the pot. Bring slowly to a boil, skimming often. Tie the celery, bouquet garni, cinnamon stick, and peppercorns in cheesecloth and add the bag to the pot along with the salt. Halve the onion, leaving the skin on, and stud one-half with the cloves. Scorch the cut side of the other half over an open flame or an electric burner. Add the onion halves to the pot. Simmer very gently uncovered, skimming occasionally, for 3 hours. The secret to a clear broth is to maintain a gentle simmer with no threat of boiling. Add hot water as needed to keep the meats always covered.

Separately wrap the carrots, leeks, turnips, and celery root in cheesecloth and tie with string. Add these vegetable bundles to the pot, pushing them down into the broth and adding more water if needed to cover them. Continue simmering until the meats and vegetables are very tender, about 1 hour longer. The meats should fall easily from a two-pronged fork. If some ingredients are done before others, remove them to a platter. Be sure there is always enough broth to cover the meats and vegetables.

Transfer the marrowbones, meats, and vegetables to a cutting board. Boil the broth until it is reduced by about half or until concentrated and well flavored, 10 to 15 minutes. Strain it into a clean bowl, discarding the onion halves and bag of aromatics, and then taste and adjust the seasoning. If you want to prepare the pot-au-feu ahead, return the meats, marrowbones, and vegetables to the strained broth and store in the refrigerator for up to 2 days.

For serving, reheat the meats, marrowbones, and vegetables in the broth if necessary. Make the croûtes. Discard the cheesecloth from the marrowbones, scoop out the marrow, and spread it on the croûtes. Discard the strings from the meats, slice, and arrange them overlapping on a large platter. Unwrap the vegetables and pile them in mounds around the meat. Cover everything with aluminum foil to keep warm.

For the first course, bring the broth back to a boil. Skim and discard the excess fat, then taste for seasoning one last time. Ladle the broth into bowls and pass the croûtes separately. For the main course, serve the meats on the platter, sprinkled with the parsley. Pass the sea salt, mustard, and cornichons in separate bowls.

= POT-AU-FEU AND ITS COUSINS =

Pot-au-Feu is recognized worldwide as a symbol of France. The enticing assortment of beef cuts and bundles of vegetables gently simmered together is the ultimate one-pot meal. Although you will find Pot-au-Feu throughout the country, there are many regional distinctions. When cabbage is added, it becomes *potée*, usually bolstered with pork and bacon. In Lorraine, the family *potée* includes summer vegetables, such as fresh white kidney beans; Savoyards throw in a sausage or two; and in a variant from the Auvergne, cabbage leaves are stuffed with ground pork and bread crumbs.

Hochepot has northern vigor with a mixture of beef, veal, and pork, all browned before simmering with the customary root vegetables. For richness, I like to include an oxtail.

Brittany's version, *kig-ha-farz*, is a monumental one-pot collection of stew beef, ham hock, oxtail, and the usual roots, together with a buckwheat pudding sweetened with prunes. The pudding is rolled in a cloth and then suspended and simmered in the broth. Not surprisingly, it is a treat you will rarely come across nowadays.

The same principle of a one-pot meal applies to several similar poultry dishes, notably Poule-au-Pot (page 107) from Béarn. It centers on a plump mature fowl—a hen that has laid eggs and runs around the farmyard, not a delicately flavored, pampered chicken fattened on corn. The *poule* is stuffed with bread crumbs flavored with liver and some ham, and then simmered with a variety of vegetables.

= SHARP AS MUSTARD =

In England, mustard is often made at home from a nippy, bright powder. But in France, the word denotes a prepared product of crushed mustard seeds, whether black, brown, or white as in *moutarde d'Alsace*. French mustard may be mild or piquant, coarse-grained or smooth, plain or flavored with aromatics such as green peppercorns or tarragon. In Burgundy, the grains are always black (the strongest and most expensive variety), stripped of their skins, ground, and mixed with wine and verjus (the juice of sour grapes), which gives *moutarde de Dijon* its acclaimed well-rounded flavor.

Other regions opt for a backing of vinegar, as in Bordeaux where the mustard is brown and mild, flavored with tarragon and a suspicion of sugar. The famous *moutarde de Meaux* is darker, sharper tasting, and rougher textured than that of Dijon because the grains are more coarsely ground and the skins are left on. In Picardy, cider vinegar lends a slight sweetness to the mustard mix. The big surprise is that the seed for almost all these mustards comes from North America, Alberta in particular. The yellow fields you see all over France are not mustard, but canola (*colza*), planted for oil.

Thank goodness my train was stuck in Lille once while en route from London. Otherwise, I might never have discovered France's most northerly city. Only an hour from Paris by high-speed train, Lille feels worlds away, with colorful, ornamented architecture in baroque and Flemish forms, and cobblestone streets with grass poking up between the cracks. The city's abundant good taste is remarkable: comfortable restaurants with handsome art on the walls and bakeries that serve coffee and invite you to sit down, rather than whisk you in and out with your morning baguette. That good taste certainly extends to the food of the whole northern region, from Flanders to Picardy and running down to Champagne.

The best way to get an overview of northern dishes is to duck into an *estaminet*, the local version of a bistro. Likely as not you will be choosing between the charms of Carbonnade de Boeuf and Pot-au-Feu. As you hesitate, you may be offered a wooden board with no less than five pâtés, each containing a different northern ingredient, such as beer, rhubarb, or redolent Maroilles cheese. No matter how hard you try to restrain yourself, you will inevitably give in to sampling a chicory ice cream or sorbet, with its irresistible hint of burnt molasses and coffee. As the *patron* confessed, "During and after the war, chicory had a bad reputation as the poor man's coffee substitute, but now we're proud of it. It's unique!"

Wazemmes, Lille's colorful Sunday market, claims to be the biggest open-air emporium in northern France, with everything from food to flea-market stands to live animals.

Northern ingredients stand out: soccer ball–sized green cabbages with light rippled leaves, pretty pink beets and rhubarb, and, of course, row upon row of Belgian endives, or *chicons* as they are called locally. Endive reigns in the north and more than half of the world's production is grown around here. The French can't seem to get enough of it for serving raw in salads with beets and nuts, wrapping in ham to gratiné, or slicing to sauté in butter, sometimes with cream. Even the roots are toasted and ground into chicory, still appreciated as a coffee substitute. Endives grow under cover in the dark, so you would be forgiven for thinking that the agriculture of the French north is nothing more than the cereals and sugar beets that stretch from horizon to horizon. The other half of the wealth is invisible!

In Lille's old quarter, I discovered À l'Huîtrière, an exquisite *poissonerie* with baskets of local mussels and oysters and a tidy display of seafood, including turbot, shrimp, and herring, all set against a backdrop of tiles and mosaics in watery blues. Nearby I spotted an unusual display of charcuterie, including a *terrine de foie à la flamande* (veal terrine with beer, spice bread, and prunes) and *petit salé lillois en terrine*. There was nothing *petit* about it, however. It was a gigantic terrine of veal with fat cornichons inside.

If you think I exaggerate the temptations of Lille, let me just say that the city's most famous son, Charles de Gaulle, regularly dispatched his chauffeur from Paris for local crisp waffles with vanilla cream.

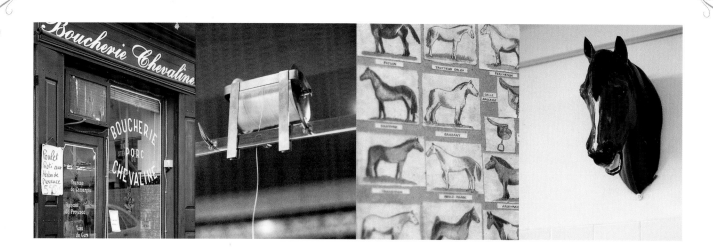

═ HUSH—IT'S HORSE ═

In many countries, the idea of eating horse provokes outrage, but not in France, where horse meat (and horse-meat pâtés and sausages) remains in demand. Most small-town markets have at least one *boucher chevaline* (horse butcher), signaled by a gilded equine profile above the front door. Cuts bear the same names as beef and look similar, though the meat is less fatty, darker, and ever-so-slightly coarse-textured. Horse meat spoils faster than beef but is naturally tender, and can be eaten very fresh, cooked or raw, within two days of butchery. If Genghis Khan did indeed start the fashion for steak tartare, as many accounts allege, the meat was probably from a Mongol steed.

Horse meat rarely appears in recipe books for the simple reason that it is a direct—and sometimes clandestine—substitute for beef. In the nineteenth century, however, the meat enjoyed a vogue at banquets, including one hosted by the city of Paris in 1865 that served a menu of horse consommé, horse meat à la mode, horse-meat fillet with mushrooms, and salad dressed with horse-meat oil! Roasts were particularly well regarded and some experts maintained that horse fillet was superior to beef. Perhaps it was, at that time. Certainly horse meat was recommended for tubercular patients, since horses, unlike cattle, were unlikely to carry the infection. Even today, horse meat is valued for its low cholesterol content.

Until recently, the great advantage of horse meat was its low price. Old cattle are not edible, but apparently meat from an elderly nag still makes acceptable eating. Before machines took over on the farm, there were plenty of aging horses around. A few French horses may still end up on the table, but today most horse meat is imported from central Europe and—surprise—North America (think of all those horses in Wyoming). It costs as much as beef, and you might think that its chief attraction had disappeared. But some eating habits die hard, and I suspect that horse meat will always have a following in France.

RÔTI DE VEAU TOURANGELLE

POT ROAST VEAL WITH HERBS AND SORREL

serves 6 to 8

The Loire region, with its capital, Tours, is known as the garden of France, home to asparagus, tender little vegetables, and greens such as sorrel. Á la tourangelle is the term for dishes garnished in this local style. What could be more delicious than the lemony bite of sorrel with a delicate roast of veal flavored with chives, tarragon, chervil, and parsley?

*Veal dries out all too easily if it is roasted in dry heat, so I prefer to cook it in a covered pot with just a little broth after browning it in butter. In France, roast veal is considered done just right when it remains moist and slightly pink (*rosé*) in the center, so that is what I suggest here. Sorrel looks like spinach and is prepared the same way, but when heated it almost dissolves to a tart purée that cries out for softening with butter and cream. (Cream also lightens the grayish tinge that can afflict plain sorrel purée.) According to season, asparagus, green peas, or braised celery and chestnuts would be an excellent accompaniment.*

ONE 3-POUND/1.35-KG BONELESS VEAL ROAST

1/2 CUP/110 G BUTTER, SOFTENED

SALT AND PEPPER

4 TO 5 TABLESPOONS CHOPPED MIXED FRESH
CHIVES, TARRAGON, CHERVIL, AND PARSLEY

3/4 CUP/175 ML DRY WHITE WINE

3/4 CUP/175 ML VEAL BROTH (SEE PAGE 373), MORE
IF NEEDED

I BOUQUET GARNI (SEE PAGE 370)

2 POUNDS/900 G SORREL

1 1/4 CUPS/300 ML CRÈME FRAÎCHE (PAGE 374) OR
HEAVY CREAM

Butterfly the roast lengthwise (cut it almost in half) so it can be opened up like a book and then lay it flat. Spread the cut surface with 3 tablespoons/45 g of the butter, sprinkle it with salt and pepper, and then with the herbs. Roll and tie it in a neat cylinder with string (see page 371). Heat the oven to 375°F/190°C.

Melt 2 tablespoons/30 g of the butter in a flameproof casserole over medium heat. Add the veal and brown thoroughly on all sides, 10 to 15 minutes. Add the wine and bring to a boil. Add the broth and bouquet garni, cover the pan, and transfer it to the oven. Cook the veal, basting from time to time, for 45 to 55 minutes. A skewer inserted in the center of the meat should be very warm but not scalding hot when withdrawn after 30 seconds, showing the meat is still moist in the center. It should register 140°F/60°C on a thermometer.

Meanwhile, cook the sorrel. Fold the leaves in half and pull off the stems. Wash the sorrel thoroughly in 1 or 2 changes of water, drain, and pat the leaves dry on a dish towel. Melt the remaining butter in a heavy pan over low heat. Add the sorrel and cook, stirring often, until it wilts. Continue cooking, and it will soften to a purée, a total of 10 to 12 minutes. Add half of the crème fraîche with salt and pepper and continue cooking until the purée just holds a shape, 3 to 5 minutes longer. Taste, adjust the seasoning, and set aside. Both the veal and sorrel may be cooked ahead and refrigerated for up to a day, leaving the veal in its casserole.

To finish, reheat the veal and sorrel separately on the stove top if necessary. Transfer the meat to a carving board and cover it with aluminum foil to keep warm. Strain the gravy into a small pan, discard the bouquet garni, and skim off any fat. Bring the gravy to a boil and, if necessary, reduce by about half until it is concentrated. Stir in the remaining crème fraîche, return to a boil, and continue boiling if necessary to thicken slightly. Taste and adjust the seasoning.

Discard the trussing strings from the veal, slice it, and arrange it overlapping on a warmed platter with the sorrel beside it. Serve the gravy separately.

BLANQUETTE DE VEAU

WHITE VEAL STEW WITH ONIONS AND MUSHROOMS

serves 4 to 6

When French television recently conducted a poll of favorite meat dishes, Blanquette de Veau was in the top five, with steak frites *and Gigot d'Agneau (page 155). I am not surprised, as its light, creamy sauce is the perfect showcase for tender veal. Traditionally all the ingredients are white: veal, baby onions, button mushrooms, white wine, and crème fraîche. The carrots that sometimes slip in should not be there. Blanquette is a homey, not luxurious dish and uses modest cuts of meat. Best is a combination of veal shoulder that has plenty of meat and pieces of breast, including rib bones for richness. It should be accompanied by boiled rice or noodles—white again.*

2 POUNDS/900 G BONELESS VEAL SHOULDER

I POUND/450 G VEAL BREAST, WITH RIB BONES

1 1/2 QUARTS/1.5 LITERS WATER, MORE IF NEEDED

I CUP/250 ML DRY WHITE WINE

I BOUQUET GARNI (SEE PAGE 370)

I GARLIC CLOVE, CHOPPED

SALT AND WHITE PEPPER

24 TO 30 BABY ONIONS (ABOUT I POUND/450 G TOTAL)

continued

8 OUNCES/225 G BUTTON MUSHROOMS, TRIMMED
AND QUARTERED

¾ CUP/175 ML CRÈME FRAÎCHE (PAGE 374) OR
HEAVY CREAM

BEURRE MANIÉ

4 TABLESPOONS/60 G BUTTER

¼ CUP/30 G FLOUR

Cut the veal shoulder into 1-inch/2.5-cm cubes, leaving the fat
and cartilage, which will dissolve during cooking to enrich the
sauce. Cut the breast into portions of 1 or 2 ribs. Put the veal in a
large saucepan with the water and bring slowly to a boil, skimming often, 10 to 15 minutes. Add the wine, bouquet garni, garlic,
salt, and white pepper, cover, and simmer, skimming and stirring
occasionally, for 1 to 1¼ hours. The veal should feel nearly tender
when you pinch a meaty piece.

Stir in the onions and mushrooms. All the ingredients should
be just covered with water. If there is too little, add more; if there
is too much, remove the lid. Continue simmering until the veal
and vegetables are tender, 20 to 25 minutes.

Transfer the meat and vegetables to a bowl with a draining spoon, and discard the bouquet garni. Bring the liquid to a
boil and boil until reduced to 4 cups/1 liter; this may take up to
20 minutes. For the beurre manié, crush the butter on a plate with
a fork and work in the flour to form a soft paste. Whisk the paste
into the simmering liquid a piece or two at a time to thicken it
lightly. You many not need all of the paste. Whisk in the crème
fraîche, bring the sauce back to a boil, and simmer for 1 minute.
Taste and adjust the seasoning. Stir in the veal and vegetables and
check the seasoning once more. Blanquette may be kept for up to
2 days in the refrigerator, and the flavor will be much improved.
Reheat it on the stove top just before serving.

CÔTES DE VEAU DIJONNAISE
VEAL CHOPS WITH MUSTARD

serves 4

*The savvy mustard makers of Dijon have done such a good marketing job
that today the town is synonymous with the classic aromatic French mustard flavored with wine and herbs. In this recipe, you can take your pick
of smooth or grainy mustard, with or without herbal or fruity flavorings.
Veal chops, particularly with this creamy sauce, suggest to me a similarly
luxurious vegetable, perhaps fresh asparagus, or fine green beans.*

4 VEAL CHOPS (ABOUT 2 POUNDS/900 G TOTAL)

SALT AND PEPPER

2 TABLESPOONS VEGETABLE OIL

6-OUNCE/170-G PIECE LEAN BACON, CUT INTO
LARDONS (SEE PAGE 371)

16 TO 18 BABY ONIONS (ABOUT 8 OUNCES/225 G
TOTAL), PEELED

I TABLESPOON/7 G FLOUR

¾ CUP/175 ML WHITE WINE, PREFERABLY
CHARDONNAY

¾ CUP/175 ML VEAL BROTH (SEE PAGE 373), MORE
IF NEEDED

I BOUQUET GARNI (SEE PAGE 370)

¼ CUP/60 ML CRÈME FRAÎCHE (PAGE 374) OR
HEAVY CREAM

2 TABLESPOONS DIJON MUSTARD, OR TO TASTE

I TABLESPOON CHOPPED FRESH PARSLEY

Season the chops on both sides with salt and pepper. Heat the oil
in a large sauté pan or frying pan over medium heat. Add the bacon
lardons and fry until lightly browned, 3 to 5 minutes. Lift them out
with a draining spoon and set them aside in a bowl. Add the onions
to the pan and sauté over medium heat, shaking the pan often so
they color evenly, until browned, 7 to 10 minutes. Remove them
with the draining spoon and set aside in a separate bowl. Lastly,
add the chops and brown them, allowing 2 to 3 minutes. Turn
them and brown the other side, 2 to 3 minutes longer. Take them
out, whisk the flour into the pan, and cook until bubbling. Add
the wine and bring to a boil, stirring constantly. Stir in the broth
and return to a boil. Stir in the lardons, then replace the chops,
pushing them down into the sauce, and add the bouquet garni.

Cover the pan and simmer over low heat for 25 minutes.
Add the onions and continue simmering until they are soft and
the chops are tender when poked with a two-pronged fork, 10 to
15 minutes longer. The cooking time will depend on the thickness
of the chops. Turn the chops from time to time and add more
broth if the sauce gets too thick.

When the chops are tender, transfer them to 4 warmed
plates. Discard the bouquet garni, stir the crème fraîche into
the sauce, and bring just to a simmer. Stir in the mustard and
parsley and take the pan from the heat. The fresh, piquant taste
of mustard turns bitter when overcooked, so mustard should not
be boiled and should always be added toward the end of cooking. Taste the sauce, adjust the seasoning, and spoon it over the
chops. Serve at once.

CÔTES DE VEAU DIJONNAISE

═ THE BULL PEN ═

The Camargue, the marshy lowlands of the Rhône delta that begins around Arles and sweeps down to the Mediterranean, is geographically distinct from Provence and Languedoc. Pink flamingos polka-dot the ponds, and pale gray Camargue horses race across the wetlands. There is no fooling with the bull of the Camargue, the belligerent black breed with its muscular neck and imposing head and horns. A larger, often creamy-spotted, black or brown breed called Brave (bull of combat) is off-limits, too. Some bulls are destined to participate in contests (no killing *à la française*), while others are the source of AOC-labeled meat (page 111). Bull meat, much deeper red than mere beef, makes a gamey, macho steak. It is also used to make dried sausages, and is the base of *gardianne de taureau*, a daube made with red wine, aromatics, olives, and citrus zest, served on Camargue rice.

Lagoons of seawater (*salins*) evaporated for salt form a necklace along the Camargue coastline (see "A Pinch of Salt," page 77). They yield some 90 percent of the salt processed in France. The flat inland landscape is checkered by windbreaks of black cypress trees and reeds that mark rice paddies unique in France. The region produces one hundred thousand tons a year, both round and long-grain varieties. The French tend to boil rice, or simmer it as a Pilaf de Riz Traditionel (page 231) flavored with herbs and spices such as saffron, often for stuffing vegetables, such as tomatoes, eggplant, and zucchini.

RAGOÛT D'AGNEAU AUX ARTICHAUTS

LAMB AND ARTICHOKE STEW

serves 6 to 8

The Italian taste for little artichokes spreads over into Provence, where they are braised for first-course salads, or combined with the excellent herb-imbued local lamb. Baby artichokes appear in early spring, at the same time as fresh fava beans, which would be my choice for an accompaniment. A squeeze of fresh lemon juice at table balances the richness of the sauce. Count on serving plenty of crusty bread on the side.

I am suggesting that you use breast of lamb here, including its bones that wonderfully enrich the sauce. An alternative is lamb shoulder, also sliced with its bones; veal breast is yet another way to go. When artichokes are very small, not more than two inches/five centimeters in diameter, they are almost totally edible except for a small hairy choke (artichokes belong to the thistle family). As a bonus, if you peel the artichoke stems, a finger length or more of central core, called the marrow, is edible, too.

ONE 4- TO 5-POUND/ABOUT 2-KG LAMB BREAST OR SHOULDER, WITH BONES

SALT AND PEPPER

2 TABLESPOONS OLIVE OIL

4 ONIONS (ABOUT 1½ POUNDS/675 G TOTAL), SLICED

1 TABLESPOON/7 G FLOUR

1 CUP/250 ML DRY WHITE WINE

2 CUPS/500 ML VEAL OR BEEF BROTH (SEE PAGE 373), MORE IF NEEDED

2 GARLIC CLOVES, CHOPPED

1 LARGE TOMATO, SEEDED AND COARSELY CHOPPED (SEE PAGE 372)

1 TABLESPOON DRIED THYME

JUICE OF ½ LEMON

8 TO 10 BABY ARTICHOKES (ABOUT 2 POUNDS/900 G TOTAL)

2 TABLESPOONS CHOPPED FRESH PARSLEY

2 LEMONS, CUT INTO WEDGES

Trim the meat, leaving in the bones and a little fat; cut the breast into sections or shoulder into 2-inch/5-cm chunks. Sprinkle them with salt and pepper. Heat the oil in a sauté pan or flameproof casserole over high heat. Working in 2 or 3 batches so the lamb is seared without drawing out the juices, brown the meat on all sides, taking 5 to 7 minutes for each batch. Remove each batch from the pan with a draining spoon and set aside.

Return the pan to medium heat, add the onions, season with salt and pepper, and cook, stirring often, until wilted and starting to brown, 8 to 10 minutes. Stir in the flour and continue to cook, stirring, until brown, 2 to 3 minutes. Add the wine, bring just to a boil, and then stir in the broth, garlic, tomato, thyme, salt, and pepper. Replace the meat, pushing it well down into the sauce. Cover the pan, bring to a boil, and simmer the lamb gently, stirring often, until it is nearly tender, about 1 hour.

Meanwhile, prepare the artichokes. Add the lemon juice to a bowl of cold water. Trim each artichoke head, cutting crosswise about halfway down to remove the tough tips. Snap off the tough outer leaves and trim any remaining tough leaf tips. Trim the cut end of each stem and then peel the stem with a vegetable peeler or small knife, taking care to remove all of the fibers. Quarter the artichokes lengthwise and scoop out the hairy central choke from each quarter with a melon baller or sharp spoon. As each artichoke quarter is trimmed, drop it into the lemon water so it does not discolor.

When the lamb is nearly tender, drain the artichokes and stir them into the pan, adding more broth if needed just to cover them. Simmer until the lamb and artichokes are very tender when pinched between a finger and thumb, 25 to 35 minutes longer. Skim off the excess fat from the surface. If the sauce seems thin, remove the lid and boil to reduce it until concentrated. Stir in the parsley. Like any ragoût, this combination of lamb and artichokes keeps well in the refrigerator for up to 3 days, or it may be frozen for up to 3 months. Wait to stir in the parsley when reheating.

Taste and adjust the seasoning of the sauce. Transfer the ragoût to a warmed serving dish and serve the lemon wedges alongside.

GIGOT DE SEPT HEURES

SEVEN HOUR LEG OF LAMB

serves 8

Versions of Gigot de Sept Heures developed where there was tough mutton—which once meant almost everywhere in France. Literally six or seven hours of gentle cooking was needed. I am always surprised how long even a leg of mature lamb, nine months old if that, must be poached just below a simmer to become tender. When cut with a spoon, the lamb should fall from the bones, a traditional test for being done. Don't hesitate to add generous amounts of vegetables to the lamb. They lose a surprising amount of volume as they cook and contribute intense flavor to the pan juices. Despite the large quantity of garlic, by the end of cooking the taste mellows to be scarcely perceptible. To make this a one-pot meal, add some unpeeled potatoes, cut into quarters, about 40 minutes before the lamb is done.

ONE 5- TO 6-POUND/ABOUT 2.5-KG LEG OF LAMB OR MUTTON

12 GARLIC CLOVES, CUT INTO STICKS

1 LARGE BOUQUET GARNI (SEE PAGE 370)

SALT AND PEPPER

4 QUARTS/4 LITERS WATER, MORE IF NEEDED

VEGETABLES

4 LEEKS (ABOUT 1 1/2 POUNDS/675 G TOTAL), WHITE AND GREEN PARTS (SEE PAGE 371)

1 SMALL CELERY ROOT (ABOUT 1 1/2 POUNDS/675 G)

4 LARGE CARROTS (ABOUT 1 1/2 POUNDS/675 G TOTAL), QUARTERED

4 TURNIPS (ABOUT 1 1/2 POUNDS/675 G TOTAL), QUARTERED

4 ONIONS (ABOUT 1 1/2 POUNDS/675 G TOTAL), QUARTERED

10 TO 15 GARLIC CLOVES

LARGE OVAL FLAMEPROOF CASSEROLE

Start preparing the lamb at least 6 hours ahead. Heat the oven to 275°F/140°C. Trim the meat of excess fat and any skin (mutton fat can be very strong). Poke holes in the meat with the point of a small knife and insert the sticks of garlic. Tie the meat as tightly as possible with string, as it will shrink during cooking. Put the lamb in the flameproof casserole with the bouquet garni, a large pinch of salt, and enough water to cover it by three-fourths. Bring the water slowly to a boil on the stove top, skimming often and taking 10 to 15 minutes. Cover the casserole and transfer it to the oven. Poach the lamb until it is almost tender when pierced with a two-pronged fork, about 4 hours. Check it every hour or so as it cooks, turning it and adding more water if too much evaporates. If the water starts to simmer, turn down the heat, as slow cooking is important to a good result.

Meanwhile, prepare the vegetables. Cut the leeks into 2-inch/5-cm lengths and tie them in several bundles with string. Peel and quarter the celery root and cut each piece in half to make 8 chunks total.

After 4 hours, or when the lamb is almost tender, lift it out. Add the leeks, celery root, carrots, turnips, onions, and whole garlic cloves to the pan and set the meat on top. Add water as necessary so the leg is half covered. Continue cooking until the meat and vegetables are very tender indeed, about 1 hour longer.

To finish the dish, lift out the lamb, put it on a platter, cover with aluminum foil, and set aside. If the vegetables are not very tender, continue simmering them, uncovered, on the stove top until they almost collapse into a fragrant mélange. Transfer them with a draining spoon to a warmed deep platter, discarding the bouquet garni. Boil the cooking broth until well reduced and concentrated; this may take up to 15 minutes. Taste and adjust the seasoning. If the lamb has cooled down, return it to the casserole and reheat it on the stove top. Discard the trussing strings from the lamb and set it on the vegetables; moisten the lamb with a little of the reduced broth and pass the rest of the broth at the table. You will not need to carve the meat, as it will fall apart into chunks with the touch of a spoon.

GIGOT D'AGNEAU À LA BRETONNE

ROAST LEG OF LAMB WITH WHITE BEANS

serves 6 to 8

Roast leg of lamb is the French cook's pride, paraded for guests or for family Sunday lunch. To make the most of this expensive cut, a gigot is invariably cooked on the bone, with a clove of garlic tucked into the shank so it permeates the whole roast. The meat may be spiked with more garlic and herbs, and is basted with butter to ensure a golden finish. However, accompaniments vary from region to region. In the south, boulangère *treatment, which calls for roasting the leg on a bed of sliced onion, potatoes, and herbs so they end brown and succulent with meat juices, is popular. When I lived on the northern coast in Normandy, my friend Françoise would roast piquant lamb from the salt marshes (*prés salés*) with little onions and baby potatoes, serving it with green beans from the garden.*

Along the coast in Brittany, fresh or dried white kidney beans simmered with a bit of tomato are customary with lamb, always with plenty of garlic—a style known as à la bretonne. *In the United States, great northern, navy, or pea beans can take their place.*

BEANS

- 2 CUPS/750 G DRIED WHITE KIDNEY BEANS
- 1 ONION, STUDDED WITH 4 WHOLE CLOVES
- 1 BOUQUET GARNI, INCLUDING 1 STALK CELERY (SEE PAGE 370)
- SALT AND PEPPER
- 2 TABLESPOONS/30 G BUTTER
- 2 ONIONS, FINELY CHOPPED
- 2 OR 3 LARGE TOMATOES (ABOUT 1 POUND/450 G TOTAL), PEELED, SEEDED, AND CHOPPED (SEE PAGE 372)
- 2 OR 3 GARLIC CLOVES, CHOPPED
- $^{1}/_{2}$ CUP/125 ML DRY WHITE WINE
- 2 TO 3 TABLESPOONS CHOPPED FRESH PARSLEY

LAMB

- ONE 4- TO 5-POUND/ABOUT 2-KG LEG OF LAMB
- 2 GARLIC CLOVES
- 1 BUNCH FRESH THYME (ABOUT $^{3}/_{4}$ OUNCE/20 G)
- 2 TABLESPOONS/30 G BUTTER

GRAVY

- $^{1}/_{2}$ CUP/125 ML DRY WHITE WINE
- 1$^{1}/_{2}$ CUPS/375 ML VEAL OR BEEF BROTH (SEE PAGE 373)

LARGE ROASTING PAN

To cook the beans, cover them generously with cold water and leave them to soak overnight. The next day, drain and put them in a large saucepan with the clove-studded onion, bouquet garni, and water to cover by at least 1 inch/2.5 cm. Cover, bring to a boil, lower the heat to a simmer, and cook until very tender, 1 to 3 hours, depending on the type and age of the beans. Add more hot water as it is absorbed to keep the beans covered in liquid, and season them with salt and pepper halfway through the cooking. At the end of cooking, they should be moist but not soupy. If they are sloppy, remove the lid 15 to 30 minutes before the end of cooking so the liquid evaporates. Discard the onion and bouquet garni.

While the beans are simmering, cook the tomatoes. Melt the butter in a small sauté pan or deep frying pan over medium heat. Add the onions and sauté until soft but not browned, 5 to 7 minutes. Stir in the tomatoes, garlic, and white wine and season with salt and pepper. Simmer over medium heat, stirring often, until nearly all the moisture has evaporated, 15 to 20 minutes. Stir the tomatoes into the cooked beans, taste, and adjust the seasoning.

To roast the lamb, heat the oven to 450°F/230°C. Prepare the lamb by trimming off any skin and all but a thin layer of fat. Cut 1 garlic clove into sticks and push the other into the lamb shank. Poke holes in the meat with the point of a small knife, and insert the sticks of garlic with small sprigs of thyme. Set the leg in the roasting pan, top with butter, salt and pepper.

Sear the meat in the very hot oven until it starts to brown, 15 to 20 minutes. Lower the heat to 375°F/190°C and continue roasting, basting often, for 40 to 50 minutes, or more if you prefer your lamb well done. Test by inserting a skewer in the thickest part of the meat; for pink lamb it should be warm to the touch when withdrawn after 30 seconds, or hot if you prefer it well done. A thermometer should register 140°F/60°C for pink meat, or 160°F/70°C for well done. If the pan juices start to scorch during roasting, add a little broth.

Transfer the lamb to a carving board, cover it loosely with aluminum foil, and leave it to stand while you make the gravy. Reheat the beans if necessary. Stir in the parsley. For the gravy, discard all but 1 tablespoon of fat from the roasting pan, add the wine, and bring to a boil on the stove top, stirring to dissolve the pan juices. Add the broth and continue boiling until the gravy is reduced and concentrated, 5 to 8 minutes. Strain into a small saucepan, taste, and adjust the seasoning.

For serving, carve the lamb into thin slices or carve the meat at the table. Set the meat on a warmed large platter, spoon the beans around it, then spoon a little gravy over the meat and serve the rest separately.

= LANGUEDOC: THE UPS AND DOWNS =

Historically, Languedoc covered a vast swath of southwestern France, though now it is more modestly defined, often coupled with Roussillon running along the Mediterranean to Spain. My image of the province is of grey limestone ranges (*causses*) stretching southward from the Massif Central, in places almost to the sea. Much of the land here is too arid and wild for settled agriculture. But sheep are raised for meat and, of course, for their milk, which is transformed into tasty little cheeses and, most famously, into blue-veined Roquefort (see "The Big Cheese," page 59).

The south-facing mountains, carpeted with fragrant herbal scrub called *garrigues*, slope to a generous band of ground that traditionally was the source of much cheap table wine, sold from gas-style pumps. Local production is now way down but quality is way up, with the Languedoc appellation including some of France's more adventurous wines. Coastal vintages making a comeback include the rich, golden muscats from Frontignan and Rivesaltes, and Banyuls, a curious and highly-regarded sweet red wine.

Artisan foods do well in the Languedoc, with foie gras ducks here, orchards and greenhouses there. On flat ground, beef cattle consume locally grown corn, and a valued tradition of corn-based dishes shows up in recipes like *millas*, a type of polenta. Local pastries include *gimblettes* (a crumbling circle flavored with candied fruits) and *oreillettes*, sweet fritters or "little ears." The giant sugared violets of Toulouse are enjoying a comeback on cakes, in jam, and as flavoring for a startlingly vivid purple aperitif.

Garlic is the signature of Languedoc, perfuming markets and hanging in every store. I think of garlic-stuffed snails grilling on the barbecue, and of thick, pungent Aioli (page 219) mandatory with Bourride (page 102), the local fish stew flavored only with garlic, onion, herbs, and olive oil, with none of the distracting tomato and saffron found in Bouillabaisse (page 99). Around here, North African influence is strong; couscous is as naturalized as pizza, and markets are perfumed with spice. Food on the coast of Languedoc is enticing—under a brilliant summer sun, sidewalk cafés do a brisk business in local fish and shellfish—though the long, flat coastline is overrun with summer crowds. I prefer the almost forgotten byways inland.

the
French Touch

INNARDS
& EXTREMITIES

CHAPTER
No. 8

French cooks are famous for never letting food go to waste, and that includes all sorts of innards and extremities. It may take an enthusiast's eye to light up at the sight of kidneys, heart, feet, and tails on the butcher's slab, but some of the most famous and sought-after traditional dishes are made from just such curiosities. For instance, *tripes à la mode de Caen*, a Norman dish from the abbey town of Caen, is a slithery mix of four different kinds of lining from a cow's stomach, together with calf's feet, all of them braced with cider and high-octane Calvados.

There is a clear pecking order for variety meats, starting at the top with calf's sweetbreads and kidneys, found fresh at the butcher on Thursdays for weekend feasting. These days some variety meats are stamped "Product of USA," and French cooks smile, believing that Americans pass up the best parts of the animal. Most small country towns boast at least one specialty butcher who will cut calf's liver to order, thick or thin. He will also pickle and simmer a whole ox tongue, an exception to the usual rule that the younger the animal, the better the bits. Just one tongue provides a sumptuous meal for ten, to serve hot with a piquant *sauce charcutière* (a variation on classic brown sauce) or cold with a caper vinaigrette. Brains, heart, oxtail, and "cheese" made from the head of a calf or pig all have their fans, and even the seemingly inedible lungs, ears, intestines, and udder find a home, often in sausages (page 187).

Don't worry, I am not suggesting you try out such esoterica at home. The handful of recipes here call for only the most popular variety meats, ones that are also easy to prepare. When choosing them in the market, use a simple test: they should be moist, look clear colored, and have no off-odor. Rounding out this short chapter is a recipe for pig's feet. They are a personal favorite of mine, and I thought you would be amused to know what is involved.

LANGUE DE BOEUF, SAUCE GRIBICHE

BEEF TONGUE WITH A PIQUANT MAYONNAISE

serves 6 to 8

Sauce Gribiche is an old friend, long overdue for a comeback. I came across it in an obscure bistro just the other day, and how happy I was! Thickened with hard-boiled egg yolk, it combines some of the richness of mayonnaise with the lightness of vinaigrette. At its best with boiled beef tongue, it complements a wide variety of cooked vegetables, too, such as carrot, cauliflower, leek, turnip, artichoke, or potato. Sauce Gribiche is also the traditional accompaniment to boiled calf's head, but I leave that to the experts.

Beef tongue is not difficult to cook. It is simply a matter of patiently waiting for up to four hours while the massive piece of meat softens to a fork-tender finish. Once cooked, the tongue is left to cool to tepid in its broth, then drained and peeled to slice for serving with Sauce Gribiche on the side. The classic accompaniment for tongue is spinach, but it would be a bit tart with this sauce, so I recommend a purée of celery root or turnips, or simply steamed baby potatoes. The cooked tongue can also be stored in the refrigerator for a few days and is just as good sliced and eaten cold, with the same piquant Sauce Gribiche.

ONE 3-POUND/1.35-KG BEEF TONGUE

POACHING LIQUID

   2 ONIONS, EACH STUDDED WITH 1 WHOLE CLOVE

   2 CARROTS, HALVED

   1 LARGE BOUQUET GARNI (SEE PAGE 370)

   2 TEASPOONS SALT

   1 TEASPOON PEPPERCORNS

   3 QUARTS/3 LITERS WATER, MORE AS NEEDED

SAUCE GRIBICHE

   3 HARD-BOILED EGGS

   3 TABLESPOONS/45 ML WHITE WINE VINEGAR

   1 TEASPOON DIJON MUSTARD

   SALT AND PEPPER

   3/4 CUP/175 ML OLIVE OR VEGETABLE OIL

   1 TABLESPOON CAPERS, RINSED AND DRAINED

   1 TABLESPOON CHOPPED CORNICHONS

   2 TABLESPOONS CHOPPED FRESH PARSLEY

   1 TABLESPOON CHOPPED FRESH CHERVIL

   1 TABLESPOON CHOPPED FRESH TARRAGON

   1 SMALL BUNCH FRESH CHIVES, FOR DECORATION

To blanch the tongue, put it in a large saucepan with cold water to cover and bring slowly to a boil, skimming often. Simmer for 10 to 15 minutes, then drain. To poach the tongue, return it to the saucepan and add the onions, carrots, bouquet garni, salt, peppercorns, and the water to cover. Cover and heat until the liquid is scarcely at a simmer. Cook the tongue until the thickest part is tender when pierced with a two-pronged fork, 3 to 4 hours. Skim the surface from time to time and add more water as needed to keep the tongue always covered. When it is done, remove the pan from the heat and let the tongue cool to tepid in the cooking broth.

For the Sauce Gribiche, separate the egg yolks from the whites. Chop the whites and set them aside. Work the yolks through a strainer into a small bowl. In a bowl, whisk together 1 tablespoon of the vinegar, the mustard, salt and pepper, and 1 teaspoon of the oil. Whisking constantly by hand or with a stand mixer, gradually pour in 1 tablespoon of the oil drop by drop; the sauce will thicken and lightly emulsify. Still whisking constantly, add the remaining oil in a slow, thin, steady stream. Stir in the chopped egg whites, capers, cornichons, parsley, chervil, tarragon, and the remaining 2 tablespoons vinegar. Taste and adjust the seasoning. The sauce may be made a day ahead and refrigerated, but the herbs should be added just before serving. After the sauce has stood for a few minutes, the oil will separate, but a few quick stirs will remix it. Note, too, that Sauce Gribiche never forms a stiff emulsion like mayonnaise, but it keeps better because the egg yolks are cooked, not raw.

When the tongue has cooled, lift it out of the broth and set on a platter. Skim the fat from the surface of the broth—there will be a thick layer to discard—and boil the broth until reduced by at least half and the flavor is concentrated, 30 to 40 minutes. Taste and adjust the seasoning. While the broth boils, peel the skin from the tongue, cut away any cartilage, and pull out any bones from the roots. The tongue and its broth may be stored in the refrigerator for 2 to 3 days.

To finish, bring the reduced broth to a boil, add the tongue, and simmer until hot throughout, 5 to 10 minutes, or longer if it has been refrigerated. Transfer the tongue to a cutting board and cut on the diagonal into thin slices, starting at the tip and slanting the knife so the slices are of uniform size. Arrange the slices, overlapping them, on a warmed platter. Return the broth to a boil, spoon some over the tongue, and top the platter with a few crossed chive blades. Pour the remaining hot broth into a bowl. Whisk the sauce to reemulsify it and transfer to a serving bowl. Serve the tongue and pass the sauce and the broth at the table.

FOIE DE VEAU LYONNAISE

CALF'S LIVER WITH ONIONS

serves 5 or 6

Lyon and the surrounding Lyonnais district have competed with Paris for centuries to be first in food. Paris is chic, sophisticated, refined; Lyon goes for hearty, accessible country cooking that is easy to love. This recipe sums it up.

6 TABLESPOONS/90 G LARD OR VEGETABLE OIL

6 LARGE ONIONS (ABOUT 2¹/₂ POUNDS/I KG TOTAL), SLICED

2 GARLIC CLOVES, CHOPPED

2 TEASPOONS SUGAR

SALT AND PEPPER

I BOUQUET GARNI (SEE PAGE 370)

5 OR 6 THICK SLICES CALF'S LIVER (ABOUT I¹/₂ POUNDS/675 G TOTAL)

³/₄ CUP/175 ML CHICKEN BROTH (SEE PAGE 373)

Melt 4 tablespoons/60 g of the lard in a frying pan over low heat. Stir in the onions, garlic, sugar (the sugar helps the onions to brown and caramelize), salt, and pepper and tuck in the bouquet garni. Press a piece of aluminum foil down on the onions, cover the pan, and sweat the onions over very low heat, stirring occasionally, until very soft, 25 to 30 minutes.

Remove the lid and foil, turn up the heat to medium, and continue cooking until the onions are caramelized and golden brown, 8 to 10 minutes longer. Stir them often so they do not scorch. Discard the bouquet garni, taste, and adjust the seasoning; set the onions aside and keep warm. They may also be refrigerated for a couple of days and reheated on top of the stove just before serving.

To finish, pat the liver slices dry on paper towels and season them with salt and pepper. Heat the remaining lard in another frying pan over high heat. Add the liver and sauté until browned, 2 to 3 minutes. Turn and brown the other side, 1 to 2 minutes longer. Do not let the liver overcook or it will be tough; it is at its best pink in the center. Transfer the liver to 5 or 6 warmed plates and pile the onions on top.

Discard the excess fat from the pan. Add the broth and bring to a boil, stirring to dissolve the pan juices. Taste for seasoning, then spoon the pan sauce over the liver and onions and serve at once.

ROGNONS À LA MOUTARDE

SAUTÉED KIDNEYS WITH MUSTARD

serves 4

You like kidneys or you don't, and for everyone, like me, who enjoys them, this recipe will be a treat. In my opinion, a quick sauté in hot butter, leaving them pink and succulent, is the best way to cook kidneys. Then comes a reduction of juices in the pan, a sumptuous thickening of cream, and a tickle of mustard.

ABOUT I¹/₄ POUNDS/600 G VEAL OR LAMB'S KIDNEYS

SALT AND PEPPER

3 TABLESPOONS/45 G BUTTER

3 TABLESPOONS/45 ML COGNAC

2 SHALLOTS, FINELY CHOPPED

¹/₂ CUP/125 ML DRY RED WINE

¹/₂ CUP/125 ML VEAL BROTH (SEE PAGE 373)

I CUP/250 ML CRÈME FRAÎCHE (PAGE 374) OR HEAVY CREAM

I TABLESPOON DIJON MUSTARD, OR TO TASTE

I TABLESPOON CHOPPED FRESH PARSLEY

Rinse the kidneys and dry on paper towels. Strip any skin from the kidneys, halve them lengthwise, and cut out the core and membrane with scissors. If using veal kidneys, slice ¾ inch/2 cm thick, and then cut the slices into ¾-inch chunks. Leave lamb's kidneys in half or cut them into ¾-inch chunks. Season the kidneys with salt and pepper.

Melt the butter in a sauté pan over high heat until the foaming stops. Add all the kidneys at once and sauté them, tossing and turning them, until they are brown on all sides but still pink inside. Allow 2 to 3 minutes for veal kidneys, 1 to 2 minutes for lamb's kidneys. Don't let them overcook or they will be tough. Pour in the Cognac and flambé it (see page 371). Using a draining spoon, transfer the kidneys to a strainer and allow them to drain, discarding any juices that escape.

For the sauce, return the pan to medium heat, add the shallots, and sauté until translucent, about 1 minute. Pour in the wine, bring to a boil, and boil until reduced by half. Add the broth and again boil until reduced by half. Whisk in the crème fraîche and bring just to a boil. Take from the heat and stir the mustard into the sauce. Taste and adjust the seasoning.

Return the kidneys to the pan and heat gently to reheat them and blend the flavors, 1 to 2 minutes. Do not allow the sauce to boil or it will be bitter and the kidneys will toughen.

Spoon the kidneys and sauce onto a warmed deep platter or 4 plates and sprinkle with the parsley. Serve at once.

FOIE DE VEAU LYONNAISE

RIS DE VEAU AUX CÈPES

SWEETBREADS WITH CÈPES

serves 4 to 6

Here is a perfect marriage. Sweetbreads are the most prized variety meat, and cèpes are often considered the finest fungus (truffles excepted). The sauce is a time-honored velouté made from the cooking liquid enriched with crème fraîche and sharpened with a squeeze of fresh lemon. Wherever cèpes grow, you will find this combination, but it is a particular specialty of Bordeaux, so I suggest using Sémillon to add depth to the sauce. A green vegetable such as fresh peas, fine green beans (haricots verts), or baby favas would be an ideal accompaniment.

2 PAIRS CALF'S SWEETBREADS (ABOUT 1¹/₂ POUNDS/ 675 G TOTAL)

SALT AND PEPPER

2 TABLESPOONS/30 G BUTTER

1 ONION, SLICED

2 TABLESPOONS COGNAC

1 CUP/250 ML DRY WHITE WINE

1 CUP/250 ML VEAL BROTH (SEE PAGE 373), MORE IF NEEDED

CÈPE VELOUTÉ SAUCE

8 OUNCES/225 G FRESH CÈPE MUSHROOMS, OR 1 OUNCE/30 G DRIED CÈPES

3 TABLESPOONS/45 G BUTTER

2 TABLESPOONS/15 G FLOUR

¹/₄ CUP/60 ML CRÈME FRAÎCHE (PAGE 374) OR HEAVY CREAM

SQUEEZE OF FRESH LEMON JUICE

Soak the sweetbreads in cold water to cover for 1 to 2 hours, changing the water once or twice. Drain, rinse, and put in a saucepan with salted water to cover. Bring slowly to a boil, lower the heat to a simmer, and cook for 10 minutes. Drain into a colander, rinse under cold running water, and drain again. Cut away the ducts from the sweetbreads and then pull off the thin coating membrane. Put the sweetbreads between 2 plates, top with a 1-pound/450-g weight, and chill until firm, 2 to 3 hours.

Melt the butter in a sauté pan or deep frying pan over medium heat. Add the onion and sauté until soft, 3 to 5 minutes. Sprinkle the sweetbreads with salt and pepper, add to the pan, and brown lightly on all sides, taking 10 to 15 minutes. Add the Cognac and flambé (see page 371). Pour in the wine and simmer for 2 minutes. Add the broth, cover, reduce the heat to very low, and poach the sweetbreads, turning them once at the midway point, until they are very tender when pierced with a two-pronged fork, 35 to 45 minutes. Lift them out of the pan, put them on a plate, and cover to keep warm. Reserve the cooking liquid.

To make the sauce, if using fresh cèpes, clean them (see page 373) and slice thickly. If using dried cèpes, rehydrate them (see page 373) and then drain well. Melt the butter in a frying pan over medium heat. Add the fresh or dried cèpes, season with salt and pepper, and sauté, stirring often, until tender, 5 to 8 minutes. If the mushrooms have rendered a lot of liquid, drain them and return them to the pan, discarding the liquid.

Stir the flour into the mushrooms off the heat. Strain in the cooking liquid from the sweetbreads and bring to a boil, stirring until the sauce thickens. If the sauce is too thick, add a little more broth. Stir in the crème fraîche, bring the sauce just to a boil, and take the pan from the heat. Season to taste with lemon juice, salt, and pepper.

Cut the sweetbreads into thick slices on the diagonal, add them to the sauce, and warm them gently for 1 to 2 minutes. Or, you may add the slices to the sauce and store the dish in the refrigerator for up to 24 hours before serving.

To finish, reheat the sweetbreads in the sauce on the stove top if necessary. Transfer the sweetbreads to 4 warmed plates, and spoon the mushrooms and sauce over and around them. Serve at once.

PIEDS DE PORC PANÉS

BROILED PIG'S FEET

serves 4 as a main course, or 8 as a first course

Once or twice a year, I come across a bistro that serves broiled pig's feet and I fall on them at once. They rival headcheese for gelatinous richness and spareribs for a finger-licking experience. Sainte-Ménehould in Lorraine is renowned for its sumptuous grilled pig's feet and the capture nearby of the fleeing Louis XVI. I have often wondered if he made a fatal pause to sample them. In traditional butcher shops, and some ethnic groceries, you will find cooked pig's feet ready to broil. To prepare them from scratch, you must first brine the pig's feet, then bind them in cheesecloth to simmer in broth. If you have to cook them yourself, you will end up with a gelatinous broth that is a great basis for such pork dishes as Cassoulet (page 178). Broiled pig's feet are usually served alone, but I find a tart green salad makes an agreeable contrast.

BRINE

    5 QUARTS/5 LITERS WATER

    2 POUNDS/900 G COARSE SALT

    1/2 CUP/110 G SUGAR

    4 LARGE PIG'S FEET (1 TO 1 1/4 POUNDS/450 TO 600 G EACH), SPLIT LENGTHWISE

    1 CUP/250 ML DRY WHITE WINE

    3 QUARTS/3 LITERS VEAL BROTH (SEE PAGE 373)

    2 ONIONS, EACH STUDDED WITH 4 OR 5 WHOLE CLOVES

    2 CARROTS

    1 TABLESPOON PEPPERCORNS

    1 LARGE BOUQUET GARNI (SEE PAGE 370)

    SALT AND PEPPER

    DIJON MUSTARD, FOR SERVING

COATING

    1/2 CUP/110 G BUTTER, MELTED

    2 CUPS/100 G FRESH BREAD CRUMBS (SEE PAGE 373)

To begin, make the brine. Combine the water, coarse salt, and sugar in a large pan over medium heat and heat, stirring occasionally, until the salt and sugar dissolve. Let the brine cool completely in the pan.

Meanwhile, put the pig's feet into a large pan of cold water, bring to a boil, and simmer for 5 minutes to blanch them. Drain and rinse with running cold water. Scrape the feet clean with a knife, rinse, and drain again. Put the feet in the cooled brine and top the feet with a heavy plate so they are fully immersed. Keep them in the refrigerator for 12 hours.

Drain and rinse the pig's feet, discarding the brine. Bind the halves of each foot together tightly with cheesecloth and string to hold the foot in its original shape. Put the wine, broth, onions, carrots, peppercorns, bouquet garni, and salt in a large saucepan and add the pig's feet, pushing them under the liquid. Cover and simmer over low heat until the meat is very soft and falling from the bones and the skin and connective tissue are very tender, 3½ to 4½ hours. (Loosen the cloth to check if a foot is ready.) Add water from time to time as needed to keep the feet always covered with liquid. Remove the pan from the heat and let the feet cool in the liquid.

When the feet are cool, lift them from the liquid, carefully unwrap the cheesecloth, and drain the feet on paper towels. Chill until firm and easy to handle, 1 to 2 hours or up to 2 days.

To finish, heat the broiler. For the coating, spread the melted butter on a large plate, and spread the bread crumbs on a second large plate. Roll the pig's feet in the butter, sprinkle them with salt and pepper, and then roll them in the bread crumbs to coat evenly. Set the feet, cut side down, on a baking sheet. Broil about 5 inches/13 cm from the heat until browned, 5 to 7 minutes. Turn and continue broiling until the feet are hot and browned on the cut side, 5 to 7 minutes longer. Serve very hot, cut side up, accompanied by the mustard.

PIG PERFECT

PORK & CHARCUTERIE

CHAPTER
No. 9

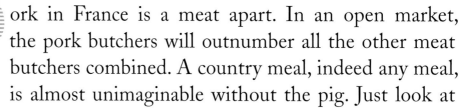

Pork in France is a meat apart. In an open market, the pork butchers will outnumber all the other meat butchers combined. A country meal, indeed any meal, is almost unimaginable without the pig. Just look at the *assiette de charcuterie* listed on so many bistro menus: a good one includes slivers of cured country ham, a slice of cooked ham *(jambon de Paris)*, a few slices of cooked garlic sausage *(saucisson à l'ail)* and dried sausage *(saucisson sec)*, and a sliver of Pâté de Campagne (page 188), all of which originate with a pig. As for sausages, I have covered a few in "Strings of Sausages" (page 187), but there are many, many more. Fresh ones are not hard to make at home. My particular favorite is Boudin Blanc (page 186), a smooth, white sausage that is both light and satisfyingly rich. (*Boudin noir*, blood sausage, is another matter, an expert's job.)

Add to these the charcuterie specialties from each region. In Burgundy, Jambon Persillé (page 177), a pretty pink terrine, comes marbled with the bright green herb, while in the south, dried sausages of every description, often rolled in wood ash, chili pepper, or *herbes de Provence*, are common. In Alsace, countless forms of wurst proliferate, their sauerkraut accompaniment sold alongside for multiple variants of Choucroute Alsacienne (page 176). The Normans and the Lyonnais like tripe, and on the Loire, it is Rillettes and Rillons (page 191)—and just about everything else you can think of.

Fresh pork itself is an inexpensive, adaptable meat, happy with herbs, garlic, fresh and dried fruits, cider, and red or white wine. Pork has a fatty reputation that is not always deserved. Some pork is lean and dries out easily, so I like to keep it moist *en cocotte*, as in Enchaud Périgourdin (page 170), or in a Norman-style apple and cream sauce. Another popular approach in France is to brine lesser cuts of fresh pork such as shoulder or hock, serving them as Petit Salé aux Lentilles (page 172), or with sauerkraut. The grand cut for salting is, of course, the ham, the imposing hindquarter of a mature animal. And without ham's cousin, bacon, such celebrated stews as Daube de Boeuf Provençale (page 139) and Boeuf Bourguignon (page 136) would lose their savor.

The other happy endings for obscure parts of the pig are pâtés and terrines, and at home I can beat a charcutier at his own game. Strictly speaking, a pâté is cooked in pastry *(pâte)* and a terrine is baked in an earthenware *(terre cuite)* mold, but nowadays the distinction counts for little. The right balance of seasoning in the ground meat mixture is key to both. A homemade Pâté de Campagne, textured but not chewy, marbled but not cloying with fat, mellowed for a few days so the seasonings highlight the plain pork, is the very essence of French country cooking.

PEBRONATA DE PORC

PORK STEW WITH RED WINE, BELL PEPPERS,
AND TOMATO

serves 6

Pebronata is a breath of the Mediterranean, challenging the senses with its vivid color, aroma, and taste. Cooking is done in three stages—pork, tomatoes, and peppers—and then all are joined in one glorious, fragrant mélange. The sauce comes from Corsica, where it is served with pork, beef, veal, game, or goat. Boiled macaroni, fusilli, shells, or bows are an excellent accompaniment to soak up the sauce, or you could opt for polenta. You will have a half cup of red wine left from the full bottle needed for this recipe—just enough for a quick glass while the dish simmers!

2 POUNDS/900 G BONELESS LEAN PORK SHOULDER

SALT AND PEPPER

2 TABLESPOONS OLIVE OIL

2 TABLESPOONS/15 G FLOUR

1½ CUPS/375 ML HEARTY RED WINE

1½ CUPS/375 ML VEAL BROTH (SEE PAGE 373), MORE
IF NEEDED

PEBRONATA SAUCE

¼ CUP/60 ML OLIVE OIL

1 ONION, CHOPPED

4 GARLIC CLOVES, CHOPPED

3 POUNDS/1.35 KG TOMATOES, PEELED, SEEDED,
AND CUT INTO STRIPS (SEE PAGE 372)

1 BOUQUET GARNI (SEE PAGE 370)

2 RED BELL PEPPERS, CORED, SEEDED, AND CUT
INTO NARROW STRIPS (SEE PAGE 370)

4 JUNIPER BERRIES, FINELY CRUSHED

1 CUP/250 ML HEARTY RED WINE

Heat the oven to 350°F/180°C. Cut the pork into 2-inch/5-cm cubes, trimming any sinew and most of the fat. Season the meat with salt and pepper. Heat the oil in a flameproof casserole over high heat. Add half of the pork cubes and brown well on all sides, taking about 3 to 5 minutes. Remove them with a draining spoon to a bowl. Brown the rest of the cubes the same way and set them aside also. Lower the heat, stir in the flour, and cook, stirring, until browned, 1 to 2 minutes. Add the wine and bring just to a boil. Stir in the broth, replace the meat, and bring to a boil. Cover, transfer to the oven, and cook until the pork is tender enough to crush easily between your finger and thumb, 1¼ to 1½ hours. Stir from time to time during cooking and add more broth if the pan seems dry.

Meanwhile, make the sauce. Heat 2 tablespoons of the oil in a large, deep frying pan over medium heat. Add the onion and sauté until starting to brown, 3 to 5 minutes. Stir in the garlic and cook for 1 minute. Add the tomatoes and bouquet garni, season with salt and pepper, and simmer over low heat until softened and reduced to a coulis, 15 to 20 minutes. To cook the peppers, heat the remaining oil in another frying pan over medium heat. Add the peppers, juniper berries, and salt and sauté, stirring often, until wilted, 8 to 10 minutes. Add the wine, bring to a boil, and boil rapidly until reduced by at least half. Stir in the tomato coulis and continue cooking over low heat until the sauce is thick and rich, 10 to 15 minutes longer. Discard the bouquet garni, taste, and adjust the seasoning.

When the pork is done, stir in the sauce and simmer for about 10 minutes to blend the flavors. Taste, adjust the seasoning, and serve directly from the casserole. Like all stews, pebronata improves on standing, so I would urge you to prepare it ahead and reheat it on the stove top. It may be kept for up to 3 days in the refrigerator, or frozen for up to 3 months.

PEBRONATA AUX AUBERGINES

EGGPLANT PEBRONATA

I have developed a delicious vegetarian version of pebronata, made with vegetable instead of veal broth, and substituting eggplant for the pork. Small eggplants are best, so plenty of dark skin is included for texture.

Trim 1½ pounds/675 g small eggplants and quarter them lengthwise; halve the quarters if large. Sprinkle generously with salt and leave for 20 minutes to draw out juices. Make the pebronata sauce as directed in Pebronata de Porc. Rinse the eggplant with cold water and dry on paper towels. Heat ¼ cup/60 ml olive oil in a large frying pan over medium heat. Add half of the eggplant pieces and sauté until browned on all sides, 8 to 10 minutes. Remove them with a draining spoon and brown the rest the same way. Return the first batch of eggplants to the pan and stir in the pebronata sauce. Cover and simmer over low heat until the eggplants are tender, 5 to 10 minutes. Taste and adjust the seasoning. Serve hot or as a salad at room temperature. Serves 4 to 6.

ENCHAUD PÉRIGOURDIN

POT-ROASTED PORK LOIN WITH CARROTS AND PARSNIPS

serves 4 to 6

Having read about Enchaud Périgourdin in an old cookbook, I was so happy to finally taste it in Périgord. Once I had tried it, I never looked back—it is so simple. The pork is spiked with sticks of garlic and then roasted en cocotte *with just a bit of broth in a covered casserole, so the meat stays moist and tasty. Carrots and parsnips are added halfway through the cooking, so they cook to just the right tenderness. The pork is also excellent cold: thin slices, spread with the jelled cooking juices and topped with some cornichons, make a robust sandwich between slices of country bread.*

2-POUND/900-G BONELESS PORK LOIN

4 OR 5 GARLIC CLOVES, CUT INTO STICKS

SALT AND PEPPER

2 TABLESPOONS/30 G LARD OR VEGETABLE OIL

2 CUPS/500 ML VEAL BROTH (SEE PAGE 373), MORE IF NEEDED

1 BUNCH FRESH THYME (ABOUT 3/4 OUNCE/20 G)

3 OR 4 CARROTS (ABOUT 12 OUNCES/330 G TOTAL), CUT INTO SLICES 3/8 INCH/1 CM THICK

6 PARSNIPS (ABOUT 1 1/2 POUNDS/ 675 G TOTAL), CUT INTO SLICES 3/8 INCH/1 CM THICK

Start preparing the pork at least 6 hours ahead of cooking. Poke evenly spaced holes all over the meat with the tip of a small knife. Insert a garlic stick in each one. Roll the pork, tie it in a neat cylinder (see page 372), and sprinkle it with salt and pepper. Refrigerate the pork for at least 6 hours or up to overnight, so the garlic permeates the meat.

The next day, heat the oven to 350°F/180°C. Heat the lard in a flameproof casserole over medium heat. Add the pork and brown well on all sides, taking about 20 minutes. Pour 1 cup/250 ml of the broth over the pork, add the thyme, and cover the pan. Roast in the oven, turning the meat occasionally, for 30 minutes. At this point, the pan juices should be brown. If not, remove the pork and boil the pan juices on the stove top until they are reduced to a glaze that will add color to the carrots and parsnips.

Stir in the carrots and parsnips with the remaining broth, sprinkle the vegetables with salt and pepper, and set the pork on top. Re-cover the pan, and continue roasting until the pork is very tender and the vegetables are done, 45 minutes to 1 hour longer. A skewer inserted into the center of the meat should be hot to the touch when withdrawn after 30 seconds, or a thermometer should register 160°F/70°C. Baste and turn the meat 2 or 3 times during cooking, and add more broth if the pan seems dry. The meat and vegetables may be refrigerated for up to 2 days.

To finish, if necessary, reheat the pork and vegetables in the casserole on the stove top over low heat, allowing 20 to 25 minutes. Transfer the meat to a carving board and cover with aluminum foil to keep warm. Lift out the vegetables with a draining spoon and spread them on a platter. Cover with foil to keep warm. Strain the pan juices into a small saucepan, and skim off any excess fat. Boil the juices to reduce and concentrate if necessary. Taste and adjust the seasoning. Discard the trussing strings from the pork and carve into thick slices. Arrange the slices, overlapping them, on the carrots and parsnips. Moisten the pork and vegetables with a little of the pan juices and serve the rest separately.

PETIT SALÉ AUX LENTILLES

LIGHTLY SALTED PORK WITH LENTILS

serves 4 to 6 as a main dish

Petit Salé is a favorite French way to transform modest cuts of pork, such as shoulder, hock, or cheek, by immersing them for just a day or two in brine, echoing the time-consuming and exacting process of curing a ham. French cooks pick up their Petit Salé from the charcutier, but you can easily make it at home. Saltpeter used to be added to help preserve the meat and give it a pink color. A substitute called curing salt, available online, is now used. Or, you can omit a preservative altogether, as I do. If the pork is to be simmered (as here), I recommend at least two days' brining. You will also find that pork for roasting will be more savory and juicy after sitting in this brine. A two-pound (1.35-kilogram) roast would need as little as twelve hours of soaking; just be sure to dry it well with paper towels before putting it in the oven.

Try to find lentils from Le Puy, in the Auvergne, for this dish. These small, flat legumes are grown on volcanic soil that gives them a sought-after blue-green tinge. A warming winter dish, Petit Salé aux Lentilles can be a main dish or a robust appetizer.

2 POUNDS/900 G BONELESS PORK SHOULDER

BRINE

    2 QUARTS/2 LITERS WATER

    2 SPRIGS FRESH THYME

    I DRIED BAY LEAF

    2 GARLIC CLOVES, SLICED

    2 TEASPOONS JUNIPER BERRIES

    I TEASPOON PEPPERCORNS

    2 WHOLE CLOVES

    I³/₄ CUPS/390 G COARSE OR KOSHER SALT

    3 TABLESPOONS/45 G SUGAR

    2 TABLESPOONS/22 G CURING SALT (OPTIONAL)

LENTILS

    I¹/₂ CUPS LENTILS (ABOUT IO OUNCES/280 G)

    I ONION, STUDDED WITH 2 WHOLE CLOVES

    I GARLIC CLOVE, CRUSHED

    I BOUQUET GARNI (SEE PAGE 370)

    SALT AND PEPPER

    2 TABLESPOONS CHOPPED FRESH PARSLEY

At least 1 day ahead, brine the pork. Roll and tie the pork (see page 372). For the brine, combine the water, thyme, bay leaf, garlic, juniper berries, peppercorns, and cloves in a saucepan. Stir in the salt, sugar, and the curing salt, if using, and heat the pan gently over low heat, stirring until the salt dissolves. Remove from the heat and let cool completely. Put the meat in a deep bowl and pour in the cooled brine. Cover and store in the refrigerator for at least 12 hours or up to a week, turning the meat from time to time. If the pork has been in the brine for up to 3 days, simply rinse it before cooking. If it has been brined for longer, soak it in cold water for 1 hour before cooking.

Rinse the pork and transfer it to a deep saucepan, brushing off any flavorings. Add water to cover, bring to a boil very slowly, and then simmer for 5 minutes. (If it has been in the brine for more than 3 days, simmer it for up to 15 minutes.) Pour off the water, leaving the pork in the pan. Cover again with cold water, top with the lid, bring to a boil, and then simmer for 1½ hours, adding water from time to time as needed so the meat remains covered. Meanwhile, pick over the lentils, discarding any stones, and wash them thoroughly.

To cook the lentils, stir them into the pork after it has cooked for 1½ hours, stirring in the onion, garlic, and bouquet garni at the same time. Simmer, uncovered, over low heat until the pork is tender when poked with a two-pronged fork, about 30 minutes longer. Transfer the pork to a carving board, cover with aluminum foil, and keep warm. The lentils should be tender but still firm and soupy with liquid (they will absorb more on standing). If a large amount of liquid remains, drain off some of it. Take out the onion, coarsely chop it, discarding the cloves, and stir it back into the lentils. Remove and discard the bouquet garni. Taste the lentils and season with salt and pepper.

Spread the lentils in a shallow serving dish and sprinkle them with the parsley. Discard the strings from the pork and carve into generous slices. Arrange the slices, overlapping them, on the lentils. Serve very hot.

Petit Salé aux Lentilles may be stored for up to 3 days in the refrigerator, but lentils overcook easily when you reheat them. If you are making the dish in advance, I advise poaching the pork until it is almost done before you add the lentils, so they are still very firm when the pork is cooked. That way, they won't overcook when they are reheated.

FILETS DE PORC NORMANDE

PORK TENDERLOINS WITH APPLE

serves 6

The favorite Norman combination of apples and cream in savory dishes is unbeatable with poultry, game birds, veal, pork, and even fish. In this interpretation, two pork tenderloins, tied together head to tail, make a luxuriously tender little roast. A wrapping of bacon keeps the pork moist and balances the sweetness of the apple, but it is still important to choose a tart variety, such as Braeburn or Rome Beauty, or you can always fall back on Granny Smith. I like to enrich the gravy with crème fraîche—Normandy, after all, is cream country—but you may omit it.

2 PORK TENDERLOINS (ABOUT 1½ POUNDS/675 G TOTAL)

6 TO 8 THIN SLICES LEAN BACON (ABOUT 6 OUNCES/170 G TOTAL)

2 TABLESPOONS/30 G LARD OR VEGETABLE OIL

2 ONIONS, SLICED

2 TART APPLES, PEELED, CORED, AND SLICED

3 TABLESPOONS/45 ML CALVADOS OR COGNAC

1½ CUPS/375 ML VEAL BROTH (SEE PAGE 373), MORE IF NEEDED

SALT AND PEPPER

¼ CUP/60 ML CRÈME FRAÎCHE (PAGE 374) OR HEAVY CREAM (OPTIONAL)

CARAMELIZED APPLE SLICES

4 TART APPLES (ABOUT 1½ POUNDS/675 G TOTAL)

¼ CUP/60 G SUGAR

4 TABLESPOONS/60 G BUTTER

Trim any skin and fat from the tenderloins. Spread half the bacon slices lengthwise and overlapping one another on a chopping board so they form a rectangle. Put the tenderloins lengthwise on top, setting them head to tail so they are the same thickness at both ends. Top with the remaining bacon strips. The meat should now be coated with strips of bacon. Insert strings under the bacon and meat and tie a neat cylinder.

Heat the oven to 350°F/180°C. Heat the lard in a shallow, flameproof casserole over medium heat. Add the pork and brown thoroughly on all sides, taking about 10 minutes. Remove and set it aside. Add the onions to the pan and cook, stirring often, until soft but not brown, 4 to 5 minutes. Stir in the two sliced apples and continue cooking until the onions and apples are browned, about 5 minutes longer.

Replace the meat, add the Calvados, and flambé it (see page 371). When the flames die, stir in the broth and bring to a boil. Transfer to the oven and roast the pork, uncovered, until tender, 50 minutes to 1 hour. A skewer inserted in the center should be hot to the touch when withdrawn after 30 seconds, or a thermometer should register 160°F/70°C. Add more broth if the pan seems dry.

When the meat is nearly tender, prepare the caramelized apple slices. Core the whole apples but do not peel them. Cut them crosswise into thick rounds, discarding the ends. Spread the sugar on a plate. Melt the butter in a large frying pan over high heat. Dip one side of each apple slice in the sugar and put, sugared side down, in the hot butter. Cook until caramelized, 4 to 5 minutes. Sprinkle the tops of the slices with the leftover sugar, turn them, and brown the other side, 2 to 3 minutes longer. Set the apple slices aside.

When the pork is done, transfer it to a carving board and cover with aluminum foil to keep warm. The apples should have softened to thicken the juices lightly. If the juices are thin, put the casserole on the stove top and boil to reduce and concentrate them, 3 to 5 minutes. To make a sauce, transfer the contents of the casserole to a food processor or blender and purée until smooth. Return to the pan, stir in the crème fraîche, if using, and bring to a boil. Taste and adjust the seasoning.

Discard the strings from the pork, carve into 8 generous slices, and divide them among 4 warmed plates. Spoon the sauce over and around the meat, and garnish each plate with the apple slices. Serve at once. The pork may also be roasted a day or two ahead, kept in the refrigerator, and reheated on the stove top. However, I would caramelize the apple slices and finish the sauce just before serving.

= CIDER AND CALVADOS =

You can recognize a cider-apple tree by its heavy tangle of branches and mass of tiny, wizened fruit. In Brittany and Normandy, the trees are everywhere: scattered in hedgerows, grouped in orchards, dotted about the fields. Driving along the country roads in autumn, the verges are piled with bags of orange, red, and yellow fruits, awaiting the cider press that rattles from farm to farm. Occasionally, the growers see a sad year when the presses never leave the barn because a late spring chill has caught the apple blossom, and with it any hope of fruit.

Peasant wisdom insists that the winds must be in the right direction and the moon in the right quarter before cider is bottled. The finest comes from a range of tart, acid, and bitter apples, two-thirds cider apples to one-third sweet, which ripen late and are already nipped by autumn frost. Just a few Norman growers have invested in the apple varieties needed for a distinctive vintage cider along the lines of vintage wines, and the vast bulk of today's commercial cider remains nondescript in name and bouquet.

In France and indeed Europe, *cidre* refers to alcoholic cider, not simple apple juice. Tradition dictates that the best way to know when cider is ready to drink is to lay a bottle flat and wait for it to explode (upright, that shouldn't happen). One up on the alcoholic scale is *pommeau*, a mix

of two-thirds fresh apple juice and one-third Calvados that is left to mature for a year or more, like Ratafia (page 357). A glass makes a pleasant aperitif.

Calvados (named after the *département* in Normandy) is a single-distillation apple brandy, bearing the same relation to cider that Armagnac has to wine. The best AOC Calvados (page 111) is aged for twelve to fifteen years in oak. Sometimes pears may be added to the apples, giving a rounder finish. "It's all in the mix and the distillation," explains Ange Giard, an artisanal producer near Domfront. He admits that most Calvados is fiery stuff, whether it is in a squat Norman jug, a slender, Loire-type flute, or a rustic earthenware pot. The custom of the *trou normand*—a generous shot glass downed in the middle of dinner to clear the palate for the final course—is a shock to the system, practically a cult. (What it does to the head is another matter.) For me, Calvados is best with coffee, on the side or poured right in, for a bracing *café Calva* on a cold morning.

In the kitchen, both cider and Calvados blend well with rich meats such as pork and duck, with kidneys, and with tripe in the renowned *tripes à la mode de Caen*. Cider can replace wine for deglazing a pan of sautéed chops, or of fish or chicken with cream. Calvados is particularly good in apple desserts, and makes a fine blaze in a flambé.

CHOUCROUTE ALSACIENNE

serves 8 to 10

If ever a glorious one-pot meal has existed, it is Choucroute Alsacienne, and regional restaurateurs make the most of it. A good bistro version unites at least three kinds of cured pork and bacon, two or three different sausages, and potatoes, all aromatic with juniper and white wine and served on a giant platter. The best sauerkraut is crisp and fresh, made at home from finely shredded raw cabbage that is salted and left to ferment a month or more. Ready-prepared sauerkraut is, of course, available canned or packaged.

Assembling the meats to flavor the sauerkraut is the major task, but cooking them is quite simple. Cured pork and sausages vary from place to place, even within Alsace, so mix and match what you can find, keeping in mind that the greater the variety, the better. Most American cities have a German or Polish specialty butcher, and there are mail-order sales, too. You should be able to find goose fat in jars. In Alsace, a medium-dry Riesling is favored for Choucroute, both for the pot and the glass. The final Alsatian touch on delivery to the table is a bracing shot of kirsch, a cherry-based local specialty. Don't hesitate to make generous amounts of Choucroute Alsacienne. Tradition dictates the platter must always be passed for seconds, and it reheats well.

4 POUNDS/1.8 KG RAW OR COOKED SAUERKRAUT

6 TABLESPOONS/90 G GOOSE FAT OR LARD

6 ONIONS (ABOUT 2 POUNDS/900 G TOTAL), CHOPPED

1 LARGE DESSERT APPLE, PEELED, CORED, AND SLICED

1-POUND/450-G PIECE LEAN BACON

1-POUND/450-G PIECE CANADIAN BACON

1-POUND/450-G PIECE SMOKED PORK LOIN

1 POUND/450 G SMOKED PORK SAUSAGES

2 TEASPOONS JUNIPER BERRIES

SALT AND PEPPER

2 BOTTLES (750 ML EACH) MEDIUM-DRY RIESLING

5 POUNDS/2.25 KG WAXY POTATOES, UNPEELED

8 TO 10 CURED PORK CHOPS (ABOUT 2 POUNDS/ 900 G TOTAL)

8 TO 10 FRANKFURTERS (ABOUT 1 POUND/450 G TOTAL)

1/2 CUP/125 ML KIRSCH

DIJON MUSTARD, FOR SERVING

VERY LARGE FLAMEPROOF CASSEROLE OF AT LEAST 10-QUART/10-LITER CAPACITY

Drain and rinse the sauerkraut with cold water, then leave it to drain in a colander. Melt 4 tablespoons/60 g of the fat in the large flameproof casserole over low heat. Add the onions and sauté, stirring occasionally, until tender but not brown, 10 to 12 minutes. Spread half of the sauerkraut over the onions, first squeezing it in your fists to extract all the water. Spread the apple, both kinds of bacon, the smoked pork loin, and smoked sausages on top. Sprinkle with the juniper berries, salt, and pepper. Cover the meat with the rest of the sauerkraut, squeezing it dry also, and pour over the wine. Cut a piece of parchment paper to fit inside the casserole and press it directly on top of the sauerkraut. Cover the pan and simmer on the stove top until the sauerkraut is tender, 1½ to 2 hours if the sauerkraut is raw and 30 minutes less if it is already cooked. Choucroute Alsacienne is excellent reheated, so do not hesitate to make it ahead. It keeps well for at least 3 days in the refrigerator, and you will have an eager audience for leftovers.

To finish, reheat the choucroute over low heat if necessary, allowing about 30 minutes. Put the potatoes in a pan of salted water to cover, top with a lid, and bring to a boil. Simmer until tender when pierced with a knife, 15 to 20 minutes. Drain the potatoes and keep them warm, peeling them just before serving. Melt the remaining 2 tablespoons/30 g fat in a frying pan over medium heat. Add the cured pork chops and sauté, turning once, until well done, 5 to 7 minutes on each side. Add them to the casserole 15 minutes before the sauerkraut is cooked. Warm the frankfurters in very hot water until heated through, 2 to 3 minutes (if boiled, they will burst). Leave them in the water to keep warm, draining just before serving.

Before going to table, pour the kirsch over the sauerkraut, taste it, and adjust the seasoning. Lift out both kinds of bacon and the pork loin and carve them in generous slices. Drain the sauerkraut well and pile it on a large warmed platter. Arrange the meats and sausages on top, with the potatoes around the edge. Pass the mustard at the table.

JAMBON PERSILLÉ

PARSLEYED HAM IN WINE ASPIC

serves 8 to 10

Half of the charm of Burgundian parsleyed ham is its color, a brilliant mosaic of pink meat set in a shimmering green aspic of white wine. My local charcutier adds lots of finely chopped shallot and a touch of garlic to the mold, and I have done the same here. I think you will like the piquant contrast of salty ham with the wine and aromatics. Full-scale Jambon Persillé is a perfectionist exercise, calling for up to six hours of simmering to fully cook the raw ham and pig's feet (they add vital gelatin). In this shorter version to make at home, I am using cooked country ham (it should be the best you can find, and not too salty) with powdered gelatin to set the aspic. I refuse, however, to cut corners on the wine, which should be a well-balanced Chardonnay with a minimum of oak.

It is the custom to mold Jambon Persillé in a deep salad bowl, so that it can be turned out and cut into wedges like a cake. I serve it with a vegetable salad such as Céleri Remoulade (page 246) as a bountiful lunch, or as part of a cold buffet.

ASPIC

I BOTTLE (750 ML) DRY CHARDONNAY

3/4 CUP/175 ML VEAL BROTH (SEE PAGE 373)

2 DRIED BAY LEAVES

2 OR 3 SPRIGS FRESH THYME

I TEASPOON PEPPERCORNS

I LARGE BUNCH FRESH CURLY-LEAF PARSLEY
(ABOUT 2 OUNCES/60 G)

1/2 CUP/125 ML BOILING WATER

3 TABLESPOONS/20 G UNFLAVORED POWDERED
GELATIN

SALT AND PEPPER

2 POUNDS/900 G COOKED COUNTRY HAM

4 SHALLOTS (ABOUT 3 OUNCES/90 G TOTAL),
FINELY CHOPPED

I OR 2 GARLIC CLOVES, CHOPPED

2-QUART/2-LITER GLASS SALAD BOWL OR OTHER
DEEP GLASS BOWL

To begin, make the aspic. Combine the wine, half of the broth, the bay leaves, thyme, and peppercorns in a saucepan, cover, and bring to a boil. Strip the parsley leaves from the stems, add the stems to the wine mixture, lower the heat, and simmer for about 30 minutes. Meanwhile, chop the parsley leaves and put them in a small heatproof bowl. Pour the boiling water over the leaves to set the color and leave them to cool.

Pour the remaining broth into a large bowl, sprinkle the gelatin on top, and leave it until softened and spongy, about 5 minutes. Strain the wine mixture into a measuring cup. There should be 3 cups/750 ml; if necessary, add a little water. Bring the wine mixture just back to a boil and pour it over the gelatin. Let stand for 1 minute, and then stir to melt and mix in the gelatin. Taste the aspic, season it with salt and pepper (remember that the ham is salty), and leave it to cool until tepid. Aspic will set quite suddenly when cold, so do not chill it.

While the aspic is cooling, pull the ham into uneven chunks, discarding the fat and any sinew (the finished dish will look best if you use your fingers rather than cutting cubes with a knife). To mold the ham, pour a layer of aspic about 3/8 inch/1 cm deep into the salad bowl. Put the bowl in the refrigerator or in a roasting pan of ice and water to chill until set. In another bowl, mix together the ham, shallots, garlic, and parsley and its liquid. Add the remaining tepid aspic and mix well. When the layer of aspic has set in the salad bowl, transfer the ham mixture to the bowl. Press the pieces of ham well below the surface of the aspic, and make sure no air bubbles are trapped beneath the ham. Cover the mold and chill until set, at least 6 hours. Jambon Persillé is a practical dish and may be stored in the refrigerator for up to 1 week. Once unmolded and cut, it should be eaten within a day.

To serve the ham, dip the bottom of the bowl in hot water for 15 to 30 seconds to loosen the aspic. Run a thin-bladed knife around the inside edge of the bowl to loosen it further, and then pull the aspic away from the sides of the bowl with your fingers to release the airlock. Unmold the ham onto a platter—it needs no decoration. Or, if you prefer, serve it directly from the bowl. Either way, cut the mold into wedges.

LE CASSOULET DE TOULOUSE

serves 12 to 16

It was in the 1930s that a legendary chef single-handedly raised Cassoulet from an obscure but agreeable country casserole to international status. Prosper Montagné, editor of the first Larousse Gastronomique *(and much else), was a native of Languedoc and devoted no fewer than sixteen hundred words to the local specialty. He distinguished three styles: "that of Castelnaudary (the earliest and most prestigious) has as a base, fresh pork, ham, pork hock, fresh sausage, and pork rind; that of Carcassone also includes leg of lamb and partridges in season; that of Toulouse includes all the Castelnaudary elements, bacon, Toulouse sausages, mutton, and confit of goose or duck."*

You will find the ingredients for Cassoulet in most upmarket supermarkets. The requisite dried large white kidney beans, the fresher the better, are a subject of much discussion around Toulouse, but almost any will do, including navy beans, cannellini, and even little pea beans. I swear that the best Cassoulet I ever tasted was made with the green kidney beans called flageolets, *totally unorthodox, but I recommend a try. Toulouse sausages are lightly seasoned sausages of fresh pork, while fully cooked garlic poaching sausages, each weighing about a pound (450 grams), need only to be reheated with the beans. Confit and goose fat come in jars.*

My version of Cassoulet de Toulouse is only slightly more modest than Prosper Montagné's, and it is perfect for a large party. All the elements, including braised lamb in a tomato sauce, are cooked separately and then assembled with the beans, ready to bake further before serving. Leftovers freeze wonderfully well for a month or two. Cassoulet is, however, a lengthy operation taking at least a day to prepare, or longer if you like the casserole to mellow for a day or two before eating.

2 POUNDS/900 G DRIED WHITE BEANS

SALT AND PEPPER

6 TO 8 LEGS DUCK OR GOOSE CONFIT (PAGE 119)

1½ POUNDS/675 G FRESH PORK SAUSAGES

ONE 1-POUND/450-G GARLIC POACHING SAUSAGE

½ CUP/50 G BROWNED BREAD CRUMBS (SEE PAGE 373)

LAMB STEW

1½ POUNDS/675 G BONELESS LAMB SHOULDER

1½ POUNDS/675 G LAMB BREAST, WITH BONES

1-POUND/450-G PIECE LEAN BACON, WITH RIND

6 TABLESPOONS/90 G GOOSE FAT OR LARD

3 ONIONS (ABOUT 1 POUND/450 G TOTAL), SLICED

2 POUNDS/900 G TOMATOES, PEELED, SEEDED, AND COARSELY CHOPPED (SEE PAGE 372)

1 CUP/250 ML MEDIUM-DRY WHITE WINE

1 QUART/1 LITER VEAL BROTH (SEE PAGE 373) OR WATER, MORE IF NEEDED

1 LARGE BOUQUET GARNI (SEE PAGE 370)

4 GARLIC CLOVES, CHOPPED

1 TABLESPOON TOMATO PASTE

LARGE FLAMEPROOF CASSEROLE, TWELVE TO SIXTEEN 8-INCH/20-CM DEEP INDIVIDUAL BAKING DISHES OR ONE 11-BY-14-INCH/28-BY-35-CM LARGE BAKING DISH

Cover the beans generously with cold water and leave them to soak overnight. The next day, drain the beans, put them in a large saucepan, and cover generously with water. Bring the beans slowly to a boil, skimming occasionally. Cover and simmer until the beans are tender. To test, lift a few on a spoon and blow on them; they should burst. Cooking can take just 1 hour or up to 3 hours, depending on the variety and age of the beans. About 20 minutes before the end of cooking, season the beans with salt (if salt is added too early, the skins will be tough).

Meanwhile, heat the oven to 350°F/180°C and make the lamb stew. Trim any cartilage and most of the fat from the lamb shoulder and cut it into 1½-inch/4-cm cubes. Cut the lamb breast, including bones, into pieces. Cut the rind from the bacon and line the casserole with the rind. Cut the bacon meat into lardons (see page 371). Heat 3 tablespoons/45 g of the goose fat in the large flameproof casserole over medium heat. Add the lardons and fry until lightly browned, 5 to 7 minutes. Take out the lardons with a draining spoon and set them aside on a large plate. Add the onions to the pan and sauté over medium heat, stirring often, until lightly browned, 7 to 10 minutes. Add them to the lardons. Increase the heat to high and melt the remaining 3 tablespoons fat. Add a few of the lamb cubes and brown well on all sides, taking 3 to 5 minutes. Set them aside on a separate plate while browning the rest. Finally, brown the pieces of lamb breast, leaving them in the pan.

Discard all but about 2 tablespoons of the fat from the casserole. Stir in the tomatoes, wine, broth, bouquet garni, garlic, tomato paste, salt, and pepper. Replace the lardons and onions and stir all together. Cover and cook the lamb breast in the oven for 30 minutes. Stir in the lamb shoulder, add more broth if the pan seems dry, and continue cooking, stirring from time to time, until all the lamb is tender, 45 to 60 minutes longer.

Cut each piece of confit in half through the joint, set the pieces in a roasting pan, and roast in the oven with the lamb until very hot and the skin is crisp, 15 to 20 minutes; set them aside with their fat. Prick the fresh sausages and brown them in a frying pan on all sides over medium heat, allowing 5 to 7 minutes so they

continued

are cooked through. Set the sausages aside on a plate. Peel the skin from the garlic sausage and cut it into slices ⅜ inch/1 cm thick.

To assemble the cassoulet, drain the cooked beans in a colander. Using a draining spoon, spread half of the beans in a layer in the bottom of the baking dish(es). Arrange the lamb pieces (reserve the sauce), fresh sausages, confit, and sliced garlic sausage on the beans, dividing everything evenly if you are using individual baking dishes. Add the remaining beans, tucking them around the meats so the meats can still be seen. Spoon the tomato sauce from the lamb over the top; the cassoulet should be moist but not soupy. Sprinkle the surface with the bread crumbs. If you like, spoon some of the fat from the confit over the bread crumbs. The cassoulet may be made 2 to 3 days ahead and kept covered in the refrigerator.

At serving time, heat the oven to 400°F/200°C. Bake the cassoulet until very hot and lightly browned, 30 to 40 minutes for individual dishes, or 1 to 1½ hours for the large dish. Serve very hot.

CAILLETTES DE LANGUEDOC
SAUSAGE PATTIES WITH LIVER AND CHARD
makes 6 caillettes, to serve 6 as a first course or 3 as a main course

Caillettes, giant meatballs made of ground pork, are a popular French charcuterie item. The pork is often mixed with ground liver and ingredients such as spinach, tomato, olives, or crumbled cooked chestnuts. Here, I am suggesting Swiss chard. Portion-sized patties are wrapped in caul fat, the veil-like stomach lining of a pig that melts during cooking and leaves an attractive lacy pattern. For an appetizer, add a salad of spicy greens; for a main course, add shell pasta or mashed potatoes. Caillettes can be served cold too, and make a good sandwich filling when sliced.

You will need to consult a specialty butcher or look on the Internet for the caul fat. Order plenty, as it freezes perfectly and is useful for enclosing all kinds of stuffings and for draping on meats or birds for roasting, acting as a baster during cooking. When I cannot find it for this recipe, I compromise by wrapping each meatball in a strip of bacon. Chicken livers may be substituted for the pork liver.

As for cooking, there is a choice: you may cook the Caillettes at once and serve them; you may prepare them up to 6 hours ahead, refrigerate them, and then bake them; or you may bake them and store them in the refrigerator for up to 3 days before serving.

1 LARGE PIECE CAUL FAT (ABOUT 6 OUNCES/170 G)

8 OUNCES/225 G LEAN PORK

8 OUNCES/225 G PORK LIVER

4 SLICES LEAN BACON (ABOUT 4 OUNCES/110 G TOTAL)

3 TABLESPOONS CHOPPED FRESH PARSLEY

1 TABLESPOON CHOPPED FRESH SAGE, PLUS 6 WHOLE LEAVES

½ DRIED BAY LEAF, CRUMBLED

SALT AND PEPPER

2 TABLESPOONS VEGETABLE OIL

SWISS CHARD

1 POUND/450 G SWISS CHARD, LEAVES ONLY

1 TABLESPOON VEGETABLE OIL

1 ONION, CHOPPED

2 GARLIC CLOVES, CHOPPED

6-BY-8-INCH/15-BY-20-CM BAKING DISH

Soak the caul fat in cold water to cover for about 30 minutes to make it pliable. Heat the oven to 375°F/190°C. Cut the pork and liver into small pieces, discarding any membrane. Chill the meats in the freezer until quite firm but not frozen, 15 to 20 minutes. Cut the bacon into small pieces and chill them also.

For the Swiss chard, bring a saucepan filled with salted water to a boil, add the leaves, and boil just until tender, 3 to 4 minutes. Drain the leaves in a colander and rinse under cold running water. Squeeze the leaves to remove excess water and coarsely chop them. Heat the oil in a frying pan over medium heat. Add the onion and sauté until soft and starting to brown, 3 to 5 minutes. Add the garlic and sauté for 1 minute. Stir in the chard and set aside.

Put half of the chilled meats and bacon in a food processor and pulse to grind until evenly chopped. Transfer to a bowl. Repeat with the remaining half, and add to the bowl. Stir in the chard mixture, parsley, chopped sage, bay leaf, salt, and pepper. Sauté a nugget of the mixture, taste, and adjust the seasoning of the rest. If the mixture is very soft, chill for about 30 minutes.

Drain the caul fat and spread it on a work surface, patching as needed to make 6 roughly square pieces. Set a sage leaf in the center of each piece. Divide the pork mixture into 6 equal portions and press each portion into a ball about the size of a small apple. Put 1 ball on top of each sage leaf. Wrap the balls in the fat, turn them so the sage leaves are on top, and pack them snugly into the baking dish. Spoon the oil on top. Bake the caillettes until well browned and a skewer inserted in the center of a ball is hot to the touch when withdrawn after 30 seconds, 40 to 50 minutes. Serve them hot or at room temperature.

SAUCISSES DE TOULOUSE, SAUCE VIN BLANC

FRESH PORK SAUSAGES WITH WHITE WINE SAUCE

makes about 10 sausages (2 pounds/900 g total)

I don't know why the space-center city of Toulouse has given its name to plain fresh pork sausages seasoned only with nutmeg, salt, pepper, and occasionally garlic. But saucisses de Toulouse *they are, throughout France. Their character comes from the addition of fatback and the coarse texture of the meat. Here, I have left the sausages plain, but herbs such as thyme, sage, or rosemary, or spices, including cumin, coriander, chili, or fennel seeds, may be added to your taste. Sausage casings are made from the pig's intestines and come in two sizes. Artificial casings are available, too, though purists flinch at their mention.*

It helps to have two people in the kitchen when stuffing sausage casings. This recipe may sound like an undertaking, but it is fun, and the results, enhanced by your personal seasonings, will have you hooked.

I¹⁄₂ POUNDS/675 G LEAN PORK

8 OUNCES/225 G PORK FATBACK

I TABLESPOON SALT, MORE IF NEEDED

I TEASPOON FINELY CRUSHED PEPPERCORNS

¹⁄₂ TEASPOON GRATED NUTMEG

2 OUNCES/60 G SMALL SAUSAGE CASINGS
(ABOUT 6 FEET/2 M)

2 TABLESPOONS VEGETABLE OIL

4 THICK SLICES COUNTRY BREAD

2 SHALLOTS, CHOPPED

³⁄₄ CUP/175 ML DRY WHITE WINE

2 TABLESPOONS CHOPPED FRESH PARSLEY

MEAT GRINDER, SAUSAGE STUFFER, OR FUNNEL

Cut the meat and fat into ½-inch/1.25-cm chunks, trimming away any membrane. Chill both the meat and fat in the freezer until quite firm but not frozen, 15 to 20 minutes (this makes them easier to grind). Work the pieces through the coarse grid of the meat grinder. (A food processor cannot be substituted. It tends to pound, rather than grind, the meat, which should remain coarse textured.) Add the salt, crushed peppercorns, and nutmeg and mix well with a wooden spoon. Chill for several hours so the spices blend. Meanwhile, soak the casings in cold water to cover for several hours until pliable.

Sauté a nugget of the sausage mixture, taste it, and adjust the seasoning of the rest. Drain the casings. Open the end of a casing and attach it to the tap. Run a slow stream of cold water through the casing to clean the inside, then repeat with the rest of the casings. Knot one end of a casing closed and push the open end over the base of the sausage stuffer or funnel. Bunch the remaining sausage casing up the tube so it no longer dangles. Work the sausage filling through the funnel into the casing, letting the casing fall as the stuffing fills. (On some machines, the stuffer is attached to the grinder so the meat passes straight into the sausage casings. In this case, work the stuffing once through the grinder and season it to taste. Add the stuffing attachment and work the stuffing again through the grinder into the casings.) Don't pack the casings too tightly or the sausages will be heavy and likely to burst during cooking. When a length of casing is stuffed, knot the top end closed. Prick any air pockets with a pin and twist at 6-inch/15-cm intervals to make individual sausages. Toulouse sausages are at their best freshly made, but they may be stored in the refrigerator for up to 24 hours.

When you are ready to cook the sausages, snip them apart with scissors. Heat the oil in a frying pan over low heat. Add the sausages and fry until browned on all sides and the center is no longer pink, 8 to 10 minutes total.

To finish, toast the bread and set each slice on a warmed plate. Arrange the sausages on top of the bread. Return the frying pan to medium heat, add the shallots, and sauté, stirring, for about 1 minute. Add the wine and boil almost to a glaze, stirring to dissolve the pan juices. Stir in the parsley and spoon the jus over the sausages. Serve at once.

MERGUEZ

SPICY LAMB SAUSAGES

Merguez sausages, brought to France by Arab immigrants, are now popular all over the country. They are made with lamb, or sometimes beef, from a halal (Islamic) butcher and flavored with harissa (a chili paste available in Moroccan groceries), cayenne pepper, and fennel seeds. The spicy sausages can accompany couscous, flavor fish soups, or even turn up on a pizza. Most often, however, they come with frites.

In the recipe for Saucisses de Toulouse, substitute 2 pounds/ 900 g lamb shoulder, carefully trimmed of all sinew, for the lean pork and fatback. After grinding, spice the meat with 4 garlic cloves, chopped; 2 teaspoons salt; 1 teaspoon ground coriander; 1 teaspoon ground cumin; 1 teaspoon fennel seeds, chopped; 1 teaspoon harissa (or any hot red pepper paste); ¼ teaspoon cayenne pepper; and ½ teaspoon crushed peppercorns. Sauté a nugget, taste, and adjust the seasoning of the rest, then stuff the sausages as directed, using small sheep's casings.

= INSPIRATION FROM NORTH AFRICA, AN ARABIC ROMANCE =

I was walking through the rose-brick streets of Albi, a town near Toulouse, on a sultry southern day, when a flashback transported me to the souks of Morocco. Not possible, I thought, but the spicy, saffron aroma was unmistakable. I was passing an archetypal North African grocery with its sacks of dried legumes and rice, tubs of olives, and pyramids of many-colored spices. In recent times, French tastes in cooking have been greatly influenced by Arab migrants, much as American tastes have been conditioned by settlers from Mexico. Although most ethnic North Africans live in cities, some have migrated to the countryside, particularly in the south, where they work the high-yield, irrigated fields that produce *primeurs*, the first early vegetables of the season, with melons and tomatoes coming close behind.

Merguez (page 181), spicy sausages of lamb or beef, are standard on French barbecues, and halal meat is available even in small towns. Restaurants hold couscous nights as an alternative to cheese fondue or mussels with frites. Striking in markets is the spread of North African spices, salted lemons, harissa (spicy hot sauce), and *warka*, the flaky Arab pastry that is a cross between phyllo and spring roll wrappers and is used for making *briks* (filled pastries). Even such Provençal dishes as *petits légumes farcis niçoise* (little stuffed tomatoes and eggplants) can be considered of Arab origin. But then, for millennia the Mediterranean has been criss-crossed by countless civilizations, and it is hardly surprising that what you find on one shore takes root on another.

= LYON: THE GASTRONOMIC HEARTLAND =

Many authorities claim that the true gastronomic heart of France lies not in Paris, but in Lyon. While the Paris area is now all bricks and mortar, an entrepôt for fine ingredients, Lyon has closer links to the countryside. If you head north, you pass through the curious marshes of the Dombes, a favorite bolt-hole for fishing and hunting, until you reach Bresse, where the world's most famous chickens are raised. To the east, you will soon be in alpine foothills, renowed for walnuts and cheese. To the west of Lyon is the Massif Central, heartland of peasant cooking. In the temperate climate south of the city, apples, pears, and stone fruits flourish, with enough heat for Provençal specialties such as melons, eggplants, and peppers. The local produce has the taste of *terroir*.

The place to find all these and other regional treats is in local markets, especially the Halles de Lyon, an indoor complex where some of the city's best charcuterie is displayed. Colette Sibilia's family has been in the business since 1925, and her five daughters will follow her. The market is a way of life for Colette, who is there every day. "It's good here. I see friends, meet people." A dozen types of *saucisson sec* are made in house. Superb cheeses, notably the creamy, soft-rind Saint-Marcellin, are sold at Renée Richard's cheese stand nearer the front of the complex. The city's farmers' market boasts one of the loveliest open-air locations in the country; from early in the morning, stalls snake along the Quai Saint-Antoine on the Saône River in the city center.

Another ideal way to sample great Lyon cooking is to eat out. The city is second only to Paris in the number and distinction of its Michelin-starred restaurants (see "French Restaurant Guides," page 199). Most of France loves to eat, but the Lyonnais have a particular taste for eating in comfort—long, leisurely lunches, roomy tables, solid chairs, and hearty dishes such as garlic sausage in red wine sauce, calf's head with sauce gribiche, Pieds de Porc Panés (page 165), and Foie de Veau Lyonnaise (page 162). The most popular fish dish is equally hearty: Quenelles Nantua (page 80) are a type of fish dumpling, cloaked in a fragrant sauce of local crayfish. Lyon's famous fresh cheese, seasoned with herbs and served with a spoon, goes under the gutsy name of cervelles de canut (*cervelles* means "brains"), and often replaces the normal cheese platter or even dessert.

To end a meal Lyon-style often calls for chocolate, an indulgence that probably came from Spain. Little cakes vary from cups of nougat filled with chocolate cream to chocolate meringues; many pâtissiers have their own special gâteau in which the chocolate is combined with almonds or perhaps chestnuts from the nearby Ardèche. Local opinion is divided on the merits of Maison Richart's stark geometric confections flavored exotically with tea and spices such as anise, now available in New York and Tokyo. Some choco-holics prefer the more voluptuous creations of Maurice Bernachon, known for the amazing chocolate froufrou that tops his *gâteau président*.

Part of what makes Lyon a gastronomic capital is, of course, the proximity to so many good wines, from the Rhône Valley to the south and Beaujolais in the north. According to one old saying, three rivers run through Lyon: the Rhône, the Saône, and the Beaujolais. Along with the wine comes a bourgeois sense of *art de vivre*. Good drink, great chefs, a reverence for tradition, a love of comfort, a passion for the table—all these combined make the inhabitants of Lyon unwavering in their appreciation for the good life.

BOUDIN BLANC

WHITE CHICKEN AND VEAL SAUSAGES

makes 6 sausages (1½ pounds/675 g total)

At their best, these are the aristocrats of sausage, delicate and so fine textured as to be almost a mousse. They consist entirely of white meat, whether veal, chicken, pork, or a mixture, and are lightly spiced, if at all. Just a few come studded, and thus perfumed, with truffle, a play on white and black. Large sausage casings, natural or artificial, are available at specialty butchers or through Internet suppliers. The boudin mixture can be ground in a food processor, but take care not to overwork it at any stage. Its delicate flavor is easily spoiled if the meat gets too warm, usually from the heat of the motor. The mixture is also particularly soft and rich, and I have found that a pastry bag with a sausage stuffer (or a very large piping tube) is easier to use than a grinder for filling the casings. As when making all sausages, two pairs of hands are helpful.

Boudins are cooked for storage, then reheated by poaching or by sauté-ing in butter (the way I like them). Most bistros serve them with fluffy puréed potatoes, or with pommes en l'air, *butter-fried apple slices that are tossed in the air to brown and caramelize evenly as they cook.*

1 OUNCE/30 G LARGE SAUSAGE CASINGS
(ABOUT 3 FEET/1 M)

1½ POUNDS/675 G LEAN BONELESS VEAL OR
BONELESS, SKINLESS CHICKEN BREASTS

¼ CUP/45 G POTATO STARCH

1 TABLESPOON SALT, MORE IF NEEDED

¾ TEASPOON WHITE PEPPER

½ TEASPOON QUATRE ÉPICES (SEE PAGE 370) OR
GROUND ALLSPICE

3 CUPS/750 ML CRÈME FRAÎCHE (PAGE 374) OR
HEAVY CREAM

3 EGGS, BEATEN TO MIX

2 TABLESPOONS/30 G BUTTER

COOKING LIQUID

3 CUPS/750 ML WATER

3 CUPS/750 ML MILK

1 CARROT, CHOPPED

1 ONION, CHOPPED

1 LEEK, WHITE PART ONLY, CHOPPED
(SEE PAGE 371)

1 STALK CELERY, CHOPPED

SALT AND PEPPER

LARGE PIPING BAG WITH LARGE PLAIN TIP

Soak the sausage casings in cold water to cover for several hours until pliable. Trim any membrane from the veal, cut the veal into ½-inch/1.25-cm chunks, and put them in a bowl. Chill the meat in the freezer until quite firm but not frozen, 15 to 20 minutes (this makes it easier to grind). Add the potato starch, salt, pepper, and *quatre épices* and stir until the cubes are coated. Stir in the crème fraîche and eggs. Divide the mixture into 2 batches. Put 1 batch in a food processor and work to a fine paste, about 30 seconds; transfer it to a bowl. Repeat with the second batch, add it to the first batch, and stir them together. Cover and chill thoroughly, at least 30 minutes. Sauté a nugget of the mixture, taste it, and adjust the seasoning of the rest. It should be quite highly seasoned.

Drain the sausage casings. Open the end of a casing and attach it to the tap. Run a slow stream of cold water through the casing to clean the inside, then repeat with the rest of the casings. Drop the large plain tip into the bottom of the piping bag. Knot one end of the casing closed and push the open end over the base of the piping tip. Bunch the remaining sausage casing up the piping tip so it no longer dangles. Spoon the veal mixture into the piping bag and twist the bag to seal it. Gently press the bag so the mixture fills the casing, letting the casing fall as it fills with stuffing. Don't pack the casing too tightly or the sausages will be heavy and are likely to burst during cooking. When a length of casing is stuffed, knot the top end closed. Prick any air pockets with a pin, and twist at 6- to 7-inch/15- to 18-cm intervals to make individual sausages.

For the cooking liquid, combine the water, milk, carrot, onion, leek, celery, salt, and pepper in a sauté pan or shallow saucepan and bring to a boil. Lower the sausages into the pan, cover, adjust the heat so the liquid is at a bare simmer, and poach for 18 to 20 minutes. The liquid should never be more than 195°F/90°C. Note that the sausages burst easily if they get too hot. Remove the pan from the heat, let the sausages cool in the liquid, and then refrigerate them. They may be made ahead and refrigerated for up to 2 days in their liquid.

Shortly before serving, fry the boudins in butter: Lift the linked cold sausages from the liquid, drain them on paper towels, and cut the sausages apart. Melt the butter in a frying pan over low heat. Add the sausages and sauté very gently, turning often, until very hot and lightly browned, 5 to 7 minutes. They quite often burst, but I like them that way. Serve at once.

= STRINGS OF SAUSAGES =

The range of sausages in France is vast: pork, beef, or lamb; fine or coarsely ground; smoked or not; fresh or dried; large or small. Furthermore, they are distinguished not only by region or *département*, but also by city or town. "In Normandy," the Michelin guide instructs us, "it is the rule to eat an *andouille* in Vire, a *boudin noir* in Mortagne-au-Perche, and a *boudin blanc* from the Avranchin."

I find the simplest way to shop for sausages at a charcuterie is to decide whether you will cook them or not. Ready-to-eat are *saucissons secs*: hard, dry sausages covered with a white bloom, or rolled in coatings such as cracked black pepper or dried herbs. Their variety is astounding: bull, boar, horse, and donkey are among the most eccentric. Some *saucissons secs* are studded with nuts, particularly hazelnuts, or flavored with garlic, or rolled in herbs. All are served in very thin slices, cut on the diagonal and with the skin removed. They are ideal with drinks, as a first course with crisp radishes, or in a baguette sandwich.

Other types of sausages must be poached, grilled, or fried. Larger sausages tend to be poached to accompany mashed potatoes, lentils, or beans. Boudin (related to *pouding*, or "pudding") can be a black, hearty blood sausage flavored with onion, or white and delicate, made from veal or chicken breast. Both are served with sautéed apples, and sometimes *aux deux pommes*, with apples and puréed potatoes. *Cervelas lyonnais* (originally containing pig's brains, or *cervelles*) is another poaching sausage weighing up to two pounds (one kilogram), studded with either pistachios or truffles. Some poaching sausages come baked in brioche and ready to slice for snacks.

Grilling and frying sausages tend to be skinnier and cook faster. Spicy, red Merguez is popular, as are tiny *chipolatas*, no thicker than a finger. If you are looking for something plain and basic, Saucisses de Toulouse (page 181) are sold all over France, as are earthy-tasting andouillettes, made from the small intestines of a pig mixed with bits of pig, calf, or beef stomach. There's even a club that celebrates their succulence, the Association Amicale d'Amateurs d'Authentiques Andouillettes (AAAAA). Even more challenging (we are, after all, talking of guts) is andouille, made from the large intestine and recognizable for its spiraled appearance and strong scent. Andouilles are usually served cold in slices as a first course, although in the north you will find them accompanied by leeks in a mustardy vinaigrette.

PÂTÉ DE CAMPAGNE

COUNTRY PÂTÉ

serves 8 to 10

This recipe for Pâté de Campagne was given to me by a traditional chef whose pâtés were renowned throughout Paris. Before departing for his annual three-week vacation in August, he would cook a few pâtés, seal them with lard, and then leave them in the unrefrigerated cellar for his return. He always maintained that these aged pâtés were the best of the whole year. Although I do agree that the longer a pâté is kept, the better it is, I make a ten-day wait my maximum.

A rich cut of pork, such as shoulder (most flavor in pork comes from the fat), is important to creating a succulent pâté. The pork belly fat I call for here should have only a little lean meat, and should not be smoked or salted.

*The terrine for baking should be literally that, a pot made of earthenware (*terre cuite*) to distribute heat slowly and evenly. Many contemporary terrine molds are made of enameled cast iron, which are fine to use, but the cooking time is often a good deal shorter. The classic accompaniment for Pâté de Campagne is cornichons, and plenty of the best crusty baguette you can find.*

8 OUNCES/225 G BARDING FAT (SEE PAGE 370)

I POUND/450 G BONELESS PORK SHOULDER

12 OUNCES/330 G PORK BELLY FAT

4 OUNCES/110 G VEAL ESCALOPES

4 CHICKEN LIVERS (ABOUT 4 OUNCES/110 G TOTAL)

PÂTE À LUTER (PAGE 190), OPTIONAL

SALAD LEAVES, FOR SERVING (OPTIONAL)

FILLING

I TABLESPOON/15 G BUTTER

I ONION, CHOPPED

2 GARLIC CLOVES, FINELY CHOPPED

I TABLESPOON SALT

I TEASPOON PEPPER

$^1/_2$ TEASPOON QUATRE ÉPICES (SEE PAGE 370) OR GROUND ALLSPICE

PINCH OF GRATED NUTMEG

2 EGGS, BEATEN TO MIX

2 TABLESPOONS COGNAC

$^1/_2$ CUP/75 G HAZELNUTS OR PISTACHIOS, TOASTED (OPTIONAL)

I DRIED BAY LEAF

I SPRIG FRESH THYME

5-CUP/1.25-LITER OVAL EARTHENWARE TERRINE WITH A LID, ELECTRIC OR HAND MEAT GRINDER

Line the terrine mold with the barding fat, reserving a piece for the top. Heat the oven to 350°F/180°C. Trim the pork, belly fat, veal, and chicken livers of membrane and any skin, and cut them into 1-inch/2.5-cm chunks. Chill all the meats in the freezer until quite firm but not frozen, 15 to 20 minutes.

While the meats are chilling, begin the filling. Melt the butter in a small frying pan over medium heat. Add the onion and sauté until soft but not brown, 3 to 5 minutes. Set aside to cool.

Work the chilled meats through the coarse grid of the meat grinder into a large bowl. (Do not use a food processor or the terrine will be heavy.) Add the cooled onion, garlic, salt, pepper, *quatre épices*, and nutmeg to the meats and stir with a wooden spoon to mix thoroughly. Beat in the eggs and Cognac, and then mix in the nuts, if using. Sauté a nugget of the mixture and taste it. At this stage, it should be quite spicy, as it will mellow later. Adjust the seasoning of the mixture. Spread the mixture in the terrine mold and smooth the top. It should fill to the rim, as it will shrink during cooking. Cover the top with the reserved barding fat, trimming it to fit the mold. Put the bay leaf and thyme sprig on top and cover the terrine with the lid. If you like, make pâte à luter and use it to seal the mold.

Line a roasting pan with a dish towel, set the terrine in it, and pour in boiling water to make a water bath (see page 373). Bring the water back to a boil on the stove top and put the pan in the oven. Cook the pâté for 1¾ to 2 hours, refilling the bath with hot water if it evaporates rapidly. (If using a metal mold, the cooking time may be shorter.) Test if the pâté is done by inserting a skewer through the hole in the lid (if necessary, break the luting paste and lift the lid to test). The skewer should be hot to the touch when withdrawn after 30 seconds, or a thermometer should register 165°F/74°C.

Take the terrine from the water bath and let it cool to tepid. Remove the lid and set a 2-pound/900-g weight on top to compress the filling. A brick wrapped in plastic wrap is an ideal size for many terrines, or set a couple of cans on a piece of cardboard cut to size. Chill the terrine until cold and firm, about 12 hours. Remove the weight, cover the mold again with the lid, and store in the refrigerator for at least 3 days before serving.

Pâté de Campagne may be served in the terrine, or unmolded and sliced. If serving in the mold, cut and remove the first piece so the slices are easier to lift out. Alternatively, unmold the pâté onto a platter, cut a few slices, and arrange them, overlapping, on the platter, with salad leaves around the edge. Pâté de Campagne always tastes best at room temperature.

clockwise from top: RILLETTES, TERRINE DE GIBIER DE LA LOIRE, PÂTÉ DE CAMPAGNE

PÂTE À LUTER
LUTING PASTE

Luting paste is a mixture of flour and water used to seal terrines and casseroles so that steam, and flavor, cannot escape. The paste should be stirred just until smooth. If it is beaten, it will become elastic and shrink during cooking.

Put 2 cups/250 g flour in a bowl and make a well in the center. Add 1 cup/250 ml water to the well and stir gently to make a soft, slightly sticky paste. Add more flour if necessary to roll the paste into a rope with your hands. Use it to seal the gap between the pot and lid.

TERRINE DE GIBIER DE LA LOIRE
GAME TERRINE

serves 10 to 12

This terrine is a showcase piece. For a formal occasion, game terrine should be unmolded and sliced to serve on individual plates with a garnish of curly endive or frisée. If you prefer to be more relaxed, leave the terrine in its mold, carving out a first slice to make access easier, and leave guests to help themselves.

1 PHEASANT, WITH LIVER (ABOUT 2 POUNDS/900 G)

2 SLICES CURED RAW HAM (ABOUT 4 OUNCES/110 G TOTAL)

6 TABLESPOONS/90 ML COGNAC

8 OUNCES/225 G BARDING FAT (SEE PAGE 370)

2 DRIED BAY LEAVES

2 SPRIGS FRESH THYME

PÂTE À LUTER (ABOVE), OPTIONAL

FILLING

8 OUNCES/225 G LEAN PORK SUCH AS LOIN

8 OUNCES/225 G PORK BELLY FAT

8 OUNCES/225 G VEAL ESCALOPES

3 CHICKEN LIVERS (ABOUT 3 OUNCES/90 G TOTAL)

3 SHALLOTS (ABOUT 2 OUNCES/60 G TOTAL), CHOPPED

1 CANNED TRUFFLE, CHOPPED, WITH ITS LIQUID (OPTIONAL)

$^1\!/_2$ TEASPOON QUATRE ÉPICES (SEE PAGE 370) OR GROUND ALLSPICE

PINCH OF GROUND CLOVES

1 TABLESPOON/22 G SALT

1 TEASPOON PEPPER

$1^1\!/_2$-QUART/1.5-LITER PORCELAIN TERRINE WITH LID, ELECTRIC OR HAND MEAT GRINDER

With a sharp, pointed knife, cut the meat from the pheasant carcass, discarding the skin and bones and keeping the breast and leg meat in pieces that are as neat as possible. Cut the ham and larger pheasant pieces into strips ½ inch/1.25 cm wide, reserving the trimmings. Spread the larger strips in a shallow dish, pour over the Cognac, cover, and leave to marinate at room temperature for 1 to 2 hours. Weigh the trimmings—there should be about 8 ounces/225 g.

Line the terrine mold with the barding fat, reserving a piece for the top. Heat the oven to 350°F/180°C. For the filling, trim the pork, pork fat, veal, and chicken livers of any membrane and cut them into chunks. Chill these meats and the reserved pheasant trimmings in the freezer until quite firm but not frozen, 15 to 20 minutes. Work the chilled meats through the fine grid of the meat grinder into a bowl. Add the shallots, truffle and its liquid (if using), *quatre épices*, cloves, salt, and pepper to the ground meats and mix well. Drain the pheasant and ham strips, reserving the Cognac marinade, and beat the marinade into the ground meat filling. Sauté a nugget and taste for seasoning. At this stage, it should be quite spicy, as it will mellow later. Adjust the seasoning of the mixture, remembering that the ham will contribute salt.

To assemble the terrine, spread one-fourth of the filling in the terrine mold and top with a layer of pheasant strips, pressing them down into the filling and making sure they do not touch the sides of the mold (otherwise the terrine tends to split when sliced). Spread them with another one-fourth of the filling and top with a layer of all the ham strips. Spread half of the remaining filling on top, top with the rest of the pheasant strips, and cover with the remaining filling, spreading it smooth. Cut the reserved barding fat in narrow strips and arrange them in a diagonal lattice on top of the meat. Put the bay leaves and thyme sprigs on top and cover the terrine with the lid. If you like, make pâte à luter and use it to seal the mold.

Line a roasting pan with a dish towel, set the terrine in it, and pour in boiling water to make a water bath (see page 373). Bring the water back to a boil on the stove top and transfer the pan to the oven. Cook the terrine for 1½ to 1¾ hours, refilling the bath with hot water if it evaporates rapidly. Note that the cooking time will vary widely depending on the shape and material of the terrine mold. Test if the terrine is done by inserting a skewer through the hole in the lid (if necessary, break the luting paste and lift the lid to test). The skewer should be hot to the touch when withdrawn after 30 seconds, or a thermometer should register 160°F/70°C.

Take the terrine from the water bath and let it cool to tepid. Remove the lid and set a 2-pound/900-g weight on top to compress the filling. A brick wrapped in plastic wrap is an ideal size for many terrines, or set a couple of cans on a piece of cardboard cut to size. Chill the terrine until cold and firm, about 12 hours. Remove the weight and cover the mold again with the lid. The forceful mix of game and Cognac in this terrine improves immeasurably if you make it at least 3 days and up to 10 days ahead, keeping it in the refrigerator.

At serving time, let the terrine come to room temperature. You may leave it in the mold to take to the table for a casual supper. For a more formal party, slice and plate it in the kitchen. I like to leave the barding fat on a game terrine, but you can discard it if you prefer.

RILLETTES
RUSTIC PORK PÂTÉ
serves 12 to 16 as a first course

Half pâté, half shredded pork, with, in this case, a bit of duck, Rillettes are simplicity itself to make. You must use high-quality pork and not skimp on fat if the pâté is to be temptingly light and bursting with pork flavor. Also, it must be made in large quantities to turn out well, so this recipe serves a crowd. However, it keeps, and freezes, well. In a menu, Rillettes take the place of a terrine or pâté, to be served with cornichons, green or black olives, and country bread.

3 POUNDS/I.35 KG LEAN PORK SHOULDER, WITH BONES

I¹⁄₂ POUNDS/675 G PORK FATBACK

2 RAW DUCK LEGS (ABOUT I POUND/450 G TOTAL)

I TABLESPOON SALT

I TABLESPOON PEPPER

3 OR 4 SPRIGS FRESH THYME

2 DRIED BAY LEAVES

I¹⁄₂ CUPS/375 ML WATER, MORE IF NEEDED

Heat the oven to 325°F/160°C. Cut the pork into 2-inch/5-cm cubes and the fat into 1-inch/2.5-cm cubes, discarding any sinew. Cut the duck legs in half through the joints. Put all the meats in a bowl and mix them thoroughly with the salt, pepper, thyme, bay leaves, and water. Transfer the mixture to a casserole; it should be almost full.

Cover, put in the oven, and cook, stirring occasionally, for 4 to 5 hours. The fat should be completely melted and clear and the meats should be very tender. Tradition has it that they should be soft enough to poke with a straw. During cooking, add a little more water if the meats threaten to stick to the bottom of the pan, but at the end of cooking all the water should have evaporated. The mixture should cook very slowly and never boil. If it appears to be cooking too fast, lower the heat.

Let the meats cool to tepid, then drain, reserving the melted fat. Spread the meats on a chopping board and discard the duck bones, thyme, and bay leaves. Using 2 forks, pull the meats into coarse shreds, then transfer them to a bowl. When the reserved fat is nearly cold and starts to set, mix it gently with the meats. Do not beat it in or the rillettes will be heavy. Taste and adjust the seasoning. Pack the rillettes into crocks or preserving jars, cover, and refrigerate for at least 2 days before serving so the flavor mellows. If sealed with a layer of melted lard, rillettes will keep in the refrigerator for up to 2 weeks or in the freezer for up to 6 months.

RILLONS
BAKED PORK CUBES

Rillons, also called *rillauds*, are a specialty of the Loire. It may sound odd to consume chunks of fatty pork all by themselves, but wait until you have a chance to try them. I add a salad of tart greens, such as *roquette* (arugula) or frisée, but in France usually only a baguette is served. Rillons can be served hot or at room temperature.

Heat the oven to 325°F/160°C. Cut 3 pounds/1.35 kg boneless breast or belly of pork into 1½-inch/4-cm cubes. Melt 2 tablespoons/30 g lard in a large sauté pan or frying pan over medium heat. Working in batches, brown the pork cubes on all sides, taking 10 to 15 minutes for each batch. Return all the cubes to the pan and add ½ cup/125 ml water, 2 teaspoons salt, 1 teaspoon pepper, 2 sprigs fresh thyme, and 2 dried bay leaves. Cover and cook in the oven until the meat is very tender but not yet falling apart, 1¼ to 1½ hours. Taste and adjust the seasoning.

Drain the rillons briefly and serve them hot or at room temperature, keeping any drippings for another use. To prepare ahead, drain the rillons while still warm and pack the meat in a crock. Melt enough lard to cover and seal them. If well sealed, rillons will keep in the refrigerator for up to 2 weeks. At serving time, heat the rillons in a frying pan to melt the fat and crisp the surface of the meat. Serves 6 to 8 as a first course.

= PORTRAIT OF A CHARCUTIER =

Ask a charcutier whom his best friend is and he will say a pig. After all, he makes use of it from snout to tail, creating dried sausages for aperitifs, fresh sausages to fry or poach, pâtés, blood sausages, pistachio-studded terrines, head-cheese, roasts, bacon, pig's feet in bread crumbs, lard, and smoked and salted hams to eat with lentils (see "The Pig Preserved," facing page). When it comes to all these goodies, and many more, the Loire region is the leader of the pack.

In the Les Halles market in Tours, I counted at least six certified master charcutiers (the term comes from *chair cuit*, meaning "cooked meat"). Franck Bourdeau's stand was one of the most impressive, with preparations ranging from andouillettes and foie gras to quiches and galantines. "We make everything ourselves," he told me, "all the sausages and terrines—and all our own sauces and pastry, too! We don't use anything industrial. We even make our own puff pastry for vol-au-vents."

What, a charcutier makes pastry? "We need to be versatile," Monsieur Bourdeau explained. "We have to understand a bit of butchery for preparing meats, we have to know how to salt and cure and season, we have to be able to cook and bake—people like to buy a few prepared salads with their meats—we must manage people, and we need to sell." No wonder his day begins at five in the morning and doesn't wrap up until seven at night! Monsieur Bourdeau divides his time between his production kitchen and the markets in and around Tours, where he loves to chat with clients and get their feedback. "It's good to hear what people tell me. It helps improve my products."

When I asked about competition at the fabulous Tours market (honestly, I have never seen so much fine charcuterie in a single place), Monsieur Bourdeau was upbeat. "There's always a market for good products. Competition keeps standards high. Our clients aren't easily fooled. There are lots of *fins gourmets*." Running my hungry eyes over the banquet that is his stand, I think he is right: there can never be too much of a good thing.

═ THE PIG PRESERVED ═

Before the invention of canning, ham, bacon, and salt pork were often the only meats available in winter; hence, the historic importance of the pig, whose inexpensive meat cures well. The process for hams involves salting (dry-salting or brining, or both), then drying in a cool, airy place, often with some smoking. Some hams are sufficiently cured to eat raw, while others must be cooked first. A typical cooked ham is the lightly salted *jambon de Paris*, a mild-tasting luncheon meat usually sold in slices. *Jambon de York* is similar, but because it is smoked and matures longer, and more slowly, it has a slightly different flavor.

Raw hams are cured in the hilly uplands and mountains of France, notably in the Ardennes, Alsace, Auvergne, Savoy, and the Basque country, where the air is brisker and drier. The production and curing methods are what give every regional ham its individuality. For instance, Bayonne ham, after dry-salting and smoking, may be rubbed with Espelette pepper. Such hams, particularly valued for their firm fat and aromatic flavor, are sliced paper-thin to eat as

a first course, often with melon or figs, or in sandwiches. Regionally, local hams are used to flavor soups and stews, such as Potage Picard (page 15) with its split peas, and to give gusto to Poulet Sauté Basquaise (page 109).

French bacon, which is made from the belly of the pig and is thickly layered with fat, is called *lard salé* or *lard fumé*, depending on whether it is salted or salted *and* smoked. Both come with the rind on, are used to give flavor and gelatin to broth and stews, and are often sold by the piece for cutting into lardons (strips) for ragoûts and to flavor such dishes as omelets. Smoked or salted bacon may also be sliced to enrich sauerkraut, or left whole and cooked in Cassoulet (page 178). Confusingly, what the French call *bacon* is what we think of as Canadian bacon or back bacon, taken from the lean meat running along the backbone. Inexpensive, meaty cuts of pork such as spareribs, hocks, and belly may also be salted to make Petit Salé (page 172), a favorite addition to dried beans or lentils.

CHEFS: THE EMPEROR PAUL BOCUSE
1926–

"So-called nouvelle cuisine usually means not enough on your plate and too much on your bill." This is the bon mot of Paul Bocuse, the French chef who was an early superstar, having trained under Fernand Point, the godfather of the nouvelle cuisine movement (page 239). Bocuse has a knack for controversy. The man whom top restaurant critics elected Chef of the Century in 1989 is also a practical joker. The story goes that when a tiresome group of tourists were dining chez Bocuse, he borrowed their cameras and snapped a picture of his entire kitchen brigade mooning the lens. Quite a rattling surprise when the diners had their film developed!

Despite his imperious personality, Bocuse has always been dead serious about good food. His own establishment, at Collonges-au-Mont-d'Or near Lyon, has had three stars since 1965. A champion of seasonal market produce, and the reinterpretation of regional recipes such as stuffed cabbage and *cervelles de canut* (fresh cheese with salt, pepper, fresh herbs, and white wine), Bocuse became the ambassador of French gastronomy to the world, and he remains an international icon.

FRENCH RESTAURANT GUIDES: STARGAZING

The French love the company of a good restaurant guide, and many people, including me, travel with more than one. For starters, there are Gault Millau, Le Bottin Gourmand, Champerand, Pudlowski, and now Zagat. The list goes on. Each has its own particular spin and a loyal band of followers, with the Michelin guide the most influential. Don't underestimate how aggressive the French can be in grading restaurants and ranking individual chefs. As one chef of the younger generation explained to me (he had worked in the United States and had just moved back to France), "Out there, people were too easy to impress. I was getting lazy. Here standards are far more demanding. I had to return. I needed that pressure."

Michelin invented the famous (or infamous) system that grades France's more ambitious restaurants with one, two, or three stars. These are awarded for the standard of a restaurant's overall hospitality, judged primarily by the quality of the food and service, and also by the comfort and style of the establishment. For the traveler, Michelin's ratings provide a general idea of what to expect. Three-star restaurants (there are about twenty-five in France) promise "exceptional cuisine, worth a special journey"; the seventy or so two-star restaurants have "excellent food, worth a detour," while establishments with one star are rated "very good in their category." There is no published list of standards; chefs second-guess, and speculate among themselves, but, consciously or not, they conform to unwritten rules, right down to table spacing and the amenities of their *toilettes*. A Michelin star—indeed, any award from a major guide—is worth too much, in terms of increased business, to be ignored.

At the top of the tree, a huge investment in infrastructure is needed—not just in linen and crystal, but in designer kitchens and the latest in porcelain and decorative kitsch. To make the business pay, chefs sell cookware, brand wines, and merchandise food. Typical is Georges Blanc at Vonnas, north of Lyon, where his restaurant and luxury-hotel business has spilled over into the entire community with a series of outlets and eateries. Vonnas used to be a sleepy Burgundian village; now you see much the same kitchen paraphernalia on sale there as you would at a shopping mall in California.

Although the past few years have seen Michelin make an effort to emphasize food over ambience, it nonetheless offers a slightly formal, conservative perspective on the restaurant scene. My own opinion is that the contents of any guide should be taken with a grain of salt: a guide is a *guide*, not a god, and no single guide is consistently right.

GREAT GAME
& GAME BIRDS

CHAPTER
No. 10

It is a fresh, sparkling morning in late September, yet I hesitate to put my head outside the door. Shots have been echoing in the woods since first light, signaling the beginning of hunting season. Hunting follows soccer as the favorite outdoor pursuit of the French, with fishing in third place. All over our *département* in northern Burgundy, village hunt clubs have spent weeks preparing for the fall assault on game birds, such as pheasant, partridge, and wild duck. Deer and wild boar still have a few weeks' reprieve, while it is open season most of the year for ground game, like rabbit and hare.

At the end of the hunting day, competition for the best of the bag can be fierce. Young game is better than old, and hunters make their pick accordingly. Last year's birds are betrayed by calluses on their feet, and deer with towering antlers may look impressive but won't taste as good. Wild boars with fearsome tusks are stuff for the taxidermist, but not for the cook. And the game needs to be aged before cooking. Almost all species are improved by hanging in a dry, airy place for a few days to tenderize and heighten the flavor of the meat.

If I am lucky I will find a wild bird or two in my local market, but most game for sale has been farm raised and comes ready for the oven. That's all the more reason to marinate it in red or white wine with all sorts of aromatics to develop fuller flavor. Remember, all game is low in fat and therefore dries out easily, and if it has led an active life, its muscles will be tough as well. Roasting or grilling is risky, advisable only with young birds or tender cuts of venison. French taste runs to pink juices for roasted birds and red rare for darker roasted meats. Like steak, game is tough and tasteless when well done.

If you want to avoid the risk, pot roasting or braising in a slow oven is a safe way to handle game, as in savory Pintade aux Choux (page 200) or the wonderful Pigeonneaux Truffés à la Crème (page 201) from Périgord.

Not all game recipes are complicated. Until comparatively recently, rabbit, hare, and small birds such as quail, or even thrush and lark, were country staples and treated as such. Faisan en Cocotte (page 200), for example, requires only a half dozen ingredients. Many such recipes can be adapted to other game or to their domesticated counterparts, substituting pork for wild boar and lamb for venison. Grapes marry well with pheasant, wild duck, or quail, and prunes with just about anything. Lapin aux Pruneaux (page 209) is a bistro best-seller. The sweet theme runs through to wines, too, with classic port and Madeira sauces on the plate, and soft Rieslings or Pinot Noirs in the glass.

Nonetheless, a few legendary game dishes are sacrosanct. Examples are *salmis*, in which birds are roasted and their bones crushed and simmered for sauce, and *civet de lièvre à la royale*, with its silky, chocolate-dark sauce thickened with blood. Nowadays, they can only be found, very occasionally, on the restaurant tables of great chefs.

CAILLES À LA BOURGUIGNONNE

BURGUNDIAN QUAIL WITH GRAPES

serves 4 as a main course, or 8 as a first course

Wild quail were once abundant in French vineyards, where they huddled around the roots and pecked at the ripening grapes. Most now are farmed, but the traditional recipes remain, featuring vine leaves and the all-important grapes. Two quail per person are usual as a main dish, or one as a first course. If you are lucky enough to find wild duck or pheasant, grapes and vine leaves are an excellent match with them, too. Count on one pheasant or duck per person; depending on their size, the roasting time will vary from twenty to forty minutes. I have perched the birds on a "nest" of grated potato, and no further accompaniment is needed.

8 QUAIL

SALT AND PEPPER

ABOUT 16 FRESH GRAPE LEAVES OR RINSED JARRED GRAPE LEAVES

2 OUNCES/60 G BARDING FAT (SEE PAGE 370), OR 8 THIN SLICES LEAN BACON

8 OUNCES/225 G SEEDLESS GREEN GRAPES

1 TABLESPOON VEGETABLE OIL

1 TABLESPOON/15 G BUTTER

3/4 CUP/175 ML CHICKEN BROTH (SEE PAGE 373), MORE IF NEEDED

2 TABLESPOONS MARC OR COGNAC

2 TEASPOONS ARROWROOT OR POTATO STARCH

2 TABLESPOONS WATER

POTATO NESTS

1 POUND/450 G BAKING POTATOES

1/4 CUP/60 ML CRÈME FRAÎCHE (PAGE 374) OR HEAVY CREAM

4 TABLESPOONS/60 G BUTTER

Wipe the quail inside and out with paper towels and sprinkle the birds with salt and pepper. Wrap each quail completely in grape leaves (you will probably need 2 leaves for each bird), and top each breast with a piece of barding fat. Tie the fat in place with string. The quail may be prepared up to 6 hours ahead and refrigerated; they should be roasted shortly before serving.

Pull the grapes from their stems. If the skins are thick and need peeling, immerse the grapes in a pan of boiling water for 30 seconds to blanch them. Drain, rinse with cold water, and peel off the skins.

Heat the oven to 400°F/200°C. Heat the oil and butter in a roasting pan over medium heat. Add the quail—they should fit in a single layer—and brown them thoroughly on all sides, 8 to 10 minutes. Transfer the pan to the oven and roast the birds, basting often, allowing 15 to 20 minutes for pink meat, or 20 to 25 minutes if you prefer them well done. To test, snip the strings from one bird and pull away one leg to see the color at the joint. It should be pink or well done, depending on your taste.

Meanwhile, make the potato nests. Peel the potatoes and coarsely grate them using a food processor or hand grater. Squeeze the shreds in a kitchen towel to remove as much water as possible and put them in a large bowl. Stir in the crème fraîche, salt, and pepper. (Work quickly so the potatoes do not discolor.) Divide the mixture into 4 equal portions if serving as a main course, or 8 portions if serving as a first course. Melt the butter in a frying pan over medium heat until the foaming stops. Drop the potato portions into the pan, spacing them well apart and flattening each portion to a round about 4 inches/10 cm across if making 4 nests, or about half the size if making 8 nests. Sauté until browned, 4 to 5 minutes. Turn them and brown the other side, 4 to 5 minutes longer. Set them aside in the pan.

When the quail are done, transfer them to a tray, cover loosely with aluminum foil, and keep them warm. Drain the excess fat from the roasting pan, add the broth, and bring to a boil on the stove top, stirring to dissolve the pan juices. Boil until reduced and concentrated, 2 to 3 minutes. Strain this gravy into a small saucepan and add the grapes and marc. Simmer over low heat until the grapes are almost tender, 1 to 2 minutes. Transfer them to a small bowl with a draining spoon. To thicken the gravy, mix the arrowroot with the water and then whisk the mixture into the simmering liquid; it will thicken at once. Add the grapes and bring the sauce almost to a boil. Thin with a little broth if necessary. Taste and adjust the seasoning.

To finish, discard the strings and barding fat from the birds. Reheat the potato nests if necessary, set them on warmed plates, and top with the quail. Spoon a few grapes and some of the sauce over the quail and pass the rest in a bowl at the table.

FAISANS EN COCOTTE BELLE FERMIÈRE

POT-ROASTED PHEASANTS WITH
CELERY ROOT AND SHALLOTS

serves 4 to 6

*My father was a hunter and my mother would cook variants of this won-
derfully adaptable recipe with whatever he brought home. Background
flavorings included bacon, shallots, or quartered onions, and winter
vegetables ranging from the celery root I suggest here, to carrots, turnips,
parsnips, and Jerusalem artichokes. Birds might be pheasant, partridge, or
pigeon. Failing that, I have been known to substitute a domestic chicken.
A contrasting side dish of peppery greens is the perfect accompaniment.*

2 PHEASANTS (ABOUT 3 POUNDS/1.35 KG EACH)

SALT AND PEPPER

1 CELERY ROOT (ABOUT 1½ POUNDS/675 G)

JUICE OF ½ LEMON

2 TABLESPOONS VEGETABLE OIL

6-OUNCE/170-G PIECE LEAN BACON, CUT INTO
LARDONS (SEE PAGE 371)

12 TO 16 SHALLOTS (ABOUT 1 POUND/450 G TOTAL),
HALVED IF LARGE

1 TABLESPOON/15 G BUTTER

2 TABLESPOONS CHOPPED FRESH PARSLEY

Heat the oven to 375°F/180°C. Wipe the pheasants inside and out
with paper towels, sprinkle them with salt and pepper, and truss
them (see page 371). Peel and quarter the celery root and cut into
1-inch/2.5-cm cubes. Sprinkle the cubes with the lemon juice, toss
to coat (this keeps them from discoloring), and put them in a bowl.

Heat 1 tablespoon of the oil in an oval flameproof casserole
over medium heat. Add the bacon lardons and fry until the fat
runs, 2 to 3 minutes. Lift them out with a draining spoon and set
aside in a bowl. Add the remaining oil to the pan. Add the celery
root and shallots and cook, stirring often, until browned, 8 to
10 minutes. Remove the vegetables from the pan and mix them
with the lardons. Melt the butter in the pan over medium heat.
Add the pheasants and brown them on all sides, taking 10 to
12 minutes.

Spread the vegetable and lardon mixture around the pheasants. Cover, transfer the pan to the oven, and cook until the
pheasants are tender, 25 to 30 minutes for pink meat, or 30 to
35 minutes for well done. Stir the vegetables occasionally during
cooking, and turn the pheasants once or twice.

Transfer the pheasants to a carving board, cover with alumi-
num foil, and leave them to stand for 5 to 10 minutes before carv-
ing. The celery root and shallots should be tender and browned.
Stir in the parsley and spread the vegetables on a warmed platter.
Cut the pheasants in half, discarding the backbones (see page 371).
Arrange them on top of the vegetables and serve.

PINTADE AUX CHOUX

BRAISED GUINEA HEN WITH CABBAGE

serves 6 to 8

*It's a toss-up whether to include guinea hen as game, in line with its dark,
musky meat, or as a domestic bird. A few guinea hens are often included
in a farmyard flock, though they are noisy, independent birds that like to
roost in trees instead of being penned in a coop. In northern France and
Champagne, the dish is made with wild partridges. Small chickens or Rock
Cornish hens can be cooked the same way.*

2 GUINEA HENS (ABOUT 3 POUNDS/1.35 KG EACH)

SALT AND PEPPER

1 SMALL HEAD GREEN CABBAGE (ABOUT 3 POUNDS/
1.35 KG)

2 TABLESPOONS/30 G LARD OR VEGETABLE OIL

4 THICK SLICES LEAN BACON (5½ OUNCES/150 G
TOTAL)

2 LARGE CARROTS, QUARTERED AND CUT INTO STICKS

1 CUP/250 ML CHICKEN BROTH (SEE PAGE 373)

½ CUP/125 ML MEDIUM-DRY WHITE WINE

1 ONION, STUDDED WITH 1 WHOLE CLOVE

1 BOUQUET GARNI (SEE PAGE 370)

12 TO 16 SMALL SMOKED COCKTAIL SAUSAGES
(ABOUT 5 OUNCES/140 G TOTAL)

2 TABLESPOONS CHOPPED FRESH PARSLEY

Wipe the hens inside and out with paper towels, sprinkle with
salt and pepper, and truss them (see page 371). Cut the cabbage
head through the stem end into 12 wedges and core each wedge.
Heat the oven to 350°F/180°C. Melt the lard in a large flameproof
casserole over medium heat. Brown the hens very thoroughly on
all sides, 8 to 10 minutes. Remove them, let the pan cool slightly,
and lay 2 of the bacon slices on the bottom. Add half of the cabbage wedges and sprinkle with salt and pepper (the bacon will add
salt). Put the hens on top, surround them with the carrots, and

then cover them with the remaining cabbage. Pour in the broth and wine. Add the onion and bouquet garni, pushing them well down into the cabbage, and top with the remaining 2 bacon slices.

Cover the casserole and braise it in the oven until the hens are tender, 1¼ to 1½ hours. To test, wiggle the thigh joints; they should move freely. Ten minutes before the end of cooking, add the sausages to the pan, pushing them well down into the cabbage so they heat through. Guinea hen with cabbage may be cooked up to 2 days ahead and kept in the refrigerator.

To finish, if necessary, reheat the hens and cabbage in a 350°F/180°C oven, allowing up to an hour for everything to be piping hot. Transfer the hens to a carving board and cover with aluminum foil to keep warm. Discard the onion and bouquet garni from the pan. Using a draining spoon, pile the cabbage, carrots, and sausages on a warmed large platter, cover, and keep warm. Set aside the bacon slices. Put the casserole on the stove top and boil the cooking juices until concentrated to make a jus, 3 to 5 minutes. Taste and adjust the seasoning. Meanwhile, cut each hen into 4 pieces (see page 371). Cut each bacon slice into 2 or 3 pieces and arrange them on the cabbage with the hens. Sprinkle with the parsley. Reheat the jus if necessary and strain it into a bowl to serve separately.

PIGEONNEAUX TRUFFÉS À LA CRÈME

POT-ROASTED SQUAB IN A TRUFFLED CREAM SAUCE

serves 4

In this luxurious recipe, pigeons are stuffed with whole truffles (albeit small ones), which permeate the meat with their intense, earthy aroma. Young, tender pigeons (squabs) are important, and the relatively short cooking time will ensure they remain pink and juicy. In fact, pigeons should be served either rosy pink or well done; they will be tough and chewy in between. My choice for the sauce would be a full-bodied, medium-dry white wine such as a Riesling or an unoaked Chardonnay. The recipe is popular in the truffle country of Périgord, served typically with Pommes Sarladaise (page 226).

4 YOUNG PIGEONS (SQUABS) (ABOUT 1 POUND/
450 G EACH)

SALT AND PEPPER

2 FRESH TRUFFLES (ABOUT 2 OUNCES/60 G TOTAL),
OR ONE 2-OUNCE/60-G JAR TRUFFLES

4 THIN SLICES BARDING FAT (SEE PAGE 370) OR
LEAN BACON

1 TABLESPOON/15 G LARD OR VEGETABLE OIL

1 TABLESPOON/15 G BUTTER

½ CUP/125 ML MEDIUM-DRY WHITE WINE

½ CUP/125 ML CHICKEN BROTH (SEE PAGE 373)

1 CUP/250 ML CRÈME FRAÎCHE (PAGE 374) OR
HEAVY CREAM

1 TO 2 TABLESPOONS MADEIRA OR COGNAC

BEURRE MANIÉ

2 TEASPOONS/10 G BUTTER

2 TEASPOONS/5 G FLOUR

Wipe the pigeons inside and out with paper towels and sprinkle them with salt and pepper. If using fresh truffles, brush them under running cold water to remove any earth, then peel them with a small knife, reserving the peelings. If using canned truffles, drain them, reserving the liquid, and peel them also. Set aside 1 truffle for the sauce. Cut the remaining truffle into 4 pieces and stuff a piece into the cavity of each pigeon. Wrap the birds in the barding fat, and truss them (see page 371).

Heat the lard and butter in a flameproof casserole over medium heat. Add the birds and brown on all sides, 8 to 10 minutes. Discard the excess fat from the pan, add the wine, and simmer for 2 to 3 minutes. Add the broth, cover, transfer the pan to the oven, and pot roast the pigeons, allowing 25 to 30 minutes for pink meat, or 50 minutes to 1 hour if you prefer the meat well done. To test, pierce a thigh with a fork; the juices should run pink or clear, depending on your taste. Meanwhile, chop the truffle peelings and slice the reserved truffle.

When the pigeons are done, remove them to a platter and cover them with aluminum foil to keep warm. For the beurre manié, crush the butter on a plate with a fork and work in the flour to form a soft paste. To thicken the sauce, pour the crème fraîche into the cooking juices and bring to a boil. Whisk in the beurre manié a piece or two at a time until the sauce coats a spoon lightly. You may not need all of the paste. Strain the sauce into a saucepan and add the truffle peelings, the Madeira, and the liquid from the canned truffles. Taste, adjust the seasoning, and keep warm.

Discard the trussing strings from the pigeons, remove the truffle quarters and set them aside. Cut each bird in half, discarding the backbone (see page 371). Arrange the halves, overlapping them, on 4 warmed plates, and spoon a little sauce over each serving. Thinly slice the truffle quarters and scatter all the truffle slices on the pigeons. Serve the remaining sauce separately.

= THE WINE HARVEST: GRAPE EXPECTATIONS =

"The *vendange* is the most important time of the year for us," says veteran Chablis vintner Michel Colbois. "The wine harvest is the culmination of a whole year's work." It is always a tricky time, too. Every autumn, wine-country people start looking at the skies and talking feverishly among themselves about the weather. "Will we get the two more weeks of sun we need?" "Is it threatening to hail?" "Is there any chance of a cold snap?"

"But the *vendange* is not what it used to be," Monsieur Colbois sighs nostalgically. "When I was married in 1947, everything was still done by hand with horse-drawn carts. The vineyards were full of pickers who used to stay on the property. We'd have thirty-five people at lunch and parties every night. I used to have guys crawling out of my *cave* at three in the morning on all fours. But they'd be back in the vineyards to pick the next morning!"

Handpicking is now done only on a small scale in France, with machines doing most of the work. "Machines are good because they collect only the fruit, not the stalks," says Monsieur Colbois, "but it's no fun. It's just you and a machine and no one to talk to." Help is not as easy to find as it once was and seasonal hiring has become expensive. "It's very difficult for a family vineyard to compete with the big houses, but I don't envy them either, particularly those with *grand cru* vineyards where it's hand labor or nothing." But small vintners do compete and, in fact, make some of the best wines around.

To mark the end of the Burgundian harvest, which even with machines remains high-volume, high-pressure work, growers traditionally decorate their vans and tractors with boughs and drive through town honking their horns. Then producers and their families get together for the *paulée*, a festive banquet with abundant food and wine. The *vendange* may not be quite what it was in the old days, but wine-country merrymaking will never go out of style.

CHEFS: THE MOTHERS OF LYON

Women have long played a historic role in Lyonnais cooking. Some five hundred years ago, Erasmus wrote of how he was entertained at a Lyonnais inn by the mistress of the inn and her daughter: ". . . so splendidly and so cheap, that I was amaz'd at it. And then after Dinner we chatted away the time so merrily, that I thought myself still at home." Travelers in the 1830s enjoyed a similar experience with Mère Guy, who was noted for her triumphant *matelote* stew, made with fish fresh from the two major rivers that bisect Lyon, the Rhône and the Saône.

In the early twentieth century, one of the most celebrated Lyon cooks was Mère Fillioux, renowned for her Quenelles Nantua (page 80) with crayfish butter. I myself spent a day in the 1980s with Mère Léa, a stout old party who shopped daily in the outdoor market on the banks of the Saône, clearing her way through crowds of shoppers with the help of a bullhorn. The roll call culminates with Mère Brazier, her former restaurant still going strong and ranked "a venerable conservatory" of tradition by the Michelin guide. It is here that you find dishes like Bresse chicken poached in broth, and the meringue dessert called Oeufs à la Neige (page 324).

Are there any *mères* left? The Lyon tourist office is firm: "Women chefs we have, but no longer any *mères*." I beg to differ. I am convinced that the robust, homey cuisine epitomized by the women cooks of Lyon may be briefly in eclipse, but it is due for a comeback any day now.

CULINARY COMMENTATORS: COLETTE
(1873–1954)

France's beloved woman of letters, Colette, was as discriminating and exacting in her quest for perfect taste as she was for *le mot juste* in her memoirs and novels. She was brought up in a poor area of Burgundy and never lost her love of the countryside, despite becoming the most *parisienne* of Parisians. Food figures prominently in her sensuous fiction, and she excelled at describing the pleasures of the table, believing that even the most banal ingredient must be chosen with care and served in its best light. "Fruit tepid, water cold in the glass: this is the way water and fruit seem best," she wrote. No doubt her country upbringing influenced her appreciation of food served au naturel.

Famously, she once said, "Away with all this slicing, this dicing, this grating, this peeling of truffles! . . . eat it like the vegetable it is, hot and served in munificent quantities." I cannot help but add that she must have been referring to the Burgundy truffle, *Tuber uncinatum*, which in Colette's time, at least, was cheap and plentiful. Food had more depth for her than just taste. Like Proust with his madeleines, she found food intensely emotional: each bite became a way of savoring a place or a moment, past or present.

CUISSOT DE CHEVREUIL ALSACIENNE AUX POIRES

ALSATIAN ROAST LEG OF VENISON WITH PEARS

serves 6 to 8

Leg of venison (the haunch) is a glorious feast, the occasion to honor good friends. It always comes with a panoply of garnishes, like the roasted pears with red currant jelly popular in Alsace. The German taste for sweetness with meat spills over to this border region, hence the sweet-tart glaze of jelly and port wine. However, even the most desirable cuts of venison are not reliably tender. Too much depends on the age of the animal and its diet.

Many cooks soak cuissot de chevreuil in a wine marinade to tenderize it. I have found that the Alsatian custom of soaking venison in milk for one or two days has a similar effect without masking the delicate taste of the young meat. As with all roasted meats, venison tastes best if cooked just before serving. Traditional accompaniments are braised red cabbage, Marrons Caramelisés (page 235), and purées of seasonal vegetables, such as butternut squash, pumpkin, or celery root.

I BONE-IN HAUNCH (LEG) YOUNG VENISON (ABOUT 5 POUNDS/2.25 KG)

8 OUNCES/225 G PORK FATBACK, CUT INTO LARDONS (SEE PAGE 371)

2 QUARTS/2 LITERS MILK, MORE IF NEEDED

3 TABLESPOONS/45 G BUTTER

SALT AND PEPPER

2$^{1}/_{2}$ CUPS/625 ML VEAL BROTH (SEE PAGE 373)

$^{1}/_{4}$ CUP/60 ML PORT

RED CURRANT GLAZE

    2 TABLESPOONS/30 G BUTTER

    $^{1}/_{4}$ CUP/60 ML PORT

    2 TABLESPOONS RED CURRANT JELLY

PEARS

    4 TO 6 FIRM PEARS (ABOUT 2 POUNDS/900 G TOTAL) SUCH AS BOSC OR ANJOU

    2 TO 3 TABLESPOONS RED CURRANT JELLY

    I TO 2 TEASPOONS GROUND CINNAMON

    3 TABLESPOONS/45 G BUTTER, MORE FOR THE BAKING DISH

LARGE ROASTING PAN

Trim any skin from the venison, leaving any fat (the meat is naturally very lean). Poke holes in the meat with the point of a knife and insert lardons of fatback. If necessary, crack the shank bone with a cleaver so the leg will fit in a roasting pan. Put the meat in a deep bowl and pour in enough milk to cover it. Cover and refrigerate for 24 to 36 hours.

Heat the oven to 450°F/230°C. Drain the venison, discarding the milk, and pat the meat dry with paper towels. Lay it in the roasting pan. For the glaze, combine the butter, port, and red currant jelly in a saucepan over medium heat until melted. Pour it over the venison. Dot the glaze-coated meat with the butter and sprinkle with salt and pepper. Roast the venison for 15 minutes.

Meanwhile, prepare the pears. Butter a baking dish. Peel and halve the pears, scooping out the core and fibrous stem. Cut a thin slice from the rounded side of each half so that it sits flat. Spoon the red currant jelly into the hollow left by the cores, sprinkle the cut surface with cinnamon, and dot with the butter. Put the pears in the buttered baking dish and bake with the venison until tender.

Continue roasting the venison until it is cooked rare or faintly pink, to your taste, 45 minutes to an hour longer. The pears may take from 45 minutes to 1¼ hours, depending on the variety and ripeness. Turn the venison 2 or 3 times as it roasts, and baste it often with the pan juices, adding a little water if the glaze starts to scorch on the pan bottom. The venison is done when a skewer inserted in the center is warm to the touch when withdrawn after 30 seconds for rare meat, or hot to the touch if you prefer it well done. A thermometer should register 130°F/55°C for rare meat or 140°F/60°C for well done. (When very well done, venison is tough, even if the animal is young.) Transfer the meat to a platter, cover loosely with aluminum foil, and keep warm. If the pears are tender when pierced with a skewer, remove and keep them warm. If not, pour a little water over them, cover the dish with foil, and continue baking until done.

For the gravy, add the broth to the roasting pan, put on the stove top, and bring to a boil, stirring to dissolve the pan juices. Lower the heat to a simmer and cook until the liquid is concentrated, 10 to 15 minutes, adding juices from the pears when they are tender. Stir in the port, taste, and adjust the seasoning.

Arrange the pears around the venison. Strain the gravy into a bowl. Carve the venison (its structure is similar to a leg of lamb, so it is carved the same way) and serve. Pass the gravy at the table.

= BURGUNDY: THE BOUNTIFUL =

I have lived in Burgundy for more than twenty-five years, so it is hard not to be biased about its attractions: stretches of sunflowers, world-famous vineyards, bright fields of mustard and rape, patches of corn for cows, windblown wheat fields up on the plateau near my home. No wonder the food here is so good, as it has been for ages. In fact, Burgundy can justly claim to be the place where serious French eating began.

Starting in the fourteenth century, when Philip the Bold extended his Duchy north by marrying Marguerite of Flanders, the Burgundian empire covered a large swath of Europe and was itself a center for creative talent. In the next century, the reigning duke added a stupendous kitchen to his palace in Dijon, the better to serve his guests. Its ample construction featured a vaulted octagonal chamber with four vast stone fireplaces sharing a common flue, and prompted the gastronome Curnonsky (page 19) to exclaim, "Some have built a hearth in their kitchen, but the dukes of Burgundy, they made a kitchen in their hearth."

Today, Burgundy retains its reputation for good cooking (not to mention its thoroughbred Pinot Noir and Chardonnay wines). Dijon remains the capital of prepared mustard. The Morvan hills are famous for their aged hams. Charolles says the same for beef; the Charolais steer answers the modern demand for a high yield of lean meat, ideal for simmering, as in Boeuf Bourguignon (page 136). The same garnish of bacon, mushrooms, and red wine is also the foundation of the regional *sauce meurette* (page 41), designed to go with eggs, fish, and brains. I have even eaten snails, a top Burgundian first course, cooked, not in the usual garlic butter, but in *sauce meurette* flavored with tarragon.

Even the French aperitif hour owes much to Burgundy. Cheese puffs called Gougères (page 50) are ubiquitous, and *kir* is named for Canon Kir, World War II Resistance hero and mayor of Dijon. Traditionally, this aperitif mixes a tablespoon of *cassis* (black currant liqueur) with dry Aligoté wine, or with *crémant* (the local sparkling wine) for a *kir royale*. For a change, any liqueur can be substituted, including *mûre* (blackberry), *framboise* (raspberry), and, my favorite, *pêche de vigne* (wild peach).

Burgundians are hearty eaters, and a local meal without cheese is almost unthinkable, preferably a wedge of the region's smelly, marc-washed Époisses (see "The Stinky Cheeses," page 49). Fruit desserts are the favorite Burgundian finale. Depending on the season, it may be a *corniotte*, a three-cornered puff pastry filled with cherry compote; a red berry soup; black currant sorbet; or pears or peaches poached in wine. Sometimes a slice of the famous Burgundian gingerbread called Pain d'Épices (page 305) will appear alongside, though not in my house, where Pain d'Épices means breakfast.

RAGOÛT DE SANGLIER
DE LA FÔRET DE FONTAINEBLEAU

RAGOÛT OF WILD BOAR
WITH JUNIPER AND WILD MUSHROOMS

serves 8

*On one memorable occasion, I was treated to this fine ragoût from the for-
mer royal forest of Fontainebleau, where wild boar still roam less than
forty miles (sixty-four kilometers) from central Paris. With local cèpes and
a notable vintage Burgundy, it was the feast of feasts. The luxurious sauce
of the ragoût invites an accompaniment of puréed potatoes or Spaëtzli
(page 230). The more robust the red wine, the better—it is used for both
marinating and to make the sauce—so I would look for a Shiraz or well-
rounded Cabernet. This recipe can be adapted to all sorts of game, including venison, hare, pheasant, pigeon, and wild duck.*

3 POUNDS/1.35 KG BONELESS WILD BOAR MEAT

2 TABLESPOONS/30 G BUTTER

2 TABLESPOONS VEGETABLE OIL

2 TABLESPOONS/15 G FLOUR

SALT AND PEPPER

1 CUP/250 ML CRÈME FRAÎCHE (PAGE 374) OR
HEAVY CREAM

1 TABLESPOON CHOPPED FRESH PARSLEY
(OPTIONAL)

MARINADE

1 BOTTLE (750 ML) ROBUST RED WINE

2 ONIONS, QUARTERED

4 SHALLOTS (ABOUT 3 OUNCES/90 G TOTAL),
HALVED

3 GARLIC CLOVES

1 LEEK, WHITE AND GREEN PARTS, CUT INTO
SLICES 3/4 INCH/2 CM THICK (SEE PAGE 371)

2 CARROTS, SLICED

1 TABLESPOON JUNIPER BERRIES, CRUSHED

2 TABLESPOONS VEGETABLE OIL

WILD MUSHROOMS

1 1/2 POUNDS/625 G WILD MUSHROOMS

3 TABLESPOONS/45 ML VEGETABLE OIL

2 GARLIC CLOVES, CHOPPED

2 SHALLOTS, CHOPPED

Trim the wild boar of skin and membrane and cut it into 1½-inch/
4-cm cubes. For the marinade, combine the wine, onions, shallots,
garlic, leek, carrots, and juniper berries in a bowl large enough to

accommodate the boar; reserve the oil. Add the boar to the marinade, stir to mix well, and spoon the oil over the meat to keep it
moist. Cover and put in the refrigerator for at least 1 day and up
to 3 days, depending on the intensity of flavor you want.

Heat the oven to 325°F/160°C. Drain the meat, reserving the
marinade (both the liquid and the vegetables), and dry the cubes
on paper towels. Heat half of the butter and oil in a flameproof
casserole over medium heat. Working in batches, add the meat
cubes and brown them on all sides, taking 4 to 5 minutes. Using
a draining spoon, set them aside in a bowl. When all of the meat
cubes are browned, add the remaining oil and butter to the pan
over high heat. Add the vegetables from the marinade, lifting
them out of the wine with a draining spoon and continuing to
reserve the liquid. Fry the vegetables until they start to brown,
8 to 10 minutes. Stir in the flour and continue cooking, stirring
often, until it is brown, 2 to 3 minutes. Stir in the reserved wine,
bring to a boil, simmer for 5 minutes and skim. Replace the meat,
pushing the cubes down into the wine and vegetables. Add salt
and pepper and cover the pan. Cook in the oven until the meat
falls easily from a two-pronged fork and you can crush a cube
between your finger and thumb, 2 to 2½ hours. Stir from time to
time during cooking and add a little water if the pan gets dry.

When the boar is nearly done, prepare the mushrooms.
Clean them (see page 373) and halve or quarter them if they are
large. Heat the oil in a frying pan over medium heat. Add the
mushrooms, season with salt and pepper, and cook, stirring often,
until all the moisture they render has evaporated and they are very
tender, 12 to 20 minutes, depending on the type of mushroom.
Two minutes before the end of cooking, stir in the garlic and shallots and continue cooking until the fragrant. Taste and adjust the
seasoning and set the pan aside.

When the meat is done, lift it out of the casserole with a
draining spoon and pile it on top of the mushrooms in the frying pan. Strain the sauce into a bowl, pressing the vegetables to
extract all the liquid. Wipe out the casserole and put the meat
and mushrooms in it. Pour in the sauce, add the crème fraîche,
and heat gently, stirring often, until the ragoût just comes to a
boil. Taste and adjust the seasoning. The ragoût may be stored in
the refrigerator for up to 3 days and the flavor will mellow. It may
also be frozen for up to 3 months.

To serve, reheat the ragoût on the stove top if necessary. It
may be served directly from the casserole or transferred to a bowl.
Sprinkle with the parsley, if you like.

MEDAILLONS DE CHEVREUIL BORDELAISE

VENISON STEAK WITH RED WINE AND SHALLOT

serves 4

The very best venison steaks, which are cut from the loin meat along the backbone, are meltingly tender and juicy and are best left well alone. In the southwest and around Bordeaux, they are simply panfried and served with a red-wine reduction sauce and a shower of crunchy chopped raw shallot. Unbeatable! For the wine sauce, a Bordeaux blend containing plenty of fruity Merlot is ideal. Here's the place for your favorite steak accompaniment—for me a mound of skinny frites.

8 VENISON MEDALLIONS (ABOUT 1½ POUNDS/
675 G TOTAL)

SALT AND PEPPER

1 TABLESPOON VEGETABLE OIL

½ CUP/110 G COLD BUTTER, CUT INTO CUBES

1½ CUPS/375 ML FRUITY RED WINE

4 SHALLOTS (ABOUT 3 OUNCES/90 G TOTAL),
FINELY CHOPPED

Shortly before serving, season the medallions with salt and pepper. Heat the oil and 1 tablespoon of the butter in a large, heavy frying pan over high heat. Add the steaks and fry until browned, 1 to 2 minutes. Turn and brown the other side, 1 to 2 minutes longer for rare venison, 2 to 3 minutes for pink meat (if cooked to well done, the venison will be tough). When pressed with your fingertip, the steak should be firm around the edge and still soft in the center. Set the steaks aside and cover loosely with aluminum foil to keep warm.

For the sauce, add the wine to the pan and boil, stirring to dissolve the pan juices, until reduced to about 2 tablespoons of glaze, 2 to 3 minutes. Whisk in the cold butter a few pieces at a time, moving the pan on and off the heat so the butter softens and thickens the sauce without melting to oil. Taste and adjust the seasoning.

To finish, arrange 2 medallions, overlapping them, on each of 4 warmed plates. Spoon the sauce over the venison and scatter the shallots thickly on top. Serve at once.

LAPIN AUX PRUNEAUX EN COCOTTE

RABBIT AND PRUNE CASSEROLE

serves 4

I live next door to a woman who runs a thriving trade raising rabbits—dozens, indeed hundreds, of them. Since there are ten rabbits in an average litter, and a grown rabbit sells for three times the price of a farm chicken, it's no wonder they proliferate in backyard hutches. The most popular way to serve a plump rabbit, aside from roasting, is to simmer it with purple prunes, their sweetness accenting the mildly gamy flavor of the meat. Lacking a rabbit, chicken is an excellent substitute in this recipe. I am suggesting a red wine for the marinade and sauce, but a medium-dry white wine would do well, too. An accompaniment of noodles or mashed potatoes soaks up the sauce and contrasts nicely with the black prunes. The pits are normally left in the prunes so they do not fall apart.

MARINADE

2 CUPS/500 ML FRUITY RED WINE

1 BOUQUET GARNI (SEE PAGE 370)

1 ONION, COARSELY CHOPPED

1 CARROT, COARSELY CHOPPED

SALT AND PEPPER

1 RABBIT (ABOUT 3 POUNDS/1.35 KG), CUT INTO
PIECES (SEE PAGE 372)

1 TABLESPOON VEGETABLE OIL, MORE IF NEEDED

1 TABLESPOON/15 G BUTTER

2 TABLESPOONS/15 G FLOUR

1 CUP/250 ML VEAL OR CHICKEN BROTH
(SEE PAGE 373), MORE IF NEEDED

2 GARLIC CLOVES, CRUSHED

6 OUNCES/170 G PRUNES

1 TO 2 TABLESPOONS CHOPPED FRESH PARSLEY

For the marinade, combine the wine, bouquet garni, onion, carrot, salt and pepper in a large, deep bowl. Add the rabbit pieces and turn them until well coated. Cover and refrigerate for at least 3 hours and up to 24 hours, stirring occasionally.

Lift the rabbit out of the marinade and dry on paper towels. Reserve the marinade, and set aside the bouquet garni. Heat 1 tablespoon oil and the butter in a sauté pan or deep frying pan over medium heat. Add the rabbit pieces and brown on all sides, taking 10 to 12 minutes. Set aside.

continued

Lift the onion and carrot out of the marinade with a draining spoon. Add more oil to the pan if it is dry and heat over medium heat. Add the onion and carrot and sauté until soft, 5 to 7 minutes. Stir in the flour and cook, stirring, until browned, 2 to 3 minutes. Stir in the marinade, bring to a boil, lower the heat to a simmer, and simmer for 2 minutes. Add the broth, garlic, and bouquet garni and season with salt and pepper. Replace the rabbit pieces in the pan, cover, and simmer, stirring and turning them once or twice, for 30 minutes. Meanwhile, cover the prunes with boiling water and leave them to soak.

After the rabbit has cooked for 30 minutes, drain the prunes and stir them into the pan. If the sauce is thick, add a little more broth. Cover and continue simmering until the rabbit is tender and falls easily from a two-pronged fork, 10 to 20 minutes longer. Discard the bouquet garni, taste, and adjust the seasoning. There should be a balance of sweet prunes, fruity wine, and a hint of black pepper. The rabbit may be cooked 2 to 3 days ahead and kept in the refrigerator.

To serve, reheat the rabbit on the stove top if necessary. It may be served directly from the pan or transferred to a bowl; sprinkle it with the parsley.

LAPIN RÔTI À LA MOUTARDE
ROAST RABBIT WITH MUSTARD
serves 4

Everywhere in France, Dijon mustard, hot or mild, with or without seeds, is used as a quick seasoning sauce when grilling or roasting. In this Provençal recipe, the mustard is bolstered with chopped herbs and plenty of garlic. Roasted tomatoes are the natural accompaniment.

3 TABLESPOONS/45 ML OLIVE OIL, MORE FOR THE ROASTING PAN

6 TABLESPOONS/120 G DIJON MUSTARD

I RABBIT (ABOUT 3 POUNDS/1.35 KG), CUT INTO PIECES (SEE PAGE 372)

2 TABLESPOONS CHOPPED FRESH BASIL

I TABLESPOON CHOPPED FRESH OREGANO OR SAVORY

I TABLESPOON CHOPPED FRESH ROSEMARY

SALT AND PEPPER

10 GARLIC CLOVES, UNPEELED

BAKED TOMATOES

    2 LARGE TOMATOES

    2 TABLESPOONS OLIVE OIL, MORE FOR BAKING DISH

    3 TABLESPOONS BROWNED BREAD CRUMBS (SEE PAGE 373)

    I GARLIC CLOVE, FINELY CHOPPED

    I TABLESPOON CHOPPED FRESH PARSLEY

ONION JUS

    2 ONIONS, FINELY CHOPPED

    3/4 CUP/175 ML MEDIUM-DRY WHITE WINE

    2 TABLESPOONS CHOPPED FRESH PARSLEY

Heat the oven to 350°F/180°C. Oil a roasting pan. Mix the 3 tablespoons oil and mustard in a small bowl, and brush the rabbit pieces generously with the mixture, reserving some for basting them as they roast. Put the rabbit pieces in the prepared pan, and sprinkle them with more oil and the basil, oregano, rosemary, salt, and pepper. Roast the rabbit until tender and golden brown, 45 minutes to 1 hour, adding the garlic cloves after the first 15 minutes. During cooking, turn the pieces from time to time, brushing them with more mustard mixture so they are always moist. Take care not to overcook the rabbit pieces or they will be dry.

For the tomatoes, core them and cut them in half through the equator. Oil a small baking dish and add the tomatoes, cut side up. In a small bowl, mix together the oil, bread crumbs, garlic, parsley, salt, and pepper, stirring to make a crumbly mixture. Spread it on the tomatoes. Bake them in the oven with the rabbit. When the skins split after 12 to 15 minutes, showing the tomatoes are tender, remove them from the oven, set aside, and keep warm.

When the rabbit pieces are done, transfer them to a platter with the garlic cloves and cover with aluminum foil to keep warm. For the onion jus, add the onions to the roasting pan and fry on the stove top over medium heat, stirring often, until golden brown, 3 to 5 minutes. Add the wine and bring to a boil, stirring to dissolve the pan juices. Taste, adjust the seasoning, and spoon the onions with their jus over the rabbit.

To serve, arrange the tomatoes around the edge of the platter. I do not advise reheating roasted rabbit because it will dry out, but you can cook it 3 or 4 hours ahead of serving, as both it and the tomatoes are excellent at room temperature.

LAPIN RÔTI À LA MOUTARDE

= THE ELUSIVE TRUFFLE =

What contributes most to the mystique and value of truffles is not growing them, but *finding* them. Truffles grow in chalky ground a few inches down in a lattice of tree roots—usually oaks, but also chestnut, hazelnut, and hornbeam. In several countries producers are now "farming" truffles in plantations, with uncertain results. It takes the keen nose of a sow or a well-trained dog to detect "black gold," and even then truffles can be gathered only one by one. This intensive labor may, in part, explain why truffle production in France is not what it used to be. "Before World War I, the annual harvest ran to 1,800 tonnes in the Périgord alone," local truffle hunter François Beaucamp told me. "Today 200 tonnes for the whole of France is a good harvest."

The most sought-after French truffles today come from Périgord and Provence. Jet black and ranging from walnut to baseball in size, *Tuber melanosporum* has an unmistakable musky taste and, at its peak, an aroma pungent enough to knock you over. They're not to everyone's taste. The veined blackish summer truffles (*Tuber uncinatum*) that are found in Burgundy, Alsace, and the Savoy don't smell as strong and have less taste, but they are half the price and still pleasant shaved and eaten raw. There is no French equivalent to the rarer white truffles (*Tuber magnatum*) of Italy's Piedmont region.

The fine black-truffle season in France runs from November to March, and that's the best time to eat them. Put one overnight in a sealed container with a dozen raw eggs, and its perfume will have penetrated right through the shells by morning. Both winter and summer truffles are exquisite shaved (or chopped) and simply added to egg dishes, pasta, or salads. Their color is valued in sauces, sausages, pâtés, and terrines, truffled foie gras terrine being a particular extravagance.

Fresh truffles lose their aroma and taste after a few days. Once brushed clean, their lifespan can be lengthened for a week or two by preserving in fat, Cognac, or Madeira. Even better is to freeze truffles, but seal them carefully; otherwise their aroma will penetrate the contents of your freezer.

the
French Touch

RUSTIC
SAUCES

CHAPTER
No. 11

Each of these rustic sauces conveys a strong sense of place. Pistou (page 220), with its basil and Parmesan cheese, could come only from Provence, and Sauce au Vin Jaune et Morilles (facing page) personifies the Jura. Moving farther north, the sauces mute and their colors pale, reflecting the softer greens and grays of the landscape. The buttery delicacy of a Breton Beurre Blanc (page 221) is a far cry from the garlic-laden Aïoli (page 219) and the olive and anchovy Tapenade (page 221) of the Mediterranean.

These rustic creations exist a world away from a smart city kitchen, with its structured cuisine and classic mother sauces. A country cook draws on local ingredients that are tasty but cheap—herbs, wine, garlic, onion, shallot—and pulls them together with butter, cream, or olive oil. There are characteristic ways of making these sauces, of course, but often the cook adds a personal twist. Rouille is a good example. Based on egg yolks and olive oil spiced with chili, Rouille can be peaceful and mild or aggressively pungent, stiff enough to hold a spoon upright or dense but fluid, tingling with garlic or fiery red with tomato paste. Some cooks like to thicken it with bread crumbs, though not me.

In the countryside, a sauce may be coarsely chopped; a coulis (smooth purée) that clings to the spoon; or so thin as to be almost a jus. It all depends on the ingredients, the whim of the cook, even the weather. Who wants a delicate broth when the temperature outside is below zero? Boundaries are few and a "sauce" is often a matter of gathering together what is on hand. What counts with a rustic sauce is not its conformity or elegance, but its impact on the palate.

SAUCE AU VIN JAUNE ET MORILLES
MOREL SAUCE WITH YELLOW WINE
makes 1½ cups/375 ml sauce to serve 4

Vin Jaune, a straw yellow wine with a lingering, maderized bite reminiscent of a dry sherry, comes from the Jura region, which borders Switzerland. Combined with the intense little morel mushrooms that pop up in woods or orchards in the spring, it makes a silken sauce for roast chicken, veal, and venison that, once tasted, is never forgotten. The wine can be hard to find, however, and I have sometimes replaced it with a dry Chardonnay laced with two to three tablespoons dry sherry. As for the mushrooms, dried morels are an excellent alternative to fresh ones, though they do not come cheap. Fresh or dried cèpes do well in this sauce, too.

8 OUNCES/225 G FRESH MORELS, OR 1 OUNCE/30 G
DRIED MORELS

2 TABLESPOONS/30 G BUTTER

SALT AND PEPPER

½ CUP/125 ML FULL-BODIED VIN JAUNE

1¼ CUPS/300 ML CRÈME FRAÎCHE (PAGE 374) OR
HEAVY CREAM

1 TEASPOON POTATO STARCH, MIXED WITH
1 TABLESPOON COLD WATER

SQUEEZE OF FRESH LEMON JUICE, MORE TO TASTE

If using fresh morels, clean them (see page 373) and dry on paper towels. If using dried morels, rehydrate them (see page 373) and then drain, reserving the soaking water. Pour the water into a measuring cup, leaving any grit behind; there should be about ½ cup/125 ml.

Melt the butter in a saucepan over medium heat. Add the fresh or dried morels, sprinkle with salt and pepper, and sauté, stirring often, until tender, about 5 minutes. If using dried morels, add the reserved soaking liquid and continue cooking until it is absorbed, 15 to 20 minutes longer. Add the Vin Jaune to the fresh or dried morels and simmer until reduced by half. Stir in the crème fraîche and bring the sauce just back to a boil. Whisk in the potato starch paste; the sauce will thicken at once. Season to taste with the lemon juice, salt, and pepper. The sauce may be kept in the refrigerator for up to 1 day, and the flavor will intensify. Serve hot.

SAUCE BORDELAISE AU VIN ROUGE
SHALLOT SAUCE WITH RED WINE
makes 1¼ cups/300 ml to serve 4

You will find versions of this invaluable little sauce all around Bordeaux. It goes with almost any meat, from beef steak to lamb to pork chops to duck breast, as well as with such vegetables as celery root. Versatile indeed! A fruity red wine, such as a Merlot or a light Bordeaux blend, is best.

1 TABLESPOON/15 G BUTTER

4 SHALLOTS (ABOUT 3 OUNCES/90 G TOTAL), CHOPPED

SALT AND PEPPER

1½ CUPS/375 ML FRUITY RED WINE

1 TABLESPOON/7 G FLOUR

2 CUPS/500 ML VEAL BROTH (SEE PAGE 373)

1 TO 2 TABLESPOONS COLD BUTTER, CUT INTO CUBES

1 TEASPOON COGNAC (OPTIONAL)

Melt the butter in a saucepan over low heat. Add the shallots, season with salt and pepper, and press a piece of aluminum foil down on the shallots. Cover the pan and sweat the shallots over very low heat, stirring occasionally, until they are very soft but not brown, 10 to 12 minutes. Discard the foil, pour in the wine, and boil, stirring occasionally, until the shallots are nearly dry, 15 to 20 minutes.

Whisk in the flour and cook, stirring, for about 1 minute. Whisk in the broth and bring the sauce to a boil, stirring constantly until it thickens. Boil the sauce until it coats a spoon and is reduced by about half, 10 to 12 minutes longer.

Take the pan from the heat and whisk in the cold butter to enrich the sauce and mellow the flavor. Taste and adjust the seasoning, adding the Cognac if you like. This sauce keeps well in the refrigerator for up to 3 days. Reheat gently before serving.

SAUCE BORDELAISE À LA CRÈME
SHALLOT SAUCE WITH WHITE WINE AND CREAM

A cousin of Sauce Beurre Blanc (page 221), this cream sauce has none of the same tendency to separate but can be reheated again and again. Traditional with lobster and crayfish, it is also delicious with fish, veal, sweetbreads, and vegetables such as asparagus and artichokes.

In the recipe for Sauce Bordelaise au Vin Rouge, substitute a medium-dry white wine such as Sémillon for the red wine, and heavy cream for the veal broth. Omit the Cognac and season the sauce to taste with fresh lemon juice just before serving. Makes 1¼ cups/300 ml sauce to serve 4.

AÏOLI

GARLIC MAYONNAISE

makes 1 1/2 cups/375 ml sauce to serve 6 to 8

Aïoli, a pungent olive oil mayonnaise flavored with garlic, is remarkably good with grilled fish, and is traditionally served with the fish stew called Bourride (page 102). For the fullest flavor, the garlic should be pounded in a mortar with the egg yolks, though most cooks now compromise by chopping the garlic as finely as possible with a knife. Le Grand Aïoli is also the name for a substantial main dish of salt cod, hard-boiled eggs, and squid, possibly snails, and cooked vegetables such as carrots, potatoes, artichokes, and green beans, all accompanied by the Aïoli sauce.

2 EGG YOLKS

2 GARLIC CLOVES, VERY FINELY CHOPPED, MORE TO TASTE

I TABLESPOON FRESH LEMON JUICE, MORE TO TASTE

SALT AND WHITE PEPPER

I 1/2 CUPS/375 ML OLIVE OIL

SMALL MORTAR AND PESTLE (OPTIONAL)

If you have the mortar and pestle, put the egg yolks, garlic, lemon juice, salt, and pepper in the mortar and pound with the pestle until the mixture thickens lightly, about 1 minute. Pounding develops the flavor of the garlic. Gradually beat in the oil a few drops at a time until the aïoli starts to thicken and emulsify. After adding about 2 tablespoons of the oil, the mixture should be quite thick. Transfer the mixture to a small bowl and continue adding the remaining oil more quickly, pouring it in a very slow, thin stream while stirring constantly with a whisk or an immersion blender. (If added too quickly, the sauce may separate.) If you are not using a mortar and pestle, whisk the sauce in a bowl from the start.

Taste and adjust the seasoning with lemon juice, salt, pepper, and with more garlic if you wish. Traditionally, the sauce should be thick enough to hold a spoon upright. Like homemade mayonnaise, aïoli may be covered tightly and stored in the refrigerator for no more than 12 hours. At serving time, let it come to room temperature before you stir it or it may separate.

SAUCE ROUILLE

RED CHILI PEPPER MAYONNAISE

makes 1 cup/250 ml sauce to serve 6

Rouille means "rust," the color of this sauce powered with garlic and red chili and traditionally made in a mortar. I think of Sauce Rouille as Provençal, though it is popular all along the Mediterranean coast with grilled fish, hard-boiled eggs, and as the mandatory accompaniment to Bouillabaisse (page 99) and Soupe de Poissons Provençale (page 18).

I FRESH RED CHILI, MORE TO TASTE

4 TO 6 GARLIC CLOVES, FINELY CHOPPED

2 EGG YOLKS

SQUEEZE OF FRESH LEMON JUICE

SALT AND PEPPER

I CUP/250 ML OLIVE OIL

I TABLESPOON TOMATO PASTE, MORE IF NEEDED

I TABLESPOON RED WINE VINEGAR

SMALL MORTAR AND PESTLE (OPTIONAL)

Cut away the green stem end from the chili, split it lengthwise, discard the seeds, and chop finely with a knife. If you have the mortar and pestle, put the garlic, egg yolks, chili, lemon juice, salt, and pepper in the mortar and pound with the pestle until the mixture thickens lightly, about 1 minute. Pounding develops the flavor of the chili and garlic. Gradually beat in the oil a few drops at a time until the sauce starts to thicken and emulsify. After adding about 2 tablespoons of the oil, the mixture should be quite thick. Transfer it to a small bowl and continue adding the remaining oil more quickly, pouring it in a very slow, thin stream while stirring constantly with a whisk or an immersion blender. (If added too quickly, the sauce may separate.) If you are not using a mortar and pestle, whisk the sauce in a bowl from the start. Work in the tomato paste and vinegar, taste, and adjust the seasoning. The sauce may be covered tightly and stored in the refrigerator for no more than 12 hours. At serving time, let it come to room temperature before you stir it or it may separate.

clockwise from top:
SAUCE AILLADE, PISTOU,
SAUCE ROUILLE, AÏOLI

PISTOU

BASIL, PARMESAN, AND GARLIC SAUCE

makes 1½ cups/375 ml sauce to serve 6 to 8

*Sea links between Italy and France have always been so easy that it is no surprise to find similar recipes all along the coastline. Pistou, pesto in Italian, is an example (*pestare *means "to pound"). The sauce was once pounded in a mortar, and a food processor has much the same effect of bruising the garlic and herbs to intensify their taste. In southern France, Pistou is served with roast lamb, as a dip for crudités, and with pasta, as well as the flavoring for a famous soup (page 16).*

4 SMALL BUNCHES FRESH BASIL (ABOUT 4 OUNCES/
110 G TOTAL)

6 GARLIC CLOVES, CUT INTO PIECES

¼ CUP/30 G PINE NUTS

1 CUP/125 G GRATED PARMESAN CHEESE

¾ CUP/175 ML OLIVE OIL

SALT AND PEPPER

Strip the basil leaves from their stems and put the leaves in a food processor with the garlic, pine nuts, Parmesan cheese, and 3 tablespoons/45 ml of the olive oil. Pulse until very finely chopped, stopping to scrape down the sides of the bowl as necessary. With the blades running, work in the remaining oil, adding it very slowly so the sauce emulsifies and thickens. Season to taste with salt and pepper. The sauce may be refrigerated for 2 to 3 days. Let it come to room temperature and whisk well before serving.

SAUCE AILLADE

GARLIC AND WALNUT SAUCE

makes 1½ cups/375 ml sauce to serve 6 to 8

Ail means "garlic," as will be evident when you taste this sauce from Languedoc, an emulsion of walnuts and walnut oil with raw garlic and parsley. Serve it with duck breast, roast pork, or grilled vegetables.

1 CUP/125 G WALNUT PIECES

8 GARLIC CLOVES, CUT INTO PIECES

2 TABLESPOONS WATER

SALT AND PEPPER

1 CUP/250 ML WALNUT OIL

2 TABLESPOONS CHOPPED FRESH PARSLEY

Put the walnut pieces and garlic in a food processor and pulse until chopped, about 1 minute. Add the water and continue working to a paste, about 1 minute longer. Season with salt and pepper. With the blades running, add the oil a few drops at a time so an emulsion forms. After about 15 seconds, when the sauce starts to stiffen, add the remaining oil in a slow, steady stream. Work in the parsley, taste, and adjust the seasoning. The sauce will keep tightly covered in the refrigerator for up to 3 days.

RAITO

RED WINE SAUCE WITH HERBS AND OLIVES

makes 3 cups/750 ml sauce to serve 8

The ancient, dark flavors of Provençal sauces such as Tapenade and Raito probably came from the eastern Mediterranean. Raito is served with fried fish, squid, or octopus, and is traditional on Christmas Eve with salt cod. This zestful sauce demands a whole bottle of fruity red wine, possibly a Côtes de Provence, to pick up the herbal notes.

2 ONIONS

2 WHOLE CLOVES

¼ CUP/60 ML OLIVE OIL

1 TABLESPOON/7 G FLOUR

1 BOTTLE (750 ML) HEARTY RED WINE

2 CUPS/500 ML BOILING WATER

1 POUND/450 G TOMATOES, PEELED, SEEDED, AND
CHOPPED (SEE PAGE 372)

3 GARLIC CLOVES

¼ CUP/30 G WALNUT PIECES, CHOPPED

1 TEASPOON FENNEL SEEDS

SALT AND PEPPER

3 OR 4 SPRIGS FRESH THYME, ROSEMARY, AND PARSLEY

3 TABLESPOONS/35 G CAPERS, RINSED AND DRAINED

⅓ CUP/65 G SALTED (DRY-CURED) BLACK OLIVES,
PITTED

Peel both onions, stud 1 onion with the cloves, and finely chop the other. Heat the oil in a saucepan over medium heat. Add the chopped onion and sauté, stirring often, until browned, 5 to 7 minutes. Whisk in the flour and cook until bubbling. Stir in the wine, water, tomatoes, whole onion, garlic, walnuts, fennel seeds, pepper, and salt (the olives will add salt later). Tie the thyme, rosemary, and parsley sprigs in a bundle with kitchen string and add them to the pan. Bring the sauce to a boil and simmer uncovered, stirring occasionally, until reduced by two-thirds, 1 to 1½ hours.

Discard the whole onion and the bundle of herbs, and then purée the sauce in a food processor (and return it to the pan) or with an immersion blender. Stir in the capers, olives, and plenty of pepper; taste and adjust the seasoning. Raito will keep tightly covered in the refrigerator for up to 3 days, and the flavor will deepen. It may also be frozen for up to 3 months. Reheat it for serving.

TAPENADE
makes 1¼ cups/300 ml sauce to serve 6 to 8

Its stark black color and vibrant flavor have earned Tapenade a lasting place on contemporary tables. The essential elements are capers, black olives, and anchovy, with olive oil and a kick of lemon. The olives you use are important. I prefer mild, dry-cured olives that are not too salty, such as those from Nyons. Olives with pits tend to have a deeper flavor, so pitting them by hand is worth the effort. Old recipes sometimes used cooked tuna instead of bread to bind the puréed mixture. It cuts the saltiness of the anchovy well and I suggest it here.

Tapenade is encouragingly versatile: it can be spread on bread, served with cooked vegetables in the manner of mayonnaise, or used as a dip for crudités. Fish topped with Tapenade and baked in the oven wakes up your palate, calling out for a glass of chilled rosé wine.

3/4 CUP/150 G SALTED (DRY-CURED) BLACK OLIVES

6 ANCHOVY FILLETS, SOAKED IN A LITTLE MILK FOR 15 MINUTES

2 OUNCES/60 G CANNED TUNA IN WATER, DRAINED, OR 2 SLICES WHITE BREAD, CRUSTS DISCARDED

2 GARLIC CLOVES, CUT INTO PIECES

3 TABLESPOONS/20 G SLICED ALMONDS

1/4 CUP/45 G CAPERS, RINSED AND DRAINED

1/2 CUP/125 ML OLIVE OIL

JUICE OF 1/2 LEMON

PEPPER

Pit the olives; drain and coarsely chop the anchovies; flake the tuna or pull the bread into pieces. Put the olives, anchovies, tuna or bread, garlic, almonds, and capers in a food processor and pulse until coarsely chopped, 1 to 2 minutes. Add 2 tablespoons of the olive oil and work to a purée. With the blades running, gradually add the remaining olive oil in a slow, steady stream so the mixture emulsifies slightly. Season with the lemon juice and plenty of

freshly ground pepper, and transfer the sauce to a bowl. It will keep tightly covered in the refrigerator for a week or more, and the flavor will blend and mellow.

SAUCE BEURRE BLANC
WHITE BUTTER SAUCE
makes 1 cup/250 ml sauce to serve 4 to 6

It is hard to believe that only fifty years ago Sauce Beurre Blanc was scarcely known outside southern Brittany and the mouth of the Loire. It was brought to Paris by a woman chef, Mère Michel, who served the classic pike with Sauce Beurre Blanc at her restaurant. The sauce makes good use of regional ingredients: white Muscadet wine, shallots, and unsalted butter from the region of Charente.

3 TABLESPOONS/45 ML WHITE WINE VINEGAR

3 TABLESPOONS/45 ML DRY WHITE WINE

2 SHALLOTS, FINELY CHOPPED

I TABLESPOON CRÈME FRAÎCHE (PAGE 374) OR HEAVY CREAM

I CUP/225 G COLD BUTTER, CUT INTO CUBES

SALT AND PEPPER

In a small, heavy pan, combine the vinegar, wine, and shallots and boil to a glaze (see page 371). Add the crème fraîche and boil again to a glaze. Whisk in the butter a few pieces at a time, moving the pan on and off the heat so the butter softens and thickens the sauce without melting to oil. Work the sauce through a strainer, or leave in the shallots, if you prefer. Taste and adjust the seasoning with salt and pepper. The sauce may be kept warm for a few minutes on a rack over a pan of warm water or in a thermos, but it should be served as soon as possible.

SAUCE BEURRE ROUGE
RED BUTTER SAUCE

A mellow version of Beurre Blanc, this sauce is based on generous amounts of red wine. A Pinot Noir is memorable in Sauce Beurre Rouge, but a simple Gamay does fine, too. Serve the sauce with poached fish, eggs, or grilled chicken breast.

In the recipe for Sauce Beurre Blanc, substitute 1 cup/ 250 ml red wine for the white wine and white wine vinegar. Boil the red wine to a glaze with the shallots, and whisk in the butter as directed. Makes 1 cup/250 ml sauce to serve 4 to 6.

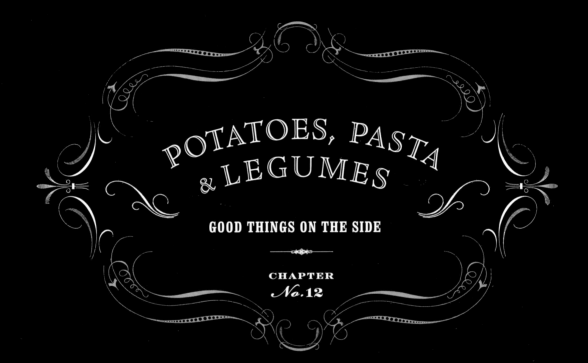

POTATOES, PASTA & LEGUMES

GOOD THINGS ON THE SIDE

CHAPTER
*No.*12

Potatoes, with bread, dominate the starch side of the French country table. It is hard to imagine a steak without frites, sausages without *pommes purée*, or duck or goose confit without crisply browned potatoes sautéed in the fat from the bird. I can tell where I am in France from the style of potatoes on my plate. The cheese and potato purée called Aligot (facing page) requires beating by a cook of muscular build,

such as you find in the Auvergne, and from the same region comes body-building Truffade (page 226), a potato cake laden with bacon and melted cheese, a poor man's version of truffled potatoes. Of course, potato dishes vary with the season, and much depends on whether the potatoes are waxy and new, or the last season's crop and hence drier and more floury. In a French supermarket, potatoes are sorted by their culinary properties, so that consumers know which ones to boil, purée, sauté, or deep-fry for frites.

In a few regions, notably in Alsace and the area around Nice, pasta is a popular alternative to potatoes, whether as noodles or in more ambitious layered or stuffed recipes, such as Ravioles (page 228), a take on Italian ravioli. Rice pops up on plates all over, particularly with fish, and has been grown for centuries in the Camargue, where the Rhône runs into the Mediterranean. In more remote rural areas, chestnuts persist as a starchy accompaniment; they were once an alternative staple to wheat in years of poor harvest. Oddly, corn grows well in much of France, but virtually all of it is fodder, and the idea

of serving corn on the cob has never caught on. "Corn is for animals," an old countryman said to me, shaking his head. But in the southwest, cornmeal may be added to bread, and appears as cornmeal mush under such names as *millas* and *broyé*.

Nowadays such dishes are thought of as sides and cooked only as a curiosity, but they were once staples, heavy puddings and pancakes intended to fill bellies. In Brittany, you may still come across *kig-ha-farz*, a buckwheat pudding wrapped in a cloth and simmered in a vast pot with stewing beef, oxtail, a ham hock, and plenty of root vegetables. *Mique*, another simmered pudding made with stale bread and sometimes with cornmeal, survives in the southwest. Other such dishes have disappeared: *l'omelette du pauvre* (poor man's omelet) from the Limousin was an unappetizing pancake of eggs watered down with milk and thickened with flour. The pork and bread crumb pancake from Toulouse called *matefaim* (hunger killer) says it all. Even within living memory, life in the countryside could be very close to the edge.

ALIGOT

POTATO AND CHEESE PURÉE

serves 6

If you ever make Aligot, you will never forget it. The combination of mashed potatoes and grated cheese, beaten over the heat for at least ten minutes so the cheese melts and then the whole finally softens to a purée that falls in ribbons from the spoon, would test a wrestler's muscles. Do not consider a handheld mixer, as the purée must be beaten by hand for the proper result. But I would advise lining up some help. This is not a light dish (though it is less dense than cheese fondue), but it is an excellent winter appetizer or accompaniment to a juicy steak. Aligot should be made with the famed Cantal cheese of the Auvergne, reminiscent of Cheddar (which can be substituted).

2 POUNDS/900 G BAKING POTATOES

SALT AND WHITE PEPPER

2 CUPS/500 ML CRÈME FRAÎCHE (PAGE 374) OR
HEAVY CREAM, MORE IF NEEDED

4 TABLESPOONS/60 G BUTTER

3¹/₂ CUPS/350 G GRATED CANTAL, GRUYÈRE, OR
WELL-AGED, SHARP CHEDDAR CHEESE

RICER OR POTATO MASHER

Peel the potatoes and cut each one into 2 or 3 uniform chunks so they will cook evenly. Put them in a pan of salted water to cover, top with a lid, and bring to a boil. Simmer until very tender when pierced with a knife, 15 to 20 minutes.

Drain the potatoes thoroughly and, while still hot, work them through the ricer into a heavy saucepan, or mash them in the saucepan with the potato masher. In a separate saucepan, bring the crème fraîche almost to a boil. Add the butter to the potatoes and beat with a wooden spoon over low heat until light and fluffy, 3 to 5 minutes. Without taking the pan from the heat, gradually beat in the hot crème fraîche. If you want to prepare Aligot ahead, stop at this point, spread the purée flat in the pan, pour a thin layer of crème fraîche on top, and leave the pan in a water bath (see page 373) to keep warm for up to 1 hour.

To finish, over medium heat, beat the cheese into the purée a handful at a time. Continue beating constantly with the wooden spoon until the mixture pulls from the sides of the pan and forms long ribbons when it falls from the spoon, 7 to 10 minutes. If it seems dry, add more crème fraîche. Add pepper, taste, and adjust the seasoning. Serve it at once, very hot from the pan, using scissors to cut it into ribbons onto each plate at the table. If left to stand, Aligot becomes very heavy.

GRATIN DAUPHINOIS

serves 6 to 8

Once tasted, never forgotten. In this superlative version of Gratin Dauphinois, the potatoes are simmered in milk, then cooked again, in cream this time, to inimitable melting softness (I use the leftover milk for soup.) I prefer this gratin quite plain, but a little bit of garlic can be rubbed in the dish before adding the potatoes and sprinkling them with genuine Gruyère. Using the authentic cheese makes all the difference, and you need only a small amount. Most important, be sure to use a floury baking potato. Gratin Dauphinois comes from the Dauphiné, just north of Provence; in faraway Normandy, cooks make a similar dish of sliced potatoes simmered in milk, blanquette de pommes de terre aux poireaux. It is flavored with leeks softened in a bit of butter; otherwise, the cooking is the same.

5 CUPS/1.25 LITERS MILK

2 POUNDS/900 G BAKING POTATOES

1¹/₂ CUPS/375 ML HEAVY CREAM

1¹/₂ CUPS/375 ML CRÈME FRAÎCHE (PAGE 374) OR
MORE HEAVY CREAM

SALT AND PEPPER

LARGE PINCH OF GRATED NUTMEG

BUTTER FOR THE BAKING DISH

³/₄ CUP/75 G GRATED GRUYÈRE CHEESE

8-BY-11-INCH/20-BY-28-CM BAKING DISH

Put the milk in a large saucepan. Peel the potatoes and cut them into slices ¼ inch/6 mm thick, preferably using a mandoline. Add them at once to the milk so they do not discolor. When all the potatoes are in the pan, bring to a boil, then simmer until almost tender, 15 to 20 minutes (potatoes take longer to cook in milk than in water). Stir often to prevent sticking.

Drain the potatoes and wipe out the pan. Return the potatoes to the pan with the heavy cream and crème fraîche. Season with salt, pepper, and nutmeg and bring just to a boil. Simmer, stirring occasionally, until very tender, 10 to 15 minutes. Do not let the potatoes boil, or the cream will curdle.

Butter the baking dish. Spread the potato mixture, which will be quite sloppy, in the prepared dish. Sprinkle the top with the cheese. Gratin Dauphinois may be prepared ahead and stored in the refrigerator for up to 2 days before continuing.

To finish, heat the oven to 350°F/180°C. Bake the gratin until piping hot throughout and browned on top, 25 to 30 minutes. Serve very hot!

LA TRUFFADE

POTATO CAKE WITH CHEESE AND BACON

serves 4

If you can't afford truffles, you indulge in Truffade, say the inhabitants of the Auvergne, notoriously among the coldest and most rugged areas of France. Often served with sausages, Truffade is a potato cake flavored with bacon and laden with cheese, a buttress against the worst weather. Nippy Cantal is the local hard cheese, and Gruyère may be substituted.

5-OUNCE/140-G PIECE LEAN BACON, CUT INTO
LARDONS (SEE PAGE 371)

2 TABLESPOONS/30 G LARD OR VEGETABLE OIL

2 POUNDS/900 G BAKING POTATOES, THINLY SLICED

SALT AND PEPPER

8 OUNCES/100 G CANTAL OR GRUYÈRE CHEESE,
DICED OR CUT INTO THIN, NARROW STRIPS

10-INCH/25-CM NONSTICK FRYING PAN

Heat the bacon lardons in a 10-inch/25-cm frying pan over medium heat until the fat runs, 2 to 3 minutes. Do not let them brown. Remove them with a draining spoon and set aside. Melt the lard in the pan, add the potatoes, and sprinkle them with pepper. The bacon may contribute enough salt. Reduce the heat to low, cover, and cook for 5 minutes. Stir in the lardons and continue to cook, uncovered, over low heat, tossing or stirring often, until the potatoes are tender and some are browned, 20 to 25 minutes. Don't worry if some of them are crushed, as they will help hold the mixture in a cake.

Stir in the cheese, taste, and adjust the seasoning. Press down on the potatoes to level them in the pan. Turn the heat to high and let them cook without stirring until the bottom is browned, 3 to 5 minutes. Press on the cake occasionally to hold it together. When done, it should be brown around the edges and starting to pull from the sides of the pan. Take the pan off the heat, run a knife around the edge to loosen the cake, and turn it out onto a warmed platter. Serve hot.

POMMES SARLADAISE

SAUTÉED POTATOES WITH GOOSE OR DUCK FAT

serves 3 or 4

The town of Sarlat in Périgord is renowned for its market selling truffles, foie gras, and confit of goose and duck. Potatoes fried in the confit fat are a local specialty, either flavored with truffles or, more economically, with garlic and herbs and called "poor man's Pommes Sarladaise." The potatoes are the traditional accompaniment to the confit itself, or will temptingly dress up your favorite steak. Look for goose fat in specialty-food stores.

2 POUNDS/900 G BAKING POTATOES

5 TABLESPOONS/75 G CONFIT FAT OR GOOSE OR
DUCK FAT

SALT AND PEPPER

1 FRESH OR CANNED TRUFFLE OR 3 GARLIC
CLOVES, CHOPPED

3 TABLESPOONS CHOPPED FRESH PARSLEY

Peel the potatoes and slice about ¼ inch/6 mm thick. Melt the fat in a large sauté pan or frying pan over medium heat. Add the potatoes with salt and pepper (take care if you are using confit fat, as it will add salt) and sauté, stirring once or twice, until nearly tender and starting to brown, 12 to 15 minutes.

Stir in the truffle (or the garlic for a poor man's version) and parsley and leave them without stirring until the undersides are brown, 5 to 7 minutes. Stir once, taste, and adjust the seasoning. Continue sautéing until the undersides are again very brown, 5 to 7 minutes more. If the potatoes are not brown enough, repeat the stirring and browning once more. Loosen the potatoes from the pan, pile them in a serving dish, and serve very hot.

LA TRUFFADE

RAVIOLES NIÇOISES

STUFFED PASTA WITH TOMATO COULIS

makes 90 to 100 ravioles to serve 8 to 10
as a main course

Ravioles, the ravioli look-alikes from around Nice near the Italian border, have recently migrated to most parts of France and grown outsize at the same time. I am skeptical about the current fad for giant ravioles, three to a portion, which are quick to shape but tricky to cook without losing the stuffing. Far more tempting are these originals, little cushions that are squares or half-moons, with comforting fillings of coarsely chopped cooked vegetables, or perhaps some meat left over from the Sunday roast, bound with a bit of gravy. I have made two filling suggestions here, with a tomato coulis for topping. Ravioles are good as a first course or main dish, and this recipe makes enough to feed a big family.

2 CUPS/500 ML FILLING OF CHOICE (RECIPES FOLLOW)

I CUP/125 G GRATED PARMESAN CHEESE

PÂTE À PÂTES FRAÎCHES

3¹/₂ CUPS/450 G FLOUR, MORE AS NEEDED

4 EGGS

I TEASPOON SALT

TOMATO COULIS

3 POUNDS/1.35 KG TOMATOES, PEELED, SEEDED, AND
CHOPPED (SEE PAGE 372)

SALT AND PEPPER

5 TABLESPOONS CHOPPED MIXED FRESH HERBS
SUCH AS THYME, OREGANO, AND PARSLEY

JUICE OF I LEMON

6 TABLESPOONS/90 ML WALNUT OIL

PASTA MACHINE, WOODEN DOWEL, LARGE PASTRY TUBE

First, choose a filling, make it, and set it aside. Make and knead the pâte à pâtes fraîches (see page 375). When the dough is smooth, continue rolling, tightening the rollers one notch each time and ending with the narrowest setting. If necessary, lightly dust the dough with flour to keep it from sticking to the rollers. Hang the strip in an airy place, and repeat with remaining pieces of dough.

Cut 1 strip of dough crosswise in half, set one-half aside, and lay the other piece on a work surface. Brush it lightly with water and put teaspoonfuls of the filling on the dough in rows at 2-inch/5-cm intervals, using about one-third of the filling. Lightly brush the other strip of dough with water and set it, wet side down, on the first. Using a small wooden dowel, press gently between each row of mounds to seal them in neat squares. To seal

the filling, press firmly around each mound with the upturned (wide) end of a large pastry tube. Cut the dough into squares with a fluted pastry wheel or a knife. Transfer the ravioles to a floured tray (do not let them touch one another). Set them aside while shaping the remaining dough and filling. Store the ravioles, uncovered, in the refrigerator for up to 3 hours. To keep them longer, arrange them in layers on parchment paper and freeze, then pack them into plastic bags and freeze for up to 1 month.

To finish, make the coulis. Put the tomatoes in a strainer and season lightly with salt and pepper. Leave for 20 minutes to drain excess liquid. Transfer the tomatoes to a saucepan and stir in the herbs, lemon juice, and oil. Taste, adjust the seasoning, and leave the saucepan over very low heat so the coulis warms to tepid.

Meanwhile, bring a very large pot of salted water to a boil. Add the ravioles and poach them just below a simmer. Cook until the pasta is tender but still firm (al dente) and the filling is hot, 3 to 4 minutes. Do not let them boil or overcook or they will burst. Drain the ravioles and pile them in a warmed deep serving dish. Top with the coulis and sprinkle with some of the grated Parmesan. Pass the rest of the cheese at the table.

FILLINGS FOR RAVIOLES

CREAM CHEESE AND HERBS: When filled with fresh cheese, ravioles are typical of the Dauphiné, the alpine region north of Provence known for its cows and rich milk. Soft goat's milk cheese may be substituted for cow's milk cheese.

Crush 1½ cups/330 g soft fresh cheese in a bowl with a fork. Work in 1½ cups/150 g grated Gruyère cheese, 3 tablespoons each chopped fresh chives and parsley, and plenty of pepper. Taste and adjust the seasoning. Stir in 1 egg to bind the filling. Makes 2 cups filling.

MEAT AND ONION: Any cooked meat is good in this filling. In Provence, leftover Daube (page 139) is popular, or you may use ham or chicken.

Finely chop 8 ounces/225 g cooked meat. Melt 3 tablespoons/ 45 g butter over medium heat. Add 2 small onions, finely chopped, and sauté until lightly browned, 3 to 5 minutes. Stir in 3 garlic cloves, chopped, and 3 tablespoons chopped fresh parsley and continue cooking for 2 minutes. Stir the meat into the onion mixture and add 3 to 4 tablespoons gravy or beef broth (see page 373) to bind it lightly. Taste and adjust the seasoning, adding a spoonful or two of Cognac or Madeira if the filling tastes bland. Makes 2 cups filling.

AUVERGNE: LA FRANCE PROFONDE

The cooking of the Auvergne is not for picky eaters. Historically a poor region, the inhabitants were long considered the most miserable in all of France. As one local cookbook says, "In calamitous times, we ate—when we had it—barley bread, as black as old leather." Many Bugnats (as the natives were called) migrated to Paris to work as cooks and servers, and a Café Bugnat is still to be found on a few street corners. First railways and then motor cars helped to bring the Auvergne out of the isolation of the high plateaus and mountains of central France, and now you can get most of the way there by highway.

Still, the Auvergne retains its wild landscape, and a cuisine to match. I remember stopping the car once on a road near Laguiole, where the pastures crest like ski slopes, to listen to what I can only describe as a dramatic silence, broken by the distant bells hung from the necks of grazing cattle. The local tawny Aubrac animals are not particularly good for milk or meat, but they are valuable because, like goats, they can survive on meager pastures. Reddish Salers cattle, named for a small Auvergnat town, are better known for their milk, most destined for cheese. The Auvergne is an outstanding cheese region, particularly famous for its blues, and also for Cantal, often paired with potatoes in the local cooking. Other staples of mountain life are dry-cured raw ham (*jambon d'Auvergne*) and dried sausages. Throughout France you will find an Auvergnat, dressed for the part in a floppy hat, doing charcuterie business at a market stand.

This is a region of simple fare, with few sauces and garnishes. The Auvergnats like soups, particularly based on cabbage, as in *oulade*, made with lard and other vegetables. Potée Auvergnate is a stew with pork sausage, potatoes, carrots, and cabbage, and there are countless savory puddings, including *pounti* or *picaussel* made from ground pork, ham, and bacon baked with green leaves and aromatics. Another local specialty is *grattons*, crisp pork cracklings that feature in *brioche aux grattons*, an egg-enriched bread for serving with aperitifs. Salt cod (page 78) has long been a staple in these mountain fastnesses in such dishes as *stoficado*, poached salt cod with potatoes, crushed with hot walnut oil, butter, garlic, parsley, eggs, and crème fraîche.

Lentilles du Puy, the region's famous tiny deep green lentils, also known as the caviar of the poor, are served with lightly salted ham pork shoulder (page 172), or on a bed of endives and walnuts. Walnuts, cracked two by two in the palm of the hand, come with aperitifs, or are tossed by the generous handful into salads already swathed in a walnut oil dressing. At a friend's house I was served cold roast beef with mayonnaise, made entirely of walnut oil (delicious!).

The cooking of the Auvergne unquestionably boasts a sense of place. And if you have just come in from a hike in the mountains or are looking out a window at a world buried in snow, robust dishes like *tripous* (mutton tripe and veal tied into packets and braised) or roasted game with a fricassée of mushrooms from the forest sound just right. Don't worry about eating too much. Your excess will be nothing the local mineral waters (see "Still and Sparkling Water," page 239) or a stop in the spa town of Vichy can't cure.

SPAËTZLI

serves 6 to 8

Half curly noodle, half dumpling—the name of this Alsatian specialty is untranslatable. Spaëtzli are quicker to make than fresh pasta, and equally versatile, taking well to any treatment that suits shells, bows, fusilli, and other absorbent pasta. They are often served with meat or game stews and other dishes with a rich sauce. In Alsace, a special press resembling a ricer with large holes is sold for Spaëtzli, but it is equally common for cooks to slice the dough in slivers, as here. For serving, they may be tossed in a tablespoon or two of fat or fried in more generous amounts until golden brown. In Alsace, goose fat would be the first choice, followed by butter.

$3^{1}/_{2}$ CUPS/450 G FLOUR, MORE FOR SHAPING

I TEASPOON SALT

2 EGGS, BEATEN TO MIX

I CUP/250 ML WATER, MORE IF NEEDED

2 TABLESPOONS/30 G GOOSE FAT OR BUTTER, MORE TO TASTE

PEPPER

For the dough, sift the flour with the salt onto a work surface and make a well in the center. Add the eggs and water to the well and mix them briefly with your fingertips. Gradually draw in the flour with your finger to make moist crumbs, adding more water if necessary. Press the crumbs together in a ball. The dough should be somewhat floppy, softer than for pasta, but not sticky. Put it in a bowl, cover, and chill for 30 minutes.

Bring a large pot of salted water almost to a boil. Generously flour the work surface. Divide the dough in half. Pat out one-half with your fist into a strip about 2 inches/5 cm wide and ⅜ inch/ 1 cm thick. Using a pastry scraper or large knife, cut it crosswise into the narrowest possible slivers and put them on a floured tray. Drop the slivers from the tray into the very hot water. The spaëtzli should not be crowded, so you may need to cook them in several batches. Simmer them until they rise to the surface and are just tender, 4 to 6 minutes. They will curl as they cook.

Meanwhile, cut the remaining dough into slivers. Heat the goose fat in a large saucepan, or in a large frying pan if you want to brown them. Lift the cooked spaëtzli out of the water with a draining spoon and drop them into the warm goose fat. Cook the remaining spaëtzli and add them to the fat. Stir to coat the spaëtzli with the fat, sprinkle with pepper, taste, and adjust the seasoning. If you prefer your spaëtzli browned, keep frying them over medium heat for 5 to 7 minutes. Transfer the spaëtzli to a warmed bowl and serve.

TOTELOTS

WARM PASTA SALAD WITH EGGS AND HERBS

serves 3 or 4 as a main course

The contemporary habit of tossing fresh pasta with vinaigrette to make a warm salad is familiar in Alsace, where squares of pasta are seasoned with shallots, garlic, and a shower of fresh parsley and then topped with rounds of hard-boiled egg. When you are short of time, the same colorful mix is good with ready-made dried pasta, such as wide noodles. In Alsace, this salad is served as an appetizer.

PÂTE À PÂTES FRAÎCHES

$2^{1}/_{2}$ CUPS/300 G FLOUR, MORE AS NEEDED

3 EGGS

I TEASPOON SALT

VINAIGRETTE

3 TABLESPOONS/45 ML VEGETABLE OIL

I TABLESPOON WHITE WINE VINEGAR

$^{1}/_{4}$ CUP/60 ML CRÈME FRAÎCHE (PAGE 374) OR SOUR CREAM

2 SHALLOTS, FINELY CHOPPED

I GARLIC CLOVE, CHOPPED

2 TABLESPOONS CHOPPED FRESH PARSLEY

SALT AND PEPPER

3 HARD-BOILED EGGS, SLICED

PASTA MACHINE

Make and knead the pâte à pâtes fraîches (see page 375). When the dough is smooth, continue rolling, tightening the rollers one notch each time and ending with the second-narrowest setting. If necessary, lightly dust the dough with flour to keep it from sticking to the rollers. Hang the strip in an airy place, and repeat with remaining pieces of dough.

Lay the dough strips on a work surface and cut each strip into 1-inch/2.5-cm squares with a large knife. Toss the squares in flour and spread them on a tray lined with a floured dry dish towel. Leave them to dry until firm, 30 minutes to 1 hour, depending on the humidity of the kitchen. They may be covered with a second dry towel and stored in the refrigerator for up to 2 days.

For the vinaigrette, in a large bowl, whisk together the oil, vinegar, crème fraîche, shallots, garlic, parsley, and salt and pepper until smooth and slightly thickened, 1 to 2 minutes.

To cook the pasta, bring a large pot of salted water to a boil, add the squares, and cook until they rise to the surface, 1 to 2 minutes. The pasta should be tender but still chewy (al dente). Drain, rinse rapidly under hot water to wash away the starch, and drain thoroughly.

To finish, add the pasta to the vinaigrette and toss to mix. Taste and adjust the seasoning. Pile the salad in a warmed bowl and decorate with the egg slices. Serve at once while still warm. If left to stand, the salad will be heavy.

PILAF DE RIZ TRADITIONEL AU FENOUIL

TRADITIONAL RICE PILAF WITH FENNEL

serves 4

In the Camargue, the delta of the Rhône River, the brilliant green of rice fields contrasts discordantly with the shimmering salt pans and black windbreaks of cypress trees. Rice has been grown here since medieval times, adding variety to the typically Mediterranean local dishes. Spices and aromatic herbs, such as rosemary, bay leaf, thyme, and oregano, are favorite flavorings. This pilaf is fragrant with fennel and saffron, a winning combination.

3 TABLESPOONS/45 ML OLIVE OIL

I FENNEL BULB (ABOUT 8 OUNCES/225 G), TRIMMED AND THINLY SLICED

I ONION, THINLY SLICED

SALT AND PEPPER

I^1/$_4$ CUPS/250 G LONG-GRAIN RICE

I TEASPOON FENNEL SEEDS

3 GARLIC CLOVES, CHOPPED

I CUP/250 ML DRY WHITE WINE

^{3}/$_4$ CUP/175 ML VEAL OR CHICKEN BROTH (SEE PAGE 373) OR WATER

LARGE PINCH OF SAFFRON THREADS, SOAKED IN 2 TO 3 TABLESPOONS BOILING WATER

4 TO 5 TABLESPOONS CHOPPED FRESH PARSLEY

Heat the oil in a sauté pan over low heat. Stir in the fennel, onion, salt, and pepper. Cover and cook, stirring occasionally, until the vegetables are tender but not brown, 15 to 20 minutes. Stir in the rice and fennel seeds, increase the heat to high, and cook, stirring constantly, until the grains are opaque, 2 to 3 minutes. Stir in the garlic, wine, broth, and the saffron and its liquid. Cover, bring to a boil, and then simmer until all the liquid is absorbed, 16 to 18 minutes.

Let the pilaf stand, off the heat, for 5 minutes without stirring, then uncover and sprinkle with the parsley. Stir the rice with a fork so as not to break up the grains, taste, and adjust the seasoning, then serve. The pilaf may be cooked up to 2 days ahead and stored in the refrigerator. Warm it over low heat on top of the stove, adding the parsley just before serving.

POISCHICHADE

CHICKPEA DIP

makes 2 cups/500 ml purée to serve 6 to 8

Poischichade is a Provençal take on popular Arab dips like hummus and eggplant caviar, and, like hummus, calls for chickpeas (otherwise known as garbanzo beans). Let's face it, no one bothers to cook them from scratch anymore, and instead most people just grab a can. Using precooked peas, this purée takes only a few minutes to make. Sweet with bell pepper and warm with chili, it makes an unusual dip for pita bread or accompaniment for grilled Merguez sausages (page 181).

I LARGE RED BELL PEPPER

TWO 15-OUNCE/420-G CANS CHICKPEAS, DRAINED AND RINSED

I TABLESPOON GROUND CUMIN

2 TEASPOONS SALT

^{1}/$_2$ TEASPOON CAYENNE PEPPER

JUICE OF I LEMON

2 TABLESPOONS OLIVE OIL, MORE IF NEEDED

PAPRIKA, FOR SPRINKLING

To peel the pepper, heat the broiler. Broil the pepper about 3 inches/7.5 cm from the heat, turning the pepper once or twice, until the skin is blistered and black, 10 to 12 minutes. Wrap the pepper loosely in plastic wrap and let cool for 5 minutes. Unwrap and then peel it and discard the core and seeds. Cut the flesh into pieces.

Combine the pepper pieces, chickpeas, cumin, salt, cayenne pepper, lemon juice, and oil in a food processor. Purée until smooth, adding more oil if necessary to make a firm yet moist paste. Taste and adjust the seasoning. Pile the poischichade in a bowl, sprinkle with the paprika, and serve. It also keeps well in an airtight container in the refrigerator for at least a week.

═ FOOD FÊTES AND FESTIVALS ═

Everywhere in the world, celebration implies food, but in France like nowhere else food also implies celebration. Year-round all over the country, there are festivals, large and small, whose entire *raison d'être* is to mark the changing seasons and enjoy some good eating. In March in Bellegarde, near Orléans, the locals whoop it up over goat by banqueting on roast kid and chèvre; in September, the town of Arleux draws forty thousand visitors with the aroma of their local smoked garlic; and violets are the star of February festivities in Toulouse, where the flower finds its way into chocolates, jams, and liqueurs. I can't begin to count the cheese festivals, nor the fêtes around everyday dishes, such as the strawberry tart fair in Corrèze or the pâté festival in Lorraine.

It makes sense to celebrate the peak season of produce, but what amazes me is that even country towns lacking a food specialty find a way to invent one. The most obscure fair I ever attended was a *festival de tartines*, literally a "toast festival." It took place on an autumnal Sunday afternoon in one of those five-houses-and-one-church hamlets in Burgundy. People had driven from miles, all for a solitary stand where local ladies spread your choice of pâté or homemade jam onto a piece of toast and hand it to you with a glass of rough red wine.

Not all festivals are for food alone, of course, but food always has a strong presence. The Christmas markets all over Alsace are a case in point. I found a charming example at Obernai, not far from Strasbourg. As I strolled past the stands, wrapped in my woollies and chewing the head off a gingerbread man, I thought to myself, "They're very cheerful, these fêtes, but what a lot of work!" For some, it means shifting from leg to leg for twelve hours a day in the freezing cold just to sell a few jars of honey or some home-smoked pork hocks. It is nice from a community standpoint, but it can't make much money. I asked local chef Dominique Bellusso as he cooked Spaëtzli over a single burner: "What brings you back here year after year?" He gave me an odd look, as if my mind was wandering. "It's fun!" he exclaimed.

The biggest upscale food fair I ever attended in France was, not surprisingly, in Paris. Called Salon Saveur, it was a sort of country affair as well, and timed for the Christmas season. Almost four hundred artisans and producers from every region had come to show their wares for four days. Amid a babble of regional accents, large crowds made their way from stall to stall, sampling olives, jams, fish stews, noodles, cheeses, nuts, cider, and more and stocking up on edible gifts for the holidays. It was a marvelous way to get an overview of local produce. Rising incomes have not swept away regional specialties; on the contrary, *produits du terroir* are valued more than ever.

= THE SCENT OF CHESTNUTS =

In winter, nothing kindles the spirit like the smell of roasting chestnuts in the street. In French provincial towns, the nuts are often sold hot in newspaper cones, a tempting sight that is hard to resist. The *chataigne*, the wild chestnut tree, with its prickly green edible fruits, is a common sight in French forests and along country lanes. Until recent times, wild chestnuts were commonly ground to make flour for bread and porridge, or boiled or grilled to eat with soup, particularly in poorer areas like the Cévennes, Périgord, Brittany, and Corsica. Spread on slatted shelves and smoked dry in special barns, the chestnuts would keep almost indefinitely.

Chataignes are not commonly sold commercially; the other type of chestnut, the *marron*, is the one we all know. Fatter and firmer than *chataignes*, *marrons* are easy to find in French supermarkets, either frozen, ready-peeled and vacuum-packed in jars, canned whole in water, or as sweetened or unsweetened purée (*crème de marrons*). The best grow in the Ardèche to the west of the Rhône Valley and are destined for the exclusive candy called *marrons glacés*. The chestnuts are shelled, peeled, and then poached in hot vanilla syrup until they take on a melting consistency. At least half fall apart en route. Once cooled, they are coated with a clear and shiny sugar glaze—and sold at an exorbitant price. No wonder!

LES HARICOTS DES VENDANGEURS

WINE PICKERS' BEANS WITH RED WINE

serves 6

My son Simon picked grapes for the harvest in Beaujolais one year and came back brown as a walnut, with fabulous stories of gargantuan breakfasts in the morning and equally large suppers at the end of the day. Kidney beans, and plenty of them, were standard fare, laced with quantities of garlic, a slab of bacon, and red wine, the cheapest ingredient of all in that abundant wine country.

1 POUND/450 G DRIED RED OR WHITE KIDNEY BEANS

6-OUNCE/170-G PIECE LEAN BACON

1 ONION, STUCK WITH 1 WHOLE CLOVE

1 LARGE BOUQUET GARNI (SEE PAGE 370)

6 TO 8 GARLIC CLOVES

SALT AND PEPPER

2 QUARTS/2 LITERS WATER, MORE AS NEEDED

1¹/₂ CUPS/375 ML ROBUST RED WINE

Cover the beans generously with cold water and leave them to soak overnight. The next day, heat the oven to 325°F/160°C. If the bacon includes rind, cut it off and put it on the bottom of a bean pot or casserole. Drain the beans, add them to the pot, and bury the bacon and onion in them. Add the bouquet garni and garlic, season with pepper, pour in the water, and cover the pot. Bake the beans until they are very soft, 2 to 4 hours, depending on the type and age of the beans. Check them from time to time and add more water if needed to keep them covered. Traditionally, beans are done if the skins of one or two burst when you blow on a spoonful. By then, the cooking liquid should have evaporated and the beans should be moist but not soupy. If there is a lot of liquid remaining, remove the lid toward the end of cooking.

When the beans are tender, stir in the wine and season with salt and pepper. (If the wine or salt are added earlier, the skins will be tough.) Cover the beans and leave them to cool for about an hour so they absorb much of the wine. Then take out the bacon, dice it, and stir it back into the beans. Do the same with the onion, discarding the clove. Scoop out the bacon rind, if using, dice it, and stir it in as well. Taste and adjust the seasoning before serving. The beans will keep well in the refrigerator for up to 2 days. Reheat them in the oven, or on the stove top if you have a flameproof bean pot or casserole.

MARRONS CARAMELISÉS

CARAMELISED CHESTNUTS

serves 4 to 6

Even better than toasted chestnuts in their jackets are whole peeled chestnuts glazed with goose fat and just a little sugar, so they are tender and deliciously toasted on the surface. Happily chestnuts coincide with the cool-weather holidays and game season; they are perfect with roast turkey, goose, and almost any game, including venison, wild boar, and pheasant. Whole peeled steamed chestnuts are available in jars, but they tend to fall apart when you try to glaze them, even though they are still delicious. For the best results, I urge you to devote the time needed to peel fresh ones.

1¹/₂ POUNDS/675 G FRESH CHESTNUTS

6 TABLESPOONS/90 G GOOSE FAT OR BUTTER

1 ONION, THINLY SLICED

SALT AND PEPPER

2 TABLESPOONS/30 G SUGAR

¹/₄ CUP/60 ML VEAL OR CHICKEN BROTH (SEE PAGE 373) OR WATER

Peel the chestnuts (see page 371). Melt half of the goose fat over medium heat in a frying pan large enough to take all the chestnuts in a single layer. Add the onion, salt, and pepper and fry, stirring often, until golden brown, 7 to 10 minutes. Transfer the onion to a bowl and set it aside. Heat the remaining fat in the pan, add the chestnuts, and shake the pan so they are coated with the fat. Sprinkle with the sugar, salt, and pepper and shake the pan again to coat them. Add the broth, cover, and cook over very low heat, stirring often, until the chestnuts are nearly tender, 20 to 30 minutes.

Uncover the pan, increase the heat to high, and continue cooking, shaking the pan often so the sugar caramelizes and the chestnuts brown evenly, 12 to 15 minutes. When they are very brown and tender, stir in the cooked onion. Taste and adjust the seasoning. The chestnuts may be cooked up to 2 days ahead and refrigerated. Reheat them on the stove top.

GALETTES BRETONNES AU SARRASIN

BRETON BUCKWHEAT GALETTES

*makes twelve 12-inch/30-cm or twenty-four
7-inch/18-cm galettes to serve 6*

The filling for a paper-thin Breton galette is always simple. The most popular, called a complet, *includes ham and egg and often a spoonful of fresh cheese. You can ask for the egg to be* brouillé, *briskly scrambled on the hot galette, or* miroir, *left untouched to bake on top. When the galette is pleated, the golden egg yolk peeps out of the crisp brown folds. One galette is a modest serving; most people eat two, sometimes even three. (If you use the smaller crêpe pan when making this recipe, four galettes is an average serving.) They go down well indeed with a pitcher of the local demi-sec cider.*

1³/₄ CUPS/225 G BUCKWHEAT FLOUR

1³/₄ CUPS/225 G UNBLEACHED WHITE FLOUR

2 TEASPOONS SALT

2 CUPS/500 ML MILK, MORE IF NEEDED

2 CUPS/500 ML WATER

¹/₂ CUP/110 G BUTTER, CLARIFIED (SEE PAGE 371)

FILLINGS (RECIPES FOLLOW)

12-INCH/30-CM FLAT, ROUND GRIDDLE PAN
OR 7-INCH/18-CM CRÊPE PAN (SEE PAGE 376)

For the batter, sift the 2 flours into a bowl and add the salt. Make a well in the center and pour 1 cup/250 ml of the milk into the well. Whisk the milk into the flour, forming a smooth paste. Whisk well for 1 minute, then add the remaining 1 cup milk in 2 batches, stirring well after each addition. Cover and let the batter rest at room temperature for 30 to 40 minutes. Stir in the water and beat again for 1 minute. If necessary, beat in more milk until the batter is the consistency of light cream. Stir in half of the clarified butter.

Warm the griddle pan or crêpe pan over medium heat until very hot, at least 5 minutes. Dip a wad of paper towel into the remaining butter and rub it over the griddle. Heat the griddle 2 minutes longer, then test the heat with a few drops of batter; they should set at once. Wipe the griddle clean with the paper towel wad, and then rub it again with butter. Ladle batter onto the center of the hot griddle pan. Using a palette knife or pastry scraper, spread it with a turn of your wrist so the griddle is thinly and completely covered, tipping the griddle to discard excess batter into a bowl. Cook the galette quickly until lightly browned on the bottom, 30 to 60 seconds. Peel the galette off the griddle and

flip it to color the other side. Note that a galette should not be browned too much, as it will be reheated with the filling. Transfer it to a plate.

If the first galette seems heavy, thin the batter with a little milk. Continue to cook the galettes, wiping the griddle clean with paper towels and rubbing it with butter as necessary to prevent sticking. Pile the finished galettes on top of one another to keep them warm. They may be tightly wrapped and stored in the refrigerator for up to 3 days or frozen for up to 3 months.

FILLINGS FOR GALETTES

GALETTE À L'OEUF (EGG GALETTE): Heat the griddle for at least 5 minutes, then rub it with clarified butter. Spread a galette on the griddle, browner side down. Break an egg in the center. For a scrambled egg: Quickly mix and spread the egg over the galette with a spatula, leaving a border at the edge. Sprinkle with salt and pepper and leave over the heat just long enough to cook the egg slightly, about 30 seconds. Fold in the edges of the galette on 4 sides to make a square with a gap in the center showing the egg. Slide it onto a warmed plate, top with a pat of salted butter, and serve hot. For an unbroken egg: Spread only the egg white on the galette and leave the yolk whole. When the egg yolk is starting to set, fold the galette up around the yolk so it is still visible, and slide the galette onto a warmed plate. Serve at once.

GALETTE AU FROMAGE (CHEESE GALETTE): Heat the griddle for at least 5 minutes, and then rub it with clarified butter. Spread a galette on the griddle, browner side down. Brush it lightly with butter and sprinkle with 2 tablespoons grated Gruyère cheese. Leave for a few seconds to heat the galette and melt the cheese, and then fold the galette as for the egg galette and slide it onto a warmed plate. Serve at once.

GALETTE AU JAMBON (HAM GALETTE): Heat the griddle for at least 5 minutes, then rub it with clarified butter. Spread a galette on the griddle, browner side down. Brush lightly with melted butter and spread a thin slice of cooked ham in the center. Leave for a few seconds to heat the galette and the ham, and then fold the galette as for the egg galette. Top it with a pat of butter, and slide it onto a warmed plate. Serve at once.

= GALETTES AND CRÊPES, THE BRETON HEAVENLY TWINS =

The divide between galettes and crêpes is part of Breton culture. A crêpe is made with white wheat flour and has a sweet filling, while a galette is savory and the batter should include some buckwheat flour. Known in French as *blé noir* or *sarassin*, buckwheat is not a wheat at all, and is instead a relative of rhubarb. In the old days, cooks had to rely on buckwheat flour because the thin soil and windy climate of Brittany did not support cereals such as wheat. The plump, misshapen buckwheat grains look like brown couscous and do not contain enough gluten to make yeast-raised breads. However, buckwheat flour makes excellent flat galettes.

Galette is an all-purpose term meaning any round thin cake or pastry. In Brittany, galettes are paper-thin, traditionally cooked on a hot griddle called a *pillig* and smoothed with a special wooden rake, or *rozell*. Much practice is needed to develop just the right flick of the wrist that spreads an even, light-as-lace coating over the whole twelve-inch (thirty-centimeter) griddle surface. I have never mastered the knack, so I use a standard crêpe pan, with a pastry scraper to spread the batter. Crêpes, using white wheat flour, are much easier to make. They are smaller than galettes and often simply rolled to eat as a snack on the run. Fillings are minimal, a sprinkling of sugar and fresh lemon juice, a spoonful of honey or jam, or Nutella, the popular chocolate and hazelnut spread.

Some cooks make their batter with milk, which turns galettes or crêpes golden, while others use water, so they are slightly crispier but grayish. Crêpes are held together with egg, but galettes, one expert told me, are lighter and thinner with no egg at all. Disagreement does not stop there. "These crêpes are so thin, so light, I wonder how some cooks do it!" I overheard a white-haired Breton matron observe as she gazed admiringly at her plate. "No, no, that's not right," replied her sister, setting down her mug of cider. "Galettes should be thicker and moister. These have no substance or taste!"

= STILL AND SPARKLING WATER =

Mineral water has always held a major place in the French diet (Louis XIV had his fine-bubbled favorite, Chateldon, shipped from central France to Versailles), but never has the bottled water market been exploited as it is today. Provincial cities have followed the lead of the metropolis in opening trendy water bars where clients taste a range of waters, just like wine. Mineral water has taken lessons from the wine industry, capitalizing on the concept of *terroir*, dreaming up clever labels, adopting a tasting vocabulary. Even though tap water often tastes as good as bottled, the French are not deterred from lugging home crates of mineral water.

There are two general categories of bottled water: *plate* (still), and *gazeuse* or *pétillante* (bubbly or sparkling). Most comes from the French Alps and the Massif Central, although Perrier, the best-known international label, surfaces on the western edges of Provence. With its trademark bright green, pear-shaped bottle and big, tingly bubbles, it is commonly served as an aperitif on lemon and ice, and widely used to dilute whiskies and the like. Sparkling Badoît, with a higher mineral content, has a finer, fizzy feel in the mouth, and bills itself as the matchless table water. Vittel and Contrexeville are high-mineral still waters, both marketing themselves as champions against obesity. Low in minerals with a pure, neutral taste are Volvic, from the Auvergne, and Evian from the French part of Lake Geneva, both ideal thirst quenchers.

Health is traditionally the key selling point for mineral waters, and Vichy is one of a number of resorts in France centered on mineral springs. Indeed, the word *spa* comes from a northern town (now in Belgium) where the fashion for what the French still call *cures* took off in the 1700s. Vichy water is said to be particularly good for the digestion; depending on whether you buy Vichy-Célestins, Vichy Saint-Yorre, or plain old Vichy, results may vary. Recently other marketing strategies have emerged in the mineral water business. The bottle for one of the latest brands on the market, a Corsican water called Saint-Georges, was designed by Philippe Starck. Chateldon water is once more the ultimate chic, available only in grand restaurants and specialty shops. One bottle is the price of a decent bottle of wine.

= CHEFS: FERNAND POINT, FATHER OF A REVOLUTION =
(1897–1955)

The duty of a good cook is to transmit everything he has learned and experienced to the next generation.

Fernand Point was the outstanding teacher and mentor of his time. He trained such culinary greats as Paul Bocuse, Alain Chapel, and Jean and Pierre Troisgros, who later together consolidated Point's philosophy and principles to create nouvelle cuisine. Point's keen interest in regional cooking, his preference for shorter cooking times, and his unwavering search for simplicity, a principle that to his mind was the hardest thing to achieve in cooking, all helped to establish the movement.

La Pyramide, Point's restaurant in the town of Vienne, south of Lyon, was a legend in its day, and so was the man. Tall, rotund, and bighearted, Point loved his clients. He was the first chef to leave the kitchen and circulate in the dining room, a practice previously unheard of. To ensure a perfect dining occasion, Point refused to serve more than fifty guests an evening. What further set him apart was his ferocious criticism of the food of his time. Although a master of classical cooking, he was not a conformist; he wanted to push cuisine forward. He believed in using the freshest ingredients; hence, he insisted on daily shopping and short menus. In fact, his own menus never had more than twenty entries and were handwritten every day. "Every morning, we start again at zero," he used to tell his apprentices, and he meant it.

POTATOES, PASTA & LEGUMES—GOOD THINGS ON THE SIDE

Tucked away in the south of France is a cozy, blue kitchen with a simple wooden table in the center and a door leading quietly out to a back garden. The walls are covered in hanging antique objects—egg beaters, ladles, a *mezzaluna*, pewter pans (all in perpetual use)—and shelves are crammed with vintage china and colorful pottery bowls (the ones with the cracks and chips have the most character). There is a wide gas stove, and a radiator with a saucer of clementine zests drying on top. It is one of the most welcoming kitchens I have ever seen—and some of the most welcoming food you can imagine comes out of it.

"It's the most important room in the house," says Martine Labro. "We're in here all the time." In such a magical room with so many aromas, tastes, and things to look at, it is no wonder. "Beauty is important in a kitchen," Martine insists. "I can't cook anything in an ugly pot. And I can't stand machines. I do everything by hand—with a mortar and pestle, a knife, a whisk—it's so much more sensual. Once someone thought they were doing me a big favor by giving me one of those electric choppers. I marched it right back to the shop unopened."

Martine exemplifies everything most of us dream a French home cook should be. "If I don't know what to make for dinner, five minutes in the market and I'll have ten ideas," Martine tells me. Her other favorite supplier is her own kitchen garden, where she grows a few vegetables and countless herbs, including five different kinds each of thyme and basil, tarragon, chives, bay, rosemary, coriander, marjoram, savory, parsley, and chervil. "I can't grow dill," Martine sighs. "The climate won't allow it. Such a disappointment!" She is proud, too, of her citrus trees: lemons, Meyer lemons, and bitter oranges. "Without lemons and fresh herbs I couldn't cook," says Martine. "I'd be completely lost."

When I bring up the wealth of exotic ingredients available in France now, Martine hesitates. "We have so many wonderful ingredients of our own, I prefer to work with them. I find if I get into exotic stuff, I scatter and my cooking becomes shallow. Every once in a while I experiment with a new taste," she admits. "But one at a time, not eight, and I work it into recipes that are already tried-and-true. For me, the exotic is a little twist. I have no use for fusion

cooking." She has even less for the supermarket. "I go to the supermarket for toilet paper," Martine says, narrowing her eyes. "There is no place that makes me lose my appetite faster. It leaves me cold."

With the best French ingredients she can find as her base and a palate of herbs, spices, oils, vinegars, and citrus to flavor them, Martine approaches her cooking like a perfumer, tasting and sniffing, adding pinches and drops of this and that. "My food is never complicated," she says, "but it does have a certain complexity of taste. For example, to dry tomatoes, I lay them on fig leaves to give them a faint and mysterious extra scent." For one of her special salads of mixed greens and vegetables, she concocts a dressing of four different oils, three vinegars, and a secret blend of garden herbs. "I'm a very instinctive cook," says Martine. "I cook with my senses."

There is another telltale sign of a French home cook: the lack of cookbooks. It is almost impossible to get a recipe out of Martine. "I never measure, so I don't know," she says, shrugging her shoulders. "The dishes are in my fingers, not my head." She does, however, have what she calls her "little red cookbook," a notebook started years ago with her recipes written on the right-hand page, and a mess of comments on the left from the many times she has made each one. Of course, she alone can translate those scribbles into her rich, moist rabbit and artichoke sauté, her pasta with mullet roe, her citrus zest tart, or her cured duck breast (right now one is dangling from a string in the cool, dark vestibule behind her kitchen door).

It has never occurred to Martine to cook professionally. Although she often entertains—"No more than six at a table, if I can help it"—her favorite cooking is for her husband and her daughter, Camille. "I cook best for family," she says. "I love the intimacy of our little dinners and the beauty of being able to cook last-minute dishes. That way we can taste things as soon as they leap out of the pan into our plates. You can't do that for crowds. Besides, I am paralyzed by speed," she admits. "I can't bear to be rushed or interrupted. Some people think I spend way too much time in this kitchen, but I tell them that it's no different from an artist in her studio. I like it in here."

VEGETABLES

A COLORFUL CROP

CHAPTER
No. 13

**U**ntil I lived in France, I did not realize the importance of vegetables in family meals. Two or three colorful sides routinely appear with the main meats, while the appetizer may be a vegetable gratin in winter or a simple vegetable salad come summertime. French country cooks are also masters of transforming garden produce into complete meals. Cabbage may be stuffed with sausage, chestnuts, onions, carrots, and bread crumbs, making a few ingredients serve a crowd. In the north, cooks braise Belgian endives and then wrap them in ham and bake them in a rich cream sauce. In the south, Ratatouille (page 261) features half a dozen Mediterranean vegetables baked together with wild herbs and sweet local garlic, substantial enough to be a main dish on a hot July day.

Nowhere are vegetables valued more than along the Mediterranean in Provence and Languedoc, where something is bound to be ready for picking in the garden year-round. Vegetables may be molded, as in Papeton d'Aubergines (page 260), or stuffed, as in Tomates Farcies au Fromage de Chèvre (page 273). Rarely are vegetables just boiled and plopped on the plate plain (not surprisingly, the French term for that is *à l'anglaise*). Even an attractive serving dish helps lift a vegetable stew from routine to remarkable, the most popular being a regional *tian* (ramekin) of earthenware for individual servings and a colorful casserole—flame red is the best seller of all time— for family-style presentation.

I have been further educated by living next to a 350-year-old vegetable garden looked after by a countryman of the old school (see "Portrait of a *Potager*," page 251). Week by week his produce reflects the seasons and the weather. When asparagus ends, that is it until next year. There never seem to be enough green peas, or tiny cherry tomatoes that are sweet as candy. Each season of the garden brings a new surprise. We think we will never see the end of green beans, then suddenly arrive plums, and next come Brussels sprouts. Over the years I have learned that mature vegetables may be tough, but they have more taste than young ones when simmered gently together until meltingly tender. The Soupe au Pistou (page 16) and Cousinat vegetable stew from Bayonne (page 265) are good examples.

Our local farmers' market opens wider horizons, and you can always tell the time of year just from the display. When the first baby onions appear, for instance, it must be April. Rumpled golden *girolle* mushrooms herald autumn and fly off the open stands in the first hour of trade. For such treasures, the best recipes are so simple that they hardly need writing down. I think of the first baby carrots and onions, glazed in butter with a sprinkling of sugar, and sturdy butternut squashes thinly sliced to roast flat on a baking sheet and spiked with herbs and brushed with oil. As the country garden changes, so does the good cook's kitchen.

LES CRUDITÉS D'ÉTÉ

RAW SUMMER SALADS

serves 4 or 5

Throughout France, a combination of salads of raw vegetables (crudités) is the happy start to eating on a hot day. The plate will include at least three vegetables of contrasting colors and textures, each one cut to retain its character and dressed with vinaigrette. Cucumber, for example, is sliced and salted so it wilts while still retaining crispness. Tomato is sliced crosswise to show the seeds, allowing its juices to blend with the dressing spooned over it. Carrot is grated into a bracing, crunchy mound.

Alternatives to these three basics include diced cooked beets (a winter choice), Olives Marinées (recipe follows), and Céleri Remoulade (page 246). That's about it, a narrow but reassuring choice. Some cooks may include a hard-boiled egg or a couple of shrimp, but for me a salade de crudités *is vegetable only. The dressing, however, is a matter of choice, and may involve a local walnut oil (my favorite), a fruity fresh-pressed olive oil, or a respectable wine vinegar. The same basic dressing is used for each vegetable, with an individual seasoning of herbs, citrus, or spices, again to your taste.*

VINAIGRETTE

¼ CUP/60 ML RED WINE OR OTHER MILD VINEGAR

I TEASPOON DIJON MUSTARD

SALT AND PEPPER

¾ CUP/175 ML NUT, OLIVE, OR VEGETABLE OIL

3 LARGE CARROTS (ABOUT 9 OUNCES/250 G TOTAL)

I CUCUMBER

3 TOMATOES (ABOUT I POUND/450 G TOTAL)

2 TABLESPOONS SHREDDED FRESH BASIL

2 TABLESPOONS CHOPPED FRESH MINT

For the vinaigrette, whisk together the vinegar, mustard, salt, and pepper in a small bowl until the salt dissolves. Gradually whisk in the oil so the dressing emulsifies and thickens slightly. Taste and adjust the seasoning.

Coarsely grate the carrots on a box grater. Put them in a bowl and toss with about one-third of the vinaigrette, setting the rest aside. Taste and adjust the seasoning of the carrots. The flavor will mellow if the carrots are left to marinate for at least 12 hours.

Shortly before serving, peel the cucumber, leaving thin, decorative stripes of the dark green peel. Thinly slice the cucumber, preferably using a mandoline. Spread the slices on a plate, sprinkle with salt, and leave for 15 to 20 minutes to draw out the juices.

Core the tomatoes and slice them into rounds, cutting through the equator. Discard the top and bottom slices and arrange the remaining slices, overlapping them, on one side of 4 plates. Sprinkle the tomatoes with salt and pepper and spoon over half of the remaining vinaigrette. Pile the grated carrots beside the tomatoes, leaving room for the cucumber.

Rinse the cucumber in a colander, drain well, and toss with the remaining vinaigrette. Taste, adjust the seasoning, and add the salad to the plates. You can prepare all of the crudités an hour or so ahead and chill them in the refrigerator. However, they are best arranged on the plates just before serving, so the dressing does not pool on the plates. At the last minute, sprinkle the tomatoes with the basil and the cucumbers with the mint.

OLIVES MARINÉES

MARINATED OLIVES

In well-tended French kitchens, you often see jars of olives marinating in olive oil with herbs, citrus zest, and perhaps a hot chili or two. The mix is arbitrary—herbal or spicy; green olives, black olives, or both—so the olives become very much a personal specialty. Here is an herbal combination I enjoy.

Combine 1 cup/250 ml olive oil; 2 sprigs each fresh thyme and rosemary; 2 dried bay leaves; 2 garlic cloves, finely chopped; some freshly ground black pepper, and a pinch of red pepper flakes in a saucepan over low heat. When the oil just simmers, remove it from the heat, stir, and leave to cool to room temperature. Taste and adjust the flavorings. Put 1½ pounds/675 g brined olives in a jar and pour the oil over them; they should be fully immersed. Allow them to cool completely, then cover and keep in a cool place for at least 1 week and for up to 2 weeks. Lift out the olives with a draining spoon for serving. The leftover oil is excellent for grilling, or you can keep the batch going by adding more olives to top it up. Makes about 1 quart/1 liter olives.

CÉLERI REMOULADE

CELERY ROOT IN MUSTARD MAYONNAISE

serves 6 to 8

*The knobbly celery roots that appear in French farmers' markets in the fall are the basis for Céleri Remoulade, one of the most famous French salads. In my opinion, there is no better way to dress this chewy, rather off-putting root than with a mustard mayonnaise (*sauce remoulade*), which turns the salad a stunning creamy white. (Some cooks add grated carrot for color, but I don't approve.) Make the salad at least 8 hours ahead if you can, as both the flavor and texture will improve. You may substitute about 1 cup/250 ml good-quality bottled mayonnaise for this olive oil version.*

MAYONNAISE À LA MOUTARDE

2 EGG YOLKS

SALT AND PEPPER

2 TABLESPOONS FRESH LEMON JUICE, MORE TO TASTE

2 TABLESPOONS DIJON MUSTARD, MORE TO TASTE

3/4 CUP/175 ML OLIVE OIL

1 CELERY ROOT (ABOUT 1 1/2 POUNDS/675 G)

Make the mayonnaise à la moutarde (see page 374). The seasoning should be quite pungent. With a chef's knife, cut the thick peel from the celery root and quarter or cut the root into eighths. Slice the pieces into julienne using a food processor. Alternatively, cut the strips by hand: thinly slice the pieces using a mandoline, then stack the slices and cut them into the thinnest possible strips using a chef's knife. As soon as the strips are cut, stir them into the mayonnaise so they do not discolor. When all are added, taste and adjust the seasoning of the salad, adding more lemon or mustard to your taste, as well as salt and pepper. The celery root will be quite chewy at first, but if you keep the salad in the refrigerator for at least 8 hours or up to 2 days, it will soften and mellow.

POIREAUX VINAIGRETTE

LEEKS VINAIGRETTE

serves 4 to 6

Leeks are sturdy, surviving all winter through hard frost. Marinated in vinaigrette, with some chopped hard-boiled egg to pick up the color, they are a popular appetizer all over France. They are best served slightly warm.

6 LEEKS (ABOUT 2 POUNDS/900 G TOTAL), BOTH WHITE AND GREEN PARTS

SALT

2 SHALLOTS, FINELY CHOPPED

1 TABLESPOON CHOPPED FRESH PARSLEY

2 HARD-BOILED EGGS, FINELY CHOPPED

VINAIGRETTE

2 TABLESPOONS WHITE WINE OR CIDER VINEGAR

1/2 TEASPOON DIJON MUSTARD

SALT AND PEPPER

1/2 CUP/125 ML VEGETABLE OIL

Trim and clean the leeks (see page 371). Reshape the leeks, divide into 2 even-sized bundles, and then tie each bundle with string, using 2 loops on each bundle. Bring a large pan of salted water to a boil, add the leeks, and simmer, uncovered, until they are very tender when poked with the point of a knife, 15 to 20 minutes (leeks should always be thoroughly cooked). Drain, rinse with warm water, and drain again thoroughly. Discard the strings and cut the leeks into 2- to 3-inch/5- to 7.5-cm lengths. Pile them on a platter or individual plates, arranging them on the diagonal, and cover to keep warm.

For the vinaigrette, whisk together the vinegar, mustard, salt, and pepper in a small bowl for 30 seconds to dissolve the salt. Gradually whisk in the oil so the dressing emulsifies and thickens slightly.

Whisk the shallots and parsley into the vinaigrette, taste, and adjust the seasoning. Spoon the dressing over the center of the leeks, leaving the ends uncoated. Sprinkle with the eggs, and serve warm or at room temperature. The leeks may be cooked and the vinaigrette made several hours ahead. Add the shallot and parsley to the vinaigrette and assemble the dish just before serving.

clockwise from top:
CHAMPIGNONS À LA GRECQUE,
POIREAUX VINAIGRETTE,
CÉLERI REMOULADE

= TRADITIONAL SALADS =

The simplicity of many of the recipes in this chapter may come as a surprise. Salads tend to be a sideline in the French countryside, something spontaneous to be enjoyed with the fresh vegetables of the moment. This doesn't mean salads don't matter. In fact, it is a rare summer meal that does not include one or two, or even a cool main-dish salad when the sun is high. There is scarcely a bistro menu that lacks crudités, for example, cold raw salads of tomato, cucumber, carrot, beet, celery root, or button mushroom dressed with vinaigrette.

Other first-course salads may feature greens, summer lettuce with a scattering of Roquefort cheese and walnuts, or with a spoonful of sautéed wild mushrooms, warm from the pan. In winter, hot bacon salad can be the perfect way to tame chewy, slightly bitter greens, such as escarole and frisée. In fact, almost anywhere in France you can recognize the season just by looking at whatever salad vegetables appear on your plate. The light pickle called *à la grecque* can be adapted in spring to baby artichokes and onions, in summer to zucchini and fennel, in winter to roots, and year-round to mushrooms.

Some salads have distinctly regional connections. Around Lyon, poached garlic sausage is served as an appetizer with warm potatoes dressed with vinaigrette. The grouping of beets, endive, mâche (lamb's lettuce), and walnuts is typical of northern regions such as Picardy and Lorraine. In Provence, many vegetable recipes are served at room temperature, in effect a salad; among them are Ratatouille (page 261) and Tian de Courgettes (page 262).

Only a few appetizer salads have expanded to become a main dish. One pioneer must be Salade Niçoise (page 253), which dates back at least to the early 1900s and Escoffier's *Le Guide Culinaire*. It was not until the 1970s, and nouvelle cuisine, that main-course salads commonly appeared on the table. Today, you will find substantial plates of chicken wings and gizzards *en confit*, or croûtes of toasted goat cheese on a bed of greens. And remember that the concept of what constitutes a main dish varies. You and I might find Oeufs Mayonnaise (page 45) or Marée de Petits Calamars et Crevettes (page 92) satisfying as a light lunch, but you won't sell that to a Frenchman born and bred in the countryside.

CHAMPIGNONS À LA GRECQUE

MEDITERRANEAN MARINATED MUSHROOMS

serves 6 as a first course

Marinated vegetable salads are a boon in hot weather, as they keep for a day or two, with the flavor improving all the time. Take the Mediterranean à la grecque preparation: a touch of tomato, wine, fresh lemon juice, olive oil, coriander seeds, and herbs. What could be more propitious? What's more, the same treatment suits a variety of vegetables, such as quartered baby artichokes, thickly sliced fennel, or florets of cauliflower or broccoli. Simply vary the cooking time. Country cooks like to see what they are getting, so they leave seeds, peppercorns, and herbs loose when serving, but you can tie them in cheesecloth to remove them later if you prefer.

1/4 CUP/60 ML OLIVE OIL

15 TO 18 BABY ONIONS OR SHALLOTS (ABOUT 8 OUNCES/225 G TOTAL)

1 POUND/450 G BUTTON MUSHROOMS, TRIMMED AND QUARTERED

1 TABLESPOON TOMATO PASTE

2 TOMATOES, PEELED, SEEDED, AND CHOPPED (SEE PAGE 372)

1 CUP/250 ML MEDIUM-DRY WHITE WINE

1 CUP/250 ML WATER

JUICE OF 1 LEMON

2 TABLESPOONS CORIANDER SEEDS

2 TEASPOONS PEPPERCORNS

2 DRIED BAY LEAVES

2 SPRIGS FRESH THYME

SALT

1 TABLESPOON CHOPPED FRESH DILL

1 TABLESPOON CHOPPED FRESH PARSLEY

Heat the oil in a large sauté pan or deep frying pan over medium heat. Add the onions and sauté until browned, 5 to 7 minutes. Add the mushrooms and stir in the tomato paste, tomatoes, wine, water, lemon juice, coriander seeds, peppercorns, bay leaves, thyme, and salt. Bring the mixture to a boil and simmer uncovered, stirring often, until the onions and mushrooms are tender, 20 to 30 minutes.

At the end of cooking, the liquid should just cover the vegetables. If there is too much, boil it for a few minutes to reduce it. Stir in the dill and parsley and let the vegetables cool. Taste and adjust the seasoning of the marinade. Serve the mushrooms and onions warm or at room temperature. They may be covered and stored in the refrigerator for several days, and the flavor will mellow.

FRISÉE AU LARD ET À L'OEUF

HOT BACON AND EGG SALAD

serves 4

As summer progresses and fall nips the air, the salad greens in my garden become chewier until suddenly it is time for hot bacon salad, which wilts the greens and adds a salty bite to their bitter-sweet taste. Lardons of smoked bacon, cut into a meaty dice, are perfect for this salad. The yolk of the lightly poached egg should burst at the touch of a fork, helping dress the green leaves.

1 HEAD ESCAROLE OR FRISÉE (ABOUT 12 OUNCES/330 G)

1/2 CUP/125 ML RED WINE VINEGAR

4 VERY FRESH EGGS

1 TO 2 TABLESPOONS VEGETABLE OIL

6-OUNCE/170-G PIECE LEAN BACON, CUT INTO LARDONS (SEE PAGE 371)

PEPPER

Discard the tough outer green leaves from the escarole and trim the root end. Separate the pale central leaves and tear any large leaves into 2 or 3 pieces. Wash and dry the leaves thoroughly and put them in a salad bowl.

To poach the eggs, bring a wide, shallow pan of water to a boil and add 3 tablespoons/45 ml of the vinegar. Crack an egg on the side of the pan and drop it into a bubbling patch of water so the white spins to coat the yolk. Repeat with the remaining eggs. Lower the heat and poach the eggs until the whites are firm to the touch but the yolks are still soft, 3 to 4 minutes. Using a draining spoon, transfer them to a bowl of cold water. They may be poached up to 6 hours ahead and refrigerated.

Just before serving, transfer the poached eggs to a bowl of hot (not boiling) water to warm through. Heat the oil in a frying pan over medium heat. Add the lardons and fry until lightly browned, 2 to 3 minutes. If the fat is excessive, pour off some of it, leaving about 4 tablespoons behind in the pan with the lardons. Pour the hot fat and lardons over the greens and toss rapidly until they are slightly wilted, 30 seconds to 1 minute. Add the remaining 5 tablespoons/70 ml vinegar to the hot pan (stand back from the fumes) and bring to a boil, stirring to dissolve the pan juices. Boil for 30 seconds to 1 minute to temper the taste of the vinegar. Pour dressing over the greens and toss again.

Sprinkle the salad with freshly ground pepper, taste, and adjust the seasoning. Transfer the salad to 4 plates. Lift out each egg with a draining spoon to top each salad. Serve at once.

═ MUSHROOMS: FROM THE GROUND UP ═

About eighty mushroom varieties grow wild in France, so it is no surprise that picking them is a national sport. You will find morels around the foothills of the Alps and the Jura, porcini cèpes in the southwest, and *girolles* and *trompettes de la mort* (both a type of chanterelle) in wooded countryside everywhere. In season, experienced locals head out with a keen eye and a basket to collect their favorites from secret spots. The rest of us make for the markets early in the morning to buy what they have gathered. Make no mistake, picking wild mushrooms is an expert's job, and one or two people die each year after an ill-judged feast. In fall and spring, the seasons for most fungi, French pharmacies display vivid posters of what, and what not, to eat.

Cèpes, sometimes called *bolets* (porcini or boletus in the United States), are often cooked in walnut oil in the southwest and make a fine accompaniment to Confit de Canard (page 119). Mustard-colored *girolles* are easy to find and delicious, but with their rumpled tops, a bit like a slept-in bed, they can be finicky to clean. Spongelike, they will spoil if soaked in water, but a quick rinse and a rub do no harm. Golden brown chanterelles, which have a lot of gills, need the same treatment, as do ivory, earlike *pleurotes* (oyster mushrooms), although they are fairly flat and thus easy to brush clean with a dry cloth.

Trumpet-shaped mushrooms the color of mourning—thus *trompettes de la mort*—need to be trimmed at the foot and slit open to remove any bugs trapped inside the bell. *Mousserons*, or fairy-ring mushrooms, need delicate handling, too, but when prepared gently in a pan with a warm cream sauce they prove that loving care is worth the effort. *Pieds de mouton* (hedgehog mushrooms) should be eaten young, as elderly ones can be slightly bitter. Take care, too, with violet *pieds bleus* (wood blewits), which are mildly toxic before cooking.

Morilles (morels) are in a class of their own. The only fungus to approach the truffle (page 212) in intensity of bouquet, morels must always be cooked because they are toxic raw. The season is short for these tall, dimple-capped spring mushrooms, and their price reflects their rarity. Any dish called *forestière* should contain morels with diced bacon, as opposed to *chasseur*, which indicates mushrooms in general. Morels, and some other wild mushrooms, particularly cèpes, are often dried—an excellent buy, I think. They need a revivifying soak in hot water, and you should, of course, keep the fragrant soaking water for soups, sauces, and broths.

It used to be that wild mushrooms were a seasonal treat, but now up to a dozen varieties are commercially grown, available year-round and undemanding to clean (see page 373). In cooking, generally speaking, different varieties of mushrooms are interchangeable, and they are especially interesting tossed together in a tangled mix. After a quick sauté in butter (with garlic and parsley or tarragon), or a simmer in a bit of broth, they are ideal heaped onto croûtes as a first-course salad, or served alongside roasted game.

= PORTRAIT OF A POTAGER =

In French, a vegetable garden is a *potager*, and soup is *potage*. They are close cousins and both represent a timeless aspect of French country life. A *potager* can be as simple as a few leeks and cabbages and an apple tree just beyond the back door. Some are allotments, leased from the town council, often in a favored spot along a riverbank. Others can be very grand indeed. One of the most magnificent I have seen is at Saint-Jean-de-Beauregard, just south of Paris.

The formal vegetable garden, with a single entrance, is spread over nearly five acres (two hectares), which are divided into four large squares by an impressive cruciform alley. Each square is lined with espaliered apple and pear trees, and is subdivided into four smaller squares bordered by flowers and filled with vegetables. Vegetables and flowers planted together are a feast for the eyes: cosmos, dahlias, and zinnias surround cabbages with large leaves, orange tomatoes dangling from their vine like bell-shaped earrings, and a patch of pink-stemmed chard.

This particular garden also has some rare coveted features in its walls. Behind one is a hidden chamber with a cabinet of glass vials filled with purified spring water. Each vial keeps a carefully manicured bunch of grapes fresh for up to six months. Farther along, at the back of another shed, is a dark, rectangular room with screened windows and slatted shelves lined with pears and apples stored like hundreds of eggs in their cartons. Each fruit stands alone, to prevent any rot from spreading. We forget how an abundance of fresh fruit year-round is an artifact of modern times.

The much humbler vegetable garden on the property where I live dates back to the 1700s, and in its day must have nourished perhaps fifty people. Today, only a handful enjoy its crop of salad greens, leeks, garlic, tomatoes, peas, corn, cabbages, onions, squash, and soft fruits. The gardener is Monsieur Milbert, now in his mid-eighties, who has dug the earth seven days a week for a half century. Almost every morning, I see him stump through the iron gate, grasping a bucket of produce by each hand.

Monsieur Milbert is one of the last of a dying breed. Never having left the land, he respects its rhythms and adheres to time-honored wisdom. For example, he is a great believer in the phases of the moon, planting when the moon waxes to encourage growth, and gathering when it wanes so that the plants have maximum vitality. But nothing gets picked until it has reached full size. I protest mildly to Monsieur Milbert that his leeks resemble rolling pins, but he won't hear of pulling them sooner. Destitute in the bad old days, he learned the hard way that baby vegetables left him undernourished. His example shows how much our gardens, beyond being simply larders, reflect who we are and the times in which we have lived.

SALADE TIÈDE DE POMMES DE TERRE, SAUCISSE À L'AIL

WARM POTATO SALAD WITH GARLIC SAUSAGE

serves 4

You can, of course, serve warm potato salad by itself, but it is good with roast chicken, for example, or a juicy pork chop. In France, however, it most often comes with succulent, pink slices of poached garlic sausage. A specialty butcher will supply poaching sausages, or you can find them on the Internet. In France, this dish is regarded as an appetizer, though for me it doubles as a main course.

1½ POUNDS/675 G SMALL WAXY POTATOES, UNPEELED

SALT AND WHITE PEPPER

¼ CUP/60 ML DRY WHITE WINE, MORE TO TASTE

1 TABLESPOON WHITE WINE VINEGAR

½ CUP/125 ML VEGETABLE OIL

2 SHALLOTS, VERY FINELY CHOPPED

ONE 1-POUND/450-G GARLIC POACHING SAUSAGE

3 TABLESPOONS CHOPPED FRESH PARSLEY

Put the potatoes in a pan of salted water to cover, top with a lid, and bring to a boil. Simmer until tender when pierced with a knife, 12 to 15 minutes. Drain the potatoes, let cool slightly, and then peel. Halve or thickly slice them into a bowl. Immediately pour the wine and vinegar over the slices and toss until absorbed. Add the oil, shallots, salt, and pepper and toss again. Try to do this with a flick of the bowl, as stirring with a spoon tends to break up the potatoes. Taste and adjust the seasoning, then leave the potatoes at room temperature for 10 to 15 minutes, covering to keep them warm. The salad may be refrigerated for up to a day and warmed in a saucepan over a water bath (see page 373).

To finish, reheat the potato salad if necessary. Immerse the sausage in a pan of very hot water. Cover and leave it to heat through, 10 to 15 minutes; do not let it boil or it will burst. Stir the parsley into the warm salad, taste, and sharpen the flavor with a little wine if needed; add more oil if it seems dry. Pile the salad on a platter. Drain the sausage, peel it, and cut it into slices ¼ inch/6 mm thick, arranging them around the potatoes. Serve the salad warm.

PETITS POIS À LA FRANÇAISE

FRESH GREEN PEAS WITH LETTUCE AND SCALLION

serves 6

These braised peas are a surprise, their green freshness accented by the acidity of the lettuce and scallion. What's more, you don't need baby peas, but rather the big fat ones of midseason. For Petits Pois à la Crème, substitute ½ cup/125 ml crème fraîche for the butter, added after the peas are cooked. Fresh peas are the perfect partner for poached salmon or roast duck. The season is short—don't miss them!

1 HEAD ROMAINE LETTUCE (ABOUT 12 OUNCES/330 G)

6 TO 8 SCALLIONS, TRIMMED

4 TABLESPOONS/60 G BUTTER, SOFTENED

1 POUND/450 G SHELLED GREEN PEAS (ABOUT 3 POUNDS/1.35 KG IN THE POD)

1 BOUQUET GARNI (SEE PAGE 370)

1 CUP/250 ML WATER, MORE IF NEEDED

2 TEASPOONS SUGAR, MORE TO TASTE

SALT AND PEPPER

Wash the lettuce, cut into quarters lengthwise, and trim the base, leaving a little of the root to hold the leaves together. Cut the white and green part of the scallions into 1-inch/2.5-cm lengths. Spread about 2 tablespoons/30 g of the butter in a large sauté pan and lay the lettuce in it. Add the scallions, peas, bouquet garni, and water; sprinkle with the sugar, salt, and pepper. Cover tightly and simmer over medium heat, shaking the pan from time to time to prevent sticking, until the peas and scallions are very tender, 30 to 45 minutes depending on the age of the peas.

Discard the bouquet garni. Lift out the lettuce quarters and cut each one in half lengthwise. Starting at the stalk end, roll up each wedge of lettuce, and then put the rolls on the peas. The dish may be kept in the refrigerator for up to 2 days.

To finish, reheat the peas if necessary. If they seem soupy, boil rapidly over high heat to evaporate some of the liquid. However, petits pois à la française should always be moist. Take the pan from the heat and add the remaining butter in small pieces, shaking the pan so the butter thickens the liquid slightly. Taste, adjust the seasoning, and serve.

SALADE NIÇOISE

serves 6

Early versions of Salade Niçoise were almost vegetarian, calling for equal amounts of green beans and potatoes, topped with quartered tomatoes, capers, olives, and anchovies, definitely an appetizer to tease the palate. By the 1950s, tuna had entered the picture, and now the salad is invariably served in main-dish portions.

HERB VINAIGRETTE

$^1/_4$ CUP/60 ML RED WINE VINEGAR

2 GARLIC CLOVES, FINELY CHOPPED

1 TEASPOON DIJON MUSTARD

SALT AND PEPPER

$^3/_4$ CUP/175 ML OLIVE OIL

1 TABLESPOON CHOPPED FRESH CHERVIL

2 TEASPOONS CHOPPED FRESH THYME

SALAD

2 POUNDS/900 G WAXY POTATOES, UNPEELED

1 POUND/450 G GREEN BEANS, TRIMMED

6 HARD-BOILED EGGS

6 SMALL TOMATOES (ABOUT 1 POUND/450 G TOTAL), PEELED (SEE PAGE 372)

TWO 6$^1/_2$-OUNCE/200-G CANS TUNA IN OLIVE OIL, OR 12 ANCHOVY FILLETS, HALVED LENGTHWISE

$^3/_4$ CUP/150 G SALTED (DRY-CURED) BLACK NIÇOIS OLIVES

For the vinaigrette, whisk together the vinegar, garlic, mustard, salt, and pepper in a large bowl for 30 seconds to dissolve the salt. Gradually whisk in the oil so the dressing emulsifies and thickens slightly. Whisk in the chervil and thyme, taste, and adjust the seasoning. Set aside.

Put the potatoes in a large pan of salted water, cutting any large ones into 2 or 3 uniform pieces so they cook evenly. Cover, bring to a boil, and simmer until tender when pierced with a knife, 15 to 20 minutes. Drain the potatoes, let cool slightly, and then peel. Cut into chunks, letting them fall into a bowl. Mix in 4 to 5 tablespoons of the vinaigrette and leave the potatoes to cool.

Meanwhile, bring a large pan of salted water to a boil. Add the beans and boil until tender but still firm, 5 to 10 minutes, depending on their size. Drain and rinse them with cold running water to set the color. Drain thoroughly and toss the beans in a bowl with 3 to 4 tablespoons of the vinaigrette. Taste and adjust the seasoning.

Cut the hard-boiled eggs lengthwise into quarters; core and cut the tomatoes into eighths. Put the tuna in a small bowl, pull into large flakes with 2 forks, and stir in 3 to 4 tablespoons of the vinaigrette. (If using anchovies, reserve.) Taste and adjust the seasoning. The ingredients may be prepared up to 2 hours ahead and kept at room temperature, but the salad is best assembled no more than a few minutes before serving.

To finish, taste the potatoes, adding more vinaigrette, salt, or pepper if needed. Spread them in a large, shallow serving bowl and arrange the green beans on top. Pile the tuna in the center and arrange the egg and tomato eighths around the edge of the dish. If using anchovies instead of tuna, top the beans with a lattice of anchovy fillets; scatter the olives on top. Spoon over any remaining vinaigrette and serve. The salad is also attractive served in individual ceramic bowls, such as pasta bowls.

SALADE TIEDE DE LENTILLES

WARM LENTIL SALAD

At its best, this salad is made with lentils still warm from simmering, tossed with a shallot vinaigrette. The salad can form a simple first course, or a main course with a slice of cooked ham or almost any kind of sausage.

Pick over 1½ cups lentils (about 10 ounces/280 g) and put them in a saucepan. Add an onion studded with 2 whole cloves; 1 garlic clove, crushed; a bouquet garni (see page 370); and salt and pepper. Add water to cover generously. Cover and simmer over low heat until tender, about 20 minutes.

Meanwhile, make a vinaigrette dressing: Whisk ¼ cup/ 60 ml red wine vinegar with 2 teaspoons Dijon mustard, salt, and pepper. Stir in 3 shallots (about 2 ounces/60 g total), finely chopped, and then whisk in ½ cup/125 ml walnut or hazelnut oil, adding it gradually so the dressing emulsifies and thickens slightly. When the lentils are tender, drain them, discarding the onion, garlic, and bouquet garni, and immediately mix them with the dressing and 2 tablespoons of chopped parsley. Taste, adjust the seasoning, and let stand 5 minutes for the flavors to blend. Serve warm or at room temperature. Serves 6.

= OLIVES AND OLIVE OIL: MEDITERRANEAN TREASURES =

Less than 1 percent of the world's olive oil comes from France, but it includes some of the best, with the finest originating from the Pays Niçois and Provence. Olive trees can survive hundreds, even thousands, of years, but they are sensitive to frost. "After the great winter of 1956, many trees died, and the ground was planted with vines," says Jean-Benoît Hugues, who runs an artisanal oil press in the Provençal hills. "Wisely, my father left his trees in to regenerate from their roots. This was my inheritance. Like me they are just past fifty, a fine age for an olive tree and a man!"

I shiver in the northern wind, but Jean-Benoît doesn't mind, as olives are pollinated by the mistral. "Where wind is lacking, olives do not bear fruit," he tells me. His oil has a characteristic taste of *terroir*, being cold pressed from four olive varieties that are picked by hand using long rakes. To extract the oil, olives are first crushed with their pits to a pulp, then pressed, washed with clear water, and separated by centrifuge. The first cold pressing yields the virgin or "green" oil, juicy, grassy, and tasting of green almonds (the best is unfiltered). The color can range from straw yellow to slightly green and the fruitiness from mild to strong, yet the flavor varies little from year to year. "It's not like wine.

The qualities of a good virgin olive oil depend not on vintage, but on the variety of olive and where they are grown," Jean-Benoît explains.

Table varieties of olives are different from those used for oil, much like the distinction between table grapes and wine grapes. The half-ripe lime-colored fruits of autumn become edible green olives, but only after salting or soaking in brine so they ferment and lose their bitterness. The queen of green olives is the little Picholine, from the Rhône delta.

Black (that is, ripe) table olives are cured in dozens of ways. Even the spice stand in my local market offers fifteen different kinds. Interesting French varieties to set out at the aperitif hour include tiny, intense black Niçois olives with seemingly outsize pits, and fat, juicy black Nyons olives, grown farther north than any others.

Olives as a flavoring can rival bacon, particularly in stews such as Daube de Boeuf Provençale (page 139). As a stand-alone ingredient, they do best puréed for Tapenade (page 221), which is even better stuffed into cherry tomatoes for serving with or without goat cheese. In the kitchen, it is important to distinguish salted (dry-cured) olives from brined ones; most recipes specify one or the other.

ARTICHAUTS BARIGOULE
STUFFED ARTICHOKES WITH PORK, OLIVES, AND THYME

serves 4

This dish, rarely found outside of Provence, is a favorite of mine, the fragrant stuffing of pork, ham, olives, and thyme just right with the characteristic bite of artichoke. To make them easy to stuff, the artichokes are first boiled so the hairy choke can be scooped out, then they are filled and braised until tender, with leaves almost falling apart. Serve the artichokes warm or at room temperature, bathed in their cooking juices. They make a robust appetizer. For me, they are a satisfying main course as well.

4 LARGE GLOBE ARTICHOKES

$^1/_2$ LEMON

1 CARROT, SLICED

1 ONION, SLICED

1 CUP/250 ML DRY WHITE WINE

1 QUART/1 LITER VEAL OR CHICKEN BROTH
(SEE PAGE 373), MORE IF NEEDED

STUFFING

1 BUNCH FRESH THYME (ABOUT $^3/_4$ OUNCE/20 G)

1 BUNCH FRESH BASIL (ABOUT $1^1/_2$ OUNCES/45 G)

1 SMALL BUNCH PARSLEY (ABOUT $1^1/_2$ OUNCES/45 G)

2 TABLESPOONS OLIVE OIL

$^1/_2$ ONION, CHOPPED

8 OUNCES/225 G GROUND PORK

2 GARLIC CLOVES, CHOPPED

1 CUP/50 G FRESH BREAD CRUMBS (SEE PAGE 373)

4 BUTTON MUSHROOMS (ABOUT 2 OUNCES/60 G
TOTAL), TRIMMED AND CHOPPED

2 OUNCES/60 G CURED RAW HAM, CHOPPED

$^1/_4$ CUP/50 G SALTED (DRY-CURED) BLACK OLIVES,
PITTED AND CHOPPED

SALT AND PEPPER

10-INCH/25-CM DEEP, ROUND CASSEROLE

Heat the oven to 350°F/180°C. Bring a large pan of salted water to a boil. Break off the stem of each artichoke and then trim the base so it sits flat. Using a serrated knife, cut off the top cone of leaves, and then trim the spiky tips of the rest with scissors. As you work, rub the cut surfaces of the artichokes with the lemon half so they do not discolor. Drop them into the boiling water and drape a dish towel on the surface so they are submerged. Simmer until partly cooked, 25 to 30 minutes. Drain the artichokes and let cool until they can be handled, then remove the choke and inside leaves with a melon baller or a sharp spoon.

Meanwhile, make the stuffing. Reserve 4 sprigs of each herb for decoration and set aside. Strip the thyme, basil, and parsley leaves from the remaining stems and chop 2 tablespoons each basil and parsley and 2 teaspoons thyme. Heat the oil in a frying pan over medium heat. Add the onion and sauté until translucent, 3 to 5 minutes. Stir in the pork and garlic, cutting the pork with a spoon to crumble it. Cook until browned, 5 to 7 minutes. Take from the heat, stir in the bread crumbs, mushrooms, ham, and olives, and leave to cool. Add the chopped herbs with some pepper and mix thoroughly. Sauté a nugget of the stuffing, taste it for seasoning, and season the rest. Salt may not be needed because the ham and olives are salty.

Fill the hollow of each artichoke with the stuffing. Reshape the artichokes and tie string around them to hold the leaves. Spread the carrot and onion in the casserole, set the artichokes upright on top, and add the wine. Set the pan over medium heat, bring to a boil, and simmer for 5 minutes. Pour over enough broth to reach halfway up the sides of the artichokes. Bring to a boil, cover the artichokes with parchment paper, and add the lid. Braise in the oven until very tender, 40 to 50 minutes. Baste with the juices from time to time, and add more broth if necessary to keep the artichokes very moist. Once cooked, they may be refrigerated in the cooking broth for up to 1 day.

To finish, reheat the artichokes on the stove top if necessary. Remove and keep them warm. Strain the cooking broth into a saucepan, bring to a boil, and taste. If it seems thin, boil to reduce and concentrate it; adjust the seasoning. Put the artichokes in warmed soup bowls, discard the strings, and pour the hot broth over them. Top each artichoke with a sprig each of thyme, basil, and parsley, and serve warm, or at room temperature in hot weather. Don't forget a spoon for the broth.

CHOU EN SURPRISE

CABBAGE STUFFED WITH SAUSAGE AND CHESTNUTS

serves 6 to 8

You don't often come across stuffed cabbage nowadays, which is a pity. I always enjoy blanching the head, pulling back the outer leaves, and then filling the center and reshaping the cabbage so the stuffing comes as a sur-prise when the cabbage is cut open like a cake. The wedges, their green leaves concealing a mixture of sausage meat and chestnuts, rest on a bed of sautéed cabbage—the perfect country meal. The greener the cabbage, the better, and curly, dark Savoy cabbage is the best of all.

I HEAD GREEN CABBAGE, PREFERABLY SAVOY
(ABOUT 2¹/₂ POUNDS/1.2 KG)

SALT AND PEPPER

I¹/₂ POUNDS/ 675 G COOKED CANNED OR VACUUM-
PACKED CHESTNUTS

2 POUNDS/900 G FRESH SPICY SAUSAGE MEAT

2 TABLESPOONS CHOPPED FRESH THYME

2 TABLESPOONS CHOPPED FRESH PARSLEY

2 QUARTS/2 LITERS BEEF OR VEAL BROTH
(SEE PAGE 373), MORE IF NEEDED

¹/₄ CUP/60 ML LARD OR VEGETABLE OIL

I ONION, CHOPPED

I CARROT, CHOPPED

2 TABLESPOONS/30 G FLOUR

Discard any damaged outer leaves from the cabbage, leaving plenty of green ones; trim the stem even with the base of the leaves. Bring a very large pan of salted water to a boil, immerse the cabbage in it, and drape a dish towel on top to keep the cabbage under the water. Simmer until the outer leaves can be easily bent back, 15 to 20 minutes. Drain the cabbage and cool it under cold running water. Gently peel back about a dozen of the outer leaves, being careful not to tear them, to reveal the heart. Using a paring knife, carefully cut out the heart and set it aside, leaving the leaves held together by the stem so they look like an empty bowl.

For the stuffing, break each chestnut into 2 or 3 pieces, crumble the sausage meat, and mix them together in a bowl with the thyme, parsley, salt, and pepper. Fry a nugget of the mixture in a small pan, taste, and adjust the seasoning of the rest.

Drape a scalded dish towel in a colander. Set the cabbage, stem side down, in the colander. Stuff the center of the cabbage with the chestnut mixture, mounding it well, and wrap the leaf ends over the stuffing to form a parcel. Gather up the towel and tie it with string to make a tight ball. Put the cabbage in a deep saucepan and add the broth almost to cover it. Drape a dish towel on top to keep the cabbage immersed and add the lid.

Put the pan over low heat, bring to a simmer, and cook the cabbage until a skewer inserted in the center is hot to the touch when withdrawn after 30 seconds, 1 to 1¼ hours. Add more broth during cooking if it evaporates rapidly. The cabbage may be cooked up to a day ahead and kept in the broth in the refrigerator. Reheat it before continuing.

Meanwhile, discard the core and ribs from the cabbage heart and shred the leaves. Melt half of the lard in a large frying pan over medium heat. Add the onion, carrot, salt, and pepper and sauté until the onion is translucent, 5 to 7 minutes. Stir in the shredded cabbage, cover, and cook gently, stirring often, until the cabbage is tender, 12 to 15 minutes. Taste and adjust the seasoning.

When the stuffed cabbage is done, lift it out using the string. Cover and set aside to keep warm. To make a sauce, strain the cooking broth, return it to the saucepan, and boil until reduced to about 2 cups/500 ml, 20 to 30 minutes. With a fork, crush the remaining lard on a plate and work in the flour to form a smooth paste. Whisk the paste into the boiling reduced broth a piece or two at a time until the sauce coats a spoon lightly. You may not need all of the paste. Taste and adjust the seasoning.

To finish, spread some of the sautéed cabbage in a bed on a warmed platter. Unwrap the stuffed cabbage and set it in the center of the platter. Pour a little of the sauce over the shredded cabbage and serve the rest separately. To serve, cut the stuffed cab-bage into wedges like a cake.

ASPERGES ET CHAMPIGNONS À LA CRÈME D'ESTRAGON

ASPERGES ET CHAMPIGNONS À LA CRÈME D'ESTRAGON

ASPARAGUS WITH MUSHROOMS IN A TARRAGON CREAM

serves 4 to 6

The Loire Valley, with its temperate climate and sandy soil, is a paradise for fine vegetables. When they reach the kitchen they are often combined, such as the green peas, lettuce, and scallions in Petits Pois à la Française (page 252), or this appealing dish of asparagus and mushrooms flavored with tarragon. This recipe makes a great first course or accompaniment to roast chicken or to a luxury meat such as veal. It is best prepared just before serving and does not take long.

I SMALL BUNCH FRESH TARRAGON (ABOUT
I OUNCE/30 G)

SALT AND PEPPER

2 POUNDS/900 G GREEN ASPARAGUS

3 TABLESPOONS/45 G BUTTER

4 OUNCES/110 G BUTTON MUSHROOMS, TRIMMED
AND THINLY SLICED

SQUEEZE OF FRESH LEMON JUICE

2 SHALLOTS, FINELY CHOPPED

3 TABLESPOONS/22 G FLOUR

$^1/_2$ CUP/125 ML CRÈME FRAÎCHE (PAGE 374) OR
HEAVY CREAM

GRATED NUTMEG

Pull the tarragon leaves from the stems and chop the leaves. Add the stems to a large, shallow pan of lightly salted water (do not oversalt the water, as it will be used for the sauce) and bring to a boil. Meanwhile, using a vegetable peeler or paring knife, peel the asparagus stems, then divide them into 4 to 6 bundles. Gather each bundle, with the tips lined up evenly, and hold them vertically, tips down. Tie each bundle with string, using 2 loops of string to hold the spears in place. Trim the cut ends even.

Immerse the bundles in the boiling water and then simmer just until tender, 6 to 8 minutes. Transfer the bundles to a colander and set aside the cooking liquid. Rinse the asparagus bundles briefly with cold running water to stop the cooking, and then leave them to drain, covered with aluminum foil to keep warm.

Melt the butter in a saucepan over medium heat. Add the mushrooms, lemon juice, salt, and pepper, press a piece of aluminum foil down over the mushrooms, cover, and cook until the mushrooms are tender, 3 to 5 minutes. Uncover, add the shallots, and cook, stirring, until any liquid the mushrooms released has evaporated. Meanwhile, measure 1 cup/250 ml of the cooking liquid. Stir the flour into the mushrooms, followed by the cooking liquid. Bring to a boil, whisking constantly until the sauce thickens slightly. Add the crème fraîche and bring just back to a boil. Take from the heat, add the chopped tarragon and a little nutmeg, taste, and adjust the seasoning.

Transfer the asparagus bundles to warmed plates and discard the strings. Spoon the sauce over the center of each bundle, leaving the stem ends and tips uncovered. Serve at once.

GRATIN DE BLETTES À LA CRÈME

GRATIN OF SWISS CHARD WITH CREAM

A favorite in southern France, Swiss chard has thick white stems and dark green leaves that resemble overgrown bok choy (red and rainbow varieties of chard are even prettier). It belongs to the beet family, and like hardy beets, it grows easily. This gratin is an excellent first course or accompaniment to fish or chicken.

In the recipe for Asperges et Champignons à la Crème d'Estragon, omit the asparagus and tarragon. Trim the stems from 1 large bunch Swiss chard (about 1½ pounds/675 g), discarding any that are wilted. If any stems seem tough, peel them with a vegetable peeler to remove the strings. Bring a large pan of salted water to a boil. Cut the chard stems crosswise into slices ½ inch/ 1.25 cm thick. Very coarsely shred the green tops. Drop the stems into the boiling water and simmer for 5 minutes. Add the green tops and continue simmering until the tops are wilted and the stems are just tender, 3 to 5 minutes longer. Drain, reserving the cooking liquid. Meanwhile, make the sauce as for the asparagus but without the tarragon. Stir the well-drained chard into the sauce, taste, and adjust the seasoning, adding lemon juice and nutmeg if needed. Pour the mixture into a buttered gratin dish, sprinkle with ½ cup/50 g grated Gruyère cheese, and brown under the broiler. Serves 4.

PAPETON D'AUBERGINES

EGGPLANT MOLD

serves 8 as a first course, or 6 as a main course

Papeton, an eggplant mold, is a specialty of Avignon in Provence, where the Catholic popes, exiled from Rome, ruled Christendom in the fourteenth century. The origins of the name are obscure, but I like to think that the glistening purple mold, rising high on the platter, echoes the shape of a papal tiara. The skins of the eggplant are used to line the mold, then filled with a zesty spiced mixture of goat cheese, yogurt, garlic, and tomato concassé. Papeton is versatile, good served warm or at room temperature, as a first or main course.

4 EGGPLANTS (ABOUT 2 POUNDS/900 G TOTAL), TRIMMED

SALT AND PEPPER

5 TABLESPOONS/75 ML OLIVE OIL, MORE FOR THE MOLD

ONE 6-OUNCE/170-G LOG SOFT GOAT CHEESE

½ CUP/125 ML PLAIN YOGURT

2 TEASPOONS GROUND CORIANDER

1 TEASPOON GROUND CUMIN

TOMATO CONCASSÉ

3 POUNDS/1.35 KG TOMATOES, PEELED, SEEDED, AND CHOPPED (SEE PAGE 372)

4 GARLIC CLOVES, CHOPPED

1 BOUQUET GARNI (SEE PAGE 370)

5-CUP/1.25-LITER CHARLOTTE MOLD (SEE PAGE 376) OR DEEP SOUFFLÉ DISH

Heat the oven to 350°F/180°C. Split 2 of the eggplants lengthwise, and score the flesh with a knife without cutting through the skin. Cut the remaining 2 eggplants into slices ¼ inch/6 mm thick. Put all the eggplants, cut side up, on a tray and sprinkle with salt to draw out the juices. Leave for 30 minutes, then rinse with water and pat dry on paper towels.

Brush the cut surfaces of the eggplants with the olive oil and lay them on 2 baking sheets, putting the halved ones cut side down. Bake until the slices are tender and fairly dry, turning them once so they brown on both sides, 15 to 20 minutes total. Take them from the oven and let cool. If the halved eggplants are not tender (cooking time depends on size), continue cooking for 10 to 15 minutes. Let them cool also. Leave the oven on.

Meanwhile, make the concassé. Put the tomatoes, garlic, bouquet garni, salt, and pepper in a saucepan. Cover and cook over very low heat for 10 minutes. Uncover and continue simmering, stirring occasionally, until the tomatoes are very thick, 12 to 15 minutes more. Taste, adjust the seasoning, and set aside.

Scoop the pulp from the halved eggplants with a spoon, taking care not to pierce the skin. Set the skins aside and coarsely chop the pulp. Crush the goat cheese in a bowl with a fork and mix in the yogurt until smooth. Stir in the eggplant pulp with the coriander, cumin, salt, and pepper. Taste and adjust the seasoning.

To assemble the papeton, oil the mold and line it with the eggplant skins, purple side outward. Spread a layer of the goat cheese mixture in the bottom and cover it with browned eggplant slices. Set aside half of the tomato concassé for serving and, using the other half, spread a thin tomato layer in the mold. Top it with more eggplant slices. Continue layering goat cheese, eggplant slices, and tomato concassé until all are used and the mold is full, ending with eggplant slices.

Cover the papeton with oiled parchment paper, oiled side down. Line a roasting pan with a dish towel, set the mold in the pan, and pour in boiling water to make a water bath (see page 373). Bring the water to a boil on the stove top and put the pan in the oven. Bake the papeton 1 to 1¼ hours, until it is firm and a skewer inserted in the center is hot to the touch when withdrawn after 30 seconds. Let cool. The papeton may be refrigerated, along with the reserved tomato concassé, for up to 2 days.

Before going to table, unmold the papeton onto a platter and let it come to room temperature. For serving, cut it into wedges like a cake and serve it with the remaining tomato concassé.

RATATOUILLE

serves 6 as a first course, or 4 as a main course

The components of classic ratatouille—eggplant, zucchini, onions, tomatoes, and bell peppers—flourish quite far north in France, but somehow this stew always tastes more vivid along the Mediterranean. The seasoning typically includes generous amounts of garlic, with herbs and spices depending on the cook's taste. Elizabeth David, author of the definitive French Provincial Cookery, *preferred coriander seeds, and I like to follow her example. I also like the vegetables to retain some texture, so I don't bother to peel them, though I do reduce them to an aromatic, savory stew in true country style. Ratatouille may be served hot or at room temperature and improves immeasurably when made a day or two ahead.*

2 SMALL EGGPLANTS (ABOUT 12 OUNCES/330 G TOTAL), TRIMMED, HALVED LENGTHWISE, AND CUT CROSSWISE INTO SLICES 3/8 INCH/1 CM THICK

12 OUNCES/330 G SMALL ZUCCHINI, TRIMMED AND CUT INTO SLICES 1/2 INCH/1.25 CM THICK

SALT AND PEPPER

1/4 CUP/60 ML OLIVE OIL

2 ONIONS, THINLY SLICED

4 GARLIC CLOVES, CHOPPED

I TABLESPOON CORIANDER SEEDS, CRUSHED

I POUND/450 G TOMATOES, SEEDED AND CHOPPED (SEE PAGE 372)

I RED BELL PEPPER, CORED, SEEDED, AND SLICED (SEE PAGE 370)

I GREEN BELL PEPPER, CORED, SEEDED, AND SLICED (SEE PAGE 370)

I LARGE BOUQUET GARNI (SEE PAGE 370)

2 TABLESPOONS CHOPPED FRESH PARSLEY

Spread the sliced eggplants and zucchini on trays, sprinkle them with salt, and leave to stand for about 30 minutes to draw out the juices. Rinse them with cold water, drain, and dry on paper towels.

Heat 2 tablespoons of the oil in a flameproof casserole over medium heat. Add the onions, salt, and pepper and sauté until translucent, 5 to 7 minutes. Take the casserole from the heat. Mix the garlic and coriander seeds with pepper and a little salt in a small bowl. Layer the eggplants, zucchini, tomatoes, and peppers in the casserole, sprinkling each layer with the garlic mixture. Spoon the remaining oil on top and push the bouquet garni into the vegetables. Cover and simmer gently over low heat until the vegetables are quite tender, stirring occasionally to mix them, 25 to 35 minutes. If the stew is too soupy, remove the lid for the last 15 minutes of cooking.

Discard the bouquet garni, taste, and adjust the seasoning. Ratatouille may be refrigerated for up to 2 days and warmed gently on the stove top before serving. Serve it in the casserole, sprinkled with the parsley.

OEUFS AU PLAT À LA RATATOUILLE
BAKED EGGS WITH RATATOUILLE

When you have leftover Ratatouille, here's how to use it:

Heat the oven to 425°F/220°C. Butter an 8-by-11-inch/ 20-by-28-cm baking dish. Spread about 4 cups/1 liter Ratatouille in the baking dish. Make 6 hollows in the mixture and crack 1 egg into each hollow. Drizzle each egg with olive oil. Bake until the egg whites are set but the yolks are still soft, 10 to 12 minutes. Serve at once. Serves 6.

= PROVENCE: SAVORING THE SUNSHINE =

As a Yorkshire girl brought up in the placid halftones of a northern landscape, my first visit to Provence came as a revelation. After a long night in the limbo of the overnight train from Paris, I lifted the blind and there it was: sharp black cypress trees, terra-cotta earth, rock-encrusted hills, all outlined by the harsh glare of a sun that was hotter, even at that hour in the morning, than anything I could have imagined. Like so many Anglo-Saxons, I was thunderstruck by the beauty of Provence.

I soon learned that the cooking is as colorful as the landscape. Typical are dishes like Ratatouille (page 261), with its mix of red tomato, black eggplant, and red and green bell peppers, or Daube (page 139), a lamb or beef stew with carrots, onions, olives, wine, and shavings of orange zest all slowly baked to aromatic perfection in a *daubière* crafted from local vivid red clay. Initiation into Provençal cooking begins with Aïoli (page 219), made by crushing mild young garlic cloves with egg yolks in an olive-wood mortar, then working in fruity green olive oil until the mayonnaise is thick enough to hold a spoon upright. Just a teaspoonful will awaken your palate, such is the intensity of southern seasoning. Pungent sauces such as Tapenade (page 221) and Rouille (page 219) are served with hard-boiled eggs, or with the local version of focaccia, called Fouace (page 292). The same assertive approach carries into cheese, which is predominantly heat-friendly goat cheese, as befits the climate.

To live in Provence is to eat fish. Local cooks grill it over herbs or bake it with vegetables in shallow earthenware dishes called *tians*. Sardines, baby squid, and bream are local favorites, and Brandade de Morue (page 78), a rich purée of salt cod with garlic and olive oil, is traditional for the feast after midnight mass on Christmas Eve. Above all, fish is puréed in soup or simmered in stews like Bouillabaisse (page 99). Meat means lamb, roasted *à la ficelle* (on a string) before the fire, or simmered in vegetable ragoûts. In the old days, beef was tough unless raised in the marshes of the Camargue, and chickens were scrawny, but supermarkets have swept away such memories. Everywhere, wild herbs from the scented hillsides, known as *maquis*, pervade the kitchen. According to Provençal lore, even a bouquet garni was originally medicinal: thyme helps the digestion, bay leaf is antiseptic, and parsley, a good source of vitamin C, is an antioxidant.

On the Mediterranean, the style of dining is different from the rest of France, and eating outdoors and cooking on the grill are habitual. Almost all foods are designed to be served warm or at room temperature, particularly little dishes of eggplant or chickpea dips, dried sausages, olives, and cooked vegetable salads in permutations of tomato, eggplant, zucchini, onion, mushroom, squash, and artichoke. All this goes perfectly with Provençal pottery and table linens in harmonious vegetable colors. "Here there is no separation between what you eat and what is beautiful," says Louisa Jones, an authority on Provence and its gardens. "For much of the year, we live among plants, among vines and olive trees, wisteria on the patio, the scents and colors of the leaves. The traditional colors of Provençal cooking are the colors of the land. The glowing golden pink of Provençal rosé wine adds yet another note of color at the table."

Dessert does not commonly round out a Provençal meal. You are much more likely to be offered fresh fruits from the Rhône Valley with a chunk of *nougat de Montélimar*; or perhaps a diamond of orange flower water–flavored almond paste called a *calisson d'Aix*, or one of the glowing whole candied fruits (see "Fruit Glacés and Fruit Confits," page 352) for which Provence is renowned. Watch also for *navettes de Marseille*, cookies of lemon or orange, and *tuiles* in the shape of a house tile, flavored with the fashionable lavender. And with them, take a tisane (page 364) to stimulate or soothe. Indeed, there is an herb tea for everything.

TIAN DE COURGETTES

ZUCCHINI GRATIN

serves 6

Tian is the Provençal name for a shallow baking dish, in various sizes and shapes, made in the local earthenware. But any ceramic baking dish of the same size or individual ceramic dishes will work well for this recipe. Unlike most gratins that call for a béchamel sauce or cream to bind the ingredients, this particular recipe uses eggs and rice. It can be prepared with a wide array of vegetables, such as spinach, Swiss chard, or broccoli rabe. Sometimes the vegetables are mixed, such as green peas with artichokes, or spinach with pumpkin. The gratin is good served hot or at room temperature, particularly in the summer.

1/4 CUP/50 G LONG-GRAIN RICE

2 POUNDS/900 G ZUCCHINI, TRIMMED AND CUT INTO SLICES 1/4 INCH/6 MM THICK

SALT AND PEPPER

6 TABLESPOONS/90 ML OLIVE OIL, MORE FOR THE DISHES

2 ONIONS, THINLY SLICED

I GARLIC CLOVE, CHOPPED

6 TABLESPOONS/60 G GRATED PARMESAN CHEESE

3 TO 4 TABLESPOONS CHOPPED FRESH BASIL OR PARSLEY

3 EGGS, BEATEN TO MIX

6 SMALL ZUCCHINI FLOWERS, FOR GARNISH (OPTIONAL)

Heat the oven to 400°F/200°C. Oil a 10-inch/25-cm *tian* or 6 individual *tians*. Bring a pot of salted water to a boil, add the rice, and simmer until tender, 10 to 12 minutes. Drain, rinse with warm water, and leave the rice to drain thoroughly. Meanwhile, sprinkle the zucchini slices with salt and pepper. Heat 3 tablespoons/45 ml of the oil in a frying pan over medium heat. Add the zucchini and sauté, stirring often, until they are just tender, 5 to 7 minutes. Drain them on paper towels, then chop coarsely and place in a bowl.

Return the pan to medium heat, add another tablespoon of the oil, and sauté the onion and garlic, stirring often, until translucent, 3 to 5 minutes. Add to the zucchini and stir in the rice, cheese, basil, and pepper. Taste, adjust the seasoning, and stir in the eggs. Spread the mixture in the dish(es) and sprinkle with the remaining 2 tablespoons oil.

Bake until set, allowing 15 to 18 minutes for individual dishes, or 25 to 30 minutes for the large one. When set, heat the broiler and brown the gratin(s), 3 to 5 minutes. The gratin(s) may be refrigerated for up to 3 days. Reheat in a 400°F/200°C oven for 10 to 15 minutes to serve hot.

If using the zucchini flowers, shortly before serving, bring a pan of salted water to a boil. Drop in the flowers and simmer until slightly wilted, 1 to 2 minutes. Drain and dry on paper towels. Place the flowers on the gratin(s) and serve hot or at room temperature directly from the dish(es).

GRATIN D'ENDIVES À L'ARDENNAISE

GRATIN OF BELGIAN ENDIVE WITH HAM

serves 6 as a first course, or 4 as a main course

Belgian endive is a winter staple in France, one of the few greens (though actually it should be snowy white) that continues all winter long. That's because it is grown indoors, in the dark, so the leaves stay bleached as if they were underground. Once they are on the grocery counter, however, endives are open to the light, so the leaves begin to curl, turning green and bitter. So for crispness and the best sweet taste, go for all-white endives and remove any spoiled leaves. When baked in a gratin like this, endive can be served as a first or main course.

6 TO 8 HEADS BELGIAN ENDIVE (ABOUT 2 POUNDS/ 900 G TOTAL)

BUTTER FOR CASSEROLE AND DISHES

I TEASPOON SUGAR

SALT AND PEPPER

6 TO 8 THIN SLICES COOKED HAM (ABOUT 12 OUNCES/ 330 G TOTAL)

1/2 CUP/50 G GRATED GRUYÈRE CHEESE

BÉCHAMEL SAUCE

2 CUPS/500 ML MILK

4 TABLESPOONS/60 G BUTTER

1/4 CUP/30 G FLOUR

PINCH OF GRATED NUTMEG

8-BY-11-INCH/20-BY-28-CM BAKING DISH

Heat the oven to 350°F/180°C. Discard any wilted leaves from the endives, wipe them, and trim the stem end. With the tip of a knife, hollow each stem so the head will cook more evenly. Butter a small casserole. Lay the endives in the casserole and sprinkle with the sugar, salt, and pepper. Cover and bake, turning them once or twice, until tender and starting to brown, 45 to 55 minutes. Set the endives aside, uncovered, until cool enough to handle. Increase the oven heat to 400°F/200°C, and butter the baking dish.

Meanwhile, make the béchamel sauce. Scald the milk in a small saucepan. Melt the butter in a separate saucepan over medium heat. Whisk in the flour and continue whisking until foaming, about 30 seconds. Take the pan from the heat, gradually whisk in the scalded milk, and season with salt and pepper. Bring the sauce to a boil, whisking constantly until it thickens, then simmer for 1 to 2 minutes. Take it again from the heat and season with the nutmeg.

Roll a slice of ham around each head of endive, and arrange the endives diagonally in the prepared baking dish. Spoon the sauce over the endives, covering them completely. Sprinkle with the cheese. The gratin may be kept in the refrigerator for up to 2 days or frozen for up to 1 month.

To finish, bake the gratin until bubbling and browned, allowing 15 to 20 minutes if the sauce is still warm, or up to 30 minutes if it has been chilled. If the gratin has not browned on top, brown the top briefly under the broiler (make sure the baking dish is flameproof). Serve very hot.

COUSINAT À LA BAYONNAISE
VEGETABLE STEW
serves 8 to 10

Cousinat is a wonderfully versatile vegetable stew that varies with the seasons. The famous smoked ham of Bayonne provides background flavor and garlic is indispensable. But otherwise all manner of roots and bulbs, greens and shoots can be added, from the baby artichokes and asparagus of spring to the eggplant and zucchini of summer to the sturdy parsnips and rutabagas of fall. Or you can take the opposite approach and cut the recipe down to a single vegetable. Cauliflower or green beans do particularly well on their own. The total cooking time of an hour and a half sounds long to modern cooks, but this is normal for tough, mature vegetables. Although they will start to disintegrate, their flavors will mellow, yielding an extraordinarily intense, meltingly soft stew. Cousinat can be a first course, or it can be an accompaniment to a simple dish, such as roast chicken or chops. With the addition of more broth, leftovers make a great soup reminiscent of minestrone.

2 TO 3 TABLESPOONS LEMON JUICE

2 OR 3 GLOBE ARTICHOKES

2 TABLESPOONS/30 G BACON FAT OR LARD

3 CUPS/330 G SHELLED FAVA BEANS, UNPEELED (ABOUT 1½ POUNDS/675 G IN THE POD)

1 POUND/450 G LARGE CARROTS, QUARTERED AND CUT INTO 2-INCH/5-CM LENGTHS

12 SCALLIONS, WHITE PART ONLY, OR 3 SMALL ONIONS, QUARTERED

8 OUNCES/225 G GREEN BEANS, TRIMMED AND HALVED CROSSWISE

2 GREEN BELL PEPPERS, CORED, SEEDED, AND CUT INTO EIGHTHS (SEE PAGE 370)

8 GARLIC CLOVES, THINLY SLICED

2 THICK SLICES DRY-CURED RAW HAM (ABOUT 8 OUNCES/225 G TOTAL), DICED

1 CUP/250 ML VEAL OR CHICKEN BROTH (SEE PAGE 373)

½ CUP/125 ML DRY WHITE WINE

2 OR 3 LARGE TOMATOES (ABOUT 12 OUNCES/330 G TOTAL), SEEDED AND COARSELY CHOPPED (SEE PAGE 372)

SALT AND PEPPER

Have ready a large bowl of water with the lemon juice added. Trim the artichoke stems even with the base of the head and snap off the tough lower leaves. Using a serrated knife, cut off the tough cone of central leaves, revealing the central hairy choke. Cut each artichoke into 6 to 8 segments. With a small knife, scoop out the choke and trim off any tough green outer leaves and fibers, so that only the tender bottom meat is left. Drop the pieces at once into the lemon water so they do not discolor.

Melt the bacon fat in a flameproof casserole. Drain the artichokes and add them to the casserole along with the favas, carrots, scallions, green beans, peppers, garlic, and ham (no salt or pepper is needed at this stage). Add the broth and bring to a boil. Cover, reduce the heat to very low, and cook gently for 30 minutes, stirring occasionally. The vegetables will steam and gradually soften. Stir in the wine and continue cooking for another 15 minutes. Stir in the tomatoes and cook for 15 minutes more. Finally, remove the lid and cook, stirring often, until the vegetables are meltingly tender and the stew is thick and moist but not soupy, 20 to 30 minutes longer.

Season with pepper, taste, and adjust the seasoning. Salt may not be needed, as the ham is salty. Cousinat improves if it is refrigerated for a day or two. Reheat it on the stove top and serve it hot or at warm room temperature.

FÈVES À LA TOURANGELLE

FRESH FAVA BEANS WITH BACON

serves 4 to 6

Fresh favas are a favorite big bean, one of the first arrivals in early spring. They have one drawback: a thick skin that needs peeling. It is a fiddly job, but the bright green, slightly crunchy bean that emerges is ample reward. Even better, when fresh lima beans are in season, they can replace favas without being peeled. Both types of bean are delicious prepared à la tourangelle, *in the fashion of Tours, the famous city on the Loire. With roast veal or spring lamb, they are unbeatable.*

3 CUPS/330 G SHELLED FAVA BEANS (ABOUT 3 POUNDS/
1.35 KG IN THE POD)

SALT AND PEPPER

3 TABLESPOONS/45 G BUTTER

4 THICK SLICES LEAN BACON (ABOUT 4 OUNCES/
110 G TOTAL), DICED

24 BABY ONIONS (ABOUT 12 OUNCES/330 G TOTAL)

2 TABLESPOONS CHOPPED FRESH CHIVES

2 TABLESPOONS CHOPPED FRESH CHERVIL OR PARSLEY

Bring a saucepan of salted water to a boil, add the fava beans, and simmer until tender but still slightly crunchy, 2 to 7 minutes, depending on their age and size. Drain, reserving ½ cup/125 ml of the cooking liquid. Rinse the beans with cold water and drain thoroughly. Peel them by pinching open the stem end of each bean with your thumbnail and popping the bean into a bowl. Set the beans aside.

For the onions, melt the butter in a frying pan over medium heat. Add the bacon and fry until lightly browned, 3 to 5 minutes. Remove the bacon with a draining spoon and set aside. Add the onions to the pan, cover, and cook over low heat, shaking the pan often so they color evenly, until the onions are lightly browned and nearly tender, 12 to 15 minutes. Return the bacon to the pan, add the reserved cooking liquid, and simmer for 5 minutes to blend the flavors. Stir in the beans, chives, and chervil and warm them for 2 to 3 minutes. Taste and adjust the seasoning. The beans may also be kept in the refrigerator for up to 1 day and reheated on the stove top; add the herbs at the last minute.

TARTINE AUX POIVRONS ET AUX PIGNONS

RED PEPPER, TOMATO, AND PINE NUT CROÛTES

serves 4 to 6

With the popularity of Italian bruschette and crostini, the French have returned to croûtes based on dark, crusty bread. Once a snack for workers in the fields, the croûtes were typically topped with no more than a rub with a cut garlic clove, a sprinkling of olive oil, and some chopped onion. Now such croûtes are crowned with cured raw ham, air-dried sausage, Pâté de Campagne *(page 188), or* Rillettes *(page 191) and served in cafés as a trendy alternative to traditional baguette sandwiches. Croûtes spread with mixtures of roasted vegetables like this one are popular, too.*

2 RED BELL PEPPERS, CORED, SEEDED, AND CUT
INTO BROAD STRIPS (SEE PAGE 370)

1 POUND/450 G CHERRY TOMATOES, STEMMED

2 ONIONS, SLICED INTO THIN CRESCENTS

8 GARLIC CLOVES, HALVED LENGTHWISE

SALT AND PEPPER

5 TABLESPOONS/75 ML OLIVE OIL

3 TABLESPOONS/30 G PINE NUTS

4 TO 6 LARGE SLICES COUNTRY BREAD, ½ INCH/
1.25 CM THICK

1 TABLESPOON BALSAMIC VINEGAR, MORE TO TASTE

2 TABLESPOONS COARSELY CHOPPED FRESH PARSLEY

2 TABLESPOONS SHREDDED FRESH BASIL

Heat the oven to 500°F/260°C. Toss the peppers, tomatoes, onions, and garlic with salt and pepper and 2 tablespoons of the oil. Spread them in a roasting pan just large enough to hold them in a single layer. Roast, stirring once, until very tender and browned, 20 to 25 minutes.

Meanwhile, spread the pine nuts in a small frying pan and toast them over medium heat, shaking and tossing often so they brown evenly, for 2 to 3 minutes; take care, as they scorch easily. Toast the bread in a wide-rack toaster, or on a baking sheet in the oven with the vegetables, allowing 10 to 15 minutes so they are golden brown. While the slices are still warm, brush generously with the remaining oil.

When the vegetables are done, toss them with the 1 table-spoon vinegar, parsley, basil, and pine nuts. Taste and adjust the seasoning, adding more vinegar if you like. Top the bread toasts with the roasted vegetables and serve at once. You may cut the vegetables and slice the bread an hour or two in advance, but the cooking must be done at the last minute.

FÈVES À LA TOURANGELLE

POTIMARRON RÔTI AUX HERBES

ROAST BUTTERNUT SQUASH WITH HERBS

serves 4

Pumpkin has long played a role on the country table in recipes such as Soupe de Potiron et Poireaux (page 24), but butternut squash is a new-comer, appearing in our local market only in the last dozen years. It goes into soup of course, it is puréed to serve with roasts and game, and I particularly like it roasted with the skin, an idea from one of my local restaurants in Burgundy.

I LARGE BUTTERNUT SQUASH (ABOUT 3 POUNDS/
1.35 KG)

2 TABLESPOONS/30 G BUTTER

2 TABLESPOONS OLIVE OIL

I TEASPOON SUGAR

SALT AND PEPPER

I BUNCH FRESH THYME (ABOUT ³/₄ OUNCE/20 G)

I BUNCH FRESH ROSEMARY (ABOUT ³/₄ OUNCE/20 G)

3 OR 4 DRIED BAY LEAVES

Heat the oven to 375°F/190°C. With a large chef's knife, cut the squash in half lengthwise and scoop out the seeds. Set each half flat on a cutting board and cut crosswise into slices ⅜ inch/1 cm thick, including the skin. Melt the butter with the oil and generously brush a heavy baking sheet. Line up the squash slices on the baking sheet and brush them also. Sprinkle with the sugar, salt, and pepper. Tuck the thyme and rosemary sprigs and bay leaves between and under the slices.

Cover with aluminum foil and cook in the oven for 30 minutes. Remove the foil and continue roasting, brushing often with the butter-oil mix, until the undersides are brown, about 15 minutes. Turn the slices and roast until they are very tender, brown, and crispy around the edges, 5 to 15 minutes longer, or 50 minutes to 1 hour total. Serve hot.

CONFIT D'OIGNONS

ONION CONFIT

serves 4 to 6

Over the years, I have tasted Confit d'Oignons cooked with wine, or spiced with cardamom or coriander, or even seasoned with soy, but I always come back to the simple original that uses just a few ingredients. At table, it plays the same role as a chutney, a fine accompaniment to ham, duck magret, pork chops, or ribs. Don't be tempted to use sweet onions. The acidity of regular yellow onions is important in giving depth of flavor to the confit.

5 TABLESPOONS/75 G BUTTER

2 POUNDS/900 G ONIONS, SLICED

I TABLESPOON/15 G SUGAR

SALT AND PEPPER

2 TABLESPOONS RED WINE VINEGAR

Melt the butter in a large sauté pan or deep frying pan over low heat. Stir in the onions with the sugar, salt, and pepper and press a piece of aluminum foil down on the onions. Cover the pan and sweat the onions over very low heat, stirring often, until they are reduced and very soft, 25 to 35 minutes. Remove the lid and foil, increase the heat to medium, and continue cooking, stirring often, until the onions are caramelized and very dark, 15 to 20 minutes longer. Stir in the vinegar, dissolving the caramel so its sweetness is balanced. Taste, adjust the seasoning, and serve hot or at room temperature. Onion confit may be tightly covered and kept in the refrigerator for a month or longer.

CONFIT D'ECHALOTES

SHALLOT CONFIT

In a more refined version of Confit d'Oignons, shallots are left whole and caramelized with a bit more sugar. Baby onions may be cooked the same way.

Peel 1 pound/450 g shallots, leaving enough root to hold them together. Melt 2 tablespoons butter in a sauté pan or frying pan over low heat and add the shallots. They should all touch the bottom of the pan. Press a piece of aluminum foil down on the shallots, cover the pan, and sweat the shallots over very low heat, shaking the pan occasionally so they color evenly, until they are tender, 25 to 35 minutes. Remove the lid and foil, sprinkle the shallots with 2 tablespoons sugar, salt, and pepper, and cook them over medium heat, shaking the pan so they color evenly, until they caramelize, 8 to 10 minutes. Serve hot or at room temperature. Serves 4.

= THE ONION FAMILY =

We all cook with the onion family, but French cooks rely on its members more than anyone else. In June, I can count at least six relatives of the family in my vegetable garden in Burgundy, including shallots, garlic, scallions, plain chives and garlic chives, and the familiar old onion itself. The only one missing is leek, a winter standby. All are alliums, members of the lily family, and it is hard to think of a savory French dish that doesn't contain a member of the onion tribe. We are so accustomed to the base note of taste lent to dishes by a bit of onion, leek, shallot, or garlic (see "Glorious Garlic," page 21) that we are more likely to notice its absence than its presence. For example, a ratatouille without the background of garlic will taste puzzlingly flat and bland.

The onion itself is the cheapest and most useful. Its strength depends on variety and origin: generally, the warmer the climate, the sweeter and fatter the bulb. The type of onion is important: for example, the mild Spanish or Bermuda onion used raw in salad gets lost in Carbonnade de Boeuf (page 137), which needs strong yellow onions to balance the flavorings of beer and mustard. The cooking method also affects an onion's flavor. Onions are sweet when gently sautéed in butter and softened almost to a purée—ideal for recipes like Zewelwai (page 280), the onion tart from Alsace. When browned, they caramelize to taste sharper and more biting, the right touch for Gratinée Lyonnaise (page 20).

Too much raw onion, for instance in salad or vinaigrette, tastes crude. This is where the shallot (not to be confused with baby onions, another handy variant) comes in. A smaller, two-lobed cousin of the onion, shallot is less acid and therefore particularly important for sauces. A minced handful in vinaigrettes adds a lively note to salads and cooked vegetables, and is essential in the wine sauce for Sauce Bordelaise au Vin Rouge (page 217) and the delicate Sauce Beurre Blanc (page 221) of Brittany and the Loire. There are two types of shallot: Small, long *échalote grise*, from the southwest, has slightly purple or beige-gray skin and is often partnered with garlic in cooking. *Échalotes rouges*, abundant in Brittany, are usually paired with onion in the northern tradition and have a milder taste and a fatter bulb. Cooking must be gentle; like garlic, chopped shallot turns bitter if sautéed too fast. Whole shallots, on the other hand, make a delicious side dish when slowly caramelized, with or without their skins.

Leeks are milder than both onions and shallots and therefore more commonly stand on their own, for example as the main filling for tarts and gratins. They are good sautéed or added to stews, and when young are often simmered and served with vinaigrette, a typical beginning to a country meal. The green tops of leeks are almost inedible, although it never hurts to add one or two to the stockpot. The same is true of onion skins, which lend color as well as flavor to broth.

The last and mildest members of the onion family include scallions (also called spring onions), chives, and garlic chives that taste as promised. All are most commonly chopped to use raw, and a country kitchen garden will include at least two of them. The elegant green stems of chives make a jazzy garnish, as do their purple cotton-ball flowers, which I love to pickle and display in a jar on the pantry shelf.

TOMATES FARCIES AU FROMAGE DE CHÈVRE

TOMATOES STUFFED WITH GOAT CHEESE

serves 4

I was given this recipe by a producer of goat cheese, a savvy marketeer who hands out recipe leaflets with every cheese he sells. Ironically named Monsieur Cochon (Mr. Pig), he is an idealist, raising his herd of 150 goats, with the help of his wife, Véronique, on herbage from his own farm. "We are producers from start to finish, from raising the goats to making the cheese to meeting our customers; that's what I enjoy," says Jean-Marie Cochon. For these stuffed tomatoes, blue cheese or soft cream cheese may be substituted for the goat cheese.

4 LARGE TOMATOES (ABOUT 1¹/₂ POUNDS/
675 G TOTAL)

SALT AND PEPPER

4 SLICES WHITE BREAD

2 TABLESPOONS OLIVE OIL

2 SMALL SOFT GOAT CHEESES (ABOUT 8 OUNCES/
225 G TOTAL)

2 GARLIC CLOVES, FINELY CHOPPED

2 TABLESPOONS CHOPPED FRESH PARSLEY

2 TABLESPOONS CHOPPED FRESH CHIVES

1 TABLESPOON CHOPPED FRESH THYME

SALAD LEAVES, FOR SERVING (OPTIONAL)

Heat the oven to 400°F/200°C. Core the tomatoes, cut shallow lids from the flower (rounded) ends, and discard them. Using a sharp spoon or melon baller, scoop out about half of the seeds from the tomatoes, taking care not to poke a hole in the bottom. Sprinkle the insides with salt and pepper. Toast the bread and stamp out the largest possible rounds from the center of each with a 3-inch/7.5-cm cookie cutter. Brush the rounds generously with some of the olive oil and set them in a single layer in a small baking dish.

For the filling, crumble the goat cheeses into a bowl, or coarsely crush them with a fork. Mix the garlic, parsley, chives, thyme, pepper, and a little salt in a small bowl, and sprinkle half of the mixture in the tomatoes. Fill the tomatoes with the crumbled cheese, mounding it so it is not packed down. Sprinkle with the remaining garlic mixture and drizzle with the rest of the olive oil. Place the tomatoes on the bread croûtes.

Bake until the cheese is very hot and the tomato skins start to split, 15 to 20 minutes. Serve the tomatoes hot on individual plates, garnished with a few salad leaves if you like.

CHANTERELLES EN PERSILLADE

CHANTERELLE MUSHROOMS WITH GARLIC AND PARSLEY

serves 4

Almost any type of wild mushroom benefits from sautéing in butter with a touch of garlic and a shower of herbs. I often mix golden chanterelles (or their close cousins, girolles*) with contrasting black* trompettes de la mort*, and whatever else is around (see "Mushrooms," page 250). The only wild mushrooms I prefer to keep separate are cèpes (porcini) and morels (which, in any case, are better simmered with some cream). Need I mention appropriate companions for wild mushrooms? They go with almost everything, from eggs to fish, meat, and poultry. But perhaps the greatest treat is a mound of sautéed wild mushrooms on spicy salad greens as an appetizer.*

1 POUND/450 G CHANTERELLE OR OTHER
WILD MUSHROOMS

4 TABLESPOONS/60 G BUTTER

2 GARLIC CLOVES, VERY FINELY CHOPPED

2 SHALLOTS, FINELY CHOPPED

SALT AND PEPPER

2 TABLESPOONS CHOPPED FRESH PARSLEY

2 TABLESPOON CHOPPED FRESH CHIVES

Clean the mushrooms (see page 373) and halve or quarter if large. Melt the butter in a large frying pan over low heat. Add the mushrooms and sprinkle with the garlic, shallots, salt, and pepper. Cover and cook, stirring occasionally, until the juices run, 5 to 10 minutes, depending on the type of mushroom. Remove the lid, increase the heat to medium, and continue cooking until all the liquid has evaporated. Stir in the parsley and chives, taste, adjust the seasoning, and serve.

= TO MARKET, TO MARKET =

No two French markets are alike. I was reminded of this one Saturday morning, when, instead of shopping at my local covered market, I decided to visit Toucy, a nearby town with a weekly open-air market that winds through cobblestone streets. The first stand I came upon was a baker, selling not only the familiar line-up of country breads, but also nearly kayak-sized *pains au levain*. Next were small tables displaying farmhouse goat cheeses, then, strangely, racks of lingerie: lime green– and cherry-colored undies, not to mention brassières apparently designed for carrying watermelons.

Whereas my regular market has several butchers (including one specializing in horse), at the Toucy market sausages and charcuterie were prominent. One Auvergnat had dried sausages heaped sky-high, some plain, others studded with nuts, or rolled in herbs or ash or pepper. My eyes wandered over a chorus of kitschy wooden cats cocking their heads at me from a distant booth, then along to a beekeeper with pots of honey. Finally they settled on a busy *charcutier*, who was funneling blood into casings for *boudin noir* sausage.

There was one more stretch of the market still to see: cages of live chickens and ducks (one cage had just-laid eggs rolling around at the bottom), plus turkeys, quails, rabbits, guinea hens, and doves, all blinking their eyes at passersby. I watched an old man with just one humble cage at his feet containing a handsome bird with herringbone plumage.

When he gave her an unexpected nudge in the behind, she hoisted herself up to reveal six fluffy, curious, chirping chicks.

I had to force myself to stop nosing around and fulfill my original mission—buying local vegetables and local oil. In the countryside, the distinction is often not made between produce grown on a small, artisan scale, and produce that is strictly organic (in French, *bio* for *biologique*). Everyone agrees that what counts most is taste. Plenty here filled the bill: stands bursting with fat new beets, shiny purple eggplants, baby leeks, carrots with dirt still clinging to them, strange squash in every imaginable shape and color. And here too was artisan oil–maker Daniel Maillaut, who handed me four bottles of exquisite walnut oil, and one of mustard. "It tastes nothing like mustard; more like peanuts," he told me. "It's delicious with herring and potato salad, or with cream and shrimp on pasta." French market vendors always know their products so well; I love their advice.

Last of all, at a mountain-produce stand decorated with suspended hams, I spotted a wedge of Emmental, moored at the end of the counter. As the man behind it cut me a slab and wrapped it neatly in paper, I could no longer contain my enthusiasm. "This is a *very* good market," I beamed, waiting for him to smile, and nod, and agree. Instead, he shrugged. "Ouf," he said. "It's a good market. I wouldn't say very good; nothing extraordinary. But I suppose it's good."

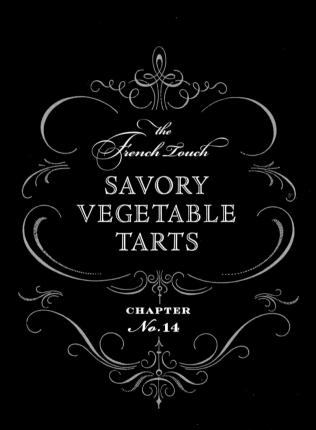

the
French Touch

SAVORY
VEGETABLE
TARTS

CHAPTER
No. 14

Savory tarts are the well-kept secret of many country bakers. In a shop window, you may be dazzled by rows of open-faced fruit tarts, but a closer look usually reveals a plump, savory offering tucked away to the side, which seems to be selling well. In Alsace, you will see Zewelwai (page 280), a creamy onion version of quiche. Northerners seize on hefty slices of Flamiche (facing page) with

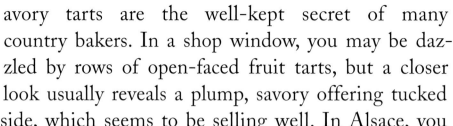

half-hidden fillings of leek or an odorous washed-rind cheese such as Maroilles. In Provence, it is likely to be Pissaladière (page 282), packed with onions and pungent with anchovy. As for quiche itself, everyone from the baker to the charcutier to the gourmet pastry shop has a trademark version. Such savory snacks are big business in France.

The shapes of these country pies and tarts are a delight. Often neatness is abandoned in favor of free-form design where the pastry is folded over the filling for a rustic effect, with no wasted trimmings. I have noticed that big, family-sized tarts are more common in the countryside, while tartlets are more popular in the city. The word *tourte* always catches

my eye, for it implies just my kind of hearty country cooking. A *tourte* is usually baked in a deep mold with a top and bottom crust.

No two savory pies look identical, but they all have two things in common: a lively, highly seasoned filling, and some type of pastry (either bread dough, simple pâte brisée, or rich, buttery pâte feuilletée). Savory *tourtes* and quiches tend to be robust, main-course material, though some tarts, such as flaky, caramelized Tarte Tatin à la Tomate (page 284), make a perfect first course. Savory tarts also do well for a light lunch or a snack on the run. In today's France, hamburgers still have stiff competition.

FLAMICHE

SAVORY YEAST BREAD WITH LEEKS AND CHEESE
makes 2 flamiches to serve 10 to 12

Flamiche comes from northern France and, like pizza, uses a yeast dough. But where pizza is laden with topping, flamiche contains just a small amount of forceful filling—typically, cooked leeks or smelly cheeses such as Munster from Alsace or Maroilles from the north, near Belgium. Baked in a deep pan, the buttery dough rises up to wrap around the filling. The dough here is enough for two flamiches, so you may prefer to halve the recipes for the leek and cheese fillings that I suggest and make one of each. For me, a green salad is the perfect accompaniment.

PÂTE À FLAMICHE

    I TABLESPOON/IO G DRY YEAST

    $^1/_4$ CUP/60 ML LUKEWARM WATER

    3$^1/_2$ CUPS/450 G FLOUR, MORE IF NEEDED

    I$^1/_2$ TEASPOONS SALT

    6 EGGS, AT ROOM TEMPERATURE

    I TABLESPOON/I5 G SUGAR

    $^3/_4$ CUP/I70 G BUTTER, SOFTENED, MORE FOR THE PANS

    FILLING OF CHOICE (RECIPES FOLLOW)

    TWO IO-INCH/25-CM MOULES-À-MANQUÉS (ROUND, SLOPING-SIDED CAKE PANS; SEE PAGE 377)

For the pâte à flamiche, sprinkle the yeast over the warm water in a small bowl and leave until dissolved, about 5 minutes. Sift the flour into a large bowl, add the salt, and make a well in the center. Break the eggs into the well and add the sugar and yeast mixture. With your fingertips, blend the ingredients in the well, and then gradually draw in the flour to make a moist, but not sticky, dough. If it is sticky, work in more flour. Turn the dough onto a lightly floured work surface and knead until smooth and very elastic, about 5 minutes. Pat it flat, spread the butter on top, and knead the two together until mixed. The dough will be very sticky at first. Alternatively, mix and knead the dough in a stand mixer fitted with the dough hook. Transfer the dough to an oiled bowl, turn it to coat the top with oil, and cover the bowl with plastic wrap. Leave to rise in a warm place until doubled in bulk, about 2 hours. If you want to prepare the dough ahead, it may be left to rise in the refrigerator for up to 12 hours. Meanwhile, make the filling.

When the dough has risen, punch it down to knock out the air and divide it in half. On a floured work surface, roll or press out each piece to a 14-inch/35-cm round. Butter the 2 cake pans

and line them with the dough, letting it drape over the rims. Spread your chosen filling over the dough and top with the custard. Fold the overhanging dough over the filling, half covering it. Leave the flamiches to rise in a warm place until well puffed, 15 to 20 minutes. Meanwhile, heat the oven to 400°F/200°C and set a shelf low in the oven.

Bake the flamiches until the crusts are browned and the fillings are set, 40 to 50 minutes. Be sure they are thoroughly browned and start to pull away from the sides of the pan, as they often seem to be done too early. If the tops brown quickly, cover them loosely with aluminum foil. Like many breads, flamiche is best eaten while still warm, but it can be kept for a few hours. Cut into wedges for serving.

FILLINGS FOR FLAMICHE

LEEK FILLING: A confit of leeks, cooked until tender in butter, then combined with eggs and crème fraîche, is a winter favorite.

While the flamiche dough is rising, trim 4 or 5 leeks (about 1½ pounds/675 g total), leaving some of the green tops, quarter them lengthwise, and then slice and clean them (see page 371). Melt 2 tablespoons/30 g butter in a frying pan over low heat, stir in the leeks with salt and pepper, and press a piece of aluminum foil down on the leeks. Cover the pan and sweat the leeks over very low heat, stirring occasionally, until very soft, 25 to 30 minutes. Do not allow them to brown. Line the cake pans with the dough as directed, and spread the leeks on top. Whisk together 2 egg yolks, 5 tablespoons/75 ml crème fraîche (page 374) or heavy cream, salt, pepper, and grated nutmeg, and spoon the custard over the leeks. Fold over the dough and bake the flamiches as described. The filling is enough for 2 flamiches.

CHEESE FILLING: The stinkier the cheese, the better for flamiche. French Munster or Maroilles is perfect.

Slice 8 ounces/225 g strong soft cheese such as French Munster or Maroilles, and discard the rinds. Line the cake pans with the dough as directed and lay the cheese on top. Whisk together 1 egg, 1 egg yolk, and ½ cup/125 ml heavy cream with plenty of salt, pepper, and grated nutmeg, and spoon the custard over the cheese. Fold over the dough and bake the flamiches as described. The filling is enough for 2 flamiches.

TARTE FLAMBÉE
BACON YEAST TART
serves 4 to 6

This Alsatian specialty, also known as flammeküche, *should really be called* tarte flammée, *or "flaming hot tart." Traditionally it was made with any plain bread dough, rolled carton-thin and baked in a scorching-hot wood-fired oven immediately after the coals had been raked out. In Alsace, Tarte Flambée is served on wooden sheets, to be eaten with your fingers, as hot as you can take it.*

PÂTE À PAIN

> 1 2/3 CUPS/200 G FLOUR, MORE AS NEEDED
>
> 1/2 TEASPOON SALT
>
> 6 TABLESPOONS/90 ML LUKEWARM WATER
>
> 1/2 TEASPOON DRY YEAST
>
> 1 EGG
>
> 1 TABLESPOON OLIVE OIL

TOPPING

> 1 TABLESPOON VEGETABLE OIL
>
> 1 CUP/250 ML CRÈME FRAÎCHE (PAGE 374) OR SOUR CREAM
>
> 2 ONIONS, VERY THINLY SLICED
>
> 6-OUNCE/170-G PIECE LEAN SMOKED BACON, CUT INTO THIN LARDONS (SEE PAGE 371)
>
> PEPPER

Make the pâte à pain (see page 375) and leave it to rise. Brush a baking sheet with the vegetable oil. When the dough has risen, knead it lightly to knock out the air. Roll out very thinly to a 12-by-15-inch/30-by-40-cm rectangle and transfer it to the prepared baking sheet. Spread the crème fraîche almost to the edge of the dough. Scatter the onions on the dough, top with the bacon lardons, and sprinkle generously with freshly ground pepper. Leave to rise in a warm place until the dough is well risen, 10 to 15 minutes. Heat the oven to 425°F/220°C and set a baking sheet on a shelf in the upper third of the oven to heat.

Set the risen tart on its baking sheet on the hot sheet in the oven and bake until the bread is browned but still soft enough to fold when you lift a corner, 15 to 20 minutes. (If it becomes crisp, the tart will be tough.) If the onions and lardons have not browned, turn on the broiler and brown the top briefly. Transfer the tart to a thin wooden board, cut into squares, and serve at once, very hot.

ZEWELWAI
ALSATIAN ONION QUICHE
serves 6 to 8

The mother of all quiches must be Quiche Lorraine (page 46); if the bacon is dropped, you get Zewelwai, a luscious onion tart rich with crème fraîche. In fact, the real difference comes from gently sweating onions (lots of them) in butter until meltingly soft and delicately sweet.

PÂTE BRISÉE

> 1 2/3 CUPS/200 G FLOUR
>
> 1 EGG YOLK
>
> 3/4 TEASPOON SALT
>
> 3 TABLESPOONS/45 ML WATER, MORE IF NEEDED
>
> 6 TABLESPOONS/90 G BUTTER, MORE FOR THE PAN

FILLING

> 2 TABLESPOONS/30 G GOOSE FAT OR BUTTER
>
> 3 ONIONS (ABOUT 1 POUND/450 G TOTAL), SLICED
>
> SALT AND PEPPER
>
> 2 EGGS
>
> 1 CUP/250 ML CRÈME FRAÎCHE (PAGE 374), THINNED WITH ABOUT 2 TABLESPOONS HEAVY CREAM
>
> PINCH OF GRATED NUTMEG
>
> 9- TO 10-INCH/23- TO 25-CM TART PAN WITH A REMOVABLE BASE

Make the pâte brisée (see page 375) and chill until firm, 15 to 30 minutes. Heat the oven to 375°F/190°C and set a baking sheet on a low shelf to heat. Roll out the dough and line the tart pan, then partially bake it blind (see page 372) on the hot baking sheet. Let the tart shell cool, and leave the baking sheet in the oven and the oven on.

For the filling, melt the goose fat in a frying pan over low heat and stir in the onions with salt and pepper. Press a piece of aluminum foil down on the onions, cover the pan, and sweat the onions, stirring often, 25 to 30 minutes. Do not allow them to brown and caramelize. Taste for seasoning and spread in the tart shell.

In a bowl, whisk together the eggs and crème fraîche. Salt the custard lightly, and add pepper and the nutmeg. Set the tart shell in its pan on the hot baking sheet and pour the custard into the shell. Bake until the filling is set and golden brown, 30 to 35 minutes. Do not overcook or the filling will curdle.

Serve warm or at room temperature. It may be baked ahead and reheated the following day.

TRUFFE EN AUMONIÈRE

TRUFFLE IN A PUFF PASTRY CASE

serves 4

In truffle-growing regions such as Périgord, astute cooks know that certain ingredients, such as port, Madeira, and foie gras, bring the savor of a fresh truffle to full bloom. That's what makes this recipe the ultimate treat. If fresh truffles are out of reach, I suggest you substitute a large button mushroom, different but still delicious. The best foie gras for this recipe comes vacuum packed and mi-cuit *(half cooked). Canned pâté de foie gras does well, too, but* mousse de foie gras *is too soft.*

PÂTE FEUILLETÉE

2 CUPS/250 G FLOUR, MORE AS NEEDED

1 CUP/225 G CHILLED BUTTER

1/2 CUP/125 ML WATER, MORE IF NEEDED

1 TEASPOON SALT

1 TEASPOON FRESH LEMON JUICE

1 EGG MIXED WITH 1/2 TEASPOON SALT, FOR GLAZE

4 FRESH TRUFFLES (ABOUT 1 OUNCE/30 G EACH)

4 TABLESPOONS/60 G BUTTER

1 SMALL ONION, DICED

1/2 CARROT, DICED

1/2 STALK CELERY, DICED

SALT AND PEPPER

3/4 CUP/175 ML VEAL BROTH (SEE PAGE 373)

2 TABLESPOONS PORT

4 OUNCES/110 G VACUUM-PACKED MI-CUIT
FOIE GRAS OR CANNED PÂTÉ DE FOIE GRAS

Make the pâte feuilletée (see page 375) and measure 1 pound/ 450 g; save the rest for another use. Chill the dough until firm, 30 minutes to 1 hour. On a floured work surface, roll out the pastry to an 11-inch/28-cm square and trim the edges to neaten them. Cut the large square into 4 equal squares. Sprinkle a baking sheet with water, transfer the dough squares to it, and chill until firm, at least 15 minutes.

Meanwhile, prepare the truffles. Brush each truffle gently under cold running water to remove any earth, then peel it with a small knife. Reserve the peelings to cook with the vegetables. Melt 2 tablespoons/30 g of the butter in a frying pan over medium heat. Add the onion, carrot, celery, salt, and pepper and sauté, stirring often, until tender, 5 to 8 minutes. Add the broth, port, and truffle peelings and simmer until the vegetables are very

tender, 12 to 15 minutes longer. Taste, adjust the seasoning, and set the pan aside to cool.

To wrap the truffles, cut the foie gras into 4 equal slices and set a slice on each square of puff pastry dough. Put a truffle on top. Drain the vegetables, reserving the cooking liquid. Sprinkle the vegetables with salt and pepper and spoon them around each truffle.

Brush the 4 corners of each pastry square with the egg glaze, bring up the corners to the top of the truffle, and pinch them together to make a little knot. Press to seal the pastry edges together. Brush the packages with the egg glaze and chill in the freezer until firm, about 15 minutes. Or you may store them in the refrigerator for up to 24 hours before continuing.

To finish, heat the oven to 475°F/240°C. Bake the packages until puffed and golden brown, 15 to 20 minutes. Meanwhile, make a jus. Boil the reserved cooking liquid to reduce to 1/2 cup/ 125 ml. Dice the remaining 2 tablespoons/30 g butter and whisk it, off the heat, into the cooking liquid, so it softens and thickens the jus without melting to oil. Taste and adjust the seasoning. Serve the truffle packages very hot, with the jus passed separately.

CHAMPIGNON EN AUMONIÈRE

MUSHROOM IN A PUFF PASTRY CASE

A plump mushroom, baked with foie gras in a pastry case, runs a surprisingly close second to a whole truffle.

In the recipe for Truffe en Aumonière, omit the truffle. Trim off the stems of 8 large button mushrooms (about 6 ounces/ 170 g total), reserving the stems. Put the mushrooms, cap down, in a buttered baking dish. Dot the mushrooms with 2 tablespoons/ 30 g butter and sprinkle with salt and pepper. Cover with aluminum foil and bake in a 350°F/180°C oven until tender and any liquid has evaporated, 15 to 20 minutes. Let them cool, then set 1 mushroom on another, bases together, to make a ball. Substitute the mushroom balls for the truffles in Truffe en Aumonière. Chop the mushroom stems and use in place of the truffle peelings in the vegetable mixture. Serves 4.

PISSALADIÈRE

ONION, ANCHOVY, OLIVE, AND TOMATO YEAST TART

serves 6

A glance at Pissaladière, a flat yeast bread from the Pays Niçois border-
ing Italy, reveals its close relationship to Neapolitan pizza. Pissaladière is
topped with much more onion and fewer tomatoes than the average pizza,
and it always includes anchovy. It can be baked in a large tart pan, or flat
on a baking sheet, as I do here. The best black olives for the topping are
brined with less salt than the classic Greek-style olive. The olives of Nyons
in northern Provence are ideal.

PÂTE À PAIN

1²/₃ CUPS/200 G FLOUR, MORE AS NEEDED

¹/₂ TEASPOON SALT

6 TABLESPOONS/90 ML LUKEWARM WATER

1 TEASPOON DRY YEAST

1 EGG

1 TABLESPOON OLIVE OIL

TOPPING

3 TABLESPOONS/45 ML OLIVE OIL, MORE FOR
BRUSHING

4 OR 5 ONIONS (ABOUT 1¹/₂ POUNDS/675 G TOTAL),
THINLY SLICED

3 GARLIC CLOVES, CHOPPED

1 TABLESPOON CHOPPED MIXED FRESH BASIL,
THYME, AND ROSEMARY

SALT AND PEPPER

12 TO 14 ANCHOVY FILLETS, SOAKED IN MILK FOR A
FEW MINUTES

2 OR 3 LARGE TOMATOES (ABOUT 1 POUND/450 G
TOTAL), PEELED (SEE PAGE 372)

¹/₂ CUP/100 G BRINED BLACK OLIVES, PITTED

Make the pâte à pain (see page 375) and leave it to rise. Meanwhile, start the topping. Heat the oil in a deep frying pan over
low heat and stir in the onions, garlic, herbs, salt, and pepper.
Press a piece of aluminum foil down on the onions, cover the
pan, and sweat the onions over very low heat, stirring occasionally,
until very soft, 25 to 30 minutes. Do not allow them to brown
and caramelize. Taste, adjust the seasoning, and set the onions
aside. Cut the anchovy fillets in half lengthwise. Cut the tomatoes
crosswise into 4 or 5 slices, discarding the core and flower ends.
Brush a baking sheet with oil.

When the dough has risen, knead it lightly to knock out the air.
Pat the dough out on the prepared baking sheet to a 12-inch/30-cm
round. Spread the onions on the dough, leaving a 1-inch/2.5-cm
border. Arrange the tomatoes to cover the onions and sprinkle with
pepper (no extra salt is needed). Make a diagonal lattice of anchovy
fillets, filling the spaces with the olives. Brush the surface of the
topping with oil. Leave to rise in a warm place until the dough is
well risen, 10 to 15 minutes. Heat the oven to 375°F/190°C.

Bake the tart until the edges are browned and quite crisp and
the topping is very hot, 25 to 35 minutes. Serve as soon as possible
after baking, hot or at room temperature.

PÂTÉ DE POMMES DE TERRE

FLAKY POTATO PIE

serves 6 to 8

Part of the charm of a savory pie or tart is to guess the filling, and Pâté de Pommes de Terre always comes as a surprise to me. It looks so glamorous, it tastes so appetizing, yet can it really be no more than a combination of two starches and some cream? In this version, the richest imaginable, the potatoes are baked inside rounds of puff pastry, then moistened with a generous amount of crème fraîche poured through a hole in the cover (see "Inimitable Crème Fraîche," page 320). The recipe comes with a tip, passed on by a friend from the Berry in central France, where Pâté de Pommes de Terre is a specialty: mix the crème fraîche with garlic and parsley and leave it overnight. This small step makes all the difference. The pie may be served as a first course, or as an accompaniment to meats.

PÂTE FEUILLETÉE

   2 CUPS/250 G FLOUR, MORE AS NEEDED

   I CUP/225 G CHILLED BUTTER

   ¹/₂ CUP/125 ML WATER, MORE IF NEEDED

   I TEASPOON SALT

   I TEASPOON FRESH LEMON JUICE

   I EGG MIXED WITH ¹/₂ TEASPOON SALT, FOR GLAZE

FILLING

   6 TABLESPOONS/90 ML CRÈME FRAÎCHE (PAGE 374) OR HEAVY CREAM

   3 GARLIC CLOVES, CHOPPED

   4 TABLESPOONS CHOPPED FRESH PARSLEY

   3 WAXY POTATOES (ABOUT I¹/₄ POUNDS/550 G TOTAL), PEELED AND THINLY SLICED

   SALT AND PEPPER

   PINCH OF GRATED NUTMEG

Make the pâte feuilletée (see page 375) and chill until firm, 30 minutes to 1 hour. Meanwhile, make the filling. Stir together the crème fraîche, garlic, and parsley and set aside. If possible, do this several hours ahead (or even the night before). Bring a saucepan of salted water to a boil. Add the potatoes and simmer until partly cooked but still firm, 3 to 5 minutes. Drain the potatoes, rinse, and drain well. Season with salt, pepper, and nutmeg and leave to cool.

Sprinkle a baking sheet with water. On a floured work surface, roll out slightly less than half the pastry to a thin 12-inch/30-cm round. Using a pan lid as a guide and a sharp knife, cut out an 11-inch/28-cm round. Roll out the remaining dough slightly thicker than the first round and cut out a 13-inch/33-cm round. Set the smaller round on the baking sheet and press it down lightly so it does not shrink. Arrange about half the potato slices in an overlapping layer on the pastry, leaving a 1-inch/2.5-cm border. Spoon about half of the crème fraîche mixture over the potatoes, reserving the rest for serving. Arrange the remaining potato slices on top, and brush the border with some of the egg glaze. Set the larger pastry round on top and press the edges of the rounds firmly together to seal them. Scallop the edge of the pie by pulling in the pastry at regular intervals with the back of a knife. Brush the top with the remaining egg glaze. Using the tip of a knife, score a 5-inch/13-cm circle on top of the pie, which will form a hat when baked. Chill the pie until firm, about 30 minutes. It may be prepared up to 1 day ahead and kept in the refrigerator.

Heat the oven to 425°F/220°C and set a shelf low in the oven. Bake the pie until puffed and golden brown, 25 to 30 minutes. A skewer inserted in the center should come out hot to the touch when withdrawn after 30 seconds. Warm the remaining crème fraîche mixture, cut the hat from the pie, and carefully pour in the crème fraîche mixture. Replace the hat and serve at once.

TARTE TATIN À LA TOMATE

TOMATO TART TATIN

serves 4 to 6

The original tarte Tatin was made with apples (page 345), but the same concept of deeply caramelized fruit turned out on a crisp pastry base has inspired today's versions featuring pear, quince, tomato, or even eggplant or Belgian endive. In Tarte Tatin à la Tomate, a drizzle of vinegar highlights the caramel, yielding an intense, savory tart to serve with crisp greens as a first course or light main dish. It also makes an excellent accompaniment to chicken or to game such as rabbit.

Don't be concerned if the tomatoes look a trifle charred when the tart is turned out, as they will taste all the better. If you have some puff pastry trimmings in your freezer, by all means use them. If not, for the small amount here, I suggest you use ready-prepared frozen dough. No special pan is needed, just two frying pans with ovenproof handles.

6 OUNCES/170 G PUFF PASTRY TRIMMINGS OR STORE-BOUGHT PUFF PASTRY

2 POUNDS/900 G PLUM TOMATOES, CORED AND HALVED LENGTHWISE

SALT AND PEPPER

¼ CUP/60 G SUGAR

¼ CUP/60 ML RED WINE VINEGAR

¼ CUP/60 ML OLIVE OIL, MORE FOR THE PAN

2 OR 3 SPRIGS FRESH ROSEMARY

2 OR 3 DRIED BAY LEAVES

I HEAD GARLIC, SEPARATED INTO CLOVES, UNPEELED

¼ CUP/60 ML RED WINE

FEW LEAVES ARUGULA OR FRISÉE, FOR GARNISH

Heat the oven to 275°F/140°C. Sprinkle the cut sides of the tomatoes with salt and pepper and set them aside. Sprinkle the sugar in a large frying pan with an ovenproof handle and cook over medium heat, stirring occasionally, until the sugar melts and toasts to golden caramel, 3 to 5 minutes. Take the pan from the heat and at once add the vinegar, standing back as it will sputter and fume. Return it to the heat, stir to dissolve the caramel, and then stir in the oil. Again take the pan from the heat and add the tomatoes, cut side down, packing them tightly so they all touch the bottom and pushing the rosemary and bay between them.

Roast the tomatoes until they are very tender and wrinkled, 2 to 2½ hours. Forty-five minutes before they are done, add the unpeeled garlic cloves to the pan. If liquid remains at the end of cooking, evaporate most of it by cooking the tomatoes briefly over high heat, taking care they do not scorch.

Oil a second frying pan with an ovenproof handle and transfer the tomatoes to it, arranging them snugly, cut side down, in a pattern. Discard the herbs and leave the garlic behind, along with any juices, in the first pan. Add the wine to the garlic and heat it, stirring to dissolve the juices and boil them down to 2 to 3 tablespoons. Pour the liquid and garlic through a strainer over the tomatoes, then push through the garlic pulp. Set the tomatoes aside to cool. The tomatoes may be cooked up to a day ahead and stored in the refrigerator.

Heat the oven to 400°F/200°C. On a floured work surface, roll out the pastry to a 10-inch/25-cm round and prick the dough so it rises evenly. Transfer it to the pan to cover the tomatoes and tuck any excess dough down around the fruit. Bake the tart until the dough has risen and is crisp and golden brown, 15 to 20 minutes. Let the tart cool for 5 minutes, then turn it out onto a platter and garnish with the arugula. Alternatively, let it cool in the pan, then turn it out and serve it at room temperature. Tarte Tatin à la Tomate may also be cooked up to 8 hours ahead and kept in the pan. Warm it briefly in the oven before turning it out.

TARTE TATIN AUX ENDIVES

ENDIVE TART TATIN

The caramelized halves of Belgian endive, arranged like a flower on the tart, are their own decoration—a perfect opening to a winter dinner.

Heat the oven to 350°F/180°C. Follow the recipe for Tarte Tatin à la Tomate, omitting the tomatoes, herbs, and garlic. Make the caramel in a 12-inch/30-cm frying pan and dissolve it in the vinegar. Trim and halve 6 to 8 small heads Belgian endive (about 2 pounds/900 g total). Pack them, cut side down, in the caramel-lined pan, sprinkle with salt and pepper, and cover with aluminum foil. Bake until the endives are tender, 45 minutes to 1 hour. Increase the oven heat to 400°F/200°C. Set the endives aside on a plate. Boil the pan juices to a glaze on top of the stove, dissolve them in the wine, and boil again down to a syrup. Replace the endives in the syrup, arranging the pieces cut side down and with stems outward like the petals of a flower. Roll out the dough, cover the endives, and bake as for Tarte Tatin à la Tomate. Serves 6 to 8.

BREADS & CAKES

THE COUNTRY BAKER

CHAPTER
No. 15

sk any French countryman, and he will tell you the most important food is bread. My neighbor Monsieur Milbert, age eighty-six, recalls that he thought nothing of eating a whole loaf or even more each day when he was young. What he has in mind from those long-ago times was a large round or oval whole-wheat loaf that remained moist and chewy for days at a time, and was bought perhaps twice a week.

The familiar baguette, literally a "wand," that we think of as so French was a city pretension, and did not become the national standard until after World War II. Within the baguette family itself, there are distinctions. A *banneton* is shorter and thicker. A *ficelle*, "string," is often sliced for croûtes, as is the slightly plumper *flute*. Large family loaves are called simply *pains*. The *bâtarde* lies halfway between a baguette and a *pain*.

Over the last fifty years in France, bread consumption per head has declined by more than half. Tastes are shifting to mixed-grain doughs, dense country loaves, and dark rye and whole-wheat breads. Shapes run to *baguettes à l'ancienne* with pointed ends, horseshoes, and plump balls slashed deeply in a lattice. Savory breads like Alsatian Tarte Flambée (page 280) and Gannat (facing page), a cheese bread from the Auvergne, rival the ubiquitous pizza, which after all is no more than bread with a savory topping. In the south, Fouace (page 292) is a savory distraction, bright with toppings of coarse salt, herbs, garlic, and grated lemon zest, singly or all at once.

It is the sweet breads that are my downfall. When I start early in the morning in France, I am in big trouble because of artisanal bakeries that offer croissants, brioches, and local specialties such as Tarte au Sucre (facing page), a great wheel of bread topped with butter and coarse sugar. Kugelhopf (page 290)

from Alsace, studded with candied peel and raisins, makes another dream breakfast paired with a *café crème*. These specialty breads vary from region to region and collectively are called Viennoiseries (page 303), just to be misleading. Lucky is the schoolchild who gets to choose a *goûter* at the pâtisserie on the way home from school. My children's choices never changed—for one a *pain au chocolat* and for the other a giant chocolate-coated meringue that exploded the minute it was bitten. And today, grown up, they haven't changed their minds.

The French don't bake much bread at home because everyone does best—or did best—buying from a bakery. However, cakes are another matter and even the busiest cook makes a cake or two. I once lived as an au pair in a French family with seven children. Not only birthdays, but also name days (each child was named after a saint) were celebrated with an identical homemade, fluffy *génoise*, the only variant being the flavor of icing chosen by the honoree. Dinner guests would be offered Maman's Gâteau Chocolat (page 304), or buttery Gâteau Breton (page 293). Other mothers from other regions whisk similar, time-honored gâteaux, ranging from spice bread in Burgundy to walnut cake in the Périgord to feather-light Biscuit de Savoie (page 298). All these cakes, and dozens more, are the pride and the signature of the cooks who make them.

GOCHTIALE

BRETON LIGHT BRIOCHE

serves 6

Where butter is made in France, you will find light, fluffy brioche breads under names like la gâche *on the Cotentin Peninsula of Normandy,* la falue *farther east,* cookeboodram *around Dunkerque near Belgium, and* kramik *in Champagne. All are made with a similar soft, floppy dough that is kneaded by lifting it off the work surface and throwing it down, first with one hand, then with the other. Small or larger quantities of butter are added after the dough has risen once. All brioche breads are best eaten fresh on the day of baking, or they may be frozen for a few months. With their high sugar or cheese content, they toast well.*

1 TABLESPOON/10 G DRY YEAST

1/2 CUP/125 ML LUKEWARM MILK

2 3/4 CUPS/330 G FLOUR, MORE IF NEEDED

1/4 CUP/60 G SUGAR

1/2 TEASPOON SALT

2 EGGS, BEATEN TO MIX

1/2 CUP/110 G BUTTER AT ROOM TEMPERATURE, MORE FOR THE PAN

1 EGG MIXED WITH 1/2 TEASPOON SALT, FOR GLAZE

6-INCH/15-CM MOULE-À-MANQUÉ (ROUND, SLOPING-SIDED CAKE PAN; SEE PAGE 377)

Sprinkle the yeast over the milk in a small bowl and let stand until dissolved, about 5 minutes. Sift the flour onto a work surface, sprinkle with the sugar and salt, and make a well in the center. Add the yeast mixture and the beaten eggs to the well. With your hand, combine the yeast mixture and eggs, then gradually work in the flour to form a smooth dough; it should be quite sticky. Knead the dough on the work surface, lifting it up and throwing it down first with one hand, then with the other, until it is very elastic and resembles chamois leather. This should take about 10 minutes, and the dough will gradually change texture until it pulls into a long rope when lifted. If necessary, work in a little more flour. Alternatively, mix and knead the dough in a stand mixer fitted with the dough hook. Transfer the dough to an oiled bowl, turn it to coat the top with oil, and cover the bowl with a damp cloth. Leave to rise in a warm place until doubled in bulk, about 1 hour.

Butter the cake pan. Knead the risen dough lightly to knock out the air. Squeeze the butter with your fist until it is pliable. Add it to the dough and knead it, first squeezing the dough and butter together with your fist until mixed, and then lifting and throwing it down, until the butter is completely incorporated, 5 to 10 minutes. (Alternatively, use the mixer.)

Lightly flour the work surface and shape the dough into a ball, folding the edges to the center. Flip the ball so the smooth side is upward and drop it gently into the prepared pan. Cover with a cloth and leave to rise in a warm place until nearly doubled, 45 minutes to 1 hour. Heat the oven to 375°F/190°C.

Brush the brioche with the egg glaze. With the point of a very sharp knife, slash a deep cross on the top of the loaf. Bake until the brioche is golden brown and starts to shrink from the sides of the pan, 25 to 35 minutes. The loaf will sound hollow when tapped on the bottom. Unmold and let cool on a rack. Cut the loaf crosswise into generous slices for serving.

BRIOCHE DE GANNAT

AUVERGNAT CHEESE BRIOCHE

If you are lucky in the Auvergne, you will be handed a chunky toasted slice of this savory bread, with a glass of the robust local wine.

Make the brioche dough as in Gochtiale, adding 1 tablespoon sugar instead of 1/4 cup/60 g. After the first rising, work in only 4 tablespoons/60 g butter. When the dough is smooth, work in 1 cup/100 g grated Cantal or Gruyère cheese, reserving 2 tablespoons for topping. Butter a 9-by-4-by-3-inch/23-by-10-by-7.5-cm loaf pan. Shape the dough into a loaf, set it in the pan, cover, and leave to rise in a warm place until the dough reaches the top of the pan, 45 minutes to 1 hour. Heat the oven to 400°F/200°C. Brush the loaf with the egg glaze and sprinkle with the reserved cheese. Bake until browned and the loaf sounds hollow when tapped on the bottom, 30 to 40 minutes. Unmold and let cool on a rack. Serves 6 to 8.

TARTE AU SUCRE

SUGAR GALETTE

Think sweet pizza and you will picture Tarte au Sucre, a great disk of bread with a crispy butter and sugar topping.

Make the brioche dough as in Gochtiale. Butter a baking sheet, and heat the oven to 400°F/200°C. Shape the dough into a ball and drop it onto the sheet. Flour your hand and pat the dough into a round or rectangle about 3/8 inch/1 cm thick with a rim at the edge. Dot the surface inside the rim with 2 tablespoons/30 g softened butter and sprinkle with 1/2 cup/100 g packed light or dark brown sugar. Let the galette rise for about 15 minutes. Bake until it has risen and is brown, 15 to 20 minutes. Serve as soon as possible for 6 to 8.

KUGELHOPF

RAISIN YEAST BREAD

makes 2 Kugelhopfs to serve 12

In Alsace, a breakfast of warm Kugelhopf is a morning ritual. I like mine to be fragrant with a bit of chopped candied peel of citron, an aromatic citrus fruit with a thick skin that candies particularly well. Sturdy metal Kugelhopf molds or fluted tube pans are easy to find, and they do a good job, but somehow the crust is never quite the same when this raisin-studded bread is baked in metal. Every time I am in Strasbourg, I buy a fluted earthenware mold for baking my own at home, and every time it seems to get broken.

1 CUP/250 ML MILK

1/2 CUP PLUS 2 TABLESPOONS/140 G BUTTER, MORE FOR THE MOLDS

3 TABLESPOONS/45 G GRANULATED SUGAR

1 TABLESPOON/10 G DRY YEAST

3 CUPS/390 G FLOUR, MORE IF NEEDED

1 TEASPOON SALT

3 EGGS, BEATEN TO MIX

3 TO 4 TABLESPOONS SLICED ALMONDS

1/2 CUP/135 G DRIED CURRANTS

1/4 CUP/65 G RAISINS

3 TABLESPOONS/45 G CHOPPED CANDIED CITRON PEEL (OPTIONAL)

CONFECTIONERS' SUGAR, FOR SPRINKLING

TWO 8-INCH/20-CM KUGELHOPF MOLDS OR TUBE PANS

Scald the milk in a small saucepan, pour about half into a small bowl, and let cool to lukewarm. Add the butter and granulated sugar to the remaining milk and continue heating, stirring until the butter melts and the sugar dissolves. Sprinkle the yeast over the lukewarm milk in a small bowl and let stand until dissolved, about 5 minutes.

Sift the flour with the salt into a large bowl and make a well in the center. Add both milk mixtures and the eggs to the well. With your hand, mix the central ingredients, and then gradually draw in the flour to make a smooth dough. It should be very soft. Cup your hand and knead the dough in a slapping motion against the side of the bowl. Continue until the dough is shiny and elastic and still clings to the sides of the bowl, about 5 minutes. Alternatively, mix and knead the dough in a stand mixer fitted with the dough hook. Cover the bowl with a damp cloth and leave to rise in a warm place until doubled in bulk, 1 to 1½ hours.

Generously butter the molds and press the sliced almonds around the sides. Knead the risen dough lightly to knock out the air. Work in the currants, raisins, and the citron peel, if using. Drop the dough by spoonfuls into the molds, dividing it evenly around the central chimney (this is important or the breads will be lopsided). Leave to rise in a warm place to the top of the molds, 45 minutes to 1 hour. Heat the oven to 375°F/190°C.

Bake the breads until they are puffed, golden brown, and pulling away from the sides of the molds, 25 to 35 minutes. Turn them out onto racks to cool. They are best eaten the day of baking, and they freeze well for up to 3 months. Sprinkle with the confectioners' sugar just before serving.

KUGELHOPF AUX LARDONS ET AUX NOIX

KUGELHOPF WITH HAM AND WALNUTS

Savory Kugelhopfs like this one are increasingly popular.

In the recipe for Kugelhopf, decrease the sugar to 2 teaspoons. Omit the sliced almonds, currants, raisins, and citron peel. Press 10 to 12 walnut halves into the flutes of the molds, and flavor the dough with ½ cup/60 g chopped walnuts, ½ cup/60 g finely diced smoked ham, and 1½ tablespoons each chopped fresh sage and thyme. Let rise and bake as for sweet Kugelhopf. Makes 2 Kugelhopfs to serve 12.

FOUACE

PROVENÇAL FLAT YEAST BREAD

serves 4

Provençal Fouace, also called fougasse, *is closely related to Italian focaccia. Both are flat breads, often flavored with such Mediterranean ingredients as chopped olives, garlic, herbs, grated citrus zest, or sun-dried tomatoes, and the dough for both is laced with nearly double the usual amount of yeast, so it rises rapidly, giving the bread an open, airy texture. Fouace is found in many shapes, too, including rounds, ovals, rectangles, wheels slashed with spokes, and this rustic leaf design.*

1 TABLESPOON/10 G DRY YEAST

$^1/_2$ CUP/125 ML LUKEWARM WATER

2 $^3/_4$ CUPS/330 G FLOUR, MORE IF NEEDED

2 EGGS

1 TEASPOON SALT

2 TEASPOONS SUGAR

2 TABLESPOONS OLIVE OIL

$^1/_4$ CUP/50 G CHOPPED PITTED BRINED BLACK OR GREEN OLIVES, 2 TABLESPOONS CHOPPED FRESH THYME OR ROSEMARY, OR GRATED ZEST OF 1 ORANGE OR 2 LEMONS

2 GARLIC CLOVES, CHOPPED (OPTIONAL)

1 EGG MIXED WITH $^1/_2$ TEASPOON SALT, FOR GLAZE

Sprinkle the yeast over half of the water in a small bowl. Sift the flour onto a work surface. Sprinkle ¼ cup/60 g of this flour over the yeast and work with your hand to make a soft, sticky paste. Leave this starter in a warm place until it starts to rise and bubble, 15 to 20 minutes.

Make a large well in the center of the sifted flour. Add the yeast starter, the remaining water, eggs, salt, sugar, oil, olives, and the garlic, if using, to the well. Briefly mix the central ingredients with your fingers, then draw in the flour using a pastry scraper. Work the ingredients with your hand to a rough dough and press it into a ball, adding more flour if it is very sticky. Flour the work surface and knead the dough until smooth and elastic, 5 to 7 minutes. Alternatively, mix and knead the dough in a stand mixer fitted with the dough hook. Transfer the dough to an oiled bowl, turn it to coat the top with oil, and cover the bowl with a damp cloth. Leave to rise in a warm place until doubled in bulk, about 1 hour.

Punch down the dough to knock out the air. Flour a baking sheet and turn the dough out onto it. With a floured fist, press it out to an oval about ¾ inch/2 cm thick. With a knife, make diagonal slits like the veins on a leaf, and pull the slits apart with your fingers. Leave to rise in a warm place until nearly doubled, 15 to 25 minutes. Heat the oven to 400°F/200°C.

Brush the bread with the egg glaze and bake until golden brown, 15 to 18 minutes. Serve the bread while still warm, leaving guests to break it into pieces at the table.

BABAS AU RHUM

RUM BABAS

makes 12 medium babas

Babas are part of French folklore, so much so that the expression tout baba *means "bowled over with delight." The story goes that one day in the eighteenth century, Duke Stanislas of Lorraine improved his morning Kugelhopf with a sprinkling of rum. The result was so delicious that he thought himself transported to Ali Baba's world of* One Thousand and One Nights. *So was born the best yeast cake of all, Baba au Rhum.*

Babas are usually baked in characteristic small, bucket-shaped molds and presented tipped on their side. Giant babas, such as you can find in Alsace and Lorraine, are tricky to soak thoroughly with the hot rum-flavored sugar syrup. For best results, make light, open-textured little yeast cakes and allow them to dry for a day or two so they absorb a maximum of syrup. Babas are often served plain, or you can decorate them with flowers fashioned from sliced almonds and a bit of candied cherry.

1 TABLESPOON/10 G DRY YEAST

3 TABLESPOONS/45 ML LUKEWARM WATER

2 CUPS/250 G FLOUR

1 TEASPOON SALT

1 TABLESPOON/15 G SUGAR

3 EGGS, BEATEN TO MIX

$^3/_4$ CUP/110 G DRIED CURRANTS

3 TABLESPOONS/45 ML DARK RUM

$^1/_2$ CUP/110 G BUTTER, SOFTENED, MORE FOR THE MOLDS

RUM SYRUP

2 CUPS/390 G SUGAR

3 CUPS/375 ML WATER

$^1/_2$ CUP/125 ML DARK RUM, MORE TO TASTE

DECORATION (OPTIONAL)

3 TO 4 CANDIED CHERRIES

4 TO 5 TABLESPOONS SLICED ALMONDS

TWELVE 7-TABLESPOON/100-ML BABA MOLDS

Sprinkle the yeast over the warm water in a small bowl and let stand until dissolved, about 5 minutes. Sift the flour, salt, and sugar into a warmed bowl, make a well in the center, and add the yeast mixture and eggs to the well. With your hand, mix the central ingredients, and then gradually draw in the flour to make a smooth dough. It should be very soft. Cup your hand and knead the dough in a slapping motion against the side of the bowl. Continue until it is shiny and very smooth, about 5 minutes. Alternatively, mix and knead the dough in a stand mixer fitted with the dough hook. Cover the bowl with a damp cloth and leave to rise in a warm place until doubled in bulk, 1 to 1¼ hours. Meanwhile, soak the currants in the rum.

Generously butter the molds, chill in the freezer until set, and butter a second time. When the dough has risen, knead it lightly to knock out the air. Add the softened butter and continue beating with your hand until the butter is incorporated, 1 to 2 minutes. Beat the currants and rum into the dough. Using 2 teaspoons, drop the dough into the prepared molds, filling them about half full and without letting dough drip onto the sides. Set the molds on a baking sheet, cover them with a dry cloth, and leave to rise in a warm place rise until the molds are full, 30 to 45 minutes. Heat the oven to 400°F/200°C.

Bake the babas until they are golden brown and have started to shrink from the sides of the molds, 20 to 25 minutes. Turn them out onto a rack to cool. If you can bake the babas a day ahead and leave them uncovered overnight, so much the better. They will dry and absorb more syrup.

For the syrup, heat the sugar and water in a sauté pan or wide, shallow saucepan over medium heat, stirring occasionally until the sugar is dissolved. Bring the syrup to a boil and boil rapidly for 2 to 3 minutes. Turn off the heat and stir in ¼ cup/60 ml of the rum. Drop the babas into the hot syrup. Turn and baste them so they absorb as much as possible, almost doubling their original size. Transfer them to a platter or individual plates with a draining spoon, laying them on their sides. If you need to soak the babas in 2 batches, reheat the syrup before adding the second batch. Reserve any leftover syrup. The babas may be soaked 4 to 6 hours ahead and kept tightly covered at room temperature.

To finish, if you like, decorate each baba with a nugget of candied cherry, surrounding it with petals of sliced almond. Sprinkle each baba with 1 teaspoon of neat rum to add fresh flavor. If any syrup remains, lace it with a bit more rum and serve it in a pitcher with the babas.

GÂTEAU BRETON

serves 8

A cross between pound cake and shortbread, Gâteau Breton seems to me richer and more luscious than either. Every pâtissier has a secret or two when making this gâteau. For one it may be a drizzle of Calvados or rum, for another it is a pinch of baking powder "to wake up the flour." This version is resolutely simple, with not even a pinch of salt to mask the pure flavor of salted butter. (If you use unsalted butter, add ½ teaspoon salt to the flour.) Calvados or rum is a possible addition. The longer you keep a Gâteau Breton—up to two weeks in an airtight container—the better it tastes. Be sure the tart pan has fluted sides, as they are traditional for this gâteau.

1 CUP/225 G SALTED BUTTER, MORE FOR THE PAN

6 EGG YOLKS, BEATEN TO MIX

2 CUPS/250 G FLOUR

1 CUP/200 G SUGAR

1 TABLESPOON CALVADOS OR RUM (OPTIONAL)

8-INCH/20-CM FLUTED TART PAN WITH REMOVABLE BASE (SEE PAGE 377)

Butter the tart pan and set aside 1 teaspoon of the egg yolks for glaze. Sift the flour onto a work surface and sweep a large well in the center with your hand. Cube the butter and put it in the well with the sugar, egg yolks, and the Calvados, if using; work them together with the fingertips of one hand until smooth. Using the fingers and heel of your hand, gradually incorporate the flour and then work the dough gently until smooth. It will be sticky at this point and must be mixed with the help of a pastry scraper.

Transfer the dough to the pan and smooth the top with your fist, dipping it in water so it does not stick. Brush the surface of the gâteau with the reserved egg yolk and mark a lattice in the glaze with the tines of a fork. Chill the gâteau until firm, at least 20 minutes. Heat the oven to 375°F/190°C.

Set the tart pan on a baking sheet and put it in the oven. Bake for 20 minutes. Reduce the heat to 350°F/180°C and continue baking until the gâteau is firm, golden brown, and the sides shrink from the edges of the pan, 20 to 25 minutes longer. Let it cool to tepid in the pan, then unmold onto a rack to cool completely. Gâteau Breton is equally good freshly baked, or kept in an airtight container for up to 2 weeks, when the texture softens and the butter flavor becomes more pronounced.

= ALSACE: ANOTHER WORLD =

Alsace is very much a world unto itself. Visiting just before Christmas one year, I felt as if I were driving through a storybook toyland: narrow roads ribboning through clusters of candy-colored stucco houses; shops crammed with carved, wooden cookie molds and hand-painted crockery; streets twinkling with fairy lights; eaves decked with boughs and garlands; bakery windows populated with gingerbread people. Alsace has its own proud traditions, its own language, and even some laws of its own, plus white wines unlike any others in France. On a quality-price basis, an Alsatian Gewürztraminer or Riesling can be one of the best bargains around.

The culinary clichés are, of course, sauerkraut and beer. The winter climate is damp and icy, so local vegetables tend to be cabbage, Brussels sprouts, and roots—just right for cold-weather appetites. As for the beer, there is surely plenty of it—after all, the brasserie originated here (see "Restaurants En Route," page 26). But there are also superb white alcohols or liqueurs distilled from the region's wonderful fruits—cherry, plum, blueberry, pear, raspberry—that brace the digestion after a heavy meal (see "Portrait of a Distiller," page 366).

On an earthier note, Alsace has nearly two hundred charcuterie specialties. *Saucisse de Strasbourg*, made of pork and beef and lightly smoked so it looks like a plump frankfurter, is everywhere. Other specialties include smoked pork in countless forms, from hocks to tenderloin, and *pâtés en croûte* filled with wild boar, venison, duck, or sweetbreads, often eaten with a small salad as a first course. The star of them all is Alsatian foie gras (page 130), sautéed with a tart fruit or served *en terrine* with a glass of late-harvest Muscat wine.

If I had to sum up Alsatian cooking in just a few dishes, I would name Choucroute (page 176), a mixture of pork and sausages served on sauerkraut, and Backoëfe (page 141), half stew and half gratin, with three kinds of meat, plus potatoes. The side dish par excellence is Spaëtzli (page 230), a twisted type of noodle. For snacks, Tarte Flambée (page 280) is standard: an ultrathin, crisp bacon-and-onion tart. Alsace has only one famous cheese: Munster, notorious in and beyond France for its stunning smell.

While the cooking of Alsace is largely sturdy and plain, the same can't be said of the baking. Here, the Alsatian sense of fantasy comes through. Best known is Kugelhopf (page 290), a brioche baked in a decorative mold and turned out like a sandcastle. *Bretzels* are knots of dough poached in boiling water and coated with coarse salt; you find them strung onto wooden rods and hanging in the bakeries. Spice breads come in every form, from doorstep-sized slabs to tiny, flat chocolate-coated stars. Local bakers sell fragrant, dollhouse-sized cookies right out of open shop fronts, and around December 6, *manilas* appear, raisin-bread men to be eaten with clementines and coffee.

= PORTRAIT OF A BOULANGER =

My most vivid images of boulanger Dominique Jan are in an old barn near my own back door. It shelters an eighteenth-century bread oven where Monsieur Jan does wonders. Before he arrives, we fire up brushwood inside the oven. By the time he comes blazing down the driveway a few hours later, his shaped croissants and loaves already risen in the back of his van, the oven temperature is just right. I have never tasted anything as magical as his wood-scented, flaky pastries hot out of that oven.

How Monsieur Jan finds the energy to visit us is beyond me. His day begins at midnight, in the nearby town of Sens. While the rest of France sleeps, he slips into his bakery to begin the doughs for baguettes (he makes eight hundred a day), for rustic country loaves, and for *pains au chocolat* and other pastries he will sell in the morning. Monsieur Jan is an anchor for the surrounding community, visited by his customers at least once and sometimes twice a day. Whereas most bakers stick to the commonplace, he also likes to make fantasy breads, things like the daisy loaf, *marguerite*, and the folded tobacco pouch, *tabatière*. He tops some breads with decorations, using rye flour for color contrast. One of my

favorites is his folkloric *épi*, slashed to resemble an ear of wheat. Although a baguette is the standard purchase, these specialty breads, along with extras like pizza and quiche, are important revenue earners for the business.

There are over thirty-five thousand boulangeries in France. "Quality still sells," Monsieur Jan tells me, when I ask how business is going. "I have a loyal following. It pays to make good bread, and I make a very good living." In a time when industrial loaves seem to be taking over the culinary landscape, this is reassuring news. I despair when I see boulangeries that have ready-to-bake loaves delivered surreptitiously to their back door. Even the sign *Artisan Boulanger* is no guarantee. "All that means is that a baker makes his own dough and bakes it in his own shop; it doesn't mean his bread is good," Monsieur Jan explains.

So, what is good bread? "It should have a shiny, dry crust, good shape, and an even texture inside so the bread can breathe," says Monsieur Jan, holding up a loaf. "And it must have taste! Anyone can recognize good bread when they taste it. You don't even need butter when you have good bread."

= BORDEAUX AND CUISINE BOURGEOISE =

If I have learned one thing over the years, it is this: where there is good wine, good food will follow. Bordeaux illustrates exactly what I mean. There are plenty of wine cellars here for tasting some of the region's finest offerings, as well as handsome, comfortable restaurants where the right thing to do is settle in for a five-hour lunch, wine-country style. The cooking is *cuisine bourgeoise*, that proud, Cordon Bleu–like realm of home cooking that draws on simple, classic recipes and high-quality ingredients. Gigot de Sept Heures (page 152), spit-roasted chicken, Pot-au-Feu (page 142) with bone marrow—these are the kinds of dishes you can expect.

Of course, there are more indigenous specialties, too. Bordeaux cooks draw on the surrounding countryside for the cèpe mushroom, which they sauté with garlic and parsley as a first course. Duck from the Landes, the sandy strip of coastline to the south, yields foie gras that the Bordelais serve with a glass of chilled, sweet Sauternes. Local cooks also make confit and use the rendered fat to fry potatoes and an omelet or two. There are oysters from the nearby Bay of Arcachon, lamb from the Landes—and, of course, red wine, which, along with shallots, is the key ingredient in dishes styled *bordelaise*, typically showcasing lobster, crayfish, calf's liver, or steak.

Bordeaux is a feast for the eyes as well as the palate. The glorious sandstone mansions that line the Gironde Estuary show off Bordeaux la Blonde at its best. Local pastry shops also offer a few special treats. At New Year, try the fruit-speckled brioche known as *gâteau des rois de Bordeaux*, or *gâteau tortillon* as locals call it. Look for *merveilles*, sugar-dusted, rum- or citrus-flavored fritters, and Cannelés (page 338), little fluted cakes, crunchy golden outside with a moist, chewy interior. As for almond-rich Financiers (recipe follows), their very name sums up the bankers and wine merchants for which the city is famous.

FINANCIERS

RICH ALMOND CAKES

serves 12

Traditionally, financiers are baked in tiny boat-shaped molds for a maximum of toasted caramel crust. However, our local pâtisserie uses muffin pans that deliver double the amount of luscious crumb. Financiers keep well for at least a week in an airtight container, and the almond flavor mellows.

1 CUP/250 G BUTTER

¾ CUP/100 G GROUND ALMONDS

¾ CUP/100 G/3½ OZ FLOUR

2 ¼ CUPS/300 G POWDERED SUGAR

8 EGG WHITES (1 CUP/250 ML)

12 MEDIUM MUFFIN TINS

Heat the oven to 425°F/220°C. Melt the butter in a saucepan and use a little to butter the molds. Sift the flour and sugar into a heavy-based saucepan and stir in the ground almonds. Whisk the egg whites until frothy, add them to the almond mixture, and mix very well. Set the saucepan over low heat and stir constantly, using the whisk, until the mixture is just warm to the touch. Remove from the heat and stir in the remaining melted butter.

Fill the molds halfway. Bake the Financiers in the oven until risen, golden brown, and starting to pull from the side of the tins, 17 to 20 minutes. Let cool 5 minutes, then unmold them onto a rack and leave to cool completely.

BISCUIT DE SAVOIE
LIGHT SPONGE CAKE
serves 8

Said to have been invented in the fourteenth century, Biscuit de Savoie must be one of the earliest documented sponge cakes. A light sponge is still the pride of one of the top chefs in France, Savoy-raised Guy Martin at the Grand Véfour in Paris. He makes his gâteaux twice a day to guarantee freshness, baking them in peaked molds coated with butter and sugar for a crisp coating. If you use soft southern flour like White Lily, which closely resembles French flour, the sponge will be even lighter. Because Biscuit de Savoie is slightly dry, it is best served with fresh berries and crème fraîche.

4 TABLESPOONS/60 G BUTTER, MELTED AND COOLED, MORE FOR THE PAN

1¼ CUPS/250 G SUGAR, MORE AS NEEDED

1 CUP/125 G FLOUR

1 CUP/175 G POTATO STARCH

PINCH OF SALT

8 EGGS, SEPARATED

GRATED ZEST OF 2 LEMONS, OR 2 TEASPOONS ORANGE FLOWER WATER

2-QUART/2-LITER PEAKED CAKE PAN SUCH AS A BUNDT PAN, PREFERABLY NONSTICK

Brush the cake pan with melted butter, sprinkle it with sugar, and discard the excess. Heat the oven to 350°F/180°C and set a baking sheet on a shelf low in the oven. Sift the flour, potato starch, and salt together 2 or 3 times.

Beat the egg yolks with half of the sugar and the lemon zest in a stand mixer fitted with the whisk attachment until thick and light, 5 to 7 minutes. The mixture should leave a thick ribbon trail when the whisk is lifted. Whisk the egg whites until stiff, using the mixer and a second bowl. With the whisk turning, gradually beat in the remaining sugar and continue beating until a stiff, glossy meringue is formed, 1 to 2 minutes. Fold the flour mixture and meringue alternately into the egg yolk mixture in 3 batches, working as lightly as possible. When the last batch is half folded, add the melted butter and continue folding until mixed.

Spoon the batter gently into the prepared cake pan. Set the pan on the baking sheet and bake the cake until it has risen, the top is browned, and it starts to pull away from the sides of the pan, 30 to 40 minutes. When pressed with your fingertip, the top of the cake should spring back. Take it from the oven, and with the tip of a knife, pull the cake away from the edge of the pan. Let cool for

5 minutes, then turn the cake out onto a rack. Sprinkle it with sugar while it is still warm so the sugar clings. Leave the cake to cool completely. Biscuit de Savoie is best served the day of baking. If you want to make it ahead, keep it in an airtight container.

QUATRE QUARTS
POUND CAKE
serves 8

Almost every European country has a version of Pound Cake, the classic combination of equal weights of butter, sugar, flour, and eggs, but the French one is subtly different. For one thing, it is usually baked as a loaf, not as a round. For another, it is often perfumed with candied fruits, or nowadays with sweet herbs such as lemon balm or verbena, or even with green tea. Quatre Quarts means "four quarters," the principle being that the eggs in the shell balance with the butter, sugar, and flour, each added one by one to the other pan of the scale so they all weigh the same. This is not as pedantic as it sounds, as equal weights (not volume measures) of the four main ingredients are vital. (As backup, I have included volume measures here, too.) Be sure all the ingredients are at room temperature before you begin. Make the cake a day ahead and it will be even better: buttery, crumbling, only lightly sweet—the ultimate home-baked indulgence.

4 EGGS

1 CUP/225 G BUTTER, MORE FOR THE PAN

1¾ CUPS/225 G FLOUR

1 TEASPOON BAKING POWDER

PINCH OF SALT

3 OUNCES/90 G CANDIED ORANGE, LEMON, OR GRAPEFRUIT PEEL, PLUS A FEW STRIPS OF CANDIED PEEL, OR 1 TABLESPOON CHOPPED FRESH LEMON BALM OR VERBENA

1 CUP PLUS 2 TABLESPOONS/225 G SUGAR

GLAZE

2 TABLESPOONS/30 G SUGAR

2 TABLESPOONS WATER

8½-BY-4½-BY-2¾-INCH/22-BY-12-BY-7-CM LOAF PAN

Let the eggs and butter come to room temperature. Butter the loaf pan, line the bottom with parchment paper, and butter the paper. Heat the oven to 350°F/180°C and set a shelf low in the oven. Sift the flour with the baking powder and salt. If using the candied peel, chop the 3 ounces and add a couple teaspoons of the flour, then thinly slice the extra strips for decoration.

Cream the butter in a stand mixer fitted with the paddle attachment. Gradually add the sugar with the paddle turning, then continue beating at medium speed until the mixture is soft and light, 3 to 5 minutes. Before adding the eggs, warm the bowl slightly in tepid water for 1 to 2 minutes. A very cold bowl can cause the mixture to separate slightly. Beat in the eggs one by one at high speed, beating well after each addition and scraping the sides of bowl to be sure all the ingredients are mixed. If the batter begins to separate, beat in a tablespoon or two of the flour. Beat in the chopped candied peel (or the herb). Using a metal spoon, fold the flour into the batter in 3 batches. Spread the batter in the prepared pan, mounding it slightly, and set the strips of peel diagonally on top, if using.

Bake the cake until it is well browned, starts to shrink from the sides of the pan, and a skewer inserted in the center comes out clean, 55 to 65 minutes. During baking, the top of the loaf will crack open slightly, like a muffin. Meanwhile, make the glaze by heating together the sugar and water, stirring until the sugar dissolves, then set aside.

When the cake is done, transfer it to a rack, top up and with its lining paper intact, and brush with the glaze while still warm. It will keep well in an airtight container for up to a week. Strip off the paper just before slicing.

GÂTEAU PITHIVIERS

PUFF PASTRY GALETTE WITH ALMOND FILLING

serves 6 to 8

Gâteau Pithiviers, named for a town just south of Paris, dates back at least two hundred years. It is instantly recognizable by its scalloped edges and domed center, marked with curved slashes to resemble the petals of a flower. On Twelfth Night (January 6), the same gâteau becomes galette des rois, *a reference to the Three Kings. In the past, the gâteau was studded with a dried kidney bean, and the lucky recipient became lord of the feast. Today, pottery shops sell painted charms to bake in the cake in place of the bean.*

PÂTE FEUILLETÉE

 2 CUPS/250 G FLOUR, MORE AS NEEDED

 1 CUP/225 G CHILLED BUTTER

 ¹/₂ CUP/125 ML WATER, MORE IF NEEDED

 1 TEASPOON SALT

 1 TEASPOON FRESH LEMON JUICE

ALMOND FILLING

 ¹/₂ CUP/110 G BUTTER

 ¹/₂ CUP PLUS 2 TABLESPOONS/125 G SUGAR

 1 EGG

 1 EGG YOLK

 1 CUP/125 G GROUND ALMONDS

 2 TABLESPOONS/15 G FLOUR

 2 TABLESPOONS RUM

 1 EGG MIXED WITH ¹/₂ TEASPOON SALT

 1 TABLESPOON/15 G SUGAR DISSOLVED IN
 2 TABLESPOONS WATER

Make the pâte feuilletée (see page 375) and chill until firm, 30 minutes to 1 hour. For the filling, cream the butter using a stand mixer fitted with the whisk attachment. Add the sugar and beat until soft and light, 2 to 3 minutes. Beat in the egg and egg yolk. Using a spoon, stir in the almonds, flour, and rum. Do not overwork the mixture or the oil will be drawn out of the almonds.

Sprinkle a baking sheet with water. On a floured work surface, roll out slightly less than half the pastry dough to a thin round. Using a pan lid as a guide and a sharp knife, cut out a 10-inch/25-cm round. Roll out the remaining dough slightly thicker than the first round, and cut out another 10-inch/25-cm round. Set the thinner round on the baking sheet and press it down lightly so it does not shrink. Mound the filling in the center, leaving a 1-inch/2.5-cm border. Brush the border with some of the egg glaze. Set the larger round on top and press the edges of the rounds firmly together to seal them. Scallop the edge of the gâteau by pulling in the pastry at regular intervals with the back of a knife. Brush the top and border with the egg glaze. Using the tip of a knife and working from the center to the edge, score the top of the gâteau in curves radiating outward like petals of a flower, without cutting through to the filling. Chill the gâteau until firm, 20 to 30 minutes. Heat the oven to 425°F/220°C.

Pierce a few holes in the center of the gâteau to allow steam to escape. Bake until puffed and brown on top, 20 to 25 minutes. Lower the oven temperature to 375°F/190°C and continue baking until the gâteau is browned underneath and around the sides and has started to shrink in size, 15 to 20 minutes longer. Five minutes before the end of cooking, brush the surface of the hot dough with the sugar glaze, and continue baking until crisp and shiny. Transfer the gâteau to a rack to cool. Serve warm or at room temperature. Gâteau Pithiviers keeps well for up to 2 days in an airtight container.

GÂTEAU PÉRIGOURDIN

WALNUT AND CARAMEL CAKE

serves 6 to 8

Walnut trees do well in the thin, stony soil of Périgord, leading to walnut pastries and cakes, including this moist, rich gâteau with a topping of crisp caramel. Like most nut cakes, this one improves when kept a day or two in an airtight container. But the topping should be added only a short time before serving, as caramel softens after a few hours in the open air.

2 SLICES DAY-OLD WHITE BREAD

I CUP/125 G WALNUT PIECES

PINCH OF SALT

1/2 CUP PLUS 2 TABLESPOONS/140 G BUTTER, MORE FOR THE PAN

2/3 CUP/140 G SUGAR

4 EGGS, SEPARATED

GRATED ZEST OF I LEMON

TOPPING

1/3 CUP/75 G SUGAR

1/4 CUP/60 ML WATER

8 WALNUT HALVES

9-INCH/23-CM ROUND CAKE PAN

Heat the oven to 325°F/160°C. Toast the bread in the oven until very dry, 6 to 8 minutes. Let it cool, leaving the oven on. Break the cooled bread into pieces and grind it to crumbs in a food processor. Add the walnuts and salt and grind to a coarse powder (the dry bread helps keep the walnuts light). Butter the cake pan, line the bottom with parchment paper, and butter the paper.

Cream the butter in a stand mixer fitted with the whisk attachment. Add half of the sugar and continue beating until the mixture is soft and light, 3 to 5 minutes. Beat in the egg yolks one by one at high speed, beating well after each addition and scraping the sides of the bowl to be sure all the ingredients are mixed. Beat in the lemon zest. Using a spoon, stir in the ground walnut mixture.

Using the mixer with another bowl, whisk the egg whites until stiff. With the whisk turning, gradually beat in the remaining sugar and continue beating until a stiff, glossy meringue is formed, 30 seconds to 1 minute. Fold about one-fourth of the meringue into the walnut mixture to lighten it, then add the walnut mixture to the remaining meringue and fold the mixtures together as lightly as possible. Spoon the batter into the prepared pan.

Bake the cake until it pulls away from the sides of the pan and a skewer inserted in the center comes out clean, 40 to 50 minutes. If the cake browns too quickly, cover it loosely with aluminum foil. Let the cake cool for 5 minutes, then turn it out onto a rack covered with a sheet of parchment paper. Strip the lining paper from the cake and leave it upside down (so it has a flat top) to cool completely, at least 1 hour.

For the topping, put the sugar and water in a small saucepan and heat gently without stirring until the sugar dissolves. Raise the heat and boil until the sugar cooks to a golden brown caramel, 3 to 5 minutes. Turn the cake top upward and set it back on the rack; set the rack on a baking sheet to catch drips. Take the caramel from the heat, let the bubbles subside, and at once pour it over the cake, spreading it with a palette knife to make a very thin layer and letting it drip down the sides. Take care, as caramel can cause serious burns. Decorate the cake at once with the walnut halves so they stick to the caramel. The caramel will become crisp as it cools. When it starts to set, mark portions in the caramel with a knife so the cake is easy to cut into wedges.

= VIENNOISERIES, THE PERFECT BREAKFAST =

Viennoiseries are those decadent French bakery breads served at breakfast: *pains au chocolat, pains au raisins,* brioche, *pains au lait,* and croissants, the most famous of all. They are made from a yeast dough with butter folded in as for puff pastry, so that the resulting "bread" rises in light, flaky layers. Most tricky of all is the Breton specialty *kouign-aman,* made from leftover bread dough layered with half its weight in both butter and sugar, a luxurious, caramelized slab that is traditional at the yearly religious festivals called *pardons.*

Croissant means "crescent," and its image as the perfect accompaniment to breakfast coffee is known worldwide. Unfortunately, its shape is no guarantee of quality. The fast-food industry has made croissants one of its emblems and markets them stuffed with ham or cheese. The true croissant, the classic of the French breakfast table, comes from another planet.

Less complicated to make, but equally rich, are brioches, containing eggs and with the butter beaten, rather than folded, into the mix. A classic brioche is built like a fat snowman with a pin head: one small ball of dough on top of another baked in a characteristic flared mold. Brioche can also be baked in a loaf pan, in one piece or several small balls. Plain, lightly sweetened versions are the breakfast and teatime preference, although festive variations may be embellished with candied or dried fruits or nuts.

Savory brioches may contain bacon or cheese and are sometimes cut into cubes to serve with drinks. Children tend to prefer *pain au lait,* similar to brioche but containing no egg. As for the name *brioche* itself, Normans still use the ancient term *brier* to describe the kneading technique. But their rights are disputed by the inhabitants of Saint-Brieuc in Brittany, the Briochains. The Briards who live in Brie can surely be discounted, as they make cheese rather than butter.

= THE VERY BEST BUTTER =

Straight milk in France wins no prizes, but the butter is brilliant. The top French butters have AOC status (page 111), meaning they are made with milk from specific cow breeds that feed on recognized pasturage. The best AOC butter from Normandy is *beurre d'Isigny,* gold and with a perfect spreading consistency. "We speak of *beurre d'Isigny* the way we talk about wines from Bordeaux or Burgundy," the Normans claim. *Beurre d'Échiré,* from the Poitou-Charentes region farther south, is the frontrunner these days, at least among food professionals. Ask a pastry chef. They love Échiré butter for its high butterfat and for its lactic acid content, which makes doughs more tender, yeast rise better, and pastries flakier, as well as giving everything a more complex taste.

Most butter in France is unsalted, although the Bretons enjoy their own salted variety—even in cooking, where it gives a distinctive tang to omelets or sautéed fish. At table in Brittany, you may be offered a choice of salt or sweet butter. In upscale restaurants throughout France these days, you will probably be offered *beurre baratte* in a fancy pot. This is hand-churned butter with a suitably artisanal appearance, but in truth such butters go rancid faster than many maître d's realize, and are not always a treat. A greater temptation is the pyramids of dairy-fresh farmhouse butter you still see in busy markets. Slapped and shaped to order with ribbed, wooden paddles, they make attractive decorative bricks for a home table. You might think that the French would go for these showy creations every time. Yet a pat of butter on the dinner table has never been commonplace, maybe on the principle that French bread is delicious on its own.

GÂTEAU AU CHOCOLAT LYONNAISE

LIGHT CHOCOLATE CAKE

serves 10 to 12

I think of this cake as chocolate mousse miraculously held together by potato starch, which yields a crisp crust and a soft and tender interior. The mixing method is quite strange, but I have always followed it to the letter and have had no trouble. The recipe comes from the back of a chocolate package I came across in Lyon, a city renowned for its chocolate fantasies. Gâteau au Chocolat Lyonnaise is served at room temperature and cuts like a sponge cake, though it tastes more like a luxurious dessert. I like to add a few fresh berries as accompaniment.

BUTTER, FOR THE PAN

8 OUNCES/225 G DARK BITTERSWEET CHOCOLATE, COARSELY CHOPPED

6 TABLESPOONS/90 ML MILK

1/2 TEASPOON VANILLA EXTRACT

1/2 CUP PLUS 2 TABLESPOONS/125 G GRANULATED SUGAR

2/3 CUP/120 G POTATO STARCH

PINCH OF SALT

2/3 CUP/90 G GROUND ALMONDS

6 EGGS, SEPARATED

COCOA POWDER OR CONFECTIONERS' SUGAR, FOR SPRINKLING

CRÈME CHANTILLY

1/2 CUP/125 ML HEAVY CREAM

1 TO 2 TABLESPOONS SUGAR

1 TABLESPOON COGNAC

10-INCH/25-CM SPRINGFORM CAKE PAN

Heat the oven to 350°F/180°C and set a shelf in the center. Butter the cake pan, line the base with parchment paper, and butter the paper.

Put the chocolate and milk in a saucepan and heat gently, stirring, until the chocolate is melted and smooth, 2 to 3 minutes. Take the pan from the heat and let the mixture cool to lukewarm. With a wooden spoon, mix in the vanilla, half of the granulated sugar, the potato starch, and the salt. In a small bowl, mix the almonds with the egg yolks, and then stir into the chocolate mixture.

In a stand mixer fitted with the whisk attachment, whisk the egg whites until stiff. With the whisk turning, gradually beat in the remaining granulated sugar and continue beating until a stiff, glossy meringue is formed, 1 to 2 minutes. Fold about one-fourth of the meringue into the chocolate mixture to lighten it, then add the chocolate mixture to the remaining meringue and fold the mixtures together as lightly as possible. Pour the batter into the prepared pan.

Bake the cake until it puffs up and the surface cracks, 24 to 28 minutes. The center should remain slightly underdone, and moisture will still cling to a skewer when you insert it in the center and withdraw it. Watch carefully, as a minute or two can make quite a difference. Let the cake cool completely before unmolding it. The cake may be served as soon as it is cool, when it will be creamy in the center. If you keep it longer, it will firm up, and it may be stored for up to 3 days in an airtight container. Whether soft or firm, it is delicious.

Shortly before serving, make the crème Chantilly (see page 374). Sprinkle the cake lightly with cocoa powder and serve the cream separately.

PAIN D'ÉPICES

BURGUNDIAN SPICE BREAD

makes 2 loaves to serve 10 to 12

Spice bread dates back to the fourteenth century and the dukedom of Burgundy, a center for the prestigious spice trade that extended from Dijon to the Flemish ports on the North Sea. Dishes at the Burgundian court were accented with precious flavors, and honey-sweetened spice bread has survived. In the old days, it was made with leftover rye bread dough, but today's simpler version uses all-purpose flour leavened with baking soda. To develop the starch in the flour so the bread turns out moist and tender, the batter must be left to stand for eight hours before baking. Once baked and cooled, the loaves should be enclosed tightly in plastic wrap and kept for at least three days, and up to a month, so the honey permeates the bread and perfumes and mellows the spices. The taste of an assertive honey, such as clover or chestnut, comes through clearly. You will find commercial Pain d'Épices all over France, but the best is still made at home.

1¼ CUPS/300 ML MILK

I CUP/225 G PACKED DARK BROWN SUGAR

1½ CUPS/450 G FULL-FLAVORED HONEY

4 CUPS/500 G FLOUR

2 TABLESPOONS FINELY CHOPPED CANDIED
ORANGE PEEL

I TEASPOON GROUND ANISEEDS

½ TEASPOON GROUND CINNAMON

½ TEASPOON GROUND CLOVES

½ TEASPOON SALT

BUTTER, FOR THE PANS

2 EGG YOLKS

2 TEASPOONS BAKING SODA

I TABLESPOON WATER

TWO 8-BY-4-BY-3-INCH/20-BY-10-BY-8-CM LOAF PANS

Heat the milk, sugar, and honey in a saucepan over low heat, stirring until the sugar dissolves. Bring just to a boil, and then set aside until tepid. Put the flour into a large mixing bowl and make a well in the center. Add three-fourths of the cooled honey mixture to the well and stir, gradually drawing in the flour to make a smooth batter. In a smaller bowl, mix the candied peel, spices, and salt. Stir the remaining honey mixture into the candied peel mixture and add this to the batter, stirring until smooth. Cover and refrigerate for 8 to 12 hours.

Heat the oven to 250°F/120°C. Butter the loaf pans, line the base and sides with parchment paper, and butter the paper. To complete the batter, mix the egg yolks, baking soda, and water in a small bowl and then stir the mixture into the batter.

Spoon the batter into the pans, filling them half full—the breads rise surprisingly high during baking—and cover them loosely with aluminum foil. Bake for 30 minutes and then remove the foil. Continue baking until a skewer inserted near the center comes out clean, 1½ to 1¾ hours more. Note that spice bread should be slightly underbaked, so it is soft in the center and has not started to shrink from the sides of the pan. Let the breads cool to tepid, then turn them out, remove the lining paper, and wrap tightly while still tepid in plastic wrap. Store for at least 3 days in an airtight container before serving.

= A TASTE OF HONEY =

In France, beehives are shifted around a bit like sheep. Along the Pyrenees, producers take their hives to the flowering *colza* (canola) fields of the plains in April, to lime and acacia trees in June, and to heather-clad mountain slopes in September. In Provence, bees feed first on wild thyme in June and then on the lavender that blooms in July and August. In Burgundy, the first-generation bees feed on acacia blossoms, then their successors on chestnut flowers, pine forests, and finally fields of sunflowers. The resulting variety in French honey is amazing. In color, it ranges from ivory to mahogany, and in texture from liquid to creamy to pasty to crystalline. Of course, each has a different taste, and the savvy cook takes great care to choose just the right kind. Chestnut honey, for example, is delicious in Madeleines (page 336), but is unusually strong and thus not to everyone's taste in a sauce for duck.

I am always happiest when I see that honey has come principally from one kind of flower—in wine terms, a varietal honey. I look for labels telling me *miel de lavande* (lavender) or *miel de romarin* (rosemary). Other select jars specify a geographical origin, such as those from Corsica or the Vosges Mountains, the only two honeys with AOC status (page 111). At the other end of the scale, generic table honey in France is a blend: *toutes fleurs*, "all flowers," the labels often read, or perhaps *miel de France*, "French honey." These undistinguished types, which are extracted from combs using high heat, lack distinction.

No matter what the flower and region, the very best honey comes when the bees first swarm after hibernation. As an old English rhyme runs, "A swarm of bees in May is worth a load of hay." Honey is unusual in savory French recipes, but it maintains a place of honor in pastry and confectionery. It is the star ingredient in the Burgundian spice bread Pain d'Épices, and it is commonly found in treats like Provençal nougat and *pâtes de fruits*.

Miel de Provence

Rémi BRUN

Apiculteur

Grand draille Nord – La Galine

13210 ST RÉMY-DE-PROVENCE

Tél. 04.90.92.28.88

Poids net 500 g   Fax 04.90.92.53.77

Récolté et mis en pot par l'apiculteur

Produit de France

MIEL DE FLEURS DE RONCE

MÛRE SAUVAGE

Sensation

Ganache lait à la Mangue
et Rhum St James

DESSERTS & ICES

A SWEET FINISH

CHAPTER
*No.*16

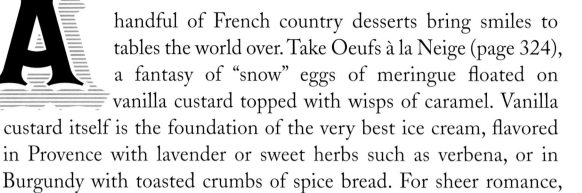

A handful of French country desserts bring smiles to tables the world over. Take Oeufs à la Neige (page 324), a fantasy of "snow" eggs of meringue floated on vanilla custard topped with wisps of caramel. Vanilla custard itself is the foundation of the very best ice cream, flavored in Provence with lavender or sweet herbs such as verbena, or in Burgundy with toasted crumbs of spice bread. For sheer romance,

try Coeur à la Crème (page 314), a heart-shaped molded cream fluffy with egg white, offset with a necklace of fresh berries, a specialty of the Loire.

Many of these desserts began local, then blossomed as their fame spread. In the south of France, you come across fritters such as the knotted Bugnes d'Arles (page 324), relatives of the *churros* of Spain and the *chiacchiere* of Italy. Pets de Nonne (page 314), fritters made of cream puff pastry dough, delight cooks as much as their guests. In the hot oil, small balls of dough double or triple in size, bobbing and flipping over as they puff, as if they were alive. Such recipes, and a handful of others, including crêpes, rank among the joys of French childhood.

All of these come to life thanks to just four basic ingredients: egg, milk, sugar, and flour. Add chocolate and the perspective widens to treats like *mousse au chocolat, marquise au chocolat,* Chocolate Soufflé (page 321), and Boule de Neige (facing page), a

snowball of dense dark chocolate cloaked in whipped cream and scattered with sugared rose petals. Nuts, particularly almonds and hazelnuts, lead in more dessert directions (see "Nuts to Crack," page 331), and fruits open a whole other chapter.

Desserts are a home cook's dream, but such indulgences are not the norm—indeed, many family meals do not include dessert at all. Most days, a bit of cheese will be followed by fruit and maybe nuts when in season. For festivals, however, country cooks welcome visitors with age-old recipes like prune-spiked Far Breton (page 357) or spicy, caramel-topped Crème Catalane (page 313). At Christmas in Provence, tables are set with *les treize desserts de Noël,* "the thirteen desserts of Christmas." Half or more are simply dried or candied fruits and nuts. But adding thirteen desserts, however plain, changes the whole momentum of a meal, transforming it into a celebration!

BOULE DE NEIGE

CHOCOLATE SNOWBALL

serves 8 to 10

Equal weights of chocolate, butter, sugar, and eggs—I was almost speech-less when I was introduced to this recipe by my friend Marielle. "But it's so good!" she exclaimed, and what could I say? The combination is cooked in a deep mold in a water bath so it sets almost to a ball. When hidden under whipped cream, it becomes an intriguing snowball with a dark, secret center. Homemade candied rose petals, or candied violets from Toulouse (available in gourmet stores), crown the surface. The snowball is tradi-tionally made in a charlotte mold, but I have baked it very successfully in a heatproof glass measuring jug.

8 OUNCES/225 G DARK BITTERSWEET CHOCOLATE, CHOPPED

1/2 CUP/125 ML BREWED ESPRESSO COFFEE

1 CUP/225 G BUTTER, CUT INTO CUBES

1 CUP PLUS 2 TABLESPOONS/230 G SUGAR

4 EGGS, BEATEN TO MIX

CANDIED ROSE PETALS (RECIPE FOLLOWS) OR CANDIED VIOLETS

CRÈME CHANTILLY

1 CUP/250 ML HEAVY CREAM

1 TO 2 TABLESPOONS SUGAR

1 TABLESPOON COGNAC, OR 1/2 TEASPOON VANILLA EXTRACT

5-CUP/1.25-LITER CHARLOTTE MOLD (SEE PAGE 376) OR HEATPROOF GLASS MEASURING JUG

Heat the oven to 350°F/180°C. Line the mold with heavy-duty aluminum foil. Put the chocolate and coffee in a saucepan and heat gently, stirring until the chocolate melts. Add the butter and sugar a little at a time, stirring after each addition until they are melted. Heat the mixture until very hot but not quite boiling. Take it from the heat and whisk in the eggs a little at a time; the heat of the mixture will cook and thicken them slightly. Strain the mixture into the mold.

Line a roasting pan with a dish towel, set the mold in the pan, and pour in boiling water to make a water bath (see page 373). Bring the water back to a boil on the stove top, and transfer the pan to the oven. Bake until a thick crust has formed on top, 30 to 40 minutes. The center of the mixture will still wobble when the mold is shaken. Remove the mold from the water bath and leave it to cool. The snowball will have risen in the oven but will shrink again as it cools. Cover and chill for at least 12 hours. It may be stored in the refrigerator for up to a week, or frozen for 3 months.

To finish, 3 or 4 hours ahead, candy the rose petals and leave them to dry. Not more than an hour before serving, hold a hot cloth around the sides of the mold for a few minutes to loosen the boule. It will be very sticky. Turn it out onto a flat platter and peel off the foil. Make the crème Chantilly (see page 374). To cover the boule, use a palette knife to coat the chocolate com-pletely with the cream, swirling it attractively. Scatter the candied rose petals on the cream, and chill until serving. At table, cut the snowball into wedges like a cake.

PÉTALES DE ROSES CONFITES

CANDIED ROSE PETALS

If you have a rosebush (pesticide-free), a few rose petals candied with sugar will dress all sorts of cakes and desserts. Violet blossoms may be candied in the same way.

Heat the oven to the lowest possible temperature, around 140°F/60°C. Line a baking sheet with parchment paper. Lightly whisk an egg white in a small bowl just until broken up. Brush the hollow upper side of single rose petals (preferably pink ones) quickly with the egg white and set them on the lined baking sheet. Sprinkle each petal very lightly with a small pinch of sugar. Bake the petals until dry and crisp, 3 to 4 hours. If thoroughly dried, they will keep in an airtight container for a couple of days.

TARTE AU FROMAGE BLANC

FRESH CHEESE TART

serves 8

French cheesecakes are creamily smooth and delicately perfumed with lemon and vanilla. They are made with a light, fresh, almost pourable cheese that has no trace of the curds of cottage cheese or ricotta, nor is it sticky like cream cheese. Called fromage frais or fromage blanc, it is available in more and more U.S. specialty markets. Whole-milk plain yogurt is a close substitute. This tart may be served on its own or with a topping of fresh berries, as I suggest here.

PÂTE BRISÉE

1 ²/₃ CUPS/200 G FLOUR

1 EGG YOLK

³/₄ TEASPOON SALT

3 TABLESPOONS/45 G SUGAR

3 TABLESPOONS/45 ML WATER, MORE IF NEEDED

6 TABLESPOONS/90 G BUTTER, MORE FOR THE PAN

1 EGG WHITE, FOR GLAZE

CHEESE FILLING

2 CUPS/450 G FROMAGE BLANC, OR 2 CUPS/ ABOUT 625 G WHOLE-MILK PLAIN YOGURT

²/₃ CUP/140 G SUGAR

2 EGGS

2 EGG YOLKS

2 TABLESPOONS/15 G FLOUR

GRATED ZEST OF 2 LEMONS

¹/₂ TEASPOON VANILLA EXTRACT

1 PINT/300 G RASPBERRIES, OR SMALL STRAWBERRIES, HULLED AND HALVED

9- TO 10-INCH/23- TO 25-CM TART PAN WITH REMOVABLE BASE (SEE PAGE 377)

Make the pâte brisée (see page 375) and chill until firm, 15 to 30 minutes. Heat the oven to 375°F/190°C and set a baking sheet on a low shelf to heat. Roll out the dough and line the tart pan, then bake it blind (see page 372) on the hot baking sheet. Lightly whisk the egg white and brush the blind-baked tart shell. Put the shell back in the oven and bake until the egg white is dry, 4 to 5 minutes. This helps prevent the moist filling from soaking into the crust. Let the tart shell cool, and leave the baking sheet in the oven and the oven on.

For the filling, put the fromage blanc in a large bowl and stir with a whisk until smooth. Beat in the sugar, then beat in the eggs and egg yolks, one at a time. Stir in the flour, lemon zest, and vanilla. Set the tart shell in its pan on the hot baking sheet. Pour the filling into the shell.

Bake for 10 minutes. Turn down the oven temperature to 325°F/160°C and continue baking until the filling is just set but not puffed, 25 to 30 minutes. To test if the tart is done, shake the pan gently to see if the filling is just set; the surface will not have started to brown. Turn off the oven, leave the door slightly open, and let the tart cool in the oven. This helps prevent cracking. When cool, after at least 2 hours, unmold the tart onto a flat platter.

The tart is best the day of baking, but it may be made a day ahead and kept tightly covered. Serve it at room temperature with a bowl of fresh berries on the side.

PETITS PIGNOLAS

PINE NUT TARTLETS

makes 12 tartlets

Until the mid-nineteenth century, the Landes region south of Bordeaux was so marshy that the inhabitants had to walk on stilts to reach their fields. Eventually pine trees were planted to reclaim the land, and pine nuts became part of the local repertoire, and with them Pignolas that taste even better than macaroons (page 336). For a decorative touch, a few pine nuts are scattered on the tarts halfway through baking. If added too soon, they will sink to the bottom of the filling.

PÂTE SUCRÉE

2 CUPS/250 G FLOUR

¹/₂ TEASPOON SALT

¹/₂ CUP/100 G SUGAR

4 EGG YOLKS

¹/₂ TEASPOON VANILLA EXTRACT

¹/₂ CUP/110 G BUTTER, MORE FOR THE MOLDS

PINE NUT FILLING

1 ³/₄ CUPS/250 G PINE NUTS

6 TABLESPOONS/90 G BUTTER

³/₄ CUP/120 G WHOLE BLANCHED ALMONDS

²/₃ CUP/140 G SUGAR

3 EGGS

¹/₄ CUP/44 G POTATO STARCH OR CORNSTARCH

1/2 TEASPOON BAKING POWDER

PINCH OF SALT

TWELVE 3-INCH/7.5-CM TARTLET MOLDS,
3 1/2-INCH/9-CM FLUTED COOKIE CUTTER

Make the pâte sucrée (see page 376) and chill until firm, 15 to 30 minutes. Meanwhile, butter the tartlet molds. Roll out the dough on a floured work surface to about 1/16-inch/2-mm thickness. Stamp out as many rounds as possible and line the tartlet molds, pressing the dough well down into the base and up the sides. Press the trimmings together and reroll the dough to stamp out the remaining rounds, for a total of 12 (you can use any extra dough for cookies). Prick the dough, set the molds on a baking sheet, and chill until firm, about 15 minutes. Heat the oven to 375°F/190°C and set a shelf low in the oven.

For the filling, spread the pine nuts on a baking sheet and toast until they just start to color, 2 to 3 minutes. Let cool. Melt the butter and leave it to cool also. Measure 1 cup/140 g of the toasted nuts and put them in a food processor, setting the rest aside. Add the almonds and sugar to the food processor and pulse until finely ground. Add the melted butter, eggs, potato starch, baking powder, and salt. Continue pulsing just until smooth.

Pour the mixture into the lined molds and bake until the batter begins to set, 10 to 12 minutes. Working quickly, take the tartlets from the oven and scatter the remaining pine nuts over the tops. Return them to the oven and continue baking until the pastry is brown and the filling is firm and puffed, 10 to 12 minutes longer. (If the tartlets begin to brown too quickly, turn the oven temperature down to 300°F/150°C.) Let the tartlets cool for 5 minutes, then unmold them carefully and transfer to a rack to cool completely. They are best eaten the day of baking, but may be stored in an airtight container for 2 to 3 days.

CRÈME CATALANE

LEMON, CINNAMON, AND FENNEL SEED CUSTARD

serves 8

This caramel-topped custard, flavored with fennel seed, cinnamon, and citrus, is a fragrant country version of crème brûlée, and far easier to make. The custard is thickened with flour, so it needs no baking, instead simply setting as it cools. The only sweetness comes from the thin caramel layer on top. A small kitchen blowtorch, available at hardware stores or kitchen supply stores, is the handiest way to toast this caramel topping, or you can use a broiler.

1 TEASPOON FENNEL SEEDS

1 QUART/1 LITER MILK

ZEST OF 1 LEMON, PARED IN STRIPS

ZEST OF 1 ORANGE, PARED IN STRIPS

1 CINNAMON STICK

2 EGGS

4 EGG YOLKS

3 TABLESPOONS/22 G FLOUR

3 TABLESPOONS/22 G CORNSTARCH

1/2 CUP/110 G DARK BROWN SUGAR, FOR TOPPING

EIGHT 5-INCH/13-CM INDIVIDUAL SHALLOW GRATIN
DISHES OR ONE 1 1/2-QUART/1.5-LITER SHALLOW
BAKING DISH; KITCHEN BLOWTORCH (OPTIONAL)

For the custard, put the fennel seeds in a small plastic bag and crush them with a rolling pin. Put them in a saucepan with the milk, lemon and orange zest, and cinnamon stick. Bring the milk just to a boil, cover, and leave to infuse over very low heat for 10 minutes. Meanwhile, in a bowl, whisk the eggs and egg yolks together until thick and light, 2 to 3 minutes, then whisk in the flour and cornstarch.

Strain the milk into the egg mixture, while stirring constantly with a whisk until smooth. Return the mixture to the pan and bring to a boil over medium heat, whisking constantly until it thickens. If any lumps form, take the pan from the heat at once and whisk the custard until smooth. Simmer the custard, stirring, until it softens slightly, showing the flour is fully cooked, 1 to 2 minutes. Take the pan from the heat and pour the custard into the gratin dishes to form a 3/8-inch/1-cm layer, smoothing the tops to make them as flat as possible. In the single large dish, the layer will be thicker. Let the custards cool, uncovered, then chill for at least 1 hour. They may be made ahead and chilled for up to a day.

To finish, sprinkle the brown sugar evenly over the cold custard with a spoon, allowing about 1 tablespoon for each dish. Light the blowtorch or heat the broiler (let the broiler preheat for at least 10 minutes). If using a blowtorch, hold the lighted torch about 3 inches/7.5 cm from each custard and heat the sugar until it melts and bubbles, forming a melted crust. If using the broiler, set the custards on a baking sheet and broil them as close as possible to the heat, allowing 30 seconds to 1 minute for the sugar to melt and form a caramel crust. Leave the custards until cool and set, 5 to 10 minutes. Serve within an hour so the caramel remains crisp.

PETS DE NONNE

CREAM PUFF FRITTERS

makes 30 to 35 fritters to serve 5 or 6

Fritters of deep-fried cream-puff pastry, topped with a dab of jam, honey, or a simple sprinkling of sugar, are beloved by all generations in France. Toddlers learn the name and no polite translation exists. It means quite simply "nun's farts" because the fritters are so light.

PÂTE À CHOUX

$^3/_4$ CUP/175 ML WATER

$^1/_2$ TEASPOON SALT

$^1/_3$ CUP/75 G BUTTER, CUT INTO CUBES

$^2/_3$ CUP/90 G FLOUR

3 TO 4 EGGS

VEGETABLE OIL, FOR DEEP-FRYING

CONFECTIONERS' SUGAR, HONEY, OR JAM, FOR SERVING

DEEP-FRYER

Make the pâte à choux (see page 374). Heat the oil to 375°F/190°C in a deep-fryer and warm the oven to low. To fry the fritters, using 2 teaspoons, drop balls of dough the size of small walnuts into the hot oil, taking care not to crowd the pan. Fry the fritters until golden on all sides, 6 to 7 minutes. The dough swells in contact with the heat, so the fritters puff and usually turn by themselves, though they may need encouragement to do so by nudging with a draining spoon. Transfer the fritters to paper towels to drain and keep warm in the oven with the door open. Be sure the oil comes back to the correct temperature before adding more fritters.

Serve the fritters at once, sprinkling them with confectioners' sugar, or passing a bowl of honey or jam.

COEUR À LA CRÈME

MOLDED FRESH CREAM CHEESE

serves 6

The perfect dessert on a hot summer day, Coeur à la Crème (also called crémets*) is made of whipped crème fraiche lightened with meringue, then left to drain in cheesecloth. Often the mixture is molded in a heart shape (*coeur*). In the Loire Valley, where this dessert is most popular, you will find porcelain molds, pierced with holes for drainage, in several sizes. An inexpensive alternative is to poke holes in a metal cake pan, heart shaped or a simple round. To provide a sweet, even fluffier contrast, the mold is traditionally served with crème Chantilly and, most important of all, fresh berries arranged in a necklace around the heart.*

2 CUPS/500 ML CRÈME FRAÎCHE (PAGE 374)

4 EGG WHITES

RASPBERRIES OR STRAWBERRIES, FOR SERVING

SUGAR, FOR SERVING

CRÈME CHANTILLY

I CUP/250 ML CRÈME FRAÎCHE OR HEAVY CREAM

I TO 2 TABLESPOONS SUGAR

$^1/_2$ TEASPOON VANILLA EXTRACT

I-QUART/I-LITER COEUR À LA CRÈME MOLD OR 6 INDIVIDUAL MOLDS; CHEESECLOTH

Line the mold(s) with cheesecloth. Whisk the chilled crème fraîche in a large bowl by hand or using a stand mixer fitted with the whisk attachment until the cream holds soft peaks. In another bowl, whisk the egg whites until stiff. Stir about one-fourth of the egg whites into the crème fraîche to lighten it, then fold the crème fraîche into the remaining whites. Spoon the mixture into the mold(s), filling well into the corners, and cover with plastic wrap. Set the mold(s) on a tray to catch the drips and place in the refrigerator for at least 8 hours. The fresh cheese keeps well for up to 36 hours, setting more firmly and acquiring more taste.

An hour or two before serving, make the crème Chantilly (see page 374). Turn the large mold out onto a flat serving dish or the individual molds onto dessert plates and peel off the cheesecloth. Arrange the berries around the edge like a necklace. Serve with separate bowls of sugar and the crème Chantilly.

COEUR À LA CRÈME

TERRINÉE DE RIZ AU CARAMEL

RICE PUDDING WITH CARAMEL

serves 4 to 6

Creamy rice pudding is a Norman specialty, baked long and slowly, some-times overnight, so it develops a deep brown crust. In a recent trend, farm-ers earn a bit extra by making dishes like this at home for the many visitors who tour the countryside. Elisabeth and Pierre Muris, for example, who live near Mont-Saint-Michel, sell takeout bowls of pudding. "Just put it in the microwave for a few minutes, it's great!" Another name for Terrinée (an allusion to the earthenware baking mold) is teurgoule. *In fact, a club called La Confrérie de la Teurgoule is dedicated just to this dish.*

In this version, the rice is simmered in milk, then baked in a dish lined with caramel. When unmolded, the pudding stands high with a gleaming gold top, a robust country version of crème caramel. Orange flower water, nutmeg, even bay leaf are alternatives to vanilla and cinna-mon as flavorings. Terrinée may be served warm or chilled, plain or with fresh berries or fruit compote.

I QUART/I LITER MILK, MORE IF NEEDED

¹/₂ CUP/100 G SHORT-GRAIN RICE

I VANILLA BEAN, SPLIT

¹/₂ TEASPOON GROUND CINNAMON

PINCH OF SALT

3 TABLESPOONS/45 G SUGAR, OR TO TASTE

3 EGGS, BEATEN TO MIX

CARAMEL

¹/₂ CUP/100 G SUGAR

¹/₄ CUP/60 ML WATER

I-QUART/I-LITER SOUFFLÉ DISH (SEE GLOSSARY)

Bring the milk to a boil in a saucepan and stir in the rice, vanilla bean, cinnamon, and salt. Simmer the rice over very low heat, uncovered, until very tender, 30 to 40 minutes. It needs stirring from time to time, particularly toward the end of cooking; if it gets very stiff, add more milk. When ready, all the milk should be absorbed, so the rice is creamy but still falls very easily from the spoon. Stir in the sugar, adding more to your taste, and leave the rice to cool to tepid. Remove the vanilla bean, rinse, and set it aside for another use. Heat the oven to 350°F/180°C.

For the caramel, have the soufflé dish nearby, and gently heat the sugar and water in a small saucepan without stirring until the sugar dissolves. Raise the heat, bring to a boil, and boil steadily without stirring until the syrup starts to color. Lower the heat and continue boiling until the syrup turns a dark caramel, 5 to 7 minutes total. Watch closely, as it will color quickly and will burn if overcooked. Take it from the heat, let the bubbles subside for about 5 seconds, and pour the caramel into the mold. At once, while the caramel is still hot and liquid, tilt and turn the mold to coat the base and sides. (Take care, as the caramel is very hot.) Leave it until set, about 5 minutes.

Stir the eggs into the cooled rice and pour it into the lined mold. Line a roasting pan with a dish towel, set the mold in it, and pour in boiling water to make a water bath (see glossary). Bring the water to a boil on the stove top, and transfer the pan to the oven. Bake the terrinée until it is just set in the center, 35 to 45 minutes. Take it from the water bath and let cool. The terrinée may be baked ahead and kept covered, in its mold, for up to 2 days in the refrigerator.

To finish, turn out the terrinée onto a deep platter. It will come out easily and a small amount of caramel sauce will form at the bottom of the dish. Serve it chilled, let it come to room temperature, or on a cold day warm it briefly in a low oven. It is delicious at any temperature.

CRÊPES AU CARAMEL ET BEURRE SALÉ

CRÊPES WITH SALTED BUTTER AND CARAMEL FILLING

makes 11 or 12 crêpes to serve 4 to 6

In their homeland of Brittany, crêpes are often eaten sprinkled simply with sugar as a snack on the run (page 238). However, this version, with its filling of caramel flavored with the region's tangy salted butter, is one you may want to enjoy on a real plate with a proper dessert spoon. To create a stunning dessert, top the crêpes with fresh berries, or with a scoop of verbena ice cream (page 325) in place of the whipped cream.

CRÊPES

I CUP/125 G FLOUR

¹/₂ TEASPOON SALT

3 EGGS

I¹/₄ CUPS/300 ML MILK

2 TABLESPOONS/30 G BUTTER, MELTED

3 TABLESPOONS/45 G CLARIFIED BUTTER (SEE GLOSSARY) OR VEGETABLE OIL, MORE IF NEEDED

SALT BUTTER CARAMEL FILLING

¹/₂ CUP/110 G SALTED BUTTER

¹/₂ CUP/125 ML HEAVY CREAM

I CUP/200 G SUGAR

¹/₂ CUP/125 ML WATER

SQUEEZE OF FRESH LEMON JUICE

PINCH OF SALT (OPTIONAL)

¹/₂ CUP/125 ML HEAVY CREAM, LIGHTLY WHIPPED, FOR SERVING

7-INCH/18-CM CRÊPE PAN (SEE PAGE 376)

For the crêpes, sift the flour and salt into a bowl. Make a well in the center and add the eggs and about half of the milk. Whisk the central ingredients until mixed, then gradually whisk in the flour to make a smooth batter. Whisk only until smooth, as the crêpes will be tough if the batter is beaten. Stir in half of the remaining milk and the melted butter. Cover the batter and leave it to stand at room temperature for 30 minutes to 1 hour so the starch in the flour expands and the batter thickens slightly.

Meanwhile, make the filling. Put the salted butter and the cream in a saucepan and heat gently until the butter melts, then set aside. Put the sugar, water, and lemon juice in a second saucepan and heat gently without stirring until the sugar dissolves. Raise the heat and boil until the sugar starts to turn golden around the edges, 5 to 7 minutes. Lower the heat and continue boiling to a deep golden brown. The caramel will darken fast. Take the pan from the heat and let it cool for 30 seconds. Add the melted butter and cream, standing back, as the caramel will sputter. Put the pan back over low heat and stir until smooth. Let the mixture cool, then taste and add a pinch of salt to sharpen the flavor if necessary. The filling will set firmly when cold, so you will need to melt it over low heat when assembling the crêpes.

To cook the crêpes, stir enough of the remaining milk into the batter so it is the consistency of thin cream. Brush the crêpe pan with some of the clarified butter and heat it until very hot. Add 2 to 3 tablespoons batter to the pan, turning it quickly so the bottom is coated evenly. Brown the crêpe over medium heat, 30 seconds to 1 minute. Loosen it with a palette knife, flip it, and brown the other side, about 30 seconds longer. Turn it out onto a plate and continue frying the remaining crêpes, brushing the pan again with clarified butter when they start to stick. (Crêpes should be fried with a minimum of butter.) Pile them one on top of another so they keep moist, and if you are serving them at once, keep them covered in a warm place. Both the filling and crêpes may be made 2 to 3 days ahead. Refrigerate the filling. To keep the crêpes, wrap them tightly and freeze them for up to 3 months.

To finish, heat the oven to 325°F/160°C. Warm the filling over low heat and bring the crêpes back to room temperature. Spread each crêpe with 1 tablespoon of the filling, roll, and arrange them in a baking dish on the diagonal. Cover the crêpes with aluminum foil and warm them in the oven for 8 to 10 minutes. Drizzle any extra caramel over the top and serve with a dollop of whipped cream.

= PORTRAIT OF A PÂTISSIER: THREE GENERATIONS, ONE PASSION =

I walk into the soothing, stone-lined interior of the oldest house in Pont Aven, a pretty town in southern Brittany, famous for its association with the painter Gauguin. A little group is quietly in place, three generations of the Jubin family. "Sit down and relax," they say. And the story begins.

Only fifty years ago, Thérèse Adelaide Rio, now in her late eighties, was running the boulangerie with her husband at Plouhinec, in the remote, forested interior of Brittany. Their wood-fired oven was at least a century old, and life was primitive, still without electricity. "Country bread was all we made," she says, "huge loaves that took six to eight hours to rise and kept up to a week. Baguette was a city luxury not seen here." The one exception was on August 15, at the Feast of the Virgin, which the village celebrated by making the famous Far Breton (page 357), a batter pudding spiked with plums to be baked in the communal oven. Each cook brought a distinctive dish as a mark of ownership (one woman used a chamber pot). "We had hundreds to bake, so we fired up the oven two or three times to get them all done. It took a day," Thérèse tells me. "The café was next door and everyone drank a glass or two while waiting. It was quite a party. When no one was looking, the dogs would nibble the puddings cooling on the ground."

Her son Dominique Jubin, now retired, takes up the story. "I was born in the bakery, as the saying goes. To have bread ready by seven in the morning, I had to knead my dough before midnight to give the *levain* [starter] time to rise." Soon Dominique was not only working through the night, as many bakers still do, but making popular pastries in the daytime, such as his giant Gâteau Breton (page 293), a variant of pound cake. Branching out, he opened a *salon de thé* next to the bakery in Plouhinec. In the 1970s, multi-grain flours came into style, and with them *pains fantaisies*. "Using seawater, I invented a loaf that needed no salt. It was very popular," Dominique tells me. "Mind you, boulangerie

and pâtisserie are very different. I don't think you can be a good pâtissier unless you are a good baker, too."

Such is the case with his son Eric, now in his mid-thirties, who apprenticed with his father and got his professional baker's certificate at age seventeen, followed by a similar pastry qualification six months later. After applying to the top pastry shops in Paris, Eric snagged first a temporary position, then a permanent one. He was working twelve hours a day, six days a week, paying his dues at minimum wage. "I was useful, I could turn my hand to anything—bread, pastry, chocolate, sugar work—and all the time I was learning." At only twenty, Eric finally landed at Fauchon in Paris, responsible for the decoration of all cakes and pastries under the legendary pastry chef Pierre Hermé.

After a few years in Brittany helping his father, Eric took jobs in Thailand, China, Qatar, and the United States. "But you cannot keep running and have a family life," he admits. So he decided to make his home in Pont Aven, in itself a small place but thronged with holidaymakers in season. Eric's almond-studded croquants, for dipping in a glass of cider or Calvados, are a favorite, as they stay crisp for weeks. His macaroons (page 336) rival those of top Parisian bakeries (which is where he learned to make them). His cakes include ribboned loaves of pound cake (page 298), all cut in individual portions in contemporary style. He has opened a section on chocolate, too.

While Eric is at work in back, his wife, Lydie, runs the front of the house. Friends drop by. The children run into the shop after school to be rewarded with one of Papa's cakes. Their grandfather visits once a week, bringing freshly churned, unpasteurized butter from an artisanal producer. Says Eric Jubin, "Here one can pause and reflect; I have time, I can take time. I can gather strawberries in the morning for my tarts at noon. There's no city in the world where I can do that."

INIMITABLE CRÈME FRAÎCHE

Crème fraîche, with its unctuous texture and tangy taste, is a key French ingredient. Sweet cream simply does not add the same piquancy and depth to dishes. This makes a difference in desserts (with my Tarte Tatin, page 346, I will take crème fraîche any day over whipped cream), and is particularly noticeable in savory dishes. For example, if the Auge Valley cider sauce for fish (page 79) is made with heavy cream instead of crème fraîche, it loses several dimensions of taste and is nowhere near as thick and velvety. Don't even think of substituting sour cream for crème fraîche, as it will separate if heated or whipped.

There are two main reasons why crème fraîche and ordinary heavy cream differ so much: one is enzymes and bacteria, and the other is butterfat. To kill harmful bacteria, few if any of today's dairy products escape pasteurization. Unfortunately, this destroys the very enzymes that add flavor and allow cream to thicken gradually on standing. However, the French have an answer to all this: to redress the balance and give pasteurized cream a rebirth, they add back lactic ferments to the crème fraîche (see recipe in the glossary, page 374). Sour cream and yogurt are low-fat cousins. Sweet cream is left as it is after pasteurization, hence its mild, sometimes flat taste.

More obviously, the thickness and flavor of cream depend on butterfat content. Sour cream has 20 percent at most, so it tastes quite sharp and breaks down easily. Sweet creams range from light, usually destined for coffee, to thick enough to whisk until fluffy, around 35 percent butterfat. Few commercial creams contain more fat, but if you are lucky, the rich cream from an artisanal dairy will be far higher. The butterfat content of crème fraîche starts at 30 percent and soars up to 50 percent for the very best AOC offerings (page 111). Crème fraîche keeps at least a couple of weeks, and while very young, it may still taste sweet and be almost pourable. After a few days, it acquires a tart, nutty flavor and will hold a spoon upright. Leave it to drain overnight in a strainer lined with cheesecloth and you will have the finest, freshest cream cheese.

The European Union has outlawed nonpasteurized cream, but France is a land of exceptions, so the statute doesn't mean none is available. You can still find crème fraîche ladled out at country markets into no-name plastic pots. Often it tastes so good that I know it cannot have been pasteurized. Almost elastic, like whipped marshmallow, true crème fraîche is, as the French say, *sans pareil*. "Pasteurization kills everything, there's nothing left," exclaims artisanal producer Francine LeSter. She exaggerates, but I know what she means.

SOUFFLÉ MOELLEUX AU CHOCOLAT

SOFT-CENTERED CHOCOLATE SOUFFLÉ

serves 4

Ask French home cooks for their special dessert and the chances are it will include chocolate, whether as a mousse or Gâteau au Chocolat (page 304). Recently, soft-centered chocolate cake has swept the board, delicious but tricky to deliver to the table just right. I much prefer this feather-light Soufflé Moelleux au Chocolat. You get the same combination of a crisp, delicate outside and soft, saucelike center, but with less trouble. I came across the recipe, an ideal showcase for the best dark chocolate, in Bayonne, where chocolate arrived from the New World in the mid-1600s.

4 OUNCES/110 G DARK BITTERSWEET CHOCOLATE, CHOPPED

1/2 CUP/125 ML HEAVY CREAM

3 EGGS, SEPARATED

1 1/2 TABLESPOONS COGNAC OR RUM

1/2 TEASPOON VANILLA EXTRACT

MELTED BUTTER, FOR THE SOUFFLÉ DISH

2 EGG WHITES

3 TABLESPOONS/45 G GRANULATED SUGAR

CONFECTIONERS' SUGAR, FOR SPRINKLING

1-QUART/1-LITER SOUFFLÉ DISH OR FOUR 1-CUP/ 250-ML SOUFFLÉ DISHES (SEE PAGE 377)

For the soufflé mixture, put the chocolate and cream in a saucepan and warm over low heat, stirring often, until the chocolate is melted. Take the pan from the heat and beat in the egg yolks so they cook and thicken the chocolate slightly (reserve the 3 egg whites for the meringue). Stir in the Cognac and vanilla. The soufflé mixture may be prepared to this point 3 to 4 hours ahead, covered, and kept at room temperature.

To finish, heat the oven to 425°F/220°C and set a shelf low in the oven. Butter the soufflé dish(es), chill in the freezer until set, and butter a second time. If using individual dishes, set them on a baking sheet. In a large bowl, whisk the 5 egg whites until stiff. Gradually add the granulated sugar and beat until a light, glossy meringue is formed, about 30 seconds. Heat the chocolate mixture until just hot to the touch, take the pan from the heat, and stir in about one-fourth of the meringue to lighten it. Add the chocolate mixture to the remaining meringue and fold the mixtures together as lightly as possible. Spoon the mixture into the prepared soufflé dish(es) and smooth the top; the dish(es) should be almost full. Run your thumb around the inside rim of the dish so the soufflé(s) will rise evenly.

Bake the soufflé(s) at once until puffed and almost doubled in volume, 12 to 15 minutes for a large soufflé, or 7 to 9 minutes for individual ones. If you shake the dish, the soufflé mixture should wobble slightly, showing it is still soft in the center. Meanwhile, line a platter with a napkin, or line individual plates with napkins. Remove the soufflé(s) from the oven, sprinkle with confectioners' sugar, and set the dish(es) on the napkin-lined plate(s). Serve the soufflé(s) at once. If serving a large soufflé, use 2 large spoons to scoop up both crisp outside and soft center onto each plate.

= THE CHARM OF CHOCOLATE =

Like many herbs and spices, chocolate was initially prized in France for its medicinal properties, which may explain why the French still have such a blissfully guilt-free attitude toward eating it. In his *Physiology of Taste*, gastronome Brillat-Savarin (page 111) claimed: "Carefully prepared chocolate is as healthful a food as it is pleasant. . . . It does not cause the same harmful effects to feminine beauty which are blamed on coffee, but is on the contrary a remedy for them." Perhaps that is why so many French cafés offer a foil-wrapped lozenge of dark chocolate with their coffee.

I like to buy from small, regional *chocolatiers* who play on local flavors. In Joel Durand's candy-box shop in Saint-Rémy-de-Provence, I sampled delicate cubes scented with rosemary and lavender. Far away in the Basque country, chocolates may be spiced up with Espelette pepper. In Lille, chocolatier George Wargnier creates chocolates tasting of beer, chicory, or spirits. When Monsieur Wargnier invited me to taste his juniper-gin ganache, he exclaimed, "That's the most diet-friendly chocolate in the house. It's so dark there's almost no cocoa butter in it, and the alcohol has

evaporated from the gin, don't worry." I was about to pop it down. "No!" he cried. "You must eat it nibble by nibble. That way your mouth heats each little bite like Cognac, and you'll taste it better."

Most French recipes call for the dark bittersweet chocolate sold in flat bars the size of your hand and marked with percentages to indicate cocoa content—at least 50 percent, and 70 to 85 percent for the darkest chocolate. This is the chocolate for homemade desserts, everything from *mousse au chocolat* to truffles, éclairs, soufflés, cakes and tarts, chocolate-covered fruits, and fondue. For serious confectionery, you will want to go to a pastry supply shop for couverture chocolate, which has a higher proportion of cocoa butter and is sold in almost tombstone-sized slabs. White chocolate is also available, but it isn't true chocolate, of course, because it contains no cocoa, just cocoa butter, sugar, and milk solids. Still, it does have its place in a hand-ful of cakes and creamy desserts. For all these chocolates, beware of low-cost imitations. You get what you pay for.

OEUFS À LA NEIGE
SNOW EGGS
makes 12 eggs to serve 6

Fashions come and go, but every French child raised on Maman's Oeufs à la Neige is hooked for life. The fluffy clouds of meringue "eggs" are set afloat on a sea of vanilla custard (crème anglaise), all drizzled with caramel—a dessert of dreams. To heighten the unreality, around Lyon the meringue is speckled all over with bright pink crushed pralines.

CRÈME ANGLAISE

> 3 CUPS/750 ML MILK
>
> I VANILLA BEAN, SPLIT
>
> 6 EGG YOLKS
>
> 5 TABLESPOONS/75 G SUGAR

MERINGUE

> 6 EGG WHITES
>
> I CUP/200 G SUGAR

CARAMEL

> $^1/_3$ CUP/75 G SUGAR
>
> $^1/_4$ CUP/60 ML WATER

Heat the milk and vanilla bean for the crème anglaise in a sauté pan or shallow saucepan over very low heat while making the meringue. For the meringue, using a hand whisk or a stand mixer fitted with the whisk attachment, whisk the egg whites until stiff. With the whisk turning, gradually beat in the sugar and continue beating until a stiff, glossy meringue is formed, 1 to 2 minutes. Dip a large metal spoon (bigger than a tablespoon) into the meringue and, with a second large spoon, shape an oval of meringue and drop it into the hot milk. Add 5 or 6 of these "eggs" to the milk and poach them over low heat, so they scarcely simmer. Do not let them boil or they will disintegrate. Poach until slightly firm, 1 to 2 minutes; turn them and poach the other side, about 1 minute. Transfer them to paper towels with a draining spoon and leave to drain (they will be speckled with seeds of vanilla). Poach the remaining eggs in the same way.

Use the milk from poaching to make the crème anglaise (see page 374) and leave it to cool, stirring occasionally so it does not form a skin, 10 to 15 minutes. Pour the cooled crème anglaise into a shallow serving bowl and pile the meringue eggs on top. They may be kept in the refrigerator, loosely covered with plastic wrap, for up to 2 hours.

To finish, make the caramel. Put the sugar and water in a small saucepan and heat gently without stirring until the sugar dissolves. Raise the heat and boil until the sugar cooks to a golden brown caramel, 3 to 5 minutes. Take it from the heat, let the bubbles subside, and with a fork or spoon drizzle the caramel over the snow eggs in a crisscross trail. Serve the snow eggs within 30 minutes so the caramel does not soften too much, spooning them into shallow bowls at the table.

BUGNES D'ARLES
PASTRY FRITTERS
makes 24 bugnes to serve 6 to 8

Throughout southern France, sweet pastry fritters are sold for snacks, often at outdoor stands as street food. Each region has its own style: the oreillettes *of Toulouse are layered like puff pastry so they curl up to resemble a little pig's ear, the* chichi-freggi *of Marseille are simply spirals of deep-fried bread sprinkled with sugar, and these bugnes from Arles are folded like a bow of ribbon.*

> 2 CUPS/250 G FLOUR, MORE IF NEEDED
>
> I $^1/_2$ TEASPOONS BAKING POWDER
>
> 3 TABLESPOONS/45 G BUTTER, AT ROOM TEMPERATURE
>
> 3 EGGS
>
> 3 TABLESPOONS/45 G GRANULATED SUGAR
>
> $^1/_2$ TEASPOON SALT
>
> I TABLESPOON RUM
>
> GRATED ZEST OF I ORANGE OR I LEMON
>
> VEGETABLE OIL, FOR DEEP-FRYING
>
> CONFECTIONERS' SUGAR, FOR SPRINKLING
>
> DEEP-FRYER

Sift the flour and baking powder onto a work surface and make a well in the center. Add the butter, eggs, granulated sugar, salt, rum, and citrus zest to the well, and mix the central ingredients thoroughly with your fingertips. With your hand, gradually work in the flour to form a dough; it should be quite sticky. Press the dough into a ball. Flour the work surface and knead the dough until it is smooth, slightly elastic, and peels easily from the work surface, about 2 minutes. If the dough is still very soft, work in a little more flour. Take care not to overwork the dough or the bugnes will be tough. Shape the dough into a ball, wrap, and chill for 30 minutes.

Roll out the dough on a floured surface to the thinnest possible rectangle. Using a fluted pastry wheel or a large knife, cut lengthwise into strips about 2½ inches/6 cm wide. Cut each strip crosswise into diamonds with sides measuring about 3 inches/ 7.5 cm. Cut a lengthwise slit 2 inches/5 cm long down the center of each diamond. Pull each of the longer points through the slit, and set the bugnes on a floured tray. Roll out the scraps, cut more diamonds, and shape more bows.

Heat the oil to 360°F/185°C in a deep-fryer. Add 5 or 6 of the bugnes, which will rise at once to the surface. When lightly browned, after about 2 to 3 minutes, turn them with a draining spoon and brown the other side, 1 to 2 minutes more. Transfer the bugnes to paper towels to drain, and sprinkle both sides generously with confectioners' sugar while still hot. Fry the rest in the same way.

Bugnes are lightest when freshly fried, but they are also fine if you keep them for a few hours at room temperature.

GLACE À LA VERVEINE
VERBENA ICE CREAM
makes 1 quart/1 liter ice cream

The basis for the very best homemade French ice cream is crème anglaise (vanilla custard sauce), often with some cream added halfway through the churning process. The creativity comes from the flavorings, which range from fresh peppermint, rose geranium, lemon balm, lemon verbena, and other garden herbs to such regional specialties as sweet, fresh cheese or toasted crumbs of Pain d'Épices (page 305), traditional in Burgundy. When the ice cream is accompanied by petits fours such as Madeleines (page 336), France comes to life in the bowl.

1 LARGE BUNCH (ABOUT 1 OUNCE/30 G) FRESH
LEMON VERBENA

2 CUPS/500 ML MILK

2 BAGS DRIED LEMON VERBENA INFUSION (OR "TEA")

PINCH OF SALT

7 EGG YOLKS

½ CUP/100 G BROWN SUGAR

1½ CUPS/375 ML HEAVY CREAM

ICE-CREAM MAKER

Pull off the fresh verbena leaves, discarding the stems. Coarsely chop the leaves and put them in a saucepan with the milk, verbena tea bags, and salt. Cover and bring almost to a boil over low heat. Leave over very low heat to infuse for 10 to 15 minutes. Strain the milk and then use it with the egg yolks and brown sugar to make crème anglaise (see page 374). Chill the custard until cold. Chill the cream and chill a container to hold the ice cream after freezing.

Freeze the custard in the ice-cream maker until almost set. Beat the cream until it holds a soft peak and stir it into the ice cream. Continue churning until the ice cream is firm. Transfer it to the chilled container, cover, and store in the freezer. The ice cream may be kept for up to a week in the freezer. After about 24 hours, it will have set very hard, so let it soften in the refrigerator for an hour before serving.

GLACE AU PAIN D'ÉPICES
SPICE BREAD ICE CREAM

Pain d'Épices is delectable broken into crumbs, toasted to develop the spices, and added to ice cream. Your favorite recipe for gingerbread, toasted as crumbs, is an excellent alternative.

Make the dried crumbs by breaking 8 ounces/225 g Pain d'Épices (page 305) to coarse crumbs with your fingers or in a food processor. Spread them on a baking sheet and toast in a 350°F/180°C oven until they are dry and crisp, 10 to 15 minutes. Let cool. Meanwhile, make 1 quart/1 liter ice cream following the recipe for verbena ice cream, omitting the verbena. Freeze it until almost firm, then stir in the spice bread crumbs with the whipped cream. Taste and add more spice, such as ground ginger or cinnamon, if you wish. Freeze the ice cream until firm. Makes 5 cups/1.25 liters ice cream.

SORBET DE MELON
makes 1 quart/1 liter sorbet

Say melon *to a Frenchman and he pictures only one variety: the round Charentais with its pale green skin and juicy, brilliant orange flesh. All other melons tend to pale into obscurity beside its intense fragrance, though a cantaloupe may be substituted. An ultraripe, fragrant melon is essential for sorbet, as chilling blankets the taste. To highlight the fruitiness, I like to add an equally fragrant sweet wine, such as a Muscat de Frontignan from the shores of the Mediterranean, but port is good, too.*

1 MELON (ABOUT 2 POUNDS/900 G)

1/4 CUP/60 G SUGAR, MORE TO TASTE

JUICE OF 1 LEMON, MORE TO TASTE

1 CUP/250 ML SWEET WHITE WINE, MORE TO TASTE

1/2 EGG WHITE, WHISKED UNTIL FROTHY

ICE-CREAM MAKER

With a sharp knife, cut a thin slice from the top and bottom of the melon so it sits flat. Pare off the peel, working from top to bottom. Halve the melon, discard the seeds, and cut the flesh into chunks. Purée the chunks in a food processor; there should be about 3 cups/750 ml. Add the sugar, lemon juice, and wine and purée again until smooth. Chill the mixture until cold. Chill a container to hold the sorbet after freezing.

Taste the mixture and add more wine, lemon juice, or sugar if needed. Freeze in the ice-cream maker until almost set. With the blades turning, add the egg white and continue churning until the sorbet is firm. Transfer it to the chilled container, cover, and store in the freezer. The sorbet may be kept for up to 24 hours in the freezer, but it will gradually harden and crystallize, so let it soften in the refrigerator for about an hour before serving.

SORBET NORMANDE
APPLE AND CALVADOS SORBET
makes 1 quart/1 liter sorbet

A French country feast is incomplete without a break in the middle (a trou *or "hole"). Traditionally, this is provided by a sharp, searing shot of the local hard spirit: Calvados in Normandy, marc in wine-growing regions, kirsch in Alsace, Cognac in Cognac, and so on. However, now that electric ice-cream makers are common, the* trou *is all the more agreeable by appearing in sorbet form. In this version from Normandy, apple cores and skins are simmered in syrup to extract the full apple flavor. If you are serving the sorbet as a traditional* trou *in the middle of a meal, the sugar should be halved. If you are serving it as dessert, I suggest* sablés *(sand cookies) as an accompaniment, as they are a Norman specialty. You can bake* sablés *using* pâte sucrée *dough (see Gâteau Basque aux Figues Fraîches, page 351). Roll out the dough ¼ inch/6 mm thick, cut out rounds, and bake until lightly browned in a 350°F/180°C oven, allowing 20 to 25 minutes.*

1 LARGE TART APPLE SUCH AS GRANNY SMITH

3 CUPS/750 ML WATER

1/2 CUP/100 G SUGAR, MORE TO TASTE

1/4 CUP/60 ML FRESH LEMON JUICE

1/4 CUP/60 ML CALVADOS, MORE FOR SERVING IF DESIRED

ICE-CREAM MAKER

Cut the apple into ½-inch/1.25-cm dice, including the peel and core. Put the pieces in a saucepan with the water and sugar and heat gently, stirring occasionally, until the sugar is dissolved. Cover, bring to a boil, and simmer over low heat until the apple pieces are softened to a pulp, 12 to 15 minutes. Let cool to tepid, then work the pulp through a strainer into a bowl. Stir in the lemon juice and Calvados, taste, and adjust the amount of sugar. Chill the mixture until cold. Chill a container to hold the sorbet after freezing.

Freeze the mixture in the ice-cream maker until very stiff. Transfer it to the chilled container, cover, and freeze for at least 30 minutes so the texture stiffens and the flavor mellows. The sorbet may be kept for up to 2 days in the freezer, but it will gradually harden and crystallize, so let it soften in the refrigerator for about an hour before serving. Scoop it into chilled glasses for serving, and drizzle a little more Calvados on top if you like.

SORBET DE MELON

= COGNAC, ARMAGNAC, AND MARC =

It was the Dutch, not the French, who first thought of Cognac. As early as the 1580s, they were Europe's preeminent producers and traders of distilled spirits. They established a foothold around Cognac and the port of La Rochelle, shipping the local wine to the many *wijnbranders* ("wine burners," that is, distillers) in Holland, hence the familiar word *brandy*. Even water was thought to be safer to drink when disinfected with brandy. It made economic sense to save on transport costs by distilling the region's wine at the source, so in due course Cognac became a center of the distillation business.

Distillation is a relatively simple process: when a fermented liquor, such as wine, is heated, it vaporizes at a lower temperature than water. However, it is not easy to get palatable results, and in olden times, spirits were distilled several times in order to expel impurities. The fact that Cognac needed to be distilled only twice was a tribute to the quality of the raw materials and the skill with which they were handled. Cognac still relies on double distilling for its unique refined flavors. Once in the bottle, distilled products like Cognac do not mature further.

Today's Cognac owes its characteristic bouquet to both particular grape varietals and the process of aging in oak casks from the nearby Limousin. The equivalent of twenty-five thousand bottles of wine is said to be lost in the town of Cognac each day through natural evaporation (as a consequence, the town's stone houses turn smoky black). Most brandy is given only two or three years to mellow, though the best may be left for up to fifty years in oak. Nowadays, almost all well-aged Cognac is mixed with younger vintages to make nonvintage blends branded by the famous houses.

A single-distilled spirit is not the same as a double-distilled one, nor should it try to be, as its very appeal lies in its earthier, harsher taste. Armagnac, produced to the southeast of Bordeaux in Gascony, is the most famous of these single distillates. Production is far smaller and more artisanal than in Cognac, with dozens of local growers advertising their *fine* along the region's winding roads. Cognac is so well branded that many labels are familiar worldwide, whereas Armagnac invites exploration and discovery.

Another French distillate is called marc, better known in international markets under the Italian name of grappa. Unlike Cognac and Armagnac, marc is distilled not from wine but from the pulp, or *marc*, left after grapes have been pressed. You will find it throughout France's major wine-producing areas, with perhaps the best coming from Burgundy and Champagne.

In cooking, Cognac and Armagnac are quite prominent in French kitchens; marc is used only occasionally, but country cooks have a penchant for its hard, musky undertones. As with wine, heat destroys subtle flavors of all these distilled alcohols, so it is a waste to use an expensive label. Cognac and Armagnac help tenderize meat in marinades; they act as a preservative in pâtés and terrines; and when added to sauces and ragoûts, they deepen and intensify the other flavors. With this in mind, they are usually added toward the end of cooking, though if simmered for a long time, they achieve a special concentration. Most spectacularly of all, Cognac and Armagnac are common in flamed dishes, an effect beloved by the traditional maître d' and mocked by chefs who call it *cinéma*.

ORANGES GIVRÉES
FROSTED ORANGES WITH ORANGE SORBET
serves 6

A Provençal indulgence, these frosted sorbet-filled oranges make a simple, eye-catching dessert. Be sure to mound the sorbet high in the orange shells so the lids sit jauntily on top. Loose-skinned mandarin oranges are best, particularly sweet little clementines during their winter season.

1 CUP/200 G SUGAR, MORE TO TASTE

1 CUP/250 ML WATER

12 MANDARIN ORANGES (ABOUT 2 POUNDS/900 G TOTAL)

1 TEASPOON ORANGE FLOWER WATER (OPTIONAL)

6 FRESH ORANGE LEAVES OR FRESH BAY LEAVES, FOR DECORATION

ICE-CREAM MAKER

Heat the sugar and water gently in a small saucepan, stirring occasionally until the sugar dissolves. Bring the syrup to a boil, simmer for 2 minutes, and then leave to cool. Cut a lid from the stem end of 6 of the oranges, then cut a very thin slice from each base so that the oranges sit flat. Scoop out the flesh with a sharp teaspoon, working over a bowl to catch the juice and taking care not to split the peel that forms a container. Chill the hollowed-out oranges and lids in the refrigerator. Purée the orange flesh in a food processor and strain the juice into the bowl. Squeeze the juice from the remaining oranges and add it to the rest. There should be about 2½ cups/625 ml juice. Stir in the cooled sugar syrup and the orange flower water, if using. Chill the mixture until cold, then taste, adding more sugar if needed.

Freeze the mixture in the ice-cream maker until set. If the mixture is too soft to shape, put it in a bowl in the freezer until stiff. Fill the hollowed-out oranges with the sorbet, mounding it very high. Set a lid on each and return the oranges at once to the freezer. They are best served within 24 hours but may be stored, tightly covered, for up to a week. The texture will harden, so transfer them to the refrigerator for an hour to soften before serving. Serve on chilled plates, poking a hole in the center of each lid and inserting an orange leaf for decoration. If any sorbet is left over, serve it separately.

GLACE AUX PRUNEAUX ET À L'ARMAGNAC
PRUNE AND ARMAGNAC ICE CREAM
makes 5 cups/1.25 liters ice cream

One year in the late summer, I visited Agen, center of French prune production, and the aromatic vanilla of the drying plums perfumed the air for miles around. This same area in southwestern France also produces the heady spirit Armagnac, and prunes preserved in it are a regional specialty.

1 CUP/150 G PITTED PRUNES, 2 CUPS/500 ML BOILING WATER, AND ½ CUP/125 ML ARMAGNAC, OR 1 QUART/ 1 LITER PRUNES IN ARMAGNAC (RECIPE FOLLOWS)

1 CUP/250 ML HEAVY CREAM

CRÈME ANGLAISE

2 CUPS/500 ML MILK

1 VANILLA BEAN, SPLIT

6 EGG YOLKS

½ CUP/100 G SUGAR

ICE-CREAM MAKER

To macerate the pitted prunes, put them in a small heatproof bowl and pour over the boiling water. Cover and leave to soak for 1 hour. (If using prunes in Armagnac, skip this step.) Meanwhile make the crème anglaise (see page 374) and chill it. Chill the cream and chill a container to hold the ice cream after freezing.

Drain the soaked prunes and put them with the Armagnac in a food processor, or use prunes in Armagnac. Purée until smooth, 30 seconds to 1 minute. Stir the purée into the cold custard. Freeze the crème anglaise in the ice-cream maker until almost set. Beat the cream until it holds a soft peak and stir it into the ice cream. Continue churning until the ice cream is firm. Transfer it to the chilled container, cover, and store in the freezer. The ice cream may be kept for up to a week in the freezer. After about 24 hours it will set very hard, so let it soften in the refrigerator for an hour before serving.

PRUNEAUX À L'ARMAGNAC
PRUNES IN ARMAGNAC

Bring 2 cups/500 ml water to a boil, pour it over 2 Ceylon tea bags (or other black tea), and leave to infuse for 5 minutes. Discard the tea bags and pour the tea over 1 cup/150 g pitted prunes in a bowl, cover, and leave to soak for 12 hours. Drain the prunes, pack into a 1-quart/1-liter jar, and pour over enough Armagnac to cover, about 1½ cups/375 ml. Cover tightly and leave to macerate for at least a week at room temperature. Makes 1 quart/1 liter prunes.

= NUTS TO CRACK =

The French love nuts in a variety of forms. Ground almonds are the basis of much French baking, replacing flour in cakes and used for frangipane tarts and marzipan candies. They may be browned before chopping or grinding, but most often are simply blanched so they pop easily out of their tough brown skins. Slivered almonds are tossed in salads or fried in butter to garnish fish. Green almonds, picked unripe in June and July, are prized for their delicate, milky flavor; upscale country restaurants often showcase them as a garnish in desserts. Runners-up in the baking department are hazelnuts, whose fragrance is always improved by toasting in the oven (this helps with peeling, too). Ground hazelnuts may replace flour in cakes, and whole or ground are often paired with chocolate in desserts. In game terrines, they add a pleasant earthy taste, and in dried sausage, they are a real treat.

I am never without walnuts in the kitchen either. The French like to pickle them whole, grind them for jam, or macerate them to make *liqueur de noix*, a local specialty of both the Dauphiné and southwestern France. Swathed in caramel, walnuts make a festive topping, and they are good ground for cake batters, although they are heavier than almonds, with a bitter edge that makes them less versatile in baking. Light toasting crisps them, but too much browning accentuates their bitterness. I lean toward walnuts for savory dishes, adding them to salads and to breads that accompany cheese, and pounding them into an unusual sauce, garlic-packed Aillade (page 220), to serve with meats. Like almonds, walnuts can be picked green, before the shell has hardened.

As for pistachios, I confess to having a kitchen cupboard crammed full of them, but not actually for cooking. A little dish of salted pistachios is the simplest of accompaniments to a welcoming drink, with everyone prying the shells apart, like mussels, and popping them down the hatch. Pistachios may be ground, but are more usually left whole in terrines, sausages, pâtés, stuffings, and desserts. Pine nuts, or *pignons*, the petite seeds of Mediterranean pine trees, are too small for satisfactory nibbling. Most often toasted and used as a garnish, they also play a starring role in recipes like Pistou sauce (page 16) and in sweet tartlets such as Petits Pignolas (page 312).

Nut oils are all the rage in French kitchens now, and shops are devoted to selling every possible kind. Unlike peanut oil, which is ideal for deep-frying, nut oils, notably walnut and hazelnut, are too delicate for high heat. They are good in marinades and above all in vinaigrette, where they can transform a familiar salad.

France has a dozen provinces but hundreds of *pays*—quite small, distinctive areas that geography or accidents of history have made particular. To move to another *pays* can be dramatic, like moving to a different state in the United States: crops, markets, accents, even living patterns may change radically. In Normandy, for example, the Pays d'Auge that is famous for apples and Calvados (page 175) looks very different from the clay-covered Pays de Bray just north of Paris that produces milk, butter, and a soft cheese called Neufchâtel.

Another *pays* that I know well is the land of chalk, or Pays de Caux, near the Channel port of Dieppe. For several summers, we lived in a picture-book village of black-and-white thatched houses clustered around a massive sixteenth-century church. The cows were black-and-white, too, with spectacle markings around their eyes, and they produced the richest milk in the whole of France, or so it seemed. Each morning the children collected a can of raw milk, still warm from the cow. The baker's brioche, made with local butter, was notable. The sea was just nearby, and we kept a tide clock in the kitchen so we would know when the sea was up and fishermen were standing by with a flapping cargo. What could be fresher than that?

Yet another face of Normandy shows at the remarkable Wednesday outdoor market in Saint-Hilaire-du-Harcouët, in the Pays du Bocage at the western end of the province. The morning livestock market for cattle, sheep, pigs, and a few goats is over by eight o'clock. Then the crowds move to the center of town, alive with cheeping birds, baby ducks, geese, chicks, scrawny pink-skinned turkeys, and handsome guinea hens. For an on-the-hoof snack, there are three types of grilled sausages, Boudin Blanc (page 185), *boudin noir*, and andouilles (those of nearby Vire are renowned throughout France). They come with frites or buckwheat galettes (page 236)—we are close to Brittany here—and the crêpe stand does such business that five well-muscled ladies are needed to keep up with trade.

Elisabeth and Pierre Muris, with their son Guillaume, go to Saint-Hilaire each week. They run a mixed farm of 170 acres (70 hectares) where they raise feed for their eighty cows. Many farms simply sell their milk to a cooperative, but the Muris family makes its own raw-milk crème fraîche, yogurt, and a fresh cheese that comes strained and smooth or with curds (*piquette*). Responsibilities are divided: Pierre delivers product and oversees business, Elizabeth is in charge of the dairy and keeps accounts, while Guillaume takes care of the farm. It is tough. "I've had no weekends off for five years," says Guillaume, "and during planting I work fourteen hours a day." I mention France's notorious thirty-five-hour work week and he first looks rueful, then grins. "My great-grandparents had this farm," he explains. "We keep adding land to it. I wouldn't have it differently."

From a bit farther west comes yet another *pays*, where François Serbonnet raises lamb on the salt marsh estuary opposite Mont-Saint-Michel. François is equally committed to the land, though he gave up being a chef only four years ago. "Cooking took up too much time in the kitchen," he says, "and I prefer to be outdoors." To qualify as the prized salt-marsh lamb, sheep are grazed on sandy pastures that flood at the equinox. Culled between four and eight months and weighing around forty pounds (eighteen kilograms), *pré salé* lamb commands up to double the price of regular lamb. Most of it comes from estuaries in Normandy and Brittany, or from Saint-Pierre and Miquelon, the French islands in the Gulf of Saint Lawrence. "The flavor of the meat is unique," explains François, "walnut with a hint of iodine." He likes his lamb grilled, with the wild sea plant called *salicorne* (samphire) on the side.

The soft landscape and temperate climate of Normandy invite easy cultivation. In the fifteenth century, farmers paid generous dispensations to the church so they could continue to consume cream and butter during Lent. A win-win situation: the Normans got to eat what they wanted, and thanks to their penance, the rest of us inherited the gothic Butter Tower of Rouen cathedral, celebrated in the glorious series of paintings by Monet. Starting with the Romans and then the Vikings, it is no wonder that Normandy has always been a prized possession.

= PETITS FOURS =

I had always considered the little cakes called petits fours to be typically Parisian, but recently I have realized that they are actually the epitome of regionalism. Each recipe included here is associated with a specific area, often with a single town. In my travels around France, I have found hundreds of petits fours, each one different from the next. Outside of Paris, the definition of petits fours expands far beyond the elaborately decorated bite-size squares of sponge cake lined up in pastry shop windows. In the countryside, any small cookie or sweet cake qualifies. Everyone has heard of Madeleines (page 336), for instance, but as far as the French are concerned, these delicate tea cakes come from Commercy, a nondescript town in eastern France that turns them out by the million.

Often there is symbolism in the shape. For instance, Scories de Vulcan (facing page), from the volcanic Massif Central, resemble rocky lava stones. Or the distinguishing feature may be a decoration, such as the buttery sand cookies

from Normandy called *sablés*, always crosshatched with the tines of a fork. An unusual ingredient or technique may be involved, as in Croquets (page 338), crisp, nut-studded fingers that are the Burgundian version of biscotti, delicious dipped in a glass of sweet wine or a bracingly black afternoon *café*. Bordeaux counters with Cannelés (page 338), fluted little caramel cakes with an intriguing chewy texture.

Fashions in petits fours can come and go, too. Cannelés are currently cutting edge, macaroons are right back in, while *tuiles* have had their day—for now. In the countryside, however, old favorites never seem to die and a good recipe is handed down from grandma. I found a bevy of Petits Pains Flamands Épicés (facing page) at Arras in the heart of Picardy, and am currently in hot pursuit of the intriguingly nutty pralines of our neighboring town of Montargis. From childhood, these sweet treats are part of the French table, appearing at lunch with desserts like Oeufs à la Neige (page 324), compote, or simply with a piece of fruit.

PETITS PAINS FLAMANDS ÉPICÉS

FLEMISH SPICED COOKIES

makes about 50 cookies

In northwestern France running up to Belgium, these delicate spiced cookies come with your cup of coffee, a reminder of the Flemish and Burgundian links with the medieval spice trade. The dough is shaped in a block, then chilled and sliced into thin wafers like a refrigerator cookie.

1²/₃ CUPS/200 G FLOUR

¹/₂ TEASPOON GROUND GINGER

¹/₂ TEASPOON QUATRE ÉPICES (SEE PAGE 370) OR GROUND ALLSPICE

PINCH OF GROUND CINNAMON

¹/₂ CUP/110 G BUTTER

¹/₂ CUP/100 G LIGHT BROWN SUGAR

¹/₂ TEASPOON BAKING POWDER

3 TABLESPOONS/15 G SLICED ALMONDS

Sift the flour, ginger, *quatre épices*, and cinnamon onto a work surface and make a well in the center. Pound the butter with your fist to soften it, then add it to the well with the brown sugar and baking powder. With your fingertips, quickly work the central ingredients until partially mixed. Using both hands, gradually draw in the flour, pulling the dough into coarse crumbs.

Divide the dough into 2 or 3 portions. Knead 1 portion on the work surface, pushing it away with the heel of your hand and gathering it up with a pastry scraper, until it is pliable and peels away easily in a single piece, 1 to 2 minutes. Knead the other portions in the same way. Press the pieces of dough together into a rectangular block 6 by 3 by 1 inch/15 by 7.5 by 2.5 cm. Wrap in plastic wrap and chill until firm enough to slice, at least 30 minutes. The dough may be frozen and sliced whenever you are ready to bake, like a refrigerator cookie.

Heat the oven to 400°F/200°C and line a baking sheet with parchment paper. Cut the dough into very thin slices and transfer them to the prepared baking sheet. Sprinkle each cookie with 2 or 3 almond slices, pressing them in lightly. Bake until golden brown, 5 to 7 minutes. Transfer the cookies to a rack to cool. They keep well for up to a week in an airtight container.

SCORIES DE VULCAN

LAVA STONES

makes about 4 dozen cookies

These lively little cookies, named for Vulcan, the Roman god of fire, have a cracked, rocky surface and crackle like a volcano as they cool. They are made in the central region of France, famous for its lava-dotted landscape. The batter is crunchy with hazelnuts and flavored with cocoa, and it must stand for at least three hours before baking. In compensation, the "stones" will keep for weeks in an airtight container. To ensure crispness, the batter uses baker's ammonia (sold in baking supply stores and on the Internet), the same curious ingredient used in Croquets de Sancerre (page 338). Like ammonia, it stings your nose and must be used in a tiny quantity. For Coffee Stones, substitute 1½ tablespoons instant espresso powder for the cocoa.

2 CUPS/280 G HAZELNUTS, PREFERABLY PEELED

¹/₂ CUP/100 G SUGAR

1¹/₂ TABLESPOONS COCOA POWDER

1 TABLESPOON/7 G FLOUR

¹/₄ TEASPOON BAKER'S AMMONIA

3 EGG WHITES

Heat the oven to 375°F/190°C. Spread the hazelnuts on a baking sheet and toast them until golden, 8 to 12 minutes. If the hazelnuts were not peeled, rub them while still hot with a rough cloth to remove the skins. Let them cool completely, then grind them very coarsely in a food processor with half of the sugar—crunchy texture is important. Pulse to work in the cocoa powder, flour, and baker's ammonia.

Set aside 2 tablespoons/30 g of the remaining sugar. Whisk 1 egg white with the remaining sugar until foamy, add it to the nut mixture in the processor, and work for a few seconds until mixed. Whisk the remaining egg whites in a bowl until soft peaks form. Gradually add the reserved 2 tablespoons sugar to the whites and continue beating until a very stiff meringue forms, 1 to 2 minutes. Add the nut mixture to the meringue and fold them together. Cover and refrigerate for at least 3 hours and up to 1 day.

When ready to bake, heat the oven to 375°F/190°C. Line a baking sheet with parchment paper. Using 2 teaspoons, set rough balls the size of a small walnut on the paper. Bake until puffed and lightly browned, 14 to 17 minutes. Let cool slightly on the paper—they will crackle like a volcano! Transfer to a rack to cool completely. When cool, the cookies will be light and crisp and have a cracked, rocky surface. They may be stored in an airtight container for a month or more.

LES MACARONS DE NANCY

ALMOND MACAROONS

makes about 16 macaroons

Macaroons were once the specialty of a convent in Nancy, capital of Lorraine. At the Revolution, the nuns were forced out into the world, and two of the sisters set up a bakery, found to this day in the rue des Soeurs Macarons. While all macaroons are based on the same three ingredients—almonds, egg whites, and sugar—they vary enormously. When made in sophisticated Parisian style with milled almond paste, the finished cakes have a fine, soft texture and crisp shell. When made at home with whole almonds, as I do here, they turn out coarse textured and chewy, with an intense almond taste and a rustic, homey look that I can never pass up. Thank heaven for the food processor. Making macaroons used to require hard labor with a pestle and mortar to obtain the correct stiff paste. Macaroons stick easily, so use a silicone sheet or parchment paper for easy removal.

I CUP/150 G WHOLE BLANCHED ALMONDS

I CUP/200 G GRANULATED SUGAR

2 EGG WHITES, WHISKED UNTIL FROTHY, MORE IF NEEDED

1/2 TEASPOON VANILLA EXTRACT

I TO 2 TABLESPOONS CONFECTIONERS' SUGAR, FOR SPRINKLING

SILICONE SHEET FOR BAKING (SEE PAGE 377)

Heat the oven to 400°F/200°C and set a shelf in the upper third of the oven. Line a baking sheet with the silicone sheet or with parchment paper. Put the almonds, granulated sugar, egg whites, and vanilla in a food processor bowl. Pulse several times until the mixture starts to pull away from the sides into a ball. Process on high speed, scraping down the sides twice, until the mixture is a smooth, sticky paste, 2 to 3 minutes. The mixture will be thick enough not to fall from a spoon, but if it seems very dry, add a little more egg white.

Moisten your hands with water, shape the mixture into balls the size of walnuts, and set them on the prepared baking sheet. Flatten them slightly with your dampened palm. Sprinkle with confectioners' sugar. Bake the macaroons until lightly browned and firm on the outside but still soft in the center, 12 to 14 minutes. Remove the baking sheet from the oven and, if using parchment paper, lift one end and at once pour a cup of water under it. The water on the hot baking sheet will form steam, loosening the macaroons. Leave them for a minute or two, then transfer to a rack to cool. They keep well for up to a week in an airtight container.

LES MADELEINES DE COMMERCY AU MIEL

HONEY MADELEINES

makes about 18 medium madeleines

Madeleines come in a palette of flavors, ranging from traditional lemon zest to orange flower water, familiar vanilla, fashionable green tea, and, my favorite, honey. I have even come across savory herb or cheese versions. The sign of a fine madeleine is a little hump, created by leaving the batter to chill and stiffen for at least two hours, and by baking in a hot oven. The batter has a tendency to stick to the traditional shell-shaped metal molds, so they should be buttered twice. The cakes also turn out fine in nonstick silicone molds, but they will never color to a crisp golden brown. For a Proustian moment, savor madeleines as he did, with a cup of tisane (page 364).

I CUP/125 G FLOUR

1/2 TEASPOON BAKING POWDER

1/2 CUP/110 G BUTTER, MELTED, MORE FOR THE MOLDS

1/2 CUP/100 G GRANULATED SUGAR

I TABLESPOON/15 G DARK BROWN SUGAR

I HEAPING TABLESPOON HONEY

GRATED ZEST OF 1/2 LEMON

2 EGGS

I EGG YOLK

METAL MADELEINE PLAQUES WITH 18 MEDIUM MOLDS

Sift the flour and baking powder into a bowl. In a large bowl, combine the melted butter, granulated sugar, brown sugar, honey, lemon zest, eggs, and egg yolk. Whisk the ingredients by hand or with a stand mixer fitted with the whisk attachment until very smooth, 1 to 2 minutes. Gradually add the flour mixture and continue whisking for 1 minute. Cover and refrigerate for at least 2 hours and up to 8 hours. Brush the molds with melted butter, chill in the freezer until set, and butter a second time.

Heat the oven to 400°F/200°C. Spoon the batter into the molds, filling them almost to the rim. Bake the madeleines until they are puffed, golden brown, and just starting to pull from the sides of the molds, 8 to 10 minutes. Note that the peaked centers will be lighter than the rest of the cakes. Turn them out onto a rack to cool. They are best eaten warm from the oven, though they may be stored in an airtight container for 2 to 3 days.

clockwise from top right:
SCORIES DE VULCAN,
MADELEINES DE COMMERCY AU MIEL,
CANNELÉS DE BORDEAUX

LES CANNELÉS DE BORDEAUX
FLUTED CARAMEL CAKES
makes 10 to 12 cannelés

Cannelés, a curious chewy cake whose flutes are drenched in caramelized sugar, eluded me for years. Two or three pâtisseries in Bordeaux claim the secret, and I bought purpose-designed fluted copper molds and followed the instructions, all to no avail. Every attempt flopped, scorched, or was disagreeably tough. Finally the answer came from my old friend Chef Chambrette, now in his eighties. "Simple," he says, "cook the egg-and-milk mixture until it curdles like overcooked crème anglaise." Cannelés are addictive. In Bordeaux, you can get them large or small, lightly golden, or toasted to a deep mahogany brown, my preference. For a deep brown surface, be sure to use metal molds—traditional ones are made of copper—and avoid the silicone molds sold by the sheet, as the batter will not brown.

2 EGG YOLKS

I CUP/200 G SUGAR

I EGG

I VANILLA BEAN

2 CUPS/500 ML MILK

MELTED BUTTER, FOR THE MOLDS

I CUP/125 G FLOUR

2 TABLESPOONS DARK RUM

I TABLESPOON VEGETABLE OIL

12 MEDIUM METAL CANNELÉ MOLDS, PREFERABLY NONSTICK

Put the egg yolks in the bowl of a stand mixer fitted with the whisk attachment and beat until mixed. Add the sugar and whisk at medium speed until coarse crumbs form, 2 to 3 minutes. Add the whole egg and continue whisking until light and the mixture holds a ribbon trail when the whisk is lifted. Split the vanilla bean lengthwise and scrape the seeds into the egg mousse (save the vanilla bean for another use). Whisk in the milk. Transfer the mixture to a saucepan and bring to a simmer over medium heat, stirring with a hand whisk until it thickens and then curdles and separates, 3 to 5 minutes. (It looks terrible, but don't worry.) Set it aside to cool, stirring often so the egg does not clump together.

Meanwhile, heat the oven to 400°F/200°C. Brush the molds with melted butter and set them on a baking sheet. When the egg mixture is cool, sift the flour on top and whisk until the batter is smooth (the curdled look will disappear). Stir in the rum and oil. Transfer the batter to a measuring jug and pour it into the molds, filling them about two-thirds full.

Bake the cannelés until they have risen and browned, 45 minutes for a light crust, or 55 minutes for a dark mahogany crust. A toothpick inserted in the center of a cake should be clean when withdrawn. Let them cool for 2 to 3 minutes, then unmold while still warm. I think cannelés are best eaten very fresh, even warm, but here Chef Chambrette and I disagree. He keeps his for several days.

CROQUETS DE SANCERRE
CRISP ALMOND FINGERS
makes 18 finger cookies

I always succumb to little cookies like these Almond Fingers, designed for dipping in a glass of sweet wine at the end of a meal. There are many versions, and most of them depend for texture (croquet means "crisp") on baker's ammonia, an obscure powder that will clear your sinuses with a single sniff. Stand back when using it, as this mystery ingredient is none other than smelling salts, the homey Victorian remedy for a fainting fit! You will find it on the Internet or in baking supply stores, and a little goes a long way. This particular recipe from the Loire dates back to the late nineteenth century.

³/₄ CUP/100 G FLOUR, MORE FOR WORKING

²/₃ CUP/140 G SUGAR

3 OUNCES/90 G WHOLE UNBLANCHED ALMONDS

¹/₂ TEASPOON BAKING POWDER

¹/₂ TEASPOON BAKER'S AMMONIA

PINCH OF SALT

I EGG, BEATEN TO MIX

2 TEASPOONS ORANGE FLOWER WATER

I EGG MIXED WITH ¹/₂ TEASPOON SALT, FOR GLAZE

Put the flour, sugar, almonds, baking powder, baker's ammonia, and salt in a food processor. Pulse the mixture to coarse crumbs so the almonds still have texture, about 30 seconds. Take care not to overwork the mixture and develop the almond oil or the croquets will be hard. Add the egg and orange flower water and work again to crumbs, 10 to 15 seconds, adding a few drops of water if they seem dry. Turn the crumbs out onto a work surface and press them together to form a ball. The dough will be quite sticky.

You will need 2 sheets of parchment paper to roll out the dough. Flour 1 sheet and then flour the dough and shape it to a square on the floured paper. Top with the second sheet. Roll out the dough to a 6-by-16-inch/15-by-40-cm rectangle. Remove the top sheet of paper and use it to line a baking sheet. Trim the edges of the dough neatly and brush the surface with the egg glaze. Cut the dough lengthwise into 6 equal strips, then cut the strips crosswise to make eighteen 5-inch/13-cm fingers. Chill them in the freezer for 30 minutes. Using a metal spatula, transfer the fingers to the prepared baking sheet. Leave the fingers, uncovered, in a cool place for 6 to 8 hours so the surface dries.

Heat the oven to 375°F/190°C. Bake the fingers until evenly golden brown, 12 to 15 minutes. Loosen them from the parchment paper with a spatula, then slide the paper with the cookies onto a rack to cool. They will keep well in an airtight container for several weeks, making them a standby in French pâtisseries.

GALETTES BRETONNES

BUTTER COOKIES

makes twelve to fourteen 3-inch/7.5-centimeter cookies

Galettes Bretonnes are an agreeably light, crumbly butter cookie that is often marketed commercially. Just a few pâtissiers make them the old way, and here's how.

2 CUPS/250 G FLOUR

$^2/_3$ CUP/140 G SUGAR

2 TEASPOONS BAKING POWDER

$^1/_2$ TEASPOON SALT

$^1/_4$ CUP/60 G BUTTER, CUT IN SMALL PIECES

1 EGG

1 TABLESPOON MILK, MORE IF NEEDED

1 EGG YOLK BEATEN TO MIX WITH 1 TABLESPOON WATER, FOR GLAZE

3-INCH/7.5-CENTIMETER COOKIE CUTTER

Put the flour, sugar, baking powder, and salt in a bowl and mix them well with your hand. Make a well in the center and add the butter, egg, and 1 tablespoon milk. Mix these central ingredients with the fingertips of one hand until they are blended. Using both hands, work in the flour until large crumbs are formed; if the crumbs seem dry, add more milk. Press the crumbs together into a ball. Wrap it in plastic and chill 15 minutes. Line a baking sheet with parchment paper.

Flour a work surface and knead the dough lightly just so it holds together. Roll it to ⅜ inch/1 cm thickness and stamp out rounds with the cookie cutter. Gather up the trimmings, flour the work surface again, and roll and cut out more cookies. Transfer them to a baking sheet, leaving room for them to spread. Brush them with egg glaze and trace an oval with the tines of a fork held upright. Chill until the dough is firm, 15 to 20 minutes. Heat the oven to 350°F/180°C. Bake the cookies in the oven until risen slightly and golden brown, 15 to 20 minutes. Transfer them to a rack—they will crisp as they cool. They can be stored in an airtight container a week or more.

FRUIT TARTS, DESSERTS, PRESERVES & LIQUEURS

France has long been a paradise for fruits, hot enough in the south to grow citrus and cool enough in the north for apples, pears, and quinces to flourish. Along the Garonne River in the southwest, I picture plums and other stone fruits, with Brittany's Plougastel Peninsula as the home of strawberries. As early as the sixteenth century, the French astrologer Nostradamus celebrated fruits with an entire book on jams.

A century later, a profusion of new fruits were nurtured by Louis XIV at Versailles. His gardener, La Quintinie, cultivated citrus trees in grand, sunlit glass houses called *orangeries*, an architectural model that still inspires us to this day.

Now we benefit from a new golden age. Never has such a range of fruits and vegetables been available all year long to such a wide market. We take for granted that we will find melons in autumn, apples and grapes in spring, and bananas, tomatoes, and even strawberries and raspberries year-round. Here in the center of France, in my small country town, the local supermarket has launched an exotica section that may include pomegranate, persimmon, fresh dates, guava, mango, lychee, and half a dozen more, looking a bit tired sometimes, but available at moderate prices. Not so long ago, all these fruits were foreign to French country cooking.

By contrast, we hear much about the disappearance of heirloom varieties, a decline taken seriously in France. Groups such as the Loire-based Société des Croqueurs de Pommes (the Apple Eaters) make a point of reviving old varieties. Alsatian cooks trap the juices from stone fruits such as plums, apricots, and cherries in a robust bread crust; in the south, lemon tart, often paired with ground almonds, reigns supreme. Tart shells filled with fresh fruit begin in strawberry season and wend their way through apricots, to end in autumn with grapes and figs. Apple tarts are featured everywhere in a dozen variations, from the renowned Tarte des Demoiselles Tatin (page 345), caramelized to a deep mahogany, to Pompet, a rustic turnover layered with thin slices of apple and sugar.

It is surely no coincidence that preserves are back in style, guaranteeing us a taste of even the most exotic fruits year-round. Gourmet stores feature boutique jars of jams and jellies, carefully styled to catch the eye. In country kitchens, flavors are given an individual twist with garden herbs like rose geranium and lemon balm. Conserves of flowers such as Gelée de Pommes et Pétales de Rose (page 360) are popular, together with sweet-sour chutneys and confits that brighten the winter table.

Another ancient way to capture the fragrance of summer fruits is to transform them into aperitifs and digestifs (page 23). It is hard to go wrong with a dash of alcohol, which is why a colorful little pick-me-up is the traditional welcome for visitors in the countryside. When mixed with sugar, fruits produce alcohol all on their own, though more often than not home brews are boosted with *alcool pour fruits*, available in French supermarkets (vodka is a good substitute). I have included a couple of liqueurs that our family makes to amuse our friends. Our drinks cupboard is a reflection of rural life and the seasons, of our tastes and pastimes.

TARTE AUX POIRES NORMANDE

NORMANDY PEAR TART WITH ALMOND FILLING

serves 6 to 8

Almonds grow far to the south, but tarts with pears baked in an almond filling are very much a Norman specialty. Often you will see them in a round tart such as this, with the pear halves fanned like the petals of a flower. Pâtisseries tend to favor a practical strip shape, with the pears packed crosswise head to tail. This allows single servings to be cut while the strip remains intact. The type of pear you use is less important than its being ripe and juicy.

PÂTE BRISÉE

1 ²/₃ CUPS/200 G FLOUR

1 EGG YOLK

³/₄ TEASPOON SALT

3 TABLESPOONS/45 ML WATER, MORE IF NEEDED

6 TABLESPOONS/90 G BUTTER, MORE FOR THE PAN

SUGAR, FOR SPRINKLING DURING BAKING

FILLING

¹/₂ CUP/110 G BUTTER

¹/₂ CUP PLUS 2 TABLESPOONS/125 G SUGAR

1 EGG

1 EGG YOLK

1 CUP/125 G GROUND ALMONDS

2 TABLESPOONS/15 G FLOUR

2 TABLESPOONS KIRSCH

3 OR 4 RIPE PEARS (ABOUT 1¹/₂ POUNDS/675 G TOTAL)

APRICOT JAM GLAZE

¹/₂ CUP/125 G APRICOT JAM

¹/₄ CUP/60 ML WATER

9- TO 10-INCH/23- TO 25-CM TART PAN WITH REMOVABLE BASE (SEE PAGE 377)

Make the pâte brisée (see page 375) and chill until firm, 15 to 30 minutes. Roll out the dough and line the tart pan (see page 372). Chill again until firm. Heat the oven to 400°F/200°C and set a baking sheet on a low shelf to heat.

For the filling, cream the butter using a stand mixer fitted with the whisk attachment. Add the sugar and beat until soft and light, 2 to 3 minutes. Beat in the egg and egg yolk. Using a spoon, stir in the almonds, flour, and kirsch. Do not overwork the

mixture or the oil will be drawn out of the almonds. Spread two-thirds of the almond cream in the chilled pastry shell.

Peel the pears, halve them, and scoop out the cores and fibrous stems using a melon baller or the point of a paring knife. Set the pear halves cut side down on a cutting board and cut them very thinly crosswise without separating the slices. Gently flatten the slices to make elongated ovals that maintain the shape of the pear half. Still keeping the slices together, lift them on a knife and arrange the halves, stem end inward, on the almond layer in a circle like the petals of a flower. Spoon the remaining almond cream into the spaces between the halves.

Bake the tart on the hot baking sheet until the pastry dough begins to brown, 10 to 15 minutes. Lower the oven heat to 350°F/180°C and continue baking until the pears are tender and the almond cream is set and browned, 20 to 25 minutes longer. About 10 minutes before the end of cooking, sprinkle the tart generously with sugar; the sugar will caramelize lightly as the tart finishes baking. Let the tart cool slightly, then loosen and remove the pan sides. Let cool completely on a rack before sliding it off the metal base. Normandy pear tart is best eaten the day of baking but may be kept for up to 2 days in an airtight container.

To finish, make the apricot jam glaze. Heat the jam with the water in a small saucepan until melted. Work the glaze through a strainer into a small bowl and return it to the pan. Warm the glaze until melted and brush a light coating over the tart. Serve at room temperature.

TARTE AUX POIRES ET CHOCOLAT

PEAR AND CHOCOLATE TART

Even simpler than Tarte aux Poires Normande is this version from the Loire Valley.

Make pâte brisée dough and line the tart pan as for Tarte aux Poires Normande. Heat the oven to 400°F/200°C and set a baking sheet on a low shelf to heat. After chilling the tart crust, sprinkle the bottom with 4 ounces/110 g bittersweet chocolate, chopped. Peel and halve 3 or 4 pears and core, slice, and flatten them as described. Set them on top of the chocolate in a flower pattern, packing them tightly. In a bowl, whisk 1 egg, 1 egg yolk, ¹/₂ cup/125 ml heavy cream, and ¹/₂ teaspoon vanilla extract to make a custard. Spoon it over the pear halves so they are lightly coated. Bake the tart for 10 minutes. Turn the heat down to 350°F/180°C and continue baking until the pastry is brown and the custard is set, 20 to 25 minutes longer. If the pears are not caramelized, brown them briefly under the broiler to highlight the scalloped pattern of slices. Serves 8.

TARTE DES DEMOISELLES TATIN

UPSIDE-DOWN CARAMELIZED APPLE TART

serves 8 to 10

In the mid-nineteenth century, the story goes, the demoiselles *Tatin were left penniless when their father died. Luckily they lived just opposite the new railroad station at Lamotte-Beuvron, a small town south of Orléans. So they took in travelers and baked the crusty dark apple tart their father had loved so much. Fortune smiled, and the Hotel Tatin is there to this day, still serving a remarkable tart baked in a wood-fired oven and topped with chunks of lightly singed caramelized apple.*

The apples must be firm and hold their shape during long cooking. I suggest Pink Lady or Golden Delicious, but there are many other suitable varieties. To ensure the all-important dark caramel, my tart is cooked first on top of the stove, patiently, so the apple halves get thoroughly drenched in the buttery caramel. Once the apples are tender and mahogany colored, I cover them with a plain pastry dough and finish the tart in the oven. The tart is best turned out and served when it is tepid, and it is hard to beat the classic accompaniment of crème fraîche, though a scoop of vanilla ice cream also does nicely.

There is even a special pan for baking the tart, a resplendent round of solid copper lined with tin, the sides sloping and high enough to contain the abundant juices the apples release as they simmer in the caramel. You will find the pan easily enough in a kitchen equipment store—at a price. Be reassured that a deep frying pan, preferably nonstick, with an oven-proof handle will perform just as well. A cast-iron skillet, ideal in shape and thickness, tends to react with acid fruits, so the tart must be turned out immediately after baking.

PÂTE BRISÉE

I ²/₃ CUPS/200 G FLOUR

I EGG YOLK

³/₄ TEASPOON SALT

3 TABLESPOONS/45 ML WATER, MORE IF NEEDED

6 TABLESPOONS/90 G BUTTER

ABOUT 5 POUNDS/2 TO 2.5 KG FIRM APPLES

¹/₂ CUP/110 G BUTTER

I ¹/₂ CUPS/300 G SUGAR

10- TO II-INCH/25- TO 28-CM TATIN MOLD

Make the pâte brisée (see page 375) and chill until firm, 15 to 30 minutes. Peel and halve the apples; scoop out the cores with a melon baller or the point of a paring knife. Melt the butter in the mold, sprinkle in the sugar, and cook over medium heat without stirring until it starts to brown and caramelize. Stir gently, then continue cooking until the caramel is deep golden brown, 6 to 8 minutes total. Let cool in the pan for 3 to 5 minutes. The butter will separate, but this does not matter.

Arrange the apples in the mold in concentric circles with the cut sides standing vertically. The caramel will help to anchor them. Pack them as tightly as possible, as they will shrink during cooking. Cook the apples over medium heat until the juice starts to run, about 8 minutes, then raise the heat and cook them as fast as possible until the underside is caramelized to a deep gold and most of the juice has evaporated, 15 to 25 minutes. With a two-pronged fork, turn the apples one by one so the upper sides are now down in the caramel. Continue cooking until this second side is brown also and almost all the juice has evaporated, 10 to 20 minutes more. The time will vary with the variety and ripeness of the apples, and can take up to 1 hour total. Let them cool to tepid while heating the oven to 400°F/200°C.

Roll out the pastry dough to a round just larger than the mold. Wrap the dough around the rolling pin and transfer it to cover the apples. Tuck the edges down around the apples, working quickly so their warmth does not melt the dough. Poke a hole in the center to allow steam to escape. Bake the tart until the pastry is firm and lightly browned, 20 to 25 minutes. Take the tart from the oven and let it cool for at least 10 minutes, or until it is tepid. Tarte Tatin may be made up to 12 hours ahead and kept in the mold in the refrigerator (if using a cast-iron skillet, the tart must be turned out immediately).

To finish, if necessary, warm the tart in the mold on the stove top before you turn it out, to soften the caramel and loosen the apples. Select a flat platter with a lip to catch any juices; invert the platter on top of the tart pan and flip the tart onto the platter. Be careful because you can be splashed with hot juice. Cut into wedges to serve.

PIQUECHAGNE

WALNUT PEAR PIE

serves 8

Pâté de Pommes de Terre (page 283) is one example of a double-crust pie from central France, and this delectable walnut pie, also known as le poirat, *is another. During baking, the dough softens to outline humpbacked quarters of pear, an appealing, natural decoration. Almonds or toasted hazelnuts can be substituted for the walnuts, and any leftover dough can be baked into delicious cookies.*

PÂTE SUCRÉE AUX NOIX

1/2 CUP/60 G WALNUT PIECES

1/2 CUP PLUS 2 TABLESPOONS/125 G SUGAR

2 CUPS/250 G FLOUR

1 EGG

1 TEASPOON GROUND CINNAMON

1/2 TEASPOON SALT

1/2 CUP PLUS 2 TABLESPOONS/140 G BUTTER, MORE FOR THE PAN

1 TO 2 TABLESPOONS SUGAR, FOR SPRINKLING

5 OR 6 FIRM PEARS SUCH AS BOSC OR ANJOU (ABOUT 2 POUNDS/900 G TOTAL)

1/3 CUP/75 ML HEAVY CREAM, LIGHTLY WHIPPED

9-INCH/23-CM TART PAN WITH REMOVABLE BASE (SEE PAGE 377), 2 1/2-INCH/6-CM ROUND PASTRY CUTTER

For the pâte sucrée aux noix, pulse the walnuts with half of the sugar in a food processor until finely ground. Do not overwork or the oil will be drawn out of the walnuts. Add the flour and pulse until mixed. Spread the nut and flour mixture on a work surface and make a well in the center. Put the egg, cinnamon, salt, and the remaining sugar in the well. Pound the butter with a rolling pin to soften it and add it to the well. Work the central ingredients together with your fingertips until thoroughly mixed and the sugar is partially dissolved. Using a pastry scraper, gradually draw in the flour and continue working with both hands, pulling the dough into coarse crumbs. Gently press the crumbs into a ball. The dough will be quite soft. Flour the work surface and work the dough, pushing it away with the heel of your hand and gathering it up with the scraper, until it is smooth, pliable, and peels easily from the surface, 1 to 2 minutes. Wrap and chill until firm, at least 30 minutes.

To shape the tart, roll out two-thirds of the dough and line the tart pan (see page 377). Peel, quarter, and core the pears and arrange the quarters in the pan in a cartwheel pattern, stem ends inward. Cover the stems with slices of any remaining pear quarters. Brush the edge of dough with water. Roll out the rest of the dough to a round the same diameter as the pan. Cut a smaller 2½-inch/6-cm round from the center with the pastry cutter, creating a ring of dough. Wrap the ring around the rolling pin and unroll it over the pears. Seal the dough edges together and flute them. Brush the top with water and sprinkle with the sugar. Chill the pie until very firm, at least 30 minutes. The pie may be kept in the refrigerator for up to 8 hours before baking.

To finish, heat the oven to 375°F/190°C and set a baking sheet to heat in the oven. Bake the pie on the hot baking sheet until the pastry is browned and the pears are tender, 30 to 40 minutes. Let the pie cool slightly, then loosen and remove the pan sides. Let cool completely on a rack before sliding it off the metal base. Piquechagne is best eaten warm on the day of baking. At serving time, pour the cream into the central opening and serve at once.

GALETTE LANDAISE

FLAKY GALETTE WITH APPLE AND ARMAGNAC

serves 6 to 8

The historic Arab influence in France remains in dishes like this galette, made with a paper-thin, stretched pastry just a tad thinner than strudel and resembling phyllo. In Mont-de-Marsan, south of Bordeaux, I attended a lesson in pulling the soft, pliable dough to a giant sheet so thin, said the pâtissier, he can read love letters through it. To work with the dough, you will need a surface at least a yard (a meter) square, and when I can, I do it in the open air, as flour gets scattered everywhere. Making it requires two people to stretch the dough thinly—not for the beginner!

The Landes is foie gras country, so the layers of the galette are brushed with goose fat (sometimes walnut oil), not butter, and flavored with a few slivers of apple, chunks of dried apricot, and Armagnac. This flaky galette, also known as pastis, estirat, *and* croustade gasconne, *calls for a pastry method unique in France, appearing in no other French recipe to my knowledge. I am including the recipe for its delectable crust and folkloric history. If you want to save time, prepared phyllo dough is an acceptable substitute for the handmade dough; allow about ½ pound/225 grams.*

PÂTE

2 ½ CUPS/300 G FLOUR

I EGG

½ CUP/125 ML WATER, MORE IF NEEDED

SQUEEZE OF FRESH LEMON JUICE

PINCH OF SALT

FILLING

½ CUP/125 ML MELTED GOOSE FAT OR WALNUT OIL,
MORE FOR THE PAN

I APPLE, PEELED, CORED, AND THINLY SLICED

4 OR 5 PITTED DRIED APRICOTS, CUT INTO 2 OR
3 PIECES

3 TO 4 TABLESPOONS ARMAGNAC

ABOUT ½ CUP/100 G SUGAR, FOR SPRINKLING

II- TO I2-INCH/28- TO 30-CM TART PAN WITH
REMOVABLE BASE (SEE PAGE 377)

For the pâte, sift the flour onto a work surface and make a well in the center. Add the egg, water, lemon juice, and salt to the well and work with your fingertips until mixed. Using a pastry scraper, gradually draw in the flour and continue working with both hands, pulling the dough into coarse crumbs. Gently press the crumbs into a ball. The dough should be very pliable and slightly moist. Flour the work surface and knead the dough, picking it up and throwing it down, until it is shiny and very elastic, 5 to 7 minutes. The dough may also be mixed and kneaded in a stand mixer fitted with the dough hook. Cover the dough with an overturned bowl and leave for about 30 minutes for the gluten in the flour to relax.

Heat the oven to 375°F/190°C. Line a baking sheet with aluminum foil and set on a low shelf in the oven to heat. Brush the tart pan with goose fat. Lightly flour a very large work surface. Cut the dough in half, leave one-half covered with the bowl, and roll out the other piece to as large a rectangle as possible. Cover it with lightly dampened towels and leave for 15 minutes. Mix the apple and apricots with the Armagnac.

Using both hands and starting from the center, pull the dough out to a paper-thin sheet, creating as few holes as possible. It helps to have two people working and it should be possible to make a 40-by-30-inch/100-by-75-cm rectangle. Trim any thick edges from the dough, and cut the sheet into 6 equal pieces, each about 14 inches/35 cm square. Never mind if a few of them have holes. Go ahead and start assembling the galette, as the dough squares dry quickly.

Set a square of dough in the tart pan, brush it lightly with goose fat, sprinkle with sugar, and add a few pieces of apple and apricots. Continue adding layers of dough, angling the points around the "clock," until all the dough squares and half the goose fat and filling are used. Then stretch the second piece of dough and finish the galette using the rest of the filling and ending with a layer of dough brushed generously with fat. Trim some of the excess dough around the edges, leaving a little to fold over to make a loose border; brush these folds also. Sprinkle the galette lightly with sugar and slash a hole in the center so steam can escape.

Set the galette on the hot baking sheet and bake until lightly browned and crisp but still moist in the center, 25 to 35 minutes. Serve warm. It may be baked a day ahead, stored in an airtight container, and warmed gently in the oven before taking to table.

POMPET

APPLE FLAKY PASTRY GALETTE

serves 8

I was happy to spot this rustic apple slice in a small pastry shop in the atmospheric market town of Revel, east of Toulouse. The region is famous for Galette Landaise (page 347), a superb flaky pastry that challenges even a professional. Pompet is a much simpler version. To make it at home, roll pâte brisée with sugar, in the manner of puff pastry, then layer it with thin apple slices—voilà! I like to use a tart apple such as Gala or Granny Smith.

PÂTE BRISÉE

    3 CUPS/390 G FLOUR

    3 EGG YOLKS

    I TEASPOON SALT

    3 TABLESPOONS/45 G SUGAR

    $^1/_4$ CUP/60 ML WATER, MORE IF NEEDED

    $^3/_4$ CUP/170 G BUTTER, MORE FOR BAKING SHEET

    ABOUT $^1/_2$ CUP/110 G SUGAR, FOR ROLLING

    I EGG MIXED WITH $^1/_2$ TEASPOON SALT, FOR GLAZE

APPLE FILLING

    2 APPLES (ABOUT 12 OUNCES/330 G TOTAL)

    GRATED ZEST OF I LEMON

    $^1/_2$ TEASPOON GRATED NUTMEG

    2 TO 3 TABLESPOONS SUGAR, FOR SPRINKLING

Make the pâte brisée (see page 375) and chill until firm, 15 to 30 minutes. Line a baking sheet with parchment paper and butter the paper.

Sprinkle the work surface with 2 to 3 tablespoons of the sugar for rolling and roll out the dough to an 11-by-24-inch/28-by-60-cm strip. Fold the rectangle into thirds to form a square and turn it 90 degrees. Sprinkle the work surface with more sugar and roll out the dough again to a strip. Peel and halve the apples; scoop out the cores with a melon baller or the point of a paring knife. Set the halves cut side down on a cutting board and thinly slice. Lightly mark the dough strip in 3 squares. Arrange half of the apple slices on the center square and sprinkle with half of the lemon zest, nutmeg, and sugar. Fold 1 dough square on top and cover it with the remaining apple slices, lemon zest, nutmeg, and more sugar (the amount you need depends on the tartness of the apples). Fold the remaining dough square on top and press the edges down lightly with the rolling pin to seal them. Prick the dough a few times with a fork so it does not rise too much in the oven. Brush the top with the egg glaze and sprinkle with a little more sugar. Set the dough on the prepared baking sheet and chill until firm, about 30 minutes.

Heat the oven to 375°F/190°C. Bake the pompet until it is brown, crisp around the edges, and the center is well done, 30 to 40 minutes. Transfer to a rack to cool, and serve warm or at room temperature. Pompet keeps well for a day or two in an airtight container.

TARTOUILLATS

FRUIT FLANS IN CABBAGE LEAVES

makes 8 tartlets

I came across this intriguing look alike of pear tartlets in a tattered old Burgundian cookbook—in spring, pitted cherries are the fruit of choice. Blanched cabbage leaves replace the usual pastry, imbuing the custard filling with a pleasant flavor of green almonds. The tartlet molds should be at least ¾ inch/2 cm deep so as to hold enough filling.

FLAN BATTER

    I CUP/125 G FLOUR

    $^1/_2$ TEASPOON SALT

    I CUP/200 GRAMS SUGAR

    4 EGGS

    I CUP/250 ML MILK

    I MEDIUM HEAD (ABOUT 2 POUNDS/900 G) GREEN CABBAGE

    BUTTER FOR THE MOLDS

    I POUND/450 GRAMS FIRM PEARS

    2 TABLESPOONS MARC OR COGNAC

    TEN $4^1/_2$-INCH/I-CM TARTLET MOLDS

For the flan batter, sift the flour into a bowl with the salt. Stir in the sugar and make a well in the center. Add the eggs and half the milk and whisk just until the mixture is smooth. Stir in the remaining milk to form a batter. Cover the bowl and let stand for 30 minutes so the starch grains in the flour swell and thicken it.

Meanwhile, bring a large pan of water to a boil. Trim the cabbage stem and immerse the head in boiling water, setting a heatproof plate on top to submerge the cabbage. Bring back to a boil and simmer the cabbage 5 minutes. Lift it out with a large fork, let cool slightly, and peel off 5 to 6 whole leaves, taking care not to tear them. Boil the cabbage again 4 to 5 minutes, drain it and peel off enough leaves to line the molds. (Use the remaining cabbage for soup.) If the stems of the cabbage leaves are large, cut them out. Butter the tartlet molds and line them with the drained leaves, pressing them down well. Heat the oven to 400°F/200°C.

Peel, quarter, and core the pears and cut them in ½-inch/ 1.25-cm chunks. Arrange them loosely in the lined molds, leaving generous space for the batter. Stir the marc into the batter, pour it into a measuring jug and fill the molds, dividing the batter evenly among them. Trim the cabbage leaves with scissors to make a neat edge and set the molds on a baking sheet. Bake them in the oven until the filling is firm and the cabbage leaves are slightly brown, 25 to 30 minutes. The filling will puff up but shrink again as it cools.

Let the tartouillats cool slightly and then unmold them onto individual plates. They are best freshly baked and can be served warm or at room temperature.

TARTE AUX FRUITS ALSACIENNE

FRUIT AND CUSTARD TART

serves 10 to 12

The local fruits in Alsace—apricots, bilberries (blueberries are a close relation), and half a dozen varieties of plum—are so juicy that cooks go to great lengths to avoid a soggy crust. They use a puffy yeast dough (popular, too, with German cooks across the Rhine) that soaks up juices from the fruit with help from a few dry bread crumbs. The creamy custard filling further encloses the fruit. No accompaniment is needed, though a scoop of ice cream won't come amiss. The tart is so eye-catching that I am suggesting you make it wheel-sized, enough for twelve at a grand occasion.

PÂTE À PAIN

　2 CUPS/250 G FLOUR, MORE AS NEEDED

　1½ TEASPOONS SALT

　1½ TABLESPOONS/22 G SUGAR

　½ CUP/125 ML LUKEWARM MILK

　1 TABLESPOON/10 G DRY YEAST

　1 EGG

　6 TABLESPOONS/90 G BUTTER, SOFTENED, MORE
　FOR THE PAN

FILLING

　2 POUNDS/900 G FRESH FRUIT SUCH AS APRICOTS,
　PLUMS, BILBERRIES, BLUEBERRIES, OR CHERRIES

　2 TABLESPOONS DRY BREAD CRUMBS (SEE PAGE 373)

　2 EGGS, BEATEN TO MIX

　¼ CUP/60 ML CRÈME FRAÎCHE (PAGE 374) OR
　HEAVY CREAM

　5 TABLESPOONS/75 G GRANULATED SUGAR

　CONFECTIONERS' SUGAR, FOR SPRINKLING

　GROUND CINNAMON, FOR SPRINKLING (OPTIONAL)

　12-INCH/30-CM TART PAN WITH REMOVABLE BASE
　(SEE PAGE 377)

Make the pâte à pain (see page 375), adding the sugar to the flour and salt, and leave it to rise. Meanwhile, prepare the fruit. Halve apricots or plums, discarding the pits; pick over and wash the bilberries or blueberries; leave the cherries whole or pit them, as you prefer. Heat the oven to 425°F/220°C and set a baking sheet on a low shelf to heat.

When the dough has risen, knead it lightly to knock out the air. Pat it flat on the work surface, spread the butter on top and continue kneading to incorporate the butter, 2 to 3 minutes. Roll out the dough about ⅜ inch/6 mm thick and line the tart pan (see page 372).

Sprinkle the bread crumbs in the tart shell and arrange the fruit, cut side up, on top, packing it closely. Bake the tart on the hot baking sheet until the dough starts to color, about 10 minutes. Meanwhile, in a bowl, whisk the eggs, crème fraîche, and granulated sugar. Pour the mixture over the fruit, lower the oven heat to 350°F/180°C, and continue baking until the pastry is browned, the fruit is tender, and the custard is set, 40 to 50 minutes longer. Take care not to overbake the tart or the custard will curdle. Like all tarts with a yeast pastry, Tarte aux Fruits Alsacienne is at its best eaten warm from the oven, though it is still good after a day or two. Just before serving, sprinkle it with confectioners' sugar and with cinnamon if you like.

= ÎLE-DE-FRANCE: CAPITAL COOKING =

The Île-de-France, the region surrounding Paris, was originally a small kingdom, in effect an island threatened by the competing dynasties of Normandy, Burgundy, and Aquitaine. Today, the area is one of the most densely populated in Europe, and it is difficult to believe that the concrete jungle surrounding Paris includes communities that once made a living cultivating asparagus (Argenteuil), peaches (Montreuil), and cherries (Montmorency). Still, these place names remain part of the culinary vocabulary, as does *à la parisienne*, a reference to mushrooms from a time when they were grown in caves near the city.

With so much of France's wealth and population concentrated in and around Paris, the Île-de-France attracts the best produce from far and wide. If you get up early enough in the morning—I mean about three o'clock—you can visit France's famous wholesale market at Rungis, near Orly Airport. It used to be located in the very center of the city, in the Les Halles district, aptly known as "the belly of France." Although the famous food pavilions were torn down, Les Halles still retains some of its old atmosphere with its famous kitchen equipment shops for the trade, such as the cluttered, old-style Dehillerin.

People from the provinces have always migrated to Paris, and they have brought edible bits of home along with them. Yet Île-de-France itself has made some important contributions to the nation's gastronomy. The region is synonymous with pastry: *gâteau Saint-Honoré*, named after the patron saint of pastry cooks; *gâteau Paris-Brest*, a choux pastry ring filled with coffee-flavored pastry cream; and *puits d'amour* (wells of love), puff pastry *bouchées* designed to hold jam, pastry cream, or flavored crème Chantilly. Other regional specialties include croissants, baguettes, and brioches, veritable ambassadors of France that are part of "continental breakfast" in hotels around the world. And Paris has been the home of frites since at least the sixteenth century, when they were sold at stalls on the Pont Neuf. In classic cookbooks, a squat French fry is still called a *pomme Pont Neuf*.

GÂTEAU BASQUE AUX FIGUES FRAÎCHES

FRESH FIG GÂTEAU

serves 8

In the Basque country, the word gâteau *usually refers to a tart, not a cake. Just to further confuse, a* gâteau *is also known locally as a* pastis, *which simply means pastry, not the anise-flavored drink. Gâteau Basque itself is a crumbly, double-crusted tart filled with either a rum-flavored pastry cream or a thick fruit purée. I prefer the fruit versions, like this one layered with a delicious fig mixture. Prune purée or Marmelade de Fruits d'Automne (page 362) make a good alternative, as does simple homemade jam.*

PÂTE SUCRÉE

> 2 CUPS/250 G FLOUR
>
> 1/2 TEASPOON SALT
>
> 3/4 CUP/150 G SUGAR
>
> I EGG
>
> I EGG YOLK
>
> I TABLESPOON RUM
>
> 1/2 CUP PLUS 3 TABLESPOONS/150 G BUTTER, MORE FOR THE PAN
>
> I EGG MIXED WITH 1/2 TEASPOON SALT, FOR GLAZE

FIG FILLING

> 12 OUNCES/330 G FRESH FIGS
>
> I TO 2 TABLESPOONS SUGAR, OR TO TASTE
>
> 2 TABLESPOONS/30 G BUTTER
>
> 1/4 CUP/60 ML PORT
>
> 1/2 CUP/60 G RASPBERRIES, OR 3 TO 4 TABLESPOONS RASPBERRY JAM
>
> 9-INCH/23-CM ROUND CAKE PAN

Make the pâte sucrée (see page 376) and chill until firm, at least 30 minutes (this particular pastry dough is quite soft). For the filling, discard the stems from the figs and cut into large chunks. Toss the figs with the sugar in a bowl. Melt the butter in a frying pan over high heat. Add the figs and cook, stirring constantly, until caramelized and very tender, 3 to 5 minutes. Add the port and flambé it (see page 371). Add the raspberries and continue cooking until the filling just falls easily from a spoon, 2 to 3 minutes. Let the mixture cool slightly. Taste, adjust the amount of sugar, and leave the filling to cool.

Roll out two-thirds of the dough to a 10-inch/25-cm round and line the cake pan (see page 372), shaping the dough about 1 inch/2.5 cm up the sides of the pan. Brush the edge of the dough with egg glaze and spread the cooled fig filling in the pan. Roll out the remaining dough to a round the same diameter as the pan. Trim it to the right size and lift it onto the filling. Press the edges of dough firmly together to seal the top and bottom layers (fluting is not traditional). Brush the top with the egg glaze and score it with the tines of a fork in a lattice (characteristic of this gâteau). Chill until firm, at least 30 minutes. Heat the oven to 375°F/190°C and set a baking sheet on a low shelf to heat.

Bake the gâteau on the hot baking sheet until golden brown and the pastry starts to pull from the sides of the pan, 35 to 45 minutes. Let the gâteau cool for 15 minutes or so in the pan, then carefully turn it upside down onto a baking sheet. Put a rack on top and turn the gâteau right side up. It is moist and fragrant the day of baking, and will become richer if you store it for a day or two in an airtight container.

GÂTEAU BASQUE AUX PRUNEAUX

GÂTEAU BASQUE WITH PRUNES

A winter classic.

Follow the recipe for Gâteau Basque aux Figues Fraîches, omitting the filling. Make the pastry dough as described. For the prune filling, put 12 ounces/330 g pitted prunes in a saucepan with 3/4 cup/175 ml water, 1 to 2 tablespoons sugar, and 1 vanilla bean, split. Cover and simmer until the prunes are very soft, 7 to 10 minutes. Let them cool to tepid, then remove the vanilla bean (keep it to use again). Pulse the prunes in a food processor to make a textured purée. Continue the gâteau as described, substituting the prune for the fig filling.

= FRUITS GLACÉS AND FRUITS CONFITS =

Candied fruits from Apt, which delighted the popes of Avignon in the fourteenth century, are still a Provençal specialty. Simple *fruits confits*, preserved without glaze, are usually sold in pieces or dice for flavoring cakes and pastries. More complex *fruits glacés* are often whole and are glazed in sugar syrup and sold as candy. At Christmas, shops all over France decorate their windows with glazed fruits, from tiny, glistening tangerines and greengage plums to small pumpkins and whole pineapples with peel and leaves intact. So much work has gone into making them that it seems sacrilege to cut them open.

In theory, any fruit can be candied, although some are more amenable than others. The peel of citrus fruit, intensely flavored and relatively dry, is the commonest choice for *fruit confit*. Soft fruits such as the strawberry are too juicy to be candied, although a highly skilled candy maker can turn a melon into a *fruit glacé*, candied and glazed in sugar. It is a question of slowly replacing the water in the fruit with sugar syrup, a process that can take up to eight days. Traditionally, fruits were left two to three months in syrup, a candying method that is rare today but still occasionally found in the south. Such handcrafted confections bear little resemblance to the sickly candied fruits found in supermarkets that taste mainly of sugar.

Almost more popular than the fruits themselves are their by-product called *berlingots*, little hard candies made by boiling leftover fruit syrup to a hard crack, then cooling and shaping it in twists. A candied melon may be treasured as a work of art, but every schoolchild is familiar with a *berlingot*.

TARTE AU CITRON
LEMON TART
serves 8

The hot Mediterranean climate of Provence is more favorable to savory dishes than to desserts based on cream and eggs. Notable exceptions include the amazing array of candied fruits in pâtisseries, sweet fritters such as Bugnes (page 324) that stand up well to the heat, and this quintessential lemon tart.

PÂTE SUCRÉE

I¹/₂ CUPS/185 G FLOUR

¹/₂ TEASPOON SALT

¹/₃ CUP/75 G SUGAR

3 EGG YOLKS

¹/₂ TEASPOON VANILLA EXTRACT

6 TABLESPOONS/90 G BUTTER, MORE FOR THE PAN

LEMON FILLING

³/₄ CUP/120 G WHOLE BLANCHED ALMONDS

³/₄ CUP/150 G GRANULATED SUGAR

3 EGGS

GRATED ZEST OF 2 LEMONS

¹/₄ CUP/60 ML FRESH LEMON JUICE

²/₃ CUP/140 G BUTTER, MELTED

CONFECTIONERS' SUGAR, FOR SPRINKLING

10-INCH/25-CM TART PAN WITH REMOVABLE BASE
(SEE PAGE 377)

Make the pâte sucrée (see page 376) and chill until firm, 15 to 30 minutes. Roll out the dough and line the tart pan (see page 372), and then chill for 30 minutes. Heat the oven to 375°F/190°C and set a baking sheet on a low shelf to heat. Bake the tart shell blind (see page 372) on the hot baking sheet and then let it cool, leaving the baking sheet in the oven and the oven on.

For the filling, pulse the almonds with 2 tablespoons of the granulated sugar in a food processor until finely ground. In a stand mixer fitted with the whisk attachment, beat the eggs and the remaining sugar until light and thick enough to leave a ribbon trail when the whisk is lifted, 3 to 5 minutes. Stir in the lemon zest, juice, and butter. Stir in the almond mixture with a spoon.

Set the tart shell on the hot baking sheet in the oven, and pour in the filling. Bake until set and golden brown, 25 to 30 minutes. Let cool, then unmold the tart onto a platter. Serve at room temperature, sprinkling with confectioners' sugar.

POIRES BELLE ANGEVINE
POACHED PEARS IN RED WINE
serves 4

Anjou, near the mouth of the Loire, is the home of the buttery Doyenne du Comice, queen of pears. It and many other beurré *pear varieties (so called for their deliciously creamy texture) were developed centuries ago in the walled garden at the provincial capital, Angers. Not surprisingly, the robust Cabernet Franc wines so characteristic of the Loire are perfect for poaching these pears. Accompany each pear with a simple cookie.*

I BOTTLE (750 ML) ROBUST RED WINE

6 TABLESPOONS/90 G SUGAR, MORE TO TASTE

ZEST OF I LEMON, PARED IN STRIPS

4 LARGE PEARS (ABOUT 2 POUNDS/900 G TOTAL),
WITH STEMS

2 TABLESPOONS RAISINS OR CHOPPED CANDIED
GINGER (OPTIONAL)

Put the wine, sugar, and lemon zest in a small, deep saucepan just large enough to hold the pears upright. Heat gently until the sugar dissolves, then bring the syrup to a boil and simmer for 2 minutes. Set it aside.

Peel the pears with a vegetable peeler, leaving the stems, and scoop out the flower indentation with the top of the peeler. (Leaving the stems on makes them easy to handle and more attractive for serving.) Using a sharp teaspoon and working from the flower end, scoop out the core inside the pear, leaving the pear whole. Cut a thin slice from the base so the pear sits upright. If you like, stuff the hollow with raisins, and lower the pear at once into the syrup so it does not discolor. Repeat with the remaining pears. Add water if necessary so the pears are covered. Weight them down with a heatproof plate to keep the wine from forming a "tidemark."

Over low heat, bring the pears slowly to a simmer and poach them until translucent and tender when pierced with the point of a knife, 15 to 25 minutes, depending on their ripeness. Leave them in the wine to cool to tepid, then transfer them to a bowl with a draining spoon and set aside.

Boil the wine syrup over high heat until concentrated and slightly thickened, 15 to 25 minutes, depending on how much water was added. You should have about 1½ cups/375 ml syrup. Taste and add more sugar if you like. Pour the hot syrup over the pears (I like to leave in the lemon zest, but you may strain it out if you prefer). They may be served hot, warm, or chilled and the flavor will differ at each stage. They may also be prepared ahead and refrigerated for up to 3 days. Serve the pears, set upright, in shallow bowls.

TARTE AU CITRON

CLAFOUTIS LIMOUSIN

CLAFOUTIS LIMOUSIN
CHERRY BATTER PUDDING
serves 6 to 8

Clafoutis comes from the Limousin, a flat agricultural area in the center of France, but versions of this simple pudding can be found all over. In the Auvergne, for example, it is known as millard, *or* flognarde *when made with pears. Clafoutis is suited to tart fruits such as apples, plums, and most famously cherries. If you follow tradition like me and leave the pits in to add a hint of bitterness, be sure to warn guests or they may crack a tooth!*

BUTTER AND GRANULATED SUGAR, FOR THE DISH

1 POUND/450 G TART CHERRIES

3 TABLESPOONS/45 ML KIRSCH OR COGNAC

CONFECTIONERS' SUGAR, FOR SPRINKLING

BATTER

1/4 CUP/60 G GRANULATED SUGAR

4 EGGS

1/4 CUP/30 G FLOUR

PINCH OF SALT

2 CUPS/500 ML MILK

1 1/2-QUART/1.5-LITER BAKING DISH

Butter the baking dish, and then sprinkle it with granulated sugar, turning and tilting the dish until evenly coated. Spread the cherries in the dish. For the batter, put the sugar in a bowl, add the eggs, and whisk until light and frothy, 1 to 2 minutes. Add the flour and salt and stir just until smooth. Do not overbeat or the pudding will be tough. Stir in the milk. The cherries and batter may be prepared an hour or two before baking and kept covered at room temperature.

Heat the oven to 375°F/190°C. If the batter has sat, it may have separated slightly, so stir to mix it, and then strain it over the cherries. Bake the pudding until browned and just set, 50 minutes to 1 hour. Let cool for 5 to 10 minutes, then sprinkle with the kirsch (the aroma from the alcohol is a treat in itself). Dust generously with confectioners' sugar and serve warm.

FAR BRETON
BATTER PUDDING WITH PRUNES

This Breton pudding is similar to Clafoutis, but more substantial, so it can be cut into wedges like a cake.

Pour boiling water over 3/4 cup/115 g pitted prunes and leave to soak for 15 to 20 minutes. Butter and sugar a 1 1/2-quart/ 1.5-liter baking dish and heat the oven to 350°F/180°C. Measure 2 1/2 cups/625 ml milk. Sift 1 cup/125 g flour with a pinch of salt into a bowl, make a well in the center, and add about half the milk. Stir with a whisk to make a smooth paste and then add the remaining milk with 2/3 cup/140 g sugar and 2 eggs, mixing well to make a smooth batter. Drain the prunes and spread them in the baking dish. Pour the batter over the prunes and bake until well browned and a skewer inserted in the center comes out dry, 1 1/2 to 1 3/4 hours. Let cool slightly, then sprinkle with 2 to 3 tablespoons rum. Cut into wedges and serve warm. Serves 6 to 8.

RATAFIA
makes 2 bottles (3 cups/750 ml each)

Have you come across Ratafia, the preferred tipple of heroines in Regency novels? It is a gentle mix of fruit juice and hard alcohol, usually composed of three parts grape juice to one part marc, Cognac, or Armagnac (page 328), the trio of spirits distilled from the grape. The resulting aperitif is pleasantly fruity, particularly when made with the favorite French Chasselas table grapes, with an eye-opening kick in the aftertaste. In cider-making areas, a version of the aperitif, using the same three-to-one proportion, is made from hard cider and its related spirit, Calvados. Ratafia is a good substitute for port in pork and game stews. Whatever version you make, the fruit juice must be fresh. Bottled pasteurized juice is not suitable. The best way is to make the juice in a food processor, as I do here.

3 POUNDS/1.35 KG SWEET RED OR GREEN GRAPES

2 CUPS/500 ML MARC, COGNAC, OR ARMAGNAC

2 BOTTLES (3 CUPS/750 ML EACH)

To make the juice, discard the stems from the grapes, rinse them, and then purée them in a food processor. Work the pulp through a food mill or strainer to extract the juice. Measure the juice; there should be about 1 quart/1 liter.

Stir together the grape juice and marc in a large bowl and use a pitcher to fill the bottles. Cap the bottles loosely and store in a cool, dark place for 6 months. The ratafia will cloud at first, then gradually clear as sediment falls to the bottom of the bottle, forming a mat. Decant the ratafia into carafes or decanters, carefully pouring the clear liqueur from the bottles and leaving the sediment behind. Seal and store in a cool place. The flavor improves with age.

LES FRUITS DU VIEUX GARÇON

OLD BACHELOR'S MACERATED FRUITS

makes 2 quarts/2 liters fruits in liqueur

For the serious country cook, bachelor or not, these fruits macerated in alcohol are a summer-long project. First into the jar go cherries. Then, as the season advances, apricots, peaches, greengage or yellow Mirabelle plums, red plums, and finally plump green or purple figs follow. Each layer is sweetened with sugar and covered with white alcohol, which in the old days was locally distilled and could taste like rocket fuel. The spirit permeates the fruit and prevents it from fermenting, while the fruit juice slowly imbues the liquid, creating a bracing liqueur. After a three-month wait, the fruits are ready to serve.

Versions of Les Fruits du Vieux Garçon can be found all over France. Where I live in Burgundy, marc is the preferred alcohol. In Alsace, you will find plums in white alcohol, in Bordeaux it may be cherries in Cognac, and in Gascony, prunes in Armagnac. For all these spirits, vodka is a neutral alternative. A tall jar is needed, preferably of glass so the brightly colored fruits are displayed, packed in layers; a large domestic canning jar does fine. The fruits should be ripe but still firm, and firm fruits do better than berries, which tend to break up.

8 OUNCES/225 G CHERRIES

8 OUNCES/225 G APRICOTS

8OUNCES/225 G WHITE PEACHES

8 OUNCES/225 G GREEN OR YELLOW PLUMS

8 OUNCES/225 G RED PLUMS

8 OUNCES/225 G RED OR GREEN FIGS

ABOUT 3 CUPS/600 G SUGAR, MORE IF NEEDED

ABOUT 1 BOTTLE (750 ML) VODKA OR COGNAC

2-QUART/2-LITER GLASS JAR

Discard the stems from the fruits and wipe the fruits with a cloth. Prick the skins with a needle so the alcohol penetrates. Large fruits such as peaches should be halved, discarding the pits. Roughly measure the fruits in a 1-quart/1-liter measuring jug, and for every cup, measure ½ cup/100 g sugar. Pack the fruits loosely in the jar and sprinkle the sugar on top. Add enough vodka just to cover the fruits. Cover the jar with a cloth or a loose lid and store in a cool, dark place.

As fruits come into season, keep adding them with more sugar and alcohol, using different colors so the layers are distinct. Taste from time to time, adding more sugar if needed. When the jar is full, seal it. If any sugar remains undissolved, turn the jar upside down to mix and dissolve the sugar. Store the fruits for at least 3 months before eating so the flavor mellows.

PÂTES DE FRAMBOISES

RASPBERRY JELLY CANDIES

makes 4 dozen/1 pound/450 g candies

My favorite French Christmas gift is a box of unassuming square candies that looks like a multicolored checkerboard. With one bite, I am back to the fragrance of fresh summer and fall fruits: golden apricots, raspberries, dusky black currants, greengage and purple plums, pears, and, last of all, tawny autumnal quinces. A whole orchard, and the passing of a twelvemonth, is right there in the box. The candies are made by simmering the fruit to a pulp, sieving it, and then cooking it with sugar to a paste. Just to be sure the paste sets, I add a little powdered pectin, available in markets or on the Internet. Tart fruits may need more sugar, and some fruits take longer to cook than others. Here I have chosen raspberries, a favorite of mine.

VEGETABLE OIL FOR THE PAN

1½ POUNDS/675 G RASPBERRIES

ABOUT 2 CUPS/400 G SUGAR, MORE FOR COATING

1 TABLESPOON/7 G POWDERED PECTIN

7-INCH/18-CM SQUARE PAN

Lightly oil the pan and line the bottom and sides with parchment paper. Put the raspberries in a saucepan, cover, and simmer over medium heat until they can easily be mashed to a pulp, 10 to 12 minutes. Let cool slightly. Work the berries through a food mill or a strainer and measure the purée; there should be about 2 cups/ 500 ml. Measure an equal volume of sugar and stir in the pectin.

Wipe out the saucepan, add the raspberry mixture, and heat gently without boiling until the sugar is dissolved, 1 to 2 minutes. Boil the mixture over medium heat, skimming occasionally and stirring often with a wooden spoon, until the paste is quite thick and registers 230°F/110°C on a sugar thermometer, 10 to 12 minutes. It needs constant stirring and it spatters, so cover your hand with a cloth. Pour the paste into the prepared pan, spread it flat with a spatula, cover, and chill for at least 2 hours.

Sprinkle a sheet of parchment paper generously with sugar, and turn out the slab of paste onto it. Sprinkle the top with sugar also. With a knife dipped in cold water, cut the paste into 1-inch/2.5-cm squares. Roll the squares all over in sugar and pack them between layers of parchment paper in an airtight container. The candies will keep for at least 1 month in a cool place.

facing page:

LES FRUITS DU VIEUX GARÇON

(VARIATION USING PEARS AND APRICOTS)

CONFITURE D'ABRICOTS AUX AMANDES

APRICOT JAM WITH ALMONDS

makes six 1-cup/250-ml jars

Apricots pair naturally with almonds—they belong to the same family—and I found this attractive recipe showcasing that match in the almond-growing valley of the Rhône. Orange-gold and unfailingly more concentrated in flavor than the fruit itself, it is one of the very best jams I know. To add a welcome tinge of bitterness, I like to crack a few apricot pits, extract the almond-shaped kernel from each one, and add the kernels to the jam. Taking another twist, you might like to try a variation: instead of the sliced almonds, add a handful of leaves of lemon balm or rose geranium, coarsely chopping them and stirring them into the jam about 10 minutes before it is ready. The aroma perfumes the kitchen as well as the pots of jam.

4 POUNDS/1.8 KG APRICOTS

JUICE OF 1 LEMON

6 CUPS/1.2 KG SUGAR

1¹/₂ CUPS/135 G SLICED ALMONDS

NUTCRACKER, PRESERVING PAN (SEE PAGE 377), SIX 1-CUP/250-ML JAM JARS

Wipe the apricots with a damp cloth. Run a knife around their circumference, through the crease, twist the halves apart, and extract the pits. Using a nutcracker, extract half a dozen kernels from the pits and coarsely chop them. Put the fruit, chopped pits, and lemon juice in a large bowl and stir in the sugar. Cover and macerate in the refrigerator for 24 hours to draw out the juice.

The next day, sterilize the jars. Tip the macerated fruit into a preserving pan and bring to a boil over medium heat, stirring often until the sugar dissolves. Boil the jam over high heat, skimming often and stirring from time to time, for 15 minutes. Stir in the almonds and continue boiling, stirring often, until the jam reaches the jell point, 10 to 15 minutes more. Characteristic double drips will fall from the spoon, and the temperature should register 220°F/105°C on a sugar thermometer.

Let the jam cool for about 5 minutes, then transfer to a heatproof measuring jug, pour into the sterilized jars, and seal. Store in a cool, dark place for up to 1 year.

GELÉE DE POMMES ET PÉTALES DE ROSE

ROSE PETAL AND APPLE JELLY

makes four 1-cup/250-ml jars

For this romantic jelly, you need a garden of full-blown pink or red roses, their petals about to fall, together with a tree of sour apples. Luckily, these demands can be simplified, as the recipe proceeds in two parts: first comes a jelly made with little crab apples (the sour apples used to make cider), then the rose petals are added and the jelly is boiled again to the jell point. Work can be minimized if you substitute a larger tart apple such as Granny Smith, or use ready-prepared apple jelly (you will need about 2 pounds/ 1 liter). Then all you must pick are the roses, the more fragrant the better. A golden pink, elusively fragrant jelly will be your reward.

APPLE JELLY

3 POUNDS/1.35 KG VERY TART APPLES

ABOUT 1¹/₂ CUPS/300 G SUGAR

2 QUARTS/2 LITERS PACKED ROSE PETALS

3 CUPS/750 ML BOILING WATER, MORE IF NEEDED

1 CUP/200 G SUGAR

JUICE OF 1 LEMON

PRESERVING PAN (SEE PAGE 377), JELLY BAG (SEE PAGE 376), FOUR 1-CUP/250-ML JELLY JARS

For the jelly, scrub the apples, especially at the blossom ends, and discard the stems. Quarter the fruits (skins and cores will add pectin to help set the jelly) and put in the preserving pan. Add water to cover barely. Bring to a boil and then simmer over low heat, without stirring, until the apples are very soft and falling apart, 45 minutes to 1 hour, depending on their ripeness.

When the apples are done, take the pan from the heat and let cool for 5 minutes. Spoon the fruit and juice into the jelly bag, or a colander lined with several layers of cheesecloth, set over a bowl. Do not press on the fruit, so the juice can drip slowly into the bowl without clouding. Leave undisturbed until the dripping stops, about 1 hour. Meanwhile, sterilize the jelly jars. Nip the white tips from the rose petals, discarding the tips. Put the petals in a large bowl and pour in the boiling water, just to cover. Cover and let steep until cool. The color of the petals will be drawn into the water. Set aside.

continued

clockwise from top right:
CONFITURE D'ABRICOTS AUX AMANDES,
GELÉE DE POMMES ET PÉTALES DE ROSE,
CONFITURE DE RHUBARBE ET FRAISES

Measure the apple juice. There will be about 2 cups/500 ml. For every 1 cup/250 ml juice, measure ¾ cup/150 g sugar and stir the sugar into the juice in the preserving pan. Bring the juice slowly to a boil, stirring occasionally until the sugar dissolves. Boil over high heat, skimming often, until the jelly reaches the jell point, 15 to 20 minutes. Characteristic double drips will fall from the spoon, and the temperature should register 220°F/105°C on a sugar thermometer. Let the jelly cool for 5 minutes.

Stir in the rose petals and their liquid, with the 1 cup/200 g sugar and the lemon juice. Heat again until the sugar dissolves, and then bring the jelly back to a boil and continue boiling over high heat, stirring often, until it reaches the jell point again, 10 to 15 minutes longer.

Let the jelly cool for about 5 minutes, then transfer it to a heatproof measuring jug, pour into the sterilized jars, and seal. Store in a cool, dark place for up to 1 year.

MARMELADE DE FRUITS D'AUTOMNE
BUTTER OF AUTUMN FRUITS WITH RAISINS AND CALVADOS
makes five 1-cup/250-ml jars

The flavors of autumn are concentrated in this intense, deep golden Norman fruit butter of apples, pears, and quinces. Looking like ancient, craggy pears, quinces are perfect in preserves, their mellow, perfumed taste developing only with long cooking. They can be hard to find, so you may substitute more of the firm pears (Bosc or Seckel are best). For a non-alcoholic butter, add a teaspoon of vanilla extract instead of the Calvados. I like to serve this fruit butter with cold ham, pork, Terrine de Gibier (page 190), and, of course, for breakfast.

3 TART APPLES (ABOUT 1 POUND/450 G TOTAL)

3 FIRM PEARS (ABOUT 1 POUND/450 G TOTAL)

3 QUINCES (ABOUT 1½ POUNDS/675 G TOTAL)

PARED ZEST STRIPS AND JUICE OF 1 LEMON

1 QUART/1 LITER WATER, MORE IF NEEDED

½ CUP/125 G GOLDEN RAISINS

3 TABLESPOONS/45 ML CALVADOS

ABOUT 4 CUPS/800 G SUGAR, MORE IF NEEDED

PRESERVING PAN (SEE PAGE 377), FIVE 1-CUP/ 250-ML JAM JARS

Wipe the apples, pears, and quinces, then quarter and core them, leaving the peel. Cut into chunks, put them in the preserving pan with the lemon zest, and add the water; it should almost cover the fruits. Simmer over medium heat until soft, 25 to 40 minutes (quinces can be very slow to cook). Set aside to cool to tepid. Put the raisins in a bowl with the Calvados, add ½ cup/125 ml hot liquid from the fruit, and leave them to macerate. Sterilize the jam jars.

When the fruit mixture is cool, purée it, with its liquid, in batches in a food processor. Measure the volume of purée—there will be about 4 cups/1 liter purée—and put the purée in the preserving pan. Stir in an equal volume of sugar. Bring the purée to a boil and boil over high heat, stirring often, until it is thick, rich, and holds a ribbon trail when the spoon is lifted, 20 to 25 minutes. Note that the purée scorches easily toward the end of cooking, and splashes as you stir.

Take the pan from the heat and let the bubbles subside. Stir in the raisins with their liquid and the lemon juice. Let the butter cool for about 5 minutes, then ladle into the sterilized jars and seal. Store in a cool, dark place for up to 1 year.

CONFITURE DE RHUBARBE ET FRAISES
RHUBARB AND STRAWBERRY JAM

Happy combinations for jam can be grouped by season, and rhubarb with strawberry is one of the first in spring.

Trim 1½ pounds/675 g rhubarb stalks, cut them into ¾-inch/ 2-cm chunks, and put them in a bowl. Hull 1 quart/600 g strawberries, washing them only if they are sandy. Cut the berries in half and mix with the rhubarb. Stir in an equal volume of sugar (about 4 cups/800 g). Cover and macerate overnight or for up to 24 hours in the refrigerator to draw out the juice. Transfer to a preserving pan and heat gently over low heat, stirring often, until the rhubarb softens to pulp and the sugar dissolves, 7 to 10 minutes. Bring the fruit to a boil and cook over high heat, skimming often and stirring from time to time, until the jam reaches the jell point, 30 to 40 minutes. Characteristic double drips will fall from the spoon, and the temperature should register 220°F/105°C on a sugar thermometer. Let the jam cool for about 5 minutes, then transfer to a heatproof measuring jug, pour into sterilized jars, and seal. Store in a cool, dark place for up to 1 year. Makes four 1-cup/250-ml jam jars.

= LOIRE: THE GARDEN OF FRANCE =

For most people, things that flow are what sum up the Loire region: the great winding river with weeping willows tossing their heads; watery reflections of grand châteaux playing on the surface; and, of course, Loire Valley wines. But, for me, an earthier side of this peaceful landscape captures the imagination and seduces the appetite. The whole valley is truly a cornucopia of fruits and vegetables, and has been since the late fifteenth century, when France's rulers took advantage of the hospitable climate. One sixteenth-century French queen gave her name, Reine Claude, to green-gage plums, and also to Reinette apples. Apricots, melons, peaches, and pears (including the Comice variety considered by many to be the finest) have all been improved by the long tradition of horticultural experimentation in the region.

As the sixteenth-century poet Pierre Ronsard remarked, "Artichokes and salad greens, asparagus, parsnips and the melons of the Loire, all are more tempting than great mounds of royal meats." After a visit to the Halles market in Tours, I realized he hadn't exaggerated. Even at the beginning of winter, stands here boast some of the finest produce I have ever seen: local mâche, pink radishes, snow white cauliflower, and copper-colored shallots. And as proof that the tradition of horticultural experimentation still exists, I also made the acquaintance of a strange little vegetable called *cerfeuil bulbeux*, which came wrapped with instructions. They looked like Jerusalem artichokes, cooked up like potatoes (only more floury), and tasted slightly of chestnuts. "You won't get anything more local than this," I was informed.

Fish is another story. Traditionally, the great Loire River was home to pike, pickerel, salmon, shad, and eels, a key ingredient in *matelote de la Loire*, a fish stew flavored with mushrooms, cream, and a local red wine. I say "traditionally" because fish is in crisis, not just in the Loire but also in the coastal areas where seafood was once abundant. Today, few supplies are local, but Loire cooks continue to prepare their favorite fish recipes, including the classic regional accompaniment Sauce Beurre Blanc (page 221).

Happily, one aspect of local gastronomy clearly doing well is poultry, game, and charcuterie. On my autumn visit, the lineup of birds seemed endless: several types of chicken, along with pheasant, quail, guinea hen, duck, partridge, and turkey. Many vendors sold poultry or rabbit "roasts": boned, stuffed with local fruits, and ready to slice—my kind of fast food! Then there are Rillettes (page 191), a pâté of pork, or better still, duck or goose, cooked until very soft, then shredded, seasoned, and mixed back into melted lard. Rillons (page 191) are closely related: chunks of pork slowly cooked until mahogany brown and very tender. All in all, considering that the Loire is also home to delicious wines, it is the perfect place for a picnic.

= A SOOTHING TISANE =

Chamomile, mint, elder flower, lime blossom, sage, verbena, lemon balm, wild thyme—the names of tisane infusions, or herb teas, read like a medieval herbal. But in France these infusions are far from being a historical curiosity, a remedy of crank doctors, or the solace of old maids. A cup of chamomile tea is said to stimulate the kidneys, sage to ease digestion, and *verveine* (lemon verbena) to soothe the liver as well as enjoying mild renown as an aphrodisiac. Commonest of all is *tilleul* (leaves of linden or lime blossom), which ensures a sound sleep and is the sovereign cure for constipation.

Most cafés offer a choice of lime blossom or mint tea, the powdered leaves trapped in dusty little bags that yield only an echo of their true bouquet. A home infusion steeped in boiling water is an infinite improvement. Every night, I make a tea with a mug full of dried *tilleul* from the trees along our lane. Fragrant infusions are a pleasing alternative to after-dinner coffee, too. One French friend of mine serves infusions of fresh rosemary branches or mint leaves to her guests. She simply crams the fresh leaves into a teapot, pours boiling water over them, and waits five minutes.

Linden trees grow all over France (source of great tisane but lousy firewood), and the little Provençal hill town of Buis-les-Baronnies has an annual *tilleul* market in July. Most chamomile comes from the Loire and is commercially grown. As for mint tea, every French garden should have its patch of spearmint, running wild over the paving stones.

= PORTRAIT OF A JAM MAKER =

My kitchen cupboard harbors at least a dozen kinds of preserves, all made from fruits in the garden. I would be smug about that if I had not met gray-haired Roseline Fontaine some years ago at Quarré-les-Tombes, a windy hill town that sounds haunted (and probably is, as it is full of megaliths marking ancient burial grounds). I will leave you to find it on your own. Madame Fontaine, the wife of the local baker, got into the jam business by accident: "We were running a café as part of my husband's shop," she told me, "and one day I left some jams on the counter to cool. So many customers asked to buy them that I thought, why not? I sold two hundred pots within three weeks and I was launched!"

My humble cupboard of *confitures* pales beside Madame Fontaine's kitchen. Floor to ceiling, her walls are lined with vivid pots, including golden tomato, purple wild peach, pink grenadine, and green damson. More exotic preserves include walnut, chestnut, pumpkin, watermelon, violet, rose, dandelion flower, and caramelized milk. To add to the complexity, she transforms jams with flavorings, such as honey, spices, vanilla, or rum. Some preserves have whimsical names, including love-in-a-cage (cape gooseberry), scratch-your-backside (rose hip), paradise jelly (wild plums and cranberry), and wedding night (apple, wild pear, and candied ginger). Definitely spooky stuff.

Madame Fontaine now sells more than two hundred different types of preserves and over twenty thousand pots a year, yet she never strays from artisanal methods. She prepares her fruits in batches of seven to nine pounds to make sure they cook fast and retain their fresh flavor. For maximum taste, she also always macerates her fruits with sugar for twenty-four hours before cooking, a trick she passed on to me. Madame Fontaine collects old cookbooks, adapting the recipes she finds to use less sugar, since today's fruits are sweeter. "Jams are not a way to use up stale ingredients," she admonishes. "The fruits must be prime, without any blemishes."

= PORTRAIT OF A DISTILLER: WATERS OF LIFE =

I chanced upon Gilbert Holl's artisanal distillery on a thread of hilly road in Alsace one chilly December. It was dusk, and what caught my eye was a gleaming copper alembic and the wheel of an old mill, treading water in a brook. A warm light filtered across the drive from the threshold of a small shop. I was out of the car and through the door in a flash.

There is real magic to liqueurs and *alcools blancs*: it always seems to me something that wizards get up to in storybooks. (How do you entice a real pear to grow inside a bottle?) An *alcool blanc* is distilled from herbs or fruits (usually just a single one) and, as its name implies, comes out colorless. The result is at least as strong as Cognac (page 328) and often a good deal rougher. A fruit liqueur has the same origins, but with fruit thrown back in. A liqueur is sweeter and softer. "Just right for women," Gilbert says. I wouldn't be so sure about that, although it is true that fruit liqueurs are more often enjoyed diluted (typically with white wine, as in a *kir*) than drunk on their own.

Gilbert is a self-taught distiller. He bought three alembics twenty-five years ago and began experimenting with marc (the French name for grappa) and summer fruits. Today, he makes no fewer than seventy varieties of distilled spirits. In addition to classics, such as black currant, plum, pear, and absinthe, he also creates more exotic essences, including pine, dandelion flower, cumin, and his signature eau-de-vie called *coeur de choucroute*, "cabbage heart." I tried a nip of that one . . . and felt it travel every inch of my throat! Gilbert told me it went well not only with choucroute but also with fish. Strange fish, in my opinion!

Industrially produced eaux-de-vie are guaranteed short-cuts to a hangover. Artisanal distillations are another breed altogether: pure fruit, clean alcohol, and lots of loving care. Gilbert's wild raspberry eau-de-vie—concentrated essence of raspberry in the form of liquid fire—is an award winner. When you learn that it takes 220 pounds (100 kilograms) of selected raspberries to make just one quart (one liter), you begin to understand what makes these boutique spirits so extraordinary. "We sell out every year," Gilbert tells me, "but we won't expand. We're artisans, and to be good you have to stay small. That's the way we want to be."

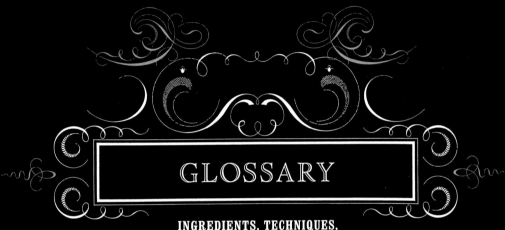

GLOSSARY

INGREDIENTS, TECHNIQUES, RECIPES & EQUIPMENT

CHAPTER
No. 18

INGREDIENTS

UNLESS OTHERWISE STATED, THE FOLLOWING IS TRUE FOR ALL THE RECIPES IN THIS BOOK:

Vegetables are medium sized and are peeled before using.

Butter is unsalted.

Eggs are large, weighing about 2 ounces/60 g each.

Sugar is U.S. granulated sugar, U.K. caster sugar, or French *sucre en poudre*.

Flour is U.S. unbleached all-purpose flour, U.K. unbleached plain flour, or French *farine type 55*; U.S. pastry flour closely resembles French *farine type 45*.

BARDING FAT

This thinly sliced pork fat is often wrapped around meat and game that has little or no natural fat. It is also used for lining terrine molds, where it helps the contents maintain a consistent level of moisture. Lightly cured bacon may be substituted.

BOUQUET GARNI

A tied bundle of aromatic herbs used for flavoring braises, ragoûts, stocks, and sauces. It should include a sprig of fresh thyme, a dried bay leaf, and several sprigs of fresh parsley. Leek greens and celery tops may also be included. If a recipe calls for a large bouquet garni, double the ingredients.

BUTTER

Most French butter (*beurre*) is unsalted, which allows the amount of salt in a dish to be controlled more easily. *Beurre demi-sel* is lightly salted and *beurre salé* has a strong salty flavor; both are most commonly table butters, though in Brittany salted butter is also popular for cooking.

FLOUR

Only a narrow range of flours is commonly available in France, including white wheat flour called *farine type 55*, and a slightly softer version, *farine type 45*, preferred by pâtissiers for light cakes, pastries, and some yeast doughs. French health-food stores sometimes carry whole-wheat flour and specialty flours, such as rye and buckwheat. U.S. white wheat flour is typically drier than French flour and has a higher gluten content, but these differences can be balanced by handling the dough lightly and increasing the liquid slightly.

ONIONS

As in most countries, onions come in half a dozen varieties in France. Most common are large onions with papery, gold-brown skins and pungent flavor, the universal choice for onion soup, onion tart, and other onion-based dishes, and for use as back-ground aromatics in braises and sauces. Large white onions are mild and less versatile. Red onions, sweetest of all, are appropriate raw in salads, though raw onion is seldom used in traditional recipes. When little onions are called for, you may use either young baby white onions or mature dry-skinned, gold-brown onions. Young ones will cook more quickly. Lastly comes a trio of aromatics, including scallions, or *oignons verts*; a coarse relative of the chive called the *cebette*; and the chive itself, or *ciboulette*.

QUATRE ÉPICES

Literally "four spices," *quatre épices* is a commercial mix of ground spices that typically includes cinnamon, clove, nutmeg, and pepper. It is most commonly used in charcuterie, with ground allspice and sometimes nutmeg an acceptable substitute.

VEGETABLE OIL

Vegetable oil is used for both frying and deep-frying. Select an oil with a mild flavor and a high flash (scorch) point. Sunflower seed oil, safflower oil, canola, and corn oil are all common in France. Peanut oil is also popular, but the French oil has a milder taste than its U.S. counterpart.

TECHNIQUES

BELL PEPPER, CORING, SEEDING, AND SLICING OR CHOPPING

Cut around the core of the pepper, twist, and pull it out. Halve the pepper lengthwise, scrape out the seeds, and cut away the protruding inside ribs. Set a pepper half, cut side down, on the board and press down with the heel of your hand to flatten it. With a large knife, slice it lengthwise into strips. For chopped peppers, bunch slices together with your hand and dice crosswise.

BIRD, CARVING

Let the cooked bird stand for 10 minutes in a warm place, then discard the trussing strings. Set the bird, back down, on a carving board. Cut the skin between the leg and breast. Using a two-pronged fork, turn the bird on its side. Cut around the "oyster" meat lying against the backbone, so the meat remains attached to the thigh. With the fork, spear the leg at the thigh and twist it up and forward, breaking the joint. Finish cutting away the leg joint and pull the leg from the carcass with the oyster meat still attached. Halve the leg by cutting through the joint, using the line of white fat as a guide. If the wishbone was not removed before cooking, cut it out. Cut horizontally above the wing joint, through to the breastbone, so you can carve a complete slice. Carve the breast in slices parallel to the rib cage. Cut off the wing, then carve the other side of the bird in the same way.

BIRD, CUTTING IN HALF, INTO 4 PIECES, AND INTO 8 PIECES

Depending on the recipe and the size of the bird, you may want to cut it in half or into 4 or 8 pieces. Set the bird, back down, on a carving board. Grasp one leg and tug it slightly so it pulls away from the body. With a sharp knife, cut the skin between the leg and body, following the outline of the thigh until the leg joint is visible. Flip the bird so you can locate the "oyster" meat lying against the backbone, and cut around it so that it remains attached to the thigh. Twist the leg sharply outward to break the thigh joint. Cut forward to detach the leg completely from the body, including the oyster. Turn the bird and repeat with the second leg. With a knife or poultry shears, cut away and remove the backbone. Cut along breastbone *to halve the carcass*. Cut off the wing tips. (Save the backbone and wing tips for the stockpot). The bird is now in *4 pieces*. To cut into *8 pieces*, divide each breast crosswise in half, cutting diagonally through the meat, then though the breast and rib bones so a portion of breast meat remains attached to each wing. Trim the ends of the rib bones. Cut the legs in half through the joint, using the white line of fat on the underside as a guide. Trim the drumsticks and any protruding bones with poultry shears.

BIRD, TRUSSING WITH STRING

Large birds such as turkey and goose, as well as smaller ducks, chickens, quail, and pigeons (squabs), can be trussed with a long piece of thin string without using a trussing needle. To make carving easier, first remove the wishbone: lift the neck skin and, with a small, sharp knife, outline the wishbone and cut it free from the breastbone. Tuck the neck skin and wings under the bird. Set the bird on its back. Pass a long string under the tail and knot it over the leg joints and around the tail, tying a double knot. Take the strings back along the body, passing them between the legs and breast. Flip the bird over onto its breast and loop the strings under each wing pinion. Tie the strings tightly, again with a double knot, and turn the bird onto its back. You will see that the legs and wings are held firmly to the body and the bird sits flat on the board.

BUTTER, CLARIFYING

Melt butter in a saucepan over low heat, skim the froth from the surface, and let cool to tepid. Pour the yellow, melted butterfat into a bowl, leaving the milky sediment at the bottom of the saucepan. When chilled, clarified butter will solidify; it may be refrigerated for up to 2 months.

CHESTNUTS, PEELING

With a small, sharp knife, slit the end of each nut. Put the nuts in a saucepan of cold water and bring just to a boil. Use a draining spoon to lift out a few nuts at a time and peel them while still hot, removing the thick outer shell and thin inner skin. If the chestnuts cool and become difficult to peel, quickly reheat them. Do not overcook them or they will soften and fall apart.

DEEP-FRYING

Deep-frying is done at a high temperature, around 375°F/190°C. Fresh oil with a high smoke point is important; peanut, safflower, and canola oils are all good choices. A traditional bath of oil is at least 2 inches/5 cm deep, so that larger ingredients, such as fish fillets, can float freely. Purpose-designed pans for deep-frying are wide enough to take plenty of fritters, with sides high enough so the bubbling oil does not spill. Electric deep-fryers are equipped with a thermostat. A sauté pan or large, shallow saucepan may be substituted.

FLAMBÉING

Flambéing with liqueurs and other spirits not only toasts and browns ingredients but also adds drama. To flambé, heat the ingredients in a shallow pan such as a frying pan. When very hot, add the alcohol. At once, light the sides of the pan with a match or carefully tip the edge of the pan to catch the gas flame. You may warm alcohol before flambéing to be sure it lights. Do not attempt to ignite too much alcohol at one time, as the flames can be fierce, and once lit, stand back from the flames. Spoon the flaming liquid over the food until the flames die, showing the alcohol has evaporated. What is left behind is concentrated flavor.

GLAZE AND JUS, MAKING

When the cooking juices of meat, poultry, or fish are boiled down, they darken and caramelize to a shiny glaze, which gives rich flavor to sauces and gravies. A glaze can also be created by adding broth to such ingredients as vegetables. After reduction, a glaze should be a deep gold and have a sticky consistency. If it has not boiled down enough, it will lack body; if it is cooked too much, it will burn. A jus is made by thinning a glaze with broth, boiling the mixture down again to a glaze, and repeating once or twice to achieve a concentrated, glossy sauce.

LARDONS

Lardons cut from a piece of slab bacon, or sometimes from other fatty pork cuts, add meaty depth of flavor at low cost. To cut lardons, trim any rind from the bacon and cut into slices ⅜ inch/ 1 cm thick. Stack the slices and cut crosswise into short strips.

LEEKS, CLEANING AND TRIMMING

Trim the root end and the top of the leek, leaving some green intact or discarding all of it, depending on the recipe. Discard the outer leaves and split the leek into quarters or halves almost through the root. Rinse the leek under running cold water, flooding it down to the root and shaking to loosen any dirt. Reassemble the layers for cooking. If the leek is to be sliced or chopped, cut it before cleaning, rinse the pieces thoroughly in a bowl of cold water, and then transfer them with your hands to a colander to drain, leaving the grit behind.

MEAT, ROLLING AND TYING

Wrap a long piece of thin string lengthwise around the meat and tie it. This stops it from curling in the oven's heat. Tie a string around the center of the meat, knot, and trim it. Repeat with a length of string near each end of the roll. Fill the gaps between the ends and center with more strings, pulling them tightly where there is more flesh and more loosely where the roll is narrow, so the meat forms an even cylinder.

MUSSELS, CLEANING

Clean mussels not more than an hour before cooking. Rinse them under cold water and drain in a colander (they will quickly die if left to soak in fresh water). With a small knife, pull off the beard (the fibrous tuft the mollusk uses to cling to rocks or pilings) and scrape the mussel shells clean of any barnacles. Gaping shells are suspect, so tap them on the counter and discard any still open or damaged, as well as with any still closed after steaming.

POACHING

Poaching means to cook in liquid that is just below a simmer, so the liquid barely ripples in one or two places rather than bubbling. Delicate foods that break up easily, such as fish and fruits, should be poached. Also, dishes such as Pot-au-Feu (page 142) are poached, so they cook very slowly and develop maximum flavor.

RABBIT, CUTTING INTO PIECES

Rabbit should be cut into equal pieces that will cook at the same speed. Trim and discard flaps of belly skin, tips of forelegs, and any other protruding bones. Using a heavy knife or cleaver, divide the rabbit crosswise into 3 sections: back legs, back, and forelegs including rib cage. Cut between the back legs to separate them, and then trim off the tail end of the backbone. Separate the forelegs in a similar fashion by chopping between the shoulders. Then cut the back (saddle) portion crosswise into 2 or 3 pieces, depending on the size of the rabbit. You should have 6 or 7 pieces. For 8 or 9 pieces, halve the back legs by cutting through the knee joint.

SAUTÉING

Sautéed food is cooked in small or thinly sliced pieces over relatively high heat in fat such as butter or oil. The fat must be hot before the food is added, and the food should cook briskly so it browns and develops a caramelized surface. Steam develops, which causes the pieces to jump—*sauter* in French—from time to time in the pan, hence the name.

SWEATING

To cook food in a little fat and no liquid over very low heat until meltingly tender. The food is chopped or thinly sliced and steams in its own juices, with parchment paper or aluminum foil pressed on top. When soft and tender, the food may be served alone or combined with other ingredients.

TART PAN, LINING

Pans with a removable base are easiest to use for shallow French-style tarts. Pâte brisée should be rolled to medium thickness (¼ inch/6 mm), pâte sucrée a little thicker, and pâte feuilletée a little thinner. Lightly butter the pan. Roll out the dough to a round about 2 inches/5 cm larger than the pan. Fold the dough loosely around the rolling pin, lift, and unroll it over the pan, being careful not to stretch it. Gently lift the edges and press the dough well into corners of the pan, using a small ball of excess dough dipped in flour. Roll the pin across the top of the pan (the metal edge is quite sharp) to cut off the excess dough. With your fingers, press the dough evenly up the sides of the pan to increase the height of the shell. Flute the edge if making a sweet tart, or leave it plain for a savory tart. Prick the base of shell all over with a fork and chill until firm.

TART SHELL, BLIND BAKING

A pastry shell is blind baked (that is, baked empty) when the filling will not be cooked in the shell, or when the filling is especially moist and might soak the pastry during baking. Heat the oven to 375°F/190°C and set a baking sheet on a low shelf to heat. Line the pan with dough as described in the previous entry and chill for at least 15 minutes. Crumple a large sheet of aluminum foil, flatten it, and line the pastry shell with it, pressing it well into the corners. Fill the shell with dried beans or rice to hold the dough in place. (The beans or rice can be kept and used again.) Bake until the edges of the dough are set and starting to brown, 15 to 20 minutes. Remove the weights and foil. If the tart shell will be filled and baked, continue baking the shell until the base is firm and dry, 4 to 5 minutes longer. If the filling does not require baking, continue baking the shell until well browned, 10 to 12 minutes longer.

TOMATOES, PEELING, SEEDING, AND CHOPPING

To peel tomatoes, core them and mark a small cross at the opposite end with the knife tip. Pour boiling water over the tomatoes and leave for 10 seconds, or until the skin starts to lift at the cross. At once, transfer the tomatoes to cold water until cool, and then drain and peel. To seed tomatoes, halve each one through its equator and squeeze each half so the seeds pop out (if you like, strain the seeds to extract the juice). To chop tomatoes, set a tomato half, cut side down, on a cutting board and slice it. Rotate the slices 90 degrees and slice again. Repeat with any remaining tomato halves, then chop them all together, coarsely or more finely as needed.

WATER BATH, USING

A water bath (*bain-marie*) is used for both cooking at steady, gentle heat and for keeping food hot or reheating it. The hot water in the bath diffuses direct heat so the food does not get too hot and remains moist from the steam.

To cook foods in a water bath: Bring a deep roasting pan of water to a boil on the stove top and set the dish, mold, or pan of food in it. The water should come at least halfway up the sides of the dish. Or, in some cases, put the dish or dishes in the roasting pan and add boiling water to reach halfway up the sides of the dish(es). Bring the water just back to a boil on the stove top and, depending on the recipe, transfer the roasting pan to a preheated oven, or continue cooking on the stove top. Count the cooking time from the moment the water comes to a boil.

To keep foods hot in a water bath: Set the dish, mold, or pan of food in a roasting pan of hot, but not boiling, water and leave over very low heat. The water should not boil, and for delicate recipes such as a butter sauce, it should remain tepid. Foods can be gently reheated this way as well.

WILD MUSHROOMS, CLEANING AND REHYDRATING

All fresh wild mushrooms need the same preparation. Pick them over to remove twigs and grass, then trim the stems. Shake and gently brush mushrooms to remove any dirt. Morels tend to be gritty, so brush each one well, splitting the stems to remove any soil inside. Rinse fresh mushrooms with cold water if they still look dirty, but never soak them because they absorb water like a sponge. Soak dried mushrooms in warm water to cover until fairly soft, about 1 hour, or in boiling water for about 30 minutes. Once rehydrated, the mushrooms may need rinsing to remove grit. The soaking water may be strained to remove grit and then added to soups or sauces for added flavor. The flavor of the same variety of fresh and dried mushrooms varies dramatically in strength, but 2 pounds/900 g of fresh mushrooms more or less equals 3½ ounces/100 g dried.

RECIPES

BREAD CRUMBS

For simplicity, use sliced white bread for bread crumbs.

Bread crumbs, browned: Discard crusts and toast bread in the oven at 350°F/180°F until golden brown, 10 to 15 minutes. Let cool and work toast to crumbs in a food processor or blender. They may be stored in an airtight container for up to 3 months.

Bread crumbs, dry white: Discard crusts and dry bread in a warm place or very low oven until crisp. Let cool and work to crumbs in a food processor or blender. They may be stored in an airtight container for up to 1 month.

Bread crumbs, fresh white: Discard crusts from fairly dry white bread and cut into large cubes. Work cubes to crumbs in a food processor or blender. Use within 1 day.

BROTH, BEEF OR VEAL

For about 2½ quarts/2.5 liters broth, roast 5 pounds/2.3 kg veal bones, or half veal bones and half beef bones, in a very hot oven for 20 minutes. Add 2 carrots, quartered, and 2 onions, quartered, and continue roasting until very brown, about 30 minutes more. Transfer the roasted bones and vegetables to a stockpot, leaving any rendered fat in the roasting pan. Add 1 bouquet garni (page 370), 1 tablespoon peppercorns, 1 tablespoon tomato purée or paste, and about 5 quarts/5 liters cold water or as needed to cover the bones and vegetables generously. Bring very slowly to a boil, skimming off any foam from the surface, and then simmer gently, uncovered, for 4 to 5 hours, skimming occasionally and adding water if necessary so the ingredients are always covered. Strain the broth and taste. If the flavor is not concentrated, boil until well reduced and flavorful. Chill and skim off any solidified fat from the surface before using. The broth may be refrigerated for up to 3 days, and freezes well for a few months.

BROTH, CHICKEN

Duck or other poultry parts or even rabbit bones may be substituted for the chicken. For about 2½ quarts/2.5 liters broth, combine 3 pounds/1.4 kg chicken backs, necks, and bones with 1 onion, quartered; 1 carrot, quartered; 1 stalk celery, cut into pieces; 1 bouquet garni (page 370); 1 teaspoon peppercorns; and about 4 quarts/4 liters cold water or as needed to cover the poultry and vegetables generously. Bring very slowly to a boil, skimming off any foam from the surface, and then simmer gently, uncovered, for 2 to 3 hours, skimming occasionally and adding more water if necessary so the ingredients are always covered. Strain the broth and taste. If the flavor is not concentrated, boil until well reduced and flavorful. Chill and skim off any solidified fat from the surface before using. The broth may be refrigerated for up to 3 days, and freezes well for a few months.

CRÈME ANGLAISE

See individual recipes for ingredient measurements. Scald milk or milk and cream with the vanilla bean, if using, splitting it to extract seeds for more flavor. Cover and leave to infuse for 10 to 15 minutes. Beat the egg yolks with the sugar until thick and pale. Stir in the hot milk and return the mixture to the pan. Heat gently, stirring with a wooden spoon, until the custard thickens enough to leave a clear trail when you draw a finger across the back of the spoon. Do not allow the custard to boil or overcook or it will curdle. At once, remove from the heat and strain into a cold bowl. If using vanilla extract, add it now. Crème anglaise may be tightly covered and refrigerated for up to 2 days. The vanilla bean may be rinsed and used again.

CRÈME CHANTILLY

See individual recipes for ingredient measurements. Chill a bowl and a whisk in the freezer. Put chilled heavy cream or crème fraîche in the cold bowl and whisk until stiff. (If the cream is not cold, it may curdle before it stiffens.) Add the sugar with the vanilla or other flavoring, and continue whisking until the cream stiffens again. Do not overbeat or it will curdle. The whipped cream may be stored in the refrigerator for an hour or two. It will separate slightly on standing, but will recombine with a few quick stirs.

CRÈME FRAÎCHE

For 1 quart/1 liter crème fraîche, stir together 3 cups/750 ml heavy cream, 1 cup/250 ml active buttermilk, and the juice of 1 lemon in a saucepan. Heat gently, stirring, until slightly cool to the touch (about 75°F/25°C). Pour the mixture into a container and partly cover the top. Keep in a warm place, 70° to 80°F/21° to 27°C, until the cream thickens and develops a slightly tart flavor, 12 to 24 hours, depending on the buttermilk culture and the temperature. Crème fraîche may be refrigerated for up to 2 weeks; it will thicken as it stands, and the flavor will intensify.

CROÛTES

Croûtes and croutons in many different styles are regularly used to provide a crisp contrast to soups and rich stews. They may be made with a country loaf, baguette, or sliced white bread, and baked, toasted, or fried in oil and/or butter. Slightly stale, dry bread is best for croûtes and most types keep well for several hours; warm them in a low oven for serving.

Croûtes, baked: Cut a baguette, country loaf, or crusty rolls into uniform slices ⅜ to ½ inch/1 to 1.25 cm thick. If you like, brush them lightly on both sides with olive oil or melted butter. Put on a baking sheet and toast in a preheated 350°F/180°C oven, turning once, until dry and lightly browned, 10 to 15 minutes. Croûtes tend to cook unevenly near the edge of the baking sheet, so move them during baking.

Croûtes, fried: Cut a baguette or country loaf as for baked croûtes, or cut shapes from sliced bread as called for in the recipe. Melt butter and/or oil to form a ¼-inch/6-mm layer in a frying pan over medium heat. A piece of bread will sizzle at once when the fat is hot enough. (Don't be tempted to skimp on the fat, or the bread will brown unevenly.) Add the bread slices and fry until browned underneath, about 1 minute. Turn and brown the other side. Transfer to paper towels to drain.

Croûtes, toasted: Cut a baguette or country loaf as for baked croûtes and toast in an electric toaster. For shaped toasted croûtes, toast slices of white or whole-wheat bread in the toaster, discard the crusts, and cut the slices in triangles or as called for in the recipe.

CROUTONS

Hearty rustic croutons are made from country bread or a baguette cut into rough ½-inch/1.25-cm cubes. More evenly shaped classic croutons are cubed from sliced white bread, with crusts discarded.

Croutons, fried: Cube the bread. Melt butter and/or oil or other fat to form a ¼-inch/6-mm layer in a frying pan over medium heat. A piece of bread will sizzle at once when the fat is hot enough. Add the bread cubes and fry, stirring constantly so they brown evenly, for 30 seconds to 1 minute. Watch closely as they scorch easily. Pour them into a strainer so the fat drains into a bowl, then spread on paper towels to drain.

Croutons, toasted: Slice bread ½ inch/1.25 thick and toast in an electric toaster. Brush with olive or nut oil or melted butter, then cut into cubes.

MAYONNAISE

See individual recipes for ingredient measurements. Have all your ingredients at warm room temperature or the mayonnaise will not thicken properly. In a small bowl, whisk the egg yolks with salt, pepper, half the vinegar or lemon juice, and the Dijon mustard, if using, until the mixture thickens slightly, 45 seconds to 1 minute. Add 1 to 2 teaspoons of the oil drop by drop, whisking constantly. The mixture should be quite thick, showing an emulsion has formed. Continue adding the oil in a slow, steady stream, whisking constantly. Stir in the remaining vinegar or lemon juice, with more mustard, salt, and pepper to taste. The mayonnaise may be covered and kept at room temperature for no more than 1 hour, or may be refrigerated for up to 12 hours. Let it come to room temperature before stirring, or it may separate.

PÂTE À CHOUX (CREAM-PUFF PASTRY DOUGH)

See individual recipes for ingredient measurements. In a large saucepan, combine the water, salt, and butter and heat gently until the butter is melted. Meanwhile, sift the flour onto a piece of parchment paper. Bring the butter mixture just to a boil (prolonged boiling evaporates the water and changes the proportions of the dough). Take from the heat and immediately add all the flour. Beat vigorously with a wooden spoon for a few moments until the mixture pulls away from the pan sides to form a ball. Beat for 30 seconds to 1 minute over low heat to dry the dough.

Beat 1 egg until mixed and set aside. Beat the remaining egg(s) into the dough, one at a time, beating thoroughly after each addition. Beat in enough of the reserved egg so the dough is shiny and just falls from the spoon. If too much egg is added, the dough will be too soft and not hold its shape. Rub the top of the dough with butter to prevent a skin from forming, and set aside until cool. Pâte à choux may be tightly covered and refrigerated for up to 12 hours before using.

PÂTE À PAIN (BREAD DOUGH)

See individual recipes for ingredient measurements. Sift the flour and salt onto a work surface and make a well in the center with your hand. Pour the water into the well, sprinkle the yeast on top, and leave until dissolved, about 5 minutes. Add the egg(s) and oil to the water and work with the fingers of one hand until mixed. Using your hand, gradually draw in the flour from the sides of the well to form a soft, floppy dough. If it sticks to your fingers, work in more flour. Flour the work surface again and knead the dough by gathering it up with your fingers and pushing it away with the heel of your hand. Continue kneading until the dough is very elastic and peels away from the surface in one piece, about 5 minutes. The dough may also be mixed and kneaded in a stand mixer fitted with the dough hook.

Transfer the dough to an oiled bowl and turn the dough so the top is oiled. Cover tightly with plastic wrap and leave to rise in a warm place until doubled in bulk, 45 minutes to 1 hour. Alternatively, the dough may be prepared ahead and left to rise for up to 12 hours or overnight in the refrigerator; let it come to room temperature before shaping.

PÂTE À PÂTES FRAÎCHES (PASTA DOUGH)

See individual recipes for ingredient measurements. Tip the flour onto a work surface and make a well in the center. Add the eggs to the well with the salt and work with the fingers of one hand until mixed. Gradually draw in the flour from the sides of the well with one hand, drawing in more as the dough thickens. Using the fingers of both hands, tear half-mixed pieces of dough into crumbs. (To make the dough in a food processor, add the ingredients to the processor bowl and work until they form small, even crumbs. Tip the crumbs onto the work surface.) If the crumbs are dry, sprinkle with 1 teaspoon water; if sticky, add 2 to 3 tablespoons more flour. When the dough is evenly mixed, press the crumbs together into a ball.

To knead the dough, set the pasta machine rollers on the widest setting. Cut the dough into 3 pieces, and cover 2 pieces with an upturned bowl. Lightly flour the third piece, press it into a rectangle, and feed it through the rollers. Fold the dough strip into thirds to make a square, give it a quarter turn, and feed again

through the rollers, dusting it with flour if it tends to stick. Continue rolling and folding until the dough is elastic, very smooth, and does not crack at the sides, 6 to 8 times. It is now ready to roll into strips and shape as described in individual recipes.

PÂTE BRISÉE (TART PASTRY DOUGH)

See individual recipes for ingredient measurements. Sift the flour onto a work surface and make a well in the center. Put egg(s) or egg yolk(s), salt, sugar (if using), and water in the well. Pound the butter with a rolling pin to soften it, add it to the well, and work the ingredients in the well with the fingers of one hand until thoroughly mixed. Using a pastry scraper, gradually draw in the flour from the sides of the well and continue working with both hands until coarse crumbs form. If the crumbs seem dry, sprinkle with another tablespoon of water; the crumbs should be soft but not sticky. Gently press the crumbs into a ball; the dough will be uneven and unblended at this point.

To blend (*fraiser*) the dough, sprinkle the work surface with flour and put the dough on it. With the heel of your hand, push the dough away from you, flattening it against the work surface. Gather it up, press it into a rough ball, and flatten it again. This flattening motion evenly blends the butter with the other ingredients without overworking the dough. Work quickly so the butter doesn't get too warm. Continue until the dough is as pliable as putty and pulls away from the surface in one piece, 1 to 2 minutes. Shape it into a ball, wrap, and chill until firm, 15 to 30 minutes. Pâte brisée may be refrigerated, tightly wrapped, for up to 2 days, or frozen for up to 3 months.

PÂTE FEUILLETÉE (PUFF PASTRY DOUGH)

See individual recipes for ingredient measurements. Have the butter already chilled. Sift the flour onto a marble slab or other cool work surface and make a well in the center. Add 2 to 3 tablespoons of the butter, cut into pieces, to the well with the water, salt, and lemon juice. Work the ingredients in the well with the fingers of one hand until thoroughly mixed. Gradually draw in the flour from the sides of the well with your hand and a pastry scraper to make crumbs. Work just until the dough is mixed, adding a little more water if it is dry. Shape the dough into a ball, wrap, and chill for 15 minutes. This dough is the *détrempe* and should be quite rough; if worked until smooth, the finished pastry will be elastic.

Lightly flour the remaining butter, put it between 2 sheets of parchment paper, and flatten it with a rolling pin. Fold the butter, replace it between the paper sheets, and continue pounding and folding until pliable but not sticky. The butter should be the same consistency as the *détrempe*. Shape the butter into a 6-inch/15-cm square and flour it lightly. Roll out the dough to a 12-inch/30-cm square, slightly thicker in the center than at the edges. Set the butter diagonally in the center of the dough, and fold the dough around it like an envelope, pinching the edges to seal the package.

Generously flour the work surface. Place the dough, seam side down, on the work surface, and lightly pound with a rolling pin to flatten it slightly. Roll out to an 18-by-6-inch/45-by-15-cm rectangle. Fold the rectangle into thirds, like a business letter. Press the ends lightly with the rolling pin to seal the edges and give the dough a quarter turn (90 degrees) so the seam is to your left. This is called a turn. Roll out the rectangle and fold again into thirds. Keep a note of the number of turns by marking a dough corner with the appropriate number of fingerprints. Wrap and chill until firm, 20 to 30 minutes.

Repeat the rolling, folding, and turning to complete 6 turns, chilling between every 2 turns. Chill the pastry until firm, 30 minutes to 1 hour, before using. It may be refrigerated for up to 3 days, or frozen for up to 3 months.

PÂTE SUCRÉE (SWEET TART PASTRY DOUGH)

See individual recipes for ingredient measurements. Sift the flour onto a work surface and make a well in the center. Put the salt, sugar, egg yolk(s) and/or whole egg, and vanilla or other flavoring in the well. Pound the butter with a rolling pin to soften it, add it to the other ingredients in the well, and work with the fingers of one hand until thoroughly mixed and the sugar is partially dissolved. Using a pastry scraper, gradually draw in the flour from the sides of the well, then work the dough and chill as for pâte brisée (page 375).

STOCK, FISH

For about 1½ quarts/1.5 liters stock, break 2 pounds/1 kg fish bones into pieces and wash thoroughly. In a stockpot, cook 1 onion, sliced, in 1 tablespoon butter until soft but not brown, 5 to 7 minutes. Add the fish bones, 1½ quarts/1.5 liters water, 1 bouquet garni (page 370), 10 peppercorns, and 1½ cups/375 ml dry white wine. Bring to a boil and simmer quite briskly, uncovered, for 20 minutes, skimming often. Strain and let cool. Fish stock may be refrigerated for up to 2 days, or frozen for up to 3 months, but it is best when freshly made.

STOCK, SHELLFISH

Proceed as for Fish Stock (previous entry), halving the amount of fish bones and adding the shells from 12 ounces/375 g shrimp with the bones. Substitute olive oil for the butter and cook 1 carrot, diced, with the onion.

EQUIPMENT

Unless otherwise stated, all the pans and bowls called for in the recipes in this book are medium sized. The diameter of pans, notably cake pans, is measured across the upper rim.

CASSEROLE

In France, the word *casserole* refers to the heavy, lidded pot in which braises and stews are cooked. A casserole resembles a Dutch oven, but comes in many more colors, shapes, and sizes, and is commonly made of enameled cast iron, so it doubles as a serving dish. The flameproof base allows you to brown foods on top of the stove, and the tight-fitting lid prevents juices that develop during cooking from evaporating. Robust earthenware casseroles such as the Provençal *daubière* are still made, but they are fragile and should not be used over direct high heat.

CHARLOTTE MOLD

Bucket shaped, with gently sloping sides and flat handles near the top to make turning out the contents easy, the charlotte mold is a classic form for molding and baking savory dishes and desserts. The mold is usually made of metal and comes in many sizes. A deep soufflé dish may be substituted.

CRÊPE PAN

This small, round frying pan has shallow sides, which makes crêpes easy to flip or turn. Traditional crêpe pans are made of steel; they must be seasoned when new, and should be wiped with a damp cloth, not washed. Nonstick crêpe pans are easy to use, but crêpes cooked in them are thicker and do not brown as well.

GRATIN DISH

Gratin dishes are shallow—no more than 2 inches/5 cm deep—which allows the contents to acquire the maximum crispy topping during baking. Shapes range from round, rectangular, and square to a popular oval that fits easily in a corner of the oven. The dish is usually heavy, so the food inside heats evenly while it toasts on top. Glazed earthenware, enameled cast iron, and heatproof glass are popular materials.

JELLY BAG

A conical jelly bag is used for draining puréed fruit to extract clear juice for jellies. The bag is made of rough, closely woven cloth, so the fruit drains slowly and the liquid emerges sparkling clear. A jelly bag should be rinsed clean in clear water, never washed with soap.

MOULE-À-MANQUÉ

The favorite French cake pan has sloping sides, so that icing easily flows down the graduated sides of the unmolded cake. It comes in many sizes, usually in metal, with or without a nonstick finish. Flexible molds of silicone are also available, but cakes baked in them do not brown well and therefore lack flavor.

OMELET PAN

Made of aluminum or steel, an omelet pan should have curved, gently sloping sides and a thick base to distribute heat evenly. The handle is angled to help fold the omelet neatly onto a plate. The pan must be seasoned when new and should be wiped with a damp cloth, not washed. A pan with a nonstick surface is easier to maintain.

PRESERVING PAN

The more quickly jams, jellies, and other preserves are cooked, the fresher and more vivid their flavor will be. Copper preserving pans spread heat rapidly and evenly, and their sloping sides allow you to reach all the corners when stirring with a wooden spoon. Large preserving pans often have two handles and a lip for pouring out the contents. Note that the copper is not lined with another metal, so it must be cleaned with coarse salt and vinegar or lemon juice not more than 30 minutes before use. A large, heavy saucepan may be substituted.

RAMEKIN

Ramekins are small baking dishes, usually porcelain, with straight sides and the shape of a soufflé dish. They come in several sizes and are used for baking individual portions, particularly in a sauce.

SAUTÉ PAN

A pan for sautéing, called in France a *plat à sauter*, resembles a frying pan with high, vertical sides. Designed for sautéing and browning foods, the sides of the pan retain a certain amount of moisture. A medium sauté pan is just right for a whole chicken, cut into pieces. Most sauté pans are made of stainless steel or anodized aluminum, and sometimes of lined copper (a luxury). They come with a lid and with handles that withstand oven heat. A skillet or deep frying pan may be substituted.

SILICONE SHEET

A flexible silicone sheet, often called by the brand name Silpat, is used to line baking sheets. Silicone creates a nonstick surface and acts as an insulator for cookies or baked goods. Parchment paper or silicone-coated parchment paper may be substituted.

SOUFFLÉ DISH

The successful soufflé depends on the classic round dish with high straight sides that guide the soufflé mixture vertically as it rises. White glazed porcelain, fluted on the outside to resemble a pleated paper case, is traditional; glass and earthenware are alternative materials. Soufflé dishes come in a variety of sizes, and are measured by volume, not diameter.

STOCKPOT

A stockpot should be taller than it is wide, with two sturdy handles. High sides ensure gradual evaporation of broth, while a comparatively narrow base means that heat spreads easily to the edges. A capacity of 12 quarts/12 liters leaves plenty of room for cumbersome bones, yet is still quite easy to lift.

TART PAN WITH REMOVABLE BASE

Shallow tart pans, with a loose base that can be pushed up free of the sides, are standard in France. They are typically round and occasionally rectangular, made of metal, and have fluted sides. U.S. pie pans may be substituted, but they hold less filling and the tart is difficult to unmold after baking. Quiche pans are heavier, often deeper, and have a fixed base; they may be made of pottery or cast iron.

TERRINE MOLD

Molds for baking pâtés and terrines are made from earthenware, porcelain, or enameled cast iron, all materials that are thick enough to diffuse oven heat. Shape varies from a long, narrow rectangle to a deep oval, and all come with a lid with a small hole so steam can escape and a skewer can be inserted to test cooking. Long terrines provide a neat loaf shape for slicing. A loaf pan may be substituted for a terrine mold, but the food does not cook as evenly.

THE COUNTRY COOKING OF FRANCE

BOOKS CONSULTED

Books about French country cooking are comparatively new, rarely earlier than 1900. After all, until quite recently, country cooking meant subsistence, living off the nearby land. Each region had characteristic ingredients; distinctive dishes based on them would surface on feast days, but they were rarely written down. In the late 19th century this began to change. *La France profonde* opened up to travelers as the train, and eventually the car, brought the provinces far closer to the city. Regionalism fascinated an increasing number of townspeople who were curious about their roots, about the essence of Frenchness and the concept of *terroir*. Rural France emerged from centuries-old obscurity and, at last, signature dishes were systematically recorded.

Prominent early French sources on country cooking from the first half of the 20th century include Curnonsky, Austin de Croze, Edouard de Pomiane, La Mazille, Simin Palay, and Madame de Saint-Ange. Closer to our own times are Michel Barbarousse, Huguette Couffignal, Robert Courtine, Roger Lallemand, Simone Morand, and Céline Vence. I find the *Guide Gourmand de la France* (Gault et Millau) a helpful companion despite its age (1970). Celebrity French chefs' books I am less impressed by; many are all glop and gloss. Most recently, the publishers Albin Michel have released an important multi-volume book series under the grandiloquent title *Inventaire du Patrimoine Culinaire de la France*. There are 19 volumes covering the French provinces, leaving one region, the Center, undone. Americans Philip and Mary Hyman are two of the key contributors to this encyclopedic series.

In the last 50 years, innumerable writers from the English-speaking world have written about French country cooking, and I would highlight books by Colman Andrews, Narcisse and Samuel Chamberlain, Elizabeth David, Jane Grigson, Robin Howe, Madeleine Kamman, Richard Olney, Waverley Root, Patricia Wells, and Paula Wolfert. As well, many cookbooks of a more general nature have regional content, not least those by Julia Child. Of course, as a whole these books are written "from the outside looking in," as mine have been, too. I'm not sure they're any the worse for that; many come out ahead of French cookbooks in terms of their usefulness in the kitchen. But then, that may merely suggest that French cooks can dispense with rebarbative recipe detail!

For titles and publication dates of these authors' works, please consult the Internet.